P9-CJI-612

THE PAPERS

of

JOHN C. CALHOUN

John Caldwell Calhoun (1782-1850)

This engraving by James B. Longacre, first published in Philadelphia in 1827, portrays Calhoun at a comparatively youthful age. The miniature bust of the statesman shown on the facing page is preserved in The South Caroliniana Library at the University of South Carolina. That bust is in the manner of another by Clark Mills, presented by the sculptor to the City of Charleston in 1846, "the most accurate and approved delineation of the expression and features of Carolina's greatest and most gifted son."

THE PAPERS

of

JOHN C. CALHOUN

Volume I, 1801-1817

Edited by

Robert L. Meriwether

Published by the University of South Carolina Press
for the South Caroliniana Society, Columbia, 1959

General

Copyright ©, 1959, by the

South Carolina Archives Department

99682

NOV 1 1960

E
337.8
C15p
v.1

Library of Congress Catalog Card Number: 59-10351

10-21-60

Manufactured in the United States of America

To

M.B.M.

THE PAPERS OF JOHN C. CALHOUN

Clara Mae Jacobs and E. L. Inabinett, *Editorial Assistants*

ADVISORY COMMITTEE, 1952–1959

Julian P. Boyd

Edgar A. Brown

Margaret L. Coit

Felix Frankfurter

Philip M. Hamer

James H. Hammond

William B. Hesseltine

Alester G. Holmes *(died, 1953)*

Allan Nevins

Robert F. Poole *(died, 1958)*

Donald S. Russell

Wendell H. Stephenson

Strom Thurmond

PUBLICATION COMMITTEE, 1952–1958

Carl L. Epting, *Chairman*

Wilfrid H. Callcott

Charles E. Cauthen

Arney R. Childs

Louise J. DuBose

J. Harold Easterby

Helen G. McCormack

Robert H. Wienefeld

Charles M. Wiltse

THE SOUTH CAROLINA ARCHIVES COMMISSION

Calhoun A. Mays, *Chairman*

Carl L. Epting, *Vice Chairman*

Charles A. Anger

Charles E. Cauthen

B. Allston Moore

Robert H. Wienefeld

J. Harold Wolfe

THE SOUTH CAROLINIANA SOCIETY

Caroline McKissick Belser, *President*

Arney R. Childs, *Vice-President*

Mary C. Simms Oliphant, *Vice-President*

E. L. Inabinett, *Secretary and Treasurer*

Mrs. David R. Coker, *Councilor*

James H. Hammond, *Councilor*

Charles Spencer McCants, *Councilor*

James O. Sheppard, *Councilor*

CONTENTS

〚〛

FOREWORD · *xv*

PREFACE · *xvii*

INTRODUCTION · *xxiii*

EDITORIAL PROCEDURE · *xxxiii*

ABBREVIATED TITLES AND LOCATION SYMBOLS · · · · · · · · · · *xxxix*

CHRONOLOGY, 1782-1817 · *xli*

1801
1. TO ANDREW PICKENS, JR., *6 September* · · · · · · · · · · · · · · · · · · · 3

1802
2. TO [. . . CALHOUN, *23 November?*] · 4

1803
3. TO ANDREW PICKENS, JR., *21 January* · · · · · · · · · · · · · · · · · · · 7
4. TO ANDREW PICKENS, JR., *23 May* · 9
5. REMARKS UPON THE QUERY: Would It Be Politic to
   Encourage the Immigration of Foreigners? *2 November* · · · · 10

1804
6. TO MRS. FLORIDE BONNEAU COLHOUN, *29 August* · · · · · · · 11
7. TO ALEXANDER NOBLE, *15 October* · 12

1805
8. TO ANDREW PICKENS, JR., *25 June* · 13
9. TO MRS. FLORIDE BONNEAU COLHOUN, *22 July* · · · · · · · · · · 15
10. TO MRS. FLORIDE BONNEAU COLHOUN, *12 August* · · · · · · · 16
11. TO MRS. FLORIDE BONNEAU COLHOUN, *9 September* · · · · · · 18

12. From Mrs. Floride Bonneau Colhoun, *14 September*   19
13. To Mrs. Floride Bonneau Colhoun, *26 September*   21
14. To Andrew Pickens, Jr., *24 November*   22
15. To Mrs. Floride Bonneau Colhoun, *23 December*   24

1806

16. To Mrs. Floride Bonneau Colhoun, *19 January*   25
17. To Mrs. Floride Bonneau Colhoun, *3 March*   26
18. To Mrs. Floride Bonneau Colhoun, *13 April*   28
19. To Mrs. Floride Bonneau Colhoun, *2 June*   29
20. To Mrs. Floride Bonneau Colhoun, *3 July*   30
21. To Mrs. Floride Bonneau Colhoun, *11 September*   31
22. To Mrs. Floride Bonneau Colhoun, *22 December*   32

1807

23. Resolutions on the Chesapeake-Leopard Affair,
    3 August   34
24. To Mrs. Floride Bonneau Colhoun, *1 October*   37

1808

25. Application for Admission to Practice in the
    Chancery Courts, *7 March*   39
26. Motion in the South Carolina House of Representatives on Compensation of the State Census Takers,
    13 December   40

1809

27. To Mrs. Floride Bonneau Colhoun, *6 April*   41
28. To Mrs. Floride Bonneau Colhoun, *25 June*   42
29. To Mrs. Floride Bonneau Colhoun, *18 July*   43
30. To Mrs. Floride Bonneau Colhoun, *1 October*   45
31. Notice in the South Carolina House of Representatives for Introduction of Justice and Limitation Bills,
    4 December   46

1810

32. To Mrs. Floride Bonneau Colhoun, *20 January*   46
33. To Mrs. Floride Bonneau Colhoun, *12 June*   48
34. To Mrs. Floride Bonneau Colhoun, *30 June*   49
35. To Mrs. Floride Bonneau Colhoun, *18 July*   50

36. To Mrs. Floride Bonneau Colhoun, *27 July*   51
37. To Mrs. Floride Bonneau Colhoun, *24 August*   53
38. To Mrs. Floride Bonneau Colhoun, *7 September*   54
39. To Mrs. Floride Bonneau Colhoun, *13 September*   56
40. To Miss Floride Colhoun, *28 September*   57

1811

41. From William Ford DeSaussure, *21 April*   58
42. To Mrs. Floride Bonneau Colhoun, *8 May*   60
43. To Mrs. Floride Bonneau Colhoun, *23 May*   60
44. To Dr. James Macbride, *10 September*   61
45. To Patrick Calhoun, *14 November*   63
46. Report on Relations with Great Britain, *29 November* 63
47. Speech on the Apportionment Bill, *5 December*   71
48. Speech on the Report of the Foreign Relations Committee, *12 December*   75
49. To Mrs. Floride Bonneau Colhoun, *21 December*   86

1812

50. Comment on the Bill for an Additional Military Force, *2 January*   87
51. Comment on Randolph's Resolution for Employment of the Army, *10 January*   89
52. To Patrick Calhoun, *24 January*   89
53. To Dr. James Macbride, *17 February*   90
54. To Mrs. John C. Calhoun, *1 March*   91
55. To Robert Cresswell, *10 March*   92
56. To Dr. James Macbride, *16 March*   93
57. Remarks on an Amendment Providing for Representation in the Louisiana Legislature for the Annexed Portion of West Florida, *19 March*   94
58. To Patrick Noble, *22 March*   95
59. Remarks on the Publication of Secret Proceedings, *7 April*   96
60. Remarks on the Bill for Importation of British Goods, *10 April*   98
61. To Dr. James Macbride, *18 April*   99
62. Comment on the Resolution for Relief of Caracas, *29 April*   100

63. To Virgil Maxcy, *2 May*   101
64. Speech on the Albany Petition for Repeal of the Embargo, *6 May*   102
65. Remarks on the Question of Restriction of Debate, *29 May*   108
66. Report on the Causes and Reasons for War, *3 June*   109
67. Bill to Declare War on Great Britain, *3 June*   125
68. To Patrick Noble, *17 June*   126
69. Speech on Suspension of Non-Importation, *24 June*   126
70. To Mrs. Floride Bonneau Colhoun, *23 November*   135
71. Speech on the Merchants' Bonds, *8 December*   136
72. To Dr. James Macbride, *25 December*   146

1813

73. Remarks on the Protection of American Seamen, *2 January*   147
74. To Patrick Calhoun, *13 January*   149
75. Speech on the Bill for an Additional Military Force, *14 January*   150
76. To Dr. James Macbride, *2 February*   162
77. Comment on the Bill to Enforce Non-Importation, *23 February*   163
78. Bill Limiting Exportation in Foreign Vessels, *26 February*   164
79. The Retaliation Bill, *26 February*   165
80. Remarks on the Seating of George Richards, Stenographer, *31 May*   168
81. Debate on Webster's Resolutions on the French Decrees, *16 June*   169
82. To Dr. James Macbride, *23 June*   177
83. Comment on the Massachusetts Memorial, *29 June*   178
84. Report and Debate on the Conduct of the Executive, *13 July*   179
85. Report on the President's Proposal of an Embargo, *21 July*   181
86. To Mrs. Ezekiel Pickens, *26 October*   182
87. Bills to Enforce Non-Importation and to Prohibit Ransoming of Vessels, *30 December*   184

1814

88. REMARKS ON POSTPONEMENT OF DISCUSSION ON NECESSITY OF THE WAR, *3 January*   185

89. DEBATE ON THE TURREAU LETTER, *11 January*   186

90. SPEECH ON THE DANGERS OF "FACTIOUS OPPOSITION," *15 January*   189

91. REMARKS ON THE MARYLAND MEMORIAL, *2 February*   201

92. RESOLUTION ON THE QUESTION OF A NATIONAL BANK, *4 February*   204

93. TO MRS. JOHN C. CALHOUN, *7 February*   205

94. REMARKS ON THE DEFENSE OF THE AMERICAN COAST, *8 February*   206

95. SPEECH ON THE LOAN BILL, *25 February*   208

96. REPORT AND BILL FOR THE REPEAL OF THE EMBARGO AND NON-IMPORTATION ACTS, *4 April*   240

97. SPEECH ON THE BILL TO REPEAL THE RESTRICTIVE SYSTEM, *6 April*   243

98. DEFENSE OF THE REPUBLICAN FOREIGN POLICY, *6 April*   249

99. SPEECH ON ENCOURAGEMENT FOR MANUFACTURES, *7 April*   252

100. SPEECH ON THE MILITARY SITUATION, *25 October*   254

101. TO ANDREW PICKENS, JR., *1 November*   260

102. REMARKS ON THE VOLUNTEER BILL, *5 November*   261

103. RESOLUTION AND REMARKS ON ARMY SUPPLIES AND DISCIPLINE, *10 November*   262

104. SPEECH ON THE UNITED STATES BANK BILL, *16 November*   263

105. DEBATE ON THE BANK BILL, *18 November*   266

106. REMARKS ON THE FORM OF SUBSCRIPTION TO THE BANK, *21 November*   269

107. REMARKS ON THE SENATE MILITIA BILL, *2 December*   271

108. RESOLUTION FOR A NEW SYSTEM OF ARMY DISCIPLINE, *24 December*   273

1815

109. TO PATRICK CALHOUN, *4 January*   274

110. TO PATRICK NOBLE, *11 February*   274

111. COMMENT ON THE BANK BILL, *13 February*   275

112. TO JOHN EWING COLHOUN, *26 February*   276

113. SPEECH ON THE MILITARY PEACE ESTABLISHMENT, *27 February*   277

114. SPEECH ON THE RESULTS OF THE WAR, *27 February*   279

115. To Mrs. Floride Bonneau Colhoun, *9 April*   283
116. From Isaac Harby, *22 May*   284
117. To Mrs. John C. Calhoun, *29 November*   286

1816

118. First Speech on the Military Academies Bill, *2 January*   287
119. Second Speech on the Military Academies Bill, *3 January*   289
120. Bill to Incorporate the Subscribers to the Bank of the United States, *8 January*   290
121. Speech on the Commercial Treaty with Great Britain, *9 January*   304
122. Speech on the Additional Revenue Report, *20 January*   314
123. Speech on the Revenue Bill, *31 January*   316
124. Speech Introducing the Bank Bill, *26 February*   331
125. Remarks on the Requirement for Specie Payment by the Bank, *28 February*   340
126. Remarks on the Need for a National Bank, *6 March*   341
127. Speech on Compensation of Members, *8 March*   343
128. Debate on the National Bank Bill, *12 March*   345
129. Speech on the Tariff Bill, *4 April*   347
130. Remarks on the Bill to Require Specie Payment, *17 April*   357
131. Debate on the Specie Payment Bill, *23 April*   359
132. To [Henry Wheaton?], *18 May*   360
133. To Alexander James Dallas, *15 June*   361
134. From Dr. John Noble, *21 August*   362
135. From William Wirt, *22 August*   364
136. To James Barrel, *22 September*   365
137. To Felix Grundy, *12 December*   365
138. Comment on a Resolution to Request the President to Suspend Execution of a Law, *13 December*   366
139. Motion for a Committee to Plan a Fund for Internal Improvements, *16 December*   367
140. Comment on a Proposed Amendment for Election of Presidential Electors, *17 December*   369
141. From Isaac Briggs, *19 December*   369
142. The Internal Improvements Bill, *23 December*   372

143. Speech on the Bill for Payment for Lost Property,
30 December — 373

1817

144. Remarks on the Bill for Payment for Lost Property,
6 January — 376

145. Debate on the Specie Payments on Stock of the
United States Bank, *7 January* — 378

146. Report on the Specie Payments on Stock of the
United States Bank, *10 January* — 380

147. First Speech on Amendments to the Compensation
Law, *17 January* — 382

148. Second Speech on Amendments to the Compensation
Law, *20 January* — 393

149. Speech on the Neutrality Bill, *25 January* — 395

150. To John Ewing Colhoun, *30 January* — 397

151. Speech on Internal Improvements, *4 February* — 398

152. From John Trumbull, *10 February* — 409

153. Speech on the Transfer of Appropriations,
14 February — 410

154. To Virgil Maxcy, *23 February* — 416

155. To John Ewing Colhoun, *27 February* — 416

156. To James Edward Colhoun, *27 October* — 417

157. To James Monroe, *1 November* — 418

158. From James Edward Colhoun, *10 November* — 419

159. To Mrs. Floride Bonneau Colhoun, *15 November* — 420

Calendar — 421

Genealogical Table — 431

Bibliography — 435

Index — 439

FOREWORD

▯

When Robert L. Meriwether died on August 24, 1958, the editing of this volume of *The Papers of John C. Calhoun* had been completed. The text of the papers, together with their notes, had been set in galley proof and checked by him. Since his death, the work of his assistants, E. L. Inabinett and Mrs. C. M. Jacobs, has consisted in seeing that his wishes were carried out. All other material was in typescript ready to go to the printer except for the index, compiled by his daughter, Margaret W. Meriwether, and the genealogical table, compiled by Mrs. Jacobs, both in accordance with his instructions. In every way this is his volume.

R. L. M. planned *The Papers of John C. Calhoun* to serve a double purpose: first, to present in typographical reproduction the most important of Calhoun's letters, reports, and speeches; and, second, by means of the Calendar of unprinted papers appended to each volume, to provide a guide to the comprehensive Calhoun Collection of the South Caroliniana Library. The building of this collection, which brings together in manuscript, photostat, or microfilm all of the known extant words of Calhoun, was R. L. M.'s great primary accomplishment. His acquisition and classification of this vast and vastly important collection will make it possible to publish, under new editorship, the succeeding volumes which he planned but could not execute.

PREFACE

In talents and energy John C. Calhoun was cast in a mold of epic proportions. From a literary viewpoint his career answers to the definition of a Greek tragedy—the story of a man of superior qualities and lofty aims in a magnificent but losing fight with an inexorable fate. To historians he has appeared in various and at times violently contrasting roles. Since the sheer power of his mind and the force of his character put him always in an important if not commanding position, it has been easy for extremists either to regard him as the shining champion of the plantation regime, or to make him the scapegoat for the sins, real or fancied, of the South.

Calhoun himself had his part in creating these difficulties of interpretation. During his career his major concern shifted from political and economic nationalism to the unending problem of protection of minorities and social orders from internal and external dangers; and, although he spoke and wrote with a clarity and directness rare in his day, the intensity with which he grappled with these issues, and his persistence in phrasing his findings in the form of basic principles, have often made it hard for students of his career to distinguish between his fundamental ideas and those policies which he adopted because of an immediate peril.

Within half-a-dozen years of Calhoun's death his devoted disciple, Richard K. Crallé, had compiled for publication a hundred and fifty of his speeches, reports, and public letters. Fifty years from the day he died J. Franklin Jameson wrote the preface to the *Correspondence of John C. Calhoun* which, like the twelve-hundred-page volume it introduced, was a tribute to the editor's own scholarship and a major contribution to a better understanding of the great Southern leader.

For correction of the merely preposterous interpretations of Calhoun which have flourished from an early date, these already published volumes should have proved ample; but for a thorough study of his forty years of intense activity in the public service they are utterly inadequate. During half of this period Calhoun was one of the major figures in the political organization which controlled the government, and a full record of those years is essential. The papers of his later life are primarily a segment of Southern history, which is subject to the defects of interpretation usually attendant on causes involved in defeat and continuing controversy. It is therefore doubly important that these papers be made readily available, lest the lack of them contribute to the continued failure to apprehend the mistakes of Calhoun and of the South of his day, and to profit by what was of enduring value in their society and civilization.

The move for a comprehensive edition of Calhoun's papers had its origin with Dr. Philip M. Hamer, Executive Director of the National Historical Publications Commission, who in 1951 listed it among the foremost needs of students of American history. The enterprise has had the benefit of his scholarship and experience, and the undertaking has profited by many courtesies extended through his office. His assistant, Miss F. Helen Beach, Archivist of the Commission, has given indispensable aid through her skill and enthusiasm in finding Calhoun papers in the National Archives and in the Library of Congress. For microfilms of the many thousands of the papers in these two great repositories, and for unfailingly cordial and helpful assistance, thanks are tendered to Dr. Wayne C. Grover, Chairman of the Publications Commission and Archivist of the United States, and to the Archives staff.

Clemson College has made the most valuable contribution of personal papers by permitting microfilming of the Clemson Collection, which includes also many hundreds of papers of the other members of the Calhoun connection. The late beloved Professor A. G. Holmes, Head of the Clemson History Department, the late President R. F. Poole, and Professor Carl L. Epting have been of great assistance in planning the project. The University of South Carolina has furnished quarters for the work and during its initial stages provided for the staff as well; for this support thanks are due to former Presidents Norman M. Smith and Donald S. Russell, Acting President Robert L. Sumwalt, and to Dean Robert H. Wienefeld. Since 1954 the editing and publication have been financed by legislative appropriation through the South Carolina Archives Department. That Department and the State Budget and Control Board deserve the thanks of all students of the period of Calhoun's life for their recognition of the significance of his papers and the opportunity presented for their publication.

Directors or custodians of libraries, archives and manuscript divisions, and their assistants, whose time at best is rarely adequate for their regular work, have cordially and generously aided in the search of their collections and in answering inquiries. In the list of collections of Calhoun correspondence one finds the Library of Congress next in importance after the National Archives and the Clemson College Library. The Library of Congress newspapers and pamphlets have also been essential sources of information. Dr. Luther H. Evans, former Librarian of Congress, and Mr. David C. Mearns, Chief of the Manuscript Division, and his staff, have been most kind and helpful. The Manuscript Division of the South Caroliniana Library of the University of South Carolina has been a major source through its collection of Calhoun Family Papers, which includes, in addition to Calhoun's own letters, several thousand letters of other members of the family, especially Senator John Ewing Colhoun and his son James Edward, Calhoun's most trusted advisor.

By notes in each volume the editor will acknowledge the kindness of custodians and collectors through whom the papers printed in that volume have been procured. But for the work as a whole he wishes here to express his grateful appreciation to persons in seven institutions, not yet listed in this preface, who have cordially aided in this enterprise: Miss Mattie Russell, Curator, and others of the staff of the Manuscript Division of Duke University Library; Mr. James W. Patton, Director, the Southern Historical Collection, University of North Carolina; Mr. Stephen T. Riley, Librarian of the Massachusetts Historical Society; Mr. R. N. Williams, 2nd, Director of the Historical Society of Pennsylvania; Mr. Robert W. Hill, Keeper of Manuscripts, New York Public Library; Lieutenant Colonel W. J. Morton, Librarian, United States Military Academy; and Mr. James T. Babb, Librarian, Mr. Robert F. Metzdorf, Curator of Manuscripts, and Miss Dorothy W. Bridgewater of the Library staff, and Professor Archibald S. Foord, Master of Calhoun College, Yale University.

Dr. Julian P. Boyd, by his masterly editing of the Jefferson Papers, has placed all persons engaged in similar work directly in his debt. Thanks for personal kindnesses are also tendered to him, and to Messrs. Lyman H. Butterfield, Leonard W. Labaree, and Ralph Ketcham of the editorial staffs of the Adams, Franklin, and Madison Papers. For their unfailing patience and skill in the work on the Calhoun Papers the editor owes a special debt of gratitude to his colleagues, Mrs. Clara M. Jacobs and Mr. E. L. Inabinett. In a real sense other departmental assistants of the South Caroliniana Library have been members of the editorial staff, for the service of that Library has been unique and indispensable. It is a privilege to work with them and to thank them—Mrs. Cornelia H. Hensley, Mrs. Margaret B. Meriwether, Mr. Harvey S. Teal, and their aides. Acknowledgments are also due to those who have shared the burden of copying, filing, and indexing the papers—Mrs. Elena I. Zimmerman, Mrs. Margaret S. Lancaster, Mrs. Jane B. Darby, Mrs. Nancy C. Meriwether, and Misses Mary Bloodworth and Naomi Williams. It is a special pleasure to acknowledge the practical assistance of Mr. Charles E. Lee, formerly of the University of South Carolina Press (now of Lee and Fawcett), on all problems of style and publication. And finally my particular appreciation for her inspired proofreading goes to Miss Margaret W. Meriwether.

For their assistance in finding Calhoun papers and procuring photocopies of them, the following friends are listed in sincere appreciation: Mrs. Mary Simms Oliphant, Miss Mary Noble, Mrs. Lila S. Holmes, Mrs. Josephine L. Hughes, Miss Louise B. Fant and Mr. H. B. Fant, and Messrs. Francis B. Simkins, George C. Taylor, and David Kohn. To the valuable collection of the late Dr. Henry Simms Hartzog, of St. Louis, we are indebted for the earliest letter of Calhoun yet found.

The Advisory Committee has furnished its full share of assistance; thanks to some of its members have already been recorded, but the editor wishes to note particularly his gratitude to Mr. Charles M. Wiltse, whose advice and help have been generously given, and whose three-volume *John C. Calhoun, Nationalist, Nullifier, Sectionalist* is an invaluable work of reference, and to Miss Margaret

L. Coit for her interest and for the aid rendered by her *John C. Calhoun, American Portrait.*

The Publication Committee of the Papers of John C. Calhoun deserves a special note of appreciation, for it was this group which met with Dr. Hamer in March 1952, adopted a resolution endorsing publication, and asked me to serve as editor. The contributions to scholarship by the members of this committee and their public service made it an honor to be associated with them in this enterprise, and their personal interest and help have been unfailing. Dr. J. H. Easterby, Director of the South Carolina Archives Department, as Secretary of the Publication Committee and its appointed representative on questions of editorial procedure, has been the editor's chief reliance in these matters and in the general problems of the work. He shares with Dr. Hamer highest credit for the initiation and success of the enterprise.

The Calhoun Papers as at present projected should run to fifteen volumes. As they are published, the South Caroliniana Library, with the co-operation of the owners of the original papers, will file the reproductions of papers, whether printed, summarized, or merely calendared, in its John C. Calhoun Collection, and these photocopies will be available to scholars through library loans. To facilitate its use each volume will be separately indexed and will have a brief introductory essay on its contents and on their significance in Calhoun's career.

INTRODUCTION

〖〗

This volume, which covers the years of Calhoun's preparation for public life and the decade of his service in the lower houses of the state and federal legislatures, makes a unit of extraordinary compactness and interest.

The papers prior to Calhoun's entry into Congress—a period appropriately climaxed by the compromise on representation in the South Carolina legislature—call for a special note or sketch, for they bear plainly the marks of the recent history of his family and of his state. The South Carolina back country society into which Patrick Calhoun's third son was born March 18, 1782, had been a scant forty years in its new home, but its dominant element during those decades was a substantial group of farmers—Scotch-Irish, German, British Colonial—who had already demonstrated the essential conservatism of the yeoman in Europe and of the independent small landowner everywhere. Their value for defense against the Indians and their moderation in the Regulator troubles of the 1760's recommended them early to the compactly organized group of planters, merchants, and professional men in the tidewater area; and before the Revolution the concession of courts and of representation, inadequate as it was, foreshadowed an eventual peace between these two divergent sections.[1] In 1769 Patrick Calhoun's neighbors made the one-hundred-and-fifty-mile journey to Prince William's Church to cast the votes which elected him to the Commons House, contending that the parish had no northwest boundary and therefore included their lands. His ready acceptance by the legislature, almost completely monopolized as it was by the tidewater, was a prophecy of the role his son was later to play in the political life of the coast country.[2]

1. Wallace, *History of S.C.*, II; Meriwether, *Expansion of S.C.*, p. 242.
2. Journal of the Commons House of Assembly, Dec. 5, 1769 (S.C. Archives Department). Compare the proceedings on the claim of the Ninety-Six settlers,

The recovery of the back country after the anarchy and destruction of the Revolution was a remarkable tribute to the stock which had settled it, but the promise of the tidewater in the Constitution of 1778 that, beginning seven years from that date, representation in the House should be based equally on white population and taxable property was not carried out.[3] The ratification of the Federal Constitution strengthened the conservatives, and for nearly a decade the Federalists governed the state with a firm hand. The piedmont had to wait for its younger generation to grow up before it could supply political leaders who could match wits with those of the older section, and Patrick Calhoun himself accepted the leadership of the coast country in the ratification of the Constitution.[4] Ninety-Six District even elected the Federalist Robert Goodloe Harper three times to Congress.[5]

Meanwhile, other members of the Calhoun connection were developing low-country interests. John Ewing Colhoun, son of Patrick's brother Ezekiel, studied law in Charleston, established himself there, and married Floride Bonneau, the daughter of a wealthy Cooper River planter. Ezekiel Pickens, John Ewing Colhoun's nephew and son of General Andrew Pickens, married a sister of Floride Bonneau, and the brothers-in-law both held up-country property in Pendleton District as well as in the tidewater. Before 1800 sons of Alexander Noble, another nephew of Patrick Calhoun, had established similar ties. John Ewing Colhoun, who was highly esteemed by his young cousin John C., after being elected United States Senator in 1800 as a Republican, broke with his party on the Judiciary bill and voted with the Federalists.[6]

who lived just east of the Calhoun community, to vote in St. Paul's Parish (*ibid.,* June 27, July 4, 20, 21, 1769). Note Patrick's committee assignments—*ibid.,* Dec. 5, 1769; Feb. 15, 16, 20, 1770.

3. Easterby, *Basic Documents of S.C., the Constitution of 1778.*

4. Note his vote, which was contrary to that of four of the six representatives from Ninety-Six, and his remark on the Constitution—*Debates . . . in the House of Representatives of S.C., on the Constitution,* p. 52, 59. Neither he nor the representative voting with him was elected to the Convention (*ibid.,* p. 83). Compare the statement about his supposed opposition to the Constitution in the 1843 *Life,* p. 4.

5. "Robert Goodloe Harper," *DAB* and *BDC.*

6. See below, Nos. 3 NOTE, and 7 NOTE, No. 22, n. 2, and No. 43; and for variant spellings of the name, No. 6 NOTE, No. 23, n. 2, and No. 26, n. 1.

Thus, when John C. Calhoun entered Yale's junior class in October 1802, following his preparation by that brilliantly successful preceptor Reverend Moses Waddel, his Republican principles were evidently strongly influenced by the doctrines—but not the policies—of the moderate Federalists. His three years of high achievement and enjoyment at Yale and the Litchfield Law School established lifelong attachments for him and gave him devoted friends. Essentially conservative himself, it was easy for him to sympathize with the New England conservatives.

Back in South Carolina, with the prestige and the practice he had acquired by his years in Connecticut and with his influential connections, he speedily gained recognition. Before he was admitted to the bar he distinguished himself by his speech and resolutions on the Chesapeake-Leopard Affair, and the next year, in the fall of 1808, he was elected to the South Carolina House of Representatives. There was no better school of politics. The House for more than a century had had an unbroken tradition of an educated and substantial membership, of careful, effective legislative procedure, and of masterful management of public affairs. Although the record of Calhoun's service in the South Carolina legislature is scanty, the assurance and skill which he later displayed in Congress showed how well he had profited by his experience.

The two sessions of the legislature in which he served were of profound significance and for no one more than Calhoun himself. At the first, it ratified the amendment to the state Constitution which, by basing representation equally on white population and taxable property, at last carried out the promise of 1778. The amendment gave the up country control of the House, the tidewater retaining the Senate, and later provided what was perhaps the best example for his doctrine of the concurrent majority. This compromise was made easier for the conservatives by the economic process which was rapidly extending the plantation regime through the state, but in part it was due to their own good political sense. It was followed the next year by another concession to democracy when the amendment for white manhood suffrage was initiated.[7]

Calhoun's entry into public life coincided with important developments in his personal fortunes. While he was at Litchfield, he

7. Cooper, *Statutes of S.C.*, I, 193-5; see also No. 26 NOTE.

had seen much of his cousin Floride, the widow of John Ewing Colhoun, and her family. In the summer of 1806 he still spoke of the fourteen-year-old daughter Floride as one of "the children." Apparently he did not see her again until the spring of 1808, when she was sixteen, and no other meeting seems to have been necessary for either. A year later, with his own success in his profession assured and Mrs. Colhoun's consent granted, the engagement became a fact, although they were not married until January 1811.[8] His feeling for his kin and friends continued as before, always warm and unaffected, but now centered in his own family.

Calhoun was elected to Congress in October 1810 from the Congressional district composed of Abbeville, Laurens, and Newberry Districts.[9] His early speeches in Congress show that he entered that body with a fairly well-rounded set of principles and policies, founded on a study of the Constitution, the ratification arguments, and the recent history of the United States. On constitutional questions he might have been described as a Madisonian Federalist. Earnestly believing in a balance of powers between the state and Federal governments and impressed with the dangers besetting the latter, he was intent on strengthening it and broadening the scope of its operations.[10] His first speech on the floor was based on the theory of divided sovereignty and separation of powers, and was in full accord with the *Federalist* essays. But his reference in that speech to the Senate as "a diplomatic corps . . . sent here to protect the state rights, and to preserve the federative principle," [11] and his silence later in the face of New England's threats of disunion, further indicate his idea of the limitations on the authority of the Federal government.

From the standpoint of politics, he was an independent Republican. He was well inclined to the administration and usually gave it and his party loyal support, but his independence showed itself

8. See Nos. 28 NOTE and 40 NOTE.

9. Charleston *City Gazette*, Oct. 22, 1810; the election days were the 8th and 9th; Cooper, *Statutes of S.C.*, V, 430. His congressional district was changed Aug. 29, 1812, to consist of Abbeville and Edgefield (*ibid.*, p. 665).

10. Note, for instance, his remark in 1812 that the union "is too weak to withstand political convulsions" (below, p. 145).

11. See No. 47 NOTE.

in occasional proposed concessions to his political opponents and in his opposition to the Republican embargoes because "the restrictive system does not suit the genius of our people." [12] But, above all, as he entered Congress, he was bent, as was the case with his fellow young Republicans, on a program of vigorous nationalism and a redemption of the country from the abuses of its rights as a neutral. An invincible determination to make his principles and policies square with fundamental right early earned him the name of metaphysician and theorist, but his practical sense extended to his politics: as one of his New England colleagues remarked in 1817, "the nation knew him to be on all important subjects the practical politician." [13]

It was Calhoun's speech of December 12, 1811, in defense of the Foreign Relations Committee's report recommending arming the United States in preparation for the war, that brought him to the front in Congress. For the moment, it was not Eastern commercial opposition which he was encountering, but John Randolph's hatred of war and strong government and devotion to the English inheritance. It was ominous that during the next six months only a fraction of the program of preparation was achieved, but the obstinate refusal of the British government to make any concession kept the administration schedule intact. It fell to the Foreign Relations Committee on April 1 to recommend a sixty-day embargo to get American vessels home, and Calhoun's defense of this measure, and the departure of Porter, the chairman of the committee, devolved on him the responsibility of the report on June 3 recommending war. In his statement of the American grievances—the violation of neutral rights by the Orders in Council and by impressment—he charged that Great Britain was really using the war with France as a means to crush American trade, and insisted that war would constitute a second declaration of independence. All these arguments had been anticipated by previous utterances of the President

12. See for instance p. 63 and 84. The quotation is on p. 131. The "restrictive system" was the name by which the complicated succession of embargoes and non-importation laws came to be known. Compare his position on the Merchants' Bonds question—No. 71.

13. *AC*13-2, p. 1620; see No. 148 NOTE.

or of the Foreign Relations Committee, but they were now more skillfully and more eloquently presented.[14]

The war on land and sea was prosecuted in an intermittent, often desultory fashion, but the contest in Congress was incessant and at times bitter. How colossal was the gamble by the young Republicans and the uneasy Madison in bringing the tragically divided country into the war was speedily made apparent by the disasters of 1812 and 1813, which were relieved only by the victories of Perry on Lake Erie and Harrison at the Thames in September and October of the latter year. But the undismayed leaders of the war party in Congress continued to devise and push through measures to raise the money and troops which might make it possible for the administration to prosecute the war to a successful finish. In January 1813 Calhoun gave his earnest support to the bill to raise 20,000 troops—which was, incidentally, the approximate number then in service—but Congress, still fearful of taxes, merely authorized new loans and issues of treasury notes. Calhoun himself and his Charleston colleague, Langdon Cheves—also a native of Abbeville District—had, six days after the declaration of war, essayed a bold move which offered hope of providing a revenue with the least opposition from a population fundamentally hostile to taxation and which promised partial appeasement of the Eastern merchants. Their proposal to repeal the embargo and non-importation acts—so hated by the merchants—and to impose high duties on imports was nearly adopted.[15] Again and again during the next two years Calhoun voiced his opposition to government embargoes on trade, but what favor he might have won in the eyes of the commercial group by his fruitless efforts to break the agricultural Republicans of their boycott habit was lost in the mounting storm of anger over the issues of the war.

When the bill for raising 20,000 soldiers was introduced, the opposition turned the debate into an argument over the whole issue of the war. Napoleonic double-dealing and French depredations on American commerce had given the Federalists ample ammunition for their insistence that Great Britain was to be preferred over her

14. See No. 66 NOTE.
15. See Nos. 69 and 77; see also Adams, *History of U.S.*, VI, 448; VII, 380.

enemy and that the Berlin and Milan decrees had never in fact or intention been repealed. Calhoun refused to be drawn into comparisons of French and British abuses of neutral rights—the favorite Federalist attack. "Were we bound to submit to England because France refused to do us justice? Had we no power of election between the ruffians?" The Orders in Council had been repealed in June 1812, leaving impressment as the one practically unassailable argument of the war party. Calhoun even more than his fellows relentlessly pressed this issue until the Federalist members were infuriated by the exposure of their indifference to the involuntary servitude of the impressed seamen—an indifference which merely reflected the English attitude toward recruiting methods and forced service in the British Navy.[16]

In turn the opposition pressed charges calculated to destroy what prestige remained to the administration, and in June 1813, Daniel Webster organized the attack. As chairman of the Foreign Relations Committee, Calhoun undertook the defense, and his blunt and forceful counter-thrusts involved him in hot personal quarrels. Despite the record of military defeat and recruiting failure, he now demonstrated what became a nearly lifelong habit—a bold optimism based rather on the need than the facts of the case.[17]

The climax came at the beginning of 1814, when the news of Napoleon's defeat at Leipzig gave notice that England was free for a major attack on the United States. Webster's demand that the administration withdraw American forces from the Canadian border and resort to purely defensive war was coupled with his defense of the tactics of the opposition. Obviously uncertain how to deal with this determined and dangerous minority, Calhoun undertook to distinguish between a factious opposition and one that was "fair and moderate." He described the former as the greatest peril of the republic but could think of no other remedy than "the good sense and virtue of the people." [18] It was, however, in the course of the war of words which raged about the bill for a loan of $25,000,000 that Calhoun made perhaps his most intense effort

16. See Nos. 75 and 95 and No. 95, n. 7.
17. See No. 81, No. 97 NOTE, No. 100, and compare No. 75 NOTE.
18. No. 90.

to weaken the opposition and to sustain the shaky war party. The bill finally passed after two months of debate, but the year 1814 was a long-drawn-out crisis, the climax of which was the British capture of Washington in August. In the autumn of that year the collapse of the government credit forced consideration of additional taxes and some form of compulsory military service, while threats of disunion became more ominous, culminating in the Hartford Convention of December.[19]

The immediate problem was the breakdown of the government's finances. During the debates on the Loan Bill, Calhoun had introduced a resolution for an inquiry into the expediency of establishing a national bank, and from November 1814 to January 1815 the fight in Congress was waged over the plan of the Secretary of the Treasury, Alexander J. Dallas, for a bank to the capital of which the government would subscribe twenty millions and from which it would borrow thirty millions. Calhoun led in the denunciation of this plan by which the government would borrow and pay interest on its own money; he insisted that the capital of the proposed bank be made up of specie and a new issue of Treasury notes, the notes of the bank to be receivable for taxes and dues to the government, but the government to have neither stock in nor control over the bank.[20] This scheme failed of passage and was rendered out of date by the news, in February 1815, of the treaty of peace; and Calhoun shifted his attention from the problem of war finances of a bankrupt government to those of a thoroughly disordered peace-time currency.

The bank question now went over to December 1815, when Calhoun, as the result of his activity the previous session, was made Chairman of the Committee on a Uniform Currency. The finances of the government were the most critical problem facing Congress, and the bank question the most difficult on which to get votes from either Republican majority or Federalist minority. Calhoun's prestige, however, was at its height. He had the support of most of the Republicans and, because of his independence during the war and his opposition to trade restrictions, had the respect of many of the

19. Nos. 95 and 100; see also No. 102, and Adams, *History of U.S.*, VIII, 287-310.
20. Nos. 92 and 104-6.

Federalists. Dallas now proposed a bank, designed on the lines of that of 1791; it was to have, however, a capital of $35,000,000, the government subscribing a fifth, but with the difference that the United States would appoint five directors, instead of none as had been the case with Hamilton's bank. On March 13, 1816, Calhoun had the satisfaction of getting the bill through the House and on April 10 it became law.[21]

Calhoun's support of the bank was for the purpose of restoring American finances and perhaps, incidentally, to strengthen the United States government. His support of a tariff which would keep the existing factories in operation was a transition to a broader program which was evidently taking shape in his mind when, on the last day of January 1816, he pleaded for an ample revenue for the government to enable it to protect the nation, provide for its development, and thus put the United States in position to fulfill its mission. The speech drew compliments from friend and foe, but perhaps the most significant was the praise of John Randolph, who, with a gentleness as effective as his usual vitriolic brilliance, reasoned with the young Southerner, and urged him to adopt "the first principles of political wisdom . . . those which respected the sovereignty of the States." [22]

The election of 1816, which retired over half the total membership of Congress, strengthened Calhoun's position in that body and in his state. The universal charge against the luckless senators and representatives in the campaign of that year was their enactment of the Compensation Law which increased the pay of members, but obviously the Congressmen were also victims of the usual reaction against war-time representative bodies. Calhoun was advised to apologize to his electorate. Instead he stood on his record, repeated the arguments he had given for the bill in Congress, and was triumphantly re-elected.[23]

It was not until December 1816 that Calhoun found himself in position to put forward his long-projected plan for beginning a nation-wide system of roads and canals—a program which, for the economic and political future of the United States, had possibilities

21. No. 120.
22. *AC*14-1, p. 844; No. 123 and NOTE.
23. No. 127, No. 134, n. 1, and No. 147.

comparable to those involved in the new tariff. He was clear enough that the future of the nation and the continuance of the union depended on transportation and communication, but on the constitutional question he had to appeal to the doctrine of implied powers. He perhaps felt that the states were amply protected by the fact that the system would certainly be a partnership between the states and central government, and evidently he anticipated no serious danger in the program.[24] The vote in the House on this bill, which closely paralleled that on the tariff, must have offered high promise to the ambitious young Congressman for his own future as for that of his country. New England voted against it, the South and West were nearly evenly divided, but New York and Pennsylvania—the powerful states to which he might look for future support—were overwhelmingly in favor of it.

Madison's veto was therefore a momentous event in the life of Calhoun as well as in that of the nation. When Calhoun came next into the field of political issues, the Erie Canal was nearly complete and New York was shifting to opposition to Federal aid to roads, while the tariff was in process of replacing improvement of transportation in the affection of Pennsylvania politicians.

On October 10, 1817, President Monroe offered Calhoun the post of Secretary of War. On December 2 he arrived in Washington with his wife and two children, and on the 8th entered on the duties of that office.[25]

24. Nos. 139, 142, and 151.
25. Wiltse, *Calhoun, Nationalist*, p. 139-42.

EDITORIAL PROCEDURE

⫼

The papers here presented follow the originals—when they are available in that form—with a minimum of changes for the purposes of print, and with no attempt to revise spelling or grammar. To correct the errors made by Calhoun's careless hand and erratic attempts at phonetic spelling would put him in a dress not his own. But, however simple this formula, the application of it has at times entailed arbitrary decisions as to the meaning of obscure or incomplete strokes of the pen, and it is too much to hope that these interpretations have always been accurate or even consistent.

Superscript letters have been brought down to the line, and any punctuation which is part of a word so abbreviated is represented by a period. Dashes and those ink marks defying analysis which were apparently intended to end sentences have been translated into periods, and when two punctuation marks appear together one has been chosen. Calhoun often rendered combinations of the letters *e, i, u, m,* and *n* by a single curving stroke of the pen; these have been spelled out. In the headings of letters the name and place, if given, are as in the original except that "Mr." and "Esq." have been omitted, and, in the interests of clarity, other titles and state names given modern abbreviations. If any part of the name or address is supplied from other sources than the immediate paper or its cover, it will be found in brackets. Endorsements and cover information which appear to be of any consequence have been relegated to footnotes, but postmarks, repetitions of address, and such bits as "By Mail" are ordinarily ignored. Salutations and other introductions to letters and papers have been printed in italics and, like letter closings, have been run in continuous lines, while signatures have been put in capitals, but, unless otherwise noted, no other liberties have been taken with them.

xxxiii

Words or letters which are illegible or lost by tears and similar mischances, but which are evident from the context, and cancellations which appear to be of any significance, are supplied in brackets in roman print. Letters or words omitted by the writer, for lack of which the sentence becomes difficult to read, interpretations of indecipherable passages and of misspellings which are incredible even for Calhoun, editorial comment, and summaries of omitted matter, are in brackets in italics. Breaks which cannot be filled are indicated by [. . .] or [. . . .] if only a few words are involved; longer gaps are similarly indicated with appended note of explanation. Editorial omissions not summarized or explained are indicated by periods without the enclosing brackets.

Papers printed from copies, except for Calhoun's speeches in Congress, the procedure for which is described below, are similarly treated, but annotated, when necessary, to indicate any previous editing. Those papers which are not printed herein but which are an integral part of the record of Calhoun's career are summarized in the Calendar. A few records, such as the slighter comments in the course of debates in the House and private claims introduced by him which at once passed out of his hands, have been ignored.

Identification of persons and things in the text has been undertaken for understanding of important points in the papers, but no attempt has been made to identify those of only casual or peripheral interest. Notes are supplied for individual papers, when they seem needed, to explain the occasion or to identify significant references. The Introduction to this volume assesses the importance, individually or in groups, of its letters and speeches in Calhoun's career. The notes carry only simplified citations to titles used, since they appear in full in the bibliography or in the list of abbreviations which precedes the text. Manuscript and newspaper sources are cited in full in the notes except for those whose abbreviations or location symbols are listed. References have been made in the notes to some of the contemporary reprints of Calhoun's papers, but there has been no attempt to make this list complete.

With the exception of his War and State Department papers, most of the surviving Calhoun correspondence is in the hand of, and signed by, the writer. Unless otherwise indicated, his papers here printed or noted are from photocopies of these originals.

Calhoun's Congressional reports and other documents are treated like the letters when the originals are available, and appear in the form in which they were introduced in the House. Annotations show the significant changes made in them in their legislative progress. When the original is not to be found, the version nearest to it has been used. The sources for nearly all of his speeches in the House, from 1811 to 1817, are the tri-weekly *National Intelligencer* and, beginning with Jan. 1, 1813, the *Daily National Intelligencer*. Citations are to the tri-weekly, which had a nation-wide circulation and is to be found in a large number of libraries. The speeches were printed in both papers, as a rule no more than a day or two apart, and without resetting the type. Calhoun's habit of intense concentration and systematic organization of his opinions and information, and his direct and forceful speech, served admirably the purposes of the *Intelligencer* reporters.[1] In consequence, the reports of his speeches, whether fragments of debate or long addresses on major issues, bear the stamp of his style, despite evidence of the reporter's usual condensation. A few of the longer papers have, in the *Intelligencer*, the caption title: "Speech of Mr. Calhoun," while several others have the heading: "The Substance of Mr. Calhoun's Speech,"[2] but the content and style of these and of his other speeches do not indicate any real line of division. That Calhoun examined or even revised the reporter's abstracts of some of his more important papers, as indicated by the editors, seems certain, but that others were "prepared for the press" by him in any other form suggests an attention to literary composition and to making records out of keeping with his bent of mind.[3]

1. See No. 36, n. 2.
2. Nos. 69, 95, and 123 are printed under the former caption, Nos. 90, 129, and 152 under the latter.
3. In 1843, when the campaign volume, *Speeches of John C. Calhoun. Delivered in the Congress of the United States from 1811 to the Present Time,* was published, it was found to contain none from his House service except that of December 1811 in defense of the war program. The *Intelligencer*, which had meanwhile become Whig and Calhoun's political foe, denounced him for suppression of his early nationalistic speeches on such subjects as the bank and the tariff. It proceeded to publish four of them—all, with slight and inconsiderable variations, accurate copies of the early versions. In reprinting No. 123 the editor declared that "The report of this Speech . . . was prepared for the press by Mr. Calhoun himself," while No. 129 he noted as "revised for the

The details of printing of these speeches depended upon the practices of the newspaper press rather than the vagaries of Calhoun's writing. Therefore, without footnote annotation, minor typographical errors have been corrected, some of the longer paragraphs broken, capitalization and abbreviation made more uniform, and, when needed for clarity, punctuation revised.[4] Gales and Seaton, printers of the *Intelligencer*, later compiled the debates and speeches in their *Annals of Congress*, the volumes for 1811 to 1817 being published in 1853 and 1854. With relatively rare lapses these are faithful copies of the *Intelligencer* and even of the rival *Federal Republican*.[5] The source notes therefore carry parallel citations to the *Intelligencer* and the *Annals*. The latter volumes also make convenient references for incidental remarks by or about Calhoun which, in the *Intelligencer*, often lie buried in solid pages of fine print. To simplify the notes and Calendar, these comments, quoted or cited there, have been referred to the *Annals* alone.

A word should be added in regard to the sixteen speeches of Calhoun from the years 1811-1817 printed by Richard J. Crallé in Volume II of his *Works of John C. Calhoun*. In the preface to the volume Crallé says that "for the comparatively few which have been preserved, the public is chiefly indebted to the Hon. Mr. Simkins, at that time a member of the House from South Carolina, who, for his own gratification, took notes and drew out the sketches (for they are by no means full reports) which appear in this collection." For the use of these Crallé thanked Francis W. Pickens.[6] "Others, belonging to the same period, have been copied from manuscripts

press by the orator himself" (*DNI*, July 12, 15, 1843). See Wiltse, *Calhoun, Sectionalist*, p. 140.

4. The record of proceedings in the *Annals* has also been checked by the *House Journal* for corrections and for occasional omissions of significant matter.

5. In compiling the *Annals*, Gales and Seaton occasionally used the opposition paper, the *Federal Republican*, to fill out gaps in the *Intelligencer*—for instance, see No. 80. For a study of the general subject, see Elizabeth G. McPherson, "History of Reporting the Debates and Resolutions of Congress," MS, 1940, University of North Carolina Library. For a brief account in print for this period see Samuel Oppenheim, *Early Congressional Debates and Reporters* (1889).

6. Pickens had studied law under Eldred Simkins and married his daughter (*BDC, DAB*).

found among the papers of Mr. Calhoun, though not in his handwriting."

In fact, the speeches of Calhoun for his House years which appear in Crallé's compilation, by their punctuation, typographical errors and other peculiarities, show that they all came, directly or by way of carefully made copies, from the *Intelligencer*, revised, however, to smooth out irregularities, real or fancied, in the original version, and occasionally to substitute words which seemed to be more in accord with Calhoun's later views.[7] Moreover, Simkins was never Calhoun's colleague in the House but was first elected as his successor. Two speeches are still to be found in manuscript in the Clemson Collection,[8] obviously copied from the *Intelligencer*. One of them appears to be in the hand of Virgil Maxcy,[9] who "compiled" the 1843 campaign volume: *Speeches of John C. Calhoun . . . from 1811 to the Present Time.*

It is even possible that all of the early speeches came to Crallé in the form of already revised copies of the *Intelligencer*, but that there was no one to tell him their sources, for Simkins died in 1832 and Maxcy was killed in the *Princeton* gun explosion in February

7. See Nos. 48 NOTE, 64 NOTE, and 95 NOTE for detailed comparison of the *Intelligencer* and *Works* versions of the speeches.

8. Nos. 113-14 and No. 124.

9. These copies may date from the preparation of Maxcy's 1831 "Biographical Memoir" of Calhoun, in which both of the speeches are discussed, one at considerable length. The copy of Grosvenor's 1817 tribute to Calhoun (see No. 147 NOTE) which Maxcy used for the Memoir has been preserved (Galloway-Maxcy-Markoe Papers, *LC*). It is similar in general appearance to the Clemson manuscripts, and is taken directly from the *Intelligencer*. The only one of Calhoun's House speeches which Maxcy included in the 1843 volume is also an obvious copy of the *Intelligencer* (see No. 48 NOTE), but with "improvements"; Crallé's version contains some, but not all, of Maxcy's emendations. Of the eight Calhoun speeches of which Maxcy seems to have had copies in 1831, seven are included in *Works*, II.

After the *Intelligencer* reprinted four of his speeches (see n. 3 above) Calhoun stated: "I was so careless as to neglect to preserve copies of my speeches or other publications prior to my election as vice president." (*DNI*, Aug. 5, 1843). Shortly before his death, he told his son "that he had retained a copy of each document he wished preserved at Fort Hill among his papers" (Andrew Pickens Calhoun to Crallé, *CC*, May 20, 1850), but these may have been the unpublished manuscripts referred to by Crallé in the preface to *Works*, VI. See Wiltse, *Calhoun, Sectionalist*, p. 111 and 140-1 on the publication of the 1843 volume.

1844. As a matter of fact, during the year 1853, when Crallé wrote his statement, Gales and Seaton, publishers of the *Intelligencer* and of the *Annals*, brought the latter work to the year 1813, and it would have required but little investigation for him to learn the sources of his copies of Calhoun's early speeches.[10]

10. Crallé was in correspondence with Gales in 1854 in regard to the authorship of the 1812 report recommending war, and was furnished with "sheets" of the *Annals* at that time (*AHR*, XIII [1907-8], 306-7).

ABBREVIATED TITLES AND LOCATION SYMBOLS

〚〛

AC [*Annals of Congress*] *Debates and Proceedings in the Congress of the United States*, 1789-1824, 42 vols., Washington, 1834-1856. Note: The first number following AC is that of the Congress, the second that of the session; the "p." references are to the numbered columns: *e. g.*, AC12-1, p. 373, refers to column 373 of the *Annals* for the First Session of the Twelfth Congress.

AHAAR *Annual Report of the American Historical Association*, Washington, 1890——

AHR *American Historical Review*, New York, 1895——

ASP *American State Papers. Documents, Legislative and Executive, of the Congress of the United States.* 38 vols., Washington, 1832-1861

BDC *Biographical Directory of the American Congress, 1774-1949*, Washington, 1950

"Biographical Memoir" "Biographical Memoir of John Caldwell Calhoun" [by Virgil Maxcy—see Wiltse, *Calhoun, Sectionalist*, p. 500], (*U.S. Telegraph*, Apr. 25, 26, 1831)

Charleston *City Gazette* *City Gazette and Commercial Advertiser*

CC John C. Calhoun Papers, Clemson College

DAB *Dictionary of American Biography*, 20 vols., New York, 1928-1936

DNI *Daily National Intelligencer*, [Washington]

House Journal *Journal of the House of Representatives of the United States* . . . . Vols. VIII and IX [12th and 13th Congresses], reprint, Washington, 1826; *Journal of the House* . . . . Fourteenth Congress [1st Session], Washington, 1815; [2nd Session], Washington, 1816

LC   Library of Congress, Manuscript Division

Life   *Life of John C. Calhoun, Presenting a Condensed History of Political Events from 1811-1843*, New York, 1843

NA   National Archives

NI   *National Intelligencer* [tri-weekly], [Washington], 1811-1817

SCHM   *South Carolina Historical and Genealogical Magazine*, I-LII, 1900-1951; and *South Carolina Historical Magazine*, LIII——, 1952——

SCL   South Caroliniana Library, University of South Carolina (if unaccompanied by other reference the citation is to the John C. Calhoun Papers)

Speeches   *Speeches of John C. Calhoun. Delivered in the Congress of the United States from 1811 to the Present Time*, New York, 1843

Wills(T)   Transcripts of South Carolina Wills, South Carolina Archives Department

Works   Richard K. Crallé, ed., *The Works of John C. Calhoun*, 6 vols., New York, 1851-1857

CHRONOLOGY, 1782-1817

1782 March 18. Birth of John Caldwell Calhoun
1795 Winter. At Moses Waddel's academy
1796 January 15. Death of father, Patrick Calhoun
1796 to 1800. At home in Ninety-Six District
1800 July 1. Enters Waddel's academy to prepare for college
1801 May 15. Death of mother, Martha Caldwell Calhoun
1802 October. Enters Yale
1804 September 12. Graduates from Yale
1804 November. Returns to South Carolina
1804 December 24. Enters law office of DeSaussure & Ford in Charleston
1805 July 22. Enters Litchfield Law School
1806 July 29. Receives diploma
1806 Fall. Returns to South Carolina and office of DeSaussure & Ford
1807 June to December. Completes legal training under George Bowie in Abbeville
1807 August 3. Drafts resolutions for Abbeville meeting on Chesapeake Affair
1807 December. Admitted to South Carolina bar; opens office in Abbeville
1808 October. Elected to South Carolina House of Representatives
1810 October. Elected to United States House of Representatives
1811 January 8. Marries Floride Colhoun
1811 October 15. Birth of son, Andrew Pickens Calhoun
1811 November 4. Twelfth Congress (first session) opens
1811 November 6. Takes seat in House
1811 November 12. Appointed second on Foreign Relations Committee
1812 April. Becomes Chairman of Foreign Relations Committee
1812 June 18. War with Great Britain declared

1812 July 6. Congress adjourns
1812 July to October. In South Carolina. Re-elected without opposition
1812 November 2. Twelfth Congress (second session) opens
1813 March 3. Congress adjourns
1813 March to May. In South Carolina
1813 May 24 to August 2. Thirteenth Congress (special session)
1813 August to November. In South Carolina
1813 December 6. Thirteenth Congress (second session) opens
1814 January 24. Birth of daughter, Floride Calhoun
1814 April 18. Congress adjourns
1814 May to October. In South Carolina
1814 August 24. British capture of Washington
1814 September 19. Thirteenth Congress (special session) opens; Calhoun late, due to sickness
1814 October. Re-elected.
1814 October 19. Takes seat in House
1814 December 15. Hartford Convention meets
1814 December 24. Treaty of Ghent signed
1815 January 8. Battle of New Orleans
1815 February 13. News of peace received in Washington
1815 March 3. Congress adjourns
1815 March to November. In South Carolina
1815 April 7. Death of daughter, Floride Calhoun
1815 December 4. Fourteenth Congress (first session) opens
1815 December 6. Becomes Chairman of Committee on a Uniform National Currency
1816 January. Birth of daughter, Jane Calhoun, who died within a year
1816 April 30. Congress adjourns
1816 May to November. In South Carolina
1816 October. Re-elected; two-thirds of House defeated
1816 December 2. Fourteenth Congress (second session) opens
1817 February 13. Birth of daughter, Anna Maria Calhoun
1817 March 3. Madison vetoes Bonus Bill; Congress adjourns
1817 March to November. In South Carolina
1817 November 1. Accepts Monroe's offer of War Department
1817 December 8. Takes oath as Secretary of War

THE PAPERS

of

JOHN C. CALHOUN

Volume I

J. C. Calhoun

1801-1817

1. To ANDREW PICKENS [JR.], Providence College, R.I.

Southampton [S.C] 6th Sept 1801.

Dr Andrew, Induced by my own inclination, and by the advice of some of my friends, I commenced the study of Lattin the 1st July 1800 at Columbia in Georgia under the Revd M. Waddel.[1] I continued to prosecute my studies at that place till March following; at which time Mr Waddel removed to this place and began to keep school here the 1st April. I am now advance[d] in the Greek as far as the Acts of the Apostles. I am now at a loss in what manner to proceed. As I am now ready to commence the study of the sciences and know not which it will be proper to study first. Therefore, if you will be so oblidging, as to transmit to me in writing, which college is in the highest repute northerly, or which in your estimation is the best, I will receive it as a particular favour. And, also, what it will be proper to study to prepare for the junior class of that college, which you shall think best. From the best information, I can acquire here, I have reason to think, that Yale college is an institution, at which an excellent education may be had. Please to let me know your opinion concerning it. Dr Andrew, forward your sentiments as soon as possible. For, as I observed before, I am at a stand to know what study first to presue; as every college has its particular rotine of study for each class.

Nothing particular has lately taken place among your relations here; except the death of my Mother, which I expect ere now you

1. In the John C. Calhoun Papers, *SCL*, there is a copy of John Martyn, . . . *Bucolicks of Virgil* (London, 1749), evidently used in Waddel's academy, which has Calhoun's name in it, apparently in his own hand, along with the names of members of the Gibert family (1802 and various dates) and of James L. "Pettigrew" (Petigru), 1805.

3

have heard. Her disolution took place on the 15th May last.[2] The doctor, who attended upon her is uncertain, what was her complaint. I never experienced so sever and unexpect[ed a] shock, as I did upon hearing her [. . .] I left her the day before her d[eath.] She appeared to be upon a fair way [to] recover. She did not apprehend any [. . .] herself. How can I express my feel[ing] when it was anounced to me the n[ext] day, that she was dead! !

James intends to begin the mercantile buiseness this fall. He has purchased a house and lot in this place. I have just recovered from a severe spell of the fever.

I remain yours sincerely and affectionately

JOHN C. CALHOUN.

1 NOTE: Andrew Pickens, Jr., was Calhoun's cousin, the son of General Andrew Pickens and Rebecca Calhoun. Rev. Moses Waddel, Calhoun's brother-in-law, maintained his school at "South Hampton on the hill above Vienna" on the Savannah River in Abbeville District (Howe, *Presbyterian Church in S.C.*, II, 141-2) from 1801 to 1804, when he moved it about four miles east to Willington (Waddel, *Memorials of the Academic Life,* p. 47-9). The letter is postmarked Southampton, S.C., Sept. 9, 1801, but the "town" did not survive the moving of the academy. This letter confirms the date and place of the beginning of Calhoun's active preparation for college given in the 1843 *Life* (p. 6), but not the statement which gives the credit for the suggestion, and the assurance of funds, to James, the second brother, who is mentioned in the letter—see, however, No. 20. For the Calhoun and Pickens families, see Genealogical Table.   SOURCE: *SCL.*

2. To [. . . CALHOUN, Abbeville, S.C.]

New Haven [*Nov.* 23?], 1802

My Dear [*Brother?*] I arrived here [about?] a week since in the sloop Albatross running between Boston & New York. I [should?]

2. The inscription on the family monument erected by Calhoun in 1844 gives the date of her death as May, 1802 ("Inscriptions from a Calhoun burying-ground," *SCHM*, XXVII [1926], 185). The cemetery is on the original tract surveyed for himself by Patrick Calhoun in 1758 and is east of and near the site of the Calhoun homestead—see Mills, *Atlas of S.C.,* Abbeville District; Meriwether, *Expansion of S.C.,* p. 135.

have come in the [. . .] but I found that I should be detained nearly a week longer in New York if I waited for it. I have not yet become acquainted with many of my class mates although you have told me so often that I ought to cultivate my social qualities more than I do. I cannot get over the repugnance which I always have to addressing perfect strangers. The class numbers about 65 among whom are some noble looking fellows. President Dwight is a very aimiable man and well calculated to perform the duties of his office. I trust that I shall like him as an instructor.

There are two large literary societies here denominated the Linonian & Brothers in Unity and between each the members of college are equally divided by the faculty. It was my lot to be assigned to the Linonian Society and I am very well pleased with [the?] decision for although knowing as yet but little of the two Societies, I [should] have chosen this if it had been let to my preference. This Society is in[*tend*]ed to promote social & literary cul[*ture*] and I am in hopes that I shall derive great benefit from it. My studies [*so*] far are very pleasant & not very difficult.

I am now rooming in Union Hall. My chum is Chris Gadsen from Cha[rles]town (you know the family) a very fine fel[*low*] not particularly given to study but does [*not*] prevent me.[1] He is a Brother in Unity consequently some dispute accoasionly rises between us in regard to the mer[*it*] of the two Societies which however is con[*fin*]ed to words. We board in commons and here you have an opportunity to see human life in all its phases of incivility & selfishness unparalleled greediness side by side and I am sorry to say that it is not at all flattering to the good quality of mankind. I [. . .][2] vant answering the purpose of an Eton fag a tall strapping fellow in the freshman class from Connecticut by the name of [. . .][3] good natured and obedient as a New Foundland dog.

I [*met*?] Uncle John in New York; he expects to be at home all this winter. [. . .] Mary is as well as usual [. . .] all my

1. Christopher Edwards Gadsden (Wallace, *Sketch of the Life and Character of Bishop Gadsden*, p. 5-6).
2. Five or six words missing.
3. A name of four or five letters illegible. "Fagging" at Yale was not abolished until 1804 (Baldwin, *Annals of Yale College*, 2nd. ed., p. 147; this citation supplied by Miss Dorothy W. Bridgewater, Yale Library, Mar. 27, 1957).

good relations there.⁴ I hope you will write my dear [brother?] as soon as convenient for I can assure you that nothing will be pleasanter than to receive letters from home. Remember me to all my friends and believe me

I remain your ever affectionate [. . . .]⁵

J. C. CALHOUN

2 NOTE: This manuscript, in unidentified hands, with the heading "New Haven Sept 23 1802 My Dear Mother," and the address "Mrs. P. C. Calhoun Abbeville C.H. South Carolina," or another paper answering to its description, was produced about 1858 in the Yale controversy as to which of the College's literary societies could claim Calhoun as a former member. Thomas R. Lounsbury later spoke of it as a forgery because of the date, which preceded Yale's opening by a month (Cross, *Connecticut Yankee*, p. 148-9). Even more to the point was the fact that Calhoun's mother died in May 1801 (see No. 1). Additional questions are raised by the closing to the paper, "Your affectionate son," by the signature "J. C. Calhoun," a form he adopted after he entered Congress, and by the figure 15 purporting to be the postage, whereas the postage to Abbeville in 1802 was 25 cents. Calhoun's answer to an inquiry in 1840 is recorded in the minutes of the Brothers in Unity (citation supplied by Miss Dorothy Bridgewater, Yale Library, Mar. 27, 1957) as follows: "during the time he was a member of Yale College he was not a member of either of the Literary Societies there. Previous to his entering coll. the mode of designating the members of these societies by lot was adopted by which he was appointed to the Linonia Society. Most of his political & personal friends being members of the Society of Brothers in Unity he preferred to belong to that Society, but the rules, then prevailing, not allowing this, he attached himself to neither of the Societies." See also Stokes, *Memorials of Eminent Yale Men*, II, 197-8.

The "letter" in its present form was written on two separate and mismatched sheets of paper. The omissions and the division of words at the edge of the paper, considered in connection with the content, suggest that the body of this manuscript is a copy made from a letter, or from a draft of a letter, of Calhoun in

4. The names are barely decipherable, and it has been impossible to identify them among Calhoun's kin.

5. In the manuscript the word "son" follows "affectionate" and is in the handwriting of the body of the letter. Assuming that the body of the manuscript is genuine the word is only to be explained as the copyist's interpretation of an indistinct closing.

which heading and closing had become indistinct, or from which they were missing. The "My Dear Mother" was written in a different hand and with much heavier strokes of the pen, and probably years later, for the ink ran deep into creases of the paper. If "Mother" was written over another word, the latter was "Brother." So far the process was probably in good faith, but the writing on the cover indicates a clumsy attempt at deception. Source: Duke University Library, Calhoun Papers.

3. To ANDREW PICKENS JR., Pendleton District, S.C.

New Haven 21st Jan. 1803

Dr Sir, After long expectation and many conjectures, I at length had the pleasure of hearing from you. I am some what surprised that you should plead want of news as part of your excuse for your long silence. You certainly know, by experience, how much pleasure it afford[s] any one far removed from his native land, to hear of the prosperity of his friends and acquaintances, how much to hear of the smallest change, and the most trivial incident, which may have taken place relative to those with whom he has been in a habit [of] intimacy. But independent of these sources of news, your sentiments upon any subject, wheather political or moral, would at any time furnish matter for a letter, which could not fail of being highly interesting. It stricks me, that your opinion of the pleasures of a collegiate life, is too exalted; and of the "scrambling world" too low. Where are all of those happy scenes within the temple of science, the bare recollection of which seems to fill your soul with ineffable pleasure! and expand your breast with a love, which embraces even its very walls! Are we not, while in college, insulated from the rest of the world; and deprived of those enjoyments and amusements, to which the human heart is so strongly enticed? Can that variety be found any where in college, without which man is miserable? Day after day presents the same unvariegated scenes; a tiresome sameness. Books, Books, Books engross our whole time and attention. Call up to your mind a student; and trace him through one day of his existence. Let it be a winter's day. Begin when the morning bell, ere yet the sun has dispeled the darkness, summons him to the chapel. In vain the warm bed entices to indulgence and the piercing cold forbids to rise; rise he must. He riseth; and has[t]ily having thrown [on] his clothes, half frozen, he repairs to chapel. He spends the day in pouring over long and abstruse mathimatical demonstrations. The sun now sinks below the westren horizon. All the world retires to rest; the student alone excepted. To him rest is a stranger. When now day has surrendered its dominions to night; not contented with that time nature has alloted man to labour, he trims his lamp, and sits down to study He studies till the clock striks twelve. Pale and meager, with a shattred constitution, he retires to bed. His sleep is short and interupted. Again the bell rings, he rises again and again goes the same round. Keep those things in view, and tell me, dear Andrew, where is the pleasure of a collegiate life. Will you place it in the approbation of his teachers, and the applause of his competitors? They are vain and unsatisfying. Will you in the gratifycation of his ambition? That ambition must be small indeed, which can be gratifyed in college. Rather then rejoice, that you have passed through college; and that you are now engaged in the buisy scenes of the "Scrambling world." You are now your own master. You are now free to the enjoyment of life. The temp[l]e of fame is now open to you. Popular renown, if to court its favour would afford you any pleasure, is now ready to attend you. You are now in that part of the journey of life, where heaven has strewed fruits and flowers with a more liberal hand. Enjoy the present moment and look back upon college, as the traveler when now he has obtained the plains turns round and views with a kind of secret plasure the craggy mountains over which he climb[ed] with much labour and fatigue.

Let me now turn from these things to one of a more serious nature, I mean the death of our honoured relation John E. Calhoun. By his death our country has lost one of its most sincere friends; and our family one of its brightest ornaments. Mr Calhoun by his sperited behaviour in the last congress gained himself much honour in N. England. Indeed the general tenour of his actions, al[t]hough not exhibited upon so elevated a stage as congress, yet have been such as to claim the gratitude of his country. It is probable, dear Andrew, that we shall follow the same presuits of life, that he did, let us therefore be ambitious to emulate his virtues and knowledge.

I am yours &c

JOHN C. CALHOUN

Remember me to your father and mother brothers and sisters and all friends.

3 NOTE: This letter is significant for its indication of Calhoun's early political ambition and conservative leanings. John Ewing Colhoun, lawyer and planter, son of Ezekiel, elder brother of John C.'s father, served several terms in the S.C. House of Representatives; he died Oct. 26, 1802 (Salley, "Calhoun Family," p. 153-4). Elected to the U.S. Senate as a Republican in 1800, he nevertheless strongly opposed the repeal of the Judiciary Act in 1802 (*AC7-1*, p. 138-45, 149), and it was obviously this "sperited behaviour" that earned the approval of the New England Federalists. For the spelling of the name see No. 6 NOTE. SOURCE: *SCL.*

4. To ANDREW PICKENS, JR., Pendleton District, S.C.

New Haven 23d May 1803.

Dr Andw. Your's dated 16th March was handed me by Mr Cheppelle upon his arrival here. Your long silence was a subject of much conjecture. But in chiding me for neglect you have fully laid open the whole mystery. It appears you have not received the answer, which, a short time after reception, I wrote to yours dated 22d Sept. The miscarriage of my answer, I hope, will satisfactorily exculpate me of any accusation of neglect, or of breach of promise.

Your opinion, I find, agrees with that, which I have frequently heard from those, who have turned their attention to the study of law, that it is both dry and laborious. This circumstance, I believe, has detered many, who were by nature and art, capacetated to shine conspicuously at the bar. But I can assure, to me it seems, that the labour and difficulty which are necessary to acquire a legal knowledge, would, so far from detering, prove the greatest stimulus to an active and vigerous persuit in the study of it. For what is a greater incitement to man than honour? Upon what does greater honour attend than upon an accurate and comprehensive knowledge of law? But why is this honour attendant on legal knowledge? Surely because it demands a strong and comprehensive mind connected with assiduous application to acquire any considerable perfection in a science so complicated, as the laws of all free and enlightened nations must necessarily be. Were the law so simple and concise as to be attainable by every one, with moderate application and abilities, where would be the honour of its acquisition?

You requested me in your last to informe you, "how I am pleased with my situation; and what is my opinion of the New Englanders in general." With my situation, I am better pleased than I expected to have been. There is, as I suppose you yourself may have experienced while residing in New England, a considerable prejudice here against both the southern states and students. However I have found a considerable number of New England students, young men of information and worth, free of prejudice. With these I associate. As to those under the influence of local prejudice I contemn and avoid. My paper is too scanty to give you my opinion at lenth of the Yankees. They are certainly more penurious, more contracted in their sentiments, and less social, than the Carolinians. But as to morality we must yield.

I am your sincere friend

JOHN C. CALHOUN

My respects to your father mother, si[s]ters, brothers and all friends.

SOURCE: Clint T. Graydon, Columbia, S.C., 1955.

5. REMARKS UPON THE QUERY: Would it be politic to encourage the immigration of forreigners into the U. States?

11 O'clock Novr. 2d. 1803

Calhoun. Probable that the emigrants from the European nations Would be drawn from the middle class of Society. Many imigrants within the knowledge of the gentleman from S. Carolina of respectable character & useful members of Society (This remark however was completly refuted by Dr. Dwight by the relation of Abraham Baldwin's remarks on his journey from Georgia to Connecticut, in which he had not seen more than 3 Native Americans in favour of the western insurrection which was then raging; but that every foreigner with whom he had conversed was rejoiced at the circumstance of the insurrection.)—The effects of forreign immigration would be the improvement of manufactures—The increase of population—diffusion of science—improvement of agriculture—&c. Forreigners would in process of time be assimulated to our own citizens—

5 NOTE: Weekly "forensic disputations" were required of juniors and seniors at Yale (note by Miss Dorothy W. Bridgewater, Yale Library, Mar. 27, 1957, with citation to Mills Day, MS Common-Place Book, 1802). John Pierpont's notebook, which reports this debate in which Calhoun took part, also includes stanzas on students, among them lines on Calhoun: "Next he to whose virtues my praises belong, Shall be for a moment the theme of my song; His soul by the ardour of honour is fir'd, And by his acquaintance he most is admird, His science extensive his manners refind, To strangers polite and to intimates kind, His mind is serene and his judgement is clear, His love for his friends is unfeign'd and sincere. By nature loves all, none willingly hates; These are of his character some feeble traits, Which incontrovertibly prove that Calhoun, Will arive at the summit of eminence soon." SOURCE: Pierpont Morgan Library, John Pierpont [Yale] College Journal, p. 1-2.

6. To MRS. FLORIDE CALHOUN, New Port, R.I.

New Haven August 29th. 1804

Dear Madam, Yesterday your friendly favor of the 23rd. Inst. came to hand. Mr. Noble [1] did suggest to me, sometime since, that you expected to spend the summer in Rhode Island, & that you would be glad to see me there, but did not mention at what place. Soon after, my Brother wrote me word that you contemplated spending it in Philadelphia. Under this uncertainty it was impossible for me to act until further information from you. This, however, as I before stated, reached me not only late, but found me ill.

I thank you, Madam, for your kind solicitude regarding the present state of my health. I am happy to assure you that I feel

1. Alexander Noble—see No. 7.

myself making some advances towards a recovery, tho' not such rapid & immediate ones, as would correspond both with the wishes of my friends, & my own impatience to recover. I flatter myself, however, that I shall have so far regained my health by Commencement that I shall be able to realize the enjoyments & participate in the labors of that Day.[2] But above all, Madam, I am anxious to recover in order that I may visit New-Port, which, with the indulgence of health, I shall do, immediately after Commencement; Until which time, and forever, believe me, Dear Madam, to be with great respect Yours

JOHN C. CALHOUN.

6 NOTE: Floride Bonneau Colhoun was the widow of John Ewing Colhoun (No. 3 NOTE). She and her sons kept the Senator's spelling of the name (her son James Edward, however, changing to Calhoun years later—*e.g.* James Edward Calhoun Papers [*SCL*], Jan. 7, 1846), but John C. often disregarded it. SOURCE: *CC.*

7. To ALEXANDER NOBLE, Charleston, S.C.

New Port 15th Oct. 1804.

Dr Alexander, From a variety of causes I have been prevented from answering your last till now. It would be superfluous to make an enumeration of all of them; but it may not be amiss to mention, that among the most considerable are, a total absence of any incident that could have been interesting, and a long and severe spell of sickness. After enjoying all most uninterupted good health, since my departure from Carolina, I was attacked in August last by a very severe dysintery which had well nigh put an end to my life. At commencement I was so low that I was unable to participate either in the pleasures or exercises of the day. The later part Sept. I arrived in this place, where I had the pleasure of finding your aunt and family well. New Port is quite a pleasant place; but it has rather an old appearance which gives some what a melancholy

2. The commencement exercises, at which he was awarded the bachelor of arts degree, and in which he was to have presented his graduation thesis (*Life*, p. 6), took place Sept. 12 (program of exercises, *Connecticut Journal—* New Haven—Sept. 20, 1804). May 4 preceding Calhoun had signed a bond for payment of all amounts due the college (Yale University Library, Yale Memorabilia Collection).

aspect. I have found no part of New England more agreeable than the Island of Rhode Island; Agreeably situated well cultivated and possessed of a good soil and one of the most delightful climates on eart[h,] it seems to possess all that can contribute to the pleasures of man. But as to the civil situation of this state and its manners, customs and moral and religious character it seems much inferior, [a]s far as my information extends, to every other part of New England. Tomorrow I set off in com[p]any with your aunt for Bost. We expect to make a short stay; not more, perhaps, than a week. I expect to return to Carolina by water; and i[n] the same vessel with your au[nt] and family. We [do] not expect to sail before the 10th or 12th of next month; as we apprehend, from accounts received from Charleston, that it would be dangerous to be there before the midle of Novr.[1] Your aunt desires to be remembered to you and the Doctor.

    I remain your friend

John C. Calhoun

Remember me to Doctor Noble and James Stedman, if he is [*in*] Charleston.

    7 NOTE: Alexander Noble was Calhoun's cousin and nephew of John Ewing Colhoun (see Genealogical Table); Dr. John Noble was his elder brother.   SOURCE: Mrs. Kathryn C. Hill, Waco, Texas, 1955.

8. To ANDREW PICKENS [JR.], Pendleton, S.C.

Havre de Grace Maryd. 25th June 1805.

Dr. Andrew, It is laid down as a maxim of prudence by many philosophers, that we ought always to make our pleasure act in subodination to our duties and obligations. Though none can deny the soundness of this rule; yet all must admit the difficulty of the practice in some cases The present, however, is one in which obligation and pleasure naturally unite. For, I write, no less in obedience to my feeling, than in conformity to your request and my promise. I would not have you conclude from this, however, that

---

1. On Dec. 24, 1804, Calhoun entered the law firm of DeSaussure and Ford in Charleston as a student (*SCHM*, XIII [1912], 177). For DeSaussure, see No. 13, n. 2.

I have much to communicate, that is new or interesting. Quite the reverse; but I am so well convinced that you will feel a plasure to hear from me, I do not hesitate to write even for that purpose alone.

As yet, our journey has been prosperous excep an accident that happened in St Thomas which your brother, as he was partaker, will give you fully.[1] We have generally both roads and accomodations good; far better both than is usually represented. This has contributed much to make the journey agreeable, which would be wholly pleasant were it not for the warm weather. However, we partly avoide this inconvenience by traveling early in the morning, and late in the evening, lying by while the day is warm. To you who are acquainted from your own observations with the country, any geogra[*phica*]l observation would be supurfluous. There is very little political information, except, what you find in the papers in this part of the union. Political agitation has both in this state and Virginia greatly subsided. It is almost as calm, as I have ever known it anywhere. The French Toulon Fleet most strongly, at present, occupies the publick. News paper readers and scriblers have formed various opinions as to its destination and success. I heard the President (I got acquainted with him at Washingn) ex[press] his opinion, that the destination w[as no]t Jamaica as commonly believed but Trinidad.[2] However this may be, it is certainly a lesson to the English that her foreign possessions are not so secure as she imagined; and has given the war a much more distracting character than it had at its commencement. Remember me to Mrs Pickens [3] to your Father, Mother brothers and sisters and to acquaintances generally. Mrs Calhoun joins her respects to you and Mrs Pickens

I am your sincere friend

JOHN C. CALHOUN

Remember me particularly to Mr Anderson Junr. and inform him I shall write him shortly.

SOURCE: *SCL.*

1. Ezekiel Pickens?—see No. 10, n. 2.
2. This call on Jefferson in Washington has been mistakenly assigned to Monticello by Starke (Jameson, *Correspondence,* p. 84)—see Wiltse, *Calhoun, Nationalist,* p. 36.
3. Andrew Pickens married Susan Wilkinson in 1804.

9. To Mrs. Floride Colhoun, New Port, R.I.

Litchfield 22d July 1805.

Dr Madam, In obedience to my feelings, no less than to your request, I embrace the first opportunity of informing you of my arrival here. From New London, I took the stage to Norwich; and thence to Hartford, where I was detained part of two days, which prevented my reaching Litchfield before Saturday evening. I found Mr Felder well, and anxiously waiting my arrival.[1] He has been here 5 weeks, and express[es] himself pleased with the place. I was peculiarly fortunate in having Judge Reeves the gentleman with whom I here study, a passenger in the stage from Hartford to this place. I delivered my letters to him; and found him on the passage open and agreeable. I have every prospect of rendering my residence here very agreeable; and I return, I assure you, with much pleasure to the cultivation of Blackston's acquaintance.

For two or three days, after I left New-Port, I felt much of that lonesome sensation, which I believe everyone experiences after departing from those with whom he has been long intimate. However by mingling and conversing with others, I have felt it much diminnished; and by a few days application to studies, which to me are highly interesting, I have no doubt it will be entirely removed. At Norwich I met with Mr. Ward; and he informed me, that his health is still in a progressive state. I have not yet had an opportunity of speaking to Sterling.[2] He resides six or seven miles out of town; but Mr Felder saw him a few days since. In conversing with him about going to the southward he observed to Mr Felder, that he was desireous of instructing in a private family. I shall, however, see him before I write again; and let you know the particulars. Mr Felder and myself room together; and both being sensible of the importance of application, [at] our age, have resolved to devote our time to solid and useful studies. With the assistence of providence and a continuation of my health I hope to

1. John M. Felder, of Orangeburg District, S.C., classmate of Calhoun at Yale (*BDC*).

2. Micah Sterling, also a Yale classmate, a native of Connecticut; he moved to Watertown, N.Y., and practiced law (*BDC*).

carry this determination into full execution. Mr Felder joins his respects to you

I remain your sincere friend

JOHN C. CALHOUN.

Remember me particularly to Mrs, Miss, and Mr Thurston; and to my acquaintances in N. Port generally. My love to Floride, John and James.[3]

9 NOTE: Calhoun came to Litchfield for training in law under Judge Tapping Reeve—see Wiltse, *Calhoun, Nationalist*, p. 35-6.   SOURCE: *CC*.

10. TO MRS. FLORIDE COLHOUN, New Port, R.I.

Litchfield 12th August 1805.

Dr Madam, On the 10th Inst. I received your's of 31st Ult, which, I assure you, both in the perusal and reception afforded me no ordinary degree of pleasure. I am sorry to hear of your indisposition; but hope, as it originated in a cold, it will be removed with the cause. I think, with Dr Turner, that the winter will be too severe for you, in your present feeble state of health. You requested me to enquire for a traveler for you;[1] I know of none at present; but shall use all deligence, should you come to a determination to return, to obtain one for you. I cannot, but look on our choice in not going through Wilmington, as extremely fortunate. This is certainly another argument in favour of your general principle that "all is for the best."

I thank you much for your affectionate mode of address, which, I assure you, is much more agreeable to my feeling than any other. Your whole actions in kindness and affection have been to me, like a mother's tenderness. I know not how, I shall make sufficient returns; unless it is by acting in a manner worthy of your friendship and esteem; which, with this assistance of him who is the author of all good resolutions and actions, I hope to do.

3. Mrs. Colhoun's children were John Ewing, Jr., Floride, and James Edward.

1. A teacher, not a traveler—see No. 12.

I feel myself much absorbed by the persuit of legal knowledge at present. In fact, in order to take the course of law lectures, not as they usually are; but as they ought to be, I find, I must devote almost the whole of my time to that purpose. I find Mr. Felder a faithful and cheering companion in the dry and solitary journey through the extensive fields of law. We both console ourselves, that in a few years we shall acquire a pretty thorough knowledge of our profession; and then our time shall be more at our own disposals. Perhaps, this is but a pleasant dream; as every succeeding year comes loaded with its own peculiar cares and buiseness.

I have reason to be thankful for a continuation of my health. I think I am rather more healthy and stout than when I left N. Port. It is some what strange, I always feel myself in the best heal[*t*]h, when stud[*y*]ing closely.

Remember me affectionately to Mrs and Miss Thurston, to Mr T. and to my acquaintances in New Port generally. Give [m]y love to Floride, Elizabeth,[2] John and James. Tell James, the first time I write to Miss ——— I shall not forget to request a kiss for him. The paper forces me to conclude. I wish you a speady return of health; and will be extremely happy to hear from you when ever it is conv[*en*]ient to write to me

I am your sincere and affectionate friend

JOHN C. CALHOUN.

Mr Felder desires to be remembered to you all.

I saw Sterling a few days since. He is desireous of instructing in a private family; but feels himself at a loss in fixing on a sum for tuition money. However should you be desireous of obtaining him please to let me know it with the particulars; also about what you think you will be willing to give; and I will engage him for you.

SOURCE: *CC.*

2. Elizabeth Bonneau Pickens, Mrs. Colhoun's niece, the daughter of Andrew Pickens' older brother, Ezekiel. See No. 86 NOTE.

11. To MRS. FLORIDE COLHOUN, New Port, R.I.

Litchfield Cont. 9th Sept. 1805.

Dr Madam, Imediately on the reception of yours in answer to my first, I hastened, to make a reply, to which, as I have received no answer, al[t]hough it is now a considerable time, I apprehend it has never reach'd New Port. The mention, which you made of your indisposition, has made me extremely anxious to hear from you; regularly on the arrival of every Eastren mail, I have visited the post office, but have uniformly had the mortification of disapointment. Indeed, I know not when, I have been so unfortunate in hearing from my friends, as I have been, since my arrival here. I have received not a scrap of a pen from either Pendleton, or Charleston, although I have writen to most of [*my*] correspondents in both of those places; and my information from Abbeville is very slight, merely that they are all well, and the season has been pleasant. About two weeks since, Mrs Brown and Lady Housten and family were here on a visit. They spent four or five days in this place; and appeared to be much pleased with Litchfield. They both enquired particularly of your health. You mentioned that Markley had been in N. Port, and would, in a short time, be here; I am much surprised in neither seeing, or hearing any thing of him since. Indeed this is rather an out of the way place; and, unless, it is now and then a Southerner from college, we rarely see any one from our end of [*the*] Union. This, al[t]hough it diminishes something from our social pleasure, yet contributes considerably to our studious habits. For, I have always found, that just in the same proportion as the number of friends and acquaintances increase around me, and a consequent opportunity of various, and interesting conversation, my attention to my studies has relaxed; but when I have only three or four, so as to make an agreeable mixture of study and social intercourse, then my attention is the most fixed, and my exertion the best directed. I have made some enquiry for a traveler should you return this fall.[1] I have heard of none except Sterling. He mentioned to me that he had a strong desire to see the Southern States; and should be very happy to accompany you, should you go and should it be agreeable on your part. I have given him no encouragement

1. See No. 10, n. 1.

to expect; but I know not that you will be able to obtain one that will suit you better. He is the same young man of whom you have heard me frequently speak. Should you return, and be unable to find one more agreeable, please to let me know, as soon as, convenient. Remember me to Mrs and Miss and Mr Thurston, and all of my acquaintances in N. Port. Give my love to Floride, Elizabeth, John and James.

I am your sincere friend

JOHN C. CALHOUN

Mr Felder joins his respects to you all.

SOURCE: *CC.*

12. From MRS. FLORIDE COLHOUN

Rhode Island—14th Septr. 1805.

Dear John, Your second Affectionate favor I have receiv'd and need not tell you what satisfaction it gave me, to hear from you, and the pleasing reflection of your prudence, which will gain you friends wherever you go, is the only compensation I can have in your absence, and a great one it is. A few days after I wrote you I came into the country about a mile out of Newport where I have remained ever since, my Health is much recover'd, the family I board with are very attentive and friendly, and I have always some of my friends with me, which makes it very agreeable, have not determin'd whether I shall return to Carolina, tho' rather expect I shall, as my Health has become so precarious, however I trust I shall be directed to do what is best, therefore feel perfectly easy. What unspeakable blessing, that I the most helpless of mortals have been brought to put my whole trust and confidence in Him who has enabled me to say *His will be done.* shou'd I be oblig'd to return Home, have some Idea of putting John and James with Mr. Backus at Bethlehem,[1] as you are acquainted with the Gentleman, will thank [*you*] for your opinion, one great inducement for me to put them there is, that they will be near you, and you cou'd sometimes see

1. The school of Rev. Azel Backus was at Bethlehem, a few miles from Litchfield (*DAB*).

them, I do not think Newport a proper place for Boys of Johns age. I am sorry to find you cant read my scrawl, you mention'd that I requested you to enquire for a traveller, but it was a private Teacher I wish'd you to get, which I must give over all Idea of, as my stay here is so uncertain. Wou'd you believe that I have not receiv'd a line from Mr. Pickens,[2] nor any of my friends in Pendleton, do let me know if you have—have receiv'd two letters from Mr. Desaussure, in his last one directed to you, which I now forward, and am asham'd that I have put it off so long, and have no other excuse to make, but a vile spirit of procrastination which always prevails me when I have a letter to write. I had nearly broke it open before I observ'd it was to you, I will thank you to write me as soon as possible, as Mr. Backus is expected here soon, I only wish I cou'd have your advice verbally, but must be content to have it by letter—since wrote the above your third favor was handed me, for which I return you many thanks. it was what I had no right to expect, as I had neglected answering your other sooner, for which I am sorry, as it has caus'd you some uneasiness, I am conscious if I receiv'd no more from my friends than I deserve, there is nothing that I cou'd expect. I have also Just had a letter from Doctor Noble he mentions that his Brother Ezekiel has suffer'd much from the Rheumatism, and that he is gone to the up Country.[3] he also says that Mr. McKleheny[4] has lost one of his Children, but had not heard a word from Mr. Pickens, this is strange, and I cannot account for it, was in hopes you had heard, but find you are in the same situation. Doctor Noble writes very pressing for me to return this winter. my paper is nearly out must conclude, your friends beg to be remember'd to you, and the Children Join me in love, remember me to Mr. Felder.

I am with every good wish Yours Affectionately

FLORIDE COLHOUN

I thank for the information respecting Mr. Sterling, have given you my reasons for not proceeding further, within.

---

2. Ezekiel Pickens, her brother-in-law and her husband's executor.

3. For Dr. John Noble, see No. 7 NOTE and his letter, Aug. 17, 1805 (*CC*).

4. Apparently Rev. James McElhenny (Howe, *Presbyterian Church,* I, 573, 611-2; *SCHM,* XXXIII [1932], 312).

12 NOTE: Of the address only Calhoun's name (spelled Colhoun) and a marginal note, "Copy of a letter to John C. C." (indicating that she had previously sent an original) appear to be in Mrs. Colhoun's hand. Calhoun's name is followed by "Litchfield/ to be forwarded by Mrs./ Sarah Blake Purcell/ New Haven/ Connecticutt/ This Letter of Consequence I forward soon this on account of/ of delay in sending on letters from/ New Haven being a Bye Post." The letter is postmarked New Port, Sept. 16. It is presumably the letter handed to Calhoun "by a gentleman from N. Haven"—see No. 13. SOURCE: *SCL.*

13. To MRS. FLORIDE COLHOUN, New Port, R.I.

Litchfield 26th Sept 1805

Dr Madam, Two days since yours of 14th Inst[1] was handed me, by a gentleman from N. Haven; which, I assure you, after so long an interval without hearing from you, afforded me no inconsiderable plasure. You mentioned to me, that you have taken your residence in the country a short distance from N. Port; and that your health is much recovered. In this stept, I think you have acted prudently; for I can not but think the air of the country considerably more saluberious, than that of the town; more espacially to one in your state of health. I hope the beneficial effect of the country air will effect a speedy and a full restoration of your health. You express your surprise, at the silence of Mr. Pickens and others of your Carolina friends; I, on my part, feel an equal astonishment; for though I have writen to most of my acquaintances there, I have as yet, received only two letters, and neither of them from Abbeville or Pendleton. How to account for this I am very much at a loss. A letter from Mr DeSaussures accompanied your last; with which I was much interested. He writes me in a very friendly and engaging manner; and expresses himself highly pleased with the account, which I gave him of his son at Princeton.[2]

1. No. 12.
2. Henry W. DeSaussure, and his son, Henry A., who was a member of the Princeton class of 1806 (Bureau of Alumni Records, Princeton). DeSaussure was a friend of Senator Colhoun and was Mrs. Colhoun's attorney (DeSaussure to Mrs. Colhoun, Dec. 31, 1802, and June 18, 1807, John E. Colhoun Papers, *SCL*). He became Chancellor in 1808 (*DAB*).

You express an idea of puting John and James with Mr. Bachcus at Bethlehem; and request my opinion on that subject. I agree with you, that N. Port is not a very fit place for boys of the age of John and James; and, should you send them else where, I know not a fiter place than Bethlehem, or a more sutiable man than Mr Bachcus The place is small and I am informed vi[r]tuous; with Mr Bachcus, I am not particularly acquainted; but he has the [marks?] of ex-amplary religion and extensive learning. You mention, as an in-duc[e]ment, that they will be near me; I do assure, that on my part I should consider it not only a duty, but as delight to pay them particular attention, should you send them to Bethlehem.

Remember me to my acquaintances in N. Port and particularly to children Mr Felder joins his respects to you and family.

I am with esteem yours &c

JOHN C. CALHOUN

A few days since Messers Darington, Cuningham and Markley passed through this place on their tour to the uper parts of New York State. I am at present in high health; and, I think, more fleshy than I was last fall.

SOURCE: *CC.*

14. TO ANDREW PICKENS [JR.], Pendleton, S.C.

Litchfield 24th. Novr. 1805.

Dr Andrew, My time is never more agreeably spent, than in the perusal of your always interesting and friendly letters. The pleasure received by yours of the 15th Sept. was not less than ordinary, but, on the contrary, after a long and anxious silence on your part, I felt myself more than usually interested. You do me injustice in supposing your letters intrude on my studious disposition; I am not so much in love with law as to feel indifferent to my friends. Many things I study for the love of study, but not so with law. I can never consider it, but as a task which my situation imposes on me. I, therefore, often lay it aside for the more delicious theme of the muses, or interesting pages of history; and always throw it away with joy to hear from my Carolina corespondents. But, I confess, from my aversion to law, I draw a motive to industry. It must be done, and the sooner the better is often my logick. You expect'd to be examined some time in this month. I wish you success; or rather, I hope, ere now I may congratulate you on your admission. Your ambition to be admited at this time is both laudable and honourable. It is high time for those selfish usurpers on the publick opinion to be painted in their true light. It is a work of patriotism and justice, and all good men will wish you success; all wise men will approbate your motive. For my part, I never could think with complasency of some up starts in that part of the state, whose thoughts and lives have been consumed in drawing down characters whose actions have afforded volumes of proof of integerty and wisdom.[1]

The work of destruction in [which these?] champions have enlisted requi[red] [. . .]tice and assiduity, with whic[h] [they?] are abundantly filled, for comple[te suc]cess. They have had their day; [the eyes?] of the people will be opened.

Some late arrivals from Europe a[re intere]sting. War between France and Au[stri]a is inevitable.[2] Bonapart's speech before the senate on his departure from Paris to take command of the army on the Rine; and the Austrian manifesto are both published. The former full of confidence in victory; the latter apparently moderate, but resolute. What will be the event time alone can ["will" *cancelled*] unfold; but I distrust the fortune of the allies. The period is certainly eventful. My respects to Mrs Pickens and my friends in Pendleton.

I am your friend

JOHN C. CALHOUN

Your seal I endeavoured to have engraved at Phia. but without success; I was told by a gentleman that he had tried for some weeks

1. Note the statements of Edward Hooker in May, 1806 ("Diary," *AHAAR,* 1896, I, 889) that in "the old District" of Ninety Six there was no more effective charge against a candidate than that he was *"one of Harper's men"* and of September following (p. 892) that "Malicious statements and letters to the injury" of Joseph and Ezekiel Calhoun were in circulation. Joseph Calhoun was then a member of the state Senate and was in November elected to Congress (*BDC*). He and Ezekiel were the sons of Calhoun's uncle William. See *DAB,* "Robert Goodloe Harper."

2. Compare Jameson's rendering of this passage and his conjectures as to the words in the missing portion of the letter (*Correspondence,* p. 99-100).

to have his; but could not find an engraver. It may be done in New York, but we stayed there only part of a day. I have not had since I arrived here a safe oppor[*tuni*]ty of sending it to N. York. It shall be done and transmited to you by the first opp[*ortuni*]ty.

SOURCE: *SCL.*

15. TO MRS. FLORIDE COLHOUN, New Port, R.I.

Litchfd. 23d. Dcr. 1805.

Dr Madam, Before receiving your's of the 12th Dcr. which on many accounts has afforded me the highest pleasure, I had concluded in my own mind that you had returned to Carolina. For, not having received an answer to my last, which I wrote immediately on the reception of your's of the 14th. of Sept., and hearing not a word by any other means I was induced to believe that you had left New Port. To be satisfied of this point I wrote to Mr. Thurston a few days since requesting him to inform me of your return to Carolina. Do attribute my long silence to this mistake rather than to any negligence.

I take great interest in the restoration of your health; at this time of so much importance to your children, while their minds are to be instructed in those principles of piety and virtue, so necessary to their happiness and usefulness. I know your solicitude for their well being; and that it is your concern for them which chiefly makes you anxious for your own health. With due care, and the assistance of a kind providence, I hope, you will find your constitution fully confirmed by spring. Nothing, I am sure, will afford greater joy to all of your friends. How very mild the season has been; the climate of New Port must have been charming for some time back. A journey thither would, had I leisure, be extremely pleasant to me. I am attached to N. Port on many accounts, and desire much to see you all. I dare say, that James has forgot his jealousy and would be glad to see me. It is a happy circumstance, that Mr Patton has opened a school so convenient. He is a man I much esteem for his many virtues and amiable character; and I have no doubt will make an excellent instructor. I have had, since I wrote you last, several letters from Carolina. They contain nothing very interesting.

I have enjoyed good health since my residence here; and hope to continue it by temperance and exercise. I tak[e] little amusement; and live a very studious life. This place is so much agitated by party feelings, that both Mr. Felder and myself find it prudent to form few connections in town. This, though some what disagreeable is not unfavourable to our studies. My love to the children.

Yours affectionately

JOHN C. CALHOUN

Mr. Felder joins his respects to you and the children.

15 NOTE: The words "party feelings" are doubtless a reference to the controversy that culminated in the April, 1806, trial and imprisonment of Selleck Osborn, editor of the Litchfield *Witness*, for abusive criticism of local Federalists. In his *New-York Patriot* of Nov. 1, 1823, Osborn, who was then supporting Calhoun for President, declared that Calhoun was the only one of the law school students who dared to march in the August 6, 1806, procession to salute him in his cell. However, Calhoun's friend John M. Felder was "Adjutant" of the procession (*The Witness*, Aug. 13, 1806, Litchfield Historical Society). Except for this letter, the record of Calhoun's stay in Litchfield indicates that his reaction to the town was uniformly pleasant. Compare also the 1879 statement of John Bissell (referred to in No. 20 NOTE). SOURCE: *CC.*

16. To MRS. FLORIDE COLHOUN, New Port, R.I.

Litchfield 19th Jany. 1806.

Dr Madam, I am so impatient to hear how the very cold weather we have had for some time back agrees with you and your family, that I write this solely to hasten your answer to my last. I cannot think N. Port near so cold as this place, which has a very high, open situation. If it is, I fear you have found, the winter very disagreeably cold. I however hope by due attention you will find your health much improved notwithst[and]ing the severity of the season. If you have not found any serious inconvenience from the weather we already have had, I think, you need not fear the remaining part of the winter; as this is the coldest month usually. We have excellent sleighing here. I was out last evening for the first time this season; and found it very agreeable. It is a mode of conveyance that the people of this state are very fond of. If you have sufficient snow in N. Port, I dare say you would find it in good weather, an exercise very conducive to your health.

Do write me how James and Elizabeth bear the cold. I dare say they have never been so rosy and full in the cheeks as this winter has made them.

I have had only one letter from Abbeville ["Carolina" *cancelled*] since I wrote you last. Brother James writes me that it had become very health[y] after a very sickly fall. Himself and family have been very unwell; but have entirely recovered. None of our friends have fallen victims to the fall sickness. How thankful we ought to be to the author of good for this high favour. Brother William had a fine son a few weeks since. James will be on to New York in the summer. I had also a letter from Alexander Noble. He expected to leave Charleston in a few days for the up country; [1] and the next summer to take a trip through the western country to New Orleans, and then, by water to New York. Mr Felder and myself are both in good health, and desire much, should we have leisure, to spend a few weeks in N. Port.

My love to the children. I am yours affectionately

JOHN C. CALHOUN

Mr. Felder joins in respects to you.
Remember me to my friends [in] N. Port.

SOURCE: *CC.*

17. To MRS. FLORIDE CALHOUN, New Port, R.I.

Litchfield 3d March 1806.

Dr Madam, Your favour of the 11th Feby. came safe; for which except of my acknowledgements. I take much pleasure in the restoration of your health; which is so necessary to the well being of your children, and so interesting to your numerous friends. I confess, I felt much anxiety on your account during the very severe

1. After the Revolution the term "upper country" began to replace "back country"—see, for instances, Jedidiah Morse, *American Geography,* p. 428, and John Drayton, *View of South Carolina,* p. 11. Calhoun was here using the abbreviated form which eventually came to be accepted; he at times bethought himself of the more correct term even though he misspelled it—see No. 22, n. 1.

weather which we have had this winter. I hope by due care, to your health during the spring months you will find your constitution compleatly restored.

You enquire if I have heard from Mr. Waddel? I have had one from him since the reception of your last letter. He has had much sickness in his family; but they are all happily restored. He writes me that his preaching has had much effect in the congregation which Mr Cummins formerly superintended.[1] On this subject he says "I never before had so much encouragement to labour in the gospel as there at present." His hopes at his other congregation were flatering; but owing to an unhappy dissension between two of its principal members his success has not been so great.

I receive with gratitude your friendly advice and anxious solicitude for my welfare on the all important subject of religion. You do me injustice to apprehend that I should receive it otherwise than a mark of the purest and highest friendship. For surely we can give no higher evidence of our friendship, than in endeavouring to promote the best interest of the subject of it. Be assured that whatever you may say on this head will be kindly received. You observe that it would give you satisfaction for me to be with you in N. Port if I could persue my studies with as much advantage there as here. Were this possible nothing would be more agreeable to my feelings. But in that case I should lose the law lectures here wholly; which would be incalculably great to me.

We have very cold weather at present. The change has been great in a few days. You will find great care necessary to keep from taking colds during the spring months, owing to the frequent and violent changes. More care will be necessary I apprehend than during the winter.

I am yours affectionately

JOHN C. CALHOUN.

Remember me to my friends in N. Port. Give my love to Floride, Elizabeth, John and James.

Mr. Felder joins his respects to you and our friends in N. Port.

SOURCE: *CC.*

1. Rev. Francis Cummins—Howe, *Presbyterian Church*, II, 145.

18. To Mrs Floride Calhoun, New Port, R.I.

Litchfield 13th April 1806.

Dr Madam, It is so long since I have heard from N. Port, that I begin to grow quite anxious to receive a letter from that quarter. Though, I have not received an answer to my last; I would again have writen had I not expected and waited to hear from you by each mail. Since my last, I have had several letters from Carolina. They contain little particular, or important. I suppose you have heard of the revival of religion in Charleston. I saw a short account of it in a New York paper by the last mail. It is an extract of a letter from a gentleman in Charleston; It mentions that a very great seriousness and attention to religion had diffused itself over the city. What a happy change to that place; which in every thing was so extremely corrupt; and particularly so inattentive to every call of religion. I hope, and think it probable, that this happy change will extend itself from the city to the country. Surely no people ever so much needed a reform as those in the parishes near Charleston.

I believe, I mentioned to you that James will come on hither in the latter part of June.[1] He is desirous of my returning with him; but I have not yet gave him an answer. However, as the course of lectures will not conclude till the fall I do not think it probable I shall. Do you think of returning in the fall? And, if you do, how by land or water? In case of your return, I should be happy so to calculate my studies as to suit your convenience. I would thank you to let me know as to those points in your next.

What a cold, disagreeable spring we have had. I fear you have experienced some inconvenience from it. But, I flatter myself, that it has been more pleasant in N. Port than here; as this is a cold, high and open situation. We have not as yet any sign of vegetation. Colds have been common. I had a very severe one; but of it I am now happily freed. I would be happy, were it consistent with my studies to visit new Port this spring. I make no doubt, I should find a visit very pleasant with my friends there. But every thing must yield to improvement at present.

I am your affectionate friend

JOHN C. CALHOUN

1. His brother James Calhoun—see Nos. 16 and 20.

Remember me to those of my acquaintance you may see. Give my love to Floride, Elizabeth, John and [J]ames. Tell James I wish to hear him read in the bible very much; and that I hope he will learn from it to be a good boy.

SOURCE: *CC.*

19. To MRS. FLORIDE COLHOUN, New Port, R.I.

Litchfield 2d. June 1806.

Dr Madam, Your last 9th May was extremely acceptable after so long an interval without hearing from N. Port. You mention that your health had not been quite so good during the spring as it had been in the winter. This from the badness of the weather since Feby might have been expected; but, I hope now, that the summer is on, you will find, as you seem to intimate in the postscript, a full restoration of your health. I regret, you cannot pay Litchfield a visit. Were it in your power, you would find the road hither good; and the country agreeable. This place is among the most pleasant towns I ever have been in. While the season is pleasant you cannot travel too much for your health. I am happy that you have obtained a private teacher worthy of discharging ["taking" *cancelled*] the important duties of education. I hope, you will find the children much benefited by his instructions. It is some time since, I had a letter from Carolina except from William. He writes nothing particular. Darington, a few days since, paid Litchfield a visit. He observed that the accounts of the revival of religion in Charleston which appeared in the papers some time since was unfounded. Every friend to religion and that place must regret it. You mention your expectation of seeing me at new Port. In August we have a vacation of three weeks ["months" *cancelled*]; at which time, if nothing intervenes, I hope to spend a few days there.

I saw in one of the Charleston's papers an account of the marriage of Miss Martin to Mr. Blanding; the same I suppose who was attentive to her sister for whom you recollect she was in morning. We expect two students from Charleston in a few days; Stroble and Frazer; I believe you are acquainted with them. Remember me to my acquaintances in N. Port; and to the children.

I am yours affectionately

JOHN C. CALHOUN

SOURCE: *CC.*

20. To MRS. FLORIDE COLHOUN, N. Port, R. I.

Litchfield 3d. July 1806.

Dr Madam; Since my answer to your last, I have received letters both from my brother James and Alexander Noble. They have relinquished the journey, which they contemplated some time since to this place. James has thought it best to wind up [hi]s marcantile buisiness in order to begin anew. This demanded his presence in Carolina; and consequently defeated his coming on to N. York.[1] Alexander Noble has intirely relinquished the buisiness of a merchant for that of a farmer. He is connected with his brother Ezekiel in the planting way. I cannot but approbate his c[h]oice; for, tho' less profitable it certainly is more peaceable and favourable to happiness. Dr Noble has purchased a plantation on Savannah river, with an expectation of leaving Charleston in a few years.[2] Since my last, we have had the pleasure of seeing Mr. Dehone, brother and two of his sisters.[3] He was here on Sunday; and preached at the episcopal c[h]urch. His Sermon was much ad[mire]d. I have had some expectation of seeing you here, as I think you would find traveling conducive to your health; and as the road and country hither are agreeable. I have never experienced so cool a summer as this has been. We have not had a day disagreeably warm. Vegetation is now not much more forward here than when we left Charleston last year. This is owing some what to the elevated situation of the place. I have a favour to ask of you which I do with reluctance owing to the many I have already received. James who has the management of my affairs and on whom I depend for remittance

1. See Nos. 16 and 18.
2. For the Nobles see No. 7.
3. Presumably Rev. Theodore Dehon, then Rector of Trinity Church, Newport; from 1809, of St. Michael's, Charleston (Dalcho, *Historical Account of the Protestant Episcopal Church in S.C.*, p. 223).

informed me in his last that owing to his concluding [hi]s buisiness he will find it more [di]fficult to meet the demands on him in Charleston and N. York during the summer than he expected; and would therefore find it some what inconvenient to make the summer remittance to me. If you can make it perfectly convenient to supply me till the fall you will oblige both my brother and myself. In case you could make it convenient, I will be able to return it during the course of the winter. Two hundred dollars will answer my present want. If it is not perfectly convenient I hope you will not put yourself to any trouble; but merely to let me know it so that I may writ on to my brother as soon as possible.

     I am yours with esteem

J OHN C. C ALHOUN

Our vacation takes place about the 20th August at which time I expect to see N. Port. Remember me to the children; and to all acquaintances.

     20 NOTE: Whether or not Mrs. Colhoun sent him the amount, he was still short of money as the vacation approached, for on Aug. 14 he provided for a bill of $49.39, for wearing apparel or materials (the largest item of which was $15 for "2 yds Super Black Sedan B cloth") by making a note for the amount (page from Stephen Dodge's ledger, with notation by John Bissell, 1879, Litchfield Historical Society.)   SOURCE: *CC.*

21. To M RS . F LORIDE C ALHOUN , New Port, R.I.

Litchfield 11th Sepr. 1806.

Dr Madam, After a tedious, and rather a disagreeable journey, I reach[*ed*] this place, without any material incident, Saturday evening. I had the pleasure of finding my friends here well; and felt a secret satisfaction on returning to a place, in which I have spent so many agreeable moments. How quickly we become attached to an agreeable residence. I assure you, I felt a considerable regret in leaving N. Port; and had I continued there much longer, at this pleasant season of the year, and with so many pleasant acquaintances, I should [*have*] left it with great reluctance. I always endeavour to make the place I reside in agreeable; from a conviction, that it is necessary to every other enjoyment. I never yet observed

31

a person to enjoy himself, who was in the habit of declaiming at the place, or at those round him. To be satisfied in this particular is something more than necessary to other enjoyments; it is itself a source of perpetual pleasure. By spreading delight on all the objects around us, it fills the soul with a secret and continual pleasure. I have no expectation of being at commencement, as the vacation is up and the lectures commenced. The present subject, on which the judge is lecturing, is an important one; and I think it my duty to make pleasure yield to interest. Remember me to all my acquaintances in New Port, particularly to Mr and Mrs Horry, Mr and Miss Thurston and Mr Ward.

  I am yours affectionately

               JOHN C. CALHOUN

Give my love to the children.

  SOURCE: *CC.*

22. To MRS. FLORIDE COLHOUN, Newport, R.I.

               Charleston 22d. Decr. 1806.

Dear Madam, Sensible that you are always desireous of hearing from me I can scarcely excuse myself In not writing till the present time. The day before I left Litchfield, I answered your last, in which I mentioned my determination to set out in a few days for Carolina by land. I proceeded to Philadelphia in the stage, where I purchased a horse and finished the remainder of the Journey on horse back, through what is generally called the uper rout. In a tour so long, without a companion, and a stranger to the road I necessarily experienced many solitary hours. My reward was the perpetual gratification of curiosity in passing through a country entirely new to me, romantick in a high degree, and abounding with many objects of considerable novelty. On my arrival in Carolina I was happy to find all my friends and relations well, with only a few instances of slight fall fevers. After spending a few weeks in Abbeville I returned to this place, where I expect to continue in Mr. Desaussure's law office till june; at which time I expect to retire to the uper country for health;[1] as it will not be safe for me with

  1. In the original Calhoun wrote "up country" and then added the "er" superscript. See No. 16, n. 1.

my no[r]thern habit to continue in Charleston. Your acquaintances here, as far as I know, are well. Mr. Macklehaney with his family spends the winter in St. Pauls. He was in Charleston a few days since but I did not see him. Mr. Pickens is at Columbia attending the session of the legislature.[2] I have not as yet seen him. It is said he is shortly to be married; I think to a Mrs Barksdale, sister to Thomas Asby, who is dead. I suppose the report is true. Since my arrival here I have been very much of a recluse. I board with the French prodestant Minister Mr. Detargney in Church ["Meeting" *cancelled*] Street.[3] It is a quiet house and answers my purpose well. At Columbia I saw Robert Anderson who was applying for admission to the bar at the constitutional court. He expects to settle at Grenvill court house. It is said, though I am loth to believe it, that his father treats him very harshly.[4] He has given him, as yet, little or no property; and would not permit him to dwell with him in the same house, tho' his son had not then prepared himself with one. I was truely sorry to hear it both on acccount of the father and the son. Robert is illy qualified to bear such treatment; and it will tend to injure his farther's reputation so much. It is attributed much to the insinuations of his mother in law. Since she is dead, I hope a good understanding will take place. I saw Mr. Horry a few days since he was well. Remember me to all acquaintances particularly to Miss and Mr Thurston

I am yours affectionately

JOHN C. CALHOUN

I am anxious to hear how the second winter agrees with you do writ me. Give my love to the children. Your friends here all fear you will desert them wholly.

SOURCE: *CC.*

2. Ezekiel Pickens, Mrs. Colhoun's brother-in-law, took his seat as Senator for the Parish of St. Thomas and St. Dennis, Dec. 2, 1806 (Senate Journal, S. C. Archives). He married Elizabeth Bonneau, Feb. 4, 1793, and Elizabeth Barksdale, Jan. 5, 1807 (*SCHM,* XXI [1920], 154; XXXIII [1932], 46).

3. Rev. Martin Detargney (*SCHM,* XXXI [1930], 67).

4. See Brackett, *Old Stone Church,* p. 150.

23. RESOLUTIONS ON THE CHESAPEAKE-LEOPARD
AFFAIR

[Abbeville, Aug. 3, 1807][1]

["Pursuant to a notification previously given the inhabitants of Abbeville District, S.C. convened at the Court-House of the same, for the purpose of expressing, together with their Fellow-citizens throughout the United States, their sentiments on the line of conduct adopted and pursued by the British Cabinet, and its subjects, towards their government.

"On motion of Mr. J. C. Colhoun, Col. Joseph Colhoun [2] was called to the Chair, and of Dr. T. Casey, Mr. S. B. Shields appointed Secretary.

"The Chairman being authorised to nominate a committee, twenty one gentlemen were selected, to report such resolutions as the nature of the circumstance appeared necessarily to require. The meeting then adjourned until 3 o'clock, when the committee thro' George Bowie,[3] Esq their Chairman, made known the following Resolves, with observations prefixed, which were unanimously received and adopted as the sentiments of the whole community:"] [4]

On all public emergencies, as it is our undoubted right, so we hold it our bounden duty to give a clear and unequivocal expression of our sentiment. The occasion which has given birth to the present meeting, imperiously enjoins a faithful discharge of this duty. We are urged by the torrent of our feelings, to give vent to an indignation deep and universal. Longer Silence illy becomes those in whom the Sovereignty of the country ultimately resides; it would be in Discord with our Esteem and Duty to the Administration of our General Government, which ought in all cases requiring vigorous exertions of the National Power to be supported, confirmed, and emboldened by a hearty co-operation of the community; it would disgrace our character Abroad, and exhibit us a degenerate

1. The date is given in the Charleston *City Gazette*, Sept. 2, 1807.
2. Joseph Calhoun was son of Calhoun's uncle William, and he so spelled his name, but it was commonly rendered Colhoun by his contemporaries—see, for instance, Accounts Audited, No. 997, May 7, 1785, S.C. Archives. For the misspelling of Calhoun's name in the South Carolina records see No. 26.
3. See No. 25.
4. The paragraphs in brackets are not in the text of Calhoun's resolutions but are the account of the meeting and are reproduced exactly as in the source.

and pusillanimous people, instead of a nation glorying in its Independence, united by a common and enthusiastic Patriotism; and resolute, by a joint exertion of strength, to maintain the united and indivisible interest of our common country. This expression of our Resentment, and determination to defend at all events our rights, cannot in the eye of an impartial world be regarded as the wanton desire of war. We have been the friends of peace. An habitual attachment to it is a deep-marked trait in our national character. Our natural humanity, the excellent and benevolent principles of our Government; and our Situation, in which the bounteous hand of Heaven has so profusely lavished its blessings, as to a place every virtuous object of enjoyment in the reach of just and honorable industry; have all concurred and combined to nourish, invigorate and confirm, this truly divine principle. As no object under Heaven, our Independence as a nation and sacred Constitution excepted, is superior in our affections to National Peace, the excellent Administration of our General Government has, with the enthusiastic approbation of a Great People, endeavoured by all laudable means; by Civility, by Humanity and Justice, to render our friendship with all people permanent and secure.

This conduct we rejoice, has in many instances been reciprocated on the part of other nations. One, however, by a series of unjust and outrageous acts, to both our individual and national rights, has evinced to the world how inveterate her hatred is to our country; how regardless she is of the laws of nations; and how inattentive to the peace and interest of her subjects. Great Britain, by her repeated gross and flagrant outrages, the impressment of our citizens, capturing our vessels, and insulting conduct in our harbours, seems determined to demonstrate, if possible, that our Love of Peace, instead of a noble principle and a generous sentiment, is only mean sufferance, and stupid insensibility; this is refuted, by well directed exertion of public energy; it is time her folly and injustice should rebound with deep inflicted wounds on herself. When on our coasts, and almost in sight of our Capital, our citizens, by her brutal violence, are murdered; a public armed vessel wholly disabled; the American Eagle struck and insulted; when unheard of indignities and outrage are offered to a humane, just, patriotic and powerful nation, every tongue should be raised to denounce the insult; every arm be stretched to avenge the injury; there should be one common Burst of National Indignation. Therefore;

Resolved, 1st. That this assembly view, with the deepest abhorrence, the unjust and murderous conduct of the British armed vessel Leopard to the United States frigate Chesapeake.

Resolved, 2nd. That it will regard as enemies of our country all, (should any be so base) who either directly or indirectly, by actions words or any means whatsoever, pretend to justify the said detestable conduct of the British.

Resolved, 3d. That the President's Proclamation has our full approbation, and that so far as our interior situation permits, we will make every possible exertion to enforce strict obedience to it.

Resolved 4th. That if the wisdom of the Government should deem a suspension of Commercial Intercourse with Great Britain and her dominions necessary, that we, emulating the glorious example of '76 and relying confidently on the resources of our country, as abundantly productive of all the necessaries and conveniencies of life, will readily renounce, as mere luxuries, all articles of foreign importation.

Resolved, 5th. That [*in*] this alarm[ing cri]sis every personal feeling and party [con]sideration ought to be immerged; [and] that we will not regard him as friendly to our country who shall endeavour to excite and foment the former differences which divided us as to the domestic administration of our government.

Resolved, 6th. That such of this assembly as are capable of military service, do consider themselves as citizen soldiers; and do pledge themselves to discharge with cheerfulness and promptitude, and at the hazard of ease, property and blood, whatever duty their country may impose.

Resolved, 7th. That it is expedient that the Militia of this State be put in a better posture of defence, and that the harbors of the United States be fortified with all possible expedition.

Resolved 8th. That the conduct of our Fellow-citizens of Norfolk,[5] and the neighbouring boroughs, is truly American, and has excited in us the most lively sense of gratitude, love and admiration.

5. A riot in Norfolk provoked British threats and these in turn brought about meetings and resolutions—see *Charleston Courier*, July 7, 1807.

Resolved, 9th. That full confidence is reposed in the Wise and Patriotic Administration of our General Government.

Resolved, 10th. That a copy of these resolutions be transmitted to the President of the United States, and to the executive of this State, by the Chairman.

Resolved, 11th. That these Resolutions be published in the Carolina Gazette, the Georgia and Carolina Gazette, and Miller's Weekly Messenger.

JOSEPH COLHOUN, Chairman
S. B. SHIELDS Secretary.

["The thanks of the assembly were unanimously tendered to the Chairman for the dignified manner in which he discharged the duties of his office; after which a short but pertinent address was delivered by Mr. J. C. Colhoun, at the conclusion of which the meeting finally adjourned."]

23 NOTE: "A committee was appointed to report to an adjourned meeting. . . . Mr. Calhoun was selected as one of the committee, and . . . was appointed by the committee chairman of the sub-committee to draught the address, and report resolutions to be submitted to the people. He was also requested by the committee to address the meeting when the resolutions should be proposed for their adoption. . . . The assemblage was very large. It was the first time he was brought before the public." (Virgil Maxcy's 1831 "Biographical Memoir"; compare the 1843 *Life,* p. 7, account.)

Alexander Bowie, George Bowie's brother, at that time eighteen years of age, was present; over forty years later he declared that Calhoun "astonished every body, and laid the foundation of that enduring popularity in his native district which he retained to the day of his death." ("Brief Sketch of Mr. Calhoun," *Camden* [S.C.] *Weekly Journal,* Oct. 24, 1854.) For Bowie see O'Neall, *Bench and Bar of S.C.,* II, 420. SOURCE: State Historical Society of Wisconsin, *Miller's Weekly Messenger* (Pendleton, S.C.), Aug. 13, 1807.

24. TO MRS. FLORIDE COLHOUN, New Port, R.I.

Abbeville 1st. Octr. 1807

Dr Madam, You will believe me, that I feel not a little anxiety to hear from you and your family, when I inform you, that I have not had a sylable of inteligence concerning you since you left

Charleston last spring. I attribute this wholly to the miscarriage of the mail; for sure am I, that you would not have permited so long a time to have passed without writing to one, who is ever anxious to hear of your well fare. So little has occured since my last to you, that I am at a loss in communicating any thing new or interesting. This Part of our state has been blessed with an extremely healthy summer. Not one of your acquaintance that I know of, that has not enjoyed good health. I have not had better health for many years. A few days since, I heard from Seneca. Your friends there are all well. We ought to feel thankful for this; more espacially as in some parts of the state it is said to be uncommonly sickly. The strangers fever is said to be unusually fatal this year in Charleston. Every paper from there brings a long catalouge of deaths. This is in part no doubt to be attributed to the nature of the climate; but a much greater part is owing to the misconduct of the inhabitants; and may be considered as a curse for their intem[p]erance and debaucheries.

I have spent on the whole a pleasant summer; and cannot but think this part of South Carolina very much improved of late; and that it still is in a state of progressive improvement. I hope in a few years, that for society, morals and info[r]mation it will be equal to any other part of the United States. Providence has given us a fine country all that is lacking is our own exertion. It gives me real pleasure to find simernaries of learning becoming so respectable and numerous. Mr. Waddel still continues to have a fine school. He is much pleased with the behaviour and progress of your Nephew. He bids fair to make an excellent scholar. Not long since, I attended an examination at Mr. Waddels with which I was much pleased, as the students appeared generally correct and well informed

I am your sincere friend

JOHN C. CALHOUN

Give my love to Floride, Elizabeth John and James; and remember me to all my friends in New Port. Your friends here would be much Pleased at your spending the winter with your family in this part of So Carolina.

J. C. C.

SOURCE: *CC.*

25. APPLICATION FOR ADMISSION TO PRACTICE IN THE CHANCERY COURTS

[7 March 1808]

State of South Carolina,

To the Honorable the Judges of the Court of Chancery of state aforesaid,

The humble pitetion of John C. Calhoun Sheweth that he is a citizen of the United States and resides in this state; that he has attained the age of twenty one years; that he has diligently read law in the offices and under the direction of certain practising attornies partly in this state and partly in that of Connecticut (viz) in the office [of] James Gold and Tapping Reeves of the state last mention[ed]; and the offices of H. W. Desaussure & Timothy Ford and George Bowie [1] of this state for the term of three years; that for the term of one year immediately preceding this application he has served a regular and diligent Clerkship in the officies of practising attornies in this state, all which will more fully appear by the annexed certificates; and that he has graduated in Yale College in the state of Connecticut. Therefore he prays your Honors that he may be admited to practice in the several courts of Chancery in this state; & your petitioner as in duty bound will ever pray.

JOHN C. CALHOUN

Be it so [*signed*] W. JAMES
W: THOMPSON.[2]

25 NOTE: Endorsed: "In Equity Exparte J C Calhoun ⎱ Petition for admittance 1808—No. 15—fild 7 March 1808."

The requirements for admission to practice in the law and equity courts were identical (Cooper, *Statutes of S.C.*, V, 521-2). For a year preceding his application for examination the candidate must have served as clerk in a law office; therefore Calhoun could not apply earlier than November or December, 1807 (note the time of his return to the state as indicated in No. 22). Maxcy's "Biographical Memoir" states that he was admitted in December, 1807, and this is confirmed by a letter to John E. Colhoun, Jr., of Jan. 20, the year of which is missing, in which Henry W. DeSaussure writes that Calhoun had been "examined & admitted to the bar"

1. For George Bowie see No. 23 and No. 29, n. 1.
2. Chancellors Waddy Thompson and William Dobein James—O'Neall, *Bench and Bar of S. C.*, I, 236, 241-2.

(DeSaussure Papers, *SCL*); DeSaussure's remark that he expected to visit Boston "perhaps in the summer of 1809" indicates that he was writing in January, 1808. SOURCE: Miss Helen C. Leonard, Spartanburg, S.C., 1953.

26. MOTION IN THE SOUTH CAROLINA HOUSE OF REPRESENTATIVES ON COMPENSATION OF THE STATE CENSUS TAKERS

December 13, 1808

[*On Motion of Mr. Colhoun*[1]]

Resolved That the Committee of priviledges and elections be required to fix the Compensation which shall be allowed in each Circuit District to the person who shall take the Census.

26 NOTE: The census was the state census of 1809 to determine the representation in the House under the constitutional amendment of 1808 (*Acts and Resolutions of S.C.*, 1808, p. 41-4). The committee's report, Dec. 16, was accepted by the House and Senate and printed in *ibid.*, p. 107-8.

Calhoun was elected from Abbeville District to the state House of Representatives in October, 1808 (Charleston *City Gazette,* Oct. 26, 1808); he took his seat Nov. 28. He was next day appointed Chairman of the Committee on Claims; he also served on a number of other committees, especially those having to do with judicial and constitutional matters, *e.g.*, Judiciary, Courts of Appeal, the Reform Bill, Equity Suits, Jurisdiction of Magistrates and the Suffrage Bill—House Journal, Nov. 29, Dec. 1, 2, 8, 1808; Nov. 29, Dec. 9, 1809. On the last date he was appointed chairman of a committee on the bill for establishing white manhood suffrage (passed by that legislature and made part of the Constitution Dec. 19, 1810—Cooper, *Statutes of S.C.*, I, 195), but it does not appear that this was more than a matter of form. He was elected trustee of the South Carolina College Dec. 12, 1809 (House Journal, Dec. 13), and attended meetings in April, 1810, and April 24-27, 29, May 1, 1811, at which last date he resigned. In these minutes likewise his name was spelled Colhoun (Minutes Board of Trustees, S.C. College).

1. Calhoun's name was consistently spelled Colhoun in the Journal, as had usually been the case with his cousin, Joseph Calhoun, who served in the state Senate and House; see also No. 23, n. 2, and No. 31.

The "Biographical Memoir" and the 1843 *Life* (p. 7) represent Calhoun as having made a speech to the caucus of Republican members, early in the session, in favor of John Langdon of New Hampshire for Vice-President, but no version of it or other reference to it has been found.   SOURCE: S.C. Archives, Journals of the House of Representatives, Dec. 13, 1808.

27. To MRS. FLORIDE CALHOUN, Charleston, S.C.

Newbury Court house 6th Aprl 1809

Dr. Madam, I regret exceedingly that I cannot carry into effect my expectation of visting Charleston before your departure thence. I have received during the circuit a considerable influx of Chancery buiseness; which as that court sets in June it will be impossible without a considerable neglect of my professional duties. I consider myself as not a little unfortunate in this disapointment; as while you were in the up country I had no opportunity excepting amidst the hurry of buiseness to spend any time in your company. I should have been glad to have conversed with you on many points: but we must all submit to those duties which call friends to a distance from one another. It is perhaps one of the most disagreable circumstance[s] in our profession, that we cannot neglect its persuit, without being Guilty at the same time of imprudence and a breach of confidence, reposed in us by our clients. I feel myself now and while I continue in the practice of the law almost as a slave chained down to a particular place and course of life. I have been very successful on the circuit in obtaining buiseness; and doubt not in a short time to have as much as I can conveniently attend to; however I still feel a strong aversion to the law; and am determined to forsake it as soon as I can make a decent independence; for I am not ambitious of great wealth.

Do let me hear from you frequently; and I on my part will promise you not to be a remiss correspondent. I [wish?] you a plesant and safe [voy]age; and that you may find your family in good health and progressed in their education. I should be glad to spend the summer northwardly were it possible; but must submit to necessity. Remember me to all friends.

I am with sentiment of esteem yours &c

JOHN C. CALHOUN

SOURCE: *CC.*

28. To Mrs. Floride Calhoun, New Port, R.I.

Abbeville 25th. June 1809

Dr Madam, After I left you at the plantation, I had a very pleasant, tho' solitary Journey, to this place. I spent a night and a day with Mr Shackleford. He is one of those who improve on acquaintance; of a liberal hospitable character, he seems to live with great ease ["hospitality" *cancelled*] and happiness in his family. At Pine Vile, I spent two days. I had the pleasure of meeting Dr McBride [1] and a number of my acquaintances, which m[a]de my stay delightful. I never was in a place where there was more appeareant equality and friendship among its inhabitants than in that ["place" *cancelled*]. I did not see the object of the Docter's affections, as she was gone to Charleston; which was of considerable regret to him and myself. She has the reputation, however, of being hansome; and, which to my mind is of much more importance, an amiable fine charecter. I felt a delightful sympathy at the prospect of my friend's happy establishment in life. It also called up strongly in my mind another subject of interest more important to myself. You know the one I alude to. It will be useless for me to conceal from you my increased anxiety on that subject. The more I reflect on it, the more indisoluably does my happiness seem to be connected with that event. If, I should finally be disappointed by any adverse circumstance, which heaven forbid, it will be by far the most unlucky accident in my life. I look for you next fall without any doubt, and at all events; and hope nothing but an impossibility will prevent you; at which time, I hope, at least, but still much more, to get rid of my anxiety. As to any disclosure if that may be necessary; I leave it wholly to your prudence; For I feel that nothing can shacke my regard. On my return I found it universally report as I conjectured. In fact to me it is quite unaccountable how thich [*such*] an impression should become so universal. Remember me to all my acquaintances to James and to ———

I am with esteem yours &c

John C. Calhoun

Do make no delay in writing to me. I expect to hear from you by the time you receive this.

1. See No. 44 note.

28 NOTE: This letter shows that Mrs. Colhoun was at her plantation, Bonneau's Ferry (the Eastern Branch of Cooper River), St. John's Berkeley, for a visit by Calhoun during May, for the Chancery Court sessions for the northwestern district were scheduled to begin June 5 (Cooper, *Statutes of S.C.*, VII, 304) and Mrs. Colhoun on June 18 wrote from Newport to Calhoun and to Henry W. DeSaussure (see his of July 3 to Ezekiel Pickens, DeSaussure Papers, *SCL*). Her letter of Sept. 2, 1809, to Andrew Pickens, Jr. (*SCHM*, IV [1903], 190-1), and DeSaussure's to Ezekiel make it clear that her daughter Floride did not come with her; and these letters and the time of Mrs. Colhoun's 1807 (see No. 24) and 1809 trips to Charleston indicate that Calhoun had not seen Floride in recent months and probably not since the spring of 1808. Starke says that Calhoun visited Mrs. Colhoun and her family at Bonneau's Ferry in the "spring" of 1808 before he was admitted to Chancery practice (Jameson, *Correspondence*, p. 86). The admission was Mar. 7 (see No. 25); but, substantiated by other evidences, Starke's statement may be taken as an approximation. Therefore Calhoun was already in love with Floride, and the encouragement that Mrs. Colhoun now gave him indicates that she was sure of her daughter's feeling in the matter. Yet, although this situation had existed for months, it is fairly obvious that she had not allowed Calhoun to ask permission to pay court to Floride; this may throw light on the touch of formality in his April letter. That Floride, wittingly or not, had something to do with her mother's suddenly granted permission is suggested by a remark in Mrs. Colhoun's September letter to Pickens on a "foolish report which prevail'd in Charleston, that Floride was engag'd to be married, and indeed they went so far as to say the event had taken place, but there was not the least foundation for such a report." That this report had not been received in Charleston as idle gossip is shown by the careful and judicious DeSaussure, who in his July letter to Ezekiel referred to "the report about F. which gave us so much uneasiness." SOURCE: *CC*.

29. TO MRS. FLORIDE CALHOUN, New Port, R.I.

Abbeville 18th July 1809.

Dr Madam, By the last mail, I received your agreeable letter of the 18th Ultimo.

Except of my hearty thanks for the promtitude of your communication; which has released my mind from no small degree of anxiety. I can scarcely describe my emotions, when I saw your well known hand writing with the New Port post mark. But the contrariety of emotion it excited of hope and fear quickly subsided into the most agreeable feeling on perusing its contents.

This language does not correspond with my former opinion on this subject. I formerly thought that it would be impossible for me to be strongly agitated in an affair of this kind; but that opinion now to me seem[s] wholly unfounded, since, as it were in the very commencement, it can produce such effects. Do let me know in your next, at what time in the fall I may expect you. The time will seem long, and, I hope, you will make your return as soon after the sickly season as possible. So unlimited is my confidence in your prudence and friendship, that to you, I make the full and entire disclosure of the most inward recesses of my thoughts; while to all the world, even to my own brothers, I am quite silent. I have a strong inclination to lay open my intention to the object of my affection by letter; if this meet with your approbation, as proper, nothing will prevent me from so doing. Will you be so good, as to let me know your sentiment, on that point; and whether, I may have your assent to such corresponde[nce].

I dined with Mr. Bowie yesterday. Mrs. Bowie is some what better than she was.[1] I saw your nephews on the 4th July. They were well. All your acquaintances here are in good health. Mr. Picken's has not passed yet on his way to Pendleton. I saw Mr. Dubose a few days since; he told me your crop looked well tho' it had been dry. Remember me to your family & all acquaintances

I am your's affectionately

JOHN C. CALHOUN

I wrote yo[u sin]ce my return from Charleston be so good [as to] inform me whether you have Reced. my letter or not

SOURCE: *CC.*

1. Presumably Mrs. George Bowie, who was Margaret, daughter of General Andrew Pickens, and therefore cousin of Calhoun and, by marriage, of Mrs. Colhoun (O'Neall, *Bench and Bar of S.C.*, II, 207).

30. To Mrs. Floride Colhoun, New Port, R.I.

Abbeville 1st October 1809.

Dr Madam, By the last mail I received yours of the first of September. How much am I indebted for that kind solicitude which you have ever evinced for my happiness. In this, the true criterion of friendship, you have exceed[*ed*] all my friends; and have ever acted more as a Parent than a simple well wisher. Never, shall I be able to make you sutiable return, for so disinterested and generous conduct.

Oh may I hope that the time is not far off, when I shall stand in a relation to you more congenial to my feelings, than that which now exists between us. It gives much fond anticipation to learn from your letter that you will revisist us next winter; and as I hope to take up your permanent residence here. If you come by water, do inform me immediately on your arrival by letter. If it should be after the twentieth of November direct your letter to Columbia; as I shall be there at the last of that month. If you return by land it is likely you will come to the upper country first. At all events I expect to see you in November or early in December.

.Your friends here are well, & except Wentworth [1] have enjoyed good health this fall. He had an attack of the fall fever; which I have no doubt he brought on by too much study and too little exercise. He is now well; and at Pendl[eton.] Our country has been healthy generally. The mail is just going so I must conclude.

I am your sincere friend

John C. Calhoun

Remember to John, James Elizabeth and all friends.

You are at liberty to read the inclosed which you will be so good, as to seal and deliver.

Source: *CC.*

1. Wentworth Boisseau. He is called Mrs. Colhoun's nephew (No. 34); the relationship has not been established, but a James Edward Boisseau, an exiled Loyalist, received a conditional bequest from her father, Samuel Bonneau (John Ewing Colhoun Papers, *SCL*).

31. Notice in the South Carolina House of Representatives for Introduction of Justice and Limitation Bills

December 4, 1809

Mr. Colhoun gave notice that on Tuesday next he would move leave to introduce the two following bills

A Bill to expedite and render more easy the administration of Justice in this State—also a bill to enable parties in certain Cases to give Copy wills in evidence & to alter the Act commonly Called the Limitation Act.

31 NOTE: On December 5, these two bills were given a first reading. The title of the second read "to give in Evidence copies of wills in actions where the Titles to Lands may come in question, & to alter and amend an act . . . for settling the Titles of the Inhabitants of this province to their possessions. . . ." It appears not to have passed the second reading. The limitation act was the one of 1712, several times amended (Cooper, *Statutes of S.C.*, II, 583-8, and X [Index to *Statutes*], 340-2).

The justice act passed Dec. 19, 1809 (*ibid.*, VII, 308-9), providing that in case of a judgment entered against a defendant on a liquidated demand, the clerk should ascertain and enter the sum due, for a fee of twenty-five cents, and in case of a summons on such a demand in which the defendant made no defense, the plaintiff should not be required to prove his demand; that a bail given to a sheriff should be entitled to the privileges of special bail. The act also changed the dates for holding court at certain court houses. SOURCE: S.C. Archives, *Journal of the House of Representatives*, Dec. 4, 1809.

32. To Mrs. Floride Calhoun, Charleston

Abbeville 20th Jan. 1810

Dr Madam; Without pretending to decide whether that maxim from which you draw so much of your sperit of risignation to the various events of this life, "that all is for the best," is in every instance true, yet I am sure that in many instances things falling out different from what we would have ordered contribute to promote our happiness. This was my case the two last days I staid at the Ferry.[1] I spent them so pleasantly; and the reflection on them since has been such a copious source of gratification and delight, that I feel myself richly rewarded for the delay, had it been for weeks. I hope, I shall forever find cause to esteem them a fortunate and happy period of my life. Should it contribute in any degree to an event, I have so much at heart, how happy a man shall I be. May He who governs all things cause it to eventuate so happily!

I had fine weather on my return; and my journey was only made disagreeable by reflecting on the increasing distance of those for whom I have so great a regard. The very day after my return proved very cloudy, weat and disagreeable. I found all of our friends well, except Mrs. A. Pickens; who is at Mr Bowie's in a very low state. I was there last night; and think she cannot survive many days. Her case is thought to be a consumption.[2]

I sent your letter to Wentworth the day after my arrival; & expect to be at Dr Waddel's myself in two or three days. I am anxious to hear from the fe[rry] and hope you have not missed [the] opportunity by Mr. Milligan. I am ve[ry] desireous to know if you have had any conversation with Mr. E. P.[3] and what he says. Tell my *much esteem'd Floride* that nothing could prevent me from the pleasure of writing, but that there is so much suspicion on the subject, that I am fearfull of the fate of a double letter endorsed in my hand writing. I hope to see you early next month; let it not be if possible, past the midle. I would recommend the road by Gibham:[4] The road from the ferry there is as good and as near as from Charleston to the same place. ["Give my most ardent," *cancelled.*]

I am with great esteem your's &c

                                                    JOHN C. CALHOUN

Tell Floride that no time, or distance can in the least abate my affection, but that absence only proves how much my happiness depends on her good opinion.

SOURCE: *CC.*

1. For the Ferry see No. 28 NOTE.
2. Mrs. Susan Wilkinson Pickens, wife of Andrew Pickens, Jr., of Pendleton, died Jan. 28, 1810 (*SCHM*, XXIV [1933], 107).
3. Presumably Ezekiel Pickens.
4. Givhans Ferry on Edisto? (See Mills, *Atlas of S.C.*, Colleton District.)

33. To Mrs. Floride Calhoun, Newport, R.I.

Abbeville 12th June 1810

Dr Madam, I regret much I could not find a private opportunity of writing to you before you sailed from Charleston. I enquired deligently but could find none; and, on enquiry, found the mail could not reach there before the 17th or eighteenth. I got up safely. I was much favoured by the weather. I would have had a lonesome journey, had it not been that my thoughts were so much absorbed by that subject so important to me; and so near my heart. How important it is, on that occasion to have the full, and entire sanction of our reason; and how delightful it is, that the more I reflect, the greater cause I see, to thank that good providence who has directed my choice. I am not much given to enthusiasm; nor to anticipate future happiness. But, I cannot, now refrain my hopes of joy. On my part, I feel the most anxious solicitude for the happiness of one, to me dearer than all others; on her's, after a careful examination, I find none but those qualities in her character, which are suited to me; and are calculated to secure lasting enjoyment. Let me add, without the least imputation of flattery, that, to be so nearly related to yourself, is a fruitful source of happiness. I know not why, from my first acquaintance with you at New-Port, I have loved you as a mother. Sure am I, that I could not from a mother experienced more kindness and tender affection. With the blessing of God I cannot but be happy; when every circumstance is so propetious. If possible, I will be in New Port next fall. I wish much that Floride would consent to that time. I will write to her about it, by my next. I think on many accounts it will be the best. If you know her sentiment I would be glad you would let me know in your next for it will be a great induceme[nt] for me to go on, if she agrees [to] that time; and what is a matter of importance, will furnish a good excuse for my leaving my professional business at the fall court. Write me immediately on receiving this. I will be very anxious till I hear of your safe arrival. I start to Laurens tomorrow morning to attend the court of Equity there. Remember me to Elizabeth if she is with you, to James and John when you see him; also to all friends.

I am with every sentiment of [esteem?] and affection

JOHN C. [CALHOUN]

SOURCE: *CC.*

34. TO MRS. FLORIDE CALHOUN

Abbeville 30th June 1810.

Dr. Madam, Yesterday I received yours dated the 16th instant; which I had been anxiously waiting for the last two mails. I am happy to hear of the health of yourself and Floride; the more so, as the season is far advanced, and must be attended with considerable hazard to both of you. I was apprehensive, that you would be detained till too late a period; but it gives me pleasure to think that you have taken your passage direct to New-Port; and in the vessel you prefered. Your party cannot fail to contribute to the pleasure of the voyage; yet I greatly fear that you have had a very disagreeable and rough one. For, since the time you were to have embarked, the wind has been almost invariably to the east, accompanied with much rain and thunder. We have had near a week of incessant rain. Savannah river and most of the other streams have been out of their banks; which has done no inconsiderable damage.

I left Dr. Waddel's two days ago. Mrs. Boisseau and your two nephews were then well. Wentworth still continues to apply himself too closely. His constitution is not suffeciently strong for the exertions which he makes.

I am glad you mentioned the subject, so near my heart, to Mr. Desaussure. It always struck me it would be proper to do so, and I should have mentioned it myself, if you had not. I am convinced he is a friend to both of us. You mention that "he will have some conversation with me on the subject." This makes me doubly anxious to see him, for whatever has the least relation to it arrests my attention. Whatever comes from the judge shall receive from me a serious consideration. I am sure it will be the dictate both of friendship and prudence. I consider him a man of great discretion. I will write you as soon as we have had the conversation; which cannot now be long. I wrote to you inclosing a letter to Floride on the 12th Instant, which I directed to New-Port. I hope you will find it on your arrival. I am with every sentiment of esteem . . . .[1]

Remember me to James, Elizabeth, if with you, and all acquaintances

SOURCE: Jameson, *Correspondence,* p. 115-6. (This letter and Nos. 43 and 109 were printed by Jameson from the originals, which have not been located.)

35. To MRS. FLORIDE CALHOUN

Abbeville 18th July, 1810

I have not yet seen the Judge, but by the last mail I had a letter from him dated at Columbia requesting me to meet him at Greenville, but I was so unfortunate as not to receive it till the day appointed for the meeting. So that all the anticipated pleasure of travelling through so pleasant a part of our State and with so pleasant a companion was defeated. I expect the Judge here in a few days and shall be punctual in writing to you. I have been looking out for some weeks past for a place to purchase so as to establish myself permanently for life. I was desirous of purchasing on the Savannah river near my relatives, but I find only one place for sale there and that at a price nearly double its value. At present I have in view a place near my brother Patrick's. It is a valuable one and as pleasant as any in that part of the State. If I purchase I may commence building immediately, but perhaps it will be best to postpone building till some time next winter, for should the event I have so much at heart take place next winter according to present arrangements and I should be elected to Congress next fall, of which I suppose there is no doubt, both my own inclination and the health of Floride would require the following summer to be spent in travel. It would scarcely be worth while to commence housekeeping for so short a time, especially as I should not be able to return to Carolina till the summer after, owing to the session of Congress. By postponing building I shall be able to consult yours and Floride's taste. Let me know your opinion on this point.

1. It is likely that Jameson here omitted no more than the signature.

35 NOTE: Calhoun in October, 1813, wrote from his new home, Bath, near the Savannah River (see No. 86, n. 1). He was in Charleston or St. John's in the spring of 1811 and spent that summer at Pendleton (Nos. 42-4). It is therefore improbable that he built or lived "near my brother Patrick's" (the original family plantation in Abbeville District) after his marriage.   SOURCE: *CC*, from transcript of MS biography of Calhoun by W. Pinckney Starke; for note on this sketch see Jameson, *Correspondence*, p. 18.

36. TO MRS. FLORIDE COLHOUN, New Port, R.I.

Abbeville 27th July 1810

Dr Madam, I think you will not call me a negligent correspondent, as I have wrote to you regularly once a fortnight since my return from St. John's.[1] I formerly was considered the most indolent in letter writing; all my friends have censured me for that fault. But, now It is my delight. I could write you by every mail, were I not apprehensive of fatiguing you by such frequent communications. Time hangs heavily on my hands; tho' I endeavour to make it pass as pleasantly as possible by close application. I have not read so intensely since I commenced the practice of law; as I have this summer.[2] Yet it is impossible to divert my thoughts from her on

1. See No. 28 NOTE.
2. An interesting confirmation of Calhoun's habit of concentration and his self-imposed mental discipline is found in the recollection of Alexander Bowie (see No. 23 NOTE) who recalled that as he read law in Abbeville the summer of 1810 he was invited to accompany Calhoun on his habitual three-mile early morning walk. To impress on his young friend "the great importance of cultivating the *power of attention,* and to encourage me in my efforts he stated that to this end he had early subjected *his* mind to such a course of rigid discipline, and had persisted without faltering, until he had acquired a perfect control over it, and that he could now confine it as long as he pleased, to any subject without wandering even for a moment; and that it was his uniform habit, when he set out alone, to walk or ride, to select a subject for reflection, and that he never suffered his attention to wander from it until he was satisfied with its examination." This process—to Bowie's mind forty-four years later—made Calhoun "the greatest thinker of his age." (*Camden* [S.C.] *Weekly Journal,* Oct. 24, 1854.)

Virgil Maxcy (see No. 63 NOTE), who was at Litchfield in 1807 (Galloway-Maxcy-Markoe Papers, Aug. 12, 1807, *LC*), described Calhoun's method in the law school debates: "He usually prepared himself by reflection on the subjects proposed for discussion, but rarely, if ever, committed to writing the arrangement of his topics, or took notes of the arguments of those who preceded him. He relied on his tenacious memory for preserving the order established in his own mind" ("Biographical Memoir").

whom they naturally concentrate. Nor do I desire so to do; were it possible; for tho', the thought of so long an absence and so great a distance makes me pensive; yet it is of a pleasant kind. It is a sweet pain. Could I suppose that she was of a fickle character I should be wretched. But then I am happy; my trust in her constancy is entire. The more I dwell on her good qualities; and compare her with others of her sex, the stronger does my reason approbate the choice of my affection; the more devoutely do I thank that good providence, who has crowned my wishes with success. Heaven has been kind to me in many instances; but I will ever consider this as the greatest of its favours. I know much happiness, or much misery is the consequence of marriage. As far as, the former can be secured by prudence, by simerlarity of character and sincerity of love, I may flatter myself with no ordinary share of bliss.

I had a letter from Dr Noble yesterday. He mentions your saling at the time appointed. This surprises me the more, that I have not heard from you. A letter is only seventeen days from Newport to this place. You I fear must have had a long passage. How impatient I am to hear from you. The next mail, I feel, will bring me a letter. I have not yet seen Judge DeSaussure. I know not what detains him. It may be he will not be here till Doctor Waddel's exehibition, which is on the 14th. next month. Andrew Pickens was here last week. He left his daughter with Mrs Bowie. They are all well in Pendleton. All friends here are well.

I am with affection your &c

JOHN C. CALHOUN

Remember me to James & tell him I will be glad he would write to me.

Dr Noble does not mention [Eliza]beth sailing with you. From that I suppose you left her. If she is with you give my best respects to her; and tell her if she will except of my offer to correspond I would take much pleasure in writing to her

SOURCE: *CC.*

37. To Mrs. Floride Colhoun, New-Port, R.I.

Abbeville 24th August 1810

Dr Madam, You see I do not stand on the punctilio of receiving an answer to my last, before I make another communication. I have only received one letter from you and not one from Floride, since you left Carolina. I, on my part, have written eight or nine. In fact, I am almost affraid of fatiguing you; but as I take a pleasure in writing, I hope you will excuse me. You know it was not so with me formerly. I aknowledge the change. However much it pleases me to write to you, yet, I believe, you must look for the cause of such frequent communications to the enclosed. If absence makes as little abatement in Floride's affection, as mine, I will have nothing to fear. It is said to be the cure of love; but I have not found it so.

Mr. Waddel had his Exehibition on the 16th. General Pickens, his wife, Andrew and several others from Pendleton were at it. They are all well. The general & Mrs. Pickens were much pleased with the visit. The summer thus far is very healthy. I begin to think this the most healthy part of our country. I never heard of so little sickness and so few death[s] in N. England, as we have had for many years past.

I wish, I could conclude my letter, as pleasantly, as I have begun. I suppose by this time you have heard of the misconduct of Wentworth Boisseau. You, and I, and the world have been much deceived in him. O how strange it is! At first I could not believe it; but when I could no longer disbelieve, I was shocked beyond measure. Even now I cannot force it out of my mind. He is blasted forever in this country. A whole life of virtue could not restore his character. It is the first instance of that crime ever heard of in this part of the world. I cannot conceive how he contracted the odious habit, except, while a sailor to the West Indies. I have not seen him; nor do I wish to do so. The last mail, I had a letter from him, in which he asked my advice. I freely gave him my opinion to leave the country, and fly to some remote part; to give up all ideas of happiness in this life, and, by a life of contrition, to make his peace with heaven. May God grant him sincere repentance.

I am with affection

JOHN C. CALHOUN

I suppose you have heard parti[cula]rly, as Dr Waddel told me
he would write to you. I c[an] not name the crime. Do not mention
any thing of it to Floride. O how it [*would*] wound her tender and
inocent heart to hear of it. His mother knows nothing of it. It must
be almost her death.

Remember me to James and tell him I would be glad he would
write to me; and I will answer every letter he may send me

J. C. C.

Source: *CC.*

38. To Mrs. Floride Colhoun, New Port, R.I.

Abbeville 7th Sepr. 1810.

Dear Madam, I join with you in expression of gratitude to that
good providence, who has so mercifully preserved the life of one
so dear to our future hopes and happiness. The perusal of your
letter filled me with joy and sympathy at the same time. Joy for
her preservation; and sympathy for the pain she must have en-
dured. How often and unmerited do we experience the kind
interferance of heaven! Had her life not been spared, how uncon-
solable would have been our condition! I know not where I should
have look[*ed*] for relief. On her all my hopes concentrate. I hope
by this time she has entirely recovered. No care, that a fond
mother's solicitude could bestow, has been wanting, I dare say, to
effect a speedy and entire cure.

By the last mail, I had a long answer from Judge DeSaussure,
to a letter I had addressed him as soon as I heard of his return
to Charleston. He is pleased to express himself in very flattering
terms of me; and to give his entire approbation to the contemplated
connection. I am not only happy in the love and esteem of your
daughter; but in the concurring assent of all our mutual friends.
This swells the cup of bliss to the full. I, in every event of my life,
seem to myself more fortunate, than I deserve. How shall I be
sufficiently gratefull? Judge DeSaussure mentions the settlement of
Floride's property. I know not, but that it will be indelicate in me
to express my opinion on that subject. The fortune is her's. I am not
directed in my choice by it. Yet, I think it a duty, that I owe to
yourself & Floride to be perfectly candid on all points. From preju-

dice, or reason, I have been always opposed to marriage settlements. I think experience and reason prove them to be unfriendly to the happiness of the marriage state; and, that they tend to produce pecuniary embarresment. In that state there should be one interest, one happiness & one destiney. That entire confidence, which is reposed by a female in the object of her choice, in placing both her honor and property in his custody give rise to the most sacred and tender regard. A marriage settlement implys a distrust. It is no safety against inevitable accident. It is a guard against the imprudence, or misconduct of the husband only. As far as children are concerned, it places them above the dependence of the parents. Nothing can be more unfriendly to their government, or character. As to property, it often tends to prevent farther accumulation; and prevent an extrication at the commencement of an embarresment. If successful in life, there is no benefit in one; if unsuccessful, what more disagreeable than to have property, but not to be able to pay just debts? It would to me, be wretched. It would be splendid poverty. You have my candid sentiment; di[c]tated, not by selfish views, but a regard to our mutual happiness. It is my duty to give it.[1]

I find it impossible for me to leave Abbeville before some time in Novr. It will then be too late to visit New Port. It is a painful necessity to me. Do let me know immediately when you expect to leave N. Port; and whether you will return by land, or water. If you return by land and can make arrangement for me to meet you I will on my part be happy so to do. I hope you will return as soon as the season will permit. I never was so anxious to see Floride and yourself.

I am with lasting affection

JOHN C. CALHOUN

Give my compliments to James and all friends in New Port. I hope you will not fail to write immediately.

I cannot omit saying a word of the wretched Went[*wor*]th. About a week ago he came privately to my office to get my aid and advice. As his character is blasted here and the crime punishable with death I advised him to fly immediately; and furnished him with money. By this time he has fled to some foreign part. O what a reverse. I

1. See No. 43 and Wiltse, *Calhoun Nationalist*, p. 50.

wish I could offer consolation to you. You have been kind and beneficient to him; but he has proved wholly unworthy of it. He seemed penitential.[2]

Source: *CC.*

39. To Mrs. Floride Colhoun, New-Port, R.I.

Abbeville 13th Sepr. 1810

Dear Madam, I know not how to express my gratitude for that almost maternal regard, which you have always exercised towards me. Such is the warmth of affection, which, I feel towards you, that I can scarcely refrain from addressing you by the endearing epithet of mother. I hope the time now will not be long, when I may with propriety use it. That day, which will put me in that endearing relation towards you will be the happiest of my life. In yours of the 20th of August, which I received yesterday, you observe, "that should it be the will of the Almighty to unite me to Floride that you only wish, she may make me as happy as I deserve." In that event it will be mine to make her happy. Should I always remain with my present feeling, which I trust in God I may, no task will be half so sweet to me, as to make her, as happy, as the conditions of this life will permit. I have no doubt, Floride will be actuated with similar feelings towards me. This mutual love must constitute the joy of the marriage state. To be united in the sacred bonds of matrimony; to regard one another, as companions mutually united for mutual happiness, for each to place their greatest joy in the happiness of the other, is to my mind the most enviable condition on earth. O that our married life may so commence, so continue and so end! And that you, our dear mother, may long continue to live, to enjoy and participate in our happiness. Your account of the almost entire restoration of Floride from the effect of her bruises was very welcome. I felt much anxiety on that subject. I was fearful, particularly, that she would not recover the use of her finger. This would have been a great misfortune to us both. Your letter before the last gave me the first information of the accident. To

2. This paragraph has been cancelled, apparently at a later time, and Jameson does not print it (see *Correspondence,* p. 16 and 120).

that letter, I wrote an answer by the last mail. I mentioned in my last, that it would not be possible for me to visit N. Port this fall. My regret at this necessity is still the greater since you mentioned in your last that it is Florides wish to return by land. Neither convenience, or profit should prevent me from going; but I found, as court approached, that my duty to be here to discharge the tr[ust] reposed in me by my clients was im[pe]rious. I hope that it will meet with your's & Floride's approbation. If I were to advise you, I would recommend you to return by water. As I shall cease issuing business after this fall, I shall have leisure to accompany you by land hereafter. Which ever way you determine, I hope you will be here by the midle of Novr. If you conclude to come by water I shall be in Charleston by the 20th of that month, at fartherest. Your friends here are all well. It blows almost a storm at this moment. I fear much damage is done on the coast. Remember me to Mrs. Banister, Dr. Dehone, John Ewing if with you and James. Also to all friends.

I am with esteem & affection

JOHN C. CALHOUN

The last account I had of Mr. Pickens he had been very sick but was on the recovery. His family was well. This was 6 or 7 weeks ago. It was healthy in Charleston the 25th. August.

SOURCE: *CC.*

40. To MISS FLORIDE COLHOUN, New Port, R.I.

Abbeville, S.C., 28 Sept., 1810

I rejoice, my dearest Floride, that the period is fast approaching when it will be no longer necessary to address you through the cold medium of a letter. At furthest it cannot be much longer than a month before I shall behold the dearest object of my hopes and desires. I am anxious to see you and my impatience daily increases. May heaven grant you a safe return. What pleasure I have experienced in your company, what delight in the exchange of sentiment, what transport in the testimonies of mutual love. In a short time this with the permission of heaven will be renewed, and I shall be happy. To be united in mutual virtuous love is the first and best bliss that God has permitted to our natures. My dearest one, may our love strengthen with each returning day, may it ripen and mellow with our years, and may it end in immortal joys. It gives me much satisfaction that time and absence make no impression on my love for you; it glows with no less ardour than at the moment of parting, which must be a happy omen of its permanent nature. When mere personal charms attract, the impression may be violent but cannot be lasting, and it requires the perpetual presence of the object to keep it alive; but when the beauty of mind, the soft and sweet disposition, the amiable and lovable character embellished with innocence and cheerfulness are united to the attractions of personal beauty, it bids defiance to time. Such, my dear Floride, are the arms by which you have conquered, and it is by these the durability of your sovereignty is established over your subject whom you hold in willing servitude.

I am much involved in business at present. Court commences in two weeks, and in a week the election for Congress will take place. My opponent is Gen. Elmore of Laurens,[1] but it is thought that I will succeed by a large majority. As soon as the result is known I will inform you. Write me before you leave New Port. I wish you a pleasant journey home. May God preserve you. Adieu my love; my heart's delight.

I am your true lover,

JOHN C. CALHOUN

40 NOTE: The Calhoun family Bible (Fort Hill, Clemson, S.C.) gives the date of the marriage as Jan. 8, 1811. SOURCE: *CC.* From the transcript of the Starke biography—see No. 35 SOURCE.

41. From W. F. DeSaussure

Charleston. April 21, 1811

My Dear Sir, It gives me very great pleasure to communicate to you favorable news of our friend John Colhoun. The letter I enclose

1. John A. Elmore (O'Neall, *Bench and Bar of S.C.,* II, 85). Calhoun's cousin, Joseph Calhoun (No. 14, n. 1), who had served two terms, did not offer for re-election (*BDC*). The election was on Oct. 8 and 9 (Charleston *City Gazette,* Oct. 8, 1810). On the 22nd the paper states: "There is no doubt of the election of this gentleman."

you from Mr Silliman arrived at one o'clock today. It holds out a very encouraging prospect.[1]

I have engaged a passage for Mrs. Colhoun in the Schooner Maria—Latham Master—at Lothrop's wharf. She sails positively on Tuesday at 12 o'clock.[2] Mr. James Hunter & his wife are the only passengers of whom the Captain knows certainly. I have informed my Aunt DeSaussure, with whom Mrs Colhoun is intimate, that Mrs C goes in this vessel, & I think it highly probable that she will go with her—as she is very anxious to go immediately. The Schooner Maria is the only vessel that goes in a day or two to N York. And as she is a good & safe vessel—and as I knew Mrs. Colhoun would be anxious to sail immediately, I thought it better to engage a passage in her than in a large ship, which is about to sail for N York—but not I fear before monday week.

I enclose you all the papers since the 18th. that I could collect. We generally destroy them at home. If you have received the previous papers, you have doubtless heard of the positive [chan]ge in *our* ministry & also of the rumoured changes.[3] One of the papers I send you contains interesting remarks upon the Regent's speech extracted from a Paris paper.

My mother joins me in presenting her best respects to yourself— Mrs. Calhoun & her mother.

I am my dear Sir with great esteem yrs

W F DeSaussure

41 NOTE: William Ford DeSaussure was son of Henry W. DeSaussure.   SOURCE: *CC*.

1. John Ewing Colhoun, elder son of the Senator, was admitted to the freshman class of Yale in 1809 (*College Catalogue . . .* 1809), where he was entrusted to Professor Benjamin Silliman, who wrote, March 8, 1811, that the youth was dangerously ill (Henry W. DeSaussure, Oct. 6, 1809, to Ezekiel Pickens; Silliman to DeSaussure, Mar. 8, 1811—DeSaussure Papers, *SCL*). See No. 43 for note of his recovery. It was apparently John Ewing of whom Silliman was thinking when he said in 1850 that he had known Calhoun when he was preparing for Yale in Newport (Fisher, *Life of Benjamin Silliman*, II, 97-8).

2. April 21 was Sunday; the letter had no place address; Calhoun and Mrs. Calhoun were presumably with her mother at Bonneau's Ferry.

3. April 1, 1811, James Monroe became Secretary of State, following the dismissal of Robert Smith (Adams, *History of U.S.*, V, 375-7). The *Charleston Courier*, Apr. 11-7, had reports on Cabinet changes.

42. To Mrs. Floride Colhoun, New Haven, Conn.

8th May 1811—Charleston.

Dr Mother, I wrote you a few days since from Columbia; and now, agreeably to my promise, I make this farther communication. It must be your first desire to know how Floride does; I therefore hasten to state that on my return from Columbia a few days since, I had the pleasure to find her in good health and sperits. She looks I think better than when you left us; and feels less sickness than what I believe is usual in her condition. We return to the country tomorrow by way of Christ church. May and Jane Righton both accompany us. I shall return myself to this place about the 20th. when I hope at fartherest we shall here from you. Mr Pickens and family arrived in town last evening. They are well. The last evening Floride, Mr Righton's family and Mr Pickens & Elizabeth went to the theatre.[1] Floride is not at all pleased; and feels no inclination to renew ["return" *cancelled*] her visit there. I was pleased to see that her good sense prevented her from being dazzled by the glare of novelty. I hope my dear mother you had a pleasant voyage; and that you on your arrival had the pleasure of finding your son quite restored. We anxiously expect your return this summer.

Floride give[s] her love to you and John Ewing. Remember me to him and all acquaintances.

I am with affection your son

[Signature cut out]

Source: *CC.*

43. To Mrs. Floride Calhoun

23d May 1811, Charleston.

My dear Mother. Since my arrival here I have had the pleasure of perusing yours of the 11th instant to Floride. Your safe arrival at New-Haven and the restoration of John's health both afford the sincerest pleasure. His recovery is almost a merical. Few have been restored to health from so low a condition. The very kind attention which he seems to have received while in his sickness must be

1. For the Rightons see *SCHM*, XXXIII (1932), 160, 164.

highly pleasant to you. Your daughter still remains in good health and sperits. I left her at Mr Pickens. we shall start for the upper country in a few days. Mrs Sterling goes with us. We expect to go by way of Pine-Ville and Columbia. The division of property in the lower country has been made. It will also be made in the upper as soon as Mr Pickens goes up. I dined with Judge DeSaussure yesterday he informed me he would transmit $600 to you today. You do not mention at what time we may expect your return; we hope as soon as possible. The rice dam gave away a few days since near the old breach The breach is a very bad [one], and will be difficult to stop. I write in haste Floride joins her love to John Ewing. Remember me to all my acquaintances who enquire after me.

43 NOTE: The "division of property" was presumably that which was made in lieu of a marriage settlement (No. 38). SOURCE: Jameson, *Correspondence*, p. 123—see No. 34 SOURCE.

44. To DR. JAMES MACBRIDE, Pine-Ville, S.C.

Abbeville 10th Sepr. 1811.

Dr MacBride, By accident, I received your letter of 1st instant a few hours since. I intended to return to Pendleton, where I have spent the summer, this morning; but was prevented by the weather. I think I scarce ever saw a more boisterous day. Your letter compensates me for the delay. Before I enter on its contents, I must do myself the pleasure to express the warm conception I have of your friendship in making the communication you have done. I have long suspected the man, or, to speake more correctly, the set of men you aluded to; but to you, I am indebted for the first direct information of the state of their feelings towards me. I have acted in publick long enough with some of them; I have marked their conduct on so many occasions, that, I think, I cannot be ignorant of their political, or private character. I have looked for opposition from them. Not from any decclerations of theirs; for they have always before me expressed a flattering approbation. The very man you mentioned sent by a brother in law, when he had as much acquaintance with me, as he now has; for I have not seen him since, expressions highly complimentary to me. No; it is a difference of principles which led me to look for that, which has followed. I love my country too much, I hope, to be subservient to their selfish views and conduct. This is my sin; this is my want of firmness; this is my dubious conduct. Had I favoured the election of such a one to a lucrative post; Had I praised such and such great men among them, no such faults would have been imputed. Want of firmness! I would have supposed it the last fault imputable to me. All know, that in the short time I have been in publick service, I have ever stood obstinate against all local, party, or factious interest. That, I often advocated unpo[p]ular questions, from a belief of their utility. I do trust that neither their censure, or that of the whole community itself will ever drive me from the path of duty. I love just renown; but, to me undeserved popularity ha[s] no charms. You have done the p[art] of the true friend to put me on my [guard] against them. As to insinuation against my capacity, speaking and writing, I do not regard them. I have never made any pretentions to excellence in either of these particulars. The praises that my friends have bestowed on me at any time in those respects, I have attributed to their partiality, rather than my merit. I have said too much on a subject that gives me no uneasiness. You ask my opinion of Rodgers & Smith. The conduct of the former meets with my full approbation. The latter has proved himself what, I have ever thought him, a weak political intriguer. May all such chara[c]ters meet with equal contempt. I am your friend

JOHN C. CALHOUN

I am happy to hear Mrs McBride is well Mrs. Calhoun was so a week since when I left home. My respects to Mrs McB Mr. Gourdine & family, Snowden & all friends.

44 NOTE: James Macbride (1784-1817), was a native of Williamsburg District, college-mate of Calhoun, physician and botanist (*Appletons' Cyclopaedia*, IV, 74); he married Eleanor, daughter of Theodore Gourdin, Mar. 4, 1811 (*SCHM*, XXXVI [1935], 69). He signed his name "Macbride." SOURCE: *LC*, James Macbride Papers.

45. To PATRICK CALHOUN, Abbeville, S.C.

Washinton 14th Novr. 1811

Dr. Brother, I send you the Int.[1] of this morning. It contains no foreign news of importance. Congress has not yet taken up any business of importance. The committees have not yet reported; and it is usual for the house to wait their reports. I expect it will be a very important session. The members are generally very anxious as to the course that will be persued. I am on the committee of foreign relations. The report of that committee will in a great measure determine the course that will be persued. It has had two meetings & I expect will report in a few days. I think there is no prospect of any commercial change for the better ["of importance" *cancelled*]; and would recommend you and my friends, if you can get a saving price for your crops to sell as soon as possible. I am inclined to think strong measures will be resorted to. Remember to Nancy, Mr & Mrs Mosely & all friends.

I am your [af]fectionate [brother]

JOHN C [Calhoun]

SOURCE: *SCL.*

46. REPORT ON RELATIONS WITH GREAT BRITAIN

November 29, 1811

The Committee to whom was referred that part of the President's message which relates to our foreign affairs, beg leave to report, in part.

That they have endeavoured to give to the subject submitted to them, that full & dispassionate consideration which is due to one so intimately connected with the interests, the peace, the safety and the honour of their country.

Your Committee will not encumber your journals and waste your patience with a detailed history of all the various matters growing out of our foreign relations. The cold recital of wrongs, of injuries and aggressions, known & felt by every member of this Union, could have no other effect than to deaden the national sensi-

1. The *National Intelligencer.*

bility, and render the public mind callous to injuries, with which it is already too familiar.

Without recurring, then, to the multiplied wrongs, of partial or temporary operation, of which we have so just cause of complaint against the two great Belligerents; your Committee will only call your attention, at this time, to the systematic aggressions of those powers, authorised by their edicts against neutral commerce; A system which, as regarded its principles, was founded on pretensions that went to the subversion of our national independence; and which, although now abandoned by one power, is, in its broad and destructive operation, as still enforced by the other, sapping the foundations of our prosperity.

It is more than five years since England & France, in violation of those principles of justice and public law, held sacred by all civilized nations, commenced this unprecedented system, by seizing the property of the citizens of the United States, peaceably pursuing their lawful commerce on the high seas.[1] To shield themselves from the odium, which such outrage must incur, each of the belligerents sought a pretext in the conduct of the other—each attempting to justify his system of rapine as a retaliation for similar acts on the part of his enemy. As if the law of nations, founded on the eternal rules of justice, could sanction a principle, which, if engrafted into our municipal codes, would excuse the crime of *one* robber, upon the sole plea, that the unfortunate object of his rapacity, was also a victim to the injustice of another ["would suffer individuals to deprecate upon the property of the community, upon the extra-ordinary plea, to be allowed to each, in his turn, that the unfortunate objects of his rapacity, were equally victims of the injustice of the others" *cancelled*]. The fact of priority could be true as to one only of the parties; & whether true or false could furnish no ground of justification.

The United States, thus unexpectedly & violently assailed by the two greatest powers in Europe, ["immediately" *cancelled*] withdrew their citizens & property from the ocean: and, cherishing the blessings of peace, although the occasion would have fully justified war, sought redress in an appeal to the justice & magnanimity of

1. "Fox's blockade" was announced May 16, 1806; Napoleon's Berlin Decree was Nov. 21, 1806 (Adams, *History of U.S.*, III, 389, 398).

the belligerents. When this appeal had failed of the success which was due to its moderation, other measures, founded on the same pacific policy, but applying to the interests instead of the justice of the belligerents, were resorted to. Such was the character of the non intercourse and non importation laws, which invited the return of both powers to their former state of amicable relations, by offering commercial advantages to the one who should first revoke his hostile edicts; and imposing restrictions on the other.

France, at length, availing herself of the proffers made equally to her and her enemy by the non importation law of May 1810, announced the repeal, on the first of the following November, of the decrees of Berlin & Milan. And it affords a subject of sincere congratulation to be informed through the official organs of the government, that those decrees are, so far at least as our rights are concerned, really & practically at an end.

It was confidently expected that this act, on the part of France, would have been immediately followed by a revocation, on the part of Great Britain, of her orders in council. If our reliance on her justice had been impaired by the wrongs she had inflicted; yet, when she had plighted her faith to the world that the sole motive of her aggressions on neutral commerce was to be found in the Berlin & Milan decrees, we looked forward to the extinction of those decrees, as the period when the freedom of the seas would be again restored.

In this reasonable expectation we have, however, been disappointed. A year has elapsed since the french decrees were rescinded, and yet, Great Britain, instead of retracing, *pari passu*, that course of unjustifiable attack on neutral rights, in which she professed to be only the reluctant follower of France, has advanced with bolder & continually increasing strides. To the categorical demands lately made by our government for the repeal of her orders in council, she has affected to deny the practical extinction of the french decrees: And she has, moreover, advanced a new & unexpected demand, encreasing in hostility the orders themselves. She has insisted, through her accredited minister, at this place, that the repeal of the orders in council must be preceded, not only by the practical abandonment of the decrees of Berlin & Milan, so far as they infringe the neutral rights of the United States; but by the renunciation, on the part of France, of the whole of her system of commercial warfare against Great Britain, of which those decrees originally formed a part.

This system is understood to consist in a course of measures, adopted by France & the other powers on the continent, subject to, or in alliance with her, calculated to prevent the introduction, into their territories, of the products & manufactures of G. Britain and her colonies; and to annihilate her trade with them. However hostile these regulations may be, on the part of France towards Great Britain; or however sensibly the latter may feel their effects, they are, nevertheless, to be regarded only as the expedients of one enemy against another, for which the United States, as a neutral power, can, in no respect, be responsible. They are, too, in exact conformity with those which Great Britain has herself adopted & acted upon, in time of peace as well as war. And it is not to be presumed that France would yield to the unauthorised demand of America what she seems to have considered as one of the most powerful engines of her present war.

Such are the pretensions upon which Great Britain founds the violation of the maratime rights of the United States—pretensions not theoretical merely, but followed up by a desolating war upon our unprotected commerce. The ships of the United States, laden with the products of our own soil & labour, navigated by our own citizens & peaceably pursuing a lawful trade are seized on our own coasts, at the very mouths of our harbours, condemned & confiscated.

Your committee are not, however, of that sect whose worship is at the shrine of a calculating averice. And while we are laying before you, the just complaints of our merchants against the plunder of their ships and cargoes, we cannot refrain from presenting to the justice & humanity of our country, the unhappy case of our impressed seamen. Although the groans of these victims of barbarity for the loss of (what should be dearer to americans than life) their liberty: Although the cries of their wives & children in the privation of protectors & parents, have, of late, been drowned in the louder clamours at the loss of property: Yet is the practice of forcing our ["impressing our" *cancelled*] mariners into the British Navy, in violation of the rights of our flag, carried on with unabated rigour & severity. If it be our duty to encourage the fair & legitimate commerce of this country by protecting the property of the merchant; then indeed, by as much as life & liberty are more estimable than ships & goods, so much more impressive is the duty to shield the persons of our seamen, whose hard and honest services are employed, equally with those of the merchants, in advancing, under the mantle of its laws, the interests of their country.

To sum up, in a word, the great causes of complaint against Great Britain, your committee need only say—That the United States as a sovereign & independent power, claim the right to use the ocean, which is the common & acknowledged highway of nations, for the purposes of transporting, in their own vessels, the products of their own soil, and the acquisitions of their own industry, to a market in the ports of friendly nations: and to bring home, in return, such articles as their necessities or convenience may require—always regarding the rights of belligerents, as defined by the established laws of nations. Great Britain, in defiance of this incontestable right, captures every american vessel bound to, or returning from, a port where her commerce is not favoured; enslaves our seamen; and, in spite of our remonstrances, perseveres in these aggressions.

To wrongs, so daring in character, and so disgraceful in their execution, it is impossible that the people of the United States should remain indifferent. We must now tamely & quietly submit, or, we must resist ["The occasion is now presented when the national The alternative is in" *cancelled*], by those means which God has placed within our reach.

Your committee would not cast a shade over the american name, by the expression of a doubt which branch of this alternative will be embraced. The occasion is now presented, when the national character, misunderstood & traduced for a time by foreign & domestic enemies, should be vindicated. If we have not rushed to the field of battle like the nations, who are led by the mad ambition of a single chief, or the averice of a corrupted court, it has not proceeded from a fear of war, but from our love of justice & humanity. That proud spirit of liberty & independence, which sustained our fathers in the successful assertion of their rights, against foreign oppression, is not yet sunk: The patriotic fire of the Revolu-

tion still burns in the american breast with a holy & unextinguish-
able flame, and will conduct this nation to those high destinies,
which are not less the reward of dignified moderation, than of exalted valour.

But we have borne with injury until forbearance has ceased to
be a virtue. The sovereignty and independence of these states,
purchased and sanctified by the blood of our fathers, from whom
we received them, not for ourselves only, but as the inheritance of
our posterity, are deliberately and systematically violated: And the
period has arrived when, in the opinion of your Committee, it is
the sacred duty of Congress to call forth the patrotism and resources of the country. By the aid of these, and with the blessing of
God, we confidently trust we shall be enabled to procure that redress, which has been sought for by justice, by remonstrance &
forbearance, in vain.

Your committee, reserving for a future report, those ulteriour
measures, which, in their opinion, ought to be pursued, would at
this time, earnestly recommend, in the words of the President,
"That the United States be immediately put into an armour & attitude demanded by the crisis, and corresponding with the national
spirit and expectations" [2] and, to this end, they beg leave to submit, for the adoption of the house, the following resolutions.

Resolved

1—That the military establishment as authorised by existing
laws, ought to be immediately completed; by filling up the ranks &
prolonging the enlistments of the troops: And that, to encourage
enlistments, a bounty in lands ought to be given, in addition to the
pay & bounty now allowed by law.

2—That an additional force of ten thousand regular troops ought
to be immediately raised, to serve for three years: And that a bounty
in lands ought to be given to encourage enlistments.

3.—That it is expedient to authorise the President, under proper
regulations, to accept the service of any number of volunteers, not
exceeding Fifty thousand: To be organized, trained & held in readi-
ness to act on such service as the exigencies of the goverment may
require

2. The committee paraphrased Madison's recommendation—see NOTE following this paper—and added the word "immediately."

4. That the President be authorised to order out, from time to time, such detachments of the Militia as, in his opinion, the public service may require.

5—That all the vessels, not now in service, belonging to the Navy & worthy of repair, be immediately fitted up & put in commission.

6. That it is expedient to permit our merchant vessels owned exclusively by resident citizens & commanded & navigated solely by citizens, to arm, under proper regulations to be prescribed by law, in self defence, against all unlawful proceedings against them on the high seas.

46 NOTE: This report is included because of the apparently large part that Calhoun had in writing it and because it represented to a great degree the program for which he contended so vigorously during the next two years. On the question of authorship, note in particular the parallel passages in Calhoun's speech of Dec. 12 and the war report of June 3, 1812 (No. 66 NOTE); see also Wiltse, *Calhoun, Nationalist,* p. 409, n. 4. The report is printed in *Works,* V, 1-7, evidently copied from the *National Intelligencer* of Nov. 30, 1811.

On Nov. 5, 1811, President Madison sent his first message to the Twelfth Congress (*AC*12-1, p. 11-5). At the close of the preceding session he and the Republican majority had accepted the dubious assurance of French officials that American neutral rights would be respected and had accordingly reenacted non-intercourse against Great Britain (Adams, *History of U.S.,* V, 350-4). He now repeated his belief in the French promises and complained of the failure of the British government to relax its Orders in Council.

Nearly buried in his review of the dangerous developments in foreign affairs, and of the problems of adjustment of American trade and industry to these conditions, was his declaration that "Congress will feel the duty of putting the United States into an armor and an attitude demanded by the crisis." He asked provision for filling the ranks of the regular army, for an auxiliary force, for volunteer corps, for detachments of militia, and (in effect) for reorganization of the militia (*AC*12-1, p. 13). On the 12th (p. 342) the House referred "so much of the President's Message as relates to the subject of our foreign relations" to a "select committee," which became the Foreign Relations Committee; Peter B. Porter of western New York was appointed Chairman, and Calhoun, who took his seat on the 6th, was given second place. The five specific requests were referred to another committee, which became the Committee on Military Affairs, David R. Williams of South Carolina, Chairman (p. 342-3).

The committee's report, presented by Porter on the 29th, was in thorough accord with Madison's message, and his requests were embodied in the first four of its six resolutions. On Dec. 6, in Committee of the Whole, the second resolution was amended by omitting the number of troops to be raised, the debate revealing a wide range of opinion as to the force which might be needed and the possibility of raising it (p. 418). The same day the House accepted the first resolution (p. 419), and on the 16th approved the amended second resolution as well as the third, fourth and fifth (p. 545-8). Disregarding the previous reference of that portion of the President's message to Williams' committee, the House now instructed Porter's to bring in bills to effect the first three. Meanwhile bills for the purposes of the first and second resolutions were introduced in the Senate (Dec. 9, p. 29-30), the first of which became law on Dec. 24 (p. 2227-8). The Senate bill, to raise 10 regiments of infantry, 2 of artillery and 1 of cavalry, to number about 25,000, was hotly debated in the House (see, for instance, p. 596, 701), but the bill was passed with little change and became law on Jan. 11 (p. 2229-34). See No. 50.

A bill to carry out the fifth resolution of Porter's Committee was enacted Mar. 30 (p. 2261-2). The committee was ordered on Dec. 19 to bring in a bill to put in effect the sixth (p. 565-6), but nothing came of it (see p. 415-6, 562, 1353-4, 1439). On the 26th (p. 583) Porter reported a bill in accordance with the third resolution—organization of a volunteer corps—which would have authorized the President to accept a force not to exceed 50,000, liable for twelve months service, the officers to be appointed by the President. There was a protracted debate over the question of the constitutionality of ordering these troops out of the country; some members voting for the bill differed among themselves on this point (*e.g.*, see p. 728, 730, 736, 741) and on the question of the appointment of officers. By the bill as it passed on the third reading Jan. 17 (p. 800-1) appointments were to be made under state laws. Calhoun did not commit himself on these issues, but voted with the majority. The volunteer act was ratified on Feb. 6 (p. 2235-7) but was a complete failure and was repealed by its 1813 substitute—see No. 75 NOTE. As amended it was not acceptable to the administration, and the prospective volunteers found more attractive the six months service in the militia organizations called for by the fourth resolution—see Monroe's criticism, Hamilton, *Writings of James Monroe*, VIII, 207-8; Adams, *History of U.S.*, VI, 389-91; and No. 75 NOTE.

Under the fourth resolution, the only one left for the Military Committee, Williams reported Feb. 6 a bill (*AC*12-1, p. 1032), authorizing the President to draft from the militia of the states their quotas of a hundred thousand men for not more than six months service. Officers were to be appointed under state laws, and whipping as a punishment of the men was forbidden. The bill was finally enacted on April 10 (p. 2267-9). Williams' bill for "classing and arming the militia," introduced in January, met opposition from the start (p. 939) and was finally rejected; Calhoun voted for this bill, which provided for issuing arms direct to the militia (p. 939, 1004, 1021-7). The committee was instructed to bring in a bill for the process of arming only (p. 1032), but this likewise was eventually lost (p. 1040, 1046, 1080, 1298). This bill would have entrusted distribution of the arms to the legislatures, and Calhoun spoke briefly against it on that account and finally voted against it (Feb. 20, 21, p. 1080, 1085).

In his speech of Dec. 6 (p. 414-7), the first in defense of his report, Porter expressly stated it to be a measure preparatory for war and in effect declared he would recommend war as soon as the preparations were sufficiently advanced unless Great Britain had meanwhile "rescinded her Orders in Council, and made some satisfactory arrangements in respect to the impressment of our seamen." See No. 59 NOTE.

With the drawing up of this report began the consultations of the war party with Secretary of State Monroe. On Dec. 7 William Lowndes of South Carolina wrote that Monroe "has given the strongest assurances that the President will cooperate zealously with Congress in declaring war, if our complaints are not redressed by May next." (Ravenel, *William Lowndes*, p. 90; see also Brant, *James Madison, President, 1809-1812*, p. 390-1, and No. 66 NOTE.) See Calhoun's defense of the report, No. 48. SOURCE: MS Report, Nov. 29, 1811, NA, RG233, 12A-C11.4; it is printed in *NI*, Nov. 30, 1811, and in *AC*12-1, p. 373-7.

47. Speech on the Apportionment Bill

December 5, 1811

Mr. Calhoun said: Before the bill had gone to the Senate, it excited but very little interest with me. All that I had heard from gentlemen on every side convinced me that it was a squabble among the several States which should bear the loss of large fractions, rather than a serious division on principle, of one ratio in preference to another. Were I governed alone by fractions, I should not rise this day; nor oppose a concurrence with the Senate, from the pride of opinion; for the ratio which the Senate have fixed, is in accordance with my vote on the original bill, although 37,000 would leave my

State with a less fraction unrepresented than 35,000: but fractions
are not my object.[1] I am not here to represent my own State alone.
I renounce the idea. And I will shew by my vote that I contend
for the interests of the whole people of this community. The present question, on concurring in the amendment of the Senate,
seemed to be totally different, and much more important than the
original one. As it now stands it is a case of disagreement between
the two Houses, and the contest is, which shall recede. A contest
of this kind (on the census bill) was one of the most serious consequences to this House. The Senate, by persistance, must force
this body either to adopt their ratio, or, if that cannot be effected,
even annihilate this branch of the Legislature. I consider this a case
of omission in our excellent Constitution—one of that kind which
must take place, perhaps, in all free constitutions, however formed;
but particularly in one like ours, formed by the foresight of wisdom,
and not by slow and successive experience. That it is a case of
omission and not foreseen, may be inferred from several parts of
the Constitution itself. The Constitution makes this House the sole
judge of the qualifications and returns of its own members. This is
supposed to vest the power so exclusively in us, that a few days
since, in a debate on the contested election from Virginia, it was
contended with much force of argument, that any law on this subject, as the Senate must participate in it, would be unconstitutional.
What is the reason? A spirit of jealousy; a manifest intention to
preserve this House from the influence of the other; and to prevent
the latter from having any control in the interior management of
this. If such caution was necessary in this particular, where the
cases must, almost necessarily, be few, and often not important,
how much more so in a question of ratio, in which that body may
add to or subtract hundreds from this—may force such a ratio on
this, as is favorable to the federative principle, and assimilate it
to the other in its formation, it may entirely annihilate this House.
Again, it is the theory of our government, and was the favorite

1. The representation and the remaining "fractions" under the several
ratios are given in a table in Niles, *Weekly Register*, I (1811-2), 237. For representation South Carolina's population in 1810 was counted as 336,569. On
a ratio of either 37,000 or 35,000 the state would have been assigned 9 representatives, but by the former calculation the remainder was 3,569, by the
latter, 21,569.

idea of all our politicians, at the time of its formation, that liberty can only exist in a division of the sovereign power; and that such division could only be permanent where each of the parts had within itself the means of protection. On this principle, the Executive and Judiciary were detached from the Legislative, and this last divided into two branches. Each of these departments has the means of self-preservation. The first has its qualified veto and its patronage; the Judiciary its independence—and each House a veto on the proceedings of the other.

In the ordinary course of legislation, this furnished ample security. Far different on the census bill. Here the whole is inverted. The veto of the Senate is no longer the means of protection to itself, but becomes a fatal means of assailing this House; it is no more a shield of defence, but a weapon of attack; and when they use it by withholding their assent, we are annihilated. This great anomaly could not have been foreseen; it must be considered as an omission. What remedy do I propose? Prevent the Senate from participating in a census bill? By no means; it would be unconstitutional; because there is no clause to that effect. I propose a means in strict unison with the Constitution, and furnished by itself. It has in this instance withheld from us the shield, but has pointed to its spirit. Let us act with a fixed determination; and not accede to the amendment of the Senate. That body, unaided by precedent, and opposed by the spirit of the Constitution, must recede. Let us follow the example of the House of Commons in England in relation to money bills, and the same effect will follow—but by no means revere that example.

The Senate, strengthened by precedent, will hereafter control us completely. On this ground they have naturally a greater capacity for struggling than we. Unless we insist in the first instance, we must ever hereafter be overpowered. What inducement can gentlemen have, to make the surrender at this time? None can be weaker, than because some of the states have, by the ratio inserted in the Senate, small fractions, and one section of the Union has by it comparatively gained.[2] Will gentlemen for this inconsiderable gain make so great a sacrifice? Particularly those from large states,

2. Use of the 35,000 ratio instead of 37,000 would have increased the East's representation by 8, but that of the South only 3.

who are the greatest gainers by fractions? For this paltry gain, more apparent than real, which can last but for 10 years, they surrender a principle of the most vital importance to them. They will enable the Senate in time to reduce them almost to the same terms of equality on this floor with the small states, as they are in the other House. Let it not be said, the Senate will always exercise this power with discretion. It is the part of political wisdom not to trust when it can make secure, and in a case of such vital importance, it will not confide in the strongest probabilities. Faith is an article of religion, but not of politics. But, sir, if any section or state of this union gained ever so much, I know not how it could justify this abandonment of principle. Who are we? The representatives of the nation; of individual rights; the trustees for the time being of that mass of power which is invested in the hands of the legislature for the protection of those rights. How then can we make a surrender consistent with the principle, with honor or with conscience, of those important rights so sacredly trusted to our keeping? Mr. Speaker—I wish the task of defending this important point had fallen to abler hands. I feel all that embarrassment which a young man, not much accustomed to speaking, must necessarily experience the first time, before such an audience, and in a place so trying to the voice as this hall. I shall be happy, if in the midst of my embarrassments, I have been intelligible, and have expressed myself, with sufficient caution, on so delicate a point.

47 NOTE: This, Calhoun's first speech in Congress, has been little regarded by students of his career. The question was on the Senate amendment to the House bill fixing the apportionment of representation under the census of 1810. Calhoun made it the occasion for an appeal to the fundamental principles of separation of powers and division of sovereignty, and in effect cited the *Federalist* essays as a source of his political philosophy.

The House committee, which reported the apportionment bill on Nov. 20, recommended a ratio of 40,000, which would have reduced the representation of Virginia by two, and that of Maryland and of three Eastern states by one each, (*AC*12-1, p. 358, 363).

Calhoun voted at least once for the committee's figure and once for 35,000; he had voted against the 37,000 ratio when the House wrote it into the bill, but now on principle supported it (p. 364-5). However, the House eventually (Dec. 18) accepted the Senate's ratio (p. 558).

In the debate John Rhea of Tennessee opposed the Senate's interference but James Fisk of Vermont protested Calhoun's "declaring war against the Senate." However, both the discussion and the vote turned on the representation of the various states (p. 404-13).

The Baltimore *American & Commercial Daily Advertiser* of Dec. 6, 1811, published a short abstract of the speech (which was copied by the *Charleston Courier*, Dec. 14, 1811) with the following significant variations from the *Intelligencer* account: "The senate was a diplomatic corps, who represented the states; who were sent here to protect the state rights, and to preserve the federative principle. The members of the house were the guardians of the national principle incorporated, and wisely incorporated into this government." "Allow the senate to interpose here, and . . . your power is annihilated." "Sir, we are the representatives of the nation; the senate represent the states. This is the theory of our government. I reverence its wisdom." "The right to negative laws was given to them as a shield of defence, not as a sword of attack; a weapon with which to prostrate at their feet the other co-ordinate branches of the government." "The House would become a cypher in the government." "[The above sketch is far from doing justice to the eloquent and animated discourse of Mr. Calhoun. It presents but an outline of the general principles which he urged with manly energy and vehemence upon the House.]" The fact that Virgil Maxcy (see No. 63) was in Baltimore at this time (Galloway-Maxcy-Markoe Papers, *LC*) suggests the surmise that he was responsible for the printing of the speech and the comment on it. SOURCE: *NI*, Dec. 14, 1811; AC12-1, p. 404-6.

48. SPEECH ON THE REPORT OF THE FOREIGN RELATIONS COMMITTEE

December 12, 1811

Mr. Calhoun—Mr. Speaker: I understood the opinion of the Committee of Foreign Relations differently from what the gentleman from Virginia (Mr. Randolph) has stated to be his impression. I certainly understood that committee as recommending the measures now before the House as a preparation for war; and such in fact was its express resolve, agreed to, I believe, by every member, except that gentleman. I do not attribute any wilful misstatement to him, but consider it the effect of inadvertency or mistake. Indeed the report could mean nothing but war or empty menace. I hope no member of this House is in favor of the latter. A bullying menacing system has every thing to condemn and nothing to recommend it—in expense it is almost as considerable as war—it excites contempt abroad, and destroys confidence here. Menaces are serious things, and, if we expect any good from them, they ought to be resorted to with as much caution and seriousness as war itself; and should, if not successful, be invariably followed by it. It was not the gentleman from Tennessee (Mr. Grundy) that made this a war question. The resolve contemplates an additional regular force; a measure confessedly improper but as a preparation for war, but undoubtedly necessary in that event. Sir, I am not insensible of the weighty importance of this question, for the first time submitted to this House, as a redress of our long list of complaints against one of the belligerents— but, according to my mode of thinking on this subject, however serious the question, whenever I am on its affirmative side, my conviction must be strong and unalterable. War, in this country, ought never to be resorted to but when it is clearly justifiable and necessary; so much so, as not to require the aid of logic to convince our reason nor the ardor of eloquence to inflame our passions. There are many reasons why this country should never resort to war but for causes the most urgent and necessary. It is sufficient that, under a government like ours, none but such will justify it in the eye of the nation; and were I not satisfied that such is our present cause, I certainly would be no advocate of the proposition now before the House.

Sir, I prove the war, should it ensue, justifiable, by the express admission of the gentleman from Virginia; and necessary, by facts undoubted and universally admitted, such as that gentleman did not pretend to controvert. The extent, duration, and character of the injuries received; the failure of those peaceful means heretofore resorted to for the redress of our wrongs, is my proof that it is necessary. Why should I mention the impressment of our seamen; depredation on every branch of our commerce, including the direct export trade, continued for years, and made under laws which professedly undertake to regulate our trade with other nations— negociation resorted to time after time, till it is become hopeless— the restrictive system persisted in to avoid war, and in the vain expectation of returning justice? The evil still grows, and in each succeeding year swells in extent and pretension beyond the preceding. The question, even in the opinion and admission of our opponents, is reduced to this single point; which shall we do, abandon or defend our own commercial and maritime rights and the personal liberties of our citizens employed in exercising them? These rights are essentially attacked, and war is the only means of redress. The gentleman from Virginia has suggested none; unless we consider the whole of his speech as recommending patient and resigned submission as the best remedy. Sir, which alternative this House ought to embrace, it is not for me to say. I hope the decision is made already, by a higher authority than the voice of any man. It is not for the human tongue to instil the sense of independence and honor. This is the work of nature; a generous nature that disdains tame submission to wrongs.

This part of the subject is so imposing, as to enforce silence even on the gentleman from Virginia. He dared not to deny his country's wrongs, or vindicate the conduct of her enemy.

Only one point of that gentleman's argument had any, the most remote, relation to this point. He would not say we had not a good cause of war, but insisted that it was our duty to define that cause. If he means that this House ought at this stage of the proceeding, or any other, to enumerate such violations of our rights, as we are willing to contend for, he prescribes a course, which neither good sense or the usage of nations warrants. When we contend, let us contend for all our rights; the doubtful and the certain; the unimportant and essential. It is as easy to struggle, or even more so, for the whole as a part. At the termination of the contest, secure all that our wisdom and valor and the fortune of the war will permit. This is the dictate of common sense; such also is the usage of nations. The single instance alluded to, the endeavor of Mr. Fox to compel Mr. Pitt to define the object of the war against France, will not support the gentleman from Virginia in his position. That was an extraordinary war for an extraordinary purpose, and could not be governed by the usual rules. It was not for conquest; or for redress of injury; but to impose a government on France, which she refused to receive; an object so detestable, that an avowal dare not be made.

Sir, here I might rest the question. The affirmative of the proposition is established. I cannot but advert, however, to the complaint of the gentleman from Virginia the first time he was up on this question. He said he found himself reduced to the necessity of supporting the negative side of the question, before the affirmative was established. Let me tell that gentleman, that there is no hardship in his case. It is not every affirmative that ought to be proved. Were I to affirm the House is now in session, would it be reasonable to ask for proof? He who would deny its truth, on him would be the proof of so extraordinary a negative. How then could the gentleman, after his admissions, with the facts before him and the nation, complain? The causes are such as to warrant, or rather make it indispensable in any nation not absolutely dependent to defend its rights by force. Let him then shew the reasons why we ought not so to defend ourselves. On him then is the burthen of proof. This he has attempted; he has endeavored to support his negative. Before I proceed to answer the gentleman particularly, let me call the attention of the House to one circumstance; that is, that almost the whole of his arguments consisted of an enumeration of evils always incident to war, however just and necessary; and that, if they have any force, it is calculated to produce unqualified submission to every species of insult and injury. I do not feel myself bound to answer arguments of the above description; and if I should touch on them, it will be only incidentally, and not for the purpose of serious refutation.

The first argument of the gentleman which I shall notice, is the unprepared state of the country. Whatever weight this argument might have, in a question of immediate war, it surely has little in that of preparation for it. If our country is unprepared, let us remedy the evil as soon as possible. Let the gentleman submit his plan; and if a reasonable one, I doubt not it will be supported by the House. But, sir, let us admit the fact and the whole force of the argument; I ask whose is the fault? Who has been a member for many years past, and has seen the defenceless state of his country even near home, under his own eyes, without a single endeavor to remedy so serious an evil? Let him not say "I have acted in a minority." It is no less the duty of the minority than a majority to endeavor to serve our country. For that purpose we are sent here; and not for that of opposition. We are next told of the expences of the war; and that the people will not pay taxes. Why not? Is it a want of capacity? What, with 1,000,000 tons of shipping; a trade of near 100,000,000 dollars; manufactures of 150,000,000 dollars, and agriculture of thrice that amount, shall we be told the country wants capacity to raise and support 10,000 or 15,000 additional regulars? No; it has the ability, that is admitted; but will it not have the disposition? Is not the course a just and necessary one? Shall we then utter this libel on the nation? Where will proof be found of a fact so disgraceful? It is said, in the history of the country 12 or 15 years ago. The case is not parallel. The ability of the country is greatly increased since. The object of that tax was unpopular. But on this, as well as my memory and almost infant observation at that time serve me, the objection was not to the tax, or its amount, but the mode of collection.[1] The eye of the nation was frightened by the number of officers; its love of liberty shocked with the multiplicity of regulations. We, in the vile spirit of imitation, copied from the most oppressive part of European laws on that subject, and imposed on a young and virtuous nation all the severe provisions made necessary by corruption and long growing chicane. If taxes should become necessary, I do not hesitate to say the people will pay cheerfully. It is for their government and their cause, and would be their interest and duty to pay. But it may be, and I believe was said, that the nation will not pay taxes, because the rights violated are not worth defending; or that the defence will cost more than the profit. Sir, I here enter my solemn protest against this low and "calculating avarice" entering this hall of legislation. It is only fit for shops and counting houses, and ought not to disgrace the seat of sovereignty by its squalid and vile appearance. Whenever it touches sovereign power the nation is ruined. It is too short sighted to defend itself. It is an unpromising spirit, always ready to yield a part to save the balance. It is too timid to have in itself the laws of self preservation. It is never safe but under the shield of honor. Sir, I only know of one principle to make a nation great, to produce in this country not the form but real spirit of union, and that is, to protect every citizen in the lawful pursuit of his business. He will then feel that he is backed by the government, that its arm

1. Calhoun evidently refers to the war-scare taxes of 1798; compare, for instance, the dispatch from Pendleton in 1803 which records a Fourth of July denunciation of those taxes (Charleston *City Gazette*, Aug. 9, 1803). The *Speeches* (p. 11) and *Works* (II, 6) consider the reference to be to the whiskey tax of eighteen years before, which had little effect on the South.

is his arms, and will rejoice in its increased strength and prosperity. Protection and patriotism are reciprocal. This is the road that all great nations have trod. Sir, I am not versed in this calculating policy; and will not therefore pretend to estimate in dollars and cents the value of national independence, or national affection. I cannot dare to measure in shillings and pence the misery, the stripes and the slavery of our impressed seamen; nor even to value our shipping, commercial and agricultural losses, under the Orders in Council and the British system of blockade. I hope I have not condemned any prudent estimate of the means of a country, before it enters on a war. This is wisdom, the other folly.

Sir, the gentleman from Virginia has not failed to touch on the calamity of war; that fruitful source of declamation by which pity becomes the advocate of cowardice; but I know not what we have to do with that subject. If the gentleman desires to repress the gallant ardor of our countrymen by such topics; let me inform him, that true courage regards only the cause, that it is just and necessary; and that it despises the pain and danger of war. If he really wishes to promote the cause of humanity, let his eloquence be addressed to Lord Wellesley or Mr. Perceval, and not the American Congress. Tell them if they persist in such daring insult and injury to a neutral nation, that, however inclined to peace, it will be bound in honor and interest to resist; that their patience and benevolence, however great, will be exhausted; that the calamity of war will ensue, and that they, in the opinion of wounded humanity will be answerable for all its devastation and misery. Let melting pity, a regard to the interest of humanity, stay the hand of injustice, and my life on it, the gentleman will not find it difficult to call off his country from the bloody scenes of war.

We are next told of the danger of war! I believe we are all ready to acknowledge its hazard and accidents; but I cannot think we have any extraordinary danger to contend with, at least so much as to warrant an acquiescence in the injuries we have received. On the contrary, I believe no war can be less dangerous to internal peace, or national existence. But we are told of the black population of the Southern States. As far as the gentleman from Virginia speaks of his own personal knowledge, I will not pretend to contradict him—I only regret that such is the dreadful state of his particular part of the country. Of the Southern section, I too have some personal knowledge, and can say, that in South Carolina no such fears in any part are felt. But, sir, admit the gentleman's statement; will a war with Great Britain increase the danger? Will the country be less able to repress insurrection? Had we any thing to fear from that quarter, which I sincerely disbelieve; in my opinion, the precise time of the greatest safety is during a war in which we have no fear of invasion—then the country is most on its guard; our militia the best prepared; and standing force the greatest. Even in our Revolution no attempts were made by that portion of our population; and, however the gentleman may frighten himself with the disorganising effects of French principles, I cannot think our ignorant blacks have felt much of their baneful influence. I dare say more than one half of them never heard of the French Revolution.

But as great as is the danger from our slaves, the gentleman's fears end not there—the standing army is not less terrible to him.[2] Sir, I think a regular force raised for a period of actual hostilities cannot be called a standing army. There is a just distinction between such a force, and one raised as a peace establishment. Whatever may be the composition of the latter, I hope the former will consist of some of the best materials of the country. The ardent patriotism of our young men, and the reasonable bounty in land, which is proposed to be given, will impel them to join their country's standard and to fight her battles; they will not forget the citizen in the soldier, and in obeying their officer learn to contemn their Constitution. In our officers and soldiers we will find patriotism no less pure and ardent than in the private citizen; but if they should be depraved as represented, what have we to fear from 25 or 30,000 regulars? Where will be the boasted militia of the gentleman? Can 1,000,000 of militia be overpowered by 30,000 regulars? If so, how can we rely on them against a foe invading our country? Sir, I have no such contemptuous idea of our militia—their untaught bravery is sufficient to crush all foreign and internal attempts on their country's liberties.

2. Calhoun's remark on the army drew on him the ire of Richard Stanford of North Carolina, who compared his remarks to those of Robert Goodloe Harper in 1798 and 1799, and the anger of Randolph, who asked if "our notions" of the value of the militia "[are] to be scourged out of us by the birch of the unfledged political pedagogues of the day?" (*AC* 12-1, p. 513, 542.)

But we have not yet come to the end of the chapter of dangers. The gentleman's imagination, so fruitful on this subject, conceives that our Constitution is not calculated for war, and that it cannot stand its rude shock. This is rather extraordinary—we must then depend upon the pity or contempt of other nations, for our existence. The Constitution, it seems, has failed in its essential part, "to provide for the common defence." No, says the gentleman from Virginia, it is competent for a defensive, but not an offensive war. It is not necessary for me to expose the error of this opinion. Why make the distinction in this instance? Will he pretend to say, that this is an offensive war; a war of conquest? Yes, the gentleman has dared to make this assertion; and for reasons no less extraordinary than the assertion itself. He says, our rights are violated on the ocean, and that these violations affect our shipping, and commercial rights, to which the Canadas have no relation. The doctrine of retaliation has been much abused of late by an unnatural extension; we have now to witness a new abuse. The gentleman from Virginia has limited it down to a point. By his system, if you receive a blow on the breast, you dare not return it on the head; you are obliged to measure and return it on the precise point on which it was received. If you do not proceed with this mathematical accuracy, it ceases to be just self-defence; it becomes an unprovoked attack. In speaking of Canada the gentleman from Virginia introduced the name of Montgomery with much feeling and interest. Sir, there is danger in that name to the gentleman's argument. It is sacred to heroism! It is indignant of submission! This calls my memory back to the time of our Revolution; to the Congress of '74 and '75. Suppose a speaker of that day had risen and urged all the arguments which we have heard on this subject; had told that Congress, "your contest is about the right of laying a tax; and that the attempt on Canada has nothing to do with it; that the war would be expensive; that danger and devastation would overspread our country, and that the power of Great Britain was irresistible." With what sentiment, think you, would such doctrines have been then received? Happy for us, they had no force at that period of our country's glory. Had they been then acted on, this Hall would never have witnessed a great nation convened to deliberate for the general good; a mighty empire, with prouder prospects than any nation the sun ever shone on, would not have risen in the West. No; we would have been vile subjected colonies; governed by that imperious rod which Britain holds over her distant provinces.

Sir, the gentleman from Virginia attributes the preparation for war to every thing but its true cause. He endeavored to find it in the probable rise of the price of hemp. He represents the people of the Western States as willing to plunge our country into war for such base and precarious motives. I will not reason on this point. I see the cause of their ardor, not in such base motives, but in their known patriotism and disinterestedness. No less mercenary is the reason which he attributes to the Southern States. He says that the non-importation act has reduced cotton to nothing, which has produced a feverish impatience. Sir, I acknowledge the cotton of our farms is worth but little; but not for the cause assigned by the gentleman from Virginia. The people of that section do not reason as he does; they do not attribute it to the efforts of their government to maintain the peace and independence of their country; they see in the low price of their produce, the hand of foreign injustice; they know well, without the market to the continent, the deep and steady current of supply will glut that of Great Britain; they are not prepared for the colonial state to which again that power is endeavoring to reduce us. The manly spirit of that section of our country will not submit to be regulated by any foreign power. The love of France and the hatred of England has also been assigned as the cause of the present measures. France has not done us justice, says the gentleman from Virginia, and how can we without partiality resist the aggressions of England. I know, sir, we have still causes of complaint against France; but it is of a different character from those against England. She professes now to respect our rights, and there cannot be a reasonable doubt but that the most objectionable parts of her decrees, as far as they respect us, are repealed. We have already formally acknowledged this to be a fact. I, however, protest against the whole of the principles on which this doctrine is founded. It is a novel doctrine, and no where to be found out of this House, that you cannot select your antagonist without being guilty of partiality. Sir, when two invade your rights you may resist both or either at your pleasure. It is regulated by prudence and not by right. The stale imputation of partiality to France is better calculated for the columns of a newspaper than for the walls of this House. I ask, in this particular, of the gentleman from Virginia, but for the same measure which he claims for himself. That gentleman is at a loss to account for, what he calls, our hatred to England. He asks how can we hate the country of Locke, of Newton, Hampden and Chatham; a country having the same language and customs with ourselves, and descending from a common ancestry. Sir, the laws of human affections are uniform. If we have so much to attach us to that country, powerful indeed must be the cause which has overpowered it.

Yes, sir, there is a cause strong enough. Not that occult courtly affection which he has supposed to be intertained for France; but it is to be found in continued and unprovoked insult and injury. A cause so manifest that the gentleman from Virginia had to exert much ingenuity to overlook it. But, sir, here I think the gentleman, in his eager admiration of that country, has not been sufficiently guarded in his argument. Has he reflected on the cause of that admiration? Has he examined the reasons of our high regard for her Chatham? It is his ardent patriotism; the heroic courage of his mind that could not brook the least insult or injury offered to his country, but thought that her interest and honor ought to be vindicated at every hazard and expence. I hope, when we are called on to admire, we shall also be asked to imitate. I hope the gentleman does not wish a monopoly of those great virtues to remain to that nation. The balance of power has also been introduced as an argument for submission. England is said to be a barrier against the military despotism of France. There is, sir, one great error in our legislation. We are ready enough to protect the interest of the states; and it should seem from this argument to watch over those of a foreign nation, while we grossly neglect our own immediate concerns. This argument of the balance of power is well calculated for the British Parliament, but not at all fitted to the American Congress. Tell them that they have to contend with a mighty power, and that if they persist in insult and injury to the American people, they will compel them to throw the whole weight of their force into the scale of their enemy. Paint the danger to them, and if they will desist from injury, we, I answer for it, will not disturb the balance. But it is absurd for us to talk of the balance of power while they by their conduct smile with contempt at our simple good-natured policy. If, however, in the contest, it should be found that they underrate us, which I hope and believe, and that we can affect the balance of power, it will not be difficult for us to obtain such terms as our rights demand. I, sir, will now conclude by adverting to an argument of the gentleman from Virginia used in debate on a preceding day. He asked why not declare war immediately. The answer is obvious; because we are not yet prepared. But, says the gentleman, such language as is here held will provoke Great Britain to commence hostilities. I have no such fears. She knows well that such a course would unite all parties here; a thing which above all others she most dreads. Besides such has been our past conduct, that she will still calculate on our patience and submission till war is actually commenced.

48 NOTE: Calhoun's, the fifth major speech in support of Porter's report (No. 46), was primarily in answer to Randolph, who, on the 9th and 10th, attacked the report on the basis of the danger from standing armies, the vulnerability of the American coastline, the possibility of slave insurrection and the iniquity of giving aid to Napoleon (*AC*12-1, p. 422, 441-55). Most of Calhoun's argument paralleled that of the committee; and with Robert Wright of Maryland (p. 468-9) and, later, Speaker Clay (p. 600), he followed it in making impressment a major issue (a stand taken by Wright in February preceding—*AC*11-3, p. 998-9, Adams, *History of U.S.*, V, 351-2, VI, 116-7). They thus strengthened the position of the United States for the time, a year hence, when impressment was to become the prime justification for continuing the war. But on the French decrees—foreseeing the pitfalls in procedure based on their supposed repeal, or perhaps scorning an involved and legalistic argument—he parted company with the President, his committee and the Republican leaders (see, for instances, *AC*12-1, p. 426, 456, 471, 486, 517) by declaring that England must be held responsible for her own transgressions without regard to those of France. The United States, he contended, must be free to choose the time and method for dealing with either antagonist.

The speech caused Thomas Ritchie of the Richmond *Enquirer* to hail Calhoun as "one of those master spirits, who stamp their name upon the age in which they live" (quoted by Wiltse, *Calhoun, Nationalist*, p. 59). It is printed in *Speeches of John C. Calhoun*, New York, 1843, p. 9-14—the only paper in the volume from Calhoun's House service—and in *Works*, II, 1-13. The *Speeches* copy follows the *Intelligencer;* for the *Works* version apparently both the *Speeches* and the *Intelligencer* were used and additional changes were made. Each version, aside from changes in punctuation and capitalization, leaves scarcely four lines out of five of the *Intelligencer* account untouched. A few of the changes are in accord with Calhoun's later emphasis—for instance, the substitution of "eyes of the people" for "eye of the nation," and "libel on the people" for "libel on the nation" (*Speeches*, 9, 11; *Works*, II, 2, 6); and "the state of apprehension in his part of the country" may have been substituted for "the dreadful state of his particular part of the country" to make Virginia seem somewhat less of a center of slave unrest (*Speeches*, p. 12; *Works*, II, 8).

There is no evidence that Calhoun made any of the changes; indeed in style they were quite out of character. The *Speeches* volume was printed for Calhoun's 1843 campaign, and the revisions were of the same type as those made in the papers published after his death in the *Works* volume. Nearly all of the revisions were for the purpose of smoothing out Calhoun's distinctly angular style. In a few cases there was real improvement, as was certainly the case when the clause "The people were startled by" replaced "the eye of the nation was frightened by." But for the most part the effect was unfortunate, for the *Intelligencer* report has all evidence of a speech vigorous, forceful, and of extraordinary power. "This is the road that all great nations have trod" was refined by these critics to make Calhoun say: "This is the way which has led nations to greatness" (*Speeches*, p. 11; *Works*, II, 7).   Source: *NI*, Dec. 19, 1811; *AC*12-1, 476-83.

49. To Mrs. Floride Colhoun Senr, Charleston, S.C.

Washington 21st Decr. 1811

Dear Mother, I received last week your affectionate letter of the 20th of the last months. It came the same day with Florides; tho' hers is dated on the 26th. It contained the first direct information I had from home; and relieved me from a load of anxiety. I left Floride and our little son [1] at so critical a period, that I almost felt an alarm at hearing from home for fear that all was not well. I feared that her anxiety of mind at my leaving her might injure her health; situated as sh[e] was; and I am sure I have great cause to be thankful that she has entirely recovered. I am as comfortably fixed here as I could be; and have nothing to render me uneasy

---

1. Andrew Pickens Calhoun, born October 15, 1811.

but my solicitude for those I have left behind. Our society is delightful. This place is quite gay, during the session; but I do not participate in it much myself. You know I never had much inclination to such enjoyment. I am invited to a ball to the French minister's on monday next; and to dine with him on Christmas day; but for political reasons have declined his invitation. I do not think at this time when a war is expected with England that much intimacy should exist with the minister of her rival; particularly as our oponents accuse us with partia[l]ity towards France.

I hop[e] you will impress on Floride the necessity of taking sufficient exerci[s]e when the weather will permit. Nothing is so conducive to health; and I think she is rather disinclined to it. Let me hear from you often. I shall not be backward in answering tho' I have a great many letters to write. Remember me to the family and all friends.

I am your affectionate son

JOHN C. CALHO[UN]

SOURCE: *CC.*

50. COMMENT ON THE BILL FOR AN ADDITIONAL MILITARY FORCE

January 2, 1812

Mr. Calhoun voted in favor of the amendment of the gentleman from Georgia,[1] though he was in favor of raising the whole 25,000 men, because he wished to carry the present measure by as large a vote as possible. He believed nothing but the most energetic course would answer any purpose. The news of the steps already taken have no doubt passed over the Atlantic. The country against whom we are taking measures, may have taken her stand. Unanimity and decision in our councils alone can save the country. He believed the public sentiment was with Congress; but if gentlemen will not, in any instance, sacrifice their opinions, but pertinaciously

1. That is, the amendment offered earlier that day by William W. Bibb; his amendment, rejected by the House, would have authorized the President, after six regiments were enlisted and officers appointed, to decide if it were necessary to make appointments of all or any officers for the remaining seven (*AC*12-1, p. 611-3). The amendment under consideration (p. 613) was really to the same effect, and was likewise rejected (p. 617).

insist upon amendment after amendment to measures brought forward for our defence, we might be forced into war before we are prepared for it. We ought either to submit, or make an energetic defence. He perceived that the public sentiment began already to doubt whether Congress was really in earnest, from the tardiness of their movements. He should vote against the proposed amendment in order to prevent farther delay.

50 NOTE: There were about 4,000 men in the regular army at this time (*AC*12-1, p. 597). The act of Dec. 24 made provision for increasing this number to the 10,000 authorized in 1808. Madison in his November message had asked also "an auxiliary force, to be engaged for a more limited term"—that is, for a shorter enlistment than the five years of the regular army. This request had been met in the Senate by a bill providing for 25,000 instead of the 10,000 desired by Madison (p. 611, 715), to be enlisted for five years, and the debate was on this bill. See No. 46 NOTE.

Monroe in June of 1812 (Hamilton, *Writings of James Monroe,* V, 206-7) charged that the opposition leaders in the Senate attempted to discredit the administration by pretended zeal for strong war measures while making enlistment more difficult by setting the term at five years—see also Adams, *History of U.S.,* VI, 147-53. But most of the House members, ignoring the difficulties in raising and financing this force, regarded the bill as an opportunity to provide an adequate army, and, like Calhoun, were eager for prompt action and at least a semblance of unity in the war program. The House passed the bill on the 6th, by a vote of 94 to 34 (*AC*12-1, p. 691). See Porter's comment, p. 701, and Clay's analysis of the situation, p. 596-8.

When Calhoun spoke, the House, while accepting the provision for the larger number, was considering amendments to economize by withholding appointment or pay of officers except when in actual service, and to authorize the President to discharge troops when they were no longer needed. The Senate rejected these amendments and on the 9th Porter moved that the House agree (p. 611, 700-1). Calhoun supported the motion, declaring that if the House were to "stickle" at this expense of twenty or thirty thousand dollars "it will show that we are not fit to manage the affairs of the nation" (p. 706-7). The House receded on all its amendments save one: on that which provided that officers be paid only for their time in service, it carried its point (p. 717-9).   SOURCE: *NI,* Jan. 4, 1812; *AC*12-1, p. 616.

51. COMMENT ON RANDOLPH'S RESOLUTION FOR EMPLOYMENT OF THE ARMY

January 10, 1812

Mr. Calhoun was not at all surprised to find gentlemen, who are opposed to putting the country in a war attitude, should endeavor by every means in their power to defeat the measures adopted. At a moment when we are calling upon the yeomanry of our country to step forward in defence of our rights, he thought such a motion very improper, and he hoped Congress would not treat it with so much respect as to suffer it to lie upon the table for a moment. The gentleman had frequently told the House he believed the army was composed of the worst materials, and he now appears to wish to bring the service into disgrace. He hoped the proposition would be disposed of without much debate.

51 NOTE: Calhoun was opposing the resolution offered by Randolph that the President be authorized to employ the regular army "when not engaged in actual service . . . in the construction of roads, canals, or other works of public utility." Randolph urged it on the ground of economy and of the health of the soldiers, and as a measure to relieve the monotony of their existence; it was rejected by the House the same day by a large majority (*AC*12-1, p. 720, 727-8). Compare Randolph's resolution of Nov. 25 preceding, looking toward abolishing corporal punishment in the army, and his accompanying declaration that the "yeomanry" of the country would not submit to it. This resolution was tabled (p. 368). SOURCE: *NI,* Jan. 14, 1812; *AC*12-1, p. 721.

52. To PATRICK CALHOUN, Abbeville, S.C.

Washington 24th Jany 1812

Dr Brother, I send you enclosed the report of the Secretary of the treasury; by which you will see his ways and means for the war.[1] I expect most of the taxes recommended will pass. I think the Stamp will be confined to bank notes. Our proportion of the direct taxes will be about $150,000. I think the scheme of collecting a good one. It will fall light on the upper country. To lay a tax is a

1. *AC*12-1, p. 848-58.

painful thing; but we must either submit or have money. I think war will be declared on the return of the Hornet;[2] it will be in March or perhaps in April. The Navy bill has been before the committee of the whole for some days back. The committee ["house" *cancelled*] has refused to grant any Naval force. I am sorry for it; because I think we could by a small Navy have peace and commerce. Such seems Mr. Monroe's opinion. He says he felt our want of a Navy in all of his negotiation. God grant that the people may have sperit to maintain our interest and honor in this momenteous period. Gen. Dearborn has been nominated by the President one of the Maj. Generals. Davy of our State is talk'd of as the other.[3] None of you write me. I think strange of it. Remember me to Nancy Mr. & Mrs Mosely and all friends.

I am your affectionate brother

J. C. CALHOUN

SOURCE: *SCL.*

53. To DR. JAMES MACBRIDE, Charleston, S.C.

Washington 16th [17?][1] Feby 1812.

Dr MacBride, You see I have grown a much more punctual correspondent than formerly. I have scarcely permited a letter of your's to rest a week unanswered. You have certainly experienced a great change of late. I am glad to find, that you have some relish for political subjects. It will make us correspond on more equal terms. Formerly the pleasure was unequal I, always fond of your persuit, the study of nature; you indifferent to mine. I do not attribute this change wholly to the cause which you do; because your friend is now an actor on the political stage; but because this is a period of the greatest moment to our country. No period since the formation of our constitution has been equally important. It is the commence-[*ment*] of a new era in our politicks. Heretofore, the conductors of our affairs, have attempted to avoid and remove difficulties by a sort of political management. They thought, that national honor and interest could both be maintained and respected, not by war, or a

2. See No. 56.
3. William R. Davie; see No. 58, n. 2.
1. See below, n. 3.

preperation for it; but by commercial arrangiments and negotiations. This might suit an inconsiderable nation, or one that had not such important rights at stake. Experience has proved it improper for us. Its effects have been distrust at home and contempt abroad. We have said, we will change; we will defend ourselves by force. I hope Congress will stick to this salutary resolve. If a majority should go back to the old stale measures, I am sure there are many that will not follow. England will not yield I expect. We will hear in a few weeks what she intends.[2] Congress will suspend any act of hostilities till then. I expect the question of war will be moved the next month. The taxes intended you have seen in the papers. The committee will report them this morning with considerable modifications.[3] The stamp will be extended only to bank notes, bills of Exchange; and notes of hand above $50 and indorsed. The tax on stills will be very moderate. It differs much from an excise. They will be published in a few days, and therefore will say no more now. Our delegation have recommended William Drayton & Andrew Pickens as Lieutenant Colonels for our state.[4]

How unusual our earthquakes—we had several shocks last night. In what will they terminate. No doubt you keep your attention directed on this unusual Phenomenon If you have made any observations do communicate them.

I am &c

J. C. CALHOUN

Remember me to Mrs. Macbride and my acquaintances in Pineville.

SOURCE: *SCL.*

54. TO MRS. FLORIDE [JOHN C.] CALHOUN, No. 2 Guignard St. [Charleston]

Washington 1st March 1812

You will no doubt, my dearest Floride, be much gratified and surprised to find the bearer of this letter in St. Johns. Mr. Cooper

2. See No. 56.
3. The committee reported on the 17th (*AC*12-1, p. 1050-6); Calhoun was probably writing on that day, for the 16th was Sunday.
4. See No. 101 NOTE.

called on me this morning in company of Mr. Talmage and informed me that he was on his way to the Southward. I was very glad to see him; as I had taken up a very favourable opinion of him from the kindness which he had bestowed on your brother when sick.

I wrote you but a few days since, and have nothing farther to communicate now. The weather is very mild and spring like this morning. I Dreamed all night the last night of being home with you; and nursing our dear son; and regreted when I awoke to find it a dream. I was in hopes that this morning's mail would bring me a letter from you; but was disapointed. It is near a month since I had one. I learned by a letter from Mr. Pickens a few days since that you were all well.

Remember me to our mother & John

I am with affection your husband

J. C. CALHOUN

54 NOTE: In the address "St. Johns" is cancelled and "No. 2. Guignard St." written in. The *Directory for the District of Charleston,* 1809, does not list Guignard St., but later directories do. SOURCE: *CC.*

55. TO ROBERT CRESSWELL, Laurens, S.C.

Washington 10th March 1812.

Dr Sir, A very important and extraordinary disclosure was made to the house yesterday, which has excited the strongest indignation here; and disconcerted the apoligists of England. A certain Mr Henery whom the British Govt. employed as an emmissary to seperate these states in the summer of 1809—during the discontents of the embargo, has made a discovery of the plot to our government. He has communicated his original commission from General Craig the govern. general of Canada, and the correspondence with the British government. The facts are undoubted. The papers were refered to the Committee on foreign relations; and Mr. Monroe attended our meeting last evening. He and Mr Pinckney [1]

1. Evidently William Pinkney, the Attorney General, recently minister to England (Adams, *History of U.S.,* VI, 20, 429); Calhoun was using the spelling of the South Carolina family.

are both acquainted with the hand writing of Lord Liverpool with whom part of the correspondence was had, and that of Craig is also authenticated. No names, of those who joined in this country the foul attempt have been disclosed. He made it one of the conditions of the discovery not to be pressed on that point. The whole correspondence will be published in a few days.

Such is the conduct we have ever to expect from England, while she retains possession of Canada—such the cause that necessiarily forces us into a state of war.

I am with much esteem yours &c

J. C. CALHOUN

55 NOTE: On Mar. 9 Madison sent to Congress the papers revealing the efforts during the year 1809 of John Henry, the British agent, to foment discord and disunion sentiment in New England (*AC*12-1, p. 1162-81). The same day the papers were ordered printed and were referred to the Committee on Foreign Relations, the report of which was delivered by Porter on the 19th (p. 1220-4). Cresswell was one of Calhoun's constituents and a member of the South Carolina Legislature; Calhoun knew him on the legal circuit (see O'Neall, *Bench and Bar of S. C.*, II, p. 251). SOURCE: *SCL.*

56. To DR. JAMES MACBRIDE, Charleston, S.C.

Washington 16th. March 1812

Dr McBride, I regret that the application of your friend Mr Couturier has come too late. All of the officers, except some of the generals, are appointed; and orders are out for the recruiting service. It is possible that in some instances resignations or other vacancies will take place. In that event, I should be happy to serve your friend.

We are all impatience here for the return of the Hornet, to determin the question of war. It is said recruiting is going on well; and I was informed yesterday at the war department, that the preperation for actual service would be very much advanced in 6 or 8 weeks. The secretary expected in that time to have 10,000 or 15,000 regulars ready for service.

The disclosure of Henery has produced much excitement here. There is no doubt of the authenticity of the documents. I make no comment; except from the peculiar formation of our government it is the greatest and most dangerous injury ["outrage" *cancelled*] that can be commited on our rights.

I am with much esteem yours &c

J. C. CALHOUN

Remember me to Mrs. McBride and my acquaintances in P. V.

56 NOTE: The *Hornet* did not arrive until May, and her dispatches made no change in the situation (Adams, *History of U.S.*, VI, 215-7). For Henry see No. 55. SOURCE: *SCL.*

57. REMARKS ON AN AMENDMENT PROVIDING FOR REPRESENTATION IN THE LOUISIANA LEGISLATURE FOR THE ANNEXED PORTION OF WEST FLORIDA

March 19, 1812

Mr. Calhoun opposed the amendment, on the ground of its incorporating in the law a principle of representation in hostility with that feature in the constitution of the new state which apportions representation in a different manner; and the convention, the body which alone could change or modify the principle of representation, was already dissolved. He suggested a mode by which the object now in contemplation could be attained, viz. by reassembling the convention.

[*The remarks of three other speakers intervene at this point.*]

Mr. Calhoun again spoke in opposition to the amendment. It proposed to annex conditions to Orleans becoming a state, of which there was nobody in existence competent to accept, the convention which framed the constitution having been dissolved. The people in question would be unrepresented only until the state government should be organized; the interval in which they would be unrepresented would be unavoidable, and, being so short, not very important. The proposed amendment would be engrafting the principle of territorial government on a state government, to which it is wholly inapplicable; it was in fact assuming to make a constitution for the people of a state, whose unalienable right it was to form a constitution for themselves.

94

57 NOTE: The bill for admitting Louisiana as a state was under consideration; on the 18th an amendment had been adopted annexing to the new state the portion of West Florida lying west of Pearl River. The question was now on an amendment offered by Richard M. Johnson, of Kentucky, providing that the annexed section send two senators and two representatives to the state legislature (*AC*12-1, p. 1216-8). The amendment was rejected (p. 1225). The Senate made the addition of territory the subject of a separate bill which became law Apr. 14; it required the state legislature, if it accepted the territory, to give it equal rights of representation (p. 1254, 1278, 1298, 2270). SOURCE: *NI*, Mar. 21, 1812; *AC*12-1, p. 1224, 1225.

58. To PATRICK NOBLE, Abbeville, S.C.

W[*ashington*] C[*ity*] 22d. March 1812

Dr Patrick, I am glad to find you so punctual a correspondent. Yesterday yours of the 4th of March came to hand. I cannot refrain from expressing my pleasure to hear of your success in your profession. You deserve success; and I doubt not you may look forward to the first honors of the profession in our state. I rejoice to hear my constituents are ready to support the cause of the country with so much Zeal; and that they so clearly perceive the necessity of Taxes. With such a state of the publick sentiment we must succeed; we will cause our rights to be respected. I think on the whole things go on well here. Congress has passed all necessary laws for a vigourous champaign. It now rest with the Executive. Their Zeal and intelligence can not now be doubted. At the commencement of the session I felt much alarm, as I thought I saw in some of the members of the cabnit a disinclination to the measures adopted and an appearant want of Zeal in most of them. The case is now very diffirent. Every exertion is making to put the country in the most respectable position. Military stores of every kind are provided or providing in New York and Vermont.

As soon as cloaths can be distributed, the recruiting service will be pushed with vigour ever where. It is doing well here now. The secretary at war thinks that he can have his preperations well advanced in 8 weeks. We have had to contend for some months past with all the intrigue of the Clinton faction.[1] They have lost ground; and I think no ground of hope is left to them of distracting our measures. Of Henery's disclosures you will see a full account in the Intelligencer. It makes a great deal of noise. Foster had dispaches from his govt. on the 20th inst. Their contents are not yet known. The rumours are various. I expect they are not important to us. Thomas Pinkny, or General Davie I expect will be made a Maj. General.[2] You ask me what I think of a military life for you. Were I a single man I would certainly take a commession. The war will be a favourite one with the country. Much honor await those who may distinguish themselves. The appointments are all disposed of now. Should you feel disposed I think the character of aid to the Maj. or a Brig. General would be a very agreeable. Davie I think will make a noble officer. Consult your own feelings.

I am with much esteem yours

J. C. CALHOUN

58 NOTE: Patrick, brother of Alexander Noble (No. 7 NOTE), and former law student of Calhoun, now his partner, was elected to the S.C. House in 1812, and was Speaker from 1818 to 1824 (*Appletons' Cyclopaedia*, IV, 528). SOURCE: *CC*.

59. REMARKS ON THE PUBLICATION OF SECRET PROCEEDINGS

April 7, 1812

Mr. Calhoun said that the member of the Committee of Foreign Relations (Mr. Randolph) to whom allusion had been made, not being in his seat, he would state how the fact just stated had occurred in the committee. That gentleman stated (said Mr. C.) that he had doubts of the power of the committee to compel him to secrecy; but the gentleman also stated that he had just returned from Baltimore, where he found the British Consul possessed the knowledge of an intended embargo, and that a great commercial house was acting on it, and therefore he did not feel it his duty to

1. See Adams, *History of U.S.*, VI, 213-5.
2. William R. Davie declined because of ill health (*Appletons' Cyclopaedia*, II, 90); Pinckney was appointed (*DAB*).

keep the secret. I, sir, was the one who made the motion that our proceeding should be confidential. After the statement made by the gentleman from Virginia, that he should feel it his duty to proclaim the fact, combined with other circumstances, I did not feel so strongly the obligation, and the motion for secrecy was waived. Under the impression that it was no longer a duty to confine the knowledge of this transaction to the bosom of the committee, I mentioned it to the gentlemen from Boston and other commercial cities, that they might be aware of the transaction; I did it from a sense of duty, that they might be as well informed on this head as other members of the House. I believe the House will see, if a committee have not power to enforce secrecy on its members in relation to its proceedings, we shall frequently be very disagreeably situated; but any such determination appearing in this case nugatory, and means being taken to diffuse the knowledge of what passed, on a consultation with others of the committee we conceived it unnecessary, as it would be unavailing, to conceal from the members, at least, what had passed in committee.

59 NOTE: Events of March destroyed any hope of change of British policy (Adams, *History of U.S.*, VI, 191-3), and in a conference of Secretary of State Monroe with the Foreign Relations Committee it was agreed that the President would ask a sixty-day embargo as a preliminary of war (AC12-1, p. 1265-6, 1593); thus this message on Apr. 1 in effect set the date for a declaration of war at about June 1. Compare Monroe's statement—Hamilton, *Writings of James Monroe*, V, 205-6. Randolph's denial that war would follow as a matter of course was sharply disputed by Felix Grundy of Tennessee and Calhoun (AC12-1, p. 1592-4).

It was evidently about this time that the committee took the action referred to by one of its members, John A. Harper of New Hampshire, in a letter to the governor of his state, William Plumer (Plumer Papers, *LC*) Apr. 29, 1812: "A few weeks since the Comee of F. Relations appointed a Sub committee to prepare a manifesto and declaration of War, of which I was one—It was agreed that each one should prepare his own draft and then compare them & make the best selection—I have completed mine."

Porter promptly brought in from the committee a bill for the purpose (AC12-1, p. 1587), and thereby carried out his pledge of Dec. 6. This embargo (p. 2262-4), which became law April 4, was designed to hold American ships, and to allow time for others to come home, pending a declaration of war (see p. 1587, 1590). It was supplemented by a bill, enacted on the 14th (p. 2269-70), to prohibit, for the duration of the embargo, exportation of specie. To a great degree the purpose of the embargo was thwarted by the Senate amendment extending it to ninety days (p. 189), and by premature publication of the plan, for on Mar. 31 the news was given out (p. 1265-6, 1593).

On the 6th a committee, appointed under a resolution passed on the 3rd to investigate any violation of secret proceedings, reported (p. 1600, 1617-9) publication of secret debates on the embargo by Nathaniel Rounsavell, an Alexandria editor, who was thereupon ordered by the House to be taken into custody. Calhoun's statement on the 7th (above) was followed by one from Josiah Quincy, of Massachusetts, that Calhoun had informed him of the impending bill. Calhoun later the same day spoke in favor of the motion, which passed, releasing Rounsavell from custody without further ado (p. 1263-74).

Apparently Calhoun protested in a private letter the reference, in the April or May elections in Massachusetts, to this service he had rendered the Eastern merchants. The Federalist *Charleston Courier* (June 3, 1812) remarked sarcastically "The young gentleman need not make himself unhappy on this score. His name is not weighty enough to have much effect on a New-England election." SOURCE: *NI*, Apr. 11, 1812; *AC*12-1, p. 1265.

60. REMARKS ON THE BILL FOR IMPORTATION OF BRITISH GOODS

April 10, 1812

Mr. Calhoun thought the motion to postpone for a few days ought to prevail. This, he said, was a mere difference of opinion between those who had the same object in view; and whatever might be the zeal of the gentlemen from Maryland and Tennessee on the great question of war, he could assure the gentlemen that they were not a whit before his honorable colleague (Mr. Lowndes) who was as determined as any gentleman on this floor or in the nation.[1] Mr. C. expressed his hope that the motion for indefinite postponement would not be pressed. He for one entertained doubts on the question, which was one that certainly admitted of doubt. It is certainly proper that our property abroad should be drawn in, in the

---

1. John Rhea of Tennessee and Robert Wright of Maryland angrily protested that the bill would wreck the war program as it had been developed thus far (*AC*12-1, p. 1300-1).

event of war. The state of public sentiment here and in England ought also to be regarded. The question was a difficult one. He hoped more respect would be shewn to his colleague's sentiments than to postpone the bill indefinitely; it was proper always to yield a little to each other.

60 NOTE: The House was considering a bill to allow the importation of goods from Great Britain contracted for prior to Feb. 1, 1811, the effective date for non-importation from England, but William Lowndes of South Carolina, who was sponsoring the bill, announced that amendments would be offered to admit all goods imported prior to Aug. 1 (*i.e.*, practically the duration of the embargo), and thus to get debts due Americans by British merchants paid in manufactures which would yield the government a large revenue in import duties (*AC*12-1, p. 1280-90). Langdon Cheves alone supported his colleague (p. 1290-5), and both declared their disapproval of the restrictive system (p. 1289, 1292).

Calhoun was trying to avoid an issue which threatened to split the war party, and delayed his own attack upon the trade restriction policy until the declaration of war (see No. 69). Lowndes approved postponement of consideration till the bill could be better understood (p. 1299-1300); the date for consideration was set at Apr. 20, but the order was disregarded (p. 1314, 1325). SOURCE: *NI*, Apr. 21, 1812; *AC*12-1, p. 1302.

61. To DR JAMES MACBRIDE, Charleston, S.C.

Washington 18th April 1812

Dr MacBride, I am sure you will give me credit for the punctuality of my correspondence, when, I inform you, that yours of the 5th inst was only recd. this morning. I see you are almost in a state of despair as to our national proceedings. I am not surprised. I am sure our proceedings must appear very slow to those who are at a distance. They are so to me; altho, by being on the spot and an actor in them, I perhaps feel and see many impediments that must be over looked by the country. This is the first war that the country has ever been engaged in; there is a great want of military knowledge; and the whole of our system has to be commenced and organised. I am sorry to say that even this does not form the greatest impediment. Our President tho a man of amiable manners and

great talents, has not I fear those commanding talents, which are
necessary to controul those about him. He permits devision in his
cabinet. He reluctantly gives up the system of peace. It is to be
hoped, that as war is now seriously determined on, the Executive
department will move with much more vigour. Without it it is impossible for Congress to proceed. The embargo is certainly a decisive stept. It is understood to be the prelude to war. I do not
expect Congress will wait its termination to declare war. A state
of suspense is a painful and dangerous one. The sooner in my opinion we are out of it the better. My respects to Mrs. Macbride and
my friends in P. Ville.

I am with esteem yours &c

J. C. CALHOUN

61 NOTE: Compare Calhoun's letter of December following
(No. 72).   SOURCE: *LC,* James Macbride Papers.

62. COMMENT ON THE RESOLUTION FOR RELIEF OF CARACAS

April 29, 1812

Mr. Calhoun expressed his regret that this proposition to aid the
cause of humanity could not be permitted to pass without the in-
termixture of party feelings, which the motion and speech of the
gentleman from Virginia, he thought, were calculated to excite. He
was opposed to the amendment, which he conceived would virtually repeal the embargo, and he hoped, as there could be no probability of adopting it, he would withdraw it. Mr. C. said he had
doubts about the latter clause of the resolution; because as to the
distress at Teneriffe, the House had no other information than a
newspaper report, whilst of the scarcity of provisions at Caraccas
they had accurate information.

[Remarks of Randolph and of Macon intervene at this point.]

Mr. Calhoun again spoke against the amendment, and in reply
to Mr. Randolph's imputation of intolerance to the minority. This
course of discussion he deprecated as not comporting with the
sacred cause of distant and oppressed humanity, &c.

100

62 NOTE: Calhoun was replying to Randolph, who proposed to amend the resolution of Nathaniel Macon of North Carolina for a direct gift of flour to sufferers from an earthquake in Caracas and ravages of locusts in Teneriffe by adding a clause lifting the embargo on vessels clearing "for any port of the aforesaid country." For accounts of the disasters see Niles, *Weekly Register,* Apr. 25 (p. 131-2) and May 2 (p. 152), 1812. Randolph protested against Calhoun's criticism and charged that the minority were treated with repeated discourtesy. A committee was ordered to bring in a bill for the purchase of provisions for Caracas at the direction of the President and to inquire into the needs of the Canary Islands. On Calhoun's motion the relief for Venezuela was fixed at $50,000. The bill became law on May 8 (*AC*12-1, p. 1351-2, 1366, 1378, 2294). SOURCE: *NI,* May 2, 1812; *AC*12-1, p. 1348-9.

63. To VIRGIL MAXCY, Annapolis, Md.

Washington 2d. May 1812.

Dr Maxcy—Should I go on to Philidelphia, as I still expect to do, I certainly shall make every exertion to visit Tulip Hill. I shall take much pleasure to see my friend in the midst of his family and enjoying those comforts, which are so delightful; but which this political life of mine has made me a stranger to for half a year. I will have business in Philidelphia about the 1st of June, so that if I go at all it will be about that time. You must not expect me, however, for fear you should be disappointed; for I would not be surprised, if about that time we should have a considerable political bustle. War, I regret, has become unavoidable. I did hope, England would have returned to a sense of justice, when she saw this country determined to avenge her wrongs. I think the friends of the country of whatever politicks, must see, that it is impossible for us to receede without the greatest injury to the character of the government. However there is no danger of that; as the same sense of the justice and necessity of the measures, which originally induced Congress to adopt them, will also coerce us to resort to that last redress of a nation's wrongs. You see I write to you freely for altho' differing from me in principle yet I know you are not a party man.

I am with much esteem your friend &c

J. C. CALHOUN

63 NOTE: Maxcy was brother of Jonathan, President of the South Carolina College, and had another brother, Milton, near Charleston. He was a classmate of Andrew Pickens at Rhode Island College, and taught in South Carolina in 1801 and 1803. He studied law with the Federalist Robert Goodloe Harper in Baltimore and began his practice there (*Appletons' Cyclopaedia,* IV, 267; MS Diary, July-Dec., 1801 [New York Public Library, MS Division, "Diaries"]; letter to Andrew Pickens, Jan. 12, 1803 [Duke University Library]). In this letter Calhoun is clearly appealing to a Federalist friend. See No. 47 NOTE.   SOURCE: *LC,* Galloway–Maxcy–Markoe Papers.

64. SPEECH ON THE ALBANY PETITION FOR REPEAL OF THE EMBARGO

May 6, 1812

Mr. Calhoun—Mr. Speaker: It is not my intention to discuss the merits of the embargo law, or to follow the gentleman from Virginia in that maze of arguments and assertions through which he has thought proper to wander. The House must be wearied, and can receive no additional light on a subject which, through the zeal of some gentlemen in opposition, has been so frequently dragged into discussion. I cannot suppose that our opponents, in their importunity, are governed by an expectation that a change will be made in the opinion of any individual of the majority. This they must see is hopeless. The measure has been too recently adopted, and after too much deliberation, to leave to the most sanguine any hope of change. To reply, then, to the arguments of gentlemen on the general merits of the embargo, would be an useless consumption of time, and an unwarranted intrusion on the patience of the House. This, as I have already stated, is not my intention; but it is my object to vindicate the motion now under discussion from unmerited censure, and to prove that it cannot be justly considered as treating the petitioners with contempt. I am aware that the right to petition this body is guaranteed by the Constitution, and that it is not less our interest than our duty to receive petitions, expressed in proper terms, as this is, with respect.

Two propositions have been made relative to the disposition of the petition now before us; one to refer to a committee—the other, that is now under discussion, to postpone the further consideration to a day beyond the termination of the embargo. It is contended, not by argument but assertion, that the former would have been more respectful to the petitioners. They have left us to conjecture the reasons. I ask, then, why would it be more respectful? Would it present stronger hopes of success, or admit as great latitude of discussion on its merits? The gentlemen know that it would not; they well know when the House wishes to give the go-by to a petition, it has been usually by the very motion which, in this instance, they advocate. On a motion of reference, debate on the merits is precluded; and, when referred, the committee, where there is no hope of success, usually lets it sleep. But, sir, I ask what is the necessity for referring this petition to a committee? What are the objects of a reference? I conceive them to be two—one to investigate some matter of fact; and the other, when a subject is much tangled with detail, to digest and arrange the parts, so that the House may more easily comprehend the whole. This body is too large for either of those operations; and, therefore, a reference is had to smaller ones. Neither of these furnish a good reason for the commitment of the present petition. The facts are not denied; and, as to detail, there is none—it ends in a point, the repeal of the embargo law—and has been so argued in opposition. This House is as fully competent to discuss its merits now, as it would be after the report of any committee; and the motion to postpone admits of the greatest latitude of discussion on its merits. This the speech of the gentleman from Virginia has proved. He has argued not only on the merits of the petition, but the embargo and almost every subject however remotely connected. I know that the motion is tantamount to that of rejection in the present instance. In fact, it has been vindicated by the mover on that ground. He has justly said, as we cannot grant the relief prayed, we ought to act with promptitude and decision, so that the petitioners may know what to expect. This motion has that character: it leaves no expectation where there can be no relief. I know, sir, we might have acted very differently; we might have spun out the hopes of the petitioners. Some may think that it would be sound policy, but in my opinion it would be unworthy of this House. Candor in our government is one of the first of political virtues. Let us always do directly what we intend shall finally be done.

Since there can be no objection to the motion now before the House, it remains to be considered whether the relief prayed ought to be granted. I am sensible that the maxim is generally correct, that individual profit is national gain; and that the party interested is the best judge of the hazard and propriety of a speculation. But there are exceptions; there are cases in which the government is the best judge—and such are those where the future conduct of government is the cause of the hazard. It certainly is the best judge of what it intends; and in those cases where it foresees a hazard, it ought in humanity to the merchants to restrain their speculations. Such is the present case. Many of our merchants labour under a delusion as to the measures of government: nor can this seem strange, since some gentlemen, even in this House, have taken up such mistaken views of things. With such conceptions of the course of events as the gentleman from New York thinks will take place, I am not surprised that he should advocate the prayer of the petition. He believes that the embargo will be permitted to expire without any hostile measure being taken against Great Britain; and that in the present state of our preparation it would be madness to think of war in sixty days or any short period. When I hear such language on this floor, I no longer wonder that merchants are petitioning you to make speculations, which in a short time must end in their ruin. I ask the gentleman from New York, who are the true friends to the petitioners—the majority who, foreseeing the hazard to which they would be exposed, restrain them from falling into the hands of British cruizers; or the minority who, by suppressing the evidence of danger, induce them to enter into the most ruinous speculations? By the one, the merchants still retain their property, depreciated, it is true, in a small degree: by the other, it will be lost to themselves and their country, and will go to augment the resources of our enemy. For, sir, let me assure the gentleman that he makes a very erroneous estimate of our preparations, and the time at which we will act. Our army and measures are not merely on paper, as he states; but, were this the proper time and subject, it could be shewn that very considerable advances have been made to put the country into the posture of defence, and to prepare our forces for an attack on our enemy. So far from being unprepared, sir, I believe that in four weeks from the time that a

104

declaration of war is heard on our frontier, the whole of Upper and a part of Lower Canada will be in our possession.[1] We will not, I hope, wait the expiration of the embargo to take our stand against England—that stand which the best interest and honor of this nation have so loudly demanded. With such a prospect, I again ask, would it be humanity or cruelty to the petitioners to grant their prayer, and, by relaxing the embargo in their favor, to entice them to certain destruction?

The gentleman from Virginia stated, to induce us to repeal the embargo law, and to make it odious, I suppose, with the community, that it operated less severely on the merchant than on the farmer and miller. He did not prove very distinctly how this unequal pressure was produced. But I understood him to say, that Eastern vessels could be had with so much facility to make shipments to any European port, and that flour had risen so much already in consequence of the embargo, that the rise in the price nearly compensated for the additional risk and price of exportation. I observe the gentleman shakes his head in disapprobation of the statement. I suppose I mistook his statement. However, I could not mistake the conclusion which he drew, that the merchants, by eluding the embargo, had prevented the depreciation of the price of wheat and flour on hand. This sir, is sufficient for my purpose. The gentleman from Virginia must know, that from the character of trade, the profit of such trade, if it really exists, cannot be confined to the merchants. It would soon raise the price of bread stuffs in the hands of the other classes of the community, and would prove that his statement of the distressed condition of the millers and farmers cannot be correct.

In his zeal against the embargo, the gentleman from Virginia says, it was engendered between the Committee on Foreign Relations and the Executive.[2] Engendered! The gentleman must be sensible of the impropriety of such language, as applied to the Executive or a committee of this House. No, sir, it was not engen-

---

1. The *Works* version of the speech (II, 13-20), omits this prediction, three times substitutes "country" for "nation," and for improvement of Calhoun's style makes a few minor changes.

2. *AC*12-1, p. 1385. Randolph had also earlier, in the debate on the embargo, declared the measure "was engendered by an extensive excitement upon the Executive" (p. 1589).

dered; but adopted by both the Executive and committee, from its manifest propriety as a prelude to war. There is no man in his reason, and uninfluenced by party feelings, but must acknowledge that a war in this country ought almost invariably to be preceded by an embargo. The very persons most loud against that measure, would be the most clamorous had it not preceded the war. There, sir, has been much false statement in relation to the embargo. I remember, when it was under discussion on a former occasion, that a gentleman then observed, he had certain information that the French minister had been importuning our government to stop the exportation of bread stuffs to the Peninsula.[3] I know not whether he intended to insinuate this as one of the causes of the embargo. Be it as it may, I do assert, from the highest authority, that no such application has ever been made directly or indirectly on the part of the French government. The assertion was of such a nature, as induced me to enquire into its correctness; and the result is such as I have stated. I can scarcely suppose, that the gentleman intended to convey the idea that French influence had anything to do with the measure. He must know that either the Executive or a majority of this body would resist with the greatest indignation any attempt to influence the measures of government; but such has been the use made of it by certain prints, either through the manner in which it was connected in debate with the embargo, or the very imperfect and unfair reports of the secret proceedings.

One would suppose, from the language of the gentleman from Virginia, that he was much in the secret of government. He says the plan now is to disband the army, and carry on a predatory war on the ocean. I can assure him, if such is the plan, I am wholly ignorant of it; and that should it be proposed it would not meet with my approbation. I am decisively of opinion that the best interests of the country will be consulted by calling out the whole force of the community to protect its rights. Should this course fail, the next best would be to submit to our enemy with as good a

3. This was Randolph, Apr. 1; the minister was M. Serurier (p. 1590). Following Calhoun's speech, Randolph said, in effect, that his statement had been made on inference (p. 1403-4). Later the same day Calhoun on information from "the highest source" repeated his denial that there had been such pressure and deplored Randolph's remarks because of the use that had been made of them (p. 1405).

grace as possible. Let us not provoke where we cannot resist. The mongrel state, neither war nor peace, is much the worst.

The gentleman from Virginia has told us much of the signs of the times. I did hope, that the age of superstition was past, and that no attempt would be made to influence the measures of government, which ought to be founded in wisdom and policy, by the vague, I may say, superstitious feelings of any man, whatever may be the physical appearances which gave rise to them. Are we to renounce our reason? Must we turn from the path of justice and experience, because a comet has made its appearance in our system, or the moon has passed between the sun and the earth? If so, the signs of the times are bad indeed. It would mark a fearful retrograde in civilization—it would prove a dreadful declension towards barbarism. Sir, if we must examine the auspices; if we must inspect the entrails of the times, I would pronounce the omens good. It is from moral, and not from brutal or physical omens that we ought to judge; and what more favorable could we desire than that the nation is, at last, roused from its lethargy and, that it has determined to vindicate its interest and honor. On the contrary, a nation so sunk in avarice, and so corrupted by faction, as to be insensible to the greatest injuries, and lost to its independence, would be a sight more portentous than comets, earthquakes, eclipses, or the whole catalogue of omens, which I have heard the gentleman from Virginia enumerate. I assert, and gentlemen know it, if we submit to the pretensions of England, now openly avowed, the independence of this nation is lost—we will be, as to our commerce, re-colonised. This is the second struggle for our liberty; and if we but do justice to ourselves, it will be no less glorious and successful than the first. Let us but exert ourselves, and we must meet with the prospering smile of heaven. Sir, I assert it with confidence, a war just and necessary in its origin, wisely and vigorously carried on, and honorably terminated, would establish the integrity and prosperity of our country for centuries.

64 NOTE: On the 6th Harmanus Bleecker of New York presented the petition of about eight hundred citizens in or near Albany asking repeal or modification of the embargo. John Rhea of Tennessee moved postponement of consideration to July 4—after the expiration of the embargo. Bleecker declared that the country could

not be prepared for war by the date of expiration of the embargo, and if war were declared, it would mean defeat and ruin. Randolph attacked the embargo because it was the precursor of war, not a means of maintaining peace as was Jefferson's, and dwelt on the hardships worked by "this blister plaster—the embargo," and the inability of the government to raise money by taxes or loans. Richard M. Johnson of Kentucky replied vigorously to Randolph before Calhoun spoke (*AC*12-1, p. 1379-95). Rhea's motion passed, 57 to 31 (p. 1413-4). For similar petitions and action see p. 1417-9. SOURCE: *NI,* May 9, 1812; *AC*12-1, p. 1395-9.

65. REMARKS ON THE QUESTION OF RESTRICTION OF DEBATE

May 29, 1812

[*Calhoun rose to make a point of order and Randolph took his seat.*]

Mr. Calhoun then said the question of war was not before the country; it was not before the House; and the gentleman was therefore speaking, as he conceived, contrary to rule, and without affording to others an opportunity to reply.

[*William M. Bibb, then presiding, overruled Calhoun's objection, on the ground that Randolph had announced intention to make a motion and that in such cases "wide range of debate" was usually allowed. Randolph thanked Calhoun for the "respite" and proceeded without stating his motion.*]

Mr. Calhoun again rose. As the gentleman had expressed his satisfaction at the rest afforded him by the former call to order, he would give him another opportunity to rest himself. He asked that the gentleman from Virginia should submit to the chair the proposition he intended to make, that the House might judge of the correctness of the course he took. If the course now taken were parliamentary, if the practice now attempted were permitted to succeed, it would be in the power of any member at any time to embarrass the proceedings of the House.

[*Speaker Clay, having resumed the chair, stated that it might be required that a motion be submitted in writing for the Speaker to decide if the remarks made applied to the subject.*]

Mr. Calhoun. I then call upon the gentleman to submit his proposition.

65 NOTE: Calhoun interrupted a long speech (*AC*12-1, p. 1451-61) in which Randolph declared he had heard rumors of a declaration of war set for June 1. In it Randolph denounced this move as submission to the French despot and as contrary to the wishes of the mercantile portion of the country. When Calhoun called upon Randolph "to submit his proposition" the affair developed into an altercation—in which Calhoun took no further part—involving Randolph, the Speaker, and other members, and was further threshed over in letters of Clay and Randolph in the *National Intelligencer* (*AC*12-1, p. 1462-79). The argument resulted in the Speaker's conclusion that the House rules should be more strictly enforced, and that, to be debated, a proposition must have a motion, a second, and a decision by the House to consider it (p. 1468-9). SOURCE: *NI*, June 16, 1812; *AC*12-1, p. 1461-2.

66. REPORT ON THE CAUSES AND REASONS FOR WAR

June 3, 1812

The Committee on Foreign Relations to whom was referred the Message of the president of the United States of the 1st of June, 1812, Report,[1]

That, After the experience which the United States have had of the great injustice of the British Government towards them, exemplified by so many acts of violence and oppression, it will be more difficult to justify to the impartial World their patient forbearance, than the measures to which it has b[e]come necessary to resort, to avenge the wrongs, & vindicate the rights and honor of the Nation. Your Committee are happy to observe, on a dispassionate review of the conduct of the United States, that they see in it no cause for censure.

1. On Apr. 6 Porter, the Chairman, presented from the Foreign Relations Committee the specie exportation bill (No. 59 NOTE), which became law Apr. 14 (*AC*12-1, p. 1617, 2269-70). On Apr. 7 he was given leave of absence for six weeks (*House Journal*, p. 278), and does not appear in House proceedings thereafter; he was at the time about to enter the military service (*DAB*). On Apr. 14 Calhoun, from that committee, presented an army bill—see Calendar.

If a long forbearance under injuries ought ever to be considered a virtue in any Nation, it is one which peculiarly becomes the United States. No People ever had stronger motives to cherish Peace: None have ever cherished it with greater sincerity and zeal.

But the period has now arrived, when the United States must support their character and station among the Nations of the Earth, or submit to the most shameful degradation. Forbearance has ceased to be a virtue. War on the one side, and peace on the other, is a situation as ruinous as it is disgraceful. The mad ambition, the lust of power, and commercial avarice of Great Britain, arrogating to herself the complete dominion of the Ocean, and exercising over it an unbounded and lawless tyranny, have left to Neutral Nations—an alternative only, between the base surrender of their rights, and a manly vindication of them. Happily for the United States, their destiny, under the aid of Heaven, is in their own hands. The crisis is formidable only by their love of peace. As soon as it becomes a duty to relinquish that situation, danger disappears. They have suffered no wrongs, they have received no insults, however great, for which they cannot obtain redress.

More than seven years have elapsed, since the commencement of this system of hostile aggression by the British Government, on the rights and interests of the United States.[2] The manner of its commencement was not less hostile, than the spirit with which it has been prosecuted. The United States have invariably done every thing in their power to preserve the relations of friendship with Great Britain: Of this disposition they gave a distinguished proof at the moment when they were made the victims of an opposite policy. The wrongs of the last War had not been forgotten at the commencement of the present one. They warned us of dangers, against which, it was sought to provide. As early as the Year 1804 the Minister of the United States at London was instructed, to invite the British Government to enter into a negotiation on all the points on which a collision might arise between the two Countries, in the course of the War, and to propose to it, an

2. Compare the "five years" of the November report (p. 64).

arrangement of their claims on fair and reasonable conditions.[3]
The invitation was accepted. A Negotiation had commenced and
was depending, and nothing had occurr'd to excite a doubt that
it would not terminate to the satisfaction of both the parties. It
was at this time, and under these circumstances, that an attack
was made, by surprise, on an important branch of the american
Commerce, which affected every part of the United States, and
involved many of their Citizens in ruin.

The Commerce on which this attack was so unexpectedly made,
was that between the United States and the colonies of France,
Spain, and other enemies of Great Britain. A Commerce just in
itself; sanctioned by the example of Great Britain in regard to
the trade with her own colonies: and sanctioned by a solemn act
between the two Governments in the last War, ["in regard to the
Trade in question" *cancelled*]: and sanctioned by the practice of
the british Government in the present War, more than two years
having then elapsed, without any interference with it.

The injustice of this attack could only be equalled by the
absurdity of the pretext alledged for it. It was pretended by the
British Government, that in case of War, her enemy had no right
to modify its colonial regulations, so as to mitigate the calamities
of War, to the inhabitants of its colonies. This pretension, peculiar
to Great Britain, is utterly incompatible with the rights of sovereignty in every independent State. If we recur to the well established, and universally admitted law of Nations, we shall find no
sanction to it, in that venerable code. The Sovereignty of every
State, is co-extensive with its dominions, and cannot be abrogated,
or curtailed in its rights, as to any part except by conquest. Neutral
Nations have a right to trade to every Port of either belligerent,
which is not legally blockaded; and in all articles which are not
contraband of War. Such is the absurdity of this pretension, that
your committee are aware, especially after the able manner in
which it has been heretofore refuted, and exposed, that they
would offer an insult to the understanding of the House, if they
enlarged on it. and if any thing could add to the high sense of the
injustice of the British Government in this transaction, it would

3. See Hamilton, *Writings of James Monroe*, IV, 170, 192-3, 233, 241-2.

be the contrast which her conduct exhibits in regard to this trade, and in regard to a similar trade by Neutrals, with her own Colonies. It is known to the World, that Great Britain regulates her own trade, in War, and in Peace, at home and in her colonies, as she finds for her interest: that in War she relaxes the restraints of her colonial system in favor of the colonies, and that it never was suggested that she had not a right to do it; or that a neutral in taking advantage of the relaxation violated a belligerent right of her enemy. But with Great Britain every thing is lawful. It is only in a trade with her enemies, that the United States can do wrong. with them all trade is unlawful.

In the Year 1793 an attack was made by the British Government on the same branch of our neutral Trade, which had nearly involved the two Countries in War. That difference however was amicably accommodated. The pretension was withdrawn ["by Great Britain" *cancelled*], and reparation made to the United States for the losses which they had suffered by it. It was fair to infer from that arrangement, that the Commerce was deemed, by the British Government, lawful, and that it would not be again disturbed.

Had the British Government been resolved to contest this trade with Neutrals, it was due to the character of the British Nation, that the decision should be made known to the Government of the United States. The existence of a negotiation, which had been invited by our Government, for the purpose of preventing differences, by an amicable arrangement of their respective pretensions, gave a strong claim to the notification, while it afforded the fairest opportunity for it. But a very different policy animated the then cabinet of England. Generous sentiments were unknown to it.[4] The liberal confidence and friendly overtures of the United States were taken advantage of to ensnare them. Steady to its purpose and inflexibly hostile to this Country, the British Government calmly looked forward to the moment, when it might give the most deadly wound to our interests. A trade just in itself, which was secured by so many strong and sacred pledges, was considered safe. Our Citizens, with their usual industry and enterprise, had embarked in it, a vast proportion of their shipping, and of their

4. This sentence also appears in *ASP* and *AC,* but not in *NI.*

capital, which were at sea under no other protection than the law of Nations, and the confidence which they resposed in the justice and friendship of the british Nation. At this period the unexpected blow was given. Many of our Vessels were seized, carried into port and condemned, by a Tribunal, which while it professes to respect the Law of Nations, obeys the mandate of its own Government in opposition to all Law.[5] Hundreds of other Vessels were driven from the Ocean, and the trade itself in a great measure suppressed.

The effect produced by this attack on the lawful Commerce of the United States, was such as might have been expected from a virtuous, independant, and highly injured people. But one sentiment pervaded the whole american Nation. No local interests were regarded, no sordid motives felt. Without looking to the parts which suffered most, the invasion of our rights was considered a common cause, and from one extremity of our union to the other, was heard the voice of an united People, calling on their Government, to avenge their wrongs, and vindicate the rights and honor of the Country.

From this period the British Government has gone on in a continued encroachment on the rights and interests of the United States, disregarding in its course, in many instances, obligations which have heretofore been held sacred by civilized Nations.

In May 1806, the whole Coast of the Continent from the Elbe to Brest inclusive was declared to be in a State of Blockade. By this Act, the well established principles of the Law of Nations, principles which have served for ages as guides, and fixed the boundary between the rights of Billigerants, and Neutrals, were violated. By the law of Nations, as recognized by Great Britain herself, no Blockade is lawful, unless it be sustained by the application of an adequate force; and that an adequate force was applied to this blockade, in its full extent, ought not to be pretended. Whether Great Britain was able to maintain legally, so extensive a blockade, considering the War in which she is engaged, requiring such extensive naval operations, is a question which it is not necessary at this time, to examine. It is sufficient

5. The admiralty court decision in the *Essex* case. See Adams, *History of U.S.*, III, 44-53, 95-102, 108-11. The phrase "in opposition to all law" also appears in *ASP* and *AC*, but not in *NI*.

to be known that such force was not applied, and this is evident
from the terms of the Blockade itself, by which, comparatively,
an inconsiderable portion of the Coast only, was declared to be
in a State of strict and rigorous blockade. The objection to the
measure is not diminished by that circumstance. If the force was
not applied, the blockade was unlawful, from whatever cause the
failure might proceed. The Belligerant who institutes the blockade
cannot absolve itself from the obligation to apply the force under
any pretext whatever. For a Belligerant to relax a blockade, which
it could not maintain, with a view to absolve itself from the obligation to maintain it,[6] would be a refinement in injustice not less
insulting to the Understanding than repugnant to the law of Nations. To claim merit for the mitigation of an evil, which the party
either had not the power or found it inconvenient to inflict would
be a new mode of encroaching on neutral rights. Your Committee
think it just to remark that this act of the British Government, does
not appear to have been adopted in the sense in which it has been
since construed. On consideration of all the circumstances attending
the measure, and particularly the character of the distinguished
Statesman who announced it, we are persuaded that it was conceived in a spirit of conciliation and intended to lead, to an accommodation of all differences, between the United States and
Great Britain. His death disappointed that hope, and the act has
since b[e]come subservient to other purposes. It has been made
by his successors a pretext, for that vast system of usurpation,
which has so long oppressed, and harassed our Commerce.[7]

The next act of the British Government which claims our attention, is the Order of Council of Jany. 7th. 1807, by which neutral
Powers are prohibited trading, from one Port to another of France,
or her allies or any other Country with which Great Britain might
not freely trade. By this order, the pretension of England, heretofore disclaimed by every other power,[8] to prohibit neutrals, disposing of parts of their Cargoes at different Ports, of the same

6. This phrase also appears in *ASP* and *AC*, but not in *NI*.
7. For "Fox's blockade" and American reaction to it, see Bemis, *Diplomatic History*, p. 147. Charles James Fox died four months later; the reference
to him reflects Monroe's impression when he was minister to England (Hamilton, *Writings of James Monroe*, IV, 411).
8. Also "disclaimed" in *ASP* and *AC*; in *NI*, "claimed."

enemy, is revived and with vast accumulation of injury. Every enemy, however great the number, or distant from each other, is considered one, and the like trade even with powers, at peace with England, who from motives of policy had excluded, or restrained her commerce, was also prohibited. In this Act the British Government, evidently disclaimed, all regard for neutral rights. Aware that the measures authorized by it, could find no pretext, in any belligerant right, none was urged. To prohibit the sale of our produce, consisting of innocent articles at any port of a belligerant, not blockaded, to consider every belligerant as one, and subject neutrals to the same restraints with all, as if there was but one, were bold encroachments. But to restrain or in any manner interfere with our Commerce with neutral Nations, with whom Great Britain was at Peace, and against whom she had no justifiable cause of War for the sole reason that they restrained or excluded from their Ports, her commerce, was utterly incompatible with the pacifick relations subsisting between the two Countries.

We proceed to bring into view the British Order in Council of Novr. 11th. 1807. which superseded every other Order, and consummated that system of hostility, on the commerce of the United States which has been since so steadily pursued. By this Order all France and her allies, and every other Country at War with Great Britain, or with which she was not at War, from which the british flag was excluded, and all the Colonies of her enemies, were subjected to the same restrictions, as if they were actually blockaded in the most strict and rigorous manner; and all trade in articles, the produce and manufacture of the said Countries and colonies, and the Vessels engaged in it, were subjected to capture and condemnation as lawful prize. To this order certain exceptions were made, which we forbear to notice, because they were not adopted from a regard to neutral rights, but were dictated by policy, to promote the Commerce of England, and, so far as they related to neutral powers, were said, to emanate from the clemency of the British Government.

It would be superfluous in your Committee to state, that by this order, the British Government declared direct and positive War against the United States. The dominion of the Ocean was completely usurped by it, all Commerce forbidden, and every flag driven from it, or subjected to capture, and condemnation, which did not subserve the policy of the British Government, by paying it a tribute and sailing under its sanction. From this period the United States have incurred the heaviest losses, and most mortifying humiliations. They have borne the calamities of War, without retorting them on its authors.

So far your Committee has presented to the view of the House, the aggressions, which have been committed under the authority of the British Government, on the Commerce of the United States. We will now proceed to other wrongs which have been still more severely felt. Among these is the impressment of our Seamen, a practice which has been unceasingly maintained by Great Britain in the wars to which she has been a party since our Revolution. Your committee cannot convey in adequate terms, the deep sense which they entertain of the injustice and oppression of this proceeding. Under the pretext of impressing British Seamen, our fellow Citizens are seized in British ports, on the high seas, and in every other quarter to which the british power extends, are taken on board british Men of War, and compelled to serve there as british subjects. In this mode our Citizens are wantonly snatched from their Country, and their families; deprived of their liberty and doomed to an ignominious and slavish bondage; compelled to fight the battles of a foreign Country and often to perish in them; our flag has given them no protection; it has been unceasingly violated and our Vessels exposed to danger by the loss of the Men taken from them. Your Committee need not remark that while this practice is continued, it is impossible for the United States, to consider themselves an independant Nation. Every new case, is a new proof of their degradation. Its continuance is the more unjustifiable, because the United States have repeatedly proposed to the British Government an arrangement which would secure to it the controul of its own people. An exemption of the Citizens of the United States from this degrading oppression, and their flag from violation, is all that they have sought.

This lawless waste of our Trade, and equally unlawful impressment of our Seamen, have been much aggravated by the insults and indignities attending them. Under the pretext of blockading the harbours of France and her allies, british squadrons have been

116

stationed on our own Coast, to watch and annoy our own trade. To give effect to the blockade of European Ports, the ports and harbours of the United States, have been blockaded. In executing these Orders of the British Government, or in obeying the spirit which was known to animate it, the Commanders of these squadrons have encroached on our jurisdiction, seized our Vessels, and carried into effect impressments within our limits, and done other acts of great injustice, violence and oppression. The United States have seen with mingled indignation and surprize, that these acts instead of procuring to the perpetrators the punishment due to unauthorized crimes, have not failed to recommend them to the favor of their Government.

Whether the British Government has contributed by active measures to excite against us the hostility of the savage tribes on our frontiers, your Committee are not disposed to occupy much time in investigating. Certain indications of general notoriety may supply the place of authentic documents, tho' these have not been wanting to establish the fact in some instances. It is known that symptoms of British hostility towards the United States have never failed to produce corresponding symptoms among those tribes. It is also well known that on all such occasions abundant supplies of the ordinary munitions of War have been afforded by the agents of British Commercial Companies, and even from British Garrisons, wherewith they were enabled, to commence that system of savage warfare on our frontiers which has been at all times indiscriminate in its effect, on all ages, sexes, and conditions and so revolting to humanity.

Your Committee would be much gratified if they could close here the detail of British wrongs, but it is their duty to recite another act of still greater malignity, than any of those which have been already brought to your view. The attempt to dismember our Union, and overthrow our excellent constitution by a secret mission the object of which was to foment discontents and excite insurrection, against the constituted authorities and laws of the Nation as lately disclosed by the Agent employed in it, affords full proof that there is no bound to the hostility of the British Government, towards the United States, no act however unjustifiable which it would not commit to accomplish their ruin.[9] This attempt excites the greatest horror, from the consideration that it was made while the United States and Great Britain were at Peace, and an amicable negotiation was depending between them, for the accommodation of their differences, thro' public Ministers regularly authorized for the purpose.

The United [*States*] have beheld with unexampled forbearance, this continued series of hostile encroachments, on their rights and interests, in the hope, that yielding to the force of friendly remonstrances, often repeated, the British Government might adopt a more just policy towards them, but that hope no longer exists. They have also weighed impartially the reasons which have been urged by the British Government in vindication of these encroachments, and found in them neither justification nor apology.

The British Government has alledged in vindication of the Orders in Council that they were resorted to, as a retaliation on France, for similar aggressions committed by her, on our neutral Trade with the British dominions. But how has this plea been supported. The dates of British and french aggressions, are well known to the World. Their origin and progress have been marked, with too wide and destructive a waste of the property of our fellow Citizens, to have been forgotten. The Decree of Berlin of Novr. 21st. 1806 was the first aggression of France in the present War. Eighteen Months had then elapsed, after the attack made by Great Britain on our neutral Trade, with the colonies of France, and her allies, and six Months from the date of the Proclamation of May 1806. Even on the 7th. of Jany. 1807, the date of the first British Order in Council, so short a term had elapsed, after the Berlin Decree, that it was hardly possible that the intelligence of it, should have reached the United States. A retaliation which is to produce its effect, by operating on a neutral power, ought not to be resorted to, 'till the neutral had justified it, by a culpable acquiescence in the unlawful act of the other belligerent. It ought to be delayed until after sufficient time had been allowed to the neutral, to remonstrate against the measure complained of, to receive an answer, and to act on it, which had not been done in

9. See No. 55 for the John Henry affair.

the present instance. And when the Order of Novr. 11th. was issued, it is well known that a Minister of France, had declared to the Minister Plenipotentiary of the United States at Paris, that it was not intended that the Decree of Berlin should apply to the United States. It is equally well known, that no american Vessel had then been condemned under it, or seizure been made, with which the British Government was acquainted. The facts prove incontestibly that the measures of France, however unjustifiable in themselves, were nothing more than a pretext for those of England. And of the insufficiency of that pretext, ample proof has already been afforded, by the British Government itself, and in the most impressive form. Altho' it was declared that the Orders in Council were retaliatory on France for her Decrees, it was also declared, and in the Orders themselves, that owing to the superiority of the British Navy, by which the fleets of France, and her allies, were confined within their own Ports, the french Decrees were considered only as empty threats.

It is no justification of the wrongs of one Power, that the like were committed by another; nor ought the fact, if true, to have been urged by either, as it could afford no proof of its love of justice, of its magnanimity or even of its courage. It is more worthy the Government of a great Nation to relieve than to assail the injured. Nor can a repetition of the wrongs by another power, repair the violated rights or wounded honour of the injured party. An utter inability alone, to resist, could justify a quiet surrender of our rights, and degrading submission to the will of others. To that condition the United States are not reduced nor do they fear it. That they ever consented to discuss with either power, the misconduct of the other, is a proof of their love of Peace, of their moderation, and of the hope which they still indulged, that friendly appeals to just and generous sentiments, would not be made to them in vain. But the motive was mistaken, if their forbearance was imputed, either to the want of a just sensibility to their wrongs, or a determination, if suitable redress was not obtained, to resent them. The time has now arrived when this system of reasoning must cease. It would be insulting, to repeat it. It would be degrading to hear it. The United States must act as an independant Nation, and assert their rights, and avenge their wrongs, according to their own estimate of them, with the party who commits them, holding it responsible for its own misdeeds, unmitigated by those of another.[10]

For the difference made between Great Britain and France, by the application of the non-importation act against England only, the motive has been already too often explained, and is too well known, to require further illustration. In the commercial restrictions to which the United States resorted, as an evidence of their sensibility, and a mild retaliation of their wrongs, they invariably placed both powers on the same footing, holding out to each in respect to itself, the same accommodation, in case it accepted the condition offered, and in respect to the other, the same restraint, if it refused. Had the British Government confirmed the arrangement, which was entered into with the British Minister in 1809, & France maintained her Decrees, with France would the United States have had to resist, with the firmness belonging to their character, the continued violation of their rights. The Committee do not hesitate to declare, that France has greatly injured the United States, and that satisfactory reparation has not yet been made for many of those injuries. But, that is, a concern, which the United States, will look to, and settle for themselves. The high character of the american people, is a sufficient pledge to the World, that they will not fail to settle it, on conditions which they have a right to claim.

More recently the true policy of the British Government towards the United States, has been completely unfolded. It has been publicly declared by those in Power, that the Orders in Council should not be repealed, until the french Government had revoked all its internal restraints on the British Commerce; and that the Trade of the United States, with France and her allies, should be prohibited, until Great Britain, was also allowed to Trade, with them. By this declaration it appears, that to satisfy the pretensions of the British Government, the United States must join Great Britain in the War with France, and prosecute the War until France

---

10. This paragraph, with its summary dismissal of the unending denunciation of French misdeeds by Randolph and the Federalists, makes a striking comparison with Madison's careful statement (*AC*12-1, p. 1629) which constitutes a lame ending to his message.

should be subdued; for without her subjugation, it were in vain, to presume, on such a concession. The hostility of the British Government to these States has been still further disclosed. It has been made manifest that the United States are considered by it as the Commercial Rival of Great Britain, and that their prosperity and growth are incompatible with her welfare. When all these Circumstances are taken into consideration, it is impossible for your Committee to doubt the Motives which have governed the British Ministry, in all its measures towards the United States since the year 1805. Equally is it impossible to doubt, longer, the course which the United States ought to pursue towards Great Britain.

From this review of the multiplied wrongs of the British Government since the commencement of the present War, it must be evident to the Impartial world, that the Contest which is now forced on the United States, is radically a Contest for their Sovereignty and Independence. Your Committee will not enlarge on any of the injuries, however great, which have had a transitory effect. They wish to call the attention of the House to those of a permanent Nature only, which intrench so deeply ["vitally" *cancelled*] on our most important Rights, and wound so extensively and vitally ["deeply" *cancelled*] our best Interests, as could not fail to deprive the United States of the principal advantages of their Revolution, if submitted to. The Controul of our Commerce by Great Britain in regulating at pleasure, and expelling it almost from the Ocean: the oppressive manner in which these Regulations have been carried into effect, by seizing and confiscating such of our vessels, with their Cargoes, as were said to have violated her Edicts, often without previous warning of their danger: the impressment of our Citizens from on board our own vessels, on the high Seas, and elsewhere, and holding them in bondage till it suited the convenience of their oppressors, to deliver them up, are encroachments of that high and dangerous tendency, which could not fail to produce, that pernicious effect. Nor would those, be the only consequences, that would result from it. The British Government might, for a while, be satisfied with the ascendancy thus gained over us, but its pretensions would soon increase. The proof which so complete and disgraceful a submission to its authority, would afford, of our degeneracy, could not fail to inspire confidence, that there was no limit to which its usurpations, and our degradation, might not be carried.

Your Committee, beleiving, that the freeborn sons of America are worthy to enjoy the liberty which their Fathers purchased at the price of so much blood and treasure, and seeing in the measures adopted by Great Britain, a course commenced and persisted in, which must lead to a loss of National character & Independence, feel no hesitation in advising resistance by force—In which the Americans of the present day will prove to the enemy and to the World, that we have not only inherited that liberty which our Fathers gave, us, but also the will & power to maintain it. Relying on the patriotism of the Nation, and confidently trusting that the Lord of Hosts will go with us to Battle in a righteous cause, and crown our efforts with success, your Committee recommend an immediate appeal to Arms.

66 NOTE: Madison's message of June 1 recommending a declaration of war, unlike his cautious statement of the preceding November, was a vigorous and effective indictment of British policy, and even began with a denunciation of impressment (AC12-1, p. 1624-9; see No. 46 NOTE). The committee's report was cast in the form of a history of Anglo-American relations since 1805. Most of the points in it were stated or indicated in Madison's briefer document, among them the significant charge that Great Britain's settled policy was to destroy American prosperity and to use this country to get control of enemy trade. See above, p. 120, AC12-1, p. 1626-7; compare also Clay's phrase, in December preceding, "to destroy a rival" (p. 601). The report, however, is characterized by a sustained eloquence obviously intended to be reminiscent of Jefferson's great indictment of 1776. The closing paragraph, the declaration that this was America's second war for independence, is strikingly similar to the corresponding passages of Calhoun's speech of May 6 and the committee's report of Nov. 29, 1811 (Nos. 46 and 64). It is interesting to note such phrases or terms as "forbearance has ceased to be a virtue," "mad ambition," "the avarice of a corrupted court" of the earlier report repeated or approximated (above, p. 67, and 68), and to compare the uncompromising hostility to England and the emphasis on the American devotion to peace, as expressed in the beginning and close of the paper, with the preface to the *Chesapeake* resolutions (No. 23). On Calhoun's motion the report was ordered to lie on the table (AC12-1, p. 1632), and Calhoun at once presented the bill declaring war (No. 67).

With the war report and the declaration the administration and
the war party reached a common goal. The difference in their
thinking and further aims is revealed by their previous history and
their approach to this point, rather than by content, tone or
emphasis of the two papers, and it was that background which
inevitably raised the question—presumably already in Calhoun's
mind (see No. 61)—if the President and these leaders would be
able to see eye to eye thereafter. See also No. 72.

Insofar as a committee report may be considered the work of
one man it seems correct to assign this paper to Calhoun. However,
Joseph Gales, the editor of the Republican, later the Whig,
National Intelligencer, shortly after Calhoun's death wrote for
Senator John J. Crittenden (*AHR,* XLIX [1943-4], 254) an article
(*AHR,* XIII [1907-8], 308-10) in which he declared that the Foreign
Relations Committee had, prior to the sending of the President's
message, "prevailed upon the Secretary," Monroe, "to prepare a
Report upon the message; which Report was presented to the
House." On Jan. 12, 1854, W. W. Moore, in answering R. K. Crallé's
inquiry about the report, declared that Gales was "positively certain" that it was "the production" of Monroe. He offered the additional evidence that it was written in the hand of Monroe's private
secretary, and quoted Gales as saying that he had recently received
a letter, from a person who was "a confidential member of the
Government" at the time of the report, confirming his impression
(*AHR,* XIII [1907-8], 306-7). In his article for Crittenden, Gales
also cited the close of the report as conclusive evidence to anyone
who had ever heard Monroe "upon the subject" that the paragraph
was his. Crallé evidently accepted Gales' statement, for he did not
print the report. Thomas H. Benton, whose *Thirty Years' View* was
published in 1854, says (I, 680) that Monroe "brought up Mr.
Madison to the war point. He drew the war report." Meigs (*Calhoun,* I, 131 n.) cites Gales and suggests that it was Benton for
whom Gales wrote the article.

Charles M. Wiltse discounts Gales' claim ("The Authorship of
the War Report of 1812," *AHR,* XLIX [1943-4], 253-9), pointing
out that use of a departmental clerk for copying was no evidence
of authorship; that Gales was a partisan of Monroe; and that as
reporter for the Senate he was somewhat out of touch with House
proceedings. He also questions the Gales argument that either the
matter or the style of the report could be cited as Monroe's. Brant
(*James Madison, President, 1809-1812,* p. 472-3) accepts Gales'
statement and adds: "Even more conclusive is the running resem-
blance in thought and language between the manifesto and the
editorials Monroe furnished to the *National Intelligencer* in April
1812. This reaches to such similarities as, in the manifesto, 'arro-

gating to herself the complete dominion of the ocean' and in the April 14 editorial, 'arrogate to her the complete dominion of the sea.'" He calls attention to two editorials printed in the *Intelligencer*, which he ascribes to Monroe (p. 434 and n. 13), and to a third, part of a corrected draft of which, in the hand of Monroe, is reproduced (opposite p. 416). He suggests that the phrase "*seven years* of British aggression" implied congressional approval of Monroe's rejected treaty of 1806.

Actually the committee's phrase was "More than seven years" and this begins the history with the *Essex* case and the seizures of 1805; see also above, n. 2. The report obviously borrows from various sources, chief of which should have been the drafts submitted by the members of the sub-committee (No. 59 NOTE). Besides his April editorials, Monroe may have made other contributions, but comparison with these editorials shows contrast rather than similarity (see *NI*, Apr. 7, 9, 14; the editorial of the 11th should be included; it makes the series nearly as long as the report). To have written the report it would have been necessary for Monroe to abandon his fixed purpose as indicated in the April editorials and clearly stated in his letter to John Taylor of June 13, 1812 (Hamilton, *Writings of James Monroe*, V, 205-12)—to achieve, by negotiation and by subordination of other issues, a relaxation of the British blockade. His editorial references to impressment, while emphatic, were brief and incidental to the charge of England's injuries to American commerce, and the repeal of the French decrees was declared to be the basis for "the difference which we now see in the relations of the United States" with Great Britain and France. It was this attitude of the administration which made the background for Madison's attempt, after the declaration of war, to reopen negotiations even before the news was received of the repeal of the Orders in Council.

The report, on the other hand, dismisses the question of the repeal of the French decrees with a passing paragraph, like Calhoun's speech of December preceding, and, in keeping with the pronouncements of the war party, directs its attack on Great Britain, makes impressment a major grievance, and offers ground for neither negotiation nor compromise. In the preliminaries of war, beginning with the work of the Foreign Relations Committee in November, Monroe was the dependence of the President and the war party for the behind-the-scenes negotiations which kept the program intact, and it was very easy, many years after, to exaggerate his part in the actual preparation of congressional papers.

The manuscript report is all in one hand except the introductory phrase and the final paragraph, both of which closely resemble that of Felix Grundy, the third member of the Committee.

The *Intelligencer* (June 20, 1812), and *ASP, For. Rel.* (III, 567-70) versions of the report were apparently made directly from the manuscript; the number of the paper—247—in the latter volume, which was printed by Gales and Seaton in 1832, is marked on pages of the manuscript. From the *Intelligencer* copy, however, there are several omissions (see above, n. 4, n. 5, and n. 6) of the type to be expected in hurried newspaper composition; the *Annals* (12-1, p. 1546-54) copy closely resembles the *ASP* version, although it, also, could have been taken from the original.   SOURCE: MS Report, June 3, 1812, *NA*, RG233, 12A-C5.1; *NI*, June 20, 1812; *AC*12-1, p. 1546-54.

67. BILL TO DECLARE WAR ON GREAT BRITAIN

[*June 3, 1812*]

[*Mr. Calhoun, from the Committee on Foreign Relations, presented a bill:*]

Be it enacted . . . that war be, and the same is hereby declared to exist, between Great Britain and her dependencies and the United States and their Territories: and that the President of the United States is hereby Authorised to use the whole land and naval force of the United States to carry the same into effect: and to issue to private armed Vessels of the United States Commissions or Letters of Marque [and g]eneral reprisal in such form as he shall think proper, and under the seal of the United States; against the Vessels, Goods and effects of the Government of Great Britain, of its subjects, and of all persons Inhabiting within any of its Territories [*or*] possessions

67 NOTE: On June 3, in secret session, "On a motion made, and leave given," Calhoun from the Foreign Relations Committee presented the above as a bill; and by a vote of 76 to 45 the House refused to reject it (*AC*12-1, p. 1632). Referred at once to a Committee of the Whole, it was reported next day without amendment, and passed on the third reading, 79 to 49 (p. 1633-7). In the Senate, also in secret session, the bill was considered from the 5th to the 17th, when it passed by a vote of 19 to 13 (p. 266-97). On the 13th the Senate amended the bill by substituting "the United Kingdom of Great Britain & Ireland & the Dependencies thereof" for "Great Britain and her dependencies"; adding "of America" to the first use of "United States"; and substituting "the said United Kingdom of

Great Britain and Ireland & the Subjects thereof" for the words
following "Government of." These changes were accepted by the
House (p. 271, 298). The act (see p. 2322-3) was signed by Madison on the 18th.   SOURCE: MS Bill, June 4, 1812 (showing also
Senate amendments), *NA*, RG233, 12A-B3 (note: the date on the
bill—June 4—is that of its passage in the House; see also *House
Journal*, p. 461, 470).

68. To PATRICK NOBLE, Abbeville, S.C.

Washington 17th June 1812

Dr Patrick, I have but a moment to inform you that war is declared
against Great Britain.[1] You will have more detailed information by
the next mail by which I expect it will be in my power to send the
decleration of war with the accompaning papers. It will be useless
to ma[ke] comments on this great [event?] made necessary by
British injustice; I hope the courage and patriotis[m] of our people,
will make it as fortunate as just.

I am with esteem yours &c

J. C. CALHOUN

SOURCE: *CC*.

69. SPEECH ON SUSPENSION OF NON-IMPORTATION

June 24, 1812

Mr. Calhoun—Mr. Speaker, I am in favor of the amendment proposed by the gentleman from Massachusetts; and, as I differ from
many of my friends on this subject, I feel it a duty to present the
reasons that will govern my vote. But, before I proceed to discuss
the question, I wish to be distinctly understood on one point—that
is, to avoid taxes forms no part of my inducement to advocate the
proposed repeal. I am ready to meet them. We are at war. It is
wisdom to make it efficient; and that system will meet with my
hearty support which renders it the most so, be it more or less
burthensome. I fear not the effect of taxes on the public mind. The
people will support any taxes short of oppression. Sir, I am not
disposed to deny that the non-importation has a very sensible effect

1. The bill passed the Senate on the third reading this day, and was signed
by the President on the 18th (No. 67 NOTE).

on the resources of the enemy; and am willing to admit that restrictions on commerce, as a means of annoyance, ought not to be neglected. I cannot, however, agree with the gentlemen who oppose this amendment, that a repeal of this act would leave the trade with Great Britain unembarrassed, or would afford a great relief to her manufacturers. A state of war is itself a severe restriction on commerce. The new and circuitous channel through which trade is compelled to flow; the additional hazard and expences incident to that state; and the double duties proposed to be laid on imports, present very serious impediments—equal, or nearly so, to the non-importation act. If, sir, in some parts of this country, English goods can now be had at 60 per cent on the invoice price, as I have been informed by some commercial gentlemen; by repealing this act you will produce no relaxation—for the expence and hazard of introduction will at least equal that per cent. By the repeal, the price of such goods will not sink; the consumption will not be increased; nor will the manufacturer be relieved. We are in the habit of thinking that prohibition in law is prohibition in fact. It is a great mistake, which I daily see contradicted in our merchants' shops lined with English manufactures. So far from entirely preventing their introduction, I believe, that to prohibit is not the most effectual mode to exclude them. I venture the assertion with confidence, that heavy duties are at least equally effectual. The greatest commercial pressure that can be obtained, I believe, will be found in duties as high as the articles introduced can bear— that is, as high as possible without smuggling. Goods can be introduced cheaper (of course more abundantly and with a greater consumption) under the non-importation act by smuggling, than under such duties. It is a fact of importance, that smuggling is more easy under the former than the latter system; and consequently can be carried on at a less price. I beg the attention of the House while I establish this point. The hazard of smuggling depends on the laws against it—their rigid execution—the public sentiment, and the interest of the mercantile class to permit it. I begin with the last, for it is the most important, as it controls the other two. Where duties are not so high as to drive the honest trader from market, the merchants as a body have an interest to prevent smuggling. Goods so introduced not only defraud the revenue, but the honest and regular trader. The higher the duty, the more powerful this principle; and in this country, where there is not much competition between many articles of foreign supply and of domestic manufacture, the duties may be made very high. In this state of things every honest merchant becomes a vigilant custom-house officer, stimulated by a sense of interest. It was this principle, which made smuggling unknown to your laws, previous to the commencement of the restrictive system. It was not the number, or vigilance of your officers. They bore no proportion to the extent of your coast. But it was hard to smuggle, where every merchant considered each bale of goods, or cask of wine so introduced, as so much loss to his profit. Very different is the effect of entire prohibition. I cannot speak of it more concisely or justly than to say it is the reverse. Under it the honest trader of necessity disappears. The desperate adventurer supplies his place. Commerce ceases to be a trade, a business of fair and regular gain; it becomes a matter of hazard and adventure. The whole class concerned in carrying it on have one common interest, to discover flaws in your revenue laws, or elude their operation; to lull the vigilance of your custom-house officers, or corrupt their integrity. Smuggling ceases to be odious. It is no longer the occupation of an insulated individual, who carefully conceals from all the world his violation of the laws. No, it becomes the business of a society, of an entire class of men—who make a jest of fraud and consider ingenuity in this lawless occupation as the highest honor. The corruption ends not here; its infectious influence spreads and contaminates public opinion. But, sir, under the operation of heavy duties only, it is reversed. Interest, it is true, controls opinion in this as well as in the other case, but it produces the opposite effect. Here the smuggler is ranked with the thief, or with that description of men, who in violation of the law live on the honest gains of others. From the merchant, the rest of the community take the impression, and the smuggler becomes universally odious. Interest has a wonderful control over sentiment. Even the more refined and elevated, the moral and religious sentiment may be considered as ultimately resting on it; not, it is true, on that of any one individual, or class of men, but on the enlarged interest of our kind. Correspondent to public sentiment will be the laws, or, what is of more importance, their execution. In all free governments the laws or their execution cannot be much above the tone of public opinion. Under the restrictive system the laws are either cried down for oppression or are not executed. Under the operation of duties only the merchant himself demands severe laws and aids in their rigid execution. He is a party concerned with his country, and has a common interest with government. He sees in the laws a friend and protector, and not an oppressor.

Sir, I think the conclusion is strong, that you cannot extend your commercial pressure on the enemy beyond, or at least much beyond, the operation of high duties. It seems to me to be the ultimate point, and, if it is a fact, that the double duties are as high as can be borne, of which I pretend not to have certain knowledge, then, the continuation of the non-importation act will not give much additional pressure. The repeal, so far from relieving the English manufacturer, will be scarcely felt in that country. It is by no means like a repeal in peace, and without additional burthens unfelt.

But, sir, I may be asked, why change, why repeal the non-importation act? If it does not produce any good, it will not much harm. As it regards our enemy, I readily admit, there is not much reason for its repeal or continuation. I feel not much solicitude on that point; but, sir, as it regards ourselves, the two systems are essentially different. In the one, the whole gain is profit to the adventurer and smuggler. The honest dealer is driven out of employ, and government is defrauded of its revenue. In the other, an honest and useful class of citizens is maintained in comfort and ease, and the treasury enriched. Even suppose the difference in the pressure on the enemy to be considerable, yet these incidental advantages ought not to be neglected. I would not give up for revenue what I suppose to be a good system; but when the effects of two measures are nearly equal in other respects, I would not overlook the exchequer. It is there, after all, we will find the fund.[1] I know the zeal and resources of the country are great; but we have not been in the habit of paying taxes; we have no system of internal revenue; and the nature of the country, and the conflict between the states and general government, render it difficult, I may say impossible, to originate one that will not excite discontent. The measure I

---

1. In *Works*, II, 25, this is revised to read: "the funds, the sinews of war."

advocate will yield you more additional revenue than the whole of the internal taxes; and this on goods which would be introduced in spite of your laws. Consider the relief it would afford you. The internal taxes might in a great measure be dispensed with; or, if we choose to give it to our gallant little navy, the millions thus gained from commerce would add considerable strength. Bestowed on our army, it would be better appointed, and enable it to act with greater vigor and promptitude. Or if you choose a different destination, you might keep down the increasing volume of public debt; a thing that ought so nearly to interest each one of us. The sum of my opinion then is, that a repeal of the non-importation act will not, under existing circumstances, afford much relief to the distresses of England, and that a commercial pressure, equally sure with an entire prohibition, and far more salutary for this country, may be produced by the operation of heavy duties. There are many who are ready to acknowledge the truth of this opinion, but fear that the effect on the public mind both here and in England would be unfortunate. They dread a change. But I will not admit, that the repeal would be a material change. One system, one fixed determination, is to resist England. Can war, can all the impediments to trade incidental to that state, be considered a change, a yielding? No, if it is a change, it is a wise one; an advancing from an inferior to a greater degree of resistance. We need not fear the effect on public opinion; if there should be any, it will be but momentary. Our duty is to pursue the wisest and the most efficient measures; it is the duty of the people to understand their character, to condemn the pernicious, and to approbate the wise. This they will finally do. Delusion cannot long exist. As to the impression on our enemy, he will not see much relief to his starving manufacturers in a war with this country. He will understand the impediments in the way of commerce. They present but little relief to his mind.

But, sir, I condemn this mode of legislating, which does not adopt or reject measures, because in themselves good or bad; but from some supposed effect they may produce on the opinion of our enemy. In all games, it is hazardous to play on the supposed ignorance of your opponent. In a few instances, it may succeed; but in most he sees your intention, and turns it against yourself.

Sir, I am in hopes if the measure I advocate should succeed, it would tend to produce harmony at home. It would go far to reconcile the mercantile class. Your restrictive measures have become odious to them—and though they may not approbate the war, yet they cannot but respect the motives which dictated it. The merchants, I hope, will come to reflect that this is the favorable moment to assert their rights. The single fact that the parts of the country most remote from the ocean and least connected with commerce have entered into this contest for commercial rights with an ardor and disinterestedness which does them the greatest honor, proves it to be, of all others, the most auspicious moment. It more than counterbalances all want of preparation. For it is more easy to prepare for war than to obtain union; and the former is not more necessary to victory than the latter. I now tell the commercial gentlemen, if their rights are not protected, their's is the fault. With hearty co-operation on their part, victory is certain.

It now remains for me to touch another and far more interesting topic of argument, and which I confess has the principal weight in the formation of my opinion on this subject. The restrictive system, as a mode of resistance, and a means of obtaining a redress of our wrongs, has never been a favorite one with me. I wish not to censure the motives which dictated it, or to attribute weakness to those who first resorted to it for a restoration of our rights. Though I do not think the embargo a wise measure, yet I am far from thinking it a pusillanimous one. To lock up the whole commerce of this country; to say to the most trading and exporting people in the world, you shall not trade; you shall not export; to break on the schemes of almost every man in society, is far from weakness, very far from pusillanimity. Sir, I confess, while I disapprove that more than any other measure, it proves the strength of your government and the patriotism of the people. The arm of despotism under similar circumstances could not coerce its execution more effectually, than the patience and zeal of the people. But, sir, I object to the restrictive system; and for the following reasons: because it does not suit the genius of our people, or that of our government, or the geographical character of our country. We are a people essentially active. I may say we are pre-eminently so. Distance and difficulties are less to us than any people on earth. Our schemes and prospects extend every where and to every thing. No passive system can suit such a people; in action superior to all others; in patience and endurance inferior to many. Nor does it suit the genius of our government. Our government is founded on freedom and hates coercion. To make the restrictive system effectual, requires the most arbitrary laws. England, with the severest penal statutes, has not been able to exclude prohibited articles; and even Bonaparte with all his power and vigilance was obliged to resort to the most barbarous laws to enforce his continental system. Burning has furnished the only effectual remedy. The peculiar geography of our country, added to the liberty of its government, greatly encreases the difficulty. With so great an extent of sea coast, with so many rivers, bays, harbors and inlets; with neighboring English provinces, which stretch for so great an extent along one of our frontiers, it is impossible to prevent smuggling to a large amount.

Besides, there are other and strong objections to this system. It renders government odious. People are not in the habit of looking back beyond the immediate cause. The farmer enquiring why he cannot get more for his produce; and he is told that it is owing to the embargo, or to commercial restrictions. In this he sees only the hands of his own government. He does not look to those acts of violence and injustice, which this system is intended to counteract. His censures fall on his government. To its measures he attributes the cause of his embarrassment; and in their removal he expects his relief. This is an unhappy state of the public mind; and even, I might with truth say, in a government resting essentially on opinion, a dangerous one. In war it is different. The privation, it is true, may be equal, or greater; but the public mind, under the strong impulses of that state of things, becomes steeled against sufferings. The difference is great between the passive and active state of the mind. Tie down a hero, and he feels the puncture of a pin; but throw him into battle, and he is scarcely sensible of vital gashes. So in war; impelled alternately by hope and fear, stimulated with revenge, depressed with shame, or elevated with victory, the people become invincible. No privation can shake their fortitude. No calamity can break their spirit. Even where equally successful, the contest is striking. War and restriction may leave the country equally exhausted; but the latter not only leaves you poor, but even when successful dispirited, divided, discontented, with diminished patriotism and the manners of a considerable portion of your people corrupted. Not so in war. In that state the common danger unites all—strengthens the bonds of society, and feeds the flame of patriotism. The national character acquires energy. In exchange for the expences of war, you obtain military and naval skill, and a more perfect organization of such parts of your government as is connected with the science of national defence. You also obtain the habits of freely advancing your purse and strength in the common cause. Sir, are these advantages to be counted as trifles in the present state of the world? Can they be measured by a monied valuation? But, it may be asked, why not unite war and restriction; and thus call the whole energy of the country into action. It is true there is nothing impossible in such an union; but it is equally true, that what is gained to the latter is lost to the former; and, sir, the reverse is also true, that what is lost to restrictions is gained to the war. My objections to restrictions without war, equally hold against them in conjunction with it. Sir, I would prefer a single victory over the enemy by sea or land, to all the good we shall ever derive from the continuation of the non-importation act. I know not, that it would produce an equal pressure on the enemy; but I am certain of what is of greater consequence, it would be accompanied with more salutary effects on ourselves. The memory of a Saratoga or Eutaw is immortal. It is there you will find the country's boast and pride; the inexhaustible source of great and heroic actions. But what will history say of restrictions? What examples worthy of imitation will it furnish posterity? What pride, what pleasure will our children find in the events of such times? Let me not be considered as romantic. This nation ought to be taught to rely on its own courage, its fortitude, its skill and virtue for protection. These are the only safe-guards in the hour of danger. Man was endued with these great qualities for his defence. There is nothing about him that indicates that he must conquer by enduring. He is not incrusted in a shell; he is not taught to rely on his insensibility, his passive suffering for defence. No, no, it is on the invincible mind; on a magnanimous nature that he ought to rely. Here is the superiority of our kind; it is these that make man the lord of the world. It is the destiny of our condition, that nations should rise above nations as they are endued in a greater degree with these shining qualities.

Sir, it is often repeated, that if the non-importation act is continued, we shall have a speedy peace. I believe it not. I fear the delusive hope. It will debilitate the springs of war. It is for this reason in part that I wish it repealed. It is the fountain of fallacious expectations. I, sir, have frequently heard another observation, with no small mortification, from some of those who have supported the war, that it is only by restriction that we can seriously affect our enemies. Why then declare war? Is it to be an appendage only of the non-importation act. If so, I disclaim it. It is an alarming idea to be in a state of war and not to rely on our courage or energy, but on a measure of peace. If the non-importation act is our chief reliance, it will soon direct our councils. Let us strike away this false hope; let us call out the resources of the nation for its protection. England will soon find that seven millions of freemen with every material of war in abundance are not to be despised with impunity. I would be full of hope, if I saw our sole reliance on the vigor of the war; but if we are to paralise it; if we are to trust in the moment of danger, to the operation of a system of peace, I greatly fear. If such is to be our course, I see not that we have bettered our condition. We have had a peace like a war; in the name of heaven let us not have the only thing that is worse, a war like a peace. I trust my fears will not be realised.

69 NOTE: On June 19 Calhoun, from the Foreign Relations Committee, presented a bill [MS, June 19, 1812, *NA*, RG233, 12A-B1] for the repeal of the embargo and specie exportation acts (No. 59 NOTE). As both were due to expire in a fortnight, his move was in effect a gesture in support of a more significant bill, introduced by his colleague Langdon Cheves the same day from the Ways and Means Committee, for a partial suspension till April 1 next of all non-importation acts. Cheves' bill was accompanied by a letter of Secretary of the Treasury Albert Gallatin to explain that the resulting imports, if duties were doubled, would provide the revenue now proposed to be raised by other taxes (*AC*12-1, p. 1510-3).

When the bill was debated (June 23) William M. Richardson, of Massachusetts, moved an amendment for direct repeal of the non-importation act of May 1, 1810, and its supplement of Mar. 2,

1811, urging it as a recognition that the restrictive system was a failure (p. 1533). The next day Calhoun made the above speech in support of the amendment, and outlined the broad basis of his appeal for unity and for a sweeping change of Republican policy. By a narrow margin the bill was indefinitely postponed (p. 1543-4). See comment of Adams (*History of U.S.*, VI, 232-4) on the significance of this speech, and Latimer, "South Carolina—A Protagonist of the War of 1812," on Calhoun, Cheves and Lowndes as defenders of merchant interests; and compare Nos. 60 and 71.

In February following Cheves renewed his effort to raise revenue by a partial suspension of the non-importation acts, but his bill was defeated by a vote of 79 to 24. Calhoun voted with Cheves but did not speak. (*AC*12-2, p. 1062-5, 1091-1100; see No. 77 NOTE.) SOURCE: *NI*, July 2, 1812; *AC*12-1, p. 1535-41.

70. To MRS. FLORIDE COLHOUN, SR., Charleston, S. C.

Washington 23d. Novr. 1812

Dr Mother, I am induced to write to you more from that sentiment of respect and affection which I hope ever to entertain for you, than any particular information which I wish to communicate. My esteem for you has rather been strengthened, than created, by the present intimate tie which through our dear Floride and little Andrew subsist between us. Your deportment long before our connection was such as to merit my warmest affection. Floride's letter to me mentions the fine health of Andrew and his disposition to feed. I think it would be advisable for her to wean him as soon as possible. You however will be the best judge. I fear to continue him longer at the breast will be neither for his or her health.

If Floride bears my absence as badly as I do hers, she must occasionally be very impatient. I know you will not fail to keep her as cheerful as possible. I often look forward with impatience for the time of my return.

I expect we shall have a warm and important session. We shall have to encounter every impediment that opposition can throw in the way.

If rice is a good price I would advise you to sell. The present prospect is in favour of its keeping up and being high; but the commercial world is at present so uncertain, that no one can anticipate the change. I would be glad to hear from you.

I am with much esteem your son

J. C. CALHOUN

SOURCE: *CC.*

71. SPEECH ON THE MERCHANTS' BONDS

December 8, 1812

Mr. Calhoun—Mr. Chairman, the subject now under discussion was first brought under the notice of Congress, by the following paragraph in the President's message at the commencement of the present session: "A considerable number of American vessels, which were in England when the revocation of the Orders in Council took place, were laden with British manufactures under an erroneous impression that the non-importation act would immediately cease to operate, and have arrived in the United States. It did not appear proper to exercise on unforseen cases of such magnitude, the ordinary power vested in the Treasury Department to mitigate forfeitures, without previously affording to Congress an opportunity of making on the subject such provision as they may think proper. In their decision they will doubtless equally consult what is due to equitable considerations and the public interest." So much of the message as has been just read, was referred to the Committee of Ways and Means. Their report constitutes the subject of our present deliberation, and of which the following is the material part:

"That on the view of the whole subject, the committee are of opinion that the Secretary of the Treasury has full power to remit or mitigate the penalties and forfeitures incurred, should an interposition in either way be called for by the circumstances of the case; and therefore recommend that it be

"*Resolved,* That it is inexpedient to legislate upon the subject, and that the petitions with the accompanying documents be referred to the Secretary of the Treasury."

My object in presenting to the view of this committee the President's message and the report, is to call their attention to a total want of accordance between them. It is almost an abuse of language to call it a report. A report ought to comprehend the subject of reference, and be to it as a conclusion is to its premises. On reading the report only, the natural conclusions would be, that we were consulted as lawyers and not as statesmen; that the point of doubt in the Executive mind turned on the construction of our acts, and not on what justice, humanity and sound policy demand. The report informs us, that the Secretary of the Treasury has power to remit or mitigate the penalties incurred, and from this fact it draws that negative proposition on which we are now deliberating. It is not a little curious to observe how formally and fully the committee have decided on this power of the Treasury Department, doubted neither by the President or Secretary, nor indeed by any one; while they overlook those interesting considerations, towards which the Executive has directed the attention of Congress, "what is due to equitable considerations and to the public interest," in relation to "unforseen cases of such magnitude." They are in truth cases of magnitude. Twenty millions of property await your decision, a sum equal nearly to half of the annual export of this country, and quite equal to the entire export in the best years of the whole country between Washington and New Orleans. It is difficult to realise magnitude when expressed in numbers only. To form a just conception we must aggregate the whole annual products of cotton, rice and tobacco, with a large proportion of the bread stuffs of this country. I would be happy to know on what principle of policy or reason so large an amount is to be left to the decision of any individual. Is more wisdom, more virtue or public confidence to be found in the Treasury Department, than in the assembled representatives of the nation?

What, sir, constitutes a feature in this report still more extraordinary and objectionable, is the apparent understanding between the committee and the Treasury Department. They coyly refuse to recommend any positive act of legislation, while they indirectly intimate what they wish and expect the Secretary of the Treasury to do; or in other words we are called on really and virtually to legislate, while we are informed that it is improper so to do. For among the documents reported by the Committee of Ways and Means, as forming the basis of their opinion, is a letter of the Secretary of the Treasury of the 23d of November which contains the following paragraph: "Upon the whole, I continue in the opinion submitted with great deference to the committee that one half of the forfeitures which would otherwise fall to the collectors ought to be remitted; but that with respect to the one half belonging to the United States, justice to the community requires, that when remitted at least an equivalent may be secured to the public for the extra profit beyond that on common exportations, which arises from the continuation of the non-importation act." Here, sir, the opinion of the Secretary is explicitly stated relative to these unforeseen cases of such magnitude, and the conclusion is irresistible, that the committee in referring them to his decision must have approved of it.

The true question, then, before the committee is not to be found in that negative resolution reported by the committee, that it is inexpedient to legislate on these cases; but in that part of the letter of the Secretary of the Treasury, which I have just read. Yes, we are now deliberating, in effect, whether it is proper to exact of the merchants their extra profit; and whether this ought to be done through the agency of the Treasury Department. I presume, the truth of this opinion will not be controverted; should it, however, ample proof will be found in almost every sentence of the report and the speeches of the gentlemen in support of it. They are literally compounded of laborious investigations to ascertain the extra profit of the merchants on their late importations.

Now, sir, without pretending to controvert the policy of taking the extra profit; I do assert, that it cannot be legally effected through the Secretary of the Treasury. It exceeds his powers. The non-importation law, under which the forfeitures accrued, refers to the act of 1797 to ascertain the powers of the Secretary in relation to cases of this kind. On reference to that act, his power will be found to be strictly a *mitigating* and *remitting* power and has for its object the remedy of an imperfection incidental to all human laws. The best worded act must comprehend many cases within the letter, that are not within its spirit or intention. In every well regulated government, an equity exists some where to remedy this object; to mitigate the rigor of the law. The act of '97 for greater security of the revenue vests this power in relation to our revenue laws in the head of the Treasury Department. The real object of those laws is to punish only the negligent or wilful violators; but, like other penal acts, they are couched in general terms, and comprehend those who by necessity or ignorance violate them. That the Treasury might be secured and the law at the same time administered in its spirit and intention only, and not its letter, this power was delegated to the Secretary of the Treasury. To establish the correctness of this exposition, I will read the act of '97.

[Here Mr. C. read the act.[1]]

Now, sir, though I admit, with the report, "that the Secretary of the Treasury has power to mitigate or remit," I do most unequivocally deny, that he has legal power to effect what is proposed to be done by the committee, to levy the extra profit. The two powers are most essentially different. The one is of a judicial and equitable character, and has for its object guilt or innocence; the other that of assessment or taxation, and has for its object not guilt or innocence, but profit. The latter is strictly a monied transaction; the former relates to the administration of the penal laws of the country. The one is administered in perfection, when due regard is had to all the circumstances as they constitute guilt or innocence, and the law applied accordingly; the other, when proper and correct estimate is made of the usual profits of trade and that on the late importation; and the difference only levied.

The power of the Secretary under the act of '97 is not arbitrary, to be exercised or not according to his pleasure; but he is bound to exercise it according to the rules of a sound discretion; if guilt appears he cannot withhold the law; if innocent he cannot apply it. The effects of the two powers strongly mark their contrariety. When circumstances of guilt or innocence only govern the Treasury in the exercise of this power, the consequence is love and reverence for the laws; but, if they are neglected, and the profit of the merchants only regarded, in the place of those sentiments will be disgust and hatred. You may indeed have a full Treasury, but you will find empty affections. More need not be said, I hope, to prove that the extra profit cannot be taken from the merchants under the power of the Treasury Department to mitigate or remit forfeitures. It is essentially a taxation; and not only is not delegated to the Secretary of the Treasury by the act of '97, but cannot be by any act of

1. *AC4-2*, p. 2953-4 (Mar. 3, 1797).

ours. It is a power, which the Constitution has sacredly deposited in Congress. It is incommunicable. I am aware, that the extra profit may be taken under the semblance of the mitigating power; that the forfeiture may be reduced to it. But this cannot change the nature of the transaction. The question will still be, is it a monied transaction, or a fair administration of the penal laws of the country? Is the object profit, or the execution of the laws? The circumstances of the case will readily decide its character. Profit and justice are not easily confounded. It is not an unusual thing for power to assume a guise; and even to appear to be the very opposite to what it really is. I impute no blame to the Committee of Ways and Means. They have overlooked the character of the power, which they wish the Secretary of the Treasury to exercise. It is an act of inadvertence, but is not the less on that account to be resisted. Precedence is a dangerous thing; and it is not unusual for executive power, even unknown to those who exercise it, to make encroachments of this kind. What has been the end of all free governments, but open force, or the gradual undermining of the legislative by the executive power? The peculiar construction of ours by no means exempts us from this evil; but on the contrary, were it not for the habits of the people, would naturally tend that way. The operation of this government is an interesting problem. I wish to see the whole in full possession of its primitive power, but all of the parts confined to their respective spheres. These, sir, are my reasons for rejecting the report of the committee.

I know, it will be said, that it is much easier to censure than advise; to reject the report than to point out what ought to be done. I am ready to acknowledge it, and to confess, that I have felt much solicitude and difficulty on this subject. But the view which the committee has presented has constituted no part of my embarrassment. I am entirely adverse to taking any part of the extra profit, whether through the agency of the Treasury Department or this House.

If our merchants are innocent, they are welcome to their good fortune; if guilty, I scorn to participate in its profit. I will never consent to make our penal code the basis of our ways and means; or to establish a partnership between the Treasury and the violators of the non-importation law. The necessity of causing our restrictive system to be respected, while in existence; and the difficulty of applying its penalties to "cases of such magnitude" constitute my embarrassment. On the one hand if the law should be enforced, thousands will be involved in ruin; on the other, if an act of grace should be done, your restrictive system will be endangered. Had the conduct of the merchants been dictated by any open contempt of the laws, or it had been entirely free from blame, our course would have been plain. None would have hesitated in the one case to have let the vengeance of the law fall on the guilty; or in the other to extend its protection to the innocent. I am ready to acknowledge, that the importers were not sufficiently circumspect and guarded. The nature of the restrictive system, the posture of affairs, the recent decision of this House on a motion to repeal the non-importation act ought to have put them on their guard. Candor also compels me to state, that I cannot admit any arguments on this question to prove the impolicy of the non-importation act; or the advantages to the community from the late importation. I can never admit as apology for the violation of the law, what was considered as an insufficient reason for its suspension; and cannot doubt that even the worst of laws ought to be respected.

But, sir, the difficulty on the other side appears to me more formidable. An indiscriminate forfeiture would, I fear, not be considered as punishment. It would be thought oppression. Punishment by the infliction of a partial evil proposes to avoid a greater; by making some the subjects of its pains, to make all of its terror. The culprits in this case are too numerous for example; particularly as the infraction of the law is of a doubtful character. This is by no means an unprecedented case; numbers have often brought impunity. It is so in the worst of crimes; even in treason, where in some instances a considerable portion of the community is involved. Some gentlemen who have felt this embarrassment, have proposed to distinguish for punishment the head and leaders of this infraction of the law. My friend from Kentucky (the Speaker) has made two favored classes; the purchasers of British goods before the 2d of February, 1811, and the shippers before the 1st of August last; that is, before the declaration of war was heard in England.[2] The

2. *AC*12-2, p. 304.

first class is favored from a supposed innocence of purchase; the other from innocence of shipments. It is not necessary to prove the error of this discrimination. If true, it does not extend as far as it ought to do. For, if innocence of purchase is a sufficient reason for exemption, how can we condemn the goods purchased before the 1st of August? For if shipments might be made before that period, surely purchases might; and if the last, then, according to the distinction in favor of purchasers before the 2d of February, they also ought to be exempted from the forfeitures. The cases then are too uniform for discrimination; and nothing remains, but to condemn or acquit the whole. I feel myself compelled to yield to the magnitude of the case. I cannot find it in me to reduce thousands to beggary by a single stroke; nor do I suppose there is one in this House in favor of so stern a policy. I am ready to acknowledge, that an act of grace will weaken the non-importation law; but that is a less evil than the alienation of the whole mercantile class. It is left us to regret, that the wise foresight of my two honorable friends and colleagues was not adopted the last session.[3] It was then proposed to suspend the law for the introduction of this very property; but it was borne down by the clamor of the day. Had that been done we would not have been reduced to the present state. Our laws would have been saved and our merchants contented.

A subject, not necessarily involved in that under discussion, has been introduced by those who have preceded me in the debate. In imitation of the example, I will be excused, I hope, in offering my sentiments on the restrictive system. It is known that I have not been a friend to that system to the extent to which it has been carried. My objection, however, is neither against the inequality, or the greatness of its pressure. It is the duty of every section to bear whatever the general interest may demand; and I, sir, am proud in representing a people pre-eminent in the exercise of this virtue. Carolina makes no complaint about the difficulties of the times. If she feels embarrassments, she turns her indignation not against her own government, but against the common enemy. She makes no comparative estimate of her sufferings with the other states. She would be even proud to be pre-eminent in suffering, if by that the

3. See NOTES to Nos. 60 and 69.

general good could be promoted, and this day she presents the
magnanimity of gaining union and energy by the pressure; and
so far from growing tired of the restrictive system, or war, as intimated by the gentleman from Kentucky, that she would willingly
bear a superadded embargo, if the public interest should demand
it.[4] But, sir, my objections are of a general and national character.
Your character, your government and country forbid a resort to
this system for a redress of wrongs. It requires a sternness of execution approaching despotism. It first creates a vast premium for its
violation; and then has to combat with the speculation, the cupidity
and capital of the whole mercantile class. To render its execution
perfect, you must not only repress the fraud, but the speculations
of the merchants; particularly that which is founded on the course
of political events. The subject before us is in point; and you will
from the same cause be involved in this very dilemma annually,
even more frequently, should the Treasury participate in the profit.
To render your system perfect, you must imitate its successful
execution in another country. Bonaparte is the only man who has a
perfect knowledge of its genius. Burning and confiscation are the
only effectual securities. A partial execution involves the most pernicious consequences. The conclusion is irresistible. The system
does not suit you. You are too enterprizing—too free—and your
coast too extended, with too many indentations of rivers, bays and
harbors. The effects of a few years' operation will change your
mercantile character. In such a state of things the honest merchant
must retire. He cannot live. His place will not be unoccupied. The
desperate adventurer and the smuggler will suceed. Unaided by the
virtue of the citizen, no law however severe its sanction will be
able to stem the torrent. There is indeed one species of restrictions,
which in a British war ought never to be neglected. Whatever
pressure can be produced on her manufacturing and commercial
interest through heavy duties ought to be effected. The reason is
obvious—it is both restriction and revenue. So much of the capital
of this country is turned towards foreign commerce, that you cannot
safely neglect this source of revenue. Nor is its restrictive character
inconsiderable. The assertion may seem strange; but I believe it
to be the highest practical and continued pressure that can be pro-

4. See AC12-2, p. 300 (Clay's speech).

duced. To say nothing of the perpetual violation of an entire prohibition by smuggling, it is subject to occasional relaxations, by
which the country becomes inundated with British goods.

At the end of the last session, I recommended high duties as a
substitute for the non-importation act. Under that system, the
quantity of goods imported would not have been greater than it
now is; but your Treasury would have been much better replen-
ished. Nor should we have had the present contest about extra
profits. It would have passed into the Treasury under the shape of
duties. High duties have no pernicious effects; and are consistent
with the genius of the people and the institutions of the country.
It is thus we would combine in the greatest degree the active resources of the country with pressure on the manufactures of the
enemy. Your army and navy would feel the animating effect. The
war would not sicken the patriot's hope, and defeat some of its
most valuable anticipated consequences. You would have the means
of filling the ranks of the regulars; and would no longer rely on the
hazardous aid of volunteers and militia. Victory, peace, and national honor, I was going to say glory, but experience has taught
me how that word is received in this House, would be the wel-
comed result of a vigorous war. But, sir, if we must have one or
the other, either all war or all restriction, I would prefer the former.
Suppose either would bring the enemy to our terms; even in their
victory they are unequal. By restriction you have nothing but the
success; but the assertion of our national rights by arms creates
those qualities which amply compensate for the privation and expense incidental to that state. Admit that the Tripolitans could
have been coerced to terms by non-importation acts, and that we
had resorted to restriction rather than arms; could we have this day
boasted of our naval victories? The Mediterranean war was the
school of our naval virtue. It has elevated the hopes of our country.
We may now look forward to the day with confidence, when we
shall be no longer insulted and injured on the high road of nations
with impunity. Besides the non-importation, as a redress of wrongs,
is radically defective. You may meet commercial restrictions with
commercial restrictions; but you cannot safely confront premedi-
tated insult and injury with commercial restrictions alone. I utter
not this from the fervor of my feelings, but it is the deliberate re-

sult of my best judgment. It sinks the nation in its own estimation; it counts for nothing what is ultimately connected with our best hopes—the union of these states. Our Union cannot safely stand on the cold calculation of interest alone. It is too weak to withstand political convulsions. We cannot without hazard neglect that which makes man love to be a member of an extensive community—the love of greatness—the consciousness of strength. So long as an American is a proud name, we are safe; but that day we are ashamed of it, the Union is more than half destroyed.

71 NOTE: The House was in Committee of the Whole on the report of the Ways and Means Committee. The bonds in question were those which had been given by owners of cargoes imported from Great Britain following the repeal, on June 23, 1812, of the Orders in Council. For the paragraph in Madison's message on the matter and its reference to the House Ways and Means Committee, see *AC12-2*, p. 15, 142. On the 25th Langdon Cheves, Chairman of that committee, presented the report which merely proposed a resolution which would leave the question in the hands of the Secretary of the Treasury (p. 198-9), but when the House began consideration of the report Cheves explained that he was not in agreement with the committee, and it was another member, Richard M. Johnson of Kentucky, who opened the debate (p. 215-35). Johnson pointed out that inasmuch as operation of the non-importation act of March, 1811, could be suspended only on proclamation of the President, these cargoes, despite the repeal of the Orders in Council, were subject to forfeiture. The Secretary of the Treasury—who was authorized under the March, 1811, law to remit the penalties, entirely or in part—considered that in the case of these cargoes the government should merely demand the portion of the merchants' expected profit which would be in excess of ordinary profits (p. 218-9).

Calhoun interpreted the law to the advantage of the merchants and contended that if the importation were a willful violation the cargoes could be confiscated, otherwise they should be released on payment of the existing duties. He scorned to aid the hard-pressed Treasury by an extra-legal partial confiscation scheme. This was the argument of Cheves, in his speech of Dec. 4 (p. 241-56), in which, however, he spoke more directly for the merchants and attacked the whole principle of the "restrictive system," pointing out the hardships to the merchants—including those among his own constituents in Charleston—and the bitterness it caused. On the 11th the committee resolution to refer the matter to the Secretary of the Treasury was rejected by a majority of three; and one by Cheves—that all penalties in the case be remitted—was lost by eight votes (p. 364), although on the 23rd a bill from the Senate to the same effect was passed (but limiting its application to goods shipped between June 23 and Sept. 15) and became law on Jan. 2 (p. 394, 404, 450-1, 1316). See also a supplementary bill from the Senate enacted Feb. 27 (p. 929, 1061-2, 1111, 1123-6, 1334-5), and Adams, *History of U.S.*, VI, 438-45.   SOURCE: *NI*, Jan. 9, 1813; *AC*12-2, p. 315-21.

72. To DR. JAMES MACBRIDE, Charleston, S.C.

Washington 25th Decbr 1812

Dr Doctor, Often have I taken up my pen to answer your letter of last summer, but have at all times found my mind in such a state of perp[*l*]exity, as to discourage me from the attempt. What I had strong reasons to fear has actually happened. Our executive officers are most incompetent men; and will let the best of causes I fear perish in their hands. We are literally boren down under the effects of errors and mismanagement. I am sorry to say that many of them lie deep; and are coeval with the existance of Mr. Jeffersons administration. The organization of the government I do not think is much to blame. Fairly administered it is a strong government. This is a source of consolation. If I could see you, I could fill a volume almost. My experience, for the short time I have been in publick life, is very great. The period has been eventful. I do believe the Executive will have to make a disgraceful peace.

The situation of your friend is by no means a pleasant one. I feel myself from peculiar considerations bound to give the administration every support towards carring on the war; when I have not the least confidence in them. As to fair open wisdom they have no[ne;] their whole art is in management.

I trust this letter for the present will be in strick confidence.

My respects to Mrs. McBride & Mr. Gourdine and family.

I am with much esteem yours &c

J. C. CALHOUN

I will be glad to hear from you.

72 NOTE: Calhoun's uneasiness and discouragement were foreshadowed by his misgivings of the previous April (No. 61). He

found comfort (see No. 76) in the replacement in January of the Secretary of War by John Armstrong and of the Secretary of the Navy by William Jones (*BDC*), but the policy embodied in Madison's diplomatic maneuvers in the summer and in his message to Congress on Nov. 4 paralyzed the war party in Congress—see No. 73 NOTE. SOURCE: *LC*, James Macbride Papers.

73. REMARKS ON THE PROTECTION OF AMERICAN SEAMEN

January 2, 1813

Mr. Calhoun observed in reply to Mr. Pearson, that he was very happy to find, that the gentleman from North Carolina, while he was unwilling to defend the Irish and Englishmen, yet was willing to promote the war for the American seamen—that the cause was a good one, and he hoped that the other gentlemen who usually acted with him, would unite to defend so brave and meritorious a class of citizens. That as to acting on the subject, he as a member of the Committee of Foreign Relations, together with some others of that committee, had it under consideration.[1] That his views did not extend farther than the proposition made by our Executive to the British government. If England would agree to reciprocal exclusion, he would agree for one to limit our protection to native-born seamen and those who are now naturalised. The subject was, however, one of very great delicacy, better fitted for negociation than legislation, and he had not fully reflected on it—but if after due deliberation, he found it could be done with propriety, it should be laid before Congress before the end of the session. That he could not agree with the gentleman from North Carolina, that we ought to rely on such provisions, and suspend in the mean time our preparations; that such conduct would be fatal, as England was a proud and high-minded nation, and that nothing could bring her to terms, but a vigorous and successful prosecution of the war.

1. Calhoun meant Pearson's proposal of a law to exclude British deserters from the American service, but the *Federal Republican* of Jan. 4 in an editorial quoted him as saying that peace was under discussion in the cabinet. On the 6th the paper recorded him as correcting, in the House on the 4th, this report "which had gone abroad." An article in the same issue sarcastically referred to Calhoun's "puzzling explanation," and insisted that the speaker had unwittingly betrayed a cabinet secret. See No. 76.

73 NOTE: Eight days after the declaration of war, and before receipt of the news of the repeal of the Orders in Council, Monroe had written to the American chargé d'affaires at London instructing him to propose an armistice based on the repeal of the Orders and discontinuance of impressment (*AC*12-2, p. 1173-5). Madison himself, while refraining from a request for a law for the purpose, had laid before Congress the correspondence on the subject which included Monroe's statement that an act would be passed excluding British seamen from American public and private vessels on condition of reciprocal action by Great Britain (p. 1174). The Foreign Relations Committee was still deadlocked over the question of presenting such a bill, and some of the opposition members now undertook to precipitate the issue by demanding the seamen's regulation bill instead of enlargement of war plans (see, for instance, p. 488). In an effective speech (p. 499-508), Joseph Pearson, a North Carolina Federalist (*BDC*), declared the repeal of the Orders in Council had left impressment as the sole avowed issue of the war, and that Great Britain, at least before the war, had shown willingness for "adjustment" of the dispute. In view of the recent negotiations he proposed, instead of an expansion of the army, a law to exclude British seamen from the maritime service and the employment and encouragement of native Americans in it (*AC*12-2, p. 503, 507).

Calhoun here stated that he would accept a bill so drastic as to exclude American citizens hereafter naturalized, and he voted for the bill in its progress through the House (see p. 1017-29, 1055, and his later comment, No. 76). But his distaste for this negotiation at the beginning of the war was made obvious by his failure to report the bill and the fact that he did not speak for it during the debate. Speaker Clay and Grundy both indicated their feeling that the administration had been over zealous in its overtures for peace (p. 602, 676).

The seamen's bill had a stormy progress through the House. At the beginning of the session John Smilie of Pennsylvania was appointed Chairman of the Foreign Relations Committee, with Calhoun second, Felix Grundy of Tennessee third (p. 142). The 1843 *Life* of Calhoun (p. 12-3) declared that at the first meeting of the committee, and on Smilie's nomination, Calhoun was elected chairman (Crallé, in *Works*, V, vi, apparently confuses this with the chairmanship of the 1811 committee). Smilie appears in House proceedings until Dec. 2 (*AC*12-2, p. 216); he died Dec. 30 (*BDC*). Calhoun in his reply to Pearson spoke as chairman of the committee, but it was Grundy who presented a bill for the regulation of seamen (*AC*12-2, p. 932-9). Charles Goldsborough, a Maryland Federalist, fourth member of the committee, ascribed authorship of it to "the

Cabinet," and declared that Grundy was "almost the only zealous patron of the bill" in the committee (p. 1048, 1052-3). As introduced in the House it was to go into effect at the end of the war and with nations making a similar arrangement with the United States; it forbade employment of any but citizens or persons who had previously applied for citizenship. The final vote in the House was 89 to 33 (p. 1055); the bill became law on March 3 (p. 1339-42), having been amended, however, to allow employment of all naturalized citizens, and persons of color, native to the United States. See Adams, *History of U.S.*, VI, 451-8 for the affair.   Source: *NI*, Jan. 12, 1813; *AC* 12-2, p. 508-9.

74. To Patrick Calhoun, Abbeville, S.C.

Washington 13th Jany 1812 [*1813*][1]

Dr brother, I have waited some time in expectation of hearing from you; and have on that account not written so soon as I should. We are no[w] engaged on the bill to raise 20,000 men for one year.[2] Its object is the reduction of Canada, and the men will be raised in the states adjacent to that frontier. The bill has raised a very warm and full discussion of the state of our foreign relations. I have not yet spoken, but expect to do so this morning. I do not know how I shall aquit myself. You saw by the papers, that considerable additions have been voted to our navy. A greater number would have been ordered, but the state of our finances would not admit. William Jones of Philidelphia has been appointed Secretary of the navy. He is said to be a very practical and competent man. General Armstrong has been nominated in the place of Eustis.[3] He has not yet pass'd the Senate.

Our late news from Europe is interesting. The French army is regaining its former position on the Peninsula; but seem to be on its retreat in Russia. What effect ["reaction" *cancelled*] it may have on our relation is difficult to say. Should the war continue another summer in Russia, I think England will be wholly engaged

1. Misdated 1812—note reference to the additional military force bill.
2. See No. 75.
3. John Armstrong and William Eustis, Secretary of War; see Calhoun's comment—No. 76.

in that quarter. Let me hear from you. Remember me to Nancy, Mr. & Mrs. Mosely and all friends.

I am your affe[*ctiona*]te brother

J. C. CALHOUN

SOURCE: *SCL.*

75. SPEECH ON THE BILL FOR AN ADDITIONAL MILITARY FORCE

January 14, 1813

Mr. Calhoun observed, that he could offer nothing more acceptable, he presumed, to the House, than a promise not to discuss the Orders in Council, French Decrees, Blockades, or Embargoes. He was induced to avoid these topics for several reasons. In the first place, they were too stale to furnish any interest to this House or country. Gentlemen who had attempted it, with whatever abilities, had failed to command attention; and it would argue very little sagacity on his part not to be admonished by their want of success. Indeed, whatever interest had been at one time attached to these subjects, they had now lost it. They have passed away; and will not soon, he hoped, return into the circle of politics. Yes, sir, as reviled as has been our country's efforts to curb belligerent injustice, as weak and contemptible as she has been represented to be in the grade of nations, she has triumphed in breaking down the most dangerous monopoly ever attempted by one nation against the commerce of another. He would not stop to enquire whether it was the non-importation act, or the menace of war, or, what was the most probable, the last operating on the pressure produced by the former. The fact is certain, that the Orders in Council of 1807 and 1809, which our opponents have often said, that England would not yield, as they made a part of her commercial system, are now no more. The same firmness, if persevered in, which has carried us thus far with success, will, as our cause is just and moderate, end in final victory. A further reason which he had not to follow our opponents into the region of documents and records, was that he was afraid of a decoy; as he was induced to believe from appearances that their object was to draw our attention from the merits of the question. Gentlemen had literally buried their arguments under a huge pile of quotations; and had wandered so far into this realm of paper, that neither the vision of this House has been, or that of the country will be, able to follow them. There the best and worst reasons share an equal fate. The truth of the one and error of the other, are covered with like obscurity.

Before he proceeded further, he would make a few observations in reply to the gentleman from Virginia (Mr. Randolph) who spoke yesterday. He complained of the desertion of his former associates from the minority principles of '98. These principles, he said, consisted in an opposition to the general government in relation to the states, and to political rights in relation to individuals.[1]

Mr. C. said he was at one moment almost induced to suspect the gentleman of a desertion of his own principles; for scarcely had he finished this part of his subject, before he passed a high-wrought eulogy on the Father of his country—on that man whose whole life indicated the strongest leaning on the side of the government of his country. He would beg the gentleman to reflect whether his definition of minority principles suited the character of Washington's administration—and, if not, with what propriety both could be praised almost in the same breath. Whether indeed the principles of '98 were such as the gentleman has represented them, he would not enquire; because not necessary to his argument. But if they are in truth those of the gentleman and his present associates, he would be happy to know with what countenance they can request the people of this country to put the government into their hands. Trust the government to those who are hostile to it! Who prefer their own interest and rights, to its interest and rights! If our opponents are in reality in favor of such principles, patriotism ought to persuade them to add one other, and that is, ever to remain in a minority. There they may perhaps be of some use, at least they will not be dangerous; but put them in power, and let them act up to what they profess, and destruction would be certain. If the gentleman from Virginia is anxious to know the real cause of the separation of his former associates from him, he must look for it in his *present* political creed, and that of those with whom he is *now united.* He will there find an article which had no

1. AC12-2, p. 782.

place in *his in* '98, and which then as well as now was reprobated by those who constitute the present majority. This article is only an enlargement of the minority principles, as defined by the gentleman; it is opposition *to our country* in relation *to England*. The proof of this article is of the same kind, and no less clear than the others. For what encroachment of England on our neutral rights, from the interruption of our carrying trade down to the moment that war was declared, which one of the innumerable insults and injuries which bursted in on us, has the opposition either not palliated or justified—and what effort of our country to resist, which has not been reprobated and opposed?

Mr. C. said that he would not multiply proof on a course of conduct the bad effect of which was too sensibly felt to be easily forgot, and the continuation of which was but too apparent in the present discussion. For what was the object of the opposition in this debate? To defeat the passage of this bill? It has been scarcely mentioned; and contains nothing to raise that storm which has been excited against it. The bill proposes to raise 20,000 men only, and that for one year; and surely there is nothing in that calculated to lay such strong hold of the jealousy or fear of the community. What then is the object of the opposition? Gentlemen certainly do not act without an intention; and wide as has been the range of debate, it cannot be so lawless as to be without an object. It was not, he repeated, to defeat the passage of this bill; no, but what was much more to be dreaded, to thwart that, which the bill proposes to contribute to, the final success of the war; and for this purpose he must do the opposition the credit to say, they have resorted to means the best calculated to produce the effect. In a free government, in the government of laws, two things are necessary for the effectual prosecution of any great measure; the law by which the executive officer is charged with the execution and vested with suitable powers; and the co-operating zeal and union of the people, who are always indispensable agents. Opposition to be successful must direct its effort against the passage of the law; or, what was more common and generally more effectual, to destroy the union and the zeal of the people. Either, if successful, is effectual. The former would in most cases be seen and reprobated; the latter, much the most dangerous, has, to the great misfortunes of republics, presented at all times a ready means of defeating the most salutary measures. To this point the whole arguments of opposition have converged. This gives a meaning to every reason and assertion, which have been advanced, however wild and inconsistent. No topic has been left untouched, no passion unessayed. The war has been represented as unjust in its origin, disastrous in its progress, and desperate in its farther prosecution. As if to prevent the possibility of doubt, a determination has been boldly asserted not to support it. Such is the opposition to the war which was admitted on all sides to be just; and which in a manner received the votes even of those who now appear to be willing to ruin the country in order to defeat its success. For let it be ever remembered, that the bill to raise the 25,000 men passed this House almost unanimously, though it was distinctly announced for what object it was intended.[2] How will gentlemen relieve themselves from this dilemma? Was it their object to embarrass the administration? Will they dare to make a confession, which will so strongly confirm the motive which has been assigned to them? A gentleman from New York (Mr. Emott) felt the awkwardness of the situation, and in his endeavor to explain has made an admission which ought ever to exclude him and his friends from power. He justified his vote on the ground that he was in favor of the force as a peace establishment. A peace establishment of 35,000 men! (Mr. Emott explained that he did not mean as a peace establishment, but that the posture of affairs at that time demanded it.) At any rate, said Mr. C. he hoped to hear nothing farther about the enormous expence of the war, since the principal expence ought to have been incurred in the gentleman's opinion, even had it not been resorted to. Well might the opposition admit the justice of the war. For years the moderation of the government, he might almost say the excessive love of peace, strove to avoid the contest. We bore all that an independent nation could bear; not indeed with patience, but in the hopes of returning justice on the part of our enemy.

Mr. C. could not omit noticing the attempt made by the gentleman from New York, to palliate the conduct of England, in re-

2. See No. 50 NOTE.

lation to one of the causes of the war; he alluded to the blockade of 1806. The gentleman contended that it was a relaxation of the law of nations in our favor; and of consequence must be considered by us in the light of a benefit. It surely cannot be necessary to trace the gentleman through his laborious discussion on this point, to expose the error of so extraordinary a conclusion. What, that, an advantage to this country, which we have struggled so much to avoid! That, a relaxation on the part of England, which she has so obstinately refused to yield! Flushed with his supposed victory on this subject, the gentleman undertook what might be considered even a more difficult task, to remove the Orders in Council as a cause of war. Mr. C. said he despaired of replying to such arguments. But it is objected that the report of the Committee of Foreign Relations has stated the orders of 1807 as a cause of war, though repealed by those of 1809. It is a sufficient justification of the report that it has stated the facts on this as well as all other points, precisely as they existed; and well might the report enumerate the orders of 1807 as a cause of war, when those of 1809 openly avow the principles of the former, and only modify their operation to the then existing circumstances. But, says another gentleman from New York, (Mr. Bleecker) we were inveigled into the war by the perfidy of France.[3] She did not fairly repeal her decrees. Be it so; and what then? Were we bound to submit to England, because France refused to do us justice? Had we no power of election between the ruffians? Where will the absurdity of such arguments end? The right to select was perfect in us; and, without reference to the conduct of France, the selection might and ought to fall on England. If, sir, the origin of the war furnish no sufficient justification for opposition to it, in vain will our opponents fly for refuge to its continuation. The Orders in Council, say they, are now no more, and why should the war be persisted in after its cause is removed? Mr. C. said his reply to this question was, that it was continued from no project of ambition, or desire of conquest; but from a cause far more sacred, the liberty of our sailors and their redemption from slavery. Yet the war is opposed, even attempted to be defeated, by the friends, connections and neighbors of these

3. Harmanus Bleecker; see *AC* 12-2, p. 621.

brave defenders of our national rights and honor. It is even asked, why should we feel so lively an interest in their fate? In vain are such arguments urged. The country will not forget its duty, the first of political duties, that of protection. Our opponents may find no motive in connection or neighborhood, but the country will in its obligation. The *friends of commerce* may evince their attachment to its profits and luxuries only; but the government will not, on that account, cease to respect the liberty of the citizen, and the enlarged interest of commerce, by protecting from English slavery the sailors, by whose toil and peril it is extended to every sea. Provided they have commerce and profit, it seems the injury and insult go for nothing with the opposition. Such a commerce may indeed bloat the country, but it will not contribute to its real strength. It subtracts more from the spirit, than it adds to the wealth of the community.

But, say our opponents, as they were opposed to the war they are not bound to support it; and so far has this opposition been carried, that we have been accused almost of violating the right of conscience in denying the right set up by gentlemen. The right to oppose the efforts of our country, while in war, ought to be established beyond the possibility of doubt, before it can be justly adopted as the basis of conduct. How conscience can be claimed in this case cannot be very easily imagined. We oppose not by laws or penalties; we only assert that the opposition experienced cannot be dictated by love of country; and is inconsistent with the duty which every citizen is under to promote the prosperity of the republic. Its necessary tendency is to prostrate the country at the feet of the enemy, and to elevate a party on the ruins of the public. Till our opponents can prove that they have a right which is paramount to the public interest, we must persist in denying the right to thwart the success of the war. War has been declared by a law of the land; and what would be thought of similar attempts to defeat any other law however inconsiderable its object? Who would dare to avow an intention to defeat its operation? Can that then be true in relation to war which would be reprobated in every other case? Can that be true which, when the whole physical force of the country is needed, withdraws half of that force? Can that be true which gives the greatest violence to party animosity? What would have been thought of such conduct in the war of the Revolution? Many good citizens friendly to the liberty of our country were opposed to the declaration at the time; could they have been justified in such opposition as we now experience? To terminate the war through discord and weakness is a hazardous experiment. But in the most unjust and inexpedient war it can scarcely be possible, that disunion and defeats can have a salutary operation. In the numerous examples which history furnishes, let an instance be pointed out, in any war, where the public interest has been promoted by divisions, or injured by concord. Hundreds of instances may be cited of the reverse. Why then, will gentlemen persist in that course where danger is almost unavoidable, and shun that where safety is almost certain?

But, sir, we are told that peace is in our power without a farther promotion of the war. Appeal not, say our opponents, to the fear, but to the generosity of our enemy. England yields nothing to her fears; stop, therefore, your preparation, and throw yourself on her mercy, and peace will be the result. We might indeed have pardon, but not peace on such terms. Those who think the war a sacrilege or a crime, might consistently adopt such a course; but we, who know it to be for the maintenance of the just rights of the community, never can. We are farther told that impressment of seamen was not considered a sufficient cause of war; and are asked why should it be continued on that account? Mr. C. observed that he individually did not feel the force of the argument; for it had been his opinion, that the nation was bound to resist so deep an injury even at the hazard of war; but, admitting its full force, the difference is striking between the commencement and the continuance of hostilities. War ought to be continued until its rational object, a permanent and secure peace, could be obtained. Even the friends of England ought not to desire the termination of the war, without a satisfactory adjustment of the subject of impressment.

It would leave the root that must necessarily shoot up in future animosity and hostilities. America can never quietly submit to the deepest of injury. Necessity might compel her to yield for a moment; but it would be to watch the growth of national strength, and to seize the first favorable opportunity to seek redress. The worst enemy to the peace of the two countries could not desire a more effectual means to propagate eternal enmity.

But it is said, that we ought to offer to England suitable regulations on this subject, to secure to her the use of her own seamen; and because we have not, we are the aggressors. He denied that we were bound to tender any regulations, or that we had not. England was the party injuring. She ought to confine her seamen to her own service; or, if that was impracticable, propose such arrangements that she might exercise her right without injury to us. This is the rule that governs all analogous cases in private life. But we have made our offer; it is, that the ship should protect the sailor. It is the most simple and only safe rule; but to secure so desirable a point, the most liberal and effectual provisions ought and have been proposed to be made on our part, to guard the British government against the evil they apprehended, the loss of her seamen.[4] The whole doctrine of protection, heretofore relied on, and still recommended by the gentleman from Connecticut, (Mr. Pitkin) is false and derogatory to our honor; and under no possible modification can effect the desirable objects of affording safety to our sailors, and securing the future harmony of the two countries.[5] Nor can it be doubted, if governed by justice, she will yield to the offer of our government, particularly if what the gentleman from New York (Mr. Bleecker) says be true, that there are 10,000 of her seamen in our service. She would be greatly the gainer by the arrangement. Experience, it is to be feared, however, will teach that gentleman that the evil lies much deeper. The use of her seamen is a mere pretence. The blow is aimed at our commercial greatness. It is this which has animated and directed all of her injurious councils towards this country. England is at the same time a trading and fighting nation; two occupations naturally at variance, and most difficult to be united. War limits the number and extent of the markets of a belligerent, makes a variety of regulations necessary; and produces heavy taxes, which are inimical to

4. *I.e.*, the condition in the armistice offer (No. 73 NOTE) that there be a stop to impressment from American ships, each power, however, excluding the other's seamen from its ships.

5. Timothy Pitkin had questioned if there was an obligation to protect a naturalized citizen against the claims of his former government when he went outside American territory (*AC* 12-2, p. 525).

the prosperity of manufactories and consequently commerce. These causes combined give to trade new channels which direct it naturally to neutral nations. To counteract this tendency, England, under various but flimsy pretences, has endeavored to support her commercial superiority by monopoly. It has been our fortune to resist with no inconsiderable success this spirit of monopoly. Her principal object in contending for the right of impressment, is to have in a great measure the monoply of the sailors of the world.[6] A fixed resistance will compel her to yield this point, as she has already done her Orders in Council. Success will amply reward our exertions. Our future commerce will feel its invigorating effects. But, say gentlemen, England will never yield this point, and every effort on our part to secure it is hopeless. To confirm this prediction and secure our reverence the prophecies of the last session are relied on. Mr. C. felt no disposition to disparage our opponents' talents in that line; but he very much doubted whether the whole chapter of woes had been fulfilled. He would, for instance, ask whether so much as related to sacked towns, bombarded cities, ruined commerce, and revolting blacks had been realized?

He was sorry to find a gentleman from Virginia (Mr. Sheffey) not yet cured of his fears in relation to this last prediction.[7] He would be glad to know what was his intention—his assertions give equal notice to the House, the enemy and the country. If danger indeed existed, he has acted with such imprudence, as ought to subject him to the censure of any reflecting man; but he would acquit the gentleman, as he did not apprehend any danger. He would not admit an increased danger from a state of war, a state in which the public force and vigilance are of necessity the greatest. But to return to the point; our cause is not so hopeless as represented by our opponents; but on the contrary, if we only persevere we have every reason, under present circumstances to anticipate ultimate success. The enemy is engaged in a contest in Europe, which requires his whole power. We have already compelled him to yield a point, which but the last year it was prophesied that he never would. The Orders in Council are now no more; that sys-

6. For impressment as a part of the British plan for trade monopoly, see No. 95 NOTE.
7. Daniel Sheffey; see *AC*12-2, p. 701.

tem by which it was vainly attempted to monopolize our trade and
to recolonize the American nation. But if England will not yield,
we can perish as well as she. Our republican virtue is as obstinate
as her imperial pride, and our duty to our citizens as unyielding
as her prerogative over her subjects. An attempt has been made to
shake our fortitude, by a cry of French alliance. It has been boldly
said, that we are already united with that country. We united with
France? We have the same cause? No; her object is dominion, and
her impulse ambition. Ours is the protection of the liberty of our
sailors. But say our opponents, we are contending against the same
country. What then? Must we submit to be outlawed by England,
in order that she may not be by France? Is the independence of
England dearer to us than our own? Must we enter the European
struggle not as an equal, consulting our peculiar interest, but be
dragged into it as the low dependent, the slave of England?

The gentleman from Virginia (Mr. Randolph) has told us that
we are contending against religion in the person of England—that
she is, in a word, the patroness of Christianity.[8] Unhappy country!
Doomed to submission to preserve the purity of religion! Doomed
to slavery that England may be independent! Because Bonaparte
is not a Protestant you must surrender your rights! Because he is
a despot you dare not resist! What does the gentleman intend? Is
it his wish, by thus dragging into the heat of political debate the
sacred cause of religion, to promote its interest or that of a faction? If the former, let him point out an instance in antient or
modern times when the junction of religion and politics has not
been fatal to the interest of both. It is this unnatural union that
has engendered the foulest progeny of human woes. History is full
of its disaster, and the gentleman is too familiar with its pages to
require a particular recital. If the gentleman's intention is not to
advance the cause of religion, but to promote the views of a party,
words cannot truly describe its real character. It is a trick that has
been, and still continues to be practised on the too easy credulity
of our nature. Its frequency however does not change its nature;
it may indeed furnish some apology, that those who practise it are
led into it without a due reflection on its character; but when understood, what can be more shocking, than that the most sacred of

8. P. 804.

all things, the medium of divine communion, our consolation as mortals, would be prostrated to the gratification of some of the worst feelings of the human heart?

Such then is the cause of the war and its continuation; and such the nature of the opposition experienced, and its justification. It remains to be seen whether the intended effect will be produced. Whether animosity and discord will be fomented, and the zeal and union of the people to maintain the rights and indispensible duties of the community will abate; or, describing it under another aspect, whether it is the destiny of our country to sink under that of our enemy or not. Mr. C. said he was not without his fears and his hopes.

On the one hand our opponents had manifestly the advantage. The love of present ease and enjoyment, the love of gain, and party zeal, were on their side. These constitute part of the weakness of our nature. We naturally lead that way without the arts of persuasion. Far more difficult is the task of the majority. It is theirs to support the distant but lasting interest of our country; it is theirs to elevate the minds of the people, and to call up all of those qualities by which present sacrifices are made to secure a future good. On the other hand, our cause is not without its hope. The interest of the people and that of the leaders of a party are, as observed by a gentleman from New York, (Mr. Stow) often at variance.[9] The people are always ready, unless led astray by ignorance or delusion, to participate in the success of the country, or to sympathise in its adversity. Very different are the feelings of the leaders; on every great measure they stand pledged against its success, and almost invariably consider that their political consequence depends on its defeat. The heat of debate, the spirit of settled opposition, and the confident prediction of disaster, are among the causes of this opposition between the interest of a party and their country; and in no instance under our own government have they existed in a greater degree than in relation to the present war. The evil is deeply rooted in the constitution of all free governments, and is the principal cause of their weakness and destruction. It has but one remedy, the virtue and intelligence of the people—it behooves them as they

9. Silas Stow—see p. 812.

value the blessings of their freedom, not to permit themselves to be drawn into the vortex of party rage. For if by such opposition the firmest government should prove incompetent to maintain the rights of the nation against foreign aggression, they will find realized the truth of the assertion that government is protection, and that it cannot exist where it fails of this great and primary object. The authors of the weakness are commonly the first to take the advantage of it, and to turn it to the destruction of liberty.

75 NOTE: In his Nov. 4 message Madison presented, in general terms, the military needs of the country (*AC*12-2, p. 14-5), but it was Monroe who outlined the plan of campaign. As Acting Secretary of War, the latter wrote, Dec. 23, 1812, to the Chairman of the Military Committee, David R. Williams, asking for higher bounties to fill out the existing regiments, and for an additional force of 20,000 twelve-months men, the officers to be appointed by the President (*ASP, Mil. Aff.*, I, 608-10).

On Feb. 13 there were nearly 19,000 men in the army (Adams, *History of U.S.*, VII, 148-9), which was practically the number for which the administration asked in November 1811. Monroe was thus revising the plan of the preceding year (see No. 46 NOTE), accepting the figure for regular troops as fixed by the January 1812 act, and calling for 20,000 twelve-months men instead of the 50,000 authorized in the volunteer bill of Feb. 6, 1812. "If a strong army is led to the field early in the spring," he declared in his letter, the British power on the continent would be destroyed and that government would realize the impossibility of reconquest.

The opposition at once attacked the proposal, asked for passage of the seamen's bill instead (No. 73 NOTE), and insisted there had been no repeal of the Berlin and Milan decrees to justify American discrimination against Great Britain (see, for instances of these charges, *AC*12-2, p. 488-9, 503, 531-2, 556, 700-1, 789). These tactics forced the majority to support the bill as an administration measure—although William Lowndes wrote at the time that not half a dozen men approved it (Ravenel, *William Lowndes*, p. 119). It was Langdon Cheves who, in the indisposition of Williams, closed the debate for his party (*AC*12-2, p. 827-43) with a powerful but studiedly moderate speech, and the bill passed, 77 to 42, being finally enacted on Jan. 29 (p. 1322-5). One section of it repealed the 1812 volunteer act. See No. 90 NOTE for extension of this enlistment.

In this carefully organized speech Calhoun made only incidental reference to the bill itself. After a preliminary appeal for recognition of the partial success already achieved by the United States, he pointed to the leaders of the opposition as the real threat to the country. He had no fear of their party as long as it was in the minority, but anticipated ruin in event of its success. For protection against this danger he could only rely upon "the virtue and intelligence of the people." Compare No. 90 NOTE, and No. 95 NOTE.

He stoutly maintained the righteousness of the American cause, effectively held up to ridicule the weak points in the opposition arguments, and frankly appraised the situation with his statement that "he was not without his fears and his hopes." See No. 74 for his letter in regard to this bill and his speech, and compare No. 90 NOTE.   SOURCE: *NI*, Mar. 20, 1813; *AC*12-2, p. 813-21.

76. To DR. JAMES MACBRIDE, Charleston, S.C.

Washington 2d. Feb 1813

Dr Macbride, You will excuse me for a very short reply to your last, when I inform you, that I expect to have the pleasure of seeing you in a few weeks. I shall be at Bonneau's ferry on the 18th of march; and I am satisfied my friend will not let many days elaps before he will gratify me with his presence. We will look for you and Mrs. Macbride the first pleasant day after the 18th.

In the mean time, I can only observe that as badly as our affairs have been managed in some respects, yet our situation is by no means so dispondent, as you have pictured it. There is an ultimate vigour in a free govt. The two fighting secretaries have been removed, which promises som[e]thing. Jones who has succeeded Hamilton is said to be very capable. Armstrong has talents and it is said skill. I regret that you or any of my friends should give the least ear to so vile and lying a paper as the F. Republican.[1] What he attributes to me in debate is an absolute falshood. An intimation which was given of an intended report of the C. of F. relation, has been turned into what you have seen. The report has since been made; and will be acted on tomorrow. The measures which it recommends are right in themselves and such as will have to be adopted whenever peace is made. But, for reasons which I will asign hereafter I feel no disposition to tak[e] an active part in it.

1. See No. 73, n. 1.

[. . .] will be contested much in [the] house. My respects to Mrs. [Macbride] and Mr. G and family.

I am with estee[m] your's &c

J. C. CALHOUN

76 NOTE: Compare Nos. 72 and 74.   SOURCE: *LC,* James Macbride Papers.

77. COMMENT ON THE BILL TO ENFORCE NON-IMPORTATION

February 23, 1813

Mr. Calhoun replied to Mr. Gold, principally to the allegation that this was not a proper time to enforce the non-importation act. He expressed his astonishment at this sentiment coming from a gentleman who, with his political friends, had the other day voted against a partial suspension of that law. For his part, if the law was to remain in force, Mr. C. thought it the duty of every man to aid in enforcing it.

[The brief remarks of five members intervene at this point.]

Mr. Calhoun again spoke in favor of the bill as going rigidly to enforce the non-importation law; because although in favor of a repeal of it, having been unable to obtain that, he was decidedly in favor of a rigorous enforcement, which was necessary to enable it to produce any pressure on the enemy.

77 NOTE: On Feb. 15 Cheves from the Ways and Means Committee introduced a bill to raise revenue by high duties and suspension of non-importation (*AC*12-2, p. 1062-5; cf. No. 69). But on Feb. 20 (p. 1099-1100) the suspending section was stricken out of the bill—Calhoun and Cheves voting against the change, Thomas R. Gold of New York voting for it—and the bill became in effect, a measure to enforce non-importation more strictly. Thereafter (see p. 1109) Calhoun supported the bill, but Gold, on the third reading, spoke against it, later (p. 1112) explaining that his original vote against suspension was because the bill was a revenue measure and "not a peace offering to commerce."   SOURCE: *NI,* Feb. 25, 1813; *AC*12-2, p. 1111.

78. Bill Limiting Exportation in Foreign Vessels

February 26, 1813

[*Mr. Calhoun, from the Committee on Foreign Relations, reported:*]

A Bill prohibiting the exportation of certain articles therein specified in foreign ships or vessels.

Be it enacted . . . That no foreign ship or vessel shall be permitted to clear out or depart from any port or place within the United States or the territories thereof having on board, any staves,[1] lumber, horses, mules, asses, neat cattle, sheep, hogs, and every species of live stock and live provisions and also every other kind of provisions whatever (sea stores only excepted)

Sect 2 . . . That If any foreign ship or vessel, shall during the continuance of this act, take on board any of the articles above enumerated, other than the provisions & sea stores necessary for the voyage, such ship or vessel and the cargo on board shall be wholly forfeited and may be seized and condemned in any court of the United States having competent Jurisdiction, and every person concerned in such unlawful shipment shall forfeit and pay a sum not exceeding　　　　dollars, nor less than　　　　dollars for every such offence.

Sect. 3. [*Penalties to be recovered as provided for by duty act of Mar. 2, 1799 and mitigated by acts of Mar. 3, 1797 and Feb. 11, 1800.*]

Sect. 4. [*The act to be effective till July 4th next.*]

78 NOTE: On the 24th President Madison sent a message (AC12-2, p. 1116-9) to Congress enclosing copies of a proclamation of the Lieutenant-Governor of Bermuda publishing an order of the British government permitting licenses for the importation into the West Indies from the United States of certain goods (listed in section 1 of the above bill) and of a paper purporting to be a circular order in general restricting licenses for the American trade to the Eastern States. The message and papers were referred to the

1. The list, from "staves" (mistakenly rendered "stores" in *Annals*) to "provisions whatsoever" is copied from the Bermuda proclamation.

Foreign Relations Committee. The House on the same day was debating a bill, forbidding American vessels to trade under a foreign license (p. 1115). On the 26th Calhoun secured the discharge of his committee from consideration of Madison's recommendation in regard to licenses (p. 1126), presumably deferring in favor of the license bill; the latter eventually passed the House (p. 1150), but was lost in the Senate (p. 121).

The same day that he moved the discharge of his committee from the question of licenses Calhoun introduced the above bill for prohibiting exports (p. 1127), and on the 27th (p. 1146) and Mar. 2 (p. 1153, 1157) defended it in remarks for which no record appears except references in the speech of an opponent, Thomas P. Grosvenor of New York (p. 1157-63), who reported Calhoun as declaring the bill was not intended as part of a system, but " 'To avenge insult'—'to retaliate on the enemy his attempts to destroy us'—'to carry to his own lips his own poisoned chalice.' " He apparently intended to quote Calhoun as speaking of the " 'degrading insults,' those 'vile invitations to treason,' " to New England, and of the " 'steady purpose in the enemy, to kindle the flames of civil war, and to dismember their happy Union.' " Grosvenor conceded to Calhoun that the British attempt "is as weak as it is wicked" but with restrained bitterness denounced the measure that would resent the insult by punishing the East with renewal of commercial restrictions. He thanked Calhoun for the confidence he expressed in the Northern States, but thought they might reply "somewhat in this manner: 'Hands off, Mr. Calhoun, if it please you; we do not dislike your compliments; indeed, we are pleased with the notes of this new tune from the South. We will do anything in reason to oblige you; but really, sir, to be complimented out of our commerce; to be flattered into poverty; to be cowed into service, is a little more than the rules of civility demand.' "

This bill likewise was lost in the Senate (p. 121). Source: MS Bill, Feb. 26, 1813, *NA*, RG233, 12A-B1; *NI*, Feb. 27, 1813; *AC*12-2, p. 1127.

79. The Retaliation Bill

Feb. 26, 1813

The Committee of Foreign Relations to whom was re-committed the Bill from the Senate entitled "An Act vesting in the President of the United States the power of retaliation in the cases therein specified,"

Report the same [1] [*as amended*]—

Be it declared and enacted . . . That, in all and every case, wherein during the present war, between the United States of America and the United Kingdom of Great Britain and Ireland, any violations of the laws and usages of War, among civilized nations, shall be done and perpetrated by those acting under authority of the British Government, on any of the citizens or persons in the land or naval service of the United States, the President of the United States is hereby authorised and required to cause full and ample retaliation to be made, according to the laws and usages of War among civilized nations, for all and every such violation as aforesaid.

Sec. 2. And be it further enacted, that in all cases where any outrage or act of cruelty and barbarity shall be practiced by any Indian or Indians in alliance with the British Government or in connexion with those acting under the authority of the said Government, on citizens of the United States or those under its protection, the President of the United States is hereby authorised and required, to cause full and ample retaliation to be done and executed on such British subjects, soldiers, seamen or marines or Indians in alliance or connexion with Great Britain, being Prisoners of War, as if the same had been done under the authority of the British Government.

Amend the title so as to read "An Act vesting in the President of the United States the power of retaliation."

79 NOTE: In his Nov. 4 message Madison had denounced British use of Indians (*AC*12-2, p. 11-2). He made no request for legislation on the subject, but his contention that the British were fully answerable "since the savages are employed with a knowledge, and even with menaces, that their fury could not be controlled" was to be construed as suggesting it. On Nov. 13, on the motion of Robert Wright, of Maryland, a committee was appointed, with Wright as chairman, to bring in a bill vesting the power of retaliation in the President (p. 149). On the 17th Wright presented such a bill which "empowered and required" the President to retaliate in case of

1. The report continues "with the following amendments—Strike out the whole of the Bill after the word 'that' in the second line, and insert the following—'in all and every case,'" etc. The intervening words have been inserted from the Senate bill.

American prisoners or impressed citizens suffering cruel treatment at the hands of British soldiers or Indians (p. 151), but the bill was rejected on the 19th by a vote of 61 to 51 (p. 154-5). Many Republicans voted against it, so wrote John A. Harper the next day (William Plumer Papers, *LC*), considering that the President already had that power. Calhoun voted with the majority.

On Feb. 2 there was introduced in the Senate a bill providing for and requiring retaliation by the President for any violation of the laws of war, but stipulating that action in every case be "to the satisfaction of a court martial" (*AC*12-2, p. 71). It had no mention of Indians. On the 18th it was sent to the House (p. 89-90) and referred to the Committee on Foreign Relations. The committee wrote a virtually new bill, the substance of which was as follows (deleted portions of the Senate bill are in brackets, followed by the committee's substitutions in italics; other insertions by the committee are also in italics): "That if any [citizen of the United States] *person or persons* in the military service of the United States, or of any individual state, . . . who has been, or shall be taken prisoner by the enemy, has been or shall be subjected to capital or other punishment . . . on the pretence of his having been born within the British dominions, or on any pretence whatever not warranted by the laws and usages of war among civilized nations, it shall be lawful for the President . . . and he is hereby *declared to be* empowered and required, in every such case, to cause retaliation, *to be made according to the laws and usages of War among civilized nations.*" The Senate clause requiring court-martial was also deleted by the committee (MS Senate Bill and MS Report of Amendments Feb. 23, 1813, *NA*, RG233, 12A-B1).

Calhoun reported the new bill on the 23rd, but on the 25th, on his motion and without debate, it was recommitted and reported again by him on the 26th in the above form (*AC*12-2, p. 1110, 1123, 1128). A new section, for retaliation for Indian outrages, was the essential difference from the bill of the 23rd and from the Senate bill. It was doubtless the result of accounts of the Raisin River massacre—see *NI*, Feb. 25—which occurred on Jan. 22 (Adams, *History of U.S.*, VII, 95-8). In the debate in the Committee of the Whole on the 27th there were objections to the enactment of a retaliation bill "arising from the opinion that such a power already existed . . . and was inseparable from sovereignty" (*AC*12-2, p. 1144), and Calhoun was asked if this bill was a declaration of law now existing or a grant to the President of a new power. He replied "that for himself he did not think the law necessary—but that there was a necessity for legislating on the subject, because of the difference of construction which gentlemen put upon the constitutional power of the executive." (*Federal Republican*, Mar. 1, 1813.) Note that the words "and required," which appear in both versions of the House bill and in that of the Senate, were stricken from it—apparently at the same time (*House Journal*, Feb. 27, 1813, p. 718-9). With additional slight verbal changes the bill was ratified, Mar. 3 (*AC*12-2, p. 1362-3; Peters, *Statutes of U.S.*, II, 829-30).

The retaliation problem was a subject of extended discussion in Madison's Dec. 7, 1813 message (*AC*13-2, p. 540-2), especially in regard to British emigrants. See also p. 785, 786, 802-3, 813. SOURCE: MS Report of Amendments, Feb. 26, 1813, and the bill as read in the Senate Feb. 2, *NA*, RG233, 12A-B1; the Senate bill as it came to the House is also in *NI*, Feb. 4, 1813, and *AC*12-2, p. 71.

80. REMARKS ON THE SEATING OF GEORGE RICHARDS, STENOGRAPHER

May 31, 1813

Mr. Calhoun denied the position that there was room sufficient, and he did not see how the Speaker could act otherwise. He thought it would be highly improper to assign him a seat on the *floor;* this would be making a priviledged stenographer, and giving him advantages which none of the others possessed. He would have an opportunity of overhearing the private conversation of members, as he would have to be placed in a situation where gentlemen resorted to express their opinions of pending measures, and then he would be able to penetrate all their measures. He thought the gallery a proper place; the debates could be as well heard in the gallery as any where, and writing be done with equal velocity. The particular qualities of ability, and impartiality had been much dwelt upon— he denied both. The debates in that paper had been confined to one side, and it was well known the gentleman did not write short hand, but was merely a notetaker, &c. He did not make use of this as an argument against the admission of Mr. Richards, but as his friends had grounded his claim upon superior talents and impartiality, he could not do less than bring the true state of the affair before the House.

80 NOTE: Thomas P. Grosvenor, of New York, had presented the petition of George Richards, reporter for the *Federal Republican,* who stated that he had been admitted during the last session, but was now excluded by the Speaker (*AC*13-1, p. 112). The im-

mediate question was on his motion to admit Richards to the floor of the House. Clay explained (p. 119) that "recent alterations" had provided for but four stenographers, and that he had assigned them in order of seniority. William Gaston, Federalist, of North Carolina, before Calhoun is recorded as speaking (p. 120), remarked that the latter had made an objection "though it had not been pressed," that Richards was not a stenographer. The heated controversy centered on Richards' partisanship, the disproportionate number of Republican reporters, and the principle of free speech. Richards' petition was rejected (p. 127), but additional provision for reporters was made later (p. 134, 153).

See Calhoun's remark in No. 76 on the *Federal Republican*. On June 1 he is recorded as speaking "with some warmth" against Richards' petition and "his high pretensions . . . . as if he had a right to be admitted!" (*AC*13-1, p. 123). Grosvenor followed with the declaration that Calhoun's charges were based on "notions which the gentleman has conjured up in his own fancy." He insisted that it was a plain matter of the right of petition (p. 125-7).

The *Intelligencer* (June 1, 1813) report of debates of May 31 noted the Richards' controversy in outline only, but on the 8th gave a column to its explanation of the case. Calhoun was mentioned in neither. The *Annals* copy of his speech was copied—with a few changes in capitalization and punctuation and one of spelling—from the *Republican*.   Source: *Federal Republican*, June 4, 1813; *AC*13-1, p. 121.

81. Debate on Webster's Resolutions on the French Decrees

June 16, 1813

Mr. Calhoun said he did not rise to oppose the passage of this resolution on account of its object; but he objected to the novelty of the form of the resolution. The resolution went further than merely asking for information; it also asks, when and by whom the information in question was received. Such form and particularity was unprecedented in such cases. He rose to ask the precise object of the gentleman in giving this form to his motion. What use was intended to be made of the information called for?

[*John Rhea moved indefinite postponement on the ground that the "existence of the repealing decree was not questioned" and that "no object could be answered" by the inquiry.*[1]]

1. *AC*13-1, p. 169.

Mr. Calhoun said he hoped the gentleman from Tennessee would not press this motion. If we advert to the transactions which have taken place since the declaration of war, we shall find that on many occasions this conversation has been made a handle of, and that a certain degree of suspicion has been attempted to be attached to the Chief Executive officer on this head.[2] A resolution had been adopted at the end of the last session, which did not include the whole object of the present resolution; and Mr. C. for his part had no indisposition to afford to gentlemen an opportunity of obtaining all the information they could wish, if asked for in a proper manner. He hoped, therefore, the gentleman would withdraw his motion.

[*Rhea thereupon withdrew his motion and Calhoun declared that the question as to the source of information suggested there might have been another channel of information; he denied there was any ground for such suspicion, and moved to strike from the first resolution the words " 'by whom and in what manner.' " Samuel McKee of Kentucky then moved instead a general motion requesting information to which Daniel Sheffey of Virginia replied; Sheffey argued that Bassano's statement was false or that Madison had suppressed a decree that could have been used to bring about repeal of the Orders in Council and thus have prevented the war. Jonathan Fisk of New York protested Sheffey's argument that the decree repeal could have brought about repeal of the Orders in Council. McKee then withdrew his motion.[3]*]

Mr. Calhoun said he had hoped that there would have been no division of opinion on this subject, that there would have been no objection to such a modification of this resolution as had been proposed by him. He would state the circumstances which he thought ought to govern gentlemen in paying some little deference to the feelings and wishes of those on this side of the House. What were the facts on which the resolutions were grounded? A few days

2. Both Webster and Thomas P. Grosvenor referred to this statement of Calhoun's as though he admitted the success of the attempt to attach suspicion to the administration—which Calhoun denied. Thus they intimated that this was giving the President an opportunity to clear himself (p. 170). Actually it was tacitly accepted by Federalist and Republican alike—although it served no one's purpose to make any point of it—that the Apr. 28, 1811, date of the repealing decree was fictitious.

3. P. 169-74; at the close of debate Calhoun withdrew his motion (p. 302).

before the end of the last session of Congress, on motion of a gentleman from Maryland, a resolution was adopted calling on the President for certain information relative to our relations with France. The President, on the next day but one, that is, on the last day of the session, made a communication, which, among other things, stated a conversation which had taken place between Mr. Barlow, our late minister to France, and the Duke of Bassano, relative to the repeal of the French decrees. Mr. Barlow expressed his surprise, when the decree of 28th April, 1811, was produced, that it had been so long concealed. The Duke of Bassano replied, that it had been communicated to our minister in France and the French minister in this country, at the time it was issued. It is fair to acknowledge that that order must have been antedated, or concealed by the French government, or communicated to the Executive, and by them concealed. Whatever form of enquiry gentlemen might think proper to adopt, by which to prove that the decree was antedated or concealed, Mr. C. was willing should be adopted. The House ought not, however, in the present stage of this business, to presume that the repealing decree had been communicated to the Executive and by him concealed. He would not attribute such motives to the gentleman from New Hampshire—he was too honorable to be actuated by them. No man who looks into his own heart and finds purity there, will be liable to misrepresent the motives of others. The resolution, as hastily read, would nevertheless convey the idea to which he had just alluded. He wished the gentleman from New Hampshire then would consent to expunge these words; and he asked it the more confidently, as the gentleman himself had shewn that those words were mere surplusage, because the object which he professed to have in view was embraced in two distinct resolutions which follow the first. If, when the President should make a reply to the resolutions thus amended, there should be any circumstance leading to a suspicion of concealment, it would be competent to any gentleman to move an additional explanatory resolution; and Mr. C. distinctly pledged himself for one, should any ambiguity appear in the reply, that he would join gentlemen in voting for further inquiry. But he had the firmest belief that nothing was withheld that was necessary to be known, and that all would be satisfactorily cleared up.

Before he sat down, he would advert to one thing. The gentleman from New Hampshire, in moving these resolves, said (according to the report of his speech in the National Intelligencer) to this
effect: that the question at issue between the governments of
America and Great Britain, on which the declaration of war turned,
was, whether the French decrees were or were not repealed. And
the gentleman from Virginia had to-day spoken to the same effect.[4]
Mr. C. said he would not, on the present occasion, go to the trouble
of dilating at large on that point; but he would observe that the
gentleman had presumed to do for us in this case what would be
considered very extraordinary to have been done in a suit at law.
He, the defendant in the action, had drawn the declaration for the
plaintiff, and pointed out the issue. This was as unfair in a political
as it would be in a legal contest. Mr. C. said he had always distinctly contended for the right to consider the injuries done to us
by each belligerent on their own ground. This had been his course,
because a different one would have been as unworthy a nation, as
it would have been unworthy of an individual. What! said he, shall
we make the right of obtaining redress from England dependent
on the justice of France? He, for his part, would take a higher, a
different ground. He saw what had led the gentleman into error—
he had mistaken the means of redress for the injury to be redressed.
This country had, indeed, in its great efforts to preserve peace and
neutrality, endeavored to get one of the belligerents to repeal its
offensive edicts, in order to induce the other to do the same. Our
government (said Mr. C.) did descend one step in passing the
act of 1810,[5] under which France did (or, as the gentlemen over
the way would say, pretended to) repeal her decrees of Berlin and
Milan. Britain did refuse to proceed *pari passu* with France in this
repeal. I will now place this question at rest for ever; this fact shall
hereafter for ever be without contradiction. England did say to
this country, even if France did repeal her decrees in relation to
us she would not repeal her Orders in Council. This she did say
by the solemn declaration of the Prince Regent, dated 21st April

4. For this remark of Webster's, see p. 150; for Sheffey's, p. 172-3.
5. The non-intercourse act of May 1, 1810.

1812.[6] No gentlemen dare hereafter reiterate the statement that if France had bona fide repealed her decrees, as regards America, England would have followed her example. Most indubitably gentlemen who so highly appreciate British faith will not discredit the evidence I produce. By some unaccountable means they have heretofore contrived to throw a cloud over it, to keep it out of sight. A further evidence in proof of my assertion is, that when there was no longer a shade of doubt hanging over the repeal of the French decrees—that is to say, for thirty-five days after the official communication to the British government of the French decree bearing date the 28th April, 1811, no repeal of the Orders in Council took place.[7] What process was going on in Britain in that interval? During these days a most laborious enquiry was in progress in the House of Commons, into the effects, beneficial or otherwise, produced on the commercial interest of Britain by her Orders in Council of 1807 and 1809; during all which time the British Ministry not only approbated and supported them, but took higher ground in relation to them than they had ever done before. They entirely *gave up* the pretended retaliatory character of the Orders in Council, they were bound to give it up. Men of common sense could no longer have defended them on that ground. The question was, in terms, whether or not our commerce, that is neutral commerce, should be made subservient to British monopoly. And how, finally, were the Orders in Council repealed? After it had been made clear as the light of the sun in Heaven, that they were injurious to British commerce.[8] Will the gentleman from Virginia now say that England would have repealed her Orders in Council, as to us, if she had been convinced that France had in the same manner revoked or modified her decrees? The gentleman dare not say it. No, sir, he dare not, because I shall prove him guilty of falsity if he does. His known integrity and candor are too great to permit him to say it. He dare not say, then, that if the French de-

6. This "declaration" made as the condition for repeal of the Orders in Council that the French decrees "be absolutely and unconditionally repealed" (*ASP, For. Rel.*, III, 430).

7. That is, from May 20 to June 23, 1812—*ibid.*, p. 433.

8. See the emphatic statements of Jonathan Russell, the American chargé at London—*ibid.*, p. 615.

cree of repeal had been known, the British orders would have been repealed, and the war thus prevented.

[*At this point Richard Stockton of New Jersey demanded of the Speaker to know if "personal threats were admissible on the floor" but Clay rejected that interpretation.*]

Mr. Calhoun continued. He wished it to be distinctly understood, that he had no personal meaning in what he said. He merely had said that the gentleman dare not, as a man of veracity, assert a fact otherwise than that fact is. He was sorry the gentleman from New Jersey, much more that the gentleman from Virginia himself should misunderstand him. I will be more particular, said Mr. C. I assert that two and two make four; and I say no gentleman dare to contradict it. I say so on conviction of the certainty of the fact. Sir, although warm in my country's cause, nothing shall ever induce me unnecessarily to wound the feelings of any gentleman in this House, more especially of the gentleman from Virginia, with whom I have never been so unfortunate as to come in collision. I may be warm, sir; I have a right to be so. I was one of the advocates of the present war. I considered the best interests and rights of the nation compromitted in the question, and I was bound to vote for it. I am therefore mortified to see it placed on ground on which it ought not to stand. I am mortified to hear the misstatements which prevail on this subject. The cause of my country is that in whose behalf I am now warm, and ever hope to be so. It is a cause on the truth and justice of which I would stake my all— though on its ultimate success I cannot, for that is yet in the womb of time.

I have condescended, sir, to view this question for a moment on the ground of the relative conduct of France and Great Britain. Not that I believe the government ought to descend, in the pursuit of a magnanimous policy, to a scholastic view, which nation has done us the first or the greatest injury. Such considerations would never enter into the view of a statesman. The question is, how we can best redress the wrongs of the country. I have ever regretted that the injuries of the belligerents should for a moment have been viewed in their retaliatory character, notwithstanding the excellence of the motive—a love of peace, and a desire to maintain it. I would have taken a higher ground, and the government, finding all their pacific efforts were in vain, were compelled at length to appeal to the last resort. An opposite view of this question appears to me ridiculous, if I dare mingle ridicule with a question of such seriousness. Is it not absurd to contend that we ought to suffer ourselves to be beaten to death, whilst engaged in abstract philosophic enquiries who gave us the first blow? In the whole of this contest of restrictions, I shall ever deem the conduct of France to have been improper. I stand here only as the assertor of American rights, the vindicator of the American cause. I will not presume that the President had received the decree in question and concealed it—and the only modification I ask of these resolutions, is to divest them of that imputation which they appear to convey. Thus modified, I shall cheerfully vote for them, to afford to gentlemen in opposition the most liberal opportunity of obtaining all the information they can wish.

81 NOTE: On July 13, 1812, Monroe received from Joel Barlow, the American Minister to France, a copy of a decree, dated Apr. 28, 1811, declaring that the Berlin and Milan decrees were to be considered, so far as concerned American vessels, nonexistent since Nov. 1, 1810. The paper had been sent to Barlow by the French Minister of Foreign Affairs on May 10, 1812 (*ASP, For. Rel.*, III, 603, 617; see Adams, *History of U.S.*, VI, 254-6). The date of the decree was obviously fictitious, but, transmitted to Lord Castlereagh on May 20, 1812, by Jonathan Russell, chargé d'affaires in London, it served as the excuse for the June 23 repeal of the Orders in Council (*ASP, For. Rel.*, III, 432, 615).

The decree put the administration in the position of having for more than a year claimed a repeal that actually did not take place until the embargo of Apr. 4, 1812, announced the intention of the United States to declare war. Evidently anticipating attacks in Congress, Madison in his Nov. 4, 1812 message to Congress, noted "the promulgation of a French decree purporting to be a definitive repeal of the Berlin and Milan decrees. This proceeding, although made the ground of the repeal of the British Orders in Council, is rendered, by the time and manner of it, liable to many objections." (*AC*12-2, p. 14.) On Jan. 18, 1813, the Senate adopted a resolution calling on the President for a copy of this decree "with such information as he may possess, concerning the time and manner of promulgating the same" (p. 54). The Federalists in the House, busy with the army bill (No. 75), did not get to a similar resolution until Mar. 1 (*AC*12-2, p. 1151), but during the debate there were ominous references to it (p. 489, 532, 556, 700-1, 789).

Madison's reply to both houses was a report from Monroe which included a copy of the decree and of the letter of Joel Barlow, of May 12, 1812, in which he repeated a declaration of the French foreign minister, the Duc de Bassano, that the repeal had been communicated at the time to Barlow's predecessor and to the French minister at Washington. Monroe did not indicate when these papers were received (*ASP, For. Rel.*, III, 602-4, 608). It was in the extra session of 1813, which began May 24, that the opposition took advantage of this opportunity to discredit the administration. On June 10 Daniel Webster, beginning, as a representative from New Hampshire, his first term in Congress, in a speech moderate in temper and courteous in form, offered five resolutions (*AC*13-1, p. 149-52), asking whether Russell had ever admitted or denied the correctness of Bassano's statement; whether the French minister to the United States had informed the government of the decree; and "in case the fact be that the first information" of the decree was Bassano's declaration to Barlow, whether an explanation of the concealment of the decree had ever been required of the French government.

It fell to Calhoun, as Chairman of the Foreign Relations Committee, to defend the administration. He began the debate with the effort to hold the proceedings to an inquiry for information, but almost immediately it became evident that the opposition was determined to use the resolutions as an introduction to their argument that Madison had been hoodwinked by, or had connived with Napoleon; that Great Britain had in good faith repealed the Orders in Council as soon as repeal of the decrees had been announced, and that the real cause of the war had been eliminated in the month in which it was declared. Calhoun's main point in reply was his vigorous contention that the repeal of the Orders in Council was due solely to the pressure from English commercial interests.

The debate continued, after Calhoun's speech, with increasing bitterness (p. 178-82, 185-301). In the course of it Thomas P. Grosvenor of New York warned Calhoun to refrain from "boisterous language" and accused him of "language both improper and indecorous." William W. Bibb, who was presiding, called Grosvenor to order, and Calhoun "rose and said, he should say nothing then, but would reply to Mr. G." (p. 200, 212). For other references to Calhoun see p. 186-8, 197, 282-3. (P. 238 refers either to a remark by Felix Grundy—p. 227—or to an unreported statement of Calhoun.) On the 18th Grundy, again second on the Foreign Relations Committee, took his turn at the defense of the administration (p. 219-29). His speech was even more effective than Calhoun's; by declaring that he would vote for the resolutions as they stood, he deprived the opposition of the argument that there was an attempt to suppress information. He pointed out that the repeal of the Orders in Council left untouched the issue of impressment. His vigorous defense of Republican policy and his scathing criticism of the Federalists turned most of their ire upon him. On the 21st Bibb stated from the chair that the Ways and Means Committee was ready to discuss its revenue bills, and asked that the debate come to a conclusion. Calhoun thereupon said that so desirous was he of this that he was willing to withdraw his motion (p. 302). The resolutions were put before the House without essential change and all passed by large majorities. Calhoun voted for all but the fourth, on which, for no apparent reason, he was silent.

For Madison's reply to the resolutions, see No. 84. SOURCE: *NI*, June 24, 1813; *AC*13-1, p. 169-71, 174-8. The speech was also printed as p. 3-8 of *The Speeches of Messrs Calhoun and Grosvenor, upon Mr. Webster's Resolutions* ["Reported for the *National Intelligencer* and the *Federal Republican*"] "Reprinted at the Courier-Office," Charleston, 1813.

82. To DR. JAMES MACBRIDE, Ash[e]ville, N.C.

Washington 23d. June 1813

Dr Sir, I regret exceedingly I had not an opportunity of seeing you, when I was last in St. Johns. It is impossible for me in the shape or extent of an ordinary letter, to communicate half the observations and speculations which I have made since the commencement of my publick life.

Party sperit is more violent than I ever knew. In what it will terminate it is impossible to conjecture. For my part my resolve is taken. No menace, no threat of disunion shall shake me, from persuing that course of measures, which I know to be for the honor and best interest of this nation. I wish them to be persued with every possible vigour; and to put it home fairly to the people, whither they will or will not make the necessary sacrafices.

I know the difficulties which oppose the best wishes of the patriot. To me they are nothing. I speak personally. I by no means dispair of the destiny of our nation or government. National greatness and perfection are of slow groth, often checked often to appearance destroied. The intelligence, the virtue and the tone of

publick sentiment are too great in this country to permit its freedom to be destroied by either domestick or foreign foes.

The application of your friend shall be attended to.

I am with esteem yours &c

J. C. Calhoun

82 NOTE: The letter was originally addressed to Macbride at
Charleston, S.C., readdressed to Salisbury Court House, then to
Asheville, and noted as forwarded by Robert Quan [?] 6 Augt 1813.
SOURCE: *LC*, James Macbride Papers.

83. Comment on the Massachusetts Memorial

June 29, 1813

Mr. Calhoun said if his vote for printing this memorial could be
conceived as in any way countenancing the doctrines it contained,
he certainly should not vote for it. He certainly never would countenance what might be considered a declaration of war by one state
against another. When he gave a vote to publish this paper, he
should do it because gentlemen had said they had not an opportunity of hearing it distinctly when it was read. As to the subject
of the remonstrance, he was ready to meet it. Congress had declared war from necessity alone, and that they would always be
willing and able to vindicate its justice and necessity, he had not
the least doubt.

83 NOTE: On June 29 Timothy Pickering presented "The
Memorial or Remonstrance of the Legislature of Massachusetts
against the war" (*AC*13-1, p. 333-41), which enlarged upon the
rights of the states as "parties to the national compact," the interests
of the commercial states, and the lack of justification for the beginning or the continuance of the war. After debate the memorial was
laid on the table (p. 341-7), and after further debate (p. 347-9) it
was ordered printed.   SOURCE: *NI*, July 1, 1813; *AC*13-1, p. 347.

84. REPORT AND DEBATE ON THE CONDUCT OF THE EXECUTIVE

July 13, 1813

The Committee of Foreign Relations to whom was referred the President's message of the 12th. inst. and the accompanying documents. Report.

That they have examined the message and documents with all the attention their importance demands. Your Committee will not indulge themselves in making the various observations which the interesting subjects brought under their consideration naturally suggest. The delay incident to such a course, connected with the lateness of the session and the advanced season of the year, forbid so wide a range; but they cannot abstain from remarking that, while the message and documents furnish strong additional proof of the justice and necessity of the war, they also present powerful motives for the steady and vigorous prosecution of it, as the surest means of a safe and honorable peace. It can now, no longer be doubted, that it was the pressure of our measures, combined with the determination of Congress to redress our wrongs by arms, and not the repeal of the French decrees, that broke down the orders in Council of 1807 and 1809; that dangerous system of monopoly by which we were, as to our commerce, in fact recolonized. Let us then persevere; and under a just providence we cannot doubt of final success. The reward is worthy of the cost and privation. It is no less than the lasting peace and independence of ourselves and our posterity.

There is another view of the subject which your committee are compelled to present to the House. It is due to justice to consider the message and documents in relation to the conduct of the Executive. They are aware, that on ordinary occasions, it is not proper for this House to express sentiments of approbation, or censure on the conduct of the President; but submit with deference, that as through this body, he is responsible to the people for the faithful discharge of his duties, there are cases in which it is not only the right, but the duty of this House to express its opinion. Such in the judgment of your committee is the present. The language of the resolutions and the motives avowed by their supporters leave no alternative. To be silent, would be to condemn. Upon a full investigation of the conduct of the Executive in relation to Great Britain and France as disclosed in the message and documents, your committee are of opinion, that a just course has been pursued towards both nations, and in no instance has the dignity, honor or interests of the United States been compromitted.

Your committee therefore recommend the adoption of the following resolution.

Resolved, That the conduct of the Executive in relation to the various subjects referred to in the resolutions of the 21st. day of June, 1813, meets with the approbation of this House.

[Calhoun moved that the report be referred to a Committee of the Whole for consideration the next day. Egbert Benson of New York moved postponement till December and declared the resolutions called for documents and explicit answers instead of Monroe's "long argument."[1]]

Mr. Calhoun could not consent to it, because he thought the subject was such as, in justice to the President, to require the decision of the House. The course adopted by the President was not unprecedented. In answer to the resolutions read the other day, Mr. Secretary Hamilton had made a long argumentative report. In this case it was peculiarly proper. Mr. C. said, when the resolutions were adopted, he had attempted to procure amendments, which would have prevented the necessity of such a report from the Secretary. He had failed in his attempts. He had foreseen this course and endeavored to prevent it. He could not agree to the postponement.

[Several members made comments and William W. Bibb of Georgia proposed tabling the report.[2]]

Mr. Calhoun assured the House that nothing was farther from his intention and that of the committee, than to introduce a discussion of the subject into the House. It was necessary and proper for the Secretary to go at length into the subject. It was equally necessary for the House to express their opinion upon the answer. This was the opinion at least of the Committee of Foreign Rela-

1. *AC*13-1, p. 435-6.
2. P. 436-8.

tions. As to any discussion, that would depend upon the manner in which the report was treated by the minority.

84 NOTE: Madison's reply to the House resolutions of June 21 (No. 81 NOTE) was a long and carefully prepared report of Monroe of July 12, presented to the House the same day (*AC*13-1, p. 433; *ASP, For. Rel.*, III, 608-12), which traversed the field Calhoun and Grundy had covered, and included a convincing array of documents. Monroe, however, recognizing that the whole war policy was still at issue, took the story back to August 1810 when Madison, in the face of complete refusal by Great Britain to make any concession, accepted the dubious promise of the Cadore letter (see Adams, *History of U.S.*, V, 255, 303-4; *ASP, For. Rel.*, III, 386-7). The day it was received Monroe's report was referred to the Foreign Relations Committee (*AC*13-1, p. 433), and on the next Calhoun made the above report.

Calhoun finally consented to consideration on the second day thereafter (p. 437-9). But on the 20th his motion to take up the report of the committee was lost, 74 to 62, with party lines split, and no action was taken (p. 470-1). See also No. 88.   SOURCE: MS Report, July 13, 1813, *NA, RG*233, 13A-D6.1; *Federal Republican,* July 16, 1813; *AC*13-1, p. 435-8.

85. REPORT ON THE PRESIDENT'S PROPOSAL OF AN EMBARGO

July 21, 1813

[*Mr. Calhoun, from the Committee on Foreign Relations, made a report*]

[*That*] it was *"inexpedient"* to pass such a law.

85 NOTE: On July 20 a confidential message from President Madison stated his inference that the British planned a combination of blockade and special licenses to neutral vessels or British vessels so disguised, and recommended an embargo on exports till the next session of Congress (*AC*13-1, p. 500). It was referred to the Foreign Relations Committee, and the minutes of the secret session as recorded in the *House Journal* of the next day state that Calhoun presented a report, which was considered in Committee of the Whole and that the House "agreed to the same, with an amendment." As adopted by the House the report was a resolution "that it would be expedient to adopt the measure submitted by the

message to the consideration of the House." The proceedings as recorded in the *Intelligencer* (July 31) differed in no material detail.

The *Intelligencer* does not give Calhoun's report, but the anti-administration *Federal Republican* states it as above with the note that Calhoun "defended his report in a concise and pertinent speech" and that Calhoun was one of the several who "skirmished smartly" in the debate.

Grundy and two other members of the committee voted for the amended report, Calhoun, the only other member voting, casting his against it, and against the bill for the embargo which Grundy brought in the next day; the bill passed the House but was lost in the Senate (p. 500-4). Calhoun later voted for a bill to prohibit American vessels trading under a British license (p. 38, 446, 483-5, 2777-9). It originated in the Senate, which had in March preceding killed the House bill to forbid vessels trading under any foreign license (see No. 78 NOTE), and was likewise reported from the Foreign Relations Committee by Grundy. Compare this procedure with that on the July 30 resolution by Thomas Newton of Virginia: on a motion by Grundy, seconded by Calhoun, consideration of prohibiting certain exports in foreign vessels was transferred from the Foreign Relations Committee to Newton's Committee of Commerce and Manufactures (*AC*13-1, p. 486-7). See No. 87 NOTE for the embargo enacted Dec. 17, 1813. SOURCE: *Federal Republican*, Aug. 13, 1813.

86. To MRS. ELIZA PICKENS, Pendleton

Bath [1] [S.C.] 26th Octr 1813

Dr. Madam, It is with regret that I find my affairs in such a posture, as to prevent me from going up with Mrs Calhoun. However I hope that the estate will suffer no prejudice by my absence from the sale, as Gen. Pickens and Mr Bowie will both be present. The estate has lost an invaluable friend in Mr. Jones. You must repair the loss as well as you can by appointing some other friend to take the management of it in the lower country.

1. Calhoun's home a mile from the Savannah River and about three miles south of Willington (Mills, *Atlas of S.C.*, Abbeville District). A plat of 840 acres, made for him May 30, 1817 (S.C. Archives) shows his house and another tract of his land adjoining. For the "once handsome house" see Moragne, *The Neglected Thread*, p. 3. His postoffice was Willington. See No. 35 NOTE.

On examination, I find it indispensable, that the estate should be in possession of some immediate fund, say to the amount of $300, or 400. There are several small debts, particularly one on Ezekiel's account at Willington, and some necessary expences which makes it unavoidable. It becomes a question how it is to be raised. I have consulted Mr Bowie on that subject. He thinks if it can be borrowed that it would be best. I wish you to show this letter to Gen. Pickens and Mr. Bowie, and to do that which with their advice shall seem expedient. I hope the estate below will be put, if possible, in such a situation as to be made productive. If that cannot be done, sales to a large amount will become unavoidable. For nothing is so injurious to an estate, as to be under the pressure of a debt bearing interest without active funds to meet at fixed periods the principal & interest. A small debt if permited to run on soon becomes heavy.

I hope you will take every care of your health; and endeavour to acquire that composure of mind which it is our duty to have at the dispensation of a just Providence.

Mrs Calhoun will deliver a letter from Dr. Smith relative to Ezekiel. I hope he will realise our expectations in his favour.

I am with sentiment of sincere friendship yours &c

J. C. CALHOUN

86 NOTE: The will of Ezekiel Pickens of St. Thomas' Parish (Wills[T] Anderson, 1, 164-9; proved Sept. 13, 1813), mentions his two marriages (to Elizabeth Bonneau and to Elizabeth Barksdale—see No. 22, n. 2), and his son Ezekiel and daughter Elizabeth Bonneau by the first marriage (who was by the will intrusted to his widow and to Mrs. Floride Colhoun for her education). He appointed his wife executrix and Andrew Pickens, Jr., John C. Calhoun, and Samuel B. Jones of Charleston as executors. See Calendar, Nov. 12, 1817.

Calhoun wrote another letter the same day—but dated it "26th Octr 1812"—to George Bowie about some details of the will. The content of the letter fixes the date. SOURCE: SCL.

87. Bills to Enforce Non-Importation and to Prohibit Ransoming of Vessels

December 30, 1813

87 NOTE: In his special message of Dec. 9 (AC13-2, p. 2031-2) Madison repeated his request of July 20 previous (No. 85 NOTE) for an embargo, declaring that supplies readily found their way to British ports, armies, and ships. He further complained that illegal importations were achieved by use of undervaluation of goods in the course of judicial proceedings against these cargoes, and "that the practice of ransoming is a cover for collusive captures." The message was referred at once to the Foreign Relations Committee (p. 2032). However, it was Grundy who carried out the President's request and presented a report for imposing an embargo. The bill passed the House on the 11th and was ratified on the 17th; Calhoun was silent in the debate, but voted for it (p. 2033-53, 2781-8). Presumably, as later claimed in the 1843 *Life*, p. 13-4, this was in the interests of party unity, and in March he refused support for embargo repeal until Madison recommended it (No. 96 NOTE). It was an exchange during the debate on removal of secrecy on the December proceedings on the embargo that brought about the near-duel between Grosvenor and Calhoun—see Wiltse, *Calhoun, Nationalist*, p. 85.

On the 30th Calhoun presented the non-importation and ransoming bills (AC13-2, p. 816-7) requested by Madison, the former forbidding delivery to the owner on bond, pending trial, of a vessel or cargo seized for violation of the non-importation laws; the other forbidding ransom by the owner or master of a ship or cargo seized by the enemy. Both passed the House (Jan. 25 and 26, p. 1134-5, 1144). Calhoun was recorded as speaking for both (p. 1131, 1135), but it was evidently the policy of the Republicans to refrain from debate, and Calhoun—though challenged on the floor to produce the evidence which, he was said to have stated, was presented to the committee—remained silent (p. 1137). Both bills, however, were lost in the Senate (p. 678, 773-4). See also No. 78.

A later bill enacted Mar. 4, 1814, for modification of the embargo was also reported by Grundy (p. 1228, 2793-5). SOURCE: MS Bills, Dec. 30, 1813, *NA*, RG233, 13A-B1; *NI*, Jan. 1, 1814; AC13-2, p. 816-7.

88. Remarks on Postponement of Discussion on Necessity of the War

January 3, 1814

Mr. Calhoun, of South Carolina said, he hoped that the motion for the 1st Monday in February would not succeed. He preferred Monday next, because it was the day designated by the gentleman himself who had first agitated this subject. Mr. C. believed that a great majority of this House and of the nation were already satisfied, in relation to the topics to be embraced by the proposed discussion. If the gentleman, however, was not satisfied himself, and wished a further opportunity to create doubts of the justice or necessity of the war, he wished to give the gentleman his own time to prove it unjust. And here, said Mr. C. if not out of order, let me set the gentleman right as to a remark he made in his preliminary observations. The gentleman called upon gentlemen on this side of the House to prove the justice of the war. That is not necessary; it has been often done before. The burthen of proof, on the presumption that our country is always in the right till the contrary be proved, now certainly rests with the gentleman from New Hampshire and his friends on that side of the House. Let the gentleman then have his own time. There were, Mr. C. said, strong reasons why gentlemen on this side of the House should agree with him in opinion on this subject. As to the great business of the session, giving vigor to the operations of the army or the navy, he hoped neither this or any other business would be permitted to interfere with it; and he pledged himself, for one, who was in favor of Monday, that he would not by his vote sanction its interference with any measure calculated to give vigor to the war. I do strongly believe, said Mr. C. that on the points agitated in the report accompanying the President's Message, there is a clear demonstration of the justice and necessity of the war, in which the Republicans of the House and of the nation have reason to rejoice, and the discussion of which will afford them further cause of exaltation.

88 NOTE: Protesting against the House acceptance of an argument as a substitute for information on specific points, Daniel Webster urged House action on Madison's July 12 report (No. 84

NOTE), and moved consideration of it in Committee of the Whole on the 10th (*AC*13-2, p. 824, 827; *House Journal*, p. 194). Calhoun had advocated action of the House in July—above, p. 180. Discussion was set for the 10th, but the question does not appear in the minutes.   SOURCE: *NI*, Jan. 4, 1814; *AC*13-2, p. 828.

89. DEBATE ON THE TURREAU LETTER

January 11, 1814

Mr. Calhoun said it was a good rule generally in cases of this kind that enquiry be granted, where it is moved in a proper manner. On such motions a very great liberality had usually prevailed in this House, which had been displayed in the vote just taken. But, as to the particular resolution before us, it is of that class which ought not to be passed in the present stage of its existence. To induce the House to pass this resolution, there ought to be three things stated. He need not suggest that this enquiry was of an unprecedented character, and varying from all usual calls on the Executive for information. To warrant the adoption, a specific object ought to be first stated; secondly, what was expected to grow out of it; and thirdly, that the object was of a character to warrant the investigation. Such enquiries as that now proposed, without these three prerequisites, would, he conceived, violate the spirit of the Constitution. By that instrument diplomacy was confided wholly to the Executive. This House had indeed the power to require information, but it was through the executive department that it ought to be sought for, and not through inquisitorial committees of this House, or on such vague statements as had been made. The inofficial mode of enquiry now proposed was a departure from the legitimate province of this body, to which he hoped the House would not accede.

[*Hanson followed Calhoun's comment with the charge that an official letter had been concealed, the offense constituting "a high misdemeanor."* [1]]

Mr. Calhoun said he now hoped the House would refuse the enquiry proposed. He had asked for a specification of the object, and had received none. He had asked for practical consequences

1. *AC*13-2, p. 890-3.

to result from it, and had received none. Mr. C. pronounced the resolution extraordinary in its character, and unprecedented in its form. The resolution went to break into the executive offices, to call *ex parte* witnesses before the House, for what purpose? For the highest purpose in the power of the House? No; for a mere inquisitorial and vexatious procedure, which is, as no such purpose is avowed, to lay no foundation for *impeachment,* the only object which would justify the application of such means. Suppose it were proved that this letter was in fact written by General Turreau, and that all the other circumstances relating to it were true, which for himself he did not credit, what did it prove? Merely that an impertinent letter had been written by a foreign minister. Did the Executive sanction it? No. What view the Executive ought to take of such a letter, or how to treat it, depended on a variety of circumstances, on which this House had not the means to form an opinion. Mr. C. said he hoped this House would not grant what was in his view a direct violation of the spirit of the Constitution. He went on, and adverted to the nice sensibility displayed by the whole phalanx on the other side of the House, yesterday, on a mere proposal for enquiry into the constitutional power of Congress to punish spies.[2] Mr. C. said he had thought for his part we had the constitutional power to enquire into that subject. He hoped on this occasion to see gentlemen consistent, and exhibit the same commendable zeal as on yesterday and join with him to secure the Constitution against an invasion of its spirit. Mr. C. expatiated on the vexatious nature of enquiries of this description tending to no practical result, &c. As to all the insinuations of French influence, and the vague declamation which the House had heard, he did not deem fit subjects of enquiry, or of so much importance as to constitute ground on which to put the Chief Magistrate under a committee of this House. Mr. C. repeated the three requisites he had before stated as necessary to justify this enquiry. If gentlemen could shew that a crime had been committed by the Executive of such a character as to make him amenable to the constitutional authority of this body, then and not till then would he consent

2. On the 10th Robert Wright of Maryland offered a resolution for an inquiry into the expediency of extending to citizens the section of the army regulations relative to spies. Calhoun voted with the majority for the Committee of the Whole to consider the resolution (p. 881-8).

to an enquiry which was equally a novelty in this House and in the history of legislation.

[*Calhoun later opposed an amendment to make the resolution a request of the President, calling, instead, for a vote on the issue of the appointment of the committee of inquiry. In the course of further argument Thomas P. Grosvenor of New York indicated that the President might deserve impeachment for his part in the affair.*[3]]

Mr. Calhoun again rose and took a rapid view of the *variety* of objects avowed by the supporters of this extraordinary motion, upon which he separately remarked. On the subject of French subserviency, which had been designated as one of the subjects of enquiry, Mr. C. ridiculed the idea of an enquiry by this House into that baseless accusation, and on a document too, which on the face of it proved, if it were permitted to prove any thing, that no such subserviency existed. The very document by which gentlemen wished to prove a French influence, cut up by the roots the fanciful absurdity—being predicated on the supposed existence of an influence of a very different character. The motion could have no other reasonable or probable object than that avowed by one of its advocates, to put down the majority—and of the weight of such a motive for such a course, the House would judge. Mr. C. recapitulated his objections to this measure, and concluded with expressing his hope of a speedy decision, as too much time had been already occupied, &c.[4]

89 NOTE: On Aug. 28, 1813, the *National Intelligencer* reprinted from the *Federal Republican* of the 25th a translation of a letter of June 14, 1809, from the French minister Turreau to Robert

3. P. 896-8.
4. As the debate continued, Calhoun was recorded as being involved in "conversation" with Grosvenor and others (p. 899). Hanson's resolution was finally rejected by a vote of 100 to 60 (p. 900). The following day, Jan. 12, debate was renewed by a motion of an administration supporter, Jonathan Roberts of Pennsylvania, for adoption of Hanson's second resolution in the form he offered it on Dec. 28, and this passed "by a large majority"; Calhoun took no part in this debate (p. 900-27). On Jan. 18 Madison replied with a report from Monroe and a letter from John Graham which merely added details (p. 1059-60). On the 24th Roberts offered a resolution that the Foreign Relations Committee inquire how Hanson, who was publisher of the *Federal Republican*, had acquired the translation; Calhoun moved a "select committee" instead, but eventually the matter was dropped (p. 1128-31, 1235-7).

Smith, Secretary of State, in which he questioned what more the
United States could have done to injure and insult France if this
country had been in alliance with Great Britain. On Sept. 4 the
Intelligencer printed a letter of Aug. 31 from John Graham, chief
clerk of the State Department, denying there had ever been such
a letter in the State Department Archives unless it was one which
Turreau had been compelled to withdraw after he, Graham, made a
translation of it for Smith. In his message to Congress of Dec. 7
Madison recommended that Congress enact a law allowing cruisers
of friendly powers to use American ports if the privilege were
reciprocated (*AC*13-2, p. 542). Alexander C. Hanson, of Maryland,
on Dec. 28 (p. 808-9) used this recommendation as his justification
for two resolutions, contending that the House should be apprised
of the relations of the United States with France before the existing
"alliance" with that country could be thus cemented. The resolutions were numbered 1 and 2, the first inquiring the manner in
which the American minister was received by the French government, the other asking for any letter of the French minister of about
June 14, 1809, prescribing the terms on which France would treat
with this country. On the 10th (p. 888) he revised his second
resolution to provide for a committee to inquire if Turreau, the
French minister, about June 14, 1809, had written such a letter.
On the 11th the separation of the two resolutions—on Calhoun's
motion of the day before, so he said—made possible the adoption
of the first without opposition (p. 890). The question was then put
on the second, and Calhoun began the debate with this protest
against the appointment of a committee of investigation instead of
a request for information.

In response to the first resolution Madison transmitted, Jan. 18,
1814, Monroe's report on the reception of William H. Crawford, the
new minister to France (p. 2096-7). SOURCE: *NI,* Jan. 13, 1814;
*AC*13-2, p. 890, 893, 898.

90. SPEECH ON THE DANGERS OF "FACTIOUS OPPOSITION"

January 15, 1814

[*Mr. Calhoun*] did not rise, he said, to examine on what terms the
President had assented to negotiate with the British government;
because he conceived it neither pertinent to the present question,
nor proper at this time. He deemed it, however, his duty to state,
that he wholly dissented from the construction, which our opponents gave to the documents connected with this subject. If a proper

opportunity should hereafter occur he would be happy to present the reasons for his opinion on this point.[1]

He was induced to occupy the time of the committee at present, to correct two essential errors, which gentlemen in the opposition have introduced into the discussion of this question; and, although not immediately connected with the merits of the bill, he thought it proper that they should be answered; because from all that he had ever heard, as well on this as former occasions, it seemed to him that they constituted the basis on which the minority rested their justification. He alluded to the character, which they gave to the war; and the claim set up in a political and constitutional point of view to justify their opposition. Gentlemen contend that this is not a defensive but an offensive war; and under that character undertake its denunciation, without ever condescending to state, what in their opinion constitutes the characteristic difference between them. He claimed the attention of the committee while he examined this point; and he hoped that it would not be considered as a mere verbal criticism, since our opponents have made the distinction the foundation of so much declamation against the war. The enquiry, in another point of view, he believed, would be useful. The people of this country have an aversion to an offensive war; which he supposed interpreted the meaning of the vehemence of the opposition on this subject; while they readily acknowledge the possible necessity and justice of one, that is defensive. It is therefore proper, that our ideas on this point should be fixed with precision and certainty. He would lay it down as an universal criterion, that a war is offensive or defensive, not by the mode of carrying it on, which is an immaterial circumstance, but by the motive and cause which led to it. If it has its origin in ambition, avarice or any of the like passions then it is offensive; [2] but if, on the contrary, to repel insult, injury or oppression, it is of an opposite character, and is defensive. The truth of this position would not require much discussion. He conceived that it might safely rely either on the authority of the best writers on the subject, or on its own internal evidence. It is only in this view that the prevalent

1. See the speech of Richard Stockton of New Jersey (*AC*13-2, p. 988-90) and No. 73 NOTE.

2. The *Intelligencer* reads: "is it offensive."

feelings on this subject can be explained. If the distinction taken is a correct one; if the two species of war are distinguishable in their cause and motive, then our aversion to the one and approbation of the other is no longer a mystery; it is founded in the nature of things. But if, on the contrary, it is true that they are distinguished by the mere accidental circumstance of the mode of carrying them on, that the scene of action should make them the one or the other, then the feelings of this country, by which it condemns or approves of either species, is a profound mystery never to be explained. In the view which he had presented, the difference between an offensive and defensive war is of the moral kind; and the American sense of justice accounts for their feelings. Their exemption from ambition and love of justice preserves them from the former; while their manly spirit and good sense will always make them cheerfully meet the other whenever it becomes necessary. What then is the character of the war in which we are now engaged? Was it dictated by avarice or love of conquest? He appealed to our opponents for a decision. They have already decided. When the resolutions of the gentleman from New Hampshire were under discussion at the last session, it was repeated till the ear was fatigued, by every one on that side of the House who took any part in the debate, that if the repeal of the Berlin and Milan decrees had been communicated in time to the British government, the Orders in Council would have been repealed; and had the last event happened, the war would not have been declared. They then have acknowledged, that the Orders in Council, and not the conquest of Canada, as they now pretend, was the cause of the war; and it would be idle to enquire whether to resist them was in its nature offensive or defensive. It would be to enquire whether they were or were not an injury to our commerce; a point he had never heard denied by the most obstinate debater. It would be equally so to examine whether the cause of continuing the war, to protect our seamen from impressment, is of an offensive or defensive character.

Very few have the hardihood to deny that it is an injury of the most serious kind, both as it regards the government, and the unhappy subjects of its operations. It involved the most sacred obligation which can bind the body politic to the citizen; he meant that of protection, due alike to all; to the beggar in the street,

much more, if susceptible of degrees, to our sailors, that class of
the community who have added so much to the wealth and renown
of this country. Having thus established the character of the war
in its origin and continuance, he would lay it down as a rule not
less clear, that a defensive war does not become offensive by being
carried beyond the limits of our territory. The motive and cause
will ever give character; all the rest are mere unessential incidents.
When once declared, the only question, even in a defensive war,
is, how can it be carried on with the greatest effect. The reverse
of this involves the most glaring absurdity. It supposes that we
had determined to compel our enemy to respect our rights; and at
the same time voluntarily renounced, what is acknowledged to be
the best and most effectual mode of producing that effect. On this
point, as well as the cause of the war, the opinion of our opponents
may be arrayed against themselves. What have they advised as to
the mode of carrying on the war? Withdraw your troops from
Canada, reduce your army and limit your operations to the ocean.
What! to the ocean! Carry the war beyond our own territory! make
it offensive! The gentlemen surely do not intend to support an
offensive war. To use their own language, it is too immoral for a
virtuous and religious people. It is then admitted, that it does not
cease to be offensive by its being waged at sea; how then can the
carrying it into Canada change its character?

Mr. C. again observed that it was a mere question of expediency
where and how the war ought to be prosecuted. For his part, so
long as it continued, he thought no effort ought to be wanting to
reduce Canada. Should success accompany our arms, we would be
indemnified for the privations and expences of the war, by the
acquisition of an extensive and valuable territory, and the permanent peace and security which it would afford a large portion of
our country; and even in the worst event, should we fail of conquest, the attempt will not be without great advantages. The war
in Canada is the best security to every part of our country. We
have a very extended, and, from the thinness of the population, in
many places weak sea coast. He did not believe that it had been
neglected as represented by the gentleman from New Hampshire; [3]
but he did believe, that many points are and must from necessity

3. Webster—see *AC*13-2, p. 941.

be without efficient protection. He would, however, ask that gentleman, how did it happen that this coast so easily assailed, by a maritime power, has sustained little or no damage, in a war that has continued upwards of eighteen months. If he is at a loss for an answer, the scheme of his political friend from Virginia, Mr. Sheffey, to confine our troops to the defensive, should it succeed, would the next summer amply explain the fact.[4] The truth is, that the war in Canada is the security of the coast. It compels the enemy to concentrate the whole of his disposable force there for the defence of his own territory. Were the absurd policy to be adopted to confine the operation of our troops within our own limits, the whole of the enemy's force in Canada would be liberated from its defence, and the entire line of our sea coast menaced with destruction. The enemy, masters on the ocean, could act with such celerity, that it would be either impossible to defend ourselves, or it must be done at an expense greater than would be necessary to reduce his possessions. Thus, even under the limited view of defence, the most effectual mode is that, which has been adopted; to carry the war into the enemy's country, and our opponents ought, according to their own distinction, to grant every aid in men and money.

Mr. C. said, that although not immediately in point, he could not refrain from observing, that of all the arguments he had ever heard since he has had the honor of a seat in this House those were by far the most extravagant which have been urged against the conquest of Canada. He has heard it characterised by every epithet which indicated vice or weakness. The advancers of such arguments surely did not reflect, that in their zeal to assail the majority, they were uttering libels on the founders of our liberty and empire. This scheme of conquest, this project of ambition, this product of folly and vice, as it has been liberally called, originated with those men to whom America owes so much; and whose wisdom and virtue is acknowledged by the world. It was by them thought an object worthy of the treasures and the best blood of the country; and finally relinquished by them with reluctance and from necessity only.

4. P. 939.

Mr. C. said, it now remained to consider the defence which gentlemen have made for their opposition to the war and the policy of their country; a subject which he conceives is of the greatest importance, not only as effecting the result of the present contest, but the lasting peace and prosperity of our country. They assume as a fact that opposition is in its nature harmless; and that the calamities which have afflicted free states have originated in the blunders and folly of the government; and not from the perverseness of opposition. Opposition, say they, is a very convenient thing; a wicked and foolish administration never fail to attribute all of their miscarriages to it; and, in confirmation of this doctrine, they appeal to Lord North's administration.[5] He did not intend to examine the particular case, to which gentlemen have with so much parade referred, as it did not fall in the course of his argument; but he thought that it could be easily proved to be essentially different, in character and consequence, from the opposition in this country. He conceived, however, that it would be proper before he examined the general position taken over the way, to make a single remark as it related to the British government on this subject. It struck him, that all arguments drawn from it on this point must be essentially erroneous. A more determined and vehement opposition there, is not only justifiable but in some measure required. The difference in the two governments in this respect results from a difference in the organization of their respective executives. In England, such is its power, patronage and consequent influence; such the veneration, which its hereditary quality and long descent possess over the subjects of that empire, that her most enlightened statesmen have ever thought that it endangered the other branches of her government, and have with much wisdom, ever since the dawn of liberty in that country, strenuously opposed its encroachments.

Very different is the case here, under a government purely republican. It presents neither the cause to justify such vehemence of opposition; nor the means of restraining it when excited. But even as applied to our government, he would readily acknowledge there was a species of opposition both innocent and useful. Opposition simply implies contrariety of opinion; and, when used in the abstract, it admitted neither censure nor praise. It cannot be said to

5. P. 942.

be either good or bad; useful or pernicious. It is not from itself, but
from the connected circumstances, that it derives its character.
When it is simply the result of that diversity in the structure of our
intellect, which conducts to different conclusions on the same subject, and is confined within those bounds which love of country and
political honesty prescribe, it is one of the most useful guardians
of liberty. It excites gentle collision, prompts to due vigilance, a
quality so indispensable and at the same time so opposite to our
nature, and results in the establishment of an enlightened policy
and useful laws. Such are its qualities when united with patriotism
and moderation. But in many instances it assumes a far different
character. Combined with faction and ambition, it bursts those
limits, within which it may usefully act, and becomes the first of
political evils. If, sir, the gentlemen on the other side of the House
intended to include this last species of opposition, as he was warranted to infer from their expression, when they spoke of its harmless character, then have they made an assertion in direct contradiction to reason, experience and all history. A factious opposition is
compounded of such elements, that no reflecting man will ever consider it as harmless. The fiercest and most ungovernable passions of
our nature, ambition, pride, rivalry and hate, enter into its dangerous composition; made still more so by its power of delusion, by
which its projects against government are covered in most instances,
even to the eyes of its victims, by the specious show of patriotism.
Thus constituted, who can estimate its force? Where can benevolent
and social feelings be found sufficiently strong to counteract its
progress? In love of country? Alas! the attachment *to a party* becomes stronger than that to *our country.* A factious opposition
sickens at the sight of the prosperity and success of the country.
Common adversity is its life; general prosperity its death. Nor is it
only over our virtuous sentiments that this bane of freedom tri-
umphs. Even the selfish passions of our nature, planted in our
bosom for our individual safety, afford no obstacle to its progress.
It is this opposition which gentlemen call harmless and treat with
so much respect; it is this moral treason, to use the language of his
friend from Tennessee (Mr. Grundy)[6] which has in all ages and
countries ever proved the most deadly foe to freedom. Nor is it

6. See below, p. 200.

then only dangerous, when it breaks forth into open treason and rebellion. Without resort to violence, it is capable in a thousand ways to counteract and deaden all of the motions of government, to render its policy wavering, and to compel it to submit to schemes of aggrandizement on the part of other governments, or, if resistance is determined on, to render it feeble and ineffectual. Do gentlemen ask for instances? Unhappily they are but too numerous. Where shall they not be found? Admired and lamented republics of antiquity! Athens, Carthage and Rome, you are the victims and witnesses of the fell spirit of factious opposition! Fatal fields of Zama and Chaeronea, you can attest its destructive cruelty! What is the history of Polybius, and that of the other historians of the free states of antiquity? What the political speeches of Cicero and the orations of Demosthenes, those models of eloquence and wisdom, but volumes of evidence attesting that an opposition founded in faction, unrestrained by moderation and a regard to the general welfare, is the most dangerous of political evils. Nor does antiquity alone testify. The history of modern times is pregnant with examples. What, he would ask, have become of the free states of modern Italy, which once flourished in wealth and power; Florence, Genoa, Venice, and many others? What of the United Provinces and Switzerland? Gone; perished under the deadly feuds of opposition. Even England, with her deep-rooted and powerful executive, has not been free from its pernicious effect. What arrested the war of Marlborough when France was so humbled, that had it been continued Europe might have been free from the danger which she has experienced from that power? What staid the conquering hand of Chatham, when before his genius and power the throne of the Bourbons trembled to its centre? The spirit of factious opposition, that common cause of calamity, that without which liberty might be eternal and free states irresistible.

Our country, as young as she is, also has her examples. In the war of the Revolution had she been united to a man; had there been no apologists of opposition; had no one opposed his will to the general determination, would the enemy ever have had a hold in our country, or would that contest have lasted for a year, or would we have been indebted to foreign aid for the establishment of our independence? Even in this war, how much has it debilitated the

196

energies of our country? The gentleman from New Hampshire, who spoke with ingenuity on this subject, told us that if we were united the Canadas would be reduced in thirty days; [7] and that in consequence of our disasters springing from our divisions, we had been disgraced. What more could he say on the fatal effect of opposition? Mr. C. appealed to that gentleman to state the cause of our divisions; and would ask him, whether, with the certain knowledge of its pernicious effect, every means that could excite opposition had not been unceasingly applied? To obviate the natural conclusion, the gentleman from New Hampshire was compelled to deny that the party now in power is a majority in this country; and to contend that the representation in this body furnishes no evidence of that fact. He argued, that many who are opposed to the war were from party motives induced to vote for those in favor of it. [8] Even admitting the argument to be well founded, which he did not think, might it not be retorted? He would be glad to know why the rule does not apply to the minority in an equal degree? Till he assigned some reason why it did not, he must continue to consider the majority here, as representing a great majority of the nation; and the minority as opposing the will of that majority.

Mr. C. said, that the pretensions and declarations of the gentlemen on the other side of the House, had compelled him to make these general observations. He knew not how else they could be met, and he thought these arguments were fraught with doctrines so erroneous and dangerous, that it was his duty to present their falsity in the best manner in his power to this House and nation. From the same sense of duty, he felt bound to offer his sentiment on a subject of great delicacy; he meant on the character of the opposition which the government has experienced since the commencement of the present difficulties in 1806, and to enquire under which of the two species of opposition, the moderate and useful, or factious and dangerous, it ought to be arranged. It was with pain he would make this enquiry. He took no pleasure in perceiving the faults of any part of our citizens, much less in presenting them to the public. His object was not to expose, but reform; to admonish of a danger so natural to free states to which all opposition even

7. AC13-2, p. 947.
8. P. 946.

of the most virtuous kind so easily degenerates, if not incessantly watched and to call on them, while yet possible to arrest its fatal career. It is important to know, that there is a stage in the progress of opposition, which gentlemen consider so harmless, which when once attained, no power can arrest; not love of country; not even the certainty of being involved in the common destruction. Has it made any progress in this country to so dangerous a state? He feared there were appearances which would justify such a belief. One of its most natural symptoms, was a settled and fixed character, which, as its object was to embarrass and weaken government, lost no opportunity to throw impediments in the way of every measure. It had two other concomitants; the one a violence and vehemence not warranted by any considerations of expediency; and the other urging of measures, which, if adopted, must lead to national ruin. It seemed to him that there were reasons to believe that the whole of these existed in the present opposition. Is it not settled and fixed? In an unexampled state of national difficulties, from the first belligerent decree against our neutral commerce down to this day, he would ask which one of all the measures of our government to resist this almost universal depredation, that has not, under one pretext or another, been opposed, ridiculed and weakened? Yes, opposed with a violence that would lead to a belief that the constituted authorities, instead of opposing the most gross and outrageous injustice, sought only the destruction of their country. Again, what have been the measures that the opposition has virtually urged? What is it at this moment? Withhold the laws; withhold the loans; withhold the men who are to fight our battles; or, in other words, to destroy public faith, and deliver the country unarmed to the mercy of the enemy. Suppose all of their objects accomplished, and what would be the situation of the country? He appealed to the people for a decision. Nor are those morbid symptoms confined to this body. The contagion has gone forth into the community, and wherever it has appeared, has exhibited the same dangerous appearances. The enquiry might be pushed much farther; but he would abstain from it, as it was to him by no means a pleasant task.

But, say the gentlemen on the other side of the House, what right have we to object? The Constitution justifies and secures them in opposition to the measures of government. They claim to be not only above laws, but beyond animadversion. It is in their eyes fair and proper that the majority who act under the undoubted and express sanction of the Constitution, should be subjected to every species of abuse and impediment; but should any one question the right or the expediency of the opposition, we hear an immediate cry of oppression. For his part, he thought that a fair and moderate opposition ought at all times to be respected; but that our Constitution authorized that dangerous and vicious species, which he had attempted to describe, he utterly denied. He called on those who made the claim to so extravagant a power to point out the article of that instrument which would warrant such a construction. Will they cite that which establishes the liberty of speech here? Its object was far different; and it furnishes not the shadow of such a power. Will they rely on its general spirit? It knows no object but the general good, and must for ever condemn all factious opposition to measures emanating from its own authority. It is then not authorized either by the letter or the spirit of the Constitution. If then our opponents have the right, it is because it is not expressly forbidden. In this sense there is no limitation to their constitutional rights. A right might be thus derived to violate the whole decalogue. The Constitution forbids almost no crimes; nor ought it to be considered in the light of a voluminous penal code, whose object was the definition and prohibition of all acts injurious to society. Even had this been the case, the argument that what is not forbid is justified, would be fallacious; for there are many acts of the most dangerous tendency (of which an unprincipled opposition is one) which in their very nature are not susceptible of that rigid definition necessary to subject them to punishment. How absurd, then, the argument, as applied to the Constitution, whose object is the mere enumeration, distribution and organization of the powers of the body politic.

Mr. C. concluded by again observing, that he was compelled by the great and dangerous errors of the gentlemen on the other side, to take a view more general, than what was usually proper, of a subject on which it was so important to think correctly; and he could not take his seat without reiterating his admonition to this body and the country, to guard against the pernicious effect of a factious opposition. Universal experience and the history of all ages furnish ample testimony of its dangerous consequences, particularly in a state of war. Could any certain remedy be applied to restrain it within the bounds of moderation, then, indeed, might our liberty be immortal. He knew of none but the good sense and the virtue of the people. The triumph of a party can be nothing to them. They can have no interest but in the general welfare.

90 NOTE: On Jan. 10 George M. Troup, of Georgia, Chairman of the Military Affairs Committee, offered three bills for strengthening the army (AC13-2, p. 872-3), the first to encourage enlistments in the regular army, the second to raise three additional regiments of riflemen (see No. 94 NOTE), the third to extend the enlistment of the twelve-months men (No. 75 NOTE) to five years or the war— the term of the regular army. The first passed the House on the third reading the day before (AC13-2, p. 979); it was ratified Jan. 27 (p. 2789-90). The debate was now on the third bill, to enlist the twelve-months men for five years and to pay them the bounty of the regulars; this bill was ratified Jan. 28 (p. 2791).

Restriction of troops to defensive warfare was proposed by Daniel Sheffey of Virginia the day before, in an amendment offered to the bill for encouraging enlistments in the regular army (p. 939). The motion was promptly rejected, but Webster the same day made so plausible an argument for the principle (p. 940-51) that Calhoun felt constrained to devote nearly half his speech to it.

His real interest, however, was in a far larger issue. As the anti-war feeling mounted in New England (see Adams, *History of U.S.*, VII, 366-7, 370-1), the campaign of the Federalist leaders in the House to break down the President and his party was waged with increasing intensity (see NOTES to Nos. 81, 88, and 89, and AC13-2, p. 912, 918, 921, 922, 955). Felix Grundy and Calhoun were the chief champions of the administration—indeed, Hanson accused the former of being "made a mouthpiece" by Calhoun (AC13-1, p. 253). Grundy in June preceding had denounced those members of the opposition who had undertaken to destroy the government's credit and to discourage enlistment, and he had raised the question if their "moral guilt" were not as great as that of the traitor (p. 225-6). "Moral treason," like his other charges, was distinctly personal and drew on him the chief fire of the Federalists (*e.g.*, p. 236, 962, 978, 1111, 1532). Actually Calhoun's accusations, though temperately expressed, were even more severe.

A year and a day earlier Calhoun had declared the opposition helpless as long as it remained a minority (No. 75 NOTE). But now he had come to regard the extreme Federalists as intent on "the destruction of the country," and, evidently referring to ominous reports from New England, added that "The contagion has gone forth into the community." Madison's description, in the tenth of the *Federalist* essays, of the danger from factions gave him a parallel for characterization of this danger, but unlike Madison, whose concern was with majority factions, Calhoun was grappling with the problem of an entrenched minority so determined that it threatened the union. Again—almost in the words of his speech of the preceding January—he could only appeal to public opinion, to "the good sense and virtue of the people."

Calhoun's earnest effort to avoid personalities, perhaps the gravity of the situation he described, moderated the Federalist response, although Richard Stockton with some propriety complained of being doomed to sit "and attend to lectures learnedly prepared" (*AC*13-2, p. 1013), and Zebulon R. Shipherd of New York remarked that the Carolinian "entertained the Committee in a manner bespeaking the authority of an apostle" (p. 1030). William Gaston of North Carolina quoted the *Federalist* to Calhoun on the danger from majority factions, and, unless there were a change of policy by the dominant party, feared for the existence of the nation (p. 1574-5, 1576). See Calhoun's reply to Gaston, below, p. 236, Sheffey's comments (*AC*13-2, p. 1325-6), and note Calhoun's remark in 1811 on state factions (No. 44).

Crallé (*Works,* II, 56) confuses the bill which was the occasion of this speech with that for encouraging enlistment in the regular army, applies that title to the speech, and dates it the 17th. He was apparently following the *House Journal* which did not list the speeches; the *Intelligencer* printed the proceedings on the 18th, but in printing the speech on the 29th gave it no date and merely headed it as Calhoun's speech on the army bill. The speech was also printed by Corse & Rounsavell, Alexandria, 1814, with a blank left in the title for the day of the month, and with the same error in regard to the bill as that in the *Works.* This printing, like that of the *Works,* evidently had its source in the *Intelligencer.* Source: *NI,* Jan. 29, 1814; *AC*13-2, 994-1002.

91. Remarks on the Maryland Memorial

February 2, 1814

Mr. Calhoun of South Carolina rose, not to debate the mere motion before the House, which he did not consider worthy of a word, but to remark on a doctrine which ought not to receive the sanction of this House. The gentleman from North Carolina, by mere abstraction, overlooked the objectionable part of the memorial. He had said, and Mr. C. agreed with him, that the people have a right to state facts; and that it is a fact that the war is about to assume a character of ferocity—a fact in which the people of that state, of the whole American people, and of the world are interested. It was not the annunciation of a fact in itself true that was objected to; but it was the character given to that fact, conveying a censure not on the government commencing in this ferocious spirit, but on the government which is acting on the defensive. This was the objection, that it imputed the blame not to the enemy, with whom it rested, but to the American government. That this memorial should speak thus, was surprizing; that it should meet with an advocate on this floor was doubly surprizing. In what manner does the memorial say this work of retaliation is to commence? By our protection of British traitors. And to this, the gentleman had said, there was no objection. Mr. Calhoun said he knew but one case in which the protection of traitors was not objectionable. If a traitor of an enemy during war flees into this country, we are not compelled to give him up. But that we are to protect "British traitors" by a course of retaliation, was what the President never thought of doing. To do so would be a contradiction of every principle of a moral character. The gentleman from New York had intimated that the President in his message had announced such a doctrine.[1] Let the gentleman point it out. Mr. C. understood the message only to embrace such as had incorporated themselves into our political society according to our laws.[2] Another part of the address, said Mr. C. the allusion to the Boston port bill, the gentleman appears to think perfectly innocent. Sir, is a measure to be judged only by its effects? It is the motive which gives character to our actions. If the Boston port bill had been passed for a proper purpose, it had not driven us into the war of the Revolution. It was the motive which then as well as now has raised the American spirit to resist British violence and usurpation, and I hope ever will. The measure of embargo, Mr. C. said, had been resorted to as a part of a system to repel encroachments by the same enemy, after a lapse of 30 years, as before drove us to war by her injustice, &c. As to the abuse of the French Em-

1. Thomas P. Grosvenor—*AC* 13-2, p. 1215-6.
2. See No. 79 NOTE.

peror, Mr. C. said he would with the gentleman from Maryland
(Mr. Archer)[3] willingly leave it to the House of Delegates of Maryland to abuse him as much as they pleased; but the correctness or
propriety of their abuse of him must, like all other things, be determined by its motive. If they merely intended to express their aversion to French tyranny, he would agree with them, and so he believed would a great majority of the American people. It was not
in this point of view he was disposed to object to this part of the
address. But it was that, in abusing the French Emperor, they
wished to justify the opposite despot over the channel, as regards
this country equally terrible and more hostile. Not only does this
memorial abuse the French Emperor, but assigns his demerits directly or by inference as a cause why we should throw ourselves
into the arms of England, our deadly enemy. Mr. C. said for these
and other reasons he should not give his vote for printing this
memorial.

[*The remarks of several speakers intervene here, among them
Grosvenor who declared his doubts "whether, according to the principles of public law, we can deliver a citizen from his allegiance to
his native country."* [4]]

Mr. Calhoun spoke in explanation. He added that he was glad
on one account, and sorry on another, that the gentleman from New
York had spoken so distinctly on one point: that persons who had
the plighted faith of the United States should not be protected—
that persons who, under sanction of our laws, have forsworn foreign
allegiance, and become citizens, should not be protected whilst
fighting under our banners beyond our territorial limits? If this
doctrine was entertained by the gentleman, he hoped it was confined to himself and had not many advocates, even in his own party.

91 NOTE: The memorial of the Maryland House of Delegates
(AC13-2, p. 1204-9) was presented by Representative Charles
Goldsborough on Feb. 2. It described the "awful condition of
national affairs," the defenseless situation of Maryland, remarked
on the "ferocity" which might be apprehended as a result of the
retaliatory measures initiated by the government in its attempt to
protect "British traitors" enlisting in the American army (see p.

3. Stevenson Archer—AC13-2, p. 1218-9.
4. P. 1223.

540-2, and No. 79), cited the French deception in the matter of the Berlin and Milan decrees (No. 81 NOTE), compared the embargo (No. 87 NOTE) to the Boston Port Bill of 1774, and urged that negotiations be carried on with the "earnest intention" of making peace. A motion to lay the memorial on the table passed (*AC*13-2, p. 1209), but a motion to print it brought about an angry debate (p. 1209-27) centering about the question if the paper was so disrespectful that it should not be printed. William Gaston of North Carolina immediately preceding Calhoun, declared the memorial only stated fact and therefore could not be considered disrespectful. The motion to print was finally defeated, Calhoun voting against it (p. 1228). SOURCE: *NI*, Feb. 3, 1814; *AC*13-2, p. 1221-2, 1227.

92. RESOLUTION ON THE QUESTION OF A NATIONAL BANK

February 4, 1814

[*Remarking that the Ways and Means Committee had, on constitutional grounds, reported against a New York petition for the establishment of a national bank,*]

Mr. C. wished to instruct the committee to enquire into the expediency of establishing a National Bank *within the District of Columbia,* the power to do which it could not be doubted came within the constitutional powers of Congress. For all practicable purposes he believed such a Bank would be as useful as that which was proposed. To come at his object, Mr. C. proposed the following motion:

Resolved, That the Committee of Ways and Means be instructed to inquire into the expediency of establishing a National Bank, to be located in the District of Columbia.

92 NOTE: The New York petition of Dec. 18, 1813, was for a bank of thirty million dollars capital, authorized to make loans to the government up to half that amount (*AC*13-2, p. 873-4). On Jan. 4 by a vote of 57 to 54 the petition was referred, over the opposition "of some who desired to refer it to a select committee," to the Ways and Means Committee; at the same time, on Calhoun's motion, it was ordered printed (p. 844). The Ways and Means Committee on the 10th reported against the petition, declaring that "the power to create corporations within the . . . States" without their consent was neither delegated by the Constitution, nor neces-

sary to put a delegated power in effect; a similar petition was received on the 20th from the merchants of Philadelphia (p. 873-4, 1058). Calhoun's resolution was agreed to without opposition (p. 1235).

On Feb. 19 (p. 1578-85) John W. Taylor, of New York, second on the Ways and Means Committee, reported a bill for establishing such a bank in Washington, although he later stated his desire for a bill "with very different provisions" (p. 1578-85, 1862). The bill proposed a bank of thirty millions capital, a fifth of it subscribed by the government, to which the bank should lend not over fifteen millions. Five of its twenty-five directors were to be appointed and removable by the President, and its notes were to be receivable for all payments to the United States. Like Calhoun's bill of 1816 (No. 120), this copied a number of sections from the act establishing the first bank of the United States (*AC1*, p. 2312-8). It was given a second reading and committed to a Committee of the Whole for the 22nd but was not taken up (*House Journal,* Feb. 19, 22, 1814, p. 304, 337, 414). On Apr. 2 (*AC13-2*, p. 1941-2) Grundy offered a resolution to appoint a committee to inquire into the expediency of establishing a national bank. A motion to add "within the District of Columbia" was lost, and Grundy's resolution passed, with himself appointed chairman and Calhoun third on the committee (Apr. 4, p. 1956). But on the 8th, on Grundy's motion (p. 2002), this committee was discharged; and on the 15th, Taylor's bill, on his own motion, was indefinitely postponed (p. 2023), thus ending the matter for the session. See No. 104.   SOURCE: *House Journal,* p. 277 (for the resolution); *NI,* Feb. 5, 1814; *AC13-2,* p. 1235.

93. To Mrs. Floride Calhoun, Willington, S. C.

Washington 7th Feb. 1814

My dearest Floride, By Dr. Casey's letter of yesterday, I had the pleasure to hear of your safe delivery of a daughter;[1] and that you had comparitively easy times. I had been waiting anxiously for mail day in expectation of such an event; and you may imagine the relief and joy it afforded me to hear not only of your safety, but the addition to our family. For both of your safety, I have all of the fond wishes of a parent and an husband. I hope your mother till you are sufficiently recovered, will be punctual in writing every mail; as my anxiety will be encreased to hear from you.

1. Their second child, Floride, born Jan. 25, who died Apr. 7, 1815. See No. 115.

As to the name, any one that you and your mother think proper will please me. It is a subject on which, I have no great choice; but my inclination would be to call her by the name which you and your mother bear.

I think there will be an earily adjournment; and am satisfied at least that the session will not be a long one. I hope Nance continues faithful to his duty; both about the house and plantation. I am glad to hear that the apple trees are planted.

Do let McGehee have his money as soon as possible.

Andrew appears to be forgot. None of the letters from home for some time mention a word of him. I hope he is doing well. Kiss him for me. Remember me to our Mother & all friends.

I am your affectionate husband

J. C. Calhoun

Source: *CC.*

94. Remarks on the Defense of the American Coast

February 8, 1814

Mr. Calhoun of South Carolina spoke in reply to Messrs. Grosvenor and Webster. He said the arguments of these gentlemen in relation to the protection of the frontier would be much better if our memories were worse. Who did not recollect the predictions so often reiterated during the first session of the twelfth Congress, that within six or at furthest twelve months after the declaration of war, our sea-coast would be depopulated, our towns destroyed, our cities burnt, and the inhabitants driven beyond the mountains? Were these predictions realized? Or rather were they not in every respect falsified?[1] So great had been the impression produced in England by the inactivity of the vast British armaments on our coasts, that it had excited the attention of the Parliament, and produced much censure. This inactivity, however, Mr. C. believed arose not from any deficiency of that spirit and enterprize which has always been considered the characteristic of British seamen, but

1. In his speech of Feb. 10 (*AC*13-2, p. 1332), Daniel Sheffey of Virginia replied with a reminder of Calhoun's 1812 prophecy of the conquest of Canada (above, p. 104-5).

was owing to the danger of attempting any thing against our fortified posts. Mr. C. was therefore surprized at the allegations of the
defenceless state of our sea-coast. The language of gentlemen had
a meaning, however. They had ever strived to make our efforts
against Canada abortive. One way to do so was to call out more
than the proportion of military force to the sea-coast, and leave the
government destitute of the necessary force to carry on operations
in the North. They would then have an opportunity to say that our
arms had failed. They were actors at the same time they were prophets; and verified their own predictions by using every effort to
bring them about, in order that they might take advantage of them.
It was very difficult to give entire protection to every part of our
sea-coast; but in the main the protection had been fully adequate
to the enterprizes of the enemy against it. The object of the accusation and clamor on this head was evidently to divert the public attention from Canada, and weaken our efforts in that quarter.

[*Calhoun was here answered by Grosvenor who repeated his
charge of the defenselessness of the coast and declared the forces
that should have defended it had been diverted to quixotic efforts
against Canada.*[2]]

Mr. Calhoun replied. He said the gentleman had very improp-
erly charged the [*majority*][3] with bringing on this discussion. The
gentleman himself had on this, as on every other occasion, introduced this topic of the defenceless state of our cities; and he would
now state a few facts on this head which should put the gentleman
down. He then entered into a view of the defence of various parts
of the coast, and the results of attacks attempted by the enemy. As
to New York in particular, he had been informed by a distinguished
naval commander, so far from not being able to resist two seventy-
fours, that few towns in the world presented so respectable a defence. The defence of our sea ports, he concluded, was not to be
credited to British forbearance. He declined entering into other
topics broached by Mr. Grosvenor, though he did in no wise
agree with him. To me, said Mr. C. it is matter of astonishment to
see American citizens in this body or elsewhere, get up and tell you
that all your objects have failed, that your situation is hopeless;

2. AC13-2, p. 1261-2.
3. The *Intelligencer* reads: "minority."

and, that instead of treating the subject with patriotic feeling, instead of exhibiting despondency at that degradation of their country which they fancifully imagine, they really appear to repeat it with delight and exultation. How, said Mr. C. do you test a friend? By his sympathy in your joys, his condolence and depression at your sorrows. How then do you prove a patriot? By his sympathy with his country's cause. If that country be in prosperity, his face beams with joy; if in adversity, it is clouded with sorrow. Does the latter comport with the manner of gentlemen in speaking thus of the situation of their country? No, sir; their countenance and manner are wholly different. Mr. C. was not however of the same opinion with the gentlemen. He still thought the country, if united, possessed the means of accomplishing all the objects of the war, protecting our seamen, and rendering our commerce secure. As to the conquest of Canada, he hoped we possessed ample means to reduce all the British provinces on this side the water, and he feared not of accomplishing the object if necessary.

94 NOTE: The debate was on the bill to raise three additional regiments of riflemen (see No. 90 NOTE), but rarely touched the subject (*AC*13-2, p. 1144-9, 1157-86, 1187-91). It passed the House in the form of a measure to convert five of the existing infantry regiments into riflemen (p. 1190), but on Feb. 8 came back from the Senate a bill to raise three additional rifle regiments (p. 1255).

On the second debate in the House, Webster criticised the misapplication of American resources and called again for defensive war while Grosvenor ridiculed the claim that the coast was really defended (p. 1258-60). On the same day the amendment was accepted and the bill became law on Feb. 10 (p. 1264, 2791-2). SOURCE: *NI*, Feb. 10, 1814; *AC*13-2, p. 1261-3.

95. SPEECH ON THE LOAN BILL

February 25, 1814

[*Mr. Calhoun rose and addressed the Chair, as follows:*]

Mr. Chairman: It is now more than two weeks since the commencement of this debate; most of which time has been consumed by the opposition in attempting to prove the bad faith, poverty, folly and injustice of our government and country: for all of their arguments and declamation, however variant and contradictory, are re-

ducible to two objections against the passage of this bill. First, that
such is the want of capital, or of public credit, that the loan cannot
be had, or it must be at an extravagant interest; and secondly, if it
could, the bill ought to be rejected, because in their opinion the
war is unjust and inexpedient. The last of these objections, I propose to discuss. To examine both at large would occupy too much
time. Without, therefore, discussing the question whether the loan
can or cannot be had, I will merely offer a few reflections incidentally connected with it. It is a little remarkable that not one of the
minority has discussed the material points on this part of the subject; I mean the question, is the money proposed to be raised by
this bill indispensible for the service of the year? and, if so, is a
loan the only, or best mode of obtaining it? The Chairman of the
Committee of Ways and Means has presented an estimate of the
expences already ordered, or which must be, by which it appears
that the sum proposed to be raised by this bill, with the other
sources of the revenue, will be absolutely necessary to meet them.
The silence of the opposition sanctions the correctness of the estimate; and as no other mode has been indicated of obtaining the
necessary supplies, this may be presumed to be the only one. It
ceases then to be a question, whether the loan can be had at this
or that interest. It is necessary; it must be had; and the rate per
centum will depend principally on the state of the money market—
and not on the arguments here. Again; on comparing the two objections, to the passage of this bill, one of them destroys all confidence in the other. Our opponents contend not only that the loan
cannot be had, but that it ought not to be granted. To defeat the
passage of this bill, or to prevent the [1] successful operation out of
this House, are the declared objects of their policy. It is true that all
have not made the latter declaration; but none, as far as my
memory serves, have disavowed it. When, then, they argue that the
loan must fail, they may be considered either as dupes to their
wishes, or what is more probable, as aiming to destroy the confidence of monied men in the public faith; for it cannot be presumed that they have any hope to defeat the passage of the bill.[2]

1. *NI*, "the"; *R&E*, p. 2, *AC*, p. 1673, *Works*, II, 70, "its." (For "*R&E*,"
see below, NOTE.)
2. Note Pickering's reply to this charge—*AC* 13-2, p. 1699.

But to proceed to the objection which I proposed to discuss. The war, say our opponents, is unjust and inexpedient, and therefore this bill ought to be rejected. The facts of the supposed injustice and inexpediency of the war, on which this objection rests, have claimed the exclusive attention of the opposition. The inference deduced from them, that they justify the rejection of this bill though far from being an intuitive proposition has received no part of their arguments or elucidation.[3] For my part, I consider it not only false but dangerous, and shall therefore not only consider the alleged injustice and inexpediency of the war, but the inference assumed from those charges. I trust with the attention of the committee to prove that both are equally unfounded. I must beg an attentive and deliberate hearing; for a correct mode of thinking on this subject, I do sincerely believe to be necessary to the lasting prosperity of our country. I say an attentive and *deliberate* hearing, for it is not sufficient that the mind be fixed on the discussion; but it should also be free from those passions and prejudices unfavorable to the reception of truth. The fact that discussion here assumes the form of debate produces a state of things unfavorable to dispassionate attention. In debate here, as between two individuals, the opposite sides are much more disposed to find objections to an argument, be it ever so clear, than to receive it with a proper degree of assent. In their zeal the interest of the country is too often forgot. Mutual recrimination, and not to discover and persuade to do what is right, is but too commonly the object.[4] I hope what I have to say will not be viewed as a mere exercise of skill in a discussion, in which those who hear me have little or no interest; but as containing principles believed to be essential to the public interest. I trust I hold in proper contempt the spirit of idle debate. Its heat and zeal are momentary. Not so with our principles and measures. On them must depend our future prosperity and happiness.

Is the war unjust and inexpedient? This is the question which I now propose to discuss. The eagerness and zeal with which our op-

3. Here and again below, n. 33, Calhoun is using "intuitive" in the sense of "self-evident" as translated in *Works*, II, 71, 95. *R&E* and *AC* follow the *NI* version.

4. *Works*, II, 71, has a free revision of this awkward sentence.

ponents endeavor to prove this point, seem to me not at all consistent with sound principles, or due love of our country. In their
zeal they often presume that we are wrong and our enemy right;
and that on us is the burthen to prove that their charges are false,
before they have attempted to prove them to be true. How contrary
this to the maxims of Roman wisdom! That wise and virtuous
people, so far from presuming their country to be wrong, considered
it as a crime in a citizen to doubt of the justice of the public cause.
In a state of war how worthy of our imitation! It was at the root
of Roman greatness. Without it a free state will ever lose much of
its peculiar and native strength; the spontaneous and concurring
zeal of its citizens. The charge of injustice and inexpediency
against the war necessarily leads me to investigate its cause. It
originated, as agreed on all sides, in certain commercial aggressions
on the part of England, and her practice of impressing American
seamen from American vessels on the high seas. Though I have
named commercial injuries first, it is my intention to give impressment the preference in the order of discussion; not only because
the war is continued for it, but because it is of greater intrinsic
importance. The life and liberty of a citizen are more important to
him and his country than his property; and consequently the obligation to protect the former more sacred than the latter. To the truth
of this position, our political institution bears testimony. A single
judicial process determines on a question of property; but it requires a double investigation, first before a grand jury and then a
petit, before the humblest and most suspected citizen can be deprived of life or liberty. This is a mode of thinking worthy of a free
people, and in fact is essential to the permanent existence of their
freedom. Yes, life and liberty, those precious gifts of Heaven, are
by our laws and constitutions guaranteed to all. They may be
abused and forfeited to the country; but cannot be torn away by
the hand of arbitrary power. Let us bear these sentiments in our
minds and bring them in our bosoms to the discussion of this
subject.

It is fortunate, that the facts connected with impressment are
few and undoubted. I set aside for the present the pretext and principle on which Great Britain acts in relation to it. None can deny
that a great number of American sailors have been impressed from

on board American vessels on the high seas, and by force compelled to serve a sovereign to whom they owe no allegiance, and to fight battles in which they have no interest. It is equally certain, that the practice is of long continuance; and that negotiation has often and in vain been resorted to for redress. I say a great number, rather than specify any particular, because I do not conceive the exact number to be material; and also, because I do not wish to incorporate any thing the least doubtful in the statement. On this point, however, the two governments are pretty well agreed. Ours estimates the entire number taken at something more than 6,000; and the British government acknowledged that at the breaking out of the war, they had sixteen hundred at least on board their public vessels.[5] After deducting from our list the dead by battles and disease, the deserters and the liberated, it will be found that theirs exceeds our estimate. To the shame of the minority, they alone have attempted to throw any doubt on this point—and to diminish the injury of the enemy below their own acknowledgment.

On this simple statement, there are two inferences so clear, that I feel it almost an insult to the understanding of this committee to state them. I must seek for my apology in the efforts of our opponents to render that doubtful which in itself is so manifest; I mean the violation of the rights and liberty of the impressed American seamen, and the correspondent duty imposed on their country to defend them. I know of no illustration of a proposition so perfectly clear. No head can be so impenetrable as not to perceive its truth; no heart so callous as not to feel its obligation. For, who is there in this community of freemen that is willing to renounce the claim of protection which he has on all, or withhold the duty which he is under to all? It is the essence of civil society. Such and so simple is the truth on which the cause of our country stands. On these essential facts and inferences we are then on all sides agreed. The obligation of the government is established. How then are we to be absolved from so sacred a duty? The impressed, the enslaved seamen have invoked the protection of their country. Shall it be extended to them, or shall it be withheld? This

5. For Lord Castlereagh's figures, see Adams, *History of U.S.*, VI, 456, VII, 19; see the reference by Robert Wright of Maryland in this debate—*AC*13-2, p. 1661.

is the question now proposed for our consideration, and which naturally introduces the various arguments of the minority on this important subject. They combat against inferences the most clear and powerful; proportionally perspicuous and strong must be the reasons to justify their conduct. I will commence with that which I believe to be most relied on; because most frequently and zealously urged in justification of our enemy. It is said that they take American seamen [6] by mistake, and not by principle; their object is to take their own seamen, but from the impossibility of distinguishing, the American seaman is impressed. The answer is plain and decisive. The argument is founded in a misconception. The duty which the country owes to the impressed sailors originates in a single fact, that they are unjustly deprived by a foreign nation of their liberty. The principle on which they are deprived of their liberty, or the manner, constitutes no part of it. Whether done by principle or mistake, it is true, may have a bearing on the continuance of the practice and its future extent. For what is done by mistake or accident generally leaves this consolation, that it will not probably occur again; but what is done by principle may be expected to continue. We have not even this hope. The evil is inveterate. The mistake, if one it is, must forever happen so long as the present practice is continued of impressing from American vessels. It, therefore, operates, as it regards us, as if it were the result of principle. I, however, deny the fact on which this justification rests. The object of England is not to take her seamen only. By recurring to official documents on this subject, it will be found, that she impresses persons on board of our vessels, who could not be mistaken for British sailors. She takes indiscriminately Dane, Dutch, Spaniard and seamen of any nation. To speak another language and to wear a different complexion are, it seems, no evidence with the British government that he is not an English sailor.

What then is the principle of that government on this subject? If we are to judge by facts, and not by pretexts, which will never be wanting, if we are simple enough to believe them, it is this: they claim, at least as far as we are concerned, that every seafaring

---

6. In *AC*, p. 1676, "citizens"; in the other three versions, "seamen."

person found on the ocean is presumptively an Englishman and bound to serve the crown of Great Britain. They admit, it is true, this presumption to be rebutted in a single case, and only in that; by the seaman proving that he belongs to the country to which the flag does under which he sails. If, for instance, the vessel is American, that he was born in the United States. The impress officer, the very person interested against him, is, however, the judge and jury who presides in this mock trial of nativity. It is thus the American flag is insulted—it is thus the American citizen is stripped of his liberty under its protection! At home, he holds his liberty under the protection of the most sacred laws; abroad— no, I will not admit the distinction, for while under our flag he is still at home—he holds life and liberty at the mercy of every in- significant drunken midshipman! But let us attend for a moment longer to the object of this principle of the British government, as illustrated by practice. A war in Europe in which England is engaged sooner or later extends to all of the other powers in that part of the globe. In consequence of her superiority at sea, the navigation and commerce of other states are destroyed, or sus- pended in a state of war; and their seamen, who cannot readily change their habits, are compelled to seek employment in foreign service. Till lately, America remaining neutral, and offering high wages, they naturally preferred ours. To this state of facts, her principle of impressing all foreign seamen was applied; and by its operation forced those who were by their own consent employed in our vessels, to serve by compulsion in her navy. Thus by a single process, under the pretext of taking her own seamen, the commerce and navigation of the world are converted into a nursery to sup- port the British navy; and the practice of impressment from neu- trals, on investigation, is discovered to be, like all of her other encroachments, a system of universal monopoly. Unless resisted by the steady and persevering efforts of other nations, she must eventually draw the commerce of the world into the vortex of her system.

It is next urged that this is an ancient custom on the part of England, and Europe generally; that it is a part of the law of

nations to impress on board of neutral vessels on the high seas.[7]
Those who urge this argument ought to substantiate it by a reference to the facts and to elementary writers on public law. Until
this is done, it cannot be considered in a stronger light than a mere
assertation. I, for my part, do not believe that it ever constituted
the custom of Europe, or that of England, till since the period of
the American war. If it were a general custom, why not recognized
by some of the many writers on the laws of nations? They minutely
state the cases in which a belligerent may enter a neutral vessel for
the purpose of search. Why not this also? None of the rights of
search would be more important and would better deserve their
attention than this, if it really were one. Their silence, then, is
decisive against the custom. I know that some English writers have
set up an old claim formed on the orders of their government; but
there is no proof of acquiescence on the part of other powers;
and, if they had, it could not be obligatory on us. The law of
nations is composed principally of usages originating in mutual
convenience. Among the nations of modern Europe who are distinguishable by their language and countenance, it is possible that
impressment on board of neutral vessels there may not be liable
to the mistakes and abuses of which we complain, and even that
it might be a mutual convenience. Such a custom, then, would not
be extraordinary. But were those nations related, as are America
and England, and if the practice must from necessity be attended
with incessant abuse, it never could exist. If our opponents, then,
had proved, and not merely asserted, such a custom, as between
us and England our country would have formed an exception. It
is not applicable to our condition; it is unequal, not reciprocal,
and attended with incessant abuse. As applied to us, then, the general usage, if there were one, ought to be removed by treaty, so
as to suit the mutual convenience of both parties; an object which
this country has ever been anxious to effect, but which has been
studiously avoided by our enemy. If, however, our opponents still
insist that it is a right under the law of nations, and must, not

7. The extremists among the opposition speakers cited international law for
the doctrine of perpetual allegiance and, therefore, for the right of a belligerent
to impress even those seamen who had been naturalized by the United States
(see for instance, p. 1015, 1389, 1508).

withstanding the argument which I have advanced, be considered as applicable to us, we may meet usage with usage; or rather doubtful uncertain usage, and opposed to reason, by that which is undoubted and founded in the very essence of civil society. If to impress in neutral vessels is an usage of England and the rest of Europe, how much more so is it to afford protection to the subjects against foreign violence! This is the usage which is certain and universal—not confined to any particular nation—not originating in accidental circumstances; all states, the most weak and contemptible, claim it; and it is so mixed into the very essence of society, that it cannot be relinquished without certain destruction. On this custom, which combines both right and duty, we may oppose any pretext or claim of our enemy.[8]

But, say some of our opponents, we are willing to defend native born American seamen, but not the naturalized.[9] I know not how those who make this distinction can answer a simple question founded on fact. American seamen, yes, sixteen hundred, at least, native born American seamen, by the acknowledgment of the British government, are impressed and held in bondage. If, then, you are willing to defend such, why not support the war now carried on solely for the defence of [10] these unfortunate citizens? What avail is the declaration, that you are willing to defend them, when you will not move a finger in their cause? But the distinction between native and naturalised is without truth or reason. It constitutes no part of the controversy between the two countries. We contended for the defence of American seamen generally; the enemy has not distinguished between the one or the other class.

8. Calhoun was evidently using Vattel's *Law of Nations.* See the 1796, New York edition, and compare two passages from Vattel: "customs consecrated by long use," (p. 56); "if that custom contains anything unjust or illegal, it is of no force" (p. 57); and note the paragraph entitled: "Of searching neutral ships" (p. 407). Compare also the definition, from Grotius, of the Law of Nations as given in the preface (p. v): "a law established by the common consent of the people."

9. See for instance, *AC*13-2, p. 1507-8, 1557.

10. In *Works*, II, 78, there is gratuitously inserted at this point: "right, outraged in the persons of these unfortunate citizens." Thomas P. Grosvenor's speech on Mar. 3 (*AC*13-2, p. 1774), near the end of the debate, included an attack on Calhoun's statement about the attitude of the minority to impressment of native seamen; the speech is not given in the *Intelligencer,* but the subject is noted in the *New York Evening Post* of Mar. 15—see n. 38 below.

He insists on continuing a custom which makes both equally liable to his oppression. We will not, we can not [11] hear of a distinction, until some security is afforded against the abuse of which we complain. Till then I can consider it only as an equivocation, which acknowledges the duty of the government to protect, but evades the discharge of it. We are told that our seamen ask no protection, and that it is strange that those who are most remote and least interested should discover the greatest anxiety for them. As to the first part of this argument, I deny its truth. The sailors have claimed our protection. They have importuned and invoked their country for it. We have had their application for protection laid before this House in the form of a document. It forms a large volume.[12] Considering the cold indifference with which we have heard their prayer, I wonder that they have not long since ceased to consider us as their guardians. But we who stand forth to discharge this sacred duty, are charged with being back-woodsmen, men who never saw a ship till convened here in our legislative capacity. Admit the fact; and what then? Such generous sympathy for those who stand connected with us only by the ties of citizenship, does honor to our country. I hope it is not strange. It is usual. Our history abounds with many instances of this sympathy of the whole with any part. When it ceases to be natural, we will cease to be one nation. It constitutes our real union. The rest is form. The wonder is, in fact, on the other side. Since it cannot be denied, that American citizens are held in foreign bondage, how strange that those who boast of being neighbors and relations, should be dead to all sympathy, or should not have the manly spirit to make a generous effort for their relief! There was a time when our opponents, to their honor, were not so cold on this subject. The venerable gentleman from Massachusetts and another gentleman high in the ranks of his party, formerly felt and spoke as we now do on it—like Americans.[13] How unhappy the change! How unaccountable! Unless indeed by the poisonous effects of the spirit

11. In *Works*, II, 78, the sense of this is changed by rendering it: "we have not—we shall not."

12. See for instance, AC13-2, p. 1509. The "volume" has not been identified; compare *ASP, For. Rel.*, III, 689.

13. See AC13-2, p. 1713 and 1725-7 for Timothy Pickering's speech of Feb. 28.

of systematic opposition—a spirit which, I lately observed on another occasion, clings more strongly to the cause of a party, than that of the country.[14]

But great frauds, say our opponents, are committed in the certificates of protection. I will not spend much time on this frivolous argument. What right has England to complain of the frauds, if they really do exist? Whether they do or not, I do not think worth the enquiry. The argument taken at the best, can have no weight except with those who think that the freeborn citizens of this country, under our flag, are to be protected like a slave by a pass in his pocket. To give weight to it we must forget our rights and duties as an independent nation. The framers of the law, under which the protections are taken out, did not intend that they should protect while navigating the ocean. The object was to identify the seamen as Americans in the ports of foreign countries; and this construction has been given to it by our government in its negociation with the British. In this view the law is not unworthy of the wisdom and independence of our country; but I can scarcely conceive a greater national degradation than the policy of affording protection to our seamen on the high seas and under our flag by a pass.[15]

On the subject of impressment one argument only remains to be replied to. The practice of taking seamen in our vessels is necessary, say our opponents, to the existence of England. I would be happy to know the reason why it is necessary. We have pledged ourselves by a law, which we offer to make the basis of a treaty, not to employ a single British sailor.[16] The provisions of the bill are ample; and we are willing to give her every reasonable security on this point. When the assertion is then made in the face of this law and disposition to exclude her seamen, that the practice of impressing on board of our vessels is necessary to her existence, it must be meant, if any thing is, in relation to American sailors. If so, before we surrender our rights and duty to the disposition of

14. No. 90.
15. The law of May 28, 1796. See J. F. Zimmerman, *Impressment of American Seamen*, p. 55-8. The frauds which Calhoun dismissed so lightly were in fact a major charge by the opposition. See, for instances, AC13-2, p. 1509, 1529, 1557, 1723.
16. See No. 73 NOTE.

a foreign power, I think it would be prudent to establish two points connected with this subject. In the first place, it ought to be clearly proved to be necessary to the existence of England. I, for one, will not agree to yield our independence on mere assertion, however respectable the authority may be by which it is made. In the next place it ought to be proved to be our duty to submit. The sense of moral obligation is peculiarly strong in the bosoms of the American people. However great the sacrifice, if our opponents can establish it to their satisfaction, to be their duty, I dare pledge myself they will make it.[17] Till both are satisfactorily proved, it would be highly unreasonable for them to demand of this country an acquiescence in a practice so ruinous. Our existence is at stake no less than hers; or rather the danger to her is imaginary; to us real and certain. An undeviating attachment to its duty is the blood and life of a free state. Habitual departure from it, must sooner or later be fatal. It infuses a poison into the system, which will corrupt and destroy. Take this very case. It is our duty, most sacredly our duty, to protect the life and liberty of our citizens against foreign oppression. Instead of doing our duty, we have for many years quietly beheld them forced into a hateful foreign service. What has been the reason of this conduct of ours? The want of power? No; a vigorous and decisive effort in the very first instance, before the enemy had learnt to be arrogant by our submission, would have strangled it in its birth. We yielded because we wished to enjoy the blessings of peace; its ease, its comforts, above all, its means of making money. The practical language of the government to the people was, it is better to be rich than to be virtuous. Can we then wonder at the alarming growth of avarice? It is to be traced back to this original sin of our government. The first American citizen impressed and not immediately liberated, was good cause, in my opinion, imperious cause of war. No calculation of gain should have prevented it. To do our duty is more important than to be rich.

Before I take my leave of this subject, I will present to the committee what I consider as a confession of the justice of our

17. *AC*, p. 1680, omits "to their satisfaction," (which is to be found in *NI* and *R&E*); *Works*, II, 81, also omits it but adds a word to make it "clearly establish."

cause, and the correctness of our policy. I allude to the habitual and obvious misstatement, which our opponents make on this subject. They say that we continue the war to compel Great Britain to renounce the right of impressing her own subjects. They must know that this is not the fact; and that it is calculated to mislead the opinion of the people. Why not state it as it really is? Why not say what they must know to be true [18] that the war is continued to protect from impressment American sailors? Is it not a fear of the public sentiment? Is it not a strong acknowledgment that the principle we contend for, if understood, would meet with kind and congenial feelings in the bosom of the American people? When the head is right, there is among a free people but little danger of the heart. When they are agreed in facts and inferences they will never disagree in sentiment.

I will now proceed to consider the next cause of the war, the injuries done by Great Britain to our commerce. It is not my intention to speak of them in the detail, or to consider them as particular acts injurious to our trading interest. This view has been often presented and is well understood. I propose to ascend to their origin and to point out the spirit and principles of the government from which they have [grown].[19] This view has not yet been taken, though it is of the most interesting nature. The detail of British injustice may rouse our indignation, but it is only by reflecting on the principles and character of her government that we can justly appreciate the extent of our danger, and the measures best calculated to counteract it. Even the repeal of her Orders in Council and the consequent suspension of commercial injuries do not strip this view of the subject of any of its interest. For, it ought ever to be remembered, that the orders rescinding the celebrated orders of 1807 and 1809, expressly retain their principle.[20] They then only slumber; and, as sure as we exist, her temper and policy will rouse them into action on the first suitable occasion, unless prevented by the firm and spirited conduct of this and other na-

18. The *NI* and *Works* versions include "must"; the other two omit it (*AC*13-2, p. 1681; *R&E*, p. 12).

19. *NI, AC*, p. 1681, and *R&E*, p. 13, read "flown"; *Works*, II, 82, "proceeded."

20. *ASP, For. Rel.*, III, 433.

tions interested in a free trade. The commercial policy of Great Britain, which has vexed and annihilated the commerce of every other nation began distinctly to develope itself in the year 1756; from which time to the present, I assert, without the fear of contradiction, she has habitually struggled to enlarge what she terms her maritime and belligerent rights on the ocean at the expence of neutrals. The assertion is predicated on historical facts, which the general information of most of the members of this committee will enable them to decide for themselves. I have neither the inclination nor the time to recite and examine the whole series in connection. I will content myself with taking a brief notice of some of the most leading and characteristic facts.

At their head, in point of time, is the order which takes its name from the year already mentioned, and which distinctly marks the commencement of this policy. The character of this celebrated rule or order is so well known as to need no comment. In the war of our Revolution, she still farther enlarged her maritime and belligerent policy, particularly in the shape of blockades, since so enormously extended. This, and other encroachments at that time, produced that association of nations called the Armed Neutrality. The object of it was to check farther encroachments, and to remedy those that already existed. It was acceded to by almost every nation in Europe. On the breaking out of the French Revolution, she in pursuit of the same policy made farther encroachments. One of the most considerable, and which was severely felt by this country, was an enlargement of articles contraband of war, so as to extend them to the numerous and important articles of bread stuffs. This was during Washington's administration, and was the principal one of that period of our history. Preparations were then made to appeal to arms for the redress of so serious an injury, but was prevented by England's agreeing to make compensation for the injuries which we had sustained. With such spirit did our government then act, although the injury then sustained dwindles into nothing compared to the present; and with so little accuracy has a gentleman from New York (Mr. Grosvenor) spoken, who not only magnified the aggressions of that period over the present, but stated that Washington was unwilling to resort to arms for redress.[21] In the present war with France, her maritime and commercial policy has hastened to its perfection. In the year 1805, it assumed an aspect most threatening to our commerce. It fell on our carrying trade, at that time in a most flourishing condition. Let it be remarked—let it be laid up in our memory—that the old rule of '56, the parent of all these aggressions, was after many years revived, and made the apology for our wrongs. Just so may we expect the revoked orders to revive. Blockades and Orders in Council followed the destruction of our carrying trade. They are too recent and too severely felt to need a particular recital. Negociation was tried—negociation failed; and the injuries continuing, have ended in the present relation between the two countries.

The English maritime and belligerent policy is not only such as I have proved it to be, but it is a policy peculiar to her, and is in opposition to the interest of the rest of the world. It is the interest and wish of all other civilized nations to ameliorate, or, if the expression is justifiable, to humanize the belligerent rights on the ocean. England stands alone. To establish this position it would be necessary to consider a little more in detail the series of facts to which I have already alluded; but as I am fearful of being tedious, I must check my inclination and confine myself to a few observations only. A signal proof of the peculiar policy of England may be found in the history of the Armed Neutrality, which had for its object, as already observed, the restriction of some of those pretended belligerent rights. Russia, Sweden, Denmark, Portugal, Spain, and even France, though then a belligerent power, acceded to it. England alone refused.[22] It may however be said, that France, too, has often committed injuries on neutral trade. The fact is admitted. But without wishing to apologize for her, I conceive there has been a marked distinction (arising out of her situation) between her conduct and England. The latter has steadily pursued a policy hostile to neutral commerce on established principles; the former has been irregular in her hostilities,

21. Grosvenor's two-hour speech on Feb. 21 and 22 is noted in *AC*13-2, p. 1587, 1589. It is described in *NI*, Feb. 24, 1814 as "able and spirited," and in the *Federal Republican* of Feb. 23 as "forcible," but was not printed in either paper.

22. This sentence is found in the other three versions, but not in *Annals*— see *AC*13-2, p. 1682.

indicating more of passion than system. Besides, she has always expressed a regret for her injuries; and represented them, however unjustifiable, as intended to counteract those of England.

It remains now to prove what is the tendency of the British maritime and commercial policy; and where, if not counteracted, it will consummate itself.[23] Reason and the general convenience of nations have for centuries established certain usages, by which belligerent powers are in many instances restrained from doing all the injury in their power to each other from a regard to the interest of others. These usages constitute the rights of neutrals, which are for the most part well defined by the many writers on the laws of nations. Under the cover of what she calls her belligerent and maritime rights, the object and tendency of the British policy is to throw off those restraints on the ocean. It is in fact to undo all that has been gained to civilization on that element, and to return to the lawless state of barbarous ages. It is the interest of every other power to restrain her within the limits of the ancient barriers; for if they are once transcended, there are no limits but what her power or interest may dictate. Neutral commerce, as such, will be annihilated. She will judge according to her pleasure what is beneficial to her enemy, and what to herself. The [*latter*] will be spared, the [*former*] destroyed.[24] Nor will the evil stop here. The waves of power are incessantly washing away the mounds that restrain them. The transition is easy from this boundless extension of her belligerent policy, to a system of universal monopoly in peace as well as war; a system which considers the ocean as her peculiar domain. I omitted, in its proper place, an argument which strongly illustrates this part of the subject; I allude to the great changes made in the British Court of Admiralty. Formerly it held jurisdiction, like all similar tribunals in other countries, under the laws of nations only.[25] It was the creature of those laws; and intended only to carry their rules into execution. They were, of course, not under the municipal laws of the country where they happened to be

23. *Works*, II, 85: "in what if not counteracted, it must terminate."

24. The *Intelligencer* version, with "latter" and "former" in reverse position, is copied by *R&E* (p. 16) but corrected by *Annals* (p. 1683); in *Works*, II, 86, the sentence is corrected and revised.

25. Note Pickering's reply to this—*AC*13-2, p. 1755.

located, as far as it regarded the rules of their decision. Thus constituted, they were one of the principal ornaments of the civilization of modern times. The whole of this is now reversed. The Courts of Admiralty receive laws as regularly from the British government, as those of Westminster. The only difference is, that the statutes of Parliament form the rules of decision to the one, and the Orders in Council to the other. It is thus, that England legislates for the ocean; and consequently for the world, on that great highway—and has her proper tribunal with commensurate jurisdiction, to carry into effect her laws. But why should I consume time to prove her maritime policy? Who is there so stupid as not to see and feel its effect? You cannot look towards her shores and not behold it. You may see it in her Parliament, her prints, her theatres and in her very songs. It is scarcely disguised. It is her pride and boast. The nature of her policy is then manifest and admitted; but it will be asked how can you counteract it? I answer, by the measures now pursued; by force, by war; not by remonstrance, not by negotiation; and still less by leaving it to itself. The nature of its growth indicates its remedy. It originated in power, has grown just in proportion as opposing power has been removed, and can only be restrained by power. Nations are for the most part not restrained by moral principles, but by fear. It is an old maxim, that they have heads but not hearts. They see their own interest, but do not sympathize for the wrongs of others. Such is the fact in relation to England. When neutrals are numerous and powerful, their rights are in some degree respected; when few and inconsiderable, despised. This last has been the unfortunate state of the world for the last twenty years. That counteracting influence, that repulsive power by which she was bound to her proper orb, has been almost wholly removed. This country alone was left to support the rights which belong to neutrals. Perilous was the condition, and arduous the task. We were not intimidated. We stood opposed to her usurpation; and by our spirit and efforts have done all in our power to save the last vestiges of neutral rights. Yes; our embargoes, non-intercourse, non-importation, and, finally war, were all manly exertions to preserve the rights of this and all other nations from the deadly grasp of the British maritime policy.

But, say our opponents, these efforts are lost—and our condition hopeless. If so, it only remains for us to assume the habit of our condition. We must submit—humbly submit—crave pardon, and hug our chains. It is not wise to provoke where we cannot resist. But let us be well assured of the hopeless nature of our condition before we sink into submission. On what do our opponents rest this despondent and slavish belief? On the recent events in Europe? I admit they are great; and well calculated to impose on the imagination. Our enemy never presented a more imposing exterior. His fortune is at the flood. But I am admonished by universal experience, that such prosperity is the most fickle of human condition. From the flood the tide dates its ebb; from the meridian the sun commences his decline. There is more of sound philosophy than fiction in the fickleness which poets attribute to fortune. Prosperity has its weakness; adversity its strength. In many respects our enemy has lost by those very changes which seem to be so much in his favor. He can now no more claim to be struggling for existence; no more to be fighting the battles of the world, and in defence of the liberties of mankind. The magic cry of French influence is lost. Hence were drawn those motives which stimulated her efforts almost to a morbid action; which united the continent to her cause, and in some degree damped the ardor of her rival in power. In this very hall we are not strangers to their magic influence. Here, even here, the cry of French influence, that baseless fiction, that phantom of faction, now banished, often resounded. I rejoice that the spell is broken by which it was attempted to bind the generous spirit of this country. The minority can no longer act under cover; but will be obliged to defend their opposition on its intrinsic merit.

It is not in this respect only, that our enemy has lost by the late events. The tremendous and exhausting conflicts of this and the preceding campaign seem at last to dispose the continental powers to peace. If they have a just conception of their true interest, and are not prevented by British gold and intrigue, a continental peace will ensue. There certainly is much alarm in England on the probability of such an event. Should it fortunately be the case—should the allies prove content with their fortune and France submit to her present limits, all Europe must speedily combine against the

British maritime policy. The great power on land being crushed, to use the language of our opponents, but more properly being forced within proper limits, the great monopolist on the ocean will, I trust, be the next object of fear and resistance. The principle of the Armed Neutrality is not and cannot be forgotten. It exists essentially in the policy of modern Europe. Ever since the discovery of the passage round the Cape of Good Hope and of this continent on which we have the proud pre-eminence of being the first great civilized power, a great change has gradually been working in Europe. For two centuries the character of that part of the world has been eminently trading and commercial. The habits of every part is formed on that state of things. There lives scarcely a human being from the ice and snows of Siberia to the sunny plains of Italy, who has not some habit, the gratification of which depends on commerce. Hence it has become an object of primary policy. All of the wars in Europe, for many years, have, with few exceptions, been more or less connected with it. The policy of every court has been to obtain commercial supplies on the best terms, and as much as possible through the agency of their own subjects. With such habits and policy, it is impossible that they can behold with indifference the monopoly of Great Britain. They will not quietly suffer the common highway of nations, intended by a kind Providence for the common intercourse and benefit of all, to be converted into a domain of her crown. No; the ocean cannot become property. Like light and air, it is insusceptible of the idea of property: Heaven has given it to man in such abundance and perfection, that no art or industry of his is needed to increase its quantity or improve its quality. All empires attempted to be raised on it must partake of the fickleness of its waves.

A policy so injurious to the common interest of mankind, must sooner or later unite the world against her. For many years, her encroachments under the dread of France, have advanced without exciting much jealousy. The attention of all the nations of Europe was exclusively directed to the maintenance of their existence, menaced by the power of France. To preserve life is more important than to acquire comfort; so to resist that power was more imperious than to oppose England. Liberated now from fear, they will soon have leisure to attend to their interest. The difference between our policy and that of other nations in this respect, is only in appearance and not reality. Each acted in a manner suitable to the circumstances under which it found itself. Attachment to France, as proclaimed by British partizans, formed no part of our policy. We were safe from the danger with which her power menaced other nations. A broad ocean was our immediate security. We resisted that power which then and now presses on us, and which will soon cause itself to be felt and resisted by all. Should the course of events be such as I have described, then will the wisdom and spirit of our country be universally applauded. Our situation was trying and responsible. We alone had to sustain all the rights and duties attached to the neutral character. We were not intimidated by its difficulties. We dared, single handed as we were, to make a stand against the favorite and obstinate policy of our enemy. The present and temporary interest of commerce was nobly surrendered for its permanent advantages. The example can scarcely fail to produce its effect; but if unfortunately we should be left alone to maintain the contest; and, if, in consequence, which may God forbid, necessity should compel us to yield for the present, yet our generous efforts will not be in vain. A mode of thinking and a tone of sentiment are excited, that must stimulate to future and more successful struggles. What we cannot effect with eight millions of people, will be done with twenty. The great cause will not be yielded: No; never! never! We cannot renounce our right to the ocean which Providence has spread before our doors; nor will we ever hold that which is the immediate gift of Heaven under the license of any nation. We have already had success worthy of our cause. The future is audibly pronounced by the splendid victories over the Guerriere Java and Macedonian. We, and all nations, are in them taught a lesson never to be forgot. Opinion is power. The charm of British naval invincibility is broken.

In this, the only just view of our contest, how pitiful appear the objections of our opponents! Some pecuniary difficulties in Massachusetts and in other places. And must we for them renounce our lasting prosperity and greatness? Have we no fortitude; no self-command? Must we, like children, yield to the impulse of present pleasure, however fatal? If the maritime parts of Massachusetts suffer let them remember that, if the war should be successful; if our future commerce and navigation should be secure, they will partake most largely in the advantages, common and great indeed to all, but peculiarly so to them.

Suppose that our opponents, who object to every thing, had been at the helm of government; and that an opposite line of policy had been pursued. No embargoes, no non-intercourses, no non-importations, no war, and, in fact, no resistance to the injuries and aggressions of Great Britain—who can be ignorant of what would have been the consequence? They would have multiplied in number and degree till our commerce would be annihilated. Un-resisted, they would constitute future principles, and our acquies-cence be construed into an acknowledgement of their truth. Then would we have felt what the experience of all ages has taught; that it is more easy to maintain than to wrest back usurped rights. Wrongs submitted to produce contrary effects in the oppressor and oppressed. Oppression strengthens and prepares for new oppres-sion; submission debases to farther submission.[26] The first wrong, by the universal law of our nature, is most easily resisted. It excites the greatest degree of union and indignation. Let that be submitted to; let the consequent debasement and loss of national honor be felt, and nothing but the grinding hand of oppression can force to resistance. I know not which to pronounce most guilty; the nation that inflicts the wrong, or that which quietly submits to it. In other respects the difference is marked. The former may be hated, but is respected, at least feared; while the latter is below pity, and any other feeling of the human heart, but sovereign contempt. In sub-mission then there is no remedy; our honor lost; our commerce under the control of our oppressor. What next? The hopes and fears (those universal instruments of government) of the whole mercantile parts of this country, and all connected interests would be turned towards Great Britain; for the power of legislation over our commerce would be virtually transferred from the American Congress to the King in Council. Need I trace the consequence? Need I paint the corrupt and debasing influence?[27] The beams of

26. The last clause of this sentence (as well as the sentence identified by n. 27 below), appears in the other three versions, but is omitted from *Annals* (p. 1687) by what appears to have been a clerical error.

27. See n. 26 above.

the mid-day sun are scarcely more clear. The very contempt which such baseness would excite, justly excite in our enemy would ensure our slavery. It is impossible to allow any right, much less independence, to that which creeps and licks the dust. Such is the condition of our nature. We must have the spirit to resist wrongs or be slaves. Such were the alternatives presented to our country; and such would have been the result of the opposite policy, now recommended and applauded by our opponents. I have now delivered all that I intended on this most interesting view of our cause.[28] It has an elevation and clearness which render it attractive to my mind. I love to dwell on it, because it imparts a steady and clear conviction of the wisdom and necessity of that course of measures, to the adoption of which it is my pride to have in part contributed. I feel how little interesting all of the common topics of opposition are after the view already taken. The descent gives a shock, which I know the committee will partake with him who is addressing them. If, however, they will continue their attention, I will offer a few observations on a subject which has made a principal figure in the speeches of our opponents.

I allude to the character which they give to this war; that it is offensive and not defensive. On this point, I spoke fully when the army bill was under consideration. What was then said has been introduced and objected to on this occasion.[29] I then stated, the difference between an offensive and defensive war consisted in the motive and cause. If, for instance, a war is forced on the nation waging it by the oppression of that against which it is declared, it would be defensive, however it might be carried on; but, if on the contrary, it originated in ambition or any improper motive, it would be offensive. This distinction is not only supported by reason, but by the declamation of our opponents. They have for almost 2 years been in the habit of denouncing offensive war. They then acknowledged that such a war is wicked, and how can it bear that character but by its cause? It seems now, that they have changed their grounds. We hear no more of the wickedness of offensive war; but, what is most strange, all their efforts are made to prove that it may be an innocent and virtuous thing. That nation, say they, is en-

28. *AC* (p. 1687) "case"; in the other three versions, "cause."
29. See No. 90 and *AC*13-2, p. 1324.

gaged in an offensive war, who first assumes a warlike attitude.
However just, however necessary the cause of assuming it, the war
is still offensive. Be it so. I care not for words. My answer is decisive. If my conception is just, that an offensive war is to be tested
by the cause, I then pronounce ours not to be of that character;
but, if your definition is correct, then an offensive war may be most
just, most virtuous and necessary, and all of your declamation
against it is idle and unmeaning rant. I tender an option, and care
not which is taken. Those who defend a bad cause act imprudently
in descending to particulars. Our opponents by doing so in this
case have furnished the best reply to their own arguments.

On expatriation and retaliation, I will say nothing. The hour is
late and I feel myself somewhat exhausted. I pass it the more
cheerfully, as the gentleman from Louisiana (Mr. Robertson) and
my colleague have replied freely to the objection on those subjects.[30]

Before I proceed farther, it will be necessary to restate the propositions with which I commenced, so that the entire chain of the
argument, both that which has already been advanced, and what
remains to be, may be distinctly seen. It will be remembered, that
I reduced all of the arguments and objections of our opponents to
the passage of this bill into two general positions.[31] First, that the
loan cannot be had, or must be had at an exorbitant interest; and
in the next, if it could be, still it ought not to be granted, because
the war is unjust and inexpedient. I also stated that the latter position comprehended the assertion of the facts of the injustice and
inexpediency of the war; and the assumed inference that they
would, if true, justify the minority in their opposition to, and rejection of the [*loan*].[32] On the alleged injustice and inexpediency of
the war, I have presented my opinion; and trust I have satisfied
the committee that its justice is demonstrably clear and its expedi-

30. Thomas B. Robertson, of Louisiana, p. 1620-7, and Langdon Cheves,
the Speaker of the House, p. 1637-50.
31. In this paragraph Calhoun was using the word "position" in its sense
of thesis or proposition. The *R&E* version follows the *Intelligencer*, the *Annals*
(p. 1688) substitutes "propositions" for "positions," and in *Works*, II, 94, the
paragraph is revised.
32. The *Intelligencer* and the *Annals* (p. 1688) have "war" for "loan"; the
R&E version (p. 24) makes the obvious correction, and *Works* (II, 94) revises
the sentence.

ency unquestionable; or rather its necessity imperious, if the preservation of the independence of the country constitutes political necessity.

But is it justifiable to withhold the loan, admitting the war to be, in the opinion of our opponents, unjust and inexpedient? This is the question now proposed to be discussed. It contains the practical consequence of all that has been said in opposition. Few propositions involve principles so deeply connected with the lasting prosperity of our republican institutions; and in which, consequently, it is more necessary to think correctly. Error here cannot be indifferent. A false mode of thinking must endanger the existence of the republic. I must then again entreat the attentive and deliberate audience of the committee, while I offer my opinion and reasons on so interesting a subject.

In considering the question, how far a war thought to be unjust or improper by any portion of the people, would warrant their opposition to it, after it is constitutionally declared, I will set out of it extreme or flagrant injustice. A war impious or sacrilegious cannot be governed by the general rules which apply to ordinary cases. At least, it is not necessary for me to consider such extreme cases, as none can impute a character of that kind to the present.

I have already stated that the sum proposed to be raised by this bill is indispensibly necessary to meet the expenses of the ensuing year; and that if it is withheld, it must communicate a fatal shock to public credit. In that event, not only the invasion of Canada would be prevented, which some gentlemen state to be their object, but the whole operations of the war, even that which is defensive in the strictest sense, would be abandoned. Officers and soldiers will no more serve in our garrisons than in Canada, without pay. It is idle to talk of preventing the reduction of the enemy's provinces only, by withholding the loan. Nor can gentlemen be serious. They have opposed every attempt to raise supplies in whatever shape it has appeared. They appear to be bold in facing bankruptcy. But have they reflected on the disastrous effects of their efforts should they be successful? The old and recent creditors of the government, the army, the navy, which they boast of cherishing, in a word, every individual would feel the calamity; for private no less than public credit would partake of the shock. I am wholly at a loss to perceive on what principle of expediency, policy or morality, such conduct can be justified. Surely it is not an intuitive proposition,[33] that because the war is simply unjust and inexpedient in the opinion of the minority, therefore they have a right to involve the country in ruin, and place it bound as a suppliant at the feet of an haughty enemy. They then ought to state some intelligible and satisfactory principle on which their conduct may be justified. I have sought with attention, but have not found the semblance of such a one. On the contrary, all the analogies of private life, as well as reason, forbid and condemn the conduct of our opponents. Suppose a father to do some act, which, in the opinion of a son, is not strictly just or proper by which he becomes involved in a contest with a stranger. Would the son be justified in taking part against him? How much less then can any party be in opposition to their country in a war with another nation; for it stands in the place of the common parent of all; and comprehends, to use the language of a member from North Carolina (Mr. Gaston) all of the charities of life.[34]

But what will be thought of the motive and conduct of the minority, when I state that much the greater part of the expenses of the war, for which this bill is intended in part to provide, has been incurred by their votes as much as by that of the majority. I hold in my hands the journal of the 1st session of the 12th Congress; by which it appears that the report of the Committee on Foreign Relations was supported, not only by the votes on this side of the House, but by a decided majority on the other. The report ended in recommending six resolutions to the adoption of the House; to fill up the old establishment; to raise 10,000 additional troops; to increase the navy; to provide for calling out of the militia; and to authorise the arming of private vessels. On the first of these there was a minority of 11 votes only; so unanimous was this House at that time! On some of the others, it is true, it was more considerable; but all met with the support of the gentlemen on the other side. What ought to be particularly noted is, when the Senate and this House disagreed on the second, to raise an additional number of regular troops, the former supporting

33. See n. 3 above.
34. AC13-2, p. 1559.

25,000 and the latter at first 10,000 men, it was increased to the Senate's number by the votes of the minority. The leading men on the side of the opposition at that time, among whom was a gentleman from Massachusetts well known in this country (Mr. Quincy) and another from New York of great influence (Mr. Emott) and many whom I now behold, voted for the report.[35] I have taken the trouble to turn down the pages where the respective votes are recorded, for the satisfaction of any member who may desire it. With what countenance can our opponents then withhold the supplies for expenses incurred by their own votes? Will they say that they knew not the object of the report? Miserable the excuse, and such as it is, not founded in fact. War with Great Britain was unequivocally announced; and even the invasion of Canada, now so hateful to them, was distinctly avowed. Was their object to embarrass and finally to put the majority out of power? Will they dare to make an avowal so disgraceful to their party? The truth is that the necessity of the war was at that time almost universally acknowledged; and as to its justice, no one doubted it. Its injustice was an invention of a period long subsequent. It is thus, that consistency, no less than reason, ought to check the minority in their opposition, and to induce them to unite with us to carry the war to a successful issue.

I would be glad to know what limits our opponents have prescribed to their opposition. If the supplies may be withheld because the war is unjust and improper in their opinion, will not the same reason justify every species of resistance both in and out of this House? If the public faith solemnly plighted—if the happiness of the country, are no checks to opposition, I see no reason why the laws or Constitution should be. Let some intelligible limitation be prescribed. I see none—to me it appears lawless. I know it will be said, is all opposition to be proscribed? Is none justifiable? We proscribe nothing. We propose no law; no restraint on the conduct of the minority. We appeal to the virtue and the intelligence of the community only. On the people must finally fall the ruinous effects of erroneous and dangerous principles. If our liberty is lost, theirs is the cost. Our Constitution supposes a degree of good sense

35. *AC*12-1, p. 691.

and virtue in them adequate to self-government. If the fact is not so, our system of government is founded in error. They only can arrest the effects of dangerous opposition. What they permanently condemn will meet with no support here.

How far the minority in a state of war may justly oppose the measures of government, is a question of the greatest delicacy. On the one side, an honest man, if he believed the war to be unjust or unwise, would not disavow his opinion; but on the contrary, an upright citizen would do no act, whatever he might think of the war, to put his country in the power of the enemy. It is this double aspect of the subject which indicates the course that reason approbates. Among ourselves at home we may contend; but whatever is requisite to give the reputation and the arms of the republic a superiority over its enemy, it is the duty of all, the minority no less than the majority, to support. Like the system of our state and general governments—within they are many; to the world but one. So it ought to be with parties; among ourselves we may divide, but in relation to other nations there ought to be only the American people. In some cases it may possibly be doubtful, even to the most conscientious, how to act. It is one of the misfortunes of differing from the rest of the community on the subject of war.

I cannot refrain from alluding to an observation made by a gentleman from North Carolina, (Mr. Gaston) connected with this view of the subject. Speaking of the reduction of Canada, he observed, that his judgment and feelings were at variance; that when he consulted the former, he believed our efforts would be unsuccessful; but when the latter, his regard to the interest of his country led him to hope for success.[36] I do not allude to this observation to point out any contradiction between it and his opposition to the passage of this bill; though I think it would be difficult to reconcile them. My object is to make an open acknowledgment to him for what I think the commencement of a more correct mode of thinking in relation to the war. I thank the gentleman for his good wishes; and that in relation to the reduction of Canada, I know it does not contain an approbation of the attempted conquest —but it comports with the conduct of a good citizen, that since

36. See *AC* 13-2, p. 1568-9.

the attempt is determined on by the constituted authority, to wish
it well. This seems to me to be in the true spirit of an honest opposition; and I hope it will be so extended as to influence the general
conduct of the minority. It is thus we may divide among ourselves,
and the national strength not be impaired. For I do not believe
with those members of the minority who assert there is no loss of
strength by their opposition. We are asked by them, why have you
not effected your objects? You command the purse and the sword
of the country, and can order whatever is necessary to be done. I
will tell you the reason—because we have not your good wishes,
it is this only which can add heart to heart. Government, it is true,
can command the arm and hand, the bone and muscle of the
nation; but these are powerless, nerveless without the concurring
good wishes of the community. He who, in estimating the strength
of a people, looks only to their numbers and physical force, leaves
out of the reckoning the most material elements of power—union
and zeal. Without these, the former is inert matter. Without these,
a free people is degraded to the miserable rabble of despotism;
but with these, they are irresistible.

The same gentleman made an assertion which I am bound to
contradict. He asserted, without attempting to prove, that this
House has degenerated into a mere registering body of executive
edicts.[37] A sense of decorum prevents me from speaking of the
charge with merited severity. I will not meet the assertion with
arguments, but assertion. It is easy to assert, but slow and difficult
to prove: it were hopeless to oppose the latter to the former—the
creeping pace of the one is no match for the winged rapidity of
the other. I then assert, that what the gentleman has said is untrue in fact. [Here Mr. Gaston entered into some explanation, and
denied the use of the word registering; and concluded by wishing
to know in what sense Mr. C. used the word untrue.] Mr. C. said,
simply as implying, that the fact is not as Mr. Gaston stated; and
that he had too much respect for him to have an allusion to any
other sense.[38]

37. Compare p. 1574.
38. Calhoun was not called to order for his statement, and in his speech on
Mar. 3 (see above, n. 10) Grosvenor cited this precedent in defense of his
declaration that when Calhoun charged "that the minority were not willing to

Some arguments and observations of mine on a former occasion, on the nature and character of opposition, have on this called forth replies from many of the minority, and particularly from the gentleman just alluded to. He asserted that a majority might also be a faction, and cited the Federalist to prove its truth; with the additional fact, that when it is one, it is far more dangerous than a factious minority.[39] If the gentleman had been more attentive, he would have found that there is nothing in my arguments that contradicts the position taken in the Federalist. What I said was in reply, and was intended to refute the assertion of our opponents on that occasion, that all the misfortunes and miseries of free states originated in the blunders and folly of majorities. The error of this opinion I then sufficiently exposed, both by experience and reason. It has found no advocate on this occasion. I will not again repeat my reasons, but simply restate, that opposition in free states is strongly inclined to degenerate into a struggle for power and ascendency, in which the attachment *to a party* becomes stronger than that *to the country*. This opinion I conceive is incontrovertibly established; in fact, the truth of it is but too manifest to all who have looked into the character of man, or who are acquainted with his history. On the contrary, I feel no disposition to deny that the majority may possibly become factious—that is, cease to consult the general interest. I claim no peculiar exemption for them—it made no part of my argument; I stated principles, but left their application to the good sense of the community. Much less do I feel disposed to contest the position that, if such a majority could and should by any misfortune exist in this country, it would be more dangerous than a factious minority. I could not doubt, for instance, that if the present minority could be swelled into a majority by the addition of one-third more to their ranks, and that they should, when in power, retain all of the principles which I hear them daily advance in this House, that they would not only be more danger-

defend the rights of native seamen, he said that which was not the truth." The Speaker held Grosvenor out of order and rejected his argument, saying that he understood Calhoun's statement "with the explanation that accompanied it, as by no means indecorous or disorderly" (*NI*, Mar. 29, 1814; letter of "A.B."; see also *AC* 13-2, p. 1774). Calhoun refused to take part in the accompanying uproar. A letter in the *New York Evening Post* (Mar. 15) gives an entirely different account of the Speaker's ruling and of Calhoun's apparent reaction.

39. See No. 90 NOTE.

ous than they now are, when their power is to divide and distract; but that it would be the greatest calamity that could befall our country.

A very important view of the subject yet remains to be presented to the committee; but I feel that the hour is too late, and I am too much exhausted to enter so fully into it as it deserves. The view alluded to is the effects of this war, which has been pronounced so ruinous by our opponents. On examination strong reasons will be found to believe, that it is daily producing the most solid and lasting advantages to the community.

It has already liberated us from that dread of British power, which was almost universal before the declaration of war. If we have done little against our enemy, he has done still less against us. What the state of public feeling was on this point, may be in some degree inferred by the debates in this House before the declaration of war. I cannot but express my surprise at an assertion of a gentleman from Virginia (Mr. Sheffey) that all of his fears and predictions had been realized.[40] Has he already forgot the speeches in which he and his friends portrayed the effects of the war in such glowing and terrific colors? Rebellion, civil war, prostrated liberty and conflagrated towns all mingled in one horrid group. [Mr. Sheffey here explained.] It seems that the gentleman has availed himself of the usual privilege of political prophets. If events turn out any thing like their prediction they are claimed as fulfilments; but if entirely opposite they are explained away.

No one who hears me, but will acknowledge that the dread of England was great and general. Her power over our hopes and our fears were too great for our complete independence, and but illy comported with the steady pursuit of our own peculiar interest. From this state the war has liberated us, I hope for ever.

We have also acquired in some degree and are progressively acquiring, what to me appears indispensable in the present state of man and the world; military skill and means, combined with the tone of thinking and feeling necessary to their use. Occasional privations are always to be encountered in the defence of national rights, and the habits necessary to meet them with fortitude are of

40. See *AC*13-2, p. 1332 and *AC*12-2, p. 680.

the greatest importance. I know how much this country is attached to peace and quiet industry. I know how delightful repose and safety are to our nature. But universal experience and the history of those nations with whom we are necessarily connected forbid me to indulge in the pleasing dream, that any degree of prudence or justice on our part can render such a state perpetual. The ambition of a single nation can destroy the peace of the world. We must then submit to the inscrutable law of our nature, which forbids the hope in this world of uninterrupted peace and enjoyment. We must also as prudent men rejoice at the acquisition of those national qualities necessary to meet the vicissitude of war when made unavoidable. Connected with this subject, I rejoice to behold the amazing growth of our manufacturing interest. I regret that I cannot present my thoughts fully on this important subject. It will more than indemnify the country for all of its losses. I believe no country, however valuable its staples, can acquire a state of great and permanent wealth, without the aid of manufactories. Reason and experience both, I conceive, support the position. Our internal strength and the means of defence are by them greatly increased. War, when forced on us hereafter, will find us with ample means; and will not be productive of that distressing vicissitude which follows it, where the industry of the country is founded on commerce, and agriculture dependent on foreign market. Even our commerce in the end will partake of the benefits. Rich means of exchange with all of the world will be furnished to it; and the country will be in a much better condition to extend to it efficient protection. I have merely suggested the topics of arguments on this important branch of our political economy: and will conclude by hoping that on some future occasion it will receive a suitable discussion.

95 NOTE: This speech in the Committee of the Whole was reported in the *Intelligencer* for Mar. 26, 1814; from this version was evidently copied the pamphlet edition of Rapine and Elliot (*Mr. Calhoun's Speech on the Loan Bill . . . February, 1814*), the *Annals* version, and that of *Works* II, 69-103. The first two copies were faithfully done save for negligible changes and those indicated in the footnotes. The *Works* version, as usual, made many minor changes for improvement of Calhoun's style, and one of the

revisions (above, n. 11) is inaccurate; several other changes which are clarifications of Calhoun's meaning, and one which is a correction of an obvious error in the *Intelligencer* (repeated by Rapine and Elliot and by the *Annals*), are indicated in the notes. In comparison of versions of the speech the Rapine and Elliot pamphlet is designated by *R&E*.

On Feb. 9 John W. Eppes of Virginia, Chairman of the Ways and Means Committee, gave a report on the finances of the government to show that the bill introduced on the 1st (*AC*13-2, p. 1199) must authorize a loan of $25,000,000 (p. 1269-71). This statement, coming on the heels of the December and January news of the collapse of Napoleon's power (Adams, *History of U.S.*, VII, 370, 372-3), caused the opposition to redouble its efforts. In the debate the loan was declared impossible, the war unjust, impressment an insufficient cause for continuing the war; retaliation was scored and the attack on Canada denounced. The administration supporters viewed the attack as a climax of the opposition to the war and out-did themselves in their efforts; the bill was certain of passage, but for the loan to meet with any measure of success it was necessary to carry it by as large a majority as possible. The veteran Jeffersonian, Nathaniel Macon of North Carolina, made the closing speech in a plea for moderation and unity, but nevertheless demanded uncompromising support for the war and for the cause of the impressed seamen (*AC*13-2, p. 1775-97). The bill passed the third reading on Mar. 3 by a vote of 97 to 55 and became law on Mar. 24 (p. 1798, 2811-2). The reports of the debate, though far from complete, fill over 500 columns of the *Annals*.

The searching analysis and rigorous reasoning, the clarity of organization and effective phrasing of this brilliant defense of the war party's position, make it perhaps the best of Calhoun's papers during his six years in the House.

In a preliminary statement he pointed out that the opposition aim was to prevent the floating of the loan, and then proceeded to his main point, the justification of the continuance of the war in order to abolish impressment. Previous statements of Calhoun and of his Republican colleagues on this issue had been riddled by the Federalists, who had pointed to the tacit acceptance of the practice by the Jefferson and Madison administrations. The Republican position was further weakened by the contemporary confusion among European nations on the right of expatriation, and by the fact that the barrier of language made impressment by the British far less of a danger to other nations. The citation to Blackstone that "'natural allegiance is perpetual'" (p. 1389), and the attempt to make impressment a part of international law, Calhoun countered with his appeal to Vattel and the international law based on custom

(n. 7 and n. 8 above). Thus impressment, like the earlier Orders in Council, was made to serve the British purpose of monopolizing the trade of the western world—a program not to be restrained by negotiations (see above, p. 224). "It originated in power . . . and can only be restrained by power." He referred hopefully to the Armed Neutrality which had brought England to terms in the Revolution, however grimly admitting the possibility of defeat; in that event he looked forward to another war. But whereas such Republican speakers as John Forsyth of Georgia and Robert Wright of Maryland threatened the East with force (*AC*13-2, p. 1609, 1670), Calhoun again, as before (see No. 90 NOTE), appealed "to the virtue and intelligence of the community only" (p. 233, above).   SOURCE: *NI*, Mar. 26, 1814; *AC*13-2, p. 1673-94.

96. REPORT AND BILL FOR THE REPEAL OF THE EMBARGO AND NON-IMPORTATION ACTS

April 4, 1814

The Committee of Foreign Relations to whom was referred the Message of the President of the 31st of March, submits to the house the following report.

Taking into consideration the great importance of the measures recommended, the Committee thinks it a duty which they owe to the House and to the Nation, to state the grounds on which their report is founded; uniting with the Executive in the policy of these measures, they wish to explain the reasons which have produced that union.

Of the past, it is unnecessary to take a review the attention of the Committee is drawn with more solicitude to the future.

Previous to the late changes in Europe the bearing of our restrictive measures was for the most part confined to our enemies; the obstructions to our commercial intercourse with the friendly powers of the world being in a manner insuperable.

At present a prospect exists of an extended commercial intercourse with them highly important to both parties, and which it may be presumed, they will find an equal interest & disposition to promote. Denmark, all Germany & Holland heretofore under the double restraint of internal regulations & external blockades & depredations from a commerce with the U States, appear by late events to be liberated therefrom

Like changes equally favourable to the commerce of this country appear to be taking place in Italy and the more eastern parts of the Mideteranean. With respect to Spain and Portugal, in the commerce with whom the United States have great interest it may be expected that commerce may be carried on without the aid heretofore afforded to the enemy. Should peace take place between France and her enemies, including Great Britain the commerce of the United States with France will fall under the same remarks.

The considerations of an internal nature which urge a repeal of these acts, at this time, are not less forcible, than those which have been already stated. Among those are the following: The Committee are persuaded that it will considerably augment the public revenue and thereby maintain the public credit: that it will enhance the price and promote the circulation of our produce, in lieu of specie, which, has of late become, so much the object of speculations tending to embarass the Government.

[*Mr. Calhoun, from the same Committee, reported:*]

A Bill To repeal an act entitled "an act laying an embargo on all ships and vessels in the ports and harbors of the United States" and so much of any act or acts as prohibit the importation of goods . . . [*the*] produce or manufacture of great britain . . . .

Sec. 1. Be it enacted . . . That the act entitled "an act laying an embargo on all ships and vessels in the ports and harbors of the United States" passed on the seventeenth day of December one thousand eight hundred and thirteen, be, and the same is, hereby repealed: Provided, That all penalties and forfeitures which have been incurred under the said act shall be recovered and distributed, and may be mitigated or remitted in like manner as if the said act had continued in full force & virtue.

Sec. 2. And be it further enacted, That so much of any act or acts as prohibits the importation of goods, wares or merchandise of the growth, produce or manufacture of Great Britain or Ireland,[1] or of any of the colonies or dependencies thereof, or of

1. On the 6th there was inserted at this point, on Calhoun's motion, a clause repealing acts prohibiting imports from ports of Great Britain or her dependencies in neutral vessels (*AC*13-2, p. 1974).

any place or country in the actual possession of Great Britain, be, and the same is hereby repealed: Provided, That all fines, penalties and forfeitures incurred by virtue of the said act or acts, shall be recovered and distributed, and may be mitigated or remitted in like manner as if the same had continued in full force & virtue: And provided also, That nothing herein contained shall be construed to authorise or permit the importation of goods, wares or merchandise, or of any article the property of, or belonging at the time of such importation, to the enemy or enemies of the United States.

Sec. 3. And be it further enacted. That no foreign ship or vessel shall receive a clearance or be permitted to depart from the United States, whose officers and crew shall not consist wholly of the citizens or subjects of the country to which such ship or vessel shall belong, or of a country in amity with the United States: & No citizen of the United States shall be permitted to depart in such ship or vessel, without a passport or permission therefor furnished under the authority and direction of the President of the United States.[2]

96 NOTE: On Mar. 2 (*AC*13-2, p. 1771-2) by a vote of 68 to 65 the House refused to consider the resolution of Robert Wright, of Maryland, to appoint a committee to inquire into the expediency of suspending the embargo. Calhoun voted against consideration of the resolution, as he likewise did on the 14th when Gaston offered a resolution for repeal of the embargo and non-intercourse laws (p. 1866-8; see No. 87 NOTE). But the collapse of Napoleon's system forced Madison to revise his own, and in his message of Mar. 31 he recommended that, in view of "the mutual interests" of the United States and the friendly foreign powers and the recent "extensive changes favorable thereto," Congress authorize the exportation of goods in vessels of the United States or of friendly

2. On the 6th William C. Bradley of Vermont moved to strike out Section 3 because it would allow a trade by neutral vessels closed to our own; Calhoun opposed the motion—our seamen should be restricted as far as possible to our own vessels (p. 1974). See No. 98, n. 1. Although Calhoun had at one point in the debate hoped that "the provisions of this bill would all go together" (p. 1973), it was on his motion, on the 12th, that the House concurred in the Senate amendments (p. 2014). Thus the bill, as finally enacted, consisted of Sections 1 and 2, the latter as amended on the 6th (above, n. 1).

An amendment to facilitate furnishing of passports was added in the form of a fourth section (*AC*13-2, p. 1992), but the Senate struck it out along with Section 3 (p. 2014).

powers; that the laws prohibiting importation of goods not the property of enemies be repealed, and that the additional duties on imports be extended for two years after peace with Great Britain instead of one as at present (AC13-2, p. 694). The same day the message was referred to Calhoun's committee (p. 1934).

Calhoun reported the repeal bill on the 4th. It was referred to the Committee of the Whole, and, on Calhoun's request, his committee was excused from consideration of the question of the additional duties (p. 1946-8). The bill became law on Apr. 14 (p. 2830). See No. 97. With the exception of the specie exportation bill of Apr. 4 (see Calendar) this was Calhoun's last Foreign Relations Committee report. Due to illness he was a month late in attendance at the next session and John Forsyth of Georgia succeeded him as chairman (AC13-3, p. 301, 304, 411; *Life*, p. 16). It was fitting that it was his bill which ended the restrictive system that he had opposed for two years (see Nos. 69, 85 and 87).   SOURCE: MS Report and Bill, Apr. 4, 1814, *NA*, RG233, 13A-D6.1, 13A-B1; *NI*, Apr. 5, 1814; AC13-2, p. 1946-7. For the act see Peters, *Statutes of U.S.*, III, 123; AC13-2, p. 2830.

97. SPEECH ON THE BILL TO REPEAL THE RESTRICTIVE SYSTEM

April 6, 1814

Mr. Calhoun of South Carolina (the Chairman of the Committee of Foreign Relations), rose to speak to the merits of the bill. In order to judge of the propriety of the measure it embraced, it would be necessary to go back to the nature and character of the war in which this nation is engaged. It was, as it had been emphatically and correctly stated, a war for Free Trade and Sailors' Rights: and, such, Mr. C. said, must be the character of every war in which this nation is engaged. We are so far removed from the European contest, that we shall never enter into the struggles for continental power in that quarter of the world. Not that we should be indifferent spectators of the events in Europe, because the changes there may have a considerable bearing on the affairs and interests of this country: but the interest we feel in these events is not of such a character as to make us a primary party in any of these contests. But one circumstance always accompanying the European struggles, will more or less involve the rights of this country in them. Of such a character is the British commercial or maritime policy, which in its effect tends to destroy the free trade of this country and also to infringe the rights of our seamen. In this point of view it is a matter of great importance that we should duly reflect on the character of the present contest, to decide what part this country ought to act, and what principles should now govern our conduct. The policy of Britain, which is to contract and limit neutral rights, and which, if not resisted, would annihilate them, will always have a strong bearing on the United States. But that policy will not stop here; it will affect the interests of every country in Europe, and place them more or less on the side of this country in resistance to the commercial policy of England.

It then becomes a matter of policy to unite those countries, interested in the cause of free trade, in the struggle which we are obliged to make against the usurpations of our enemy. In this point of view the most liberal and generous policy ought to be pursued by us as to the other powers of Europe, and particularly to the great northern powers of Sweden and Russia. But it might be said our past measures contradict this leading principle of policy. Mr. C. thought not. The restrictive system sprung from an unusual state of things: it was a pacific policy arising from the extraordinary state of the world at the time we embarked in it—and of course was a temporary rather than a permanent policy. On looking back to its origin, gentlemen would find it to be such as he had stated. It originated at a moment when every power on the continent of Europe was arrayed against Great Britain, and no one country in Europe was then interested in the support or defence of neutral rights. There was scarcely a port in Europe, which, at the commencement of our restrictive system, was not occluded to British commerce. In this state of things, the United States, in order to avoid war, not having taken the resolution at that time to declare war, resorted to the restrictive system—resorted to it because the extraordinary state of the European world presented a prospect that the strong pressure of this system on Great Britain might save the nation from a war into which we have since been reluctantly drawn. Such was the character of the embargo measure, originating from the posture of the world at that day, when it was resorted to without the prospect of its producing an impression on any neutral power—for there were then no neutrals. Gentlemen might say, that in this view of the restrictive system, it ought to have terminated at the commencement of the war. To be candid, Mr. C. said that was his opinion; and, when a motion was made by a gentleman from Massachusetts to that effect, he (Mr. C.) had advocated it on the ground that the restrictive policy was opposed to war. That motion was not successful, but it was rejected by a majority of one vote, so many members of the Republican party agreeing with him in that opinion as almost to have carried the question at that time.[1] But why was the system not then terminated? The reasons would be obvious to all who reverted to the circumstances of that time. The state of the world which originally induced the system, which gave great energy to it, continued in its pristine vigor. All Europe was still occluded to British commerce; the war between Russia and France had not broken out—Russia had not then opened her ports to British commerce. This was then the governing motive which prevented the repeal of that system. Had the state of the world then been what it now is; had all the European world, France excepted, been open to British commerce; had there existed neutral nations on the continent of Europe, of very great power and influence; Mr. C. said, had this state of things then existed, there was the strongest reason to believe, from the small minority against the resolution of the gentleman from Massachusetts to which he had alluded, the restrictive system would have been terminated by the war. As to his own views of that system, Mr. C. said he thought it ought to have terminated in war earlier than it did. In this respect he had disagreed with gentlemen on the other side of the House, with whom he had then voted. They wished for neither war nor restriction.

But, said Mr. C. let us now attend to the present state of the world. What is the condition of England? As between us and Great Britain, there are many nations of great power now in a neutral condition. Russia, Sweden, all Germany, Denmark, Spain, for even she may be considered neutral—and perhaps Holland. Under the entire change in the circumstances of Europe, ought not the restrictive system then to terminate? Indubitably—indubitably, he said, because all the reasons which justified and

1. See No. 69.

recommended its continuance had ceased. It was originally resorted to as a pacific measure; having declared war, as a war measure it was continued, and was a forcible measure, because all
Europe was shut against our enemy. All Europe being now open
to her, that reason has ceased. Suppose we were to persist in the
measure. Does any one believe that England will feel the measure
as she did when the continent was shut? Certainly not. But in
addition to that consideration, the fact is that we are now contending for free trade, and ought to propitiate as much as possible
every nation which has the same interest as ourselves in its maintenance. In one word, it is our interest to attach the friendship of
Russia, Sweden, Holland, Denmark, and of all nations who have
a deep interest in free trade, to the cause of America. Mr. C. felt
a strong impression, that if we opened our ports to them, and the
maritime usurpations of Britain continued, they would in time
make common cause with America; that in time their weight would
be thrown into the scale with us to counteract the policy of Britain.
It would not be decorous or wise for the United States standing
up for the freedom of trade, to pursue a course of policy calculated
to irritate those nations with whom we may have common cause.
What had the Emperor of Russia said in relation to our war with
Britain, when apprized of it? He had expressed his solicitude for
trade with America, and regretted that our difference with Great
Britain would interrupt it. This sentiment he had expressed at the
moment when all France and her allies marched against him, and
he did not know how soon France would plant her standard in his
capital. That sentiment must have still greater influence with him
now, when his enemy is repelled. The same feeling which governed the Emperor of Russia in this respect must in a greater
or less degree govern every nation on the continent of Europe,
whose interests are the same. In the proposition which had been
made to France on the part of the allies, a solicitude had been
evinced on this subject, which, if this country shews a disposition
to extend the benefits of its commerce to the European continent,
must have weight in the British cabinet.

We ought never to forget, Mr. C. said, the reason which had
forced us into war. Anxious to maintain our neutral position and
enjoy the benefits of neutral trade, we had for years closed our

eyes against the aggressions on the part of the enemy. Sufferance on our part had provoked only further injury, which had forced us to arms in defence of neutral rights and free trade. Under this view of the subject, he hoped this committee would duly appreciate the necessity of conciliating those nations whose interests were now the same as ours, with whom we have now some trade, and in future may expect it to be greatly extended. But it might be said England would not permit this trade. To what situation, Mr. C. asked, would she then be reduced? To an alternative the most awkward and perplexing. She must either keep up her present mere cruising or paper blockade of our sea coast, to prevent the entrance of those neutrals, or modify her system of paper blockade in favor of all neutrals. Will not a persistance in her present illegitimate blockade, and capture at sea of neutral vessels destined for the United States, irritate and vex those nations, and detach them from the cause of Great Britain? If, on the other hand, she modifies her blockade in their favor, Mr. C. said, we may carry on a lucrative trade to the continent of Europe, not beneficial to England, but very much so to the United States. The very option which will thus be presented will embarrass the British cabinet, and have a stronger tendency to produce peace than ten years continuence of the present system, when the prospect of its producing any pressure has become so very faint.

Mr. C. said he would ask of gentlemen on the same side of the House with himself, whether, if the restrictive system were now off, there would be ten votes in the House in favor of putting it on? He contended there would not. If it were to expire on the 10th of the month, would there be ten votes in favor of its renewal? He believed not. If the House would in neither case embrace it under present circumstances, there was the strongest reason to presume that in its judgment the restrictive system is not now operative and wise. What then, he asked was the objection to repealing it? A regard to consistency. He knew, he said, that regard ought always to be had to that valuable trait in governments or men. But it was not the duty of men to regulate their conduct without any regard to events. True wisdom consists in properly adapting your conduct to circumstances. Two things may change our conduct in any particular point: a change of our own opinion, or of exterior circumstances, which entirely change the reason of our former conduct. Men cannot always go straight forward, but must regard the obstacles which impede their course. Inconsistency consists in a change of conduct when there is no change of circumstances which justify it. Those who adapt their conduct to a change of circumstances, act not inconsistently but otherwise. They would be inconsistent if they persisted in a course of measures after the reasons which called for them had so changed as to require a course directly the reverse. Mr. C. said he respected the firmness of many friends around him, because it indicated their determination to persevere in any system and adhere to any measure which they believed the interest of their country to require. But, according to the view which he had taken, he did not view such a persistance in the restrictive system to be the dictate either of wisdom or sound policy. There were many other observations which he might make on this subject, which he should at present forbear to urge. As to the manufacturing interest, in regard to which some fears had been expressed, the resolution voted by the House yesterday was a strong pledge that it would not suffer the manufacturers to be unprotected in case of a repeal of the restrictive system.[2] Mr. C. said he hoped at all times and under every policy they would be protected with due care. All further remarks he reserved until he should hear the objections to the bill.

97 NOTE: This was Calhoun's speech, in Committee of the Whole, introducing his bill to repeal the embargo and non-importation acts (No. 96). Since the declaration of war the sworn enemy of this "restrictive system," Calhoun was now in the agreeable position, as spokesman for the administration, of advocating repeal. His speech was a tactful review of the reasons that had hitherto moved Madison and his supporters, a plain statement of his own position, and an effective presentation of the possibilities that lay in repeal. In the face of the panic in Washington caused by Napoleon's collapse (see Adams, *History of U.S.*, VII, 393-4, VIII, 10), Calhoun spoke with optimism and enlarged upon Madison's suggestion that this was the opportunity, now that most of the European countries were no longer at war with Great Britain, to

2. The resolution of Samuel D. Ingham of Pennsylvania that the Secretary of the Treasury report at the next session "a general tariff of duties," which was adopted that day (AC13-2, p. 1959-61).

force the latter to allow the trade or to antagonize the Continent.
SOURCE: *NI,* Apr. 7, 1814; *AC*13-2, p. 1962-5.

98. SPEECH IN DEFENSE OF THE REPUBLICAN
FOREIGN POLICY

April 6, 1814

Mr. Calhoun said he wished, before the committee rose, to make a
few remarks in reply to what had fallen from the gentleman from
New Hampshire. That gentleman had said that it was now proved
that the policy of the restrictive system was not truly American. If
the gentleman meant that the continuance of that system had not
been dictated exclusively by a sense of the interests of this country
as affected by the state of other powers, he asserted that which
materially differed from the fact. If the gentleman meant that it
had grown out of the state of the world, he was right. The system
most indubitably grew out of the state of the world. The gentleman had not made the discovery he appeared to suppose; because
this circumstance had been repeatedly avowed and never concealed. The gentleman had said that our measures should not be
governed by the state of affairs in Europe; that it was our true
policy to be independent of her—in other words, that no man was
fit to be a statesman who knew any thing of England, of Russia,
or of any other power of Europe. Mr. C. said, that while he admitted we ought not to form "entangling alliances" with other
powers, yet not to regulate our conduct in relation to commercial
matters by the state of affairs in Europe, would be a course of
policy imprudent and unwise. Every measure adopted in respect
to foreign commerce must be predicated on a knowledge of the
state of Europe. If not, we had better at once adopt the terrapin
policy gentlemen have so much reprobated, and have not a cock-
boat or sail on the ocean.

The whole fallacy of the gentleman's argument (said Mr. C.)
consists in this: the gentleman considers our measures as co-operating with those of the Emperor of France, and desires to produce
the impression that we have common views and the same object
with France. Such is not the fact. But the people of the United
States, in pursuit of their own interest, have a right to seize on

circumstances, however produced, whether by England, France or Russia, and suit their commercial policy thereto. This was a position which Mr. C. said he should never renounce; and he thought no man who should deliberately consider the subject would differ from him in opinion. In this point of view we have co-operated with France; we have seized on passing events, and adopted measures applicable to the circumstances of the times and adapted to the policy of the country. Whatever there may be criminal or foreign in such policy, Mr. C. said he would readily assume. As to the stale charge of French influence again insinuated at this day, he could not be expected to notice it; he detested and contemned it. It was ridiculous: it had nothing to do with this or any other question in this House, or with the policy of the government. The object of the government had been to control the maritime and commercial policy of the enemy: in this respect the war and the restrictive system were identified—they were merely different means of asserting the same end, the noble end of the liberty of the seas, free trade and sailors' rights. Whether the one or the other should be pursued, or both, was a matter of election, to be decided by the exercise of a sound discretion. No imputation of improper foreign influence can be sustained against the government for seizing on circumstances arising from the state of either France or England to adapt our measures accordingly. Even England regulates her conduct by that of France. And when nations regulate their policy by the circumstances of their enemies, might not we, whilst neutrals, regulate our conduct according to the circumstances of the belligerents? The restrictive system and this war have a common policy—to maintain our rights and compel the enemy to respect our just claims.

It was believed by politicians on all sides that, owing to the situation of the world, the restrictive system was one which had, prior to the war, saved our commerce from foreign control and subjection, which had prevented us from being in fact recolonized. Suppose the policy of the gentleman had been pursued, and we had forgotten Europe, and been indifferent to British exactions and oppressions. What would have been the result? Our commerce would have been placed under the direction of England; it would have been carried on for her benefit; she would have kept on monopolizing and monopolizing, until not only our carrying trade, but our direct trade, and even our coasting trade would have been destroyed. We had commenced resistance by the restrictive system. It would have been wiser, Mr. C. said, in his opinion, if we had begun with war, and if he had then been a member of this House he would have preferred that course. That the two systems of war and restriction were consistent with each other was all that he contended for. We were now, he said, in pursuit of the good old policy to which we have been compelled to resort, of resisting by war the maritime oppressions of Britain, which began with the rule of '56, and gained strength in the power and ambition with which the administration of Chatham inspired the councils of England. It had continued growing until it had compelled this country to leave the sweets and ease of neutrality to encounter the hazards and hardships of war. What would be lost by giving up the restrictive system, Mr. C. said would be made up by increased vigor to the war. We should still be able to coerce the enemy; we could still act and act more strongly on his provinces; we could commit depredations on his commerce by our privateers —and the very circumstance of war existing with Great Britain, together with the operation of the double duties, would still retain, as to her, two-thirds of the commercial restrictions which now exist. I hope (said Mr. C.) the gentleman will not assert that this House or the government has co-operated in the views of France. I hope the gentleman believes us to be too honorable men for that, and that we stand on American ground. History will view the conduct of this government in that light—and will record that we acted by ourselves, unconnected and uncontrolled by *any* foreign nation.

[*After remarks of several other speakers the bill was reported to the House. William C. Bradley, of Vermont, immediately repeated a motion, made earlier that day, to strike out Section 3 because it would benefit the farmer and merchant, but would be ruinous for the manufacturer and the seaman.*[1]]

1. *AC*13-2, p. 1974, 1983. Bradley's motion was lost next day by a vote of 78 to 70 (p. 1986-7), but the section was stricken out by the Senate—see No. 96, n. 2.

Mr. Calhoun said he, as a grower of produce, should certainly feel an interest in striking out that section, as it was the interest of the planter to let commerce run in any channel it might wear for itself. But it was deemed advisable to retain our seamen as much as possible from foreign and in our own service. As to the manufacturing interest, it could not be considered as disregarded, when there existed a duty of 50 per cent on the invoice duty of foreign goods. If this was not encouragement, he knew not what was. The vote of the House yesterday required a general tariff to be laid before it conveyed a pledge that the manufacturing interest should be protected. Double duties would not protect it properly; double duties on coffee and sugar offered no encouragement to the manufacture of broadcloth. He hoped to see manufactures encouraged by appropriate duties, and had no idea of their being left without such protection.

98 NOTE: The House was still in Committee of the Whole on No. 96. Calhoun was replying to Webster, whose speech (*AC*13-2, p. 1965-73) was a biting satire on the restrictive measures—which he declared were not "a purely American policy" but "an humble imitation of the continental system of France"—and a cautious demand for a consistent course in regard to American manufactures. Calhoun's final comment, however, was in answer to Bradley. SOURCE: *NI*, Apr. 7, 1814; *AC*13-2, p. 1976-8, 1983-4.

99. SPEECH ON ENCOURAGEMENT FOR MANUFACTURES

April 7, 1814

Mr. Calhoun of South Carolina said he hoped the motion would not prevail. He thought the gentleman was mistaken in supposing that our infant manufacturing institutions would be embarrassed by this measure. What was the encouragement which they now received from the government? The *ad valorem* duties now averaged about 33 1/3 per cent. Most of the importations being in neutral bottoms, the discriminating duty of 10 per cent. on such importations in foreign vessels would make it 43 per cent. and when were added to this the freight and other expenses incident to a state of war, the actual duty on foreign and premium to domestic manufactures could not be less than *fifty per cent*. Was it wise to extend to our manufactures further encouragement than this? During a state of war, too great a stimulus was naturally given to manufactures—a stimulus so great that it could not be expected to be continued in a time of peace; and when peace comes, come when peace will, the vicissitude which manufacturers must experience will be much greater and injurious to them, if besides the double duties the restrictive system were retained, than it ought to or would otherwise be. The great requisite to the due encouragement of manufactures now was, that certain manufactures in cottons and woolens, which have kindly taken root in our soil, should have a moderate but permanent protection ensured to them. He knew not how that object could be better effected than by the scheme of establishing a new tariff of duties, which this House had shewn a determination to adopt. To continue the present non-importation system merely to protect manufactures, when they received already so much protection, would be dangerous instead of beneficial to them.

Another circumstance than those he had adverted to now operated to encourage manufactures—the heavy expenditure for the clothing of our army. The government could and did regulate those expenditures as far as possible for the encouragement of manufactures. Having replied to the main point of the gentleman's argument, he would not follow him through the whole of his remarks. As to her manufactures, Mr. C. said, that all Europe was open to the enemy. The very circumstance of this demand for her manufactures which destroyed the efficiency of our non-importation system, by enhancing their price in the British market would furnish additional encouragement to our manufactures. Could it be expected, under the present circumstances of the world, that our non-importation, violated as it constantly was by smuggling and simulated papers, could produce much effect? He believed not. All the arguments he had yesterday urged applied as forcibly to this provision of the bill as to that which contemplated a repeal of the embargo. He hoped all the provisions of the bill would be permitted to share the same fate.

[*In answer to McKim's further plea Calhoun pointed out the extreme difficulty of enforcing a non-importation law.*]

99 NOTE: The repeal bill (No. 96) was now before the House (No. 98 NOTE); Calhoun was speaking to the motion of Alexander McKim of Maryland to strike out Section 2 and was replying to McKim's plea for American manufactures. Section 2 permitted importation of British manufactures if they were not enemy-owned, and McKim argued that the double duties now in existence would be entirely inadequate against the flood that would be released by the repeal. The most elaborate argument for the manufacturer, however, was made by Elisha R. Potter, of Rhode Island (AC13-2, p. 1992-2000). See Calhoun's Apr. 6 comment on the tariff (above, p. 248) and his 1816 speech, No. 129.   SOURCE: NI, Apr. 9, 1814; AC13-2, p. 1989-91.

100. SPEECH ON THE MILITARY SITUATION

October 25, 1814

[Mr. Calhoun] did not rise to consider whether the war was originally just and necessary; or whether the administration had abandoned the original objects of the contest; much less whether the opposition—according to the very modest declaration of the member from New Hampshire (Mr. Webster) possessed all of the talent and confidence of the country.[1] His object was to call the attention of this House to the necessity of prompt and vigorous measures for the prosecution of the war. If ever a body of men held the destinies of a country in their hands, it was that which he was now addressing. You have for an enemy a power the most implacable and formidable; who, now freed from any other contest, will, the very next campaign, direct the whole of his force against you. Besides his deep rooted enmity against this country, which will urge him to exertion, the enemy is aware of the necessity, on his part, to bring the contest to a speedy termination. He dreads its continuance: for he well knows, that should it be maintained by us with vigor, for only a few years, there will be other parties to the struggle, which may again involve him in a war with all Europe. He then will put forth, from spite and policy, the whole of his strength the very next summer to crush us if possible, by one mighty effort. To meet this state of things, the whole of our resources will have to be called into action; and, what is of equal

1. For Webster's speech of Oct. 24, see AC13-3, p. 459-65.

importance, with such promptitude, as to be ready to act as soon as the season will admit.

What then are the duties, which devolve on this House, and which must be performed in order that we may be in a state of desirable preparation to meet and maintain the struggle? This is the question which he proposed to consider, not indeed in detail, or with great accuracy, but generally, in order that we may be aware of the urgent necessity for dispatch. First, then, it will be absolutely necessary to pass these tax resolutions, or some others of equal vigor, into laws. Our finances it is acknowledged are much deranged; and it is also admitted on all sides, that they can only be restored by a vigorous system of taxes. Has any member estimated how much time this will consume. It is now the 25th of October, and we have not passed even the resolutions; at the same rate of proceeding, to settle all the complexity of the detail of the bills, and pass them into laws will require months. In the next place, it will be necessary, (he presumed no member could doubt it) to take the state of the circulating medium into consideration; and to devise some measure to render it more safe, and adapted to the purposes of finance. The single fact, that we have no proper medium commensurate in its circulation with the Union, that it is all local, is calculated to produce much embarrassment in the operation of the Treasury. But, sir, after we have passed the taxes and established an adequate circulating medium, which must of necessity, with the closest attention, consume much time, much still will remain to be done. The army to which the President has so strongly called our attention has not yet claimed a moment of our time. He would not pretend to anticipate the plan, which the Military Committee would doubtless submit to this House, but he would state what appeared to him indispensable to give the greatest effect with the most economy, to our arms. He did not wish to be understood [*to advocate*] parsimony, but that which gave to the amount expended the greatest effect.

The enemy at present presses the war both on our seaboard and interior frontier. The nature of the war on either, will, if properly considered, indicate the mode, that it ought to be met and resisted. On the seaboard it must be strictly defensive. The enemy can make no permanent conquest of any importance there; but he hopes, by alarming and harassing the country, and putting us to an enormous expence in defending it, to break the spirit of the nation, and bring it to his own terms. The only remedy in our hand, without a marching force, is to fortify as strongly as possible the cities and exposed points, and to garrison them with a sufficient number of experienced regular troops. In case of an attack, they are to be aided by militia of the cities and adjacent country called out on the occasion *en masse* which can be done without much vexation or expence. It is thus by having respectable garrisons of regular troops, aided as he has stated, and supported by strong works, we will afford more security, and will save millions of expence. The present militia force he supposed in actual service could not be much short of 100,000. Less than half that number of regulars could be made abundantly adequate to the defence of our seaboard.

On the Canada frontier the war must assume an opposite character. If we wish to act with effect, it must there be wholly offensive. He did hope the miserably stale and absurd objections against offensive operations in Canada had ceased, till he heard yesterday the member from New Hampshire (Mr. Webster). It was so obviously the cheapest and most effectual mode of operating on our enemy, that thinking men, he believed with little exception of all parties, had agreed in its expediency. For, suppose that we should have at the opening of the next campaign a sufficient force on the Canada frontier for its reduction; and what would then be the result? Either our enemy must call off the whole of his force to defend himself in that quarter, or he must permit it to fall into our possession. Either event would be desirable. If the enemy should adopt the former, as in all probability he would be compelled to do, our seaboard would be freed from danger and alarm, and we would have the further advantage of meeting him on equal terms. He would no longer be aided by his maritime superiority. If however, he should not strengthen himself in Canada, but continue the war on the coast, it would be still more to our advantage. The reduction of his possessions, besides shedding a glory on our arms, and producing both here and in England the happiest effects in our favor, would enable us to maintain the struggle with half the expense in men and money. After so desirable an event our efforts might be almost exclusively directed to the defence of the seaboard, and the war would assume a new aspect highly favorable to this country.

To cause so desirable a state of things, a regular force of at least 50,000 men ought to be ready to act against Canada by the first of May or June, at farthest. If they could be immediately raised and marched to their proper depots for training, they could in a few months be well trained for service. He was well assured that the brilliant battles of Bridgewater and Chippawa were won by men, three fourths of whom had not been in the ranks more than four months. With skilful officers, and with the aptitude of the Americans to acquire the military art, the finest army in a few months might be formed.[2] He said, he could not refrain from congratulating this House and country on the acquisition we had made in so short a time of military skill. It was wonderful, almost incredible, that, in a year or two, with very little opportunity, such generals should be formed as have the last Summer led our army to glory. No country under all of these circumstances ever in so short a time developed so much military talent. Put under their command without delay a sufficient force well appointed, and you will then find yourselves in the road to honor and secure peace. But can this be done by idle debate, by discussing the origin of the war, and the relative talent and virtue of the two great parties in this country? *Now* is our time, not for debate, but action. Much is to be done. We have not a moment to lose. Time is to us every thing, men, money, honor, glory, and peace. Should we consume it in debate, and let the moments for preparation glide away, our affairs must be irretrievably ruined. Compare what remains to be done with the time for action; and it is certain that to act promptly is as important as to act at all. Under these impressions, he hoped, that the House would pass this day on all the resolutions; and that they would be referred back to the committee to report bills immediately; and that whatever was needful to our early and complete preparation would be promptly dispatched. The enemy is already arrived and as soon as permitted by the season, will strike with deadly intention; let us be ready to receive and return the blow with redoubled force. We are placed in circumstances the

2. Note Adams, *History of U.S.*, VIII, 28, 44-5, on the significance of Chippawa and the record of Winfield Scott's brigade; cf. No. 118, n. 1.

most urgent and imperious. Our supposed weakness has tempted the enemy to make his extraordinary demands.[3]

Who that bears the heart of an American can think of them without the most just indignation? Surrender the Lakes to his controul; renounce the fisheries, that nursery for seamen; cede a part of Maine, and all beyond the Greenville line, and recognize the Indians as their allies, and under their protection. Such is his language. He relies not so much on his own strength as our weakness and disunion. Let it be our most serious business by vigor and promptitude to baffle and destroy his vain hopes. If we fail, it will not be for the want of means, but because we have not used them. We have generals and troops that have proved themselves an over match for the choicest of the enemy's battalions, commanded by her most boasted officers. To this evidence of skill and courage, superadd preparations on our part equal to our resources; by this means you will make him sensible of his presumption, and listen to terms of peace honorable to both nations. He has it in his power at all times to make such a peace. Every member who hears me, knows this to be the fact, notwithstanding the unjust and unfounded insinuations of the member from New Hampshire (Mr. Webster) to the contrary. He observed again, that England dreaded a continuance of the contest. The affairs of Europe are far from being settled. Her relation in a commercial point of view is calculated to raise up powerful enemies on the continent. Should she be foiled and disgraced here, which she must be, if we but do our duty, the opportunity so favorable to humble her will be seized. Of these facts she is sensible; and our very preparation for a vigorous war will make her dread the contest.

But suppose, instead of vigorous and prompt preparation, we consume our time in debate here, and permit our affairs to go on in the consequent slow and feeble way. Where is the man so blind as to believe that England will limit her views by her present demands, as extravagant as they are? We are already told, that she will proportion her future demands to the relative situation of the two countries. She neither expected nor desired peace on the terms which were offered. Her bosom is repossessed with the am-

3 See *ASP, For. Rel.*, III, 708-10; the papers are published in *NI*, Oct. 11.

bition and projects that inspired her in the year '76. It is the war of the Revolution revived—we are again struggling for our liberty and independence. The enemy stands ready, and eagerly watches to seize any opportunity which our feebleness or division may present, to realize his gigantic schemes of conquest. In this struggle for existence, he must intreat the members of the opposition, though they can reconcile it to their conscience to stand with folded arms and coldly look on, not to impede by idle and frivolous debate the efforts of those who are ready by every sacrifice to maintain the independence of the country. The subject is weighty—he felt himself pressed on all sides by the most interesting topics; but he would abstain from farther observation, lest he who admonished against the consumption of the time of the House in long debate, should set an example of it in himself. The time is precious. He felt that he owed an apology for consuming so much as he had done.

100 NOTE: On the 10th John W. Eppes of Virginia, Chairman of the Ways and Means Committee, submitted a report (*AC*13-3, p. 378-81) which began weeks of debate and finally evolved into a series of revenue bills. The report was prefaced with the statement that loans were an "uncertain" resource and the terms on which they could be received undesirable. Indeed, just a month later the Treasury had to suspend payment of interest on bonds (Adams, *History of U.S.*, VIII, 244-5). This left taxes and Treasury notes as the source of money for the war. The committee proposed, by increases in the existing internal revenue taxes and the addition of other articles to the list, to raise $11,635,000. Before the report was considered Eppes presented a letter from the new Secretary of the Treasury, A. J. Dallas (*AC*13-3, p. 401-10), proposing a different schedule of taxes, to produce about the same amount, and establishment of a national bank of fifty millions capital. Debate on the report on the 21st, 22nd and 24th consisted mainly of discussion of individual items and of attacks by the opposition.

The debate was now in the House. Calhoun's insistent call for action, the first speech of the session in general defense of the war program, came the day after one of Webster's sweeping attacks on the administration (p. 459-65). SOURCE: *NI*, Nov. 3, 1814; *AC*13-3, p. 465-9.

101. To Lt. Col. Andrew Pickens, Pendleton, S.C.

Washington 1st Novr 1814

Dr Andrew, I have but a moment to acknowledge the receipt of your letter by the last mail; and to inform you of the result of my conversation with Col. Monroe relative to your case. He stated that he did not think it possible that you could be reinstated; but that should new corps be raised, that your resignation would cause no impediment to an appointment. I found that he was not ignorant of your name; and that he was very favourably impressed with your character as an officer. I regret much from the turn which our national affairs have taken that you are out of the army. Every exertion is making to get men and money. I hope our exertion will be on a scale commensurate with the publick exigincies. Steps will be reported in the Senate and our house immediately to fill up and increase the present establishment.[1] They will be vigourous. The period of militia duty will be extended at least for 2 years; and those companies will be exempted from draught who will furnish a certain number for the U.S. service. Landed bounty will be extended to 300 acres; and will comprehend those furnished in lieu of a draught. The sentiment is universal almost that men must be had.

We have no late news except the arrival of the Peacock at New York. The rumour of her having sunk a sloop is unfounded. The federal party is now divided; but will soon unite to justify all of the claims of England. How strange! They threaten a devision in N. England and many here dread it.

I am &c

J. C. Calhoun

101 NOTE: Pickens was commissioned Lieutenant-Colonel, Tenth Infantry, Mar. 12, 1812; transferred to the Forty-Third Infantry, Apr. 6, 1814; resigned June 15, 1814 (Heitman, *Historical Register . . . U.S. Army*, I, 790). SOURCE: *SCL.*

1. See Nos. 100 and 102.

102. REMARKS ON THE VOLUNTEER BILL

November 5, 1814

Mr. Calhoun of South Carolina remarked that the military force by which we can operate consists of two descriptions: the regular force, whose general character is mercenary, the soldiers enlisting for the sake of the bounty and subsistence; drafted militia called into service under legal obligations; and volunteers, brought into the field by patriotic motives only. If volunteers were to be obtained only by the greatness of the inducements or the amount of compensation held out, why call for volunteers at all? Mr. C. said he would not consent to derogate from the motives of those who volunteer by supposing them to be altogether actuated by such motives. There were temptations of one kind held out to those who enlist in the regular army, and of another to those who volunteer. Love of country is the boast, it is the jewel of the volunteer corps. They are unfit for the tug of war, for its drudgery and fatigue. They are peculiarly adapted to cases of emergency, of great personal danger, but not great fatigue. We must rely on regulars to be enlisted, and, if not to be had in sufficient numbers, on those who shall be drafted from the whole body of the militia.[1] These two constitute the bone and muscle of the army. If great reliance had been placed on a volunteer force, why had another bill been reported by the Military Committee, with extraordinary provisions for filling the ranks of the army? Certainly, the volunteers had only been considered a co-operating or subsidiary force, the regulars being the basis. A body of volunteers, for instance, might individually and collectively possess the same spirit as the little army under General Brown, but they could not be expected to render the same kind of services.[2]

102 NOTE: In his message to Congress of Sept. 20 Madison called for legislation "for filling the ranks of the regular Army and . . . enlarging the provision for special corps, mounted and un‚ mounted, to be engaged for longer periods of service than are due from the militia," and for provision for "classing and disciplining" the militia to assure more energetic and efficient service (*AC*13-3,

1. See Calhoun's remarks on militia, No. 107.
2. Jacob Brown—see Adams, *History of U.S.*, VIII, 34.

p. 14). On Oct. 27 George M. Troup, Chairman of the Military
Committee, offered three bills—the first for dividing the free male
population into "classes" of twenty-five men, each class being required to supply a recruit for the army; the second authorizing the
President to accept organizations of volunteers; the third providing
for forty additional regiments for frontier defense (p. 482). Accompanying papers from Secretary of War Monroe called for filling the
ranks of the existing establishment, to its complement of 62,448
"with the least possible delay," and pointed out the desperate military plight of the country (p. 482-91). See No. 107 NOTE.

The volunteer bill was taken up on Nov. 2 (*AC*13-3, p. 518);
minimum term of service was set at twelve months, and provision
made that a volunteer serving for two years should be exempt from
militia duty for the remainder of the war (p. 519-21). The bill was
debated in the House on the third reading on the 4th, but various
objections, including that to the two-year exemption, in which Calhoun and Webster joined, put it back in the Committee of the
Whole (p. 525), where on Calhoun's motion the two-year exemption was stricken from the bill (p. 527).

On the 5th the bill was again in the House where Joseph H.
Hawkins of Kentucky urged restoration of the exemption to make
the service appeal to the west "where these men were expected to
be had" (p. 531; see also p. 539). It was to this plea that Calhoun
was speaking. As eventually revised and ratified, Jan. 27, 1815 (p.
1896-9) it was an act for acceptance of two corps, one of state
troops, the other of volunteers, each limited to 40,000 and the men
serving at least twelve months. The act had no provision for exemption from militia service.   SOURCE: *NI*, Nov. 8, 1814; *AC*13-3, p.
531-2.

103. RESOLUTION AND REMARKS ON ARMY SUPPLIES AND DISCIPLINE

November 10, 1814

Mr. Calhoun of South Carolina offered for consideration the following resolutions:

Resolved, That the Committee on Military Affairs be directed
to inquire into the expediency of changing the present mode of
supplying the Army by contract, into some other, better calculated
for a state of war.

Resolved, That the Secretary of War be directed to inform the
House whether the Army of the United States is trained by any

one uniform system of discipline; and if not, what are the causes that have prevented it, and whether any legislative provision is necessary to effect the same.

Mr. Calhoun said, it was not necessary to state to the House, that, next to having an army, to have it well supplied and well trained was an object of the greatest importance. He had been informed, from a source to be relied on, that the present mode of supplying the army, whilst it subjected the public to speculations by the contractors, was frequently on great emergencies found wholly inefficient. One of the most important enterprises in the South would have failed in consequence of the deficiency of the contractor, had not the difficulty been overcome by the great energy of the commanding general on that occasion.[1] There was, he had also understood, a variance in the discipline of the army, in consequence of five or six different systems employed in the training of the army. So great was this variance, that no large body of our army, Brown's command perhaps excepted, could be properly exercised together.

103 NOTE: The resolutions were agreed to; and on Jan. 24, 1815, Troup, from the Military Affairs Committee, reported a bill for subsisting the army by authorizing appointment of "commissaries of subsistance." This bill passed the House on the third reading Feb. 7 (*AC*13-3, p. 1101, 1131), but was lost in the Senate (p. 230, 232, 237). In the War Department records, Confidential and Unofficial Letters Sent (*NA*, RG107) there is a copy of a letter from Monroe to Calhoun, Dec. 23, 1814, stating the preference of Generals Scott and Gaines for supply by commissaries, and Monroe's belief that the officers generally were of this opinion. See No. 108 on the army discipline resolution. SOURCE: *House Journal*, p. 522 (for the resolutions); *NI*, Nov. 12, 1814; *AC*13-3, p. 550-1.

104. SPEECH ON THE UNITED STATES BANK BILL

November 16, 1814

Mr. Calhoun then, in a very ingenious and elaborate speech, common justice to which requires it to be published at length, laid before the House his views on this subject, and the reasons why he

---

1. See, for instance, Bassett, *Correspondence of Andrew Jackson*, I, 333-7.

should propose a total change in the features of the bill. The motion he now made was one of limited character, but such a one as he proposed to follow up by other amendments, or by distinct legislative provisions, which should together embrace a plan of which the following is a brief outline: The capital of the bank remaining unchanged, at fifty millions, the payments of subscriptions to this capital stock to be made in the proportion of one-tenth in specie [which he afterwards varied to six-fiftieths][1] and the remainder in specie, or in Treasury notes to be hereafter issued; subscriptions to be opened monthly in the three last days of each month, beginning with January next, for certain proportions of the stock until the whole is subscribed—payment to be made at the time of subscribing; the shares to consist of one hundred instead of five hundred dollars each; the United States to hold no stock in the bank, nor any agency in its disposal, nor control over its operations, nor right to suspend specie payments.[2] The amount of Treasury notes to be subscribed, viz. forty-five millions, to be provided for by future acts of Congress, and to be disposed of in something like the following way, viz. fifteen millions of the amount to be placed in the hands of the agents, appointed for the purpose, or in the hands of the present Commissioners of the Sinking Fund, to go into the stock market, to convert the Treasury notes into stock; another sum, say five millions, to be applied to the redemption of the Treasury notes becoming due at the commencement of the ensuing year; the remaining twenty millions he proposed to throw into circulation as widely as possible. They might be issued in such proportions monthly as to be absorbed in the subscriptions to the bank at the end of each month, &c. This operation, he presumed, would raise the value of Treasury notes perhaps 20 or 30 per cent. above par, being the value of the privilege of taking the bank stock, and thus afford at the same time a bonus and an indirect loan to the government; making unnecessary any loan by the bank until its extended circulation of paper shall enable it to make a loan which shall be advantageous to the United States. The Treasury notes so to be issued to be redeemable in stock at 6 per cent. dis-

1. The brackets and enclosed words are in the *NI*.
2. The Fisk bill included authority for the President of the United States to suspend specie payment by the bank.

posable by the bank at its pleasure, and without the sanction of government; to whom neither is the bank to be compelled to loan any money.

This, it is believed, is, in a few words, a fair statement of the *projet* of Mr. Calhoun, which he supported by a variety of explanations of its operations, &c. the notes of the bank, when in operation, to be received exclusively in the payment of all taxes, duties, and debts to the United States.[3] The operation of this combined plan, Mr. C. conceived, would be to afford, 1. Relief from the immediate pressure on the Treasury; 2. A permanent elevation of the public credit; and, 3. A permanent and safe circulating medium of general credit. The bank should go into operation, he proposed, in April next. He concluded his exposition by a motion, the effect of which is to deprive the United States of any share in the stock of the bank, and to change the proportions of specie and paper in which it shall be payable to *one-tenth* in *specie,* and *nine-tenths* in *Treasury notes.*

104 NOTE: See No. 92. The report of the Ways and Means Committee, made on Oct. 18 (*AC*13-3, p. 401), was accompanied by a letter from the new Secretary of the Treasury, A. J. Dallas, of Oct. 17 (p. 401-9), proposing a national bank of fifty millions capital, of which the government should subscribe two-fifths, to be paid in 6 per cent bonds ("stock"), the President to appoint annually five of the fifteen directors and to designate one of them to be president of the bank. The three-fifths to be subscribed by private capital was to include six millions in gold or silver, six in Treasury notes and twelve in 6 per cent "stock" issued since war was declared. The bank was to lend the government thirty millions, at 6 per cent interest.

On Oct. 24 the House by a vote of 66 to 40 committed itself to a national bank (p. 457-8), and a bill in general accord with the above proposals of Dallas was introduced by Jonathan Fisk of New York on Nov. 7 (p. 534-5; see *NI,* Nov. 10, 1814, for an abstract). Significant differences were authority to the President to suspend specie payment by the bank, and that it proposed he appoint five of the twenty-five directors but have no right to appoint the president. Several provisions, however—such as the appointment of directors, prohibition on "mercantile speculations" and that its notes

3. Calhoun probably had in mind the revision he secured on the 19th (No. 106 NOTE), which left the government free to withdraw this privilege.

should be receivable in all payments to the U.S.—were to be found in Taylor's bill of February preceding (No. 92 NOTE) and were not in Dallas' plan. The bill would have revived the United States Bank but with drastic changes to meet the war emergency. Due to illness (*Life*, p. 16) Calhoun was a month late in reaching Congress this session, and John Forsyth of Georgia became Chairman of the Foreign Relations Committee; James Clark of Kentucky was given the second place (*AC*13-3, p. 304). On Feb. 11, 1815, Calhoun was appointed to Clark's place after the latter was given a leave of absence (p. 1148), but this appointment was not renewed at the next session, and Calhoun became Chairman of the Committee on a Uniform Currency (*AC*14-1, p. 377).

In the preceding session Calhoun had been concerned in moves to establish such a bank (No. 92), and was now free to take the lead in this project. His speech came in the course of the debate, in the Committee of the Whole, on the second section of the bill, which detailed the form of the private subscriptions. In his speech in the Senate, Oct. 3, 1837, on the Treasury note bill (*Works*, III, 125-9; Wiltse, *Calhoun, Nationalist*, p. 94-6), Calhoun declared that his support for the 1814 bill was sought by Dallas and by many of his own "political friends," but that after careful study he concluded that the government would be merely borrowing its own notes and paying interest twice.

In the face of the desperate military and financial plight of the United States Calhoun elected to concentrate his effort on finances. By this succinct outline he sketched a bank which should—chiefly by absorbing the Treasury notes—rescue the government from its war-time bankruptcy and provide a stable currency. He proposed, however, no government control nor government grant other than to give the notes of the bank the monopoly of Federal financial transactions. His motion, which was the concluding sentence of his speech, was passed in the committee the next day by a majority of "about sixty votes" (*AC*13-3, p. 613). See No. 111 and, for the result of the controversy, Nos. 105 and 106.   SOURCE: *NI*, Nov. 17, 1814; *AC*13-3, p. 587-8.

105. DEBATE ON THE BANK BILL

November 18, 1814

Mr. Calhoun of South Carolina remarked, that he looked upon the decision of the House on yesterday [1] as indicating a disposition on the part of the House to change the whole nature of the bill, now

1. No. 104 NOTE.

before a Committee of the Whole, for incorporating the subscribers to the Bank of the United States of America. As many amendments in detail would be required, he thought the most proper way to act on the bill would be to re-commit it for amendment to a select committee.

[*Opposed by Wright of Maryland and Lowndes of South Carolina, Calhoun withdrew his motion and later moved to strike out the third section which proposed subscription by the United States of twenty millions in 6 per cent stock.*[2]]

Mr. Calhoun said the principle of his motion had been decided by the amendment which had been made to the 2nd section. Consistency required that the House, after deciding as they did yesterday, should now strike out this section.

[*Wright denied Calhoun's contention and urged government interest in the bank for protection of agriculture and manufacturing against the merchant and foreign influence.*[3]]

Mr. Calhoun, finding, as he said, from the course of the debate, that the eyes of the committee had been so entirely directed to the main object of the amendment adopted yesterday, that they had overlooked the part of it to which this section had reference, rose to explain the reasons of this present motion. Whether the provision now under consideration should be struck out or retained, he contended, depended on the situation of the nation. He was clearly of opinion, that, in the present situation of the nation, it ought to be struck out. One great object of this bank was to afford the means of relieving the nation from difficulties under which it now laboured. By striking out this section, the government would not, he said, lose the advantages it would derive from retaining it, inasmuch as the twenty millions, instead of being vested by the United States in stock, would assume the shape of Treasury notes, and in reality produce the effect, by their absorption in the bank, of an immediate loan to the government. Which, he asked, does the United States now most want—a capital, or the use of a capital? He said he should be glad, indeed, abstractedly, that the United States should possess a share in the capital of the bank; he should be glad the United States should possess a capital in the bank on which they

2. *AC*13-3, p. 614; the House accepted this amendment (p. 632).
3. P. 614-5.

could draw one, two or three per cent. more interest than they had to pay for it. But we want still more the *use* of the capital. If any gentleman could conceive the situation of the country to be such that we could lock up instead of using these twenty millions of capital, he would vote against this amendment. The capital, he said, would not be lost to the United States but would assume for them the most active and most efficient form, by means of the Treasury notes, which, being put into circulation and absorbed by the government, would effect an immediate loan to the government. But, it had been said, unless the United States held some share in the bank, it would fall into the hands of our enemies. Mr. C. said he did not think so harshly as the gentleman from Maryland of the commercial interest; in the large, he believed that great interest to be American, notwithstanding some exceptions might be found to that character. But even if such a disposition as was feared by the gentleman should exist, it would not be controlled by retaining the present provisions of the bill; because the twenty directors could always vote down the five proposed to be appointed by the Executive, if there should arise a contest between the government and the bank. But there was another means of protecting the government against the bank, more potent and certain than any such provisions: let the United States retain the power over its deposits, and over the receipt of the bank notes in payment of duties and debts to the government, and it would possess a sufficient control over the bank.

[*At this point John Forsyth of Georgia renewed his earlier argument that the government should subscribe stock.[4]*]

Mr. Calhoun said, that if fifteen millions of the forty-four millions of Treasury notes were applied, as he had suggested,[5] to the purchase of stock, and five millions to the redemption of Treasury notes falling due at the commencement of the next year, there would be no difficulty in disposing of the remainder of them. He said, to vest 20 millions in the capital stock of the bank would be acting like a man, without a dollar in his pocket, offering to lend out money at an interest lower than he has to pay for it for his use. If the demands of the Treasury during the next year did not require

4. P. 616; see also p. 614.
5. In his speech of the 16th, No. 104.

the whole of these notes, Mr. C. said a part could be retained until the year after, and thus provision be made for two years. If the subscriptions were received monthly in twelve instalments, there would never be out at one time more than two millions, much less than the amount of Treasury notes now in circulation. There would be no doubt, he thought, of their being sought for with avidity.

105 NOTE: The House was continuing the debate, in the Committee of the Whole, on the bank bill (No. 104). The development of opposition caused Calhoun now to reinforce his argument that his plan to keep the government out of the capital of the bank would be a means of using the bank to absorb the Treasury notes. Toward the end of the day's debate his motion to strike out the third section passed in the committee, 79 to 53 (*AC*13-3, p. 618). See No. 106.   SOURCE: *NI*, Nov. 19, 1814; *AC*13-3, p. 613-6.

106. REMARKS ON THE FORM OF SUBSCRIPTION TO THE BANK

November 21, 1814

Mr. Calhoun said, in reply to these remarks, that it was a sound rule in legislation, not to act with a view to benefit one or another party, but with a view to promote the national good. If a bank was to be erected to prop up this or that party, Mr. C. said, it should not receive his sanction. In moving the amendment, he said, he had not been governed by views of so limited a character. He had regarded the nation as a nation, and not as divided into two political parties. The subscription was equally open to both parties; and although the monied class attached to the ruling party might be exhausted, the farming interest was not in so miserable a situation. Mr. C. was not willing to recognize the correctness of the picture which the gentleman had drawn of the great Republican party as exhausted and moneyless. Although there was great capital on one side, so there was on the other; and it is our boast that the yeomanry, the substantial part of our population, are on that side of the question to which we belong. The very amendments proposed, and now objected to, present the opportunity to every capitalist, however inconsiderable, to share in the capital of the bank, &c. and to disseminate its benefits all over the country, &c. As to the control over the bank, Mr. C. contended that the amendments, retaining the power over deposits and of making the bills receivable for the revenue or otherwise, gave the government a greater control than it before possessed over the operations of the bank, &c. Legislation on party principles, he said, must ever re-act on the party pursuing it. He would therefore not resort to it. No, said he; rather let us act on national, on great principles.

106 NOTE: See Nos. 104 and 105. In the debate in Committee of the Whole on the 19th Calhoun had successfully defended the right of the government to inspect the proceedings of the bank, and got stricken from the bill sections making the notes of the bank receivable in all payments to the government (thus reserving to the government the right to decide the matter), and the section authorizing the President to suspend specie payment. He defeated a motion by Lowndes, who was generally supporting him, to reduce the capital to thirty-five millions (AC13-3, p. 621-2).

On this day, the 21st (p. 626-9), the House debated the reported bill and "the amendments to the second section, which embrace the principle of Mr. Calhoun's amendment, and which put the second section in the following shape:

"Sec. 2. . . . That it shall be lawful for any person, copartnership, or body politic, to subscribe for so many shares of the said capital stock of the said bank, as he, she, or they, shall think fit; and the sums respectively subscribed shall be payable in the manner following, that is to say: *six millions of dollars* in gold or silver coin of the United States; or in gold coin of Spain, or the dominions of Spain, at the rate of one hundred cents for every twenty-eight grains and sixty-hundredths of a grain of the actual weight thereof, or in other foreign gold or silver coin, at the several rates prescribed by the first section of an act regulating the currency of foreign coins in the United States, passed tenth day of April, one thousand eight hundred and six; and *forty-four millions* of dollars thereof in such gold or silver coin as aforesaid, or in Treasury notes now authorized, or to be authorized, to be issued in the year one thousand eight hundred and fifteen."

For the italicized words there was substituted: "on each share twelve dollars" and "eighty-eight," which made no change in proportions. Calhoun was now replying to James Fisk's protest that the bank would be controlled by the monied Federalists (p. 629-31).

On the 25th Lowndes moved, in view of the hopeless disagreement, recommitment of the bill to a special committee. Calhoun supported this motion, remarking that the division was "confined neither to party nor locality" and that he was "extremely anxious that the bank should be established" (p. 643-4). However, the committee—with Lowndes, Fisk and Calhoun in the first, second and third places, respectively—was equally unable to agree and Nov. 28 (p. 651-4) returned the bill as it was, with a letter from Dallas vigorously opposing the proposed method of using Treasury notes. In the final debate Alexander C. Hanson, of Maryland, one of the Federalist extremists, denounced the bill declaring that a scheme "so absurd and visionary, could have been looked for from no other quarter than that which produced it"; and he rejoiced "that gentlemen on the other side of the House have at last . . . the courage . . . to pursue . . . an *ignis fatuus* (Mr. Calhoun) no further . . . . It was this same bold and false prophet who led us into Canada to conquer free trade and sailors' rights . . ." (p. 657-8). Calhoun followed "in reply to some points of Mr. Hanson's speech, and in energetic defence of the bill," and the Speaker had to call both speakers to order in the effort to exclude personalities from the debate (p. 665). The House finally refused, by a vote of 104 to 49, to advance the bill even to a third reading (p. 685-6). On the bill and its final defeat see Wiltse, *Calhoun, Nationalist*, p. 94-6; Walters, *Dallas*, p. 194-6; Catterall, *Second Bank of the U.S.*, p. 11-4. See No. 111 for the next attempt.   Source: *NI*, Nov. 22, 1814; *AC*13-3, p. 631.

107. Remarks on the Senate Militia Bill

December 2, 1814

Mr. Calhoun briefly replied to the call made upon him by Mr. Troup for the reason why he preferred acting on the bill, that reason he thought was very obvious; that the bill, having met the approbation of the Senate, would, if it passed this House, immediately become a law. Policy appeared to him to require a preference of this bill to that reported by the committee of this House. If the Senate send us one bill, and we, instead of acting on it, send them another, it would place the two Houses in an awkward predicament. It seemed to him, he said, that the whole argument of the gentlemen against this bill was misplaced. This bill, as well as the gentleman's bill, would produce a certain number of recruits for the regular army. Should the bill reported by the gentleman prevail, it would give us either regulars or money; if this bill should pass, we shall have regulars or good militia. Both bills were calculated to produce regulars, if they could be obtained by purchase. If absolute certainty was the object of the gentleman, it could only be obtained by resorting to a regular and fair system of conscription. To the result of any other system, whether that reported by the Military Committee of this House, or that now under consideration, some uncertainty must attach. The bill from the Senate promising as much certainty as that reported in this House, he hoped it would be gone through with and finally passed.[1]

107 NOTE: When the volunteer bill (No. 102) was taken up Troup stated that his committee understood that "through some channel or other, another plan" would be presented to the House, and he was therefore postponing "for a few days" the other bills brought in by his committee (AC13-3, p. 519). Finally, on Dec. 2 his first army bill was considered, along with two Senate bills, one providing for enlarging the existing encouragement for enlistment in the army, the other to authorize the President to call out 80,430 militia, but with provision for exemptions of militia "classes" which furnished their quotas of recruits for the regular army (*House Journal*, p. 560; see AC13-3, p. 705). Troup began the debate on the Senate militia bill with the statement that it was not referred to his committee, but had, on Calhoun's motion (which does not appear in the *NI* proceedings or in the *House Journal*) come directly to the House and that doubtless Calhoun was prepared to explain it. He stated his own preference for the committee's bill; and in February following explained his failure to introduce his bill earlier, stating that the committee, after canvassing opinion in both houses, had become convinced that no effective measure for filling the regular army "could be . . . resorted to" (p. 1129-30). Troup's speech (p. 705-12) was followed immediately by Calhoun's statement.

In the course of the debate on the militia bill Calhoun approved a successful motion to eliminate a section putting limitations on service of the militia outside their states (p. 714).

The bill passed the House Dec. 14 (p. 928), but was eventually lost in the Senate (p. 141). The other Senate bill—offering larger bounties for enlistment in the regular army—was innocuous enough to reach enactment on Dec. 10 (p. 1837-8). Thus the administration

1. On Dec. 22, in debate on the expense involved, Calhoun repeated his opinion that the bill would produce a regular force; if not, at least a militia force superior, because of their longer term, to ordinary militia (AC13-3, p. 974).

was left to fight the war with 34,000 regulars, and the ordinary militia. See Adams, *History of U.S.*, VIII, 264-81.   Source: *NI*, Dec. 3, 1814; *AC*13-3, p. 712.

108. Resolution for a New System of Army Discipline

December 24, 1814

Mr. Calhoun, from the committee to whom was referred on the 23d ultimo, the report of the Secretary of War, relating to an uniform system of discipline for the Army of the United States, reported the following resolution:

Resolved, That the Secretary of War be directed to appoint a Board of Officers, to modify "the rules and regulations for the field exercise and manoeuvres of the French Infantry," as translated by Macdonald,[1] so as to make them correspond with the organization of the Army of the United States, and to make such additions and retrenchments as may be thought proper; and to lay the same, as soon as possible, before this House.

108 NOTE: On Nov. 23, 1814, the Speaker laid before the House the report of Monroe requested by Calhoun's resolution of Nov. 10 (No. 103), and on Calhoun's motion it was referred to a committee of which he was appointed chairman (*AC*13-3, p. 638; *NI*, Nov. 24, 1814; *House Journal*, p. 542). Monroe's report, dated Nov. 22, was to the effect that there was no uniform system of discipline in the army and suggested appointment of "a Board of General and Field Officers, to digest and report" such a system (*AC*13-3, p. 638).

Calhoun's resolution of Dec. 24 was agreed to (p. 989); but apparently the news of peace in February following caused the project, in effect, to be laid aside—see *Memoirs of Lieut.-General Scott*, I, 207.   Source: *House Journal*, p. 615. See also *NI*, Dec. 29, 1814; *AC*13-3, p. 988-9.

1. John MacDonald, *Rules and Regulations for the Field Exercise and Manoeuvres of the French Infantry;* translated from the French. 2 vols. London, 1803.

109. To PATRICK CALHOUN

Washington 4th Jan 1814 [*1815*].[1]

Dear Brother, I was very glad to hear from you by your letter of 17th Decr. My acquaintances generally do not write me sufficiently often and I may bring the same charge against you and the rest of our brothers.

I think the price of cotton will again rise. There is no doubt of a great failure on the Mississippi. The consumption of cotton in our own factories is estimated at 100,000 bales, which must be more than one third of the quantity produced. The fall in England seems to me to have risen from temporary causes. On the whole if you do not wish the money, I would advise you to wait the spring market.

I wish you would mention to James to enter my sulky for me. I value it at $100. The plated harness costing $20, making $120 which I gave for both.

The opinion of the naval offices is that the Wasp is not lost. They think that the reportd engagement between her and the British frigate that went into Lisbon in so shattered a condition cannot be true; as she was not at that time in those seas. Their impression is that the engagement was with a privateer and that the Wasp is in the Pacifick ocean. I trust it may be true. There is a good deal of talk of the next President. The New Yo[rkers] wish to start Tomkins; but I [think] they cannot succeed. My [im]pression is that Monroe wi[ll be] the man. My respect to Nancy and family and all acquain[tances].

SOURCE: Jameson, *Correspondence,* p. 126-7—see No. 34 SOURCE.

110. To PATRICK NOBLE, Abbeville, S.C.

Washington 11th Feb 1815

Dear Patrick, I have but [a] moment to inform you that the Orleans mail has just brought the glorious news that the British have evacuated the Island of Orleans. They acknowledge their loss to be

1. The date, 1815, is clear from his reference to the "Wasp"—see Adams, *History of U.S.,* VIII, 193.

4,000 with Packenham and Gibbs killed and Kean dangerously wounded. The mail is just closing.

I am &c

J. C. Calhoun

Source: *SCL.*

111. Comment on the Bank Bill

February 13, 1815

Mr. Calhoun in a pithy speech of moderate length, expressed himself in favor of commitment, though friendly only to two of the proposed instructions, viz. the reduction of the interest on loans to the government, and striking out the old stock. He assigned the reasons also why the plan of a bank now before the House did not meet his approbation.

111 NOTE: On Dec. 9 a bank bill, conforming in general to that desired by Dallas (see No. 104) was received from the Senate (*AC*13-3, p. 799). This bill reduced the proposed government subscription to one-fifth, increased the amount of Treasury notes that might be paid in for stock, and provided that the government might borrow thirty millions from the bank (p. 226). Calhoun apparently took no part in the debate, except to state his opposition to the bill in its present form, and voted against it (p. 1025, 1030); but finally, after amendments were made which would have set the capital at thirty millions, five of it in specie, fifteen in Treasury notes, and ten in "war stock," he voted for it (p. 1040, 1044). This bill was vetoed by Madison (p. 189-91, Jan. 30). Whereupon another was put through the Senate, but Calhoun declared in his 1837 speech (*Works*, III, 127-8) that at the time he informed the authors of the bill that it was still unacceptable. The new bill was given the second reading in the House on Feb. 13 when the changes were considered to which Calhoun addressed the remarks above. On Feb. 14 the bill was laid on the table (*AC*13-3, p. 1153). In his 1837 speech (*Works*, III, 129) Calhoun said that this was on his motion and was the result of the news of peace, and that at once the bank proponents offered to come to his terms; this he refused, notifying them that he would now insist on provision for "speedy restoration of specie payments." On Feb. 17 on the motion of Lowndes, the bill was indefinitely postponed (*AC*13-3, p. 1167-8) after, so Calhoun stated (*Works*, III, 129), more fruitless overtures had been made to him. See Catterall, *Second Bank of U.S.*, p. 14-7; Walters, *Dallas,*

p. 196-7; Adams, *History of U.S.*, VIII, 257-60; Wiltse, *Calhoun, Nationalist*, p. 98-100; and No. 120.   SOURCE: *NI*, Feb. 14, 1815; AC13-3, p. 1150.

112. To CAPT. JOHN E. CALHOUN, Carlisle, Pa.

Washington 26th Feb 1815.

Dear John, I regret that your departure from this place was so suudden [*sudden*] as not to give me an opportunity of seeing you; and tho', it has afforded me extreme delight that the just and necessary war which we had been compeled to wage with England has been brought to a termination so advantageous and glorious to our country, yet I would have been much pleased if you could have had an opportunity of acquiring that honor which I am confident you would, had the war lasted another campaign. The most active means had been put in operation to reduce the Canadas the next summer, and I believe, with such officers and soldiers as we have they would have succeeded.

As to your future course; my advice would be not to continue in the army during peace; but I would not resign. The probability is that the military establishment will be much reduced; and it is preposed to give every captain who will be thrown out by such reduction 640 acres of land and three months pay. If you should resign, you would loose this compensation, which the country thinks fit to give to those who have served her. You had better write to the secretary at war that you had entered the service of the country, with an intention to render what service you could during the war, and that it was not your desire to continue in during peace, and that you would desire to be ranked among those officers, who would be put out of service by the reduction of the army.

I am yours &c

J. C. CALHOUN

My respect to Captain Carrington

112 NOTE: John Ewing Colhoun was commissioned Captain, Third Rifle, Mar. 17, 1814; resigned Mar. 11, 1815 (Heitman, *Historical Register . . . U.S. Army*, I, 317).   SOURCE: CC.

113. SPEECH ON THE MILITARY PEACE
ESTABLISHMENT

February 27, 1815

Mr. Calhoun said, it appeared to him, that on the question of fixing the military peace establishment, the House were rather acting in the dark, having before them neither the estimates nor the facts on which they were founded. In determining the amount of the military establishment, he said, the House ought to take into view three objects, and graduate the force to be retained accordingly: The proper maintenance and garrison of our military posts and fortresses; the retention of so large a force as would keep alive military science, and serve as a seminary for that purpose; and the adaptation of our military force to the policy of the enemy in regard to this country. As regarded either of these objects, it appeared to him the House was not in possession of information to enable it to act understandingly. What force would be necessary to guard our seaports, to protect our Northwestern and Western frontiers from Indian hostility? Of this there was no estimate, but every thing was left to conjecture. As to the second point, practical military men ought to be consulted whether it would be proper to keep up a military force to maintain military science. The next question was the most important: Have we a sufficient knowledge of the force and policy of the enemy to authorize a reduction of our military force? He contended we had not. What would be the feelings of England on receiving intelligence of the late events, he did not know. Whether the soreness of her recent defeat would produce a disposition to remain at peace or to retaliate, no gentleman could say. If there was any doubt on the subject, we ought to act with caution in reducing our military establishment. What course the enemy will pursue we cannot determine; whether he will keep up a small peace establishment or a large military force, we do not know. It ought to be recollected, that he has abundance of military means, and that living is as cheap in Canada as in England. If the enemy should keep up a force on our borders of 30 or 40 thousand men, instead of reducing it to four or five thousand, would it be wise for us wholly to disarm? It would not. Mr. C. said he deprecated such a state of things; but, if the enemy should retain a large force in service in our vicinity, it would be highly impolitic for us to reduce ours as low as is proposed.[1] The gentleman from Virginia (Mr. Jackson)[2] had on a former day, remarked that our situation was particularly felicitous in having no enemy immediately in our neighborhood. But, it ought to be borne in mind that the most powerful nation in Europe possessed provinces adjoining our territory, into which she could readily pour an armed force. He hoped that nation never would, but it might do so. Suppose, with forty thousand men, he chose, without notice, to make a hostile movement against our territory: every strong position on the Niagara frontier would fall at once into his hands, and the very expence we wish to avoid must be quadrupled to enable us to regain them. Having neither estimates nor facts, as he had before remarked, the House ought to act cautiously. It is easier to keep soldiers than to get them; to have officers of skill and renown in your possession, than to make them. Let us wait awhile before we reduce our army to a mere peace establishment.

113 NOTE: On the 22nd (*AC*13-3, p. 1177), Troup, from the Military Affairs Committee, presented a bill to fix the peace-time military establishment at 10,000 men—the proportion of infantry, artillery and riflemen to be determined by the President, the engineer corps to be retained, and the command to include two major generals and four brigadiers. The House was now considering an amendment, adopted in the Committee of the Whole (p. 1204) to reduce the number to six thousand—a measure already vigorously debated in the committee and by the House. The House agreed to the reduction, Calhoun voting against it (p. 1251-2), but the act, as approved Mar. 3 (p. 1934-5) provided for 10,000 men and for two major generals and two brigadiers. See No. 114, and, for note on a copy of this speech in the Clemson Collection, No. 114 NOTE. SOURCE: *NI*, Mar. 14, 1815; *AC*13-3, p. 1215-6.

1. Pickering attacked this statement (*AC*13-3, p. 1219); Calhoun explained (p. 1219-20) that he meant it as "a case to show a policy of keeping up a respectable military force" and that the loss of Detroit, for lack of adequate force, had occasioned more than half the expense of the war.
2. John G. Jackson, p. 1208.

114. Speech on the Results of the War

February 27, 1815

Mr. Calhoun was more and more convinced of the inexpediency of breaking up at once our whole military establishment. Had they before them, he asked, or could they have at this session, the necessary estimates whereon to fix the peace establishment? If they had, there would probably be little difference of opinion on the subject; but they had not. Gentlemen had said, that to retain so great a force would imply a suspicion of the good faith of Great Britain in regard to the peace. His reply to that argument was, that, if the largest number now proposed be agreed to, we shall reduce our army to one-sixth of the amount of our war establishment; that is to say, from sixty to ten thousand men, and ultimately perhaps from ten thousand to six. He rose now, however, principally to reply to the argument that our ratification of the treaty of peace amounted to an abandonment to Great Britain of the right of impressment, &c.—to an abandonment of "free trade and sailors' rights." [1] In the first place, he denied the position that this country had ever set up a claim to the immunity of the flag. We had always been ready to make any arrangement by which our own seamen should be protected. Although the government perhaps ought to have done so, it never made it a point, that the flag should protect every thing under it. It had said, however, that unless the flag did protect all sailing under it, it would be difficult to remedy the abuse of the search for persons. We offered the rule that the flag should protect the seamen, as one subject to modification. [2] This government had always been willing to make such reciprocal regulations as should in this respect secure to each nation its rights. The celebrated seamen's bill, as it was generally called, was the result of a disposition of this sort. [3] We have denied the right of Great Britain to take any other than her own seamen: and have we made any stipulation, express or implied, by which we yielded the right of

1. Richard Stockton, of New Jersey, argued that making a treaty without mention of impressment meant abandonment of that claim and also declared that the United States claimed the flag protected all persons on merchant ships (*AC*13-3, p. 1226-9).

2. Compare Calhoun's remark, above, p. 157.

3. See No. 73 NOTE.

our citizens to exemption from impressment by her authority? On the contrary, said Mr. C. I maintain that that right is substantially and forever fixed. We have exhibited, during this war, a power and an energy of character which will prevent any power from hereafter finding it expedient to take our or any other seamen from our decks.

Mr. C. added, he had no doubt but Great Britain would be willing to guard against future collision on that subject, to enter into reciprocal arrangements which shall preclude hereafter any necessity or pretence for searching our merchant vessels for her seamen. There is no abandonment on our part, by the treaty, of any right. He had seen assertions to the contrary in newspapers; but he never expected to have heard it gravely said on this floor, that it would be something like a violation of the treaty if we should hereafter resist the practice of impressment of our seamen. The war, Mr. C. said, had effected all its great objects. The British claim of impressment, which we resisted, ended with the European war. It was a claim resulting from a state of war. That state ceasing, the operation of the claim ceased, and there was no necessity for a treaty stipulation against a claim which was extinct. If war should again break out in Europe, and that claim be revived (which he believed it would not) we shall be in a better condition than ever to assert the rights of our citizens; though, he believed, we have made such an impression on the British nation, that it will never feel the same disposition hereafter that it has formerly evinced to encroach on our rights, which are now better secured than by paper or parchment stipulations. They are secured and settled by the vigor and energy of the American people, who will again be ready to draw the sword if Britain again encroaches on our dearest rights.

[*Alexander C. Hanson, of Maryland, here replied to Calhoun's "extraordinary assertions."* [4]]

4. AC13-3, p. 1237-45. Hanson quoted (p. 1240) a paragraph (AC12-2, p. 934) of Grundy's report of Jan. 29, 1813, accompanying the seamen's bill, to the effect that the war should be prosecuted until a stop to impressment of American seamen was assured (see No. 73 NOTE). He charged the doctrine to Calhoun as chairman of the committee. He also attacked Calhoun's contention that instead of demanding immunity for the flag, the United States had fought only for protection of American seamen (AC13-3, p. 1240-2; his citations were from Monroe's letter of Apr. 15, 1813, to the peace commissioners— p. 1289, 1297-8). Calhoun arose immediately in reply to Hanson (p. 1245-6).

Mr. Calhoun again rose. Nothing, he said, was more easy than by taking detached parts of papers, and omitting to take circumstances into view, entirely to misrepresent any question. If the gentleman last up, who had quoted a part of the instructions to our ministers, had read a little more of that report, he would have perceived the gross error of the construction he had put upon it; for he would have found that our ministers were authorized to have made a treaty, containing a stipulation respecting impressment, to terminate at the conclusion of a peace in Europe—the object being to guard against the possible continuance of the practice of impressment during the war in Europe.[5] He would have further seen, that, when that peace took place, the necessity for such a stipulation ceased. What (said Mr. C.) was the injury which we complained of, and what was the claim of the enemy? The claim of the enemy was, that he had a right, in time of war, to enter on board American (neutral) vessels, and to judge who were American and who British seamen, and to take therefrom whomsoever he thought proper. What was the ground of complaint on our side? That the enemy, in the exercise of this pretended right, frequently took American seamen, to the detriment of the commerce, and deprivation of the personal liberty of American citizens. At the time those instructions were expedited to our ministers, there was a war raging in Europe, which no gentleman then pretended to think would come to a termination in many years. It appeared to be a contest, which would endure for a series of years, having already, with little intermission, lasted twenty years. Those statements and those instructions, a part of which had been quoted, were then given, respecting the question of impressment as springing out of a state of war; and it was at that time the report was made to this House, proclaiming the necessity of unceasing resistance of so grievous an injury.

That state of war, Mr. C. continued, having ceased, and with it the evil of impressment, there was no necessity to continue the war on that account. And, had we continued the war on that account, what then would have been the language of the gentleman and his friends? That statesmen go to war for practical injuries; that, as Great Britain never impresses in time of peace in Europe, in the

5. P. 1298.

present state of things to have continued the war on that ground
would have been fighting to resist a speculative claim, on the part
of the British government, which in practice had ceased. To have
done so would have been unwise, and would have met the severest
reprobation of the gentlemen on that side of the House. Every body
who heard him knew, Mr. C. said, that such would have been the
clamor rung from one end of the country to the other. Any one
who adverted to the very document, of which the gentleman had
read a part, will find his whole argument answered by it (taking in
connexion with it the circumstances of the world) as completely
and demonstrably as any proposition in Euclid. The idea that we
had relinquished our right in this respect, because it was not recited in the treaty, was, in his opinion, preposterous. It could not
be maintained by the semblance of an argument. It is not at all
affected by it, unless that it is fortified by the events of the present
war, and the spirit with which it has been waged, which will probably make foreign powers more careful of invading our rights. The
benefit of the claim to Britain can never compensate for the injury
she might sustain by provoking us to war, in resistance of it, and
in defence of the personal liberty of the citizens. In the late war,
this nation has acquired a character which will secure respect to its
rights. If ever an American citizen should be forcibly impressed,
Mr. C. said he should be ready again to draw the sword in his
defence: and no government could prosper that would, with impunity, permit such a damnable violation of the personal rights of
its citizens. Government itself is only protection; and they cannot
be separated. I feel pleasure and pride, said Mr. C. in being able
to say, that I am of a party which drew the sword on this question,
and succeeded in the contest: for, to all practical purposes, we
have achieved complete success.

114 NOTE: A copy of Nos. 113-14, in a hand resembling Virgil
Maxcy's, is in the Clemson Collection. (See p. xxxvii and No. 124
NOTE.) Both were made from the *Intelligencer,* or possibly from
intervening copies, and have minor revisions which Crallé used in
Works, II, 117-23. The changes are typical of the improvements
on Calhoun's style already noted in comments on the *Works* versions
of the early papers. In this speech (p. 280) Calhoun had the word
"power" occurring twice in the same sentence, and near the close
of his speech he referred to a violation as "damnable." In the manu-

script copy the second "power" is changed to "nation" and "damnable" to "flagrant." Crallé used both corrections. SOURCE: *NI,*
Mar. 16, 1815; *AC*13-3, p. 1235-6, 1245-6.

115. To MRS. FLORIDE CALHOUN, Charleston

Bath [*S.C.*] 9th April 1815.

My dear Mother, Floride wrote to you by Mr. Shackleford that all
were well. We at that time little calculated that in three days, we
should experience the heaviest calamity that has ever occured to
us. It is no less than the death of our interesting and dearest
daughter. She was in the bloom of health on Wednesday morning
the 6th inst. and was a corps the next day. She was taken with a
vomiting and fever very suddenly about eleven o'clock and died
about an hour by sun the next morning. We suspected no danger
till about midnight and even then except a wildness in her eyes
the symtoms were not very distressing. We became much alarmed
about day; and sent of a dispach for Dr Casey but he was gone to
Augusta. Every thing was done which we thought could be of
service but in vain. Thus early was stached [*snatched*] from us in
the bloom of life, our dear child ["she" *cancelled*] whom provide[nce] seemed, but a few hours before, to destine to be our comfort and delight. So healthy so cheerful, so stought; every prognostick of health and long life. She had just began to talk and walk;
and progressed so fast in both as to surprise every one. She could
hardly step when I returned on the 20th of March and before her
death she could run all over the house. But why should I dwell on
these once flattering appearances? She is gone alas! from us for
ever; and has left behind nothing but our grief and tears. So fixed
in sorrow is her distressed mother that every topick of consolation,
which I attemp to offer but seems to grieve her the more. It is in
vain I tell her it is the lott of humanity; that almost all parents have
suffered equal calamity; that Providence may have intended it in
kindness to her and ourselves, as no one can say what, had she
lived, would have been her condition, whither it would have been
happy or miserable; and above all we have the consolation to know
that she is far more happy than she could be here with us. She
thinks only of her dear child; and recalls to her mind every thing

that made her interesting, thus furnishing additional food for her grief.

We will expect you up as soon as your business will permit. Floride desires her love to you. Our respects to all friends.

I am with affection yours &c

J. C. CALHOUN

SOURCE: *CC.*

116. From ISAAC HARBY

Chston May 22d 1815

Dr Sir During the last sitting of Congress I took the liberty of addressing you, as well as several other Members of Congress from this State, on a subject which no doubt is fresh in your reccollection. On Mr Cheves's return to this place he informed me that the strong reccommendation given to Mr Dallas by all the members that I wrote to, led him to believe that my object would be attained, & Judge Johnson who, when at Washington took a very active part in my favor did so strongly believe that Mr Dallas (then acting) had consented to my Solicitation, that he expressed Great astonishment that I had not heard from the Department on the Subject. Mr Cheves, being now a private Citizen & Judge Johnson absent the State I again take the liberty of addressing you on the Subject.

The "Southern Patriot" being honored with your patronage You can judge how far it is entitled to the consideration of those whose cause it advocates from principle.

The mercantile community & their dependents, compose the bulk & chief support, of public Journals, in our large commercial Cities. They are opposed to the administration, & consequently to every paper that will not sacrifice its independence, & become a mere machine to be moved in such manner as they will point out. Believg. as I do that the present Administration is not only best calculated to secure to the people their liberty & happiness, but is also highly instrumental in keeping down a restless Faction, advocating these Opinions & not disposed to "trim" as many public Journals (even under the patronage of Government) styled republican think proper to do, I am by no means a favorite, (as a Journalist) with the men, notoriously known as the Enemies of the Administration.

The "Patriot" has a very General Circulation throughout the State, & its patrons are among the best friends to the Country. I need not however say to You the great advantage that results in having a share of the patronage of Government, it gives a character to the paper thus patronised, & is the mean of drawing to it other support.

I am certain that it will be admitted, no paper has been better exerted in the Republican Cause & none in this State speaks a language so bold to the Opposition party. It is not for me to express an Opinion as to the ability which Conducts the "Patriot" it has this however to be proud of, that its Editorial matter, frequently fills the Columns, of the most respectable & able republican prints throughout the Union.

If Sir it comports with yr feelings, you would essentially serve me by reminding Mr Dallas or Mr Monroe of the strong & highly respectable reccomendation which my application had & which I believe has not been acted on, merely because more important business occupied the attention of the Department. While I assure You that if I should succeed, I would gratefully appreciate the honorable distinction, so on the Contrary should I be supposed unworthy that distinction, I will not loose of my exertion in supporting those measures, which in my estimation are best calculated to secure the happiness of our beloved Country.

I am Sir with most profound respect, Yr very Obt St

ISAAC HARBY.

Editor "Southern Patriot"

116 NOTE: This correspondence also includes a Jan. 31, 1816, letter of endorsement of Harby's application, signed by Calhoun and all but one of the South Carolina delegation. Calhoun wrote a separate recommendation June 17, 1815 (Iowa State Department of History and Archives). Harby was successful in his application; the *Patriot* on Feb. 14, 1816, began publication of the laws of this session. SOURCE: *NA,* RG59, General Records of State Department, Correspondence on Publication of the Laws.

117. To MRS. FLORIDE CALHOUN, Charleston, S.C.

Washington 29th Novr. 1815.

My dear wife, I arrived at this place yesterday; having performed the journey in a shorter time than what I expected by several days. At Raleigh in North Carolina I met with John Taylor which as it afforded company made the journey more pleasant [1] The last 53 miles is performed by a steam boat; nothing can be superior to that mode of conveyance w[he]ther we regard the safety, ease or expedition of traveling. You are moved on rapidly without being sensible of it. I hope by another session there will be one from Charleston to this place.

The more I reflect on it, I am the better satisfied you ought to go to Charleston at the time of your labour. St John's appears to me to be very inconvenient. I will write to Dr. McBride to attend to you; and I am certain that he will omit nothing that his skill and ["patience" *cancelled*] attention ["Science" *cancelled*] can contribute to make your time safe and easy.[2]

I hope Andrew has lost his fever. I should [fe]el much anxiety for him if it should continue after the Winter fairly sets in. I would fear that he would not get clear of it till spring Do not fail to write by every mail. I am anxious to hear from you all. Remember me affectionately to your mother and brothers. Kiss our dear son for me and tell him how much his father loves him.

Believe me to be your affectionate husband,

JOHN C. CALHOUN

SOURCE: *CC.*

1. John Taylor, Representative from South Carolina, and Calhoun attended the first day of the session, Dec. 4 (*House Journal,* p. 6).
2. The Calhoun family Bible (Fort Hill, Clemson, S.C.) gives the birth of Jane Calhoun, Jan. 1816, but not her death, which must have occurred before the spring of 1817—see No. 156.

118. First Speech on the Military Academies Bill

January 2, 1816

Mr. Calhoun said, the only question really before the House at this time appeared to be, what was the best mode to produce a national spirit. That policy, he said, which creates the best political system; which promotes the national prosperity; which provides efficiently for the national security; that policy, by the effect of which every part of the country feels itself secure, whilst commerce is prosperous, and agriculture and manufactures are protected; that, he said, was the policy which would certainly create a true national feeling. Every thing in opposition to such a policy would end in sectional feelings. Applying these general remarks to the present question, what, he asked, was the object of the bill? To establish a military school. What was the object of this school? To contribute to the national security, by the diffusion of military knowledge. Whether one great central school was better calculated to produce this effect, than several separate schools, was the question. Mr. C. said he believed it would not. If we had a central great school, as now proposed, it would principally be filled with the sons of wealthy men: of great and influential men, others would not have the means of sending their sons abroad for education—for, here, certainly, the allowance by the government would not cover the expences of the young men. Where, in this country, shall we look for genius and talent? Most indubitably in the middle ranks, in the lower ranks in preference to the higher; not that these classes actually contain a greater portion of talent, but that they have stronger stimulants to its exertion. Rich men, being already at the top of the ladder, have no further motive to climb. It is that class of the community who find it necessary to strive for elevation, that furnishes you with officers. Look, said Mr. C. at the officers who distinguished themselves in service during the late war. Were there among them the sons of wealthy men or of great men? If there were any such, Mr. C. said he knew of none. The rule he applied was a general one. If the school were established here, the means of support afforded by the government to the cadets would not cover their expences; men in moderate circumstances would be unable to send their sons, and the country would be deprived of their valuable services. The

Academy would be in a great measure filled by the sons of the wealthy and influential men within four hundred miles of this place. Mr. C. said he believed the provisions of this bill were more important than any yet on the table of the House, and as important as any that would come before the House at the present session. The way to render the nation secure, is not by maintaining a large foreign army, very expensive and a little dangerous; it is not thus you will keep up a proper military spirit; but by military education. Upon the officers of armies in a great measure depends, particularly in a free government, the success of war. Free governments always afford materials for soldiers. Of the celebrated brigade of Scott,[1] Mr. C. said, three-fourths of the privates had not been in service more than six months. All that was wanted to make soldiers amongst us was education, which the private can soon acquire; but the making of *officers* is the work of time, particularly in the present state of the science of war—and it was proper, therefore, to provide amply for that object. In time of war, Mr. C. said, we ought to get *soldiers* speedily—we ought to come into the population at once, by the measure so much reprobated at the last session from the other side of the House.[2] Mr. C. was in favor of establishing more than one additional military school, in order to diffuse, as far as possible, military science. This, he said, would secure us against invasion from abroad, and, by making the militia formidable, against despotism at home. It was in this way that militia would be made more efficient than in any other. At present, the number of academies proposed to be established might be sufficient; but he hoped that they would be progressively increased, and that it would not be long before we should have one in every considerable state in the Union. Mr. C. compared the feelings of the House now and previous to the war. Now, he said, we see every where a nationality of feeling; we hear sentiments from every part of the House in favor of union, and against a sectional spirit. What had produced this change? The glory acquired by the late war, and the prosperity which had followed it. Let us direct our attention, then, said he,

1. On Scott's brigade see No. 100, n. 2, and the comment on Calhoun's remark by Samuel S. Conner, of Massachusetts, AC14-1, p. 760.

2. See No. 107 NOTE.

to the objects calculated to accomplish the prosperity and greatness of the nation, and we shall certainly create a national spirit.

118 NOTE: On Dec. 26 (*AC*14-1, p. 402) the Military Affairs Committee, reporting on the portion of the President's message recommending the enlargement of the military academy and the establishment of others (p. 15), brought in a bill providing for academies in the District of Columbia, at Mt. Dearborn in South Carolina and at Newport in Kentucky, the number of cadets at all the academies not to exceed 800. The House was then, Jan. 2, in Committee of the Whole; the same day (p. 435) the bill was amended to provide for one additional academy only. See No. 119. SOURCE: *NI*, Jan. 11, 1816; *AC*14-1, p. 430-1.

119. SECOND SPEECH ON THE MILITARY ACADEMIES BILL

January 3, 1816

Mr. Calhoun also opposed the reduction of the number of cadets; because, if the present number were retained, it would afford ample room for a proper selection of officers. In another point of view, he thought it materially necessary to retain the proposed number. The whole population of the United States is composed of men active, vigorous and spirited. With good officers to lead them, you may at any time make out of any portion of them active, good soldiers. What is requisite to make our militia efficient? Military knowledge, only, said Mr. C. The cadets will many of them return to the body of the people, and become a part of the militia. Suppose a renewal of the struggle between us and the nation with whom we were recently at war; suppose she should put forth her whole strength to crush this young country; we shall then find the use of having men qualified to lead our citizens to meet her invading foe. The whole population of the country becomes an efficient force, because it has among it men properly educated and qualified to lead an army into the field. Every citizen of a free country, and of course of this country, said Mr. C. has two duties to perform; the duty of defending his country by arms if necessary, and the duty of voting and thus participating in the management of the affairs of his country. Every young man of ardent feeling will desire to qualify himself for their proper performance. These are duties which every citizen ought zealously to perform, and from which, if the people ever shrink, our nation will not long have existence. Mr. C. appealed to the history of republics, which had so often lost their liberties from the indisposition of the citizens to perform their share of military duty. It ought to be the object of a wise government to resist a tendency towards apathy in the people; to diffuse military science. The dependence on regular force merely was a contracted idea, which he hoped this House would not give into. The army, Mr. C. said, was, and ought always to be, a respectable part of the military force of the nation; but a well organized militia is its bulwark—and they are but a rabble without discipline. Hence the necessity for the free diffusion of military science. He hoped, therefore, the largest number of cadets proposed to be authorized, would be agreed to.

119 NOTE: Earlier in the day, while the House was considering, in Committee of the Whole, the additional academies bill (No. 118), Calhoun offered a motion to provide for three, but this was lost (*AC*14-1, p. 437). The debate was now in the House, and Calhoun was objecting to the proposal to reduce the number of cadets. The figure was set at 600, however, and the bill returned to the Military Committee for appropriate revision (p. 450). It was later reported but was not taken up by the House (p. 515, 1235). SOURCE: *NI,* Jan. 13, 1816; *AC*14-1, p. 448-9.

120. BILL TO INCORPORATE THE SUBSCRIBERS TO THE BANK OF THE UNITED STATES

January 8, 1816

[*Mr. Calhoun, from the committee on that part of the President's message which relates to an uniform national currency, reported:*]

A Bill to incorporate the Subscribers to the Bank of the United States.

Sect 1.   Be it enacted &c. That a Bank of the United States of America shall be established with a capital of Thirty five millions of dollars divided into Three hundred and fifty thousand shares of one hundred dollars each share: but Congress may at any time hereafter augment the capital of the said Bank to a sùm not exceeding Fifty Millions of dollars in such manner as shall be by law provided.[1] Seventy thousand shares amounting to the sum of seven Millions of dollars, part of the capital of the said Bank shall be subscribed and paid for by the United States, in the manner hereinafter specified: And Two hundred and eighty thousand shares, amounting to the sum of Twenty eight millions of dollars shall be subscribed and paid for by individuals, companies or Corporations in the manner hereinafter specified.

Sect. 2. And be it further enacted &c. That subscriptions for the sum of Twenty eight millions of dollars towards constituting the capital of the said Bank shall be opened on the first monday in June next at the following places: that is to say at [*Washington, D.C., and one place named in each state—blanks for New Jersey and Ohio places—by three commissioners for each place, appointed by the President, subscriptions to be received each day from ten till four until the following Saturday; the commissioners to send the subscriptions to the Philadelphia commissioners and transcript to the Secretary of the Treasury; in case of over-subscription the Philadelphia commissioners to apportion shares (but allowing each subscriber at least one share); if under-subscription, to continue to receive them.*][2]

Sect. 3. And be it further enacted &c. That it shall be lawful [*for subscriptions to be received—no one for more than 3,000 shares—and paid for as follows: $7,000,000 in gold or silver coin, and $21,000,000 in gold or silver coin or in the funded debt of the United States—that portion bearing 6 per cent interest to be received at par value, that bearing 3 per cent at $65 per $100, and that bearing 7 per cent at $106.51.*] And the payments of the said subscriptions shall be made and compleated by the subscribers respectively at the times and in the manner following: that is to

1. This clause, for increase of the capital, was stricken out of this section (which became Section 1 of the act) on Feb. 29—see No. 126 NOTE.

2. In Section 2 of the act, Portland, Maine, was added, the New Jersey and Ohio places designated, and that of Connecticut changed (House amdt.); the term for subscription was extended to twenty days exclusive of Sundays, and provision made for five Philadelphia commissioners (Senate amdts.). In reapportionment in case of over subscription the commissioners were to reduce the largest subscriptions "in such manner as that no subscription shall be reduced in amount while any one remains larger" (House amdt.), but no place was to have its total reduced below 3,000 shares (Senate amdt.).

say: at the time of subscribing there shall be paid Five dollars on each share in gold or silver coin as aforesaid and Twenty five dollars more in coin as aforesaid or in Funded debt as aforesaid: [*this process to be repeated in 6 months and again in 12 months*]; and at the expiration of eighteen calendar months there shall be paid the further sum of ten dollars in gold or silver coin as aforesaid.[3]

Sect. 4. And be it further enacted &c. That at the time of subscribing to the capital of the said Bank as aforesaid each and every subscriber shall deliver to the Commissioners at the place of subscribing as well the amount of their subscriptions respectively in coin as aforesaid as the Certificates of Funded debt for the funded debt proportion of their respective subscriptions, together with a Power of Attorney authorizing the said Commissioners or a majority of them to transfer the said Stock in due form of law to "The President Directors and Company of the Bank of the United States of America" as soon as the said Bank shall be organized. Provided always that if in consequence of the apportionment of the shares in the capital of the said Bank among the Subscribers . . . any subscriber shall have delivered to the Commissioners at the time of subscribing a greater amount of gold or silver coin and Funded Debt than shall be necessary to compleat the payments for the share or shares to such subscribers apportioned as aforesaid, the Commissioners shall [*on application return the excess. There follows provision for deposit of the subscriptions and pay for the commissioners.*][4]

Sect. 5. And be it further enacted &c. That it shall be lawful for the United States to pay and redeem the Funded debt subscribed to the capital of the said Bank at the rates aforesaid, in such sums and at such times as shall be deemed expedient anything in any Act or Acts of Congress to the contrary thereof notwithstanding. And it shall also be lawful for the President Directors and Company of the said Bank to sell and transfer for gold and silver coin or bullion the Funded debt subscribed to the capital of the said Bank as aforesaid. Provided always that they shall not

3. The act (Section 3) made the coin requirements in the second and third payments $10 each (House amdt.). See *AC* 14-1, p. 1121, 1203, for Calhoun's comment and motion on the schedule of payments, and p. 1121 for his comment on the rate for the 6 per cent stock.
4. This section became Section 4 of the act.

sell more thereof than the sum of two millions of Dollars in any one year: nor sell any part thereof at any time within the United States without previously giving notice of their intention to the Secretary of the Treasury and offering the same to the United States at the current price not exceeding the rates afo[*resai*]d.[5]

Sect. 6. And be it further enacted &c. That at the opening of the Subscription to the capital Stock of the said Bank the Secretary of the Treasury shall subscribe [*for the United States the 70,000 shares in gold or silver coin, Treasury notes, or 6 per cent stock, in seven equal annual payments, the first at the opening of the subscription—however, with approval of the President and consent of the corporation, paying any or all of the amounts in advance.*] [6]

Sect. 7. And be it further enacted &c. That the Secretary of the Treasury with the approbation of the President of the United States shall from time to time select and designate the mode of paying for the said subscription of the United States to the capital of the said Bank as aforesaid And if payment thereof or of any part thereof be made in Public Stock bearing interest at the rate of six per centum per annum as aforesaid the said interest shall be payable qua[*r*]terly to commence from the time of making such payment on account of the said subscription and the principal of the said Stock shall be redeemable in any sums and at any periods which the Government shall deem fit. And the Secretary of the Treasury shall from time to time cause the certificates of such Public Stock to be prepared and made in the usual form and shall pay and deliver the same to the President, Directors and Company of the said Bank at or as soon as conveniently may be after the time and times hereinbefore prescribed for the payment of the said subscription of the United States to the capital of the said Bank as aforesaid: or at such other time and times as may be

5. The act (Section 5) required the offer to be made for a period of at least 15 days (Senate amdt.).

6. This section and Section 7 were replaced in the act by the revised Section 6, which set the date for payment of the entire government subscription at Jan. 1, 1817; eliminated the Treasury notes as a means of payment; changed the interest on stock to 5 per cent (payable quarterly); made the principal redeemable by the government at its option; and authorized the bank to sell the stock for coin, no more than $2,0000,000 in any one year (House amdt.). See No. 125 NOTE.

agreed upon in pursuance of the authority hereinbefore given to anticipate the payments of the said subscription as aforesaid. And if payment of the said subscription of the United States to the capital of the said Bank as aforesaid or of any part thereof shall be made in Treasury Notes [*such notes shall not bear interest, shall be receivable for all payments to the United States and to the bank, and may be re-issued if so received; but a portion shall be cancelled yearly so that the entire amount issued shall be cancelled within 8 years.*]

Sect. 8. And be it further enacted &c. That if any person shall falsely make forge or counterfeit [*the treasury notes*] every such person shall be deemed and adjudged guilty of felony: and being thereof convicted by due course of law shall be sentenced to be imprisoned and kept to hard labour, for a period not less than three years, nor more than ten years, and be fined in a sum not exceeding Five Thousand dollars.[7]

Sect. 9. And be it further enacted &c. That the Subscribers to the said Bank of the United States of America, their Successors and assigns shall be and are hereby created a corporation and body politic by the name and style of "The President Directors and Company of the Bank of the United States" and shall so continue until [*Mar. 3, 1836*] and by that name shall be and are hereby made able and capable in law, to have purchase . . . goods chattels and effects of whatsoever kind, nature, and quality to an amount not exceeding in the whole Fifty five Millions of dollars, including the amount of the capital Stock aforesaid: and the same to sell grant demise alien or dispose of, to sue and be sued . . . in all courts and places whatsoever . . . and also to ordain, establish and put in execution such bye laws and ordinances and regulations as they shall deem necessary and convenient for the government of the said corporation, not being contrary to the constitution and laws of the United States: and generally to do and execute all and singular the acts matters and things, which

7. This section was omitted from the act by reason of the elimination of the Treasury notes (see above, n. 6). Section 18 of the act provided similar penalties for counterfeiting bills and notes of the bank, and added a clause to the effect that state courts were not excluded from jurisdiction over these offenses; Section 19 of the act provided for further protection against counterfeiting (House amdts.).

to them it shall or may appertain to do: subject neverthless to the rules regulations, restrictions, limitations and provisions hereinafter priscribed and declared.[8]

Sect 10. And be it further enacted &c. That for the management of the affairs of the said Corporation there shall be twenty five Directors, five of whom shall be annually appointed by the President of the United States by and with the advice and consent of the Senate, and twenty of whom shall be annually elected at the Banking House in the City of Philadelphia on the first Monday of January in each year by the qualified Stockholders of the capital of the said Bank and by a plurality of votes then and there actually given according to the scale of voting hereinafter prescribed. . . . And the Board of Directors annually at the first meeting after their election in each and every year shall proceed to elect one of the five Directors appointed by the President of the United States to be President of the Corporation who shall hold the said office during the same period for which the Directors are appointed and elected as aforesaid. . . . And Provided also that in case [*of failure to make appointment or hold an election, the directors or president to continue in office until appointment or election, and*] in case of the death resignation or removal of the President of the said Corporation the Directors shall proceed to elect another President from the Directors appointed by the President of the United States as aforesaid: and in case of the death resignation or absence from the United States or removal of a Director from office the vacancy shall be supplied by the President of the United States or by the Stockholders as the case may be. But the President of the United States alone shall have power to remove the President of the Bank or any of the Directors appointed by him as aforesaid.[9]

8. This became Section 7 of the act which, however, defined the court clause to include state courts "having competent jurisdiction" and any circuit court of the United States. See AC14-1, p. 1204-5.

9. The corresponding section (8) of the act, stipulated that the five directors be stockholders of the corporation (see p. 1139), not more than three of them residents of any one state; it eliminated the requirement that the president of the bank be elected from one of the five appointed directors, and likewise the authority of the President to remove the president of the bank (House amdts.). The Senate added the amendment that any director of the bank or of one of its branches should lose his place if he became director of another bank. See NOTES to Nos. 125 and 126.

Sect. 11. And be it further enacted &c. That as soon as the sum of [*$8,400,000 of subscription received, exclusive of that of the government, the Philadelphia commissioners to give at least 30 days notice, in each place in which subscriptions made, of election of the 20 directors, and the President of the United States authorized to appoint the 5 directors during this session; the directors to elect a president of the bank from one of the five appointed directors, and all to serve until the first Monday in January ensuing.*] [10]

Sect. 12. And be it further enacted &c. That the Directors for the time being shall have power to appoint such officers, clerks and servants under them as shall be necessary for executing the business of the said corporation, and to allow them such compensation for their services respectively as shall be reasonable: and shall be capable of exercising such other powers and authorities for the well governing and ordering of the affairs of the said corporation as shall be prescribed fixed and determined by the laws regulations and ordinances of the same.[11]

Sect. 13. And be it further enacted &c. That the following rules, restrictions limitations and provisions shall form and be fundamental articles of the constitution of the said Corporation to wit.[12]

1. The number of votes to which the Stockholders shall be entitled, in voting for Directors, shall be according to the number of Shares he she or they respectively shall hold in the proportions following: that is to say; for one share and not more than two shares one vote: for every two shares above two and not exceeding ten, one vote: for every four shares above ten and not exceeding thirty one vote: for every six shares above thirty and not exceeding sixty one vote: for every eight shares above sixty and not exceeding one hundred, one vote: and for every ten shares above one hundred, one vote But no person, copartnership or body politic shall be entitled to a greater number than thirty votes: and after the first election no share or shares shall confer a right of voting which shall not have been holden three calendar months previous to the day

10. The corresponding section (9) of the act relieved these appointees of the requirement of being stockholders.

11. Section 10 of the act.

12. This "rules" section, 13, became Section 11 of the act.

of election. And Stockholders actually resident within the United States and none other may vote in elections by proxy. But no person shall give in the whole a greater number of votes as Proxy, and in his own right, than he would be entitled to give in his own right only, according to the proportion of voting hereinbefore prescribed.[13]

2. Not more than three fourths of the Directors elected by the Stockholders, and not more than four fifths of the Directors appointed by the President of the United States who shall be in office at the time of an annual election shall be elected or appointed for the next succeeding year,[14] but the Director who shall be the President at the time of an election may always be reappointed by the President of the United States, and be re-elected President of the Bank by the Directors thereof.

3. None but a resident citizen of the United States shall be a Director: nor shall a Director be entitled to any emolument. But the Stockholders may make such compensation to the President, for his extraordinary attendance at the Bank, as shall appear to them reasonable.[15]

4. Not less than seven directors shall constitute a board for the transaction of business, of whom the President shall always be one except in case of sickness or necessary absence, in which case his place may be supplied by any other director whom he by writing under his hand shall depute for that purpose. And the director so deputed, may do and transact all the necessary business belonging to the office of the President of the said corporation, during the continuance of the sickness or necessary absence of the President.[16]

5. A number of Stockholders not less than sixty who together shall be proprietors of one thousand shares or upwards shall have power at any time to call a general meeting of the Stockholders for purposes relative to the institution, giving at least ten weeks notice

13. The last sentence was omitted from Section 11, subsection 1 of the act (House amdt.).

14. The Senate amended this clause. Section 11, subsection 2 of the act forbade directors holding office for more than three years of four in succession.

15. Section 11, subsection 3 of the act substituted "stockholder, resident citizen" for "resident citizen," and "directors" for "stockholders" (House amdts.). See also No. 126, and No. 126, n. 1.

16. Subsections 4, 5, 6, and 7 of Section 13 of the bill were not amended and retained the same subnumbers in Section 11 of the act.

in two public newspapers of the place where the Bank is seated and specifying in such notice the object or objects of such meeting.

6. Every Cashier or Treasurer, before he enters upon the duties of his office shall be required to give bond, with two or more sureties, to the satisfaction of the Directors in a sum not less than fifty thousand Dollars, with a condition for his good behavior and the faithful performance of his duties to the corporation.

7. The lands tenements and heriditaments which it shall be lawful for the said Corporation to hold, shall be only such as shall be requisite for its immediate accommodation in relation to the convenient transacting of its business, and such as shall have been bona fide mortgaged to it by way of security or conveyed to it in satisfaction of debts previously contracted in the course of its dealings or purchased at sales, upon judgements which shall have been obtained for such debts.

8. The total amount of debts which the said corporation shall at any time owe, whether by bond bill note or other contract over and above the debt or debts due for money deposited in the bank, shall not exceed the sum of Fifty Millions of Dollars unless the contracting of any greater debt shall have been previously authorized by a law of the United States. In case of excess the Directors under whose Administration it shall happen shall be liable for the same in their natural and private capacities. . . . But this provision shall not be construed to exempt the said corporation or the lands tenements goods or chattels of the same from being also liable for and chargeable with the said excess.[17]

Such of the said directors who may have been absent when the said excess was contracted or created or who may have dissented from the resolution or act, whereby the same was so contracted or created may respectively exonerate themselves from being so liable by forthwith giving notice of the fact, and of their absence or dissent to the President of the United States and to the Stockholders at a general meeting which they shall have power to call for that purpose.

9. The said Corporation shall not directly or indirectly deal or trade in any thing except bills of Exchange gold or silver bullion,

---

17. The act, Section 11, subsection 8, set the limit at $35,000,000 (House amdt.).

or in the sale of goods really and truly pledged for money lent and not redeemed in due time or goods which shall be the proceeds of its lands. It shall not be at liberty to purchase any public debt whatsoever: nor shall it take more than at the rate of six per centum per annum, for or upon its loans or discounts.[18]

10. No loan shall be made by the said Corporation for the use or on account of the Government of the United States, to an amount exceeding Five hundred thousand dollars or of any particular state to an amount exceeding Fifty thousand dollars or of any foreign prince or state, unless previously authorized by a law of the United States

11. The Stock of the said Corporation shall be assignable and transferable according to such rules as shall be instituted in that behalf by the laws and ordinances of the same.

12. The Bills obligatory and of credit under the seal of the said Corporation which shall be made to any person or persons shall be assignable by endorsement thereupon under the hand or hands of such person or persons and his her or their executors or administrators and of his her or their assignee or assignees and so as absolutely to transfer and vest the property thereof in each and every assignee or assignees successively, and to enable such assignee or assignees and his her or their executors or administrators to maintain an action thereupon in his her or their own name or names. And the Bills or Notes which may be issued by order of the said Corporation [*payable to any person or bearer, to be binding and assignable or negotiable, in same manner*] and those which are payable to Bearer shall be assignable and negotiable by delivery only.[19]

13. Half yearly dividends shall be made of so much of the profits of the Bank as shall appear to the Directors advisable and once in every three years, the directors shall lay before the Stockholders, at a general meeting for their information, an exact and

18. Subsections 9, 10, and 11 of Section 13 of the bill were unchanged in Section 11 of the act.

19. To Section 11, subsection 12 of the act was added the restriction on these bills that none be for a sum less than $5,000, and the proviso that all bills or notes of the bank should be made payable on demand other than those for $100 or more payable to order, which might be made payable for a period not over 60 days (Senate amdts.).

particular statement of the debts which shall have remained unpaid after the expiration of the original credit for a period of treble the term of that credit, and of the surplus of the profits, if any, after deducting losses and dividends. If there shall be a failure in the payment of any part of any sum subscribed to the capital of the said Bank by any person copartnership or body politic, the party failing shall lose the benefit of any dividend which may have accrued prior to the time for making such payment and during the delay of the same.[20]

14. The directors of the said Corporation shall establish a competent office of discount and deposite in the District of Columbia, whenever any law of the United States shall require such an Establishment:[21] [*and may establish similar offices in other places, or employ other banks—approved by the Secretary of the Treasury— for the purpose.*] Thirteen managers or directors of every office established as aforesaid shall be annually appointed by the Directors of the Bank to serve one year: they shall chuse a President from their own number: each of them shall be a citizen of the United States and not more than three fourths of the said managers or directors in office at the time of an annual appointment, shall be reappointed for the next succeeding year: but the President may be always re-appointed.

15. The officer at the head of the Treasury Department of the United States . . . may require, not exceeding once a week, [*statements of the capital stock, debts due the bank, deposits, notes in circulation, specie on hand, and may inspect accounts*]. Provided That this shall not be construed to imply a right of inspecting the account of any private individual or individuals with the Bank.[22]

20. Section 13, subsection 13 of the bill was unchanged in Section 11 of the act.
21. Through Senate amendment of the bill at this point, Section 11, subsection 14 provided that after the whole capital of the bank should have been paid up, the directors should establish such offices—when applied for by the legislature and required by law of Congress—in each state in which 2,000 shares of stock were subscribed or held; the directors were to be residents of the state, territory or district and were to hold office for no more than three years of four in succession. The House had previously amended the section to require that the directors be no more than thirteen, nor less than seven in number.
22. This became, unchanged, Section 11, subsection 15 of the act. For subsections 16 and 17, added to Section 11 of the act, see below, n. 29.

Sect. 14. [*Penalty on trading by or for the corporation contrary to provisions of the act—treble the amount involved.*][23]

Sect 15. [*Penalty on persons responsible for loans by the bank exceeding $500,000 to the United States government or $50,000 to a state, or a loan to any foreign prince or state (unless authorized by law), treble the amount involved.*]

Sect. 16. And be it further enacted &c. That the Bills or Notes of the said Corporation originally made payable, or which shall have become payable on demand shall be receivable in all payments to the United States, unless otherwise directed by Act of Congress.

Sect. 17. And be it further enacted &c. That during the continuance of this Act and whenever required by the Secretary of the Treasury the said Corporation shall give the necessary facilities for transferring the public funds from place to place [24] and for distributing the same in payment of the public creditors, without charging commissions or claiming allowance on account of difference of exchange and shall also do and perform the several and respective duties of the commissioners of loans for the several states, or of any one or more of them [25] at the times, in the manner and upon the terms prescribed by the Secretary of the Treasury.

Sect. 18. And be it further enacted &c. That the said Corporation shall not at any time suspend or refuse to pay the notes thereof in gold or silver coin upon demand according to the contract and promise of such Notes. [*Cancelled: provision that the bank pay six per cent interest on notes if specie payment were refused, and a penalty of $5,000 and forfeiture of his stock on each director assenting to the refusal or suspension.*] Provided always nevertheless that upon the representation of the said Corporation Congress shall have power to authorize the suspension or refusal aforesaid for a time to be limited by law: and that during the recess of Congress it shall be lawful for the President of the United States upon a like

23. Section 14, 15, 16 of the bill became, unchanged, Sections 12, 13, 14 of the act.

24. Section 17 of the bill became Section 15 of the act, which added at this point "within the United States, or the Territories thereof" (House amdt.).

25. Section 15 of the act substituted for the remainder of the section: "whenever required by law" (House amdt.).

representation to authorize such suspension for a term which shall not exceed six weeks after the opening of the next ensuing session of Congress:[26] [*Cancelled:a qualification of the above omitted penalties.*]

Sect 19. And be it further enacted &c. That in consideration of the exclusive priveliges and benefits conferred by this Act upon the said Bank the President Directors and Company thereof shall pay to the United States out of the corporate funds thereof the sum of one million and five hundred thousand dollars in three equal payments: that is to say, Five hundred thousand dollars at the expiration of two years, Five hundred thousand dollars at the expiration of three years, and five hundred thousand dollars at the expiration of four years, after the said Bank shall be organized and commence its operations in the manner hereinbefore provided.[27]

Sect. 20. And be it further enacted &c. That no other Bank shall be established by any future law of the United States during the continuance of the corporation hereby created for which the faith of the United States is hereby pledged: Provided, Congress may renew existing charters for banks in the District of Columbia not increasing the capital thereof:[28] and may grant charters if they deem it expedient, to any banking associations now in operation in the said District, and renew the same not increasing the capital thereof. And not withstanding the expiration of the term for which the said corporation is created, it shall be lawful to use the corporate name, style and capacity for the purpose of suits for the final settlement and liquidation of the affairs and accounts of the corporation and for the sale and disposition of their estate, real personal and mixed but not for any other purpose, or in any other

26. Section 18 of the bill, because of the addition of a new Section 16 in the act (see below, n. 29), became Section 17. The revised section in the act required the bank to meet in specie all its obligations, including deposits, upon demand—providing for payment of a 12-per-cent-interest penalty until the demand was met; Congress might regulate the whole process by law. The provision permitting suspension by Congress and the President was omitted. See No. 125 NOTE.

27. Section 19 of the bill became Section 20 of the act.

28. For the remainder of this sentence the act, Section 21, substituted the provision that Congress might also establish any other bank or banks in the District of capital not exceeding a total of $6,000,000.

manner whatsoever: nor for a period exceeding two years after the expiration of the said term of incorporation.[29]

120 NOTE: In his annual message on Dec. 5 Madison recommended (*AC*14-1, p. 15) that Congress provide for a uniform currency, establishing, if necessary for the purpose, a national bank. On Dec. 6 Calhoun was appointed chairman of the committee on this subject (p. 377). See No. 111 NOTE for the bank bills of the previous session, and No. 124 for beginning of the debate and action in the House.

On Dec. 24, 1815, Secretary of the Treasury Dallas wrote to Calhoun acknowledging the latter's letter of the 23rd in which Calhoun stated that the Committee on the Currency "had determined that a National Bank is the most certain means of restoring to the nation a specie circulation," and asking his opinion on six points. Dallas' letter and his outline of the proposed bank partly resembled his communication of a year before (No. 104 NOTE) but was shorn of its war-time provisions and was now patterned on the act establishing the First Bank, the distinctive differences being that he proposed that the government have five of the twenty-five directors, that the president of the bank come from the number appointed by the President, and that the Secretary of the Treasury should appoint the presidents of the branch banks. (MS, *NA*, RG233, 14A-E1, Original Reports, Treasury Department, No. 151; the outline appears in *NI*, Jan. 9, 1816, and the letter and outline in *ASP, Finance*, III, 57-61 and *AC*14-1, p. 505-14.) In outline the bill introduced by Calhoun even more closely duplicated the provisions of the 1791 act, and drew upon it for the wording of a number of sections (see No. 92 NOTE), but by meticulously detailed provisions and restrictions enormously expanded all previous plans. Calhoun accepted Dallas' proposals that the president of the main bank be one of the Presidential appointees (however leaving the directors of the branch banks to elect their own), that only Congress could suspend specie payment except in recess of Congress when the

29. The following sections and subsections were added to the act: Section 16—requiring deposits of the money of the United States to be made in the bank or its branches unless the Secretary of the Treasury should order otherwise, in which case he must report his reasons to Congress at its next session (House amdt.); Section 22—providing that Congress might declare the act void if subscriptions should fail to make possible establishment by April next (apparently a Senate amdt.); Section 23—for possible inspection of the books of the bank by committees of either house of Congress (Senate amdt.—see *AC*14-1, p. 276-7); Section 11, subsection 16—forbidding a stockholder, unless he were a citizen of the United States, to vote for a director (House amdt.); and Section 11, subsection 17—ordering that no note be issued for less than $5 (Senate amdt.).

President might do so, and that the bank pay for its charter and privileges a bonus of a million and a half dollars.

The significant changes made in the course of the debate in the House and Senate were the striking out of the clause allowing expansion of the capital to fifty millions, and of the requirement that the president of the bank be one of the directors appointed and removable by the President, the elimination of the authority of President or Congress to suspend specie payment, and the addition of the provision that government funds be deposited in the bank or in its branches unless the Secretary of the Treasury should order otherwise.

On the bank, see Catterall, *Second Bank of the U.S.*, p. 18-21; Wiltse, *Calhoun, Nationalist*, p. 108-11; Walters, *Dallas*, p. 210-2. Source: MS Bill, Jan. 8, 1816, *NA*, RG233, 14A-B1; see *ibid.* for the printed copies (with manuscript amendments) as the bill passed the House on Mar. 14 and the Senate on Apr. 3; "House amdt." and "Senate amdt." in the footnotes refer to these copies. The bill was printed in *AC*14-1, p. 494-505, and an outline in *NI*, Jan. 9, 1816. For the act as it was approved Apr. 10, 1816, see *AC*14-1, p. 1812-25; Peters, *Statutes of U.S.*, III, 266-77.

121. Speech on the Commercial Treaty with Great Britain

January 9, 1816

Mr. Calhoun observed, that the votes on this bill had been ordered to be recorded; and that the House would see, in his peculiar situation, a sufficient apology for his offering his reasons for the rejection of the bill. He had no disposition to speak on this bill; as he felt contented to let it take that course, which, in the opinion of the majority, it ought, till the members were called on by the order of the House to record their votes.

The question presented for consideration is perfectly simple, and easily understood; is this bill necessary to give validity to the late treaty with Great Britain? It appeared to him, that this question is susceptible of a decision, without considering whether a treaty can in any case set aside a law; or, to be more particular, whether the treaty which this bill purposes to carry into effect, does repeal the discriminating duties. The House will remember, that a law was passed at the close of the last session, conditionally repealing those duties.[1] That act proposed to repeal them in relation to any nation, which would on its part agree to repeal similar duties as to this country. On the contingency happening, the law became positive. It has happened, and has been announced to the country that England has agreed to repeal. The President, in proclaiming the treaty, has notified the fact to the House and country. Why then propose to do that by this bill, which has already been done by a previous act? He knew it had been said in conversation, that the provisions of the act were not as broad as the treaty. It did not strike him so. They appeared to him to be commensurate. He would also reason from the appearance of this House, that they were not very deeply impressed with the necessity of this bill. He never, on any important occasion, saw it so indifferent. Whence could this arise? From the want of importance? If, indeed, the existence of the treaty depended on the passage of this bill, nothing scarcely could be more interesting. It would be calculated to excite strong feelings. We all know how the country was agitated when Jay's Treaty was before this House. The question was on an appropriation to carry it into effect; a power acknowledged by all to belong to the House; and on the exercise of which, the existence of the treaty was felt to depend. The feelings manifested corresponded with this conviction.

Not so on this occasion. Farther, the treaty has already assumed the form of law. It is so proclaimed to the community; the words of the proclamation are not material; it speaks for itself; and if it means any thing, it announces the treaty as a rule of public conduct, as a law exacting the obedience of the people. Were he of the opposite side, if he indeed believed this treaty to be a dead letter till it received the sanction of Congress, he would lay the bill on the table and move an enquiry into the fact, why the treaty has been proclaimed as a law before it had received the proper sanction. It is true, the Executive has transmitted a copy of the treaty to the House; but has he sent the negotiation? Has he given any light to judge why it should receive the sanction of this body? Do gentlemen mean to say that information is not needed; that though we have the right to pass laws to give validity to

1. AC13-3, p. 1934.

treaties, yet we are bound by a moral obligation to pass such laws? To talk of the right of this House to sanction treaties, and at the same time to assert that it is under a moral obligation not to with-hold that sanction, is a solecism. No sound mind that understands the terms, can possibly assent to it. He would caution the House, while it was extending its powers to cases which he believed did not belong to it, to take care lest it should lose its substantial and undoubted power. He would put it on its guard against the dangerous doctrine, that it can in any case become a mere registering body. Another fact, in regard to this treaty. It does not stipulate that a law should pass to repeal the duties proposed to be repealed by this bill, which would be its proper form, if in the opinion of the negotiators a law was necessary; but it stipulates in positive terms for their repeal without consulting or regarding us.

Mr. C. here concluded this part of the discussion, by stating that it appeared to him from the whole complexion of the case, that the bill before the House was mere form and not supposed to be necessary to the validity of the treaty. It would be proper how-ever, he observed, to reply to the arguments which have been urged on the general nature of the treaty-making power, and as it was a subject of great importance, he solicited the attentive hearing of the House. It is not denied, he believed, that the President with the concurrence of two thirds of the Senate have a right to make commercial treaties; it is not asserted that this treaty is couched in such general terms as to require a law to carry the details into exe-cution. Why then is this bill necessary? Because, say gentlemen, that the treaty of itself, without the aid of this bill, cannot exempt British tonnage and goods imported in their bottoms, from the operation of the law, laying additional duties on foreign tonnage and goods imported in foreign vessels; or, giving the question a more general form, because a treaty cannot annul a law. The gen-tleman from Virginia, (Mr. Barbour,) who argued this point very distinctly, though not satisfactorily, took as his general position, that to repeal a law is a legislative act, and can only be done by law; that in the distribution of the legislative and treaty making power the right to repeal a law fell exclusively under the former.[2]

2. For Philip P. Barbour's argument see AC14-1, p. 478-82.

How does this comport with the admission immediately made by him, that the treaty of peace repealed the act declaring war? If he admits the fact in a single case, what becomes of his exclusive legislative right? He indeed felt that his rule failed him, and in explanation assumed a position entirely new; for he admitted that when the treaty did that which was not authorised to be done by law, it did not require the sanction of Congress, and might in its operation repeal a law inconsistent with it. He said, Congress is not authorized to make peace; and for this reason a treaty of peace repeals the act declaring war. In this position, he understood his colleague [3] substantially to concur. He hoped to make it appear that, in taking this ground, they have both yielded the point in discussion. He would establish, he trusted, to the satisfaction of the House, that the treaty-making power, when it was legitimately exercised, always did that which could not be done by law; and that the reasons advanced to prove that the treaty of peace repealed the act making war, so far from being peculiar to that case, apply to all treaties. They do not form an exception but in fact constitute the rule. Why then, he asked, cannot Congress make peace? They have the power to declare war. All acknowledge this power. Peace and war are the opposites. They are the positive and negative terms of the same proposition; and what rule of construction more clear, than that when a power is given to do an act, the power is also given to repeal it? By what right do you repeal taxes, reduce your army, lay up your navy, or repeal any law but by the force of this plain rule of construction? Why cannot Congress then repeal the act declaring war? He acknowledged with the gentleman, they cannot, consistently with reason. The solution of this question explained the whole difficulty. The reason is plain; one power may make war; it requires two to make peace. It is a state of mutual amity succeeding mutual hostility; it is a state that cannot be created but with the consent of both parties. It required a contract or a treaty between the nations at war. Is this peculiar to a treaty of peace? No, it is common to all treaties. It arises out of their nature and not from any accidental circumstance attaching itself to a particular class. It is no more or less than that Congress cannot

3. William Lowndes (p. 494, 525). Randolph devoted his speech (p. 533-8) to a reply to Calhoun denying that a treaty could invalidate a law.

make a contract with a foreign nation. Let us apply it to a treaty of commerce, to this very case. Can Congress do what this treaty has done? It has repealed the discriminating duties between this country and England. Either could by law repeal its own. But by law they could go no farther; and for the same reason that peace cannot be made by law. Whenever then an ordinary subject of legislation can only be regulated by contract, it passes from the sphere of the ordinary power of making laws, and attaches itself to that of making treaties, wherever it is lodged. All acknowledge the truth of this conclusion where the subject on which the treaty operates is not expressly given to Congress. But in other cases they consider the two powers as concurrent; and conclude from the nature of such powers that such treaties must be confirmed by law. Will they acknowledge the opposite, that laws on such subjects must be confirmed by treaties? And if, as they state, a law can repeal a treaty when concurrent, why not a treaty a law? Into such absurdities do false doctrines lead.

The truth is, the legislative and treaty-making power, are never in the strict sense concurrent. They both may have the same subject, as in this case commerce; but they discharge functions as different in relation to it in their nature, as their subject is alike. When we speak of concurrent powers, we mean when both can do the same thing; but he contended, that when the two powers under discussion were confined to their proper sphere, not only the law could not do what could be done by treaty, but the reverse was true; that is, they never are nor can be concurrent powers. It is only when we reason on this subject that we mistake; in all other cases the common sense of the House and country decide correctly. It is proposed to establish some regulation of commerce; we immediately enquire, does it depend on our will; can we make the desired regulation without the concurrence of any foreign power; if so, it belongs to Congress, and any one would feel it to be absurd to attempt to effect it by treaty. On the contrary, does it require the consent of a foreign power; is it proposed to grant a favor for a favor, to repeal discriminating duties on both sides? It is equally felt to belong to the treaty power; and he would be thought insane who would propose to abolish the discriminating duties in any case, by an act of the American Congress. It is calculated, he felt, almost to insult the good sense of the House, to dwell on a point apparently so clear. What then would he infer from what had been advanced? That according to the argument of gentlemen, treaties, producing a state of things inconsistent with the provisions of an existing *law*, annul such provisions. But as he did not agree with them in the view which they took, he would here present his own for consideration. Why then has a treaty the force which he attributed to it? Because it is an act in its own nature paramount to laws made by the common legislative powers of the country. It is in fact a law and something more, a law established by *contract* between independent nations. To analogise it to private life, law has the same relations to treaty, as the resolution taken by an individual to his contract. An individual may make the most deliberate promise—he may swear it in the most solemn form, that he would not sell his house or any other property he may have; yet, if he would afterwards sell, the sale would be valid in law; he would not be admitted in a court of justice to plead his oath against his contract. Take a case of government in its most simple form, where it was purely despotic, that is, all power lodged in the hands of a single individual. Would not his treaties repeal inconsistent edicts?

Let us now ascend from the instances cited, to illustrate the nature of the two powers, to the principle on which the paramount character of a treaty rests. A treaty always affects the interests of two; a law only that of a single nation. It is an established principle of politics and morality, that the interest of the many is paramount to that of the few. In fact, it is a principle so radical, that without it no system of morality, no rational scheme of government, could exist. It is for this reason, that contracts or that treaties, which are only the contracts of independent nations, or to express both in two words, that *plighted faith* has in all ages and nations been considered so solemn. But it is said, in opposition to this position, that a subsequent law can repeal a treaty; and to this proposition, he understood that the member from North Carolina (Mr. Gaston) assented.[4] Strictly speaking, he denied the fact. He knew that a law might assume the appearance of repealing a treaty; but

4. William Gaston, p. 490.

he insisted it was only in appearance, and that, in point of fact, it was not a repeal. Whenever a law was proposed, declaring a treaty void, he considered that the House acted not as a legislative body, but *judicially*. He would illustrate his ideas. If the House is a moral body, that is, if it is governed by reason and virtue, which it must always be presumed to be, the only question that ever could occupy its attention, whenever a treaty is to be declared void, is whether, under all of the circumstances of the case, the treaty is not already destroyed, by being violated by the nation with whom it is made, or by the existence of some other circumstance, if other there can be. The House determines this question, is the country any longer bound by the treaty? Has it not ceased to exist? The nation passes in judgment on its own contract; and this, from the necessity of the case, as it admits no superior power to which it can refer for decision. If any other consideration moves the House to repeal a treaty, it can be considered only in the light of a violation of a contract acknowledged to be binding on the country. A nation may, it is true, violate its contract; they may even do this under the form of law; but he was not considering what might be done, but what might be rightfully done. It is not a question of power, but of right.

Why are not these positions, in themselves so clear, universally assented to? Gentlemen are alarmed at imaginary consequences. They argue not as if seeking for the meaning of the Constitution; but as if deliberating on the subject of making one; not as members of the legislature, and acting under a constitution already established, but as that of a convention about to frame one. For his part, he had always regarded the Constitution as a work of great wisdom, and, being the instrument under which we existed as a body; it was our duty to bow to its enactments, whatever they may be, with submission. We ought scarcely to indulge a wish that its provisions should be different from what they in fact are. The consequences, however, which appear to work with so much terror on the minds of the gentlemen, he considered to be without any just foundation. The treaty-making power has many and powerful limits; and it will be found when he came to discuss what those limits are, that it cannot destroy the Constitution, our personal liberty, involve us without the assent of this House in war, or grant away our money. The limits he proposed to this power, are not the same, it is true; but they appeared to him much more rational and powerful than those which were supposed to present effectual guards to its abuse. Let us now consider what they are? The grant of the power to make treaties, is couched in the most general terms. The words of the Constitution are, that the President shall have power, by and with the advice and consent of the Senate, to make treaties, provided two-thirds of the Senators present concur. In a subsequent part of the Constitution, treaties are declared to be the surpreme law of the land. Whatever limits are imposed on those general terms ought to be the result of the sound construction of the instrument. There appeared to him but two restrictions on its exercise; the one derived from the nature of our government, and the other from that of the power itself. Most certainly all grants of power under the Constitution must be controlled by that instrument; for, having their existence from it, they must of necessity assume that form which the Constitution has imposed. This is acknowledged to be true of the legislative power, and it is doubtless equally so of the power to make treaties. The limits of the former are exactly marked; it was necessary to prevent collision with similar co-existing state powers. This country is divided into many distinct sovereignties. Exact enumeration here is necessary to prevent the most dangerous consequences. The enumeration of legislative powers in the Constitution has relation then not to the treaty power, but to the powers of the state. In our relation to the rest of the world the case is reversed. Here the states disappear. Divided within, we present the exterior of undivided sovereignty. The wisdom of the Constitution, appears conspicuous. When enumeration was needed, there we find the powers enumerated and exactly defined; when not, we do not find what would be vain and pernicious. Whatever then concerns our foreign relations; whatever requires the consent of another nation, belongs to the treaty power; can only be regulated by it; and it is competent to regulate all such subjects; provided, and here are its true limits; such regulations are not inconsistent with the Constitution. If so they are void.

No treaty can alter the fabric of our government, nor can it do that which the Constitution has expressly forbad to be done; nor can it do that differently which is directed to be done in a given mode, and all other modes prohibited. For instance, the Constitution says, no money "shall be drawn out of the Treasury but by an appropriation made by law." Of course no subsidy can be granted without an act of law; and a treaty of alliance could not involve the country in war without the consent of this House. With this limitation it is easy to explain the case put by my colleague, who said, that according to one limitation a treaty might have prohibited the introduction of a certain description of persons before the year 1808, notwithstanding the clause in the Constitution to the contrary. Mr. C. said, that he would speak plainly on this point; it was the intention of the Constitution that the slave trade should be tolerated till the time mentioned. It covered him with confusion to name it here; he felt ashamed of such a tolerance, and took a large part of the disgrace, as he represented a part of the Union, by whose influence it might be supposed to have been introduced.[5] Though Congress alone is prohibited by the words of the clause from inhibiting that odious traffic, yet his colleague would admit that it was intended to be a general prohibition on the *government of the Union.* He perceived his colleague indicated his dissent. It will be necessary to be more explicit. Here Mr. C. read that part of the Constitution, and showed that the word "Congress" might be left out, in conformity to other parts of the Constitution without injury to the sense of the clause; and he insisted the plain meaning of the parties to the Constitution, was, that the trade should continue till 1808, and that a prohibition by treaty would be equally against the spirit of the instrument.

Besides these constitutional limits, the treaty power, like all powers, has others derived from its object and nature. It has for its object, contracts with foreign nations; as the powers of Congress have for their object whatever can be done in relation to the powers delegated to it without the consent of foreign nations. Each in its proper sphere operates with general influence; but when they became erratic, then they were portentous and dangerous. A treaty never can legitimately do that which can be done by law; and the converse is also true. Suppose the discriminating duties repealed

5. Calhoun during this year was buying slaves in the domestic market— see No. 135.

on both sides by law, yet what is effected by this treaty would not even then be done; the plighted faith would be wanting. Either side might repeal its law without breach of contract. It appeared to him that gentlemen are too much influenced on this subject by the example of Great Britain. Instead of looking to the nature of our government they have been swayed in their opinion by the practice of that government to which we are but too much in the habit of looking for precedents. Much anxiety has recently been evinced to be independent of English broadcloths and muslins; he hoped it indicated the approach of a period when we should also throw off the thraldom of thought. The truth is, but little analogy exists between this and any other government. It is the pride of ours to be founded in reason and equity; all others have originated more or less in fraud, violence or accident. The right to make treaties in England, can only be determined by the practice of that government; as she has no written constitution. Her practice may be wise in regard to her government, when it would be very imprudent here. Admitting the fact to be, then, that the King refers all commercial treaties affecting the municipal regulations of the country to Parliament, for its sanction, the ground would be very feeble to prove that to be the intention of our Constitution. Strong difference exists between the forms of the two governments. The King is hereditary; he alone, without the participation of either House of Parliament, negotiates and makes treaties; they have no constitution emanating from the people, alike superior to the legislature and the King. Not so here. The President is elected for a short period, he is amenable to the public opinion, he is liable to be impeached for corruption, he cannot make treaties without the concurrence of two thirds of the Senate, a fact very material to be remembered, which body is in like manner responsible to the people at periods not very remote; above all, as the laws and Constitution are here perfectly distinct, and the latter is alike superior to laws and treaties, the treaty power cannot change the form of government, or encroach on the liberties of the country, without encroaching on that instrument, which so long as the people are free, will be watched with vigilance.

121 NOTE: On Dec. 29 Forsyth, Chairman of the Foreign Relations Committee, introduced a bill making the changes involved

in the treaty of July 3, 1815 with Great Britain, abolishing discriminating tonnage dues on American and British vessels (*AC*14-1, p.
419-20). The question at issue was whether or not a bill were
necessary to put the treaty in effect. Calhoun declared that the act
of Mar. 3, 1815, covered the case. The issue having been raised,
however, of conflict between a treaty and a law of Congress, he
undertook a definitive answer to the question. He contended that
the treaty-making power, limited by the Constitution to objectives
and methods not forbidden directly or indirectly by the Constitution, was distinct from the law-making power and thus independent
of the House. Since neither power could invade the sphere reserved
for the other, the bill should be rejected. Calhoun's argument drew
much attention from other speakers—see p. 533-8, 555, 560, 563,
623, 634.

The bill passed the third reading on the 13th, Calhoun voting
against it (p. 674). Meanwhile a Senate bill which arrived at the
same objective by declaring of no effect all discriminating duties
in conflict with the treaty was received and eventually enacted
instead (p. 884, 897, 1057-8, 1798).   SOURCE: *NI*, Jan. 23, 1816;
*AC*14-1, p. 526-33.

122. SPEECH ON THE ADDITIONAL REVENUE
REPORT

January 20, 1816

Mr. Calhoun was in favor of the motion for the committee to rise;
because, he said, this was a question involving momentous considerations. On the ways and means depended every measure of
the government. On the decision of the questions now before the
committee depended the question whether a liberal and enlightened policy should characterize the measures of the government.
Gentlemen ought therefore to proceed with caution. If gentlemen
were of opinion that our navy ought not to be gradually improved;
that preparation ought not to be made during peace for preventing
or meeting war; that internal improvements should not be prosecuted—if these were their sentiments, they were right in desiring
to abolish all taxes. If they thought otherwise, it was absurd, it
was preposterous to say, that we should not lay taxes on the people. Mr. C. said gentlemen ought not to give into the contracted
idea, that taxes were so much money taken from the people: properly applied, the money proceeding from taxes, was money put out

to the best possible interest for the people. He wished, he said, to see the nation free from external danger and internal difficulty. With such views, he could not see the expediency of abolishing the system of finance established with so much labor and difficulty. It was a subject which ought to be approached seriously and deliberately. The broad question was now before the House, whether this government should act on an enlarged policy; whether it would avail itself of the experience of the last war; whether it would be benefited by the mass of knowledge acquired within the few last years; or whether we should go on in the old imbecile mode, contributing by our measures nothing to the honor, nothing to the reputation of the country. Such would not be his course. He believed this great people, daily acquiring character and strength, would excite the jealousy of foreign powers. He had no hostility to the power to which he had particular reference; but he had a friendship for his own country. He thought it due to the wisdom of its councils, and to its security, that it should be well prepared against possible assaults from abroad. If danger should come, we shall then be ready to meet it. If it never come, we shall derive a sufficient consolation from a knowledge of our security. In this view of the magnitude of this topic, and to give gentlemen on every side an opportunity of speaking on the question which is now opened, which is to decide whether we are to travel downward, or to raise the nation to that elevation to which it ought to aspire, he should vote for the committee's rising.

122 NOTE: On Jan. 9 (AC14-1, p. 516-22) William Lowndes, Chairman of the Ways and Means Committee, presented a report on the revision of the revenue system. Adverting to Europe's armaments and twenty-year habit of war, and the need for rapid payment of the debt, he called for "a considerable revenue," suggesting import duties as the chief but not the sole source. The report proposed a revenue of twenty-five millions, about nine and a half millions of it for national defense, "internal improvement," and payment on the public debt. There were twelve resolutions, the first of which was a recommendation for continuance of the additional duties until June 30 next, and until a new tariff should be enacted; the sixth, for reduction of the direct tax to provide only three million dollars; the tenth, for a 42 per cent increase in the permanent import duties. On the 18th (p. 693) the House adopted the first

resolution, setting the expiration date at June 30, and on Jan. 23 (p. 737) approved the 42 per cent addition, to be effective until a new tariff might be adopted. The act incorporating these provisions was ratified Feb. 5 (p. 1795-6). On the 20th began the long fight on the direct tax; the debate this day, in Committee of the Whole, was chiefly a fruitless wrangle between Clay, the Speaker, and Randolph (p. 720-30); the day's session ended shortly after Calhoun's speech. See No. 123.   SOURCE: *NI*, Jan. 23, 1816; *AC*14-1, p. 728-9.

123. SPEECH ON THE REVENUE BILL

January 31, 1816

Mr. Calhoun commenced his remarks by observing, that there were in the affairs of nations, not less than that of individuals, moments, on the proper use of which depended their fame, prosperity and duration. Such he conceived to be the present situation of this nation. Recently emerged from a war, we find ourselves in posession of a physical and moral power of great magnitude; and, impressed by the misfortunes which have resulted from want of forecast heretofore, we are disposed to apply our means to the purposes most valuable to the country. He hoped, that in this interesting situation, we should be guided by the dictates of truth and wisdom only, that we should prefer the lasting happiness of our country to its present ease, its security to its pleasure, fair honor and reputation, to inglorious and inactive repose.

We are now called on to determine what amount of revenue is necessary for this country in time of peace; this involves the additional question, what are the means which the true interests of this country demand? The principal expence of our government grows out of measures necessary for its defence; and in order to decide what those measures ought to be, it will be proper to enquire what ought to be our policy towards other nations, and what will probably be theirs towards us? He intentionally laid out of consideration the financial questions, which some gentlemen had examined in the debate; and also the question of retrenchments, on which he would only remark, that he hoped, whatsoever of economy entered into the measures of Congress, they would be divested of the character of parsimony.

Beginning with the policy of this country, it ought, he said, to correspond with the character of its political institutions. What then is their character? They rest on justice and reason. Those being the foundations of our government, its policy ought to comport with them. It is the duty of all nations, especially of one whose institutions recognize no principle of force, but appeal to virtue for their strength, to act with justice and moderation; with moderation approaching to forbearance. In all possible conflicts with foreign powers, our government should be able to make it manifest to the world, that it has justice on its side. We should always forbear, if possible, until all should be satisfied, that when we take up arms, it is not for the purpose of conquest, but maintaining our essential rights. Our government, however, is also founded on equality; it permits no man to exercise violence; it permits none to trample on the rights of his fellow citizen with impunity. These maxims we should also carry into our intercourse with foreign nations, and as we render justice to all, so we should be prepared to exact it from all. Our policy should not only be moderate and just, but as high minded as it is moderate and just. This, said Mr. C. appears to me the true line of conduct. In the policy of nations, said he, there are two extremes: one extreme in which justice and moderation may sink into feebleness—another in which that lofty spirit, which ought to animate all nations, particularly free ones, may mount up to military violence. These extremes ought to be equally avoided: but of the two, he considered the first far the most dangerous, far the most fatal. There were, he said, two splendid examples of nations which had ultimately sunk by military violence— the Romans in ancient time, the French in modern.

But how numerous were the instances of nations gradually sinking into nothingness through imbecility and apathy. They have not indeed struck the mind as forcibly as the instance just mentioned; because they have sunk ingloriously, without any thing in their descent to excite either admiration or respect. I consider the extreme of weakness not only the most dangerous of itself, said Mr. C. but as that extreme to which the people of this country are peculiarly liable. The people are, indeed, high minded; and, therefore, it may be thought my fears are unfounded. But they are blessed with much happiness; moral, political and physical: these operate

317

on the dispositions and habits of this people, with something like
the effects attributed to southern climates—they dispose them to
pleasure and to inactivity, except in pursuit of wealth. I need not
appeal to the past history of the country; to the indisposition of
this people to war from the commencement of the government—
arising from the nature of our habits, and the disposition to pursue
those courses which contribute to swell our private fortunes. We
incline, not only from the causes already mentioned, but from the
nature of our foreign relations, to that feeble policy, which I consider as more dangerous than the other extreme. We have, it is
true, dangers to apprehend from abroad—but they are far off, at
the distance of three thousand miles: which prevents that continued
dread which they would excite if in our neighborhood. Besides,
we can have no foreign war which we should dread, or ought to
fear to meet, but a war with England; but a war with her breaks
in on the whole industry of the country, and affects all its private
pursuits. On this account we prefer suffering very great wrongs
from her, rather than to redress them by arms. The gentleman from
Pennsylvania asked if the country did forbear till it felt disgrace,
whose fault was it?[1] Not, he said, that of the administrations of
Washington and Adams; for neither of them had left it so. A few
words, said Mr. C. on this point. The fault was principally in
neither of our several administrations, in neither of the two great
parties. It arose from the indisposition of the people to resort to
arms, from the reason already assigned. It arose also from two incidental circumstances—the want of preparation, and the untried
character of our government in war. But there were other circumstances connected with the party to which the gentleman belongs,
which caused the country to forbear too long. That party took
advantage of the indisposition of the people to an English war, and
preached up the advantages of peace when it had become ignominious; and until we had scarcely the ability to defend ourselves.

The gentleman from Pennsylvania further said, if peace had not
been made when it was, we should not have been here deliberating
at this time.[2] This assertion is an awful one, if true. If the nation
was on the verge of ruin, the defects which brought it to that situ-

1. Joseph Hopkinson; see *AC*14-1, p. 799.
2. P. 795.

ation ought to be known, probed and corrected, even if they rose out of the Constitution. But, Mr. C. said, it is an assertion that ought not to be lightly made. The effects are dangerous; for what man hereafter, with such consequences before his eyes, would venture to propose a war? If such were the admitted fact, a future enemy would persist in war, expecting the country to sink before his efforts: his arms would be steeled, his exertions nerved against us. The position was in every view, one of that dangerous bearing on the future relations of the country, that it ought not to be admitted without the strongest proof. What, said Mr. C. was the fact? What had been the progress of events for a few months preceding the termination of the war? At Baltimore, at Plattsburg, at New Orleans, the invaders had been signally defeated; a new spirit was diffused through the whole mass of the community. Can it be believed then, that the government was on the verge of dissolution? No, sir; it never stood firmer on its basis than at that moment. It was true, indeed, we labored under great difficulties; but it is an observation made by a statesman of great sagacity, Edmund Burke, when Pitt was anticipating the downfall of France through her finances, that an instance is not to be found of a high-minded nation sinking under financial difficulties—and it would have been exemplified in our country had the war continued. Men on all sides began to unite in defence of the country; parties in this House began to rally on this point, and if the gentleman from Pennsylvania had been a member at that time, he also, from what he has said, would have taken that ground. The gentleman had taken a position on this point as erroneous as it was dangerous; and, Mr. C. said, he had thought proper thus to notice it.

As a proof, said Mr. C. that the situation of the country naturally inclines us to too much feebleness rather than too much violence, I refer to the fact, that there are on this floor, men who are entirely opposed to armies, to navies, to every means of defence. Sir, if their politics prevail, the country will be disarmed, at the mercy of any foreign power. On the other side, sir, there is no excess of military fervor, no party inclining to military despotism: for, though a charge of such a disposition has been made by a gentleman in debate, it is without the shadow of foundation.[3] What is the fact

3. Randolph (see p. 685, 721-3) or Benjamin Hardin of Kentucky (p. 749)?

in regard to the army? Does it bear out his assertion? Is it even proportionally larger now than it was in 1801–2, the period which the gentleman considers as the standard of political perfection? It was then about 4000 men; it was larger in proportion than an army of 10,000 men would now be. The charge of a disposition to make this a military government, exists only in the imaginations of gentlemen; it cannot be supported by facts: it is contrary to proof and to evidence.

Having dismissed this part of the subject, Mr. C. proceeded to consider another part of it, in his opinion equally important, viz.: What will be the probable policy of other nations? With the world at large, said he, we are now at peace. I know of no nation with which we shall probably come into collision, unless it be with Great Britain and Spain. With both of these nations we have considerable points of collision: I hope this country will maintain, in regard to both of them, the strictest justice: but with both these nations there is a possibility, sooner or later, of our being engaged in war. As to Spain, I will say nothing, because she is the inferior of the two, and those measures which apply to the superior power, will include also the inferior. I shall consider our relations then with England only.

Peace now exists between the two countries. As to its duration, I will give no opinion, except that I believe the peace will last the longer for the war which has just ended. Evidences have been furnished during the war of the capacity and character of this nation, which will make her indisposed to try her strength with us on slight grounds. But, what is the probable course of events respecting the future relations between the two countries? England is the most formidable power in the world. She has the most numerous army and navy at her command. We, on the contrary, are the most growing nation on earth; most rapidly improving in those very particulars in which she excels. This question then presents itself: will the greater power permit the less to attain its destined greatness by natural growth, or will she take measures to disturb it? Those who know the history of nations, will not believe that a rival will look unmoved on this prosperity. It has been said, that nations have heads, but no hearts. Every statesman, every one who loves his country, who wishes to maintain the dignity of that country, to see it attain the summit of greatness and prosperity, regards the progress of other nations with a jealous eye. The English statesmen have always so acted. I find no fault with them on that account, but rather to point it out as a principle which ought also to govern our conduct in regard to them. Will Great Britain permit us to go on in an uninterrupted march to the height of national greatness and prosperity? I fear not. But, admitting the councils on that side of the water to be governed by a degree of magnanimity and justice, the world has never experienced from them, and I am warranted in saying never will, may not some unforeseen collision involve you in hostilities with Great Britain? Gentlemen on the other side have said, that there are points of difference with that nation, (existing prior to the war) which are yet unsettled. I grant it. If such, then, be the fact, does it not shew that points of collision remain—that whenever the same condition of the world that existed before the war shall recur, the same collisions will probably take place? If Great Britain sees the opportunity of enforcing the same doctrines we have already contested, will she not seize it?

Admitting this country to maintain that policy which it ought; that its councils be governed by the most perfect justice and moderation, we yet see, said Mr. Calhoun, that by a difference of views on essential points, the peace between the two nations is liable to be jeopardized. I am sure, that future wars with England are not only possible, but, I will say more, that they are highly probable—nay, that they will certainly take place. Future wars, I fear, with the honorable Speaker,[4] future wars, long and bloody, will exist between this country and Great Britain: I lament it—but I will not close my eyes on future events; I will not betray the high trust reposed in me; I will speak what I believe to be true. You will have to encounter British jealousy and hostility in every shape, not immediately manifested by open force or violence, perhaps, but by indirect attempts to check your growth and prosperity. As far as they can, they will disgrace every thing connected with you; her reviewers, paragraphists and travellers will assail you and your institutions, and no means will be left untried to bring you to contemn yourselves, and be contemned by others. I thank my

4. See p. 787.

God, they have not now the means of effecting it which they once had. No; the late war has given you a mode of feeling and thinking which forbids the acknowledgment of national inferiority, that first of political evils. Had we not encountered Great Britain, we should not have had the brilliant points to rest on which we now have. We, too, have now *our* heroes and illustrious actions. If Britain has her Wellington, we have our Jacksons, Browns and Scotts. If she has her naval heroes, we have them not less renowned, for they have snatched the laurel from her brows. It is impossible that we can now be degraded by comparisons; I trust we are equally above corruption and intrigue; it only remains then to try the contest by force of arms.

Let us now, said Mr. C. consider the measures of preparation which sound policy dictates. First, then, as to extent, without reference to the kind: They ought to be graduated by a reference to the character and capacity of both countries. England excels in means all countries that now exist, or ever did exist; and has besides great moral resources—intelligent and renowned for masculine virtues. On our part our measures ought to correspond with that lofty policy which becomes freemen determined to defend our rights. Thus circumstanced on both sides, we ought to omit no preparation fairly in our means. Next, as to the species of preparation, which opens subjects of great extent and importance. The navy most certainly, in any point of view, occupies the first place. It is the most safe, most effectual, and the cheapest mode of defence. For, let the fact be remembered, our navy costs less per man, including all the amount of extraordinary expenditures on the Lakes, than our army. This is an important fact, which ought to be fixed in the memory of the House; for, if that force be the most efficient and safe, which is at the same time the cheapest, on that should be our principal reliance. We have heard much of the danger of standing armies to our liberties—the objection cannot be made to the navy. Generals, it must be acknowledged, have often advanced at the head of armies to imperial rank and power; but in what instance had an admiral usurped on the liberties of his country? Put our strength in the navy for foreign defence, and we shall certainly escape the whole catalogue of possible ills, painted by gentlemen on the other side. A naval power attacks that country, from whose hostility alone we have any thing to dread, where she is most assailable, and defends this country where it is weakest. Where is Great Britain most vulnerable? In what point is she most accessible to attack? In her commerce—in her navigation. There she is not only exposed, but the blow is fatal. There is her strength; there is the secret of her power. Here, then, if ever it become necessary, you ought to strike.

But where are *you* most exposed? On the Atlantic line; a line so long and so weak, that you are peculiarly liable to be assailed in it. How is it to be defended? By a navy, and by a navy alone can it be efficiently defended. Let us look back to the time when the enemy was in possession of the whole line of the sea coast, moored in your rivers, and ready to assault you at every point. The facts are too recent to require to be painted—I will only generally state that your commerce was cut up; your specie circulation destroyed; your internal communications interrupted, your best and cheapest high way being entirely in possession of the enemy; your ports foreign, the one to the other; your treasury exhausted, in merely defensive preparations and militia requisitions, not knowing where you would be assailed, you had at the same moment, to stand prepared at every point. A recurrence of this state of things, so oppressive to the country, in the event of another war, could be prevented only by the establishment and maintenance of a sufficient naval force. Mr. C. said he had thought proper to press this point thus strongly, because, though it was generally assented to that the navy ought to be increased, he found that assent too cold, and the approbation bestowed on it too negative in its character. It ought, it is said, to be gradually increased. If the navy is to be increased at all, let its augmentation be limited only by your ability to build, officer and man. If it is the kind of force most safe, and at the same time most efficient to guard against foreign invasion, or repel foreign aggression, you ought to put your whole force on the sea side. It is estimated that we have in our country eighty thousand sailors. This would enable us to man a considerable fleet, which, if well directed, would give us the habitual command on our own coast, an object, in every point of view, so desirable. Not that we ought, hastily, without due preparation, under present circumstances, build a large number of vessels; but we ought to commence preparation, establish docks, collect timber and naval stores, and, as soon as the materials are prepared, we ought to commence building, to the extent which I have mentioned. If any thing can preserve the country in its most imminent dangers from abroad, it is this species of armament. If we desire to be free from future wars, as I hope we may, this is the only way to effect it. We shall have peace then, and what is of still higher moment, with perfect security.

In regard to our present military establishment, Mr. C. said, it was small enough. That point the honorable Speaker had fully demonstrated: it was not sufficiently large at present to occupy all our fortresses.[5] Gentlemen had spoken in favor of the militia, and against the army. In regard to the militia, said Mr. C. I would go as far as any gentleman, and considerably further than those would who are so violently opposed to our small army. I would not only arm the militia, but I would extend their term of service, and make them efficient. To talk about the efficiency of militia called into service for six months only, is to impose on the people; it is to ruin them with false hopes. I know the danger of large standing armies, said Mr. C. I know the militia are the true force; that no nation can be safe at home and abroad, which has not an efficient militia; but the time of service ought to be enlarged, to enable them to acquire a knowledge of the duties of the camp, to let the habits of civil life be broken. For though militia, freshly drawn from their homes, may in a moment of enthusiasm, do great service, as at New Orleans, in general they are not calculated for service in the field, until time is allowed for them to acquire habits of discipline and subordination. Your defence ought to depend on the land, on a regular draft from the body of the people. It is thus in time of war the business of recruiting will be dispensed with; a mode of defending the country every way uncongenial with our republican institutions; uncertain, slow in its operation and expensive, it draws from society its worse materials, introducing into our army, of necessity, all the severities, which are exercised in that of the most despotic government. Thus compounded, our army in a great degree, lose that enthusiasm which citizen-soldiers,

5. P. 788.

conscious of liberty, and fighting in defence of their country, have ever been animated.

All free nations of antiquity entrusted the defence of the country, not to the dregs of society, but to the body of citizens; hence that heroism which modern times may admire but cannot equal. I know that I utter truths unpleasant to those who wish to enjoy liberty without making the efforts necessary to secure it. Her favor is never won by the cowardly, the vicious or indolent. It has been said by some physicians that life is a forced state; the same may be said of freedom. It requires efforts; it presupposes mental and moral qualities of a high order to be generally diffused in the society where it exists. It mainly stands on the faithful discharge of two great duties which every citizen of proper age owes the republic; a wise and virtuous exercise of the right of suffrage; and a prompt and brave defence of the country in the hour of danger. The first symptom of decay has ever appeared in the backward and negligent discharge of the latter duty. Those who are acquainted with the historians and orators of antiquity know the truth of this assertion. The least decay of patriotism, the least verging towards pleasure, and luxury will there immediately discover itself. Large standing and mercenary armies then become necessary; and those who are not willing to render the military service essential to the defence of their rights, soon find, as they ought to do, a master. It is the order of nature and cannot be reversed. This would at once put an adequate force in your hands, and render you secure. I cannot agree with those who think that we are free from danger, and need not to prepare for it, because we have no nation in our immediate neighborhood to dread. Recollect that the nation with whom we have recently terminated a severe conflict, lives on the bosom of the deep; that although three thousand miles of ocean intervene between us, she can attack you with as much facility as if she had but 200 or 250 miles over land to march. She is as near you as if she occupied Canada instead of the islands of Great Britain. You have the power of assailing as well as being assailed; her provinces border on our territory, the dread of losing which if you are prepared to attack them will contribute to that peace which every honest man is anxious to maintain as long as possible with that country.

Mr. C. then proceeded to a point of less but yet of great importance—he meant, the establishment of roads and opening canals in various parts of the country. Your country, said he, has certain points of feebleness and certain points of strength about it. Your feebleness should be removed, your strength improved. Your population is widely dispersed. Though this is greatly advantageous in one respect, that of preventing the country from being permanently conquered, it imposes a great difficulty in defending your territory from invasion, because of the difficulty of transportation from one point to another of your widely extended frontier. We ought to contribute as much as possible to the formation of good military roads, not only on the score of general political economy, but to enable us on emergencies to collect the whole mass of our military means on the point menaced. The people are brave, great and spirited: but they must be brought together in sufficient number, and with a certain promptitude to enable them to act with effect. The importance of military roads was well known to the Romans: the remains of their roads exist to this day, some of them uninjured by the ravages of time. Let us make great permanent roads, not like the Romans, with views of subjecting and ruling provinces, but for the more honorable purposes of defence; and connecting more closely the interests of various sections of this great country. Let any one look at the vast cost of transportation during the war, much of which is chargeable to the want of good roads and canals, and he will not deny the vast importance of a due attention to this object.

Mr. C. proceeded to another topic—the encouragement proper to be afforded to the industry of the country. In regard to the question, how far manufactures ought to be fostered, Mr. C. said it was the duty of this country, as a means of defence, to encourage the domestic industry of the country, more especially that part of it which provides the necessary materials for clothing and defence. Let us look at the nature of the war most likely to occur. England is in the possession of the ocean; no man, however sanguine, can believe that we can deprive her soon of her predominance there. That control deprives us of the means of maintaining our army and navy cheaply clad. The question relating to manufactures must not depend on the abstract principle, that industry left to pursue its own course, will find in its own interest all the encouragement that is necessary. I lay the claims of the manufacturers entirely out of view, said Mr. C.—but on general principles, without regard to their interest, a certain encouragement should be extended at least to our woollen and cotton manufactures.

There was another point of preparation which, Mr. C. said, ought not to be overlooked—the defence of our coast, by means other than the navy, on which we ought to rely mainly but not entirely. The coast is our weak part, which ought to be rendered strong, if it be in our power to make it so. There are two points on our coast particularly weak, the mouths of the Mississippi and the Chesapeake Bay, which ought to be cautiously attended to, not however neglecting others. The administration which leaves these two points in another war without fortification, ought to receive the execration of the country. Look at the facility afforded by the Chesapeake Bay to maritime powers in attacking us. If we estimate with it the margin of rivers navigable for vessels of war, it adds 1400 miles at least to the line of our sea coast; and that of the worst character, for when an enemy is there, it is without the fear of being driven from it: he has besides the power of assaulting two shores at the same time, and must be expected on both. Under such circumstances no degree of expense would be too great for its defence. The whole margin of the bay is besides an extremely sickly one, and fatal to the militia of the upper country. How it is to be defended, military and naval men will best judge, but I believe that steam frigates ought at least to constitute a part of the means; the expense of which however great, the people ought and would cheerfully bear.

There were other points to which, Mr. C. said, he might call the attention of the committee, but for the fear of fatiguing them. He would mention only his views in regard to our finance, as connected with preparatory measures. A war with Great Britain, said he, will immediately distress your finances, as far as your revenue depends on imports. It is impossible during war to prepare a system of internal revenue in time to meet the defect thus occasioned. Will Congress then leave the nation wholly dependent on foreign commerce for its revenue? This nation, Mr. C. said, was rapidly changing the character of its industry. When a nation is agricultural, depending for supply on foreign markets its people may be taxed through its impost almost to the amount of its capacity. The nation was however rapidly becoming to a considerable extent a manufacturing nation. We find that exterior commerce (not including the coasting trade) was every day bearing less and less proportion to the entire wealth and strength of the nation. The financial resources of the nation will therefore daily become weaker and weaker, instead of growing with the nation's growth, if we do not resort to other objects than our foreign commerce for taxation. But, gentlemen say, the moral power of the nation ought not to be neglected, and that moral power is inconsistent with *oppressive taxes* on the people. It certainly is with oppressive taxes, but to make them so they must be both heavy and unnecessary. I agree, therefore, with gentlemen in their premises; but not in their conclusion, that because an oppressive tax destroys the whole moral power of the country, there ought therefore to be *no* tax at all. Such a conclusion is certainly erroneous. Let us, said Mr. C. examine the question, whether a tax laid for the defence, security and lasting prosperity of a country, is calculated to destroy the moral power of this country. If such be the fact, as indispensable as I believe these taxes to be, I will relinquish them; for of all the powers of the government the power of a moral kind is most to be cherished. We had better give up all our physical power, than part with that. But what is moral power? The zeal of the country, and the confidence in the administration of its government. Will it be diminished by laying taxes wisely, necessarily and moderately? If you suppose the people intelligent and virtuous, it cannot be admitted. But if a majority of them are ignorant and vicious, then it is probable a tax laid for the most judicious purpose may deprive you of their confidence. The people, I believe, are intelligent and virtuous. The wiser then you act; the less you yield to the temptation of ignoble and false security, the more you attract their confidence. The very existence of your government proves their intelligence: for, let me say to this House, that if one who knew nothing of this people were made acquainted with its government and with the fact that it had sustained itself for thirty years, he would know at once that this was a most intelligent and virtuous people. Convince the people that measures are necessary and wise, and they will maintain them. Already they go far, very far before this House in energy and public spirit. If ever measures of this description become unpopular, it will be by speeches here. Are any willing to lull the people into false security? Can they withdraw their eyes from facts menacing the prosperity, if not the existence of the nation? Are they willing to inspire them with sentiments injurious to their lasting peace and prosperity?

The subject is grave; it is connected with the happiness and existence of the country. I do most sincerely hope that this House are the *real agents of the people:* they are brought here not to consult their ease and convenience, but their general defence and common welfare. Such is the language of the Constitution.

I have faithfully, in discharge of the sacred trust reposed in me by those for whom I act, pointed out those measures which our situation and relation to the rest of the world, render necessary for our security and lasting prosperity. They involve no doubt much expence; they require considerable sacrifices on the part of the people; but are they on that account to be rejected? We are called on to choose; on the one side is great ease it is true, but on the other the security of the country. We may dispense with the taxes; we may neglect every measure of precaution, and feel no *immediate* disaster; but in such a state of things what virtuous, what wise citizen, but what must look on the future with dread! I know of no situation so responsible, if properly considered, as ours. We are charged by Providence not only with the happiness of this great and rising people, but in a considerable degree with that of the human race. We have a government of a new order, perfectly distinct from all which has ever preceded it. A government founded on the rights of man, resting not on authority, not on prejudice, not on superstition, but reason. If it succeed, as fondly hoped by its founders, it will be the commencement of a new era in human affairs. All civilized governments must in the course of time conform to its principles. Thus circumstanced can you hesitate what course to choose? The road that wisdom points, leads it is true up the steep, but leads also to security and lasting glory. No nation, that wants the fortitude to tread it, ought ever to aspire to greatness. Such ought and will certainly sink into the list of those that have done nothing to be known or remembered.

It is immutable; it is in the nature of things. The love of present ease and pleasure, indifference about the future, that fatal weakness of human nature, has never failed in individuals or nations to sink to disgrace and ruin. On the contrary, virtue and wisdom, which regard the future, which spurn the temptations of the moment, however rugged their path, end in happiness. Such are the universal sentiments of all wise writers, from the didactics of the philosophers to the fictions of the poets. They agree that pleasure is a flowery path, leading off among groves and meadows, but ending in a gloomy and dreary wilderness; that it is the syren's voice, which he who listens to is ruined; that it is the cup of Circe, which he who drinks, is converted into a swine. This is the language of fiction, reason teaches the same. It is my wish to elevate the national sentiment to that which every just and virtuous mind possesses. No effort is needed here to impel us the opposite way; that also may be but too safely trusted to the frailties of our nature. This nation is in a situation similar to that which one of the most beautiful writers of antiquity paints Hercules in his youth: He represents the hero as retiring into the wilderness to deliberate on the course of life which he ought to choose. Two goddesses approached him; one recommending to him a life of ease and pleasure; the other of labor and virtue. The hero adopted the counsel of the latter, and his fame and glory are known to the world. May this nation, the youthful Hercules, possessing his form and muscles, be enspired with similar sentiments and follow his example.

123 NOTE: The opposition to William Lowndes' revenue report (No. 122 NOTE) concentrated on his proposal for continuation of three millions of the direct tax. The furious attacks by the opposition alarmed Calhoun for the future of the whole program— the program that was intended, to use his words from his short speech of the 20th (No. 122), to make "the nation free from external danger and internal difficulty." The eloquent appeal to American patriotism in this speech of Jan. 31, 1816, is to be compared to his war report of June, 1812, and his speech of February, 1814, on the loan bill. Unlike Clay (see his speech, *AC*14-1, p. 776-92), Calhoun made no reference to the possible military problems involved in the South American wars, but sketched an even broader program of national defense—by army, navy and coast-defense, by internal

improvements, and by encouragement of manufactures. Compare his statement in his tariff speech (No. 129).

The debate was still in the Committee of the Whole. On Feb. 6 (*AC*14-1, p. 917) the House agreed to the tax for one year, and the bill became law on Mar. 5 (p. 1798-1800).

John Randolph's tribute (p. 840), generous and effective, though in vigorous dissent, was only the most conspicuous evidence of the favor in Congress in which Calhoun found himself at the close of the war—see, for instance, p. 442, 555, 760, 846-7, 909, and compare the reactions to his speeches on the compensation law (Nos. 146 and 148). Randolph's speech was much more than was usual in Congress a direct reply to a speaker (p. 840-6); it was likewise a significant commentary on Calhoun's political philosophy: "I must say, in the abstract, I was pleased with the gentleman's speech, said Mr. R.— but, I have long believed there was a tendency in the administration of this Government, in the system itself indeed, to consolidation, and the remarks made by the honorable gentleman from South Carolina have not tended to allay any fears I have entertained from that quarter. Make this a simple integral Government, said Mr. R., and I subscribe to the doctrines of the honorable gentleman; because they are drawn from the same fountain from which I have drawn my own principles. Mr. R. said he was glad to see that the gentleman had not raked in the kennels (he would say) of democracy, for the principles of which he had formed his political creed." (P. 840-1.) "When speaking of the value of our form of Government, the gentleman might have added to his remarks, Mr. R. said, that whilst in its federative character it was good, as a consolidated Government it would be hateful; that there were features in the Constitution of the United States, beautiful in themselves when looked at with reference to the federative character of the Constitution, which were deformed and monstrous when looked at with reference to consolidation. The gentleman was too deeply read in Aristotle, too well versed in political lore, to deny the fact." (P. 841.)   Source: *NI*, Apr. 11, 1816; *AC*14-1, p. 829-40.

124. Speech Introducing the Bank Bill

February 26, 1816

Mr. Calhoun rose to explain his views of a subject so interesting to the Republic, and so necessary to be correctly understood, as that of the bill now before the committee. He proposed at this time only to discuss general principles, without reference to details. He was aware, he said, that principle and detail might be united; but he should at present keep them distinct. He did not propose to comprehend in this discussion, the power of Congress to grant bank charters; nor the question whether the general tendency of banks was favorable or unfavorable to the liberty and prosperity of the country; nor the question whether a National Bank would be favorable to the operations of the government. To discuss these questions, he conceived, would be an useless consumption of time. The constitutional question had been already so freely and frequently discussed, that all had made up their minds on it. The question whether banks were favorable to public liberty and prosperity, was one purely speculative. The fact of the existence of banks, and their incorporation with the commercial concerns and industry of the nation, proved that enquiry to come too late. The only question was, on this hand, under what modifications were banks most useful, and whether the United States ought or ought not to exercise the power to establish a bank. As to the question whether a National Bank would be favorable to the administration of the finances of the government, it was one on which there was so little doubt, that gentlemen would excuse him if he did not enter into it. Leaving all these questions then, Mr. C. said, he proposed to examine the cause and state of the disorders of the national currency, and the question whether it was in the power of Congress, by establishing a National Bank, to remove those disorders. This, he observed, was a question of novelty and vital importance; a question which greatly affected the character and prosperity of the country.

As to the state of the currency of the nation, Mr. C. proceeded to remark—that it was extremely depreciated, and in degrees varying according to the different sections of the country, all would assent. That this state of the currency was a stain on public and private credit, and injurious to the morals of the community, was so clear a position as to require no proof. There were, however, other considerations arising from the state of the currency not so distinctly felt, not so generally assented to. The state of our circulating medium was, he said, opposed to the principles of the Federal Constitution. The power was given to Congress by that instrument in express terms to regulate the currency of the United

States.[1] In point of fact, he said, that power, though given to Congress, is not in their hands. The power is exercised by banking institutions, no longer responsible for the correctness with which they manage it. Gold and silver have disappeared entirely; there is no money but paper money, and that money is beyond the control of Congress. No one, he said, who referred to the Constitution, could doubt that the money of the United States was intended to be placed entirely under the control of Congress. The only object the framers of the Constitution could have in view in giving to Congress the power "to coin money, regulate the value thereof and of foreign coin," must have been to give a steadiness and fixed value to the currency of the United States. The state of things at the time of the adoption of the Constitution, afforded Mr. C. an argument in support of his construction. There then existed, he said, a depreciated paper currency, which could only be regulated and made uniform by giving a power for that purpose to the general government. The states could not do it. He argued, therefore, taking into view the prohibition against the states issuing bills of credit, that there was a strong presumption this power was intended to be exclusively given to Congress.

Mr. C. acknowledged there was no provision in the Constitution by which states were prohibited from creating the banks which now exercised this power; but, he said, banks were then but little known—there was but one, the Bank of North America with a capital of only 400,000 dollars; and the universal opinion was, that bank notes represented gold and silver, and that there could be no necessity to prohibit banking institutions under this impression, because their notes always represented gold and silver, and they could not be multiplied beyond the demands of the country. Mr. C. drew the distinction between banks of deposit and banks of discount, the latter of which were then but little understood, and their abuse not conceived until demonstrated by recent experience. No man, he remarked, in the Convention, much talent and wisdom as it contained, could possibly have foreseen the course of these insti-

1. Note that while Calhoun was thus reported to have claimed, incorrectly, for Congress the power to regulate the currency under "express terms" of the Constitution, he followed this statement almost immediately by an accurate quotation from the section.

tutions; that they would have multiplied from one to two hundred and sixty; from a capital of 400,000 dollars to one of eighty millions; from being consistent with the provisions of the Constitution, and the exclusive right of Congress to regulate the currency, that they would be directly opposed to it; that so far from their credit depending on their punctuality in redeeming their bills with specie, they might go on ad infinitum in violation of their contract, without a dollar in their vaults. There had, indeed, Mr. C. said been an extraordinary revolution in the currency of the country. By a sort of under-current, the power of Congress to regulate the money of the country had caved in, and upon its ruin had sprung up those institutions which now exercised the right of making money for and in the United States—for gold and silver are not the only money, but whatever is the medium of purchase and sale, in which bank paper alone was now employed, and had, therefore, become the money of the country. A change, great and wonderful, has taken place, said he, which divests you of your rights, and turns you back to the condition of the Revolutionary War, in which every state issued bills of credit, which were made a legal tender, and were of various value.

This then, Mr. C. said, was the evil. We have in lieu of gold and silver a paper medium, unequally but generally depreciated, which affects the trade and industry of the nation; which paralyzes the national arm; which sullies the faith, both public and private, of the United States; a paper no longer resting on gold and silver as its basis. We have indeed laws regulating the currency of foreign coin; but they are under present circumstances a mockery of legislation, because there is no coin in circulation. The right of making money, an attribute of sovereign power, a sacred and important right, was exercised by two hundred and sixty banks, scattered over every part of the United States, not responsible to any power whatever for their issues of paper. The next and great enquiry was, he said, how this evil was to be remedied? Restore, said he, these institutions to their original use; cause them to give up their usurped power; cause them to return to their legitimate office of places of discount and deposit; let them be no longer mere paper machines; restore the state of things which existed anterior to 1813, which was consistent with the just policy and interests of the country;

cause them to fulfil their contracts, to respect their broken faith; resolve that every where there shall be an uniform value to the national currency; your constitutional control will then prevail.

How then, he proceeded to examine, was this desirable end to be attained? What difficulties stood in the way? The reason why the banks could not now comply with their contract was that conduct which in private life frequently produces the same effect. It was owing to the prodigality of their engagements without means to fulfil them; to their issuing more paper than they could possibly redeem with specie. In the United States, according to the best estimation, there were not in the vaults of all the banks more than fifteen millions of specie, with a capital amounting to about eighty two millions of dollars: hence the cause of the depreciation of bank notes—the excess of paper in circulation beyond that of specie in their vaults. This excess was visible to the eye, and almost audible to the ear; so familiar was the fact, that this paper was emphatically called *trash,* or *rags.* According to estimation, also, he said, there were in circulation at the same date, within the United States, two hundred millions of dollars of bank notes, credits, and bank paper, in one shape or other. Supposing thirty millions of these to be in possession of the banks themselves, there were perhaps one hundred and seventy millions actually in circulation, or on which the banks draw interest. The proportion between the demand and supply which regulates the price of every thing, regulates also the value of this paper. In proportion as the issue is excessive, it depreciates in value—and no wonder, when, since 1810 or 1811, the amount of paper in circulation had increased from 80 or 90 to 200 millions. Mr. C. here examined the opinion entertained by some gentlemen, that bank paper had not depreciated, but that gold and silver had appreciated, a position he denied by arguments founded on the portability of gold and silver which would equalize their value in every part of the United States, and on the facts, that gold and silver coin had increased in quantity instead of diminishing, and that the exchange with Great Britain had been (at gold and silver value) for some time past in favor of the United States. Yet, he said, gold and silver were leaving our shores. In fact, we have degraded the metallic currency; we have treated it with indignity, it leaves us, and seeks an asylum on foreign shores. Let it become again the basis of bank transactions, and it will re-visit us.

Having established, as he conceived, in the course of his remarks, that the excess of paper issues was the true and only cause of depreciation of our paper currency, Mr. C. turned his attention to the manner in which that excess had been produced. It was intimately connected with the suspension of specie payments; they stood as cause and effect: first, the excessive issues caused the suspension of specie payments; and advantage had been taken of that suspension to issue still greater floods of it. The banks had undertaken to do a new business, uncongenial with the nature of such institutions: they undertook to make long loans to government, not as brokers, but as stockholders—a practice wholly inconsistent with the system of specie payments. After shewing the difference between the ordinary business of a bank in discounts, and the making loans for twelve years, Mr. C. said, indisputably the latter practice was a great and leading cause of the suspension of specie payments. Of this species of property (public stock) the banks in the United States held on the 30th day of September last, about eighteen and a half millions, and a nearly equal amount of Treasury notes, besides stock for long loans made to the state governments, amounting altogether, to within a small amount of forty millions, being a large proportion of their actual capital. This, he said, was the great cause of the suspension of specie payments.

Had the banks (he now discussed the question) the capacity to resume specie payment? If they have *the disposition,* he said, they may resume specie payments. The banks are not insolvent, he said: they never were more solvent. If so, the term itself implies, that, if time be allowed them, they may before long be in a condition to resume payment of specie. If the banks would regularly and consentaneously begin to dispose of their stock, to call in their notes for the Treasury notes they have, and moderately curtail their private discounts; if they would act in concert in this manner, they might resume specie payments. If they were to withdraw by the sale of a part only of their stock and Treasury notes, twenty-five millions of their notes from circulation, the rest would be appreciated to par, or nearly, and they would still have 15 millions of stock disposable to send to Europe for specie, &c. With thirty millions of dollars in their banks, and so much of their paper withdrawn from circulation, they would be in a condition to resume payments in specie. The only difficulty, that of producing concert, was one which it belonged to Congress to surmount. The indisposition of the banks, from motives of interest, obviously growing out of the vast profits most of them have lately realized, by which the stockholders have realized from 12 to 20 per cent. on their stock, would be, he shewed, the greatest obstacle. What, he asked, was a bank? An institution, under present uses, to make money. What was the instinct of such an institution? Gain, gain; nothing but gain; and they would not willingly relinquish their gain from the present state of things, which was profitable to them, acting as they did without restraint, and without hazard. Those who believed that the present state of things would ever cure itself, Mr. C. said, must believe what is impossible; banks must change their nature, lay aside their instinct, before they will aid in doing what it is not their interest to do. By this process of reasoning, he came to the conclusion, that it rested with Congress to make them return to specie payments, by making it their interest to do so. This introduced the subject of the National Bank.

A national bank, he said, paying specie itself, would have a tendency to make specie payments general, as well by its influence as by its example. It will be the interest of the national bank to produce this state of things, because otherwise its operations will be greatly circumscribed, as it must pay out specie or national bank notes; for he presumed one of the first rules of such a bank would be to take the notes of no bank which did not pay in gold and silver. A national bank of 35 millions, with the aid of those banks which are at once ready to pay specie, would produce a powerful effect all over the Union. Further, a national bank would enable the government to resort to measures which would make it unprofitable to banks to continue the violation of their contracts, and advantageous to return to the observation of them. The leading measure of this character would be to strip the banks refusing to pay specie of all the profits arising from the business of the government, to prohibit deposits with them, and to refuse to receive their notes in payment of dues to the government. How far such measures would be efficacious in producing a return to specie payments, he was unable to say—but it was as far as he would be willing to go at the present session. If they persisted in refusing to resume payments in specie, Congress must resort to measures of a deeper tone, which they had in their power.

The restoration of specie payments, Mr. C. argued, would remove the embarrassments on the industry of the country, and the stains from its public and private faith. It remained to see whether this House, without whose aid it was in vain to expect success in this object, would have the fortitude to apply the remedy. If this was not the proper remedy, he hoped it would be shewn by the proposition of a proper substitute, and not opposed by vague and general declamation against banks. The disease, he said, was deep; it affected public opinion—and whatever affects public opinion touches the vitals of the government. Hereafter, he said, Congress would never stand in the same relation to this measure in which they now did. The disease arose in time of war—the war had subsided, but left the disease, which it was now in the power of Congress to eradicate—but, if they did not now exercise the power, they would become abettors of a state of things which was of vital consequence to public morality, as he shewed by various illustrations. He called upon the House, as guardians of the public weal, of the health of the body politic which depended on the public morals, to interpose against a state of things which was inconsistent with either. He appealed to the House too as the guardians of public and private faith. In what manner, he asked, were the public contracts fulfilled? In gold and silver, in which the government had stipulated to pay? No; in paper issued by these institutions; in paper greatly depreciated; in paper depreciated from 5 to 20 per cent. below the currency in which the government had contracted to pay &c. He added another argument—the inequality of taxation in consequence of the state of the circulating medium, which, notwithstanding the taxes were laid with strict regard to the constitutional provision for their equality, made the people in one section of the Union pay perhaps one fifth more of the same tax than those in another. The Constitution having given Congress the power to remedy these evils, they were, he contended, deeply responsible for their continuance.

The evil he desired to remedy, Mr. C. said, was a deep one; almost incurable, because connected with public opinion, over which banks have a great control—they have in a great measure a control over the press; for proof of which he referred to the fact that the present wretched state of the circulating medium had scarcely been denounced by a single paper within the United States. The derangement of a circulating medium, he said, was a joint thrown out of its socket; let it remain for a short time in that state, and the sinews will be so knit, that it cannot be replaced— apply the remedy soon, and it is an operation easy though painful. The evil grows, whilst the resistance to it becomes weak; and, unless checked at once, will become irresistible. Mr. C. concluded the speech of which the above is a mere outline, which the imagination of the reader must fill up, by observing, that he could have said much more on this important subject, but he knew how difficult it was to gain the attention of the House to long addresses.

124 NOTE: Calhoun's was the opening speech, in the Committee of the Whole, on the bank bill (reported by him on Jan. 8— No. 120). In it he concentrated on the practical problems created by the country's financial chaos. However, by assuming that the phrase of the Constitution covering the coinage of money and the regulation of its value could be considered as synonymous with his own words "to regulate the currency" (see above, n. 1), he undertook to put his bill in the best constitutional light.

In the debate which immediately followed, Calhoun objected to a motion of John Sergeant of Pennsylvania to reduce the capital to $20,000,000, declaring the figure in the bill to be in accordance with its functions (AC14-1, p. 1066-7). On the 28th this motion was defeated by a vote of 74 to 49 (p. 1108). See No. 125.

A manuscript copy of this speech, in an unidentified hand, is in the Clemson College collection. It shows the same evidence of transcription from the *Intelligencer* as Nos. 113 and 114—see No. 114 NOTE.   SOURCE: *NI*, Feb. 27, 1816; AC14-1, p. 1060-6.

125. REMARKS ON THE REQUIREMENT FOR SPECIE PAYMENT BY THE BANK

February 28, 1816

Mr. Calhoun then rose, and in an energetic manner vindicated the bill, and his views of it, from the attack which had been made on them. He said, no man in the House would reprobate more than he the establishment of a bank which was not a specie bank. A bank not to pay specie, he said, would be an instrument of deception; it would have no character or feature of a bank—he should regard it with disgust and abhorrence. This bank, he asserted in reply to contrary assertions, if established, would be a specie bank. He professed himself ready to remedy any defects which should be pointed out; but he hoped the committee would not be influenced to destroy its essential features by such vague arguments as had been urged against them. This was to be a specie bank, or he would have nothing to do with it. He called upon gentlemen not to give way to objections to the details of the bill made by those who were altogether inimical to the establishment of any bank; their arguments, he intimated, ought to be received with suspicion, because their views of the subject might be supposed to be warped by their hostility to the project altogether. Mr. C. then spoke at length in explanation and reply to those gentlemen who had preceded him in the debate. In regard to the estimation of paper in circulation, &c. he took occasion to say, that he and General Smith had not widely differed in opinion on that head, when they came to understand terms.[1] Mr. C. said he had not specified the particular items in his estimate of the amount of bank issues and transactions—his object had been merely to shew, without descending to particulars, that the banks had over-traded. He referred, for illustration, to the Bank of Washington, reputed a prudent bank, which on a capital of 350,000 dollars, what with stock and discounts to individuals drew interest on 800,000 dollars. His object, he said,

1. Samuel Smith of Maryland on the 27th (*AC*14-1, p. 1070-4) spoke in general support of the bill but urged gentler pressures on the state banks and contended they had not issued excessive amounts of paper. On Mar. 5 (p. 1139) Smith, in the committee, got an amendment adopted forbidding the appointment by the President of more than three directors from any one state (No. 120, Sec. 10).

when up before, was to prove that the banks generally had done a business which would authorize them to divide at the enormous rate of fourteen and an half per cent, on their capital paid in, &c. &c.

125 NOTE: The debate of the 27th and 28th, in the Committee of the Whole (*AC*14-1, p. 1070-89, 1091-1108), was on Sergeant's motion of the 26th to reduce the capital to $20,000,000 (No. 124 NOTE), but the discussion centered as much about the question of specie payment. Sergeant (*AC*14-1, p. 1074-81) defended the state banks, charged that the proposed bank was subject to the same weakness, and denied that it could maintain specie payment (see No. 120, Sec. 18).

Webster vigorously attacked the bill (*AC*14-1, p. 1091-4), contending that the need of the country was specie currency and that the proposed bank would do nothing toward establishing it. Joseph Hopkinson of Pennsylvania (p. 1095-1105) stoutly defended the state banks in general, but not "that miserable litter of forty-two" chartered by the Pennsylvania legislature (p. 1102). The specie issue was raised again in the committee on Mar. 6 (p. 1155), when a motion was made to deprive the President of the authority during recess of Congress to suspend specie payment. Calhoun thereupon offered to support a motion to extend the restriction to Congress also, and next day (p. 1157-8) this was adopted.

On Mar. 4 Smith moved to strike out Treasury notes, as a form of payment, from Section 6 (to which Calhoun assented), to make the interest on government stock five instead of six per cent, and to set the date for delivery of the subscription at the bank at Jan. 1, 1817 (No. 120, Sec. 6). Smith's motions were adopted (*AC*14-1, p. 1136).   SOURCE: *NI*, March 2, 1816; *AC*14-1, p. 1107.

126. REMARKS ON THE NEED FOR A NATIONAL BANK

March 6, 1816

Mr. Calhoun rose to make a remark or two in reply to his friend (Mr. Robertson). He almost despaired of the passage of the bill, after some of the indications which he had witnessed, and began to doubt whether any bill would pass at all on the subject. For himself, Mr. C. said, his anxiety for the measure was not extreme— but as long as there was a lingering hope of its success, he should omit no effort to make it an efficient remedy for the evils of the present currency. If, after making it suit, as far as possible, the taste of every one, gentlemen determined to oppose it, it was time for them to look out for some other remedy. Mr. C. said, he felt deeply the evil of the disordered state of our currency, and the necessity of a cure. In devising that cure, difficulties were to be expected. The direction of the bank he knew had been made a *sine qua non* by some gentlemen on one side of the House, and he was sorry to find it was one also with some on the other. It was a fate peculiar to great measures, to fall in their details. The obstinacy of gentlemen in matters of what they deemed principle, was honorable to them, but he feared it would be fatal to the bill. He lamented it—the disorders were so deep, so great, that justice to the country called for a remedy at the hands of the government. If gentlemen would seriously consider the character and power and nature of the evil—two hundred and sixty banks issuing almost as many millions of depreciated paper—they must see the necessity of co-operating in the measure of relief. The necessity for union was great and urgent, for the disease was almost incurable—it was a leprosy on the body politic—&c.

[*A motion was made to restrict directors of branch banks to natives.*[1]]

Mr. Calhoun objected to the amendment. It was the first time, he said, that any attempt had been made in this country to discriminate between native and naturalized citizens. The Constitution recognised no such distinction, except in the eligibility to the highest office in the government, and he could see no reason for introducing on this occasion so odious and unprecedented a distinction.

126 NOTE: The bank bill was still in the Committee of the Whole—see No. 125. Calhoun's bill was an attempt at compromise between the advocates of government and private control, and the question had already come to an issue. On Feb. 29 Calhoun accepted the motion of Daniel Cady of New York to strike out the clause allowing Congress to increase the capital to $50,000,000 (AC14-1, p. 1109; see No. 120, Sec. 1), but protested against Cady's

1. A motion by Randolph was adopted (AC14-1, p. 1152) to require that to be a director the "citizen"—see No. 120, Sec. 13, subsection 3—must be a "native"; this was followed by another to extend the restriction to directors of the branch banks. The second motion was defeated (AC14-1, p. 1155) and, in the House on Mar. 11, Calhoun got Randolph's amendment rejected also (p. 1201).

next motion to eliminate the government's contribution, declaring that "he should consider the success of it as tantamount to a decision to strike out the first section of the bill." He followed up this statement by the declaration that the government stood to make 2 per cent by putting this stock in the bank—the difference between its payments of interest and what it would receive from the bank (p. 1110). Cady's motion was defeated next day (p. 1119).

On the 4th and 5th (p. 1137) a motion by Timothy Pitkin of Connecticut to strike out the five appointed directors (No. 120, Sec. 10) had been debated, but finally failed (AC14-1, p. 1137, 1139; see also No. 128 NOTE). Calhoun objected to this motion and was supported by several members. Now, on the 6th, Samuel Smith moved that Section 10 be amended to allow the president to be elected from any of the directors (p. 1151). Calhoun made no objection, as he thought that clause "not necessary to give the Government a due control over the concerns of the bank: and that it would still retain as much influence as would serve every beneficial purpose." Thomas B. Robertson of Louisiana thereupon spoke against the motion saying he wished "an institution of national character." "He adverted to the liberality which had been manifested by the chairman . . . and thought the principle of accommodation might be carried too far." Smith's motion passed the same day (p. 1152). SOURCE: *NI*, Mar. 7, 1816; *AC14-1*, p. 1152-3.

127. SPEECH ON COMPENSATION OF MEMBERS

March 8, 1816

Mr. Calhoun said, so far as this bill proposed to increase the compensation to members, he was in favor of it; because he thought the present pay very inadequate to the dignity of the station, and far short of the time, labor and sacrifice required. He thought 1500 dollars would be found not sufficient, and would prefer, on the ground of a due compensation as well as regard to principle 2500 dollars. He said on principle, for in the fixing the pay of members heretofore, it had not been sufficiently attended to. Our extent, population and wealth made a strong executive necessary; and we accordingly find the framers of our Constitution have made that the preponderating part of our government. It constitutes a branch of the legislature, and has besides the whole patronage of government, while the other branches have naked power only without patronage or influence. He did not complain of any undue influence of executive power now; he wished not to be so understood, as he was speaking solely in relation to the constitutional powers of the president. The best and wisest men in this country have always thought his power so great as to render it ultimately dangerous. What then is to be done? To weaken it, would be to weaken the country; perhaps to endanger it.

The only safe control, is in the character, experience and intelligence of this House. Whenever this House is properly composed, when it contains a sufficient number of men of ability, experience and integrity it of necessity will give direction to public affairs; but a weak and inexperienced House necessarily falls under executive control. The increased pay is calculated to draw men of abilities into this House; and, what is of equal importance, to keep them here till they are matured by experience. What is the usual fact? Young men of genius, without property, for in four instances in five such is the case with genius, are elected; being tempted into public service by the honorable desire of acquiring distinction in the service of the country they remain here till they have acquired some experience and begin to be useful to the country; but are finally compelled to return to private life, from the inadequacy of the pay. It is a great public misfortune; it is highly injurious to the proceedings of this House. Ever since he had known the body, there had been no want of talent; but the want of experience had often been felt. If we are wise, we will as far as possible attract and secure abilities and integrity in the *public service*. Providence intended them, as the best gift to the nation, for that purpose; and any people, as they use or neglect them, flourish or decay. Another view of this subject, connected with the great extent of our Republic, made it expedient. A majority of the members come from three to eight hundred miles. In serving the country, they are not only obliged to be absent a great part of the year from their families; but what is almost equally distressing, to be absent a *great distance*. We serve at the expense of the best sympathies of our nature; we are far removed from the centre of that system of social feelings, which at once constitutes the solace and ornament of our nature. The best dispositions are the most sensible to this sacrifice; and are by it most likely to be driven out of the councils of the nation. This state of things ought to be counteracted as far as possible; the condition of a member ought to be made more desirable than at present; he ought at least to be able to have his family about him, which he cannot, at the present pay, without ruin, unless he be a man of property. For these reasons he thought the measure a wise one, and to be highly republican. It had for a long time been felt to be necessary. It was worthy of the disinterested gallantry of the member who had introduced it.

127 NOTE: On the 4th (AC14-1, p. 1127-30) Richard M. Johnson of Kentucky, "hero of the battle of the Thames," offered a resolution for appointment of a committee to inquire into the expediency of paying members by the session instead of by the day, contending that it was the per diem method which protracted the sessions by causing "the constant and never-ending debate" (p. 1127). On the 6th he introduced the bill changing the compensation from $6 a day to $1500 per session (p. 1150). Calhoun's speech was on the third reading in the House. The bill passed the same day, by a vote of 81 to 67, and became law on the 19th (p. 1188, 1801). See Wiltse, *Calhoun, Nationalist,* p. 112-3, 124-5, and No. 147 and No. 134 n. 1. SOURCE: *NI,* May 4, 1816; AC14-1, p. 1183-4. The *NI* copy incorrectly dates it Mar. 9; see *NI,* Mar. 9, and *House Journal,* Mar. 8.

128. DEBATE ON THE NATIONAL BANK BILL

March 12, 1816

[Calhoun was supporting an amendment to relieve the bank of a proposed penalty of forfeiture of its charter for failure to pay notes in specie.]

It was with much reluctance, Mr. C. said, that he opposed any provision which the House had deemed necessary to perfect the bill; but in the present instance he was compelled to make an objection. The fundamental character of this bank was, that it should pay its notes in gold or silver coin; and a sufficient penalty was provided to effect that end. It is a good rule in law, said Mr. C. that where you attach a separate penalty to a particular violation of a law, you weaken the general penalty; and as he thought the general penalty would attach in the case without this special provision, which would, therefore, weaken the general sanctions of the bill, he hoped it would be stricken out.

[*The amendment was adopted accordingly, but Randolph at once moved to increase the penalty for non-payment of specie from ten to twenty per cent.*]

Mr. Calhoun repeated the reluctance with which he objected to any motion which, in the opinion of the gentleman who made it, would improve the bill; but he had thought that even the propriety of *ten* per cent. contemplated by the bill, was very questionable, as he doubted whether that provision might not produce combinations against the bank, which were so anxiously guarded against. Every man acquainted with the subject knows, that no bank can at all times possess the means of meeting a general run upon it; and he submitted it to the House, whether such a provision as was now proposed, would not be dangerous to the institution, by inviting a run on it, and thereby producing a suspension of payment. He admitted that it was all-important to the benefit anticipated from the bank, that it should pay its notes, at all times, in specie; and he thought that end already secured by other sanctions sufficiently guarded. This bank, said Mr. C. is no more than a part of the commercial community in which it is established, and any embarrassment of the bank must press also on the whole commercial community; that community would be the first to give way in such a case, and this would produce a run on the bank, and compel the stoppage of payment. If the amendment would produce a greater certainty of specie payments, it might be proper; but believing that it might defeat its own object, and produce that which it was intended to guard against, he thought it dangerous, &c.

128 NOTE: This was the final debate on the bank bill (see No. 126). Randolph's motion failed (*AC*14-1, p. 1203). The same day Bolling Hall of Georgia moved to apply the bonus to internal improvements (p. 1204-5); Calhoun in reply "declared his approbation of the object, but feared the adoption of the amendment might drive off some who would otherwise support the bill. Unfortunately for us, he said, there was not a unanimous feeling in favor of internal improvement, some believing this not the proper time to commence that work; and such a provision might deprive the bill of some friends, which at present was the main object of his solicitude." He replied to a proposal to locate the bank in New York by saying that he supposed the members had already made

up their minds, and that he hoped Philadelphia would be the final choice (p. 1205).

Later in the day William Mayrant of South Carolina moved that the five government directors be paid salaries (he suggested $3,000) and be forbidden loans from the bank in order to make the government's influence independent as well as strong. Calhoun objected on the ground that the salary would have to be very large to induce "a commercial man of any standing to forego the benefits of the bank," and the loans could be secured through friends anyway; the motion was defeated (p. 1206-7). On the 13th, Alney McLean of Kentucky moved that no branch be established in a state except under a law of that state (p. 1208-9). Calhoun replied "that this motion appeared to involve an inquiry into the Constitutional power of Congress to establish banks in the States." He wished to avoid the question now. "When the necessity arose for discussing the question, he should be prepared to meet it." (P. 1209.)

On Mar. 13, as the debate drew to a close (p. 1207-11), Pitkin renewed his motion to eliminate the government's directors (p. 1209); see No. 126 NOTE. Calhoun's comment (AC14-1, p. 1210) showed his anxiety over the possible breakdown of the support gained for the bill by the compromise, but the next day, after a hectic final session and "a few remarks" by Calhoun, it passed on the third reading by 80 to 71 (p. 1219). In the Senate the bill was debated from Mar. 25 to Apr. 3, when it passed (p. 235-81). On the 4th Calhoun proposed that the question be put on the Senate amendments as a whole, as "they were not important" (p. 1327). On the 5th Calhoun defeated the attempt to delay consideration until his committee reported on specie payment (p. 1337-8; see No. 130). Randolph's re-opening of the whole question of the constitutionality, expediency and danger of the bill brought from Calhoun the remark that the bill had been maturely considered and fairly passed (p. 1338), and the same day the Senate amendments were approved (p. 1344). SOURCE: *NI*, Mar. 14, 1816; *AC*14-1, p. 1202-3.

129. SPEECH ON THE TARIFF BILL

April 4, 1816

[*Mr. Calhoun, replying to Mr. Randolph, said:*]

The debate heretofore on this subject, has been on the degree of protection which ought to be afforded to our cotton and woollen manufactures; all professing to be friendly to those infant establishments, and to be willing to extend to them adequate encouragement. The present motion assumes a new aspect. It is introduced professedly on the ground, that manufactures ought not to receive any encouragement; and will, in its operation, leave our cotton establishments exposed to the competition of the cotton goods of the East Indies, which, it is acknowledged on all sides, they are not capable of meeting with success, without the proviso proposed to be stricken out by the motion now under discussion. Till the debate assumed this new form, he had determined to be silent; participating, as he largely did, in that general anxiety which is felt, after so long and laborious a session, to return to the bosom of our families. But on a subject of such vital importance, touching, as it does, the security and permanent prosperity of our country, he hoped that the House would indulge him in a few observations. He regretted much his want of preparation—he meant not a verbal preparation, for he had ever despised such, but that due and mature meditation and arrangement of thought, which the House is entitled to on the part of those who occupy any portion of their time. But whatever his arguments might want on that account in weight, he hoped might be made up in the disinterestedness of his situation. He was no manufacturer; he was not from that portion of our country supposed to be peculiarly interested. Coming, as he did, from the South, having, in common with his immediate constituents, no interest, but in the cultivation of the soil, in selling its products high, and buying cheap the wants and conveniencies of life, no motive could be attributed to him, but such as were disinterested.

He had asserted, that the subject before them was connected with the security of the country. It would, doubtless, by some be considered a rash assertion; but he conceived it to be susceptible of the clearest proof; and he hoped, with due attention, to establish it to the satisfaction of the House.

The security of a country mainly depends on its spirit and its means; and the latter principally on its monied resources. Modified as the industry of this country now is, combined with our peculiar situation and want of a naval ascendancy; whenever we have the misfortune to be involved in a war with a nation dominant on the ocean, and it is almost only with such we can at present be, the monied resources of the country, to a great extent, must fail. He took it for granted, that it was the duty of this body to adopt those measures of prudent foresight, which the event of war made necessary. We cannot, he presumed, be indifferent to dangers from abroad, unless, indeed, the House is prepared to indulge in the phantom of eternal peace, which seemed to possess the dream of some of its members. Could such a state exist, no foresight or fortitude would be necessary to conduct the affairs of the Republic; but as it is the mere illusion of the imagination, as every people that ever has or ever will exist, are subjected to the vicissitudes of peace and war, it must ever be considered as the plain dictate of wisdom, in peace to prepare for war. What, then, let us consider constitute the resources of this country, and what are the effects of war on them? Commerce and agriculture, till lately, almost the only, still constitute the principal sources of our wealth. So long as these remain uninterrupted, the country prospers; but war, as we are now circumstanced, is equally destructive to both. They both depend on foreign markets; and our country is placed, as it regards them, in a situation strictly insular; a wide ocean rolls between. Our commerce neither is or can be protected, by the present means of the country. What, then, are the effects of a war with a maritime power—with England? Our commerce annihilated, spreading individual misery, and producing national poverty; our agriculture cut off from its accustomed markets, the surplus product of the farmer perishes on his hands; and he ceases to produce, because he cannot sell. His resources are dried up, while his expences are greatly increased; as all manufactured articles, the necessaries, as well as the conveniences of life, rise to an extravagant price. The recent war fell with peculiar pressure on the growers of cotton and tobacco, and other great staples of the country; and the same state of things will recur in the event of another, unless prevented by the foresight of this body.

If the mere statement of facts did not carry conviction to any mind, as he conceives it is calculated to do, additional arguments might be drawn from the general nature of wealth. Neither agriculture, manufactures or commerce, taken separately, is the cause of wealth; it flows from the three combined; and cannot exist without each. The wealth of any single nation or an individual, it is true, may not *immediately* depend on the three, but such wealth always presupposes their existence. He viewed the words in the

349

most enlarged sense. Without commerce, industry would have no
stimulus; without manufactures, it would be without the means of
production; and without agriculture, neither of the others can subsist. When separated entirely and permanently, they perish. War
in this country produces, to a great extent, that effect; and hence,
the great embarrassment which follows in its train. The failure
of the wealth and resources of the nation necessarily involved the
ruin of its finances and its currency. It is admitted by the most
strenuous advocates, on the other side, that no country ought to
be dependent on another for its means of defence; that, at least,
our musket and bayonet, our cannon and ball, ought to be of
domestic manufacture. But what, he asked, is more necessary to
the defence of a country than its currency and finance? Circumstanced as our country is, can these stand the shock of war? Behold
the effect of the late war on them. When our manufactures are
grown to a certain perfection, as they soon will under the fostering
care of government, we will no longer experience these evils. The
farmer will find a ready market for his surplus produce; and what
is almost of equal consequence, a certain and cheap supply of all
his wants. His prosperity will diffuse itself to every class in the
community; and instead of that languor of industry and individual
distress now incident to a state of war, and suspended commerce,
the wealth and vigor of the community will not be materially
impaired. The arm of government will be nerved, and taxes in the
hour of danger, when essential to the independence of the nation,
may be greatly increased; loans, so uncertain and hazardous, may
be less relied on; thus situated, the storm may beat without, but
within all will be quiet and safe.

To give perfection to this state of things, it will be necessary
to add, as soon as possible, a system of internal improvements, and
at least such an extension of our navy, as will prevent the cutting
off our coasting trade. The advantage of each is so striking, as not
to require illustration, especially after the experience of the recent
war. It is thus the resources of this government and people would
be placed beyond the power of a foreign war materially to impair.
But it may be said that the derangement then experienced, resulted
not from the cause assigned, but from the errors or the weakness
of the government. He admitted, that many financial blunders were

committed, for the subject was new to us; that the taxes were not laid sufficiently early, or to as great an extent as they ought to have been; and that the loans were in some instances injudiciously made; but he ventured to affirm, that had the greatest foresight and fortitude been exerted, the embarrassment would have been still very great; and that even under the best management, the total derangement which was actually felt, would not have been postponed eighteen months, had the war so long continued. How could it be otherwise? A war, such as this country was then involved in, in a great measure dries up the resources of individuals, as he had already proved; and the resources of the government are no more than the aggregate of the surplus incomes of individuals called into action by a system of taxation. It is certainly a great political evil, incident to the character of the industry of this country, that, however prosperous our situation when at peace, with an uninterrupted commerce, and nothing then could exceed it, the moment that we were involved in war the whole is reversed. When resources are most needed; when indispensible to maintain the honor; yes, the very existence of the nation, then they desert us. Our currency is also sure to experience the shock; and becomes so deranged as to prevent us from calling out fairly whatever of means is left to the country. The result of a war in the present state of our naval power is the blockade of our coast, and consequent destruction of our trade. The wants and habits of the country, founded on the use of foreign articles, must be gratified; importation to a certain extent continues, through the policy of the enemy, or unlawful traffic; the exportation of our bulky articles is prevented too, the specie of the country is drawn to pay the balance perpetually accumulating against us; and the final result is a total derangement of our currency.

To this distressing state of things there were two remedies, and only two; one in our power immediately, the other requiring much time and exertion; but both constituting, in his opinion, the essential policy of this country; he meant the navy, and domestic manufactures. By the former, we could open the way to our markets; by the latter we bring them from beyond the ocean, and naturalize them. Had we the means of attaining an immediate naval ascendancy, he acknowledged that the policy recommended by this bill, would be very questionable; but as that is not the fact—as it is a period remote, with any exertion, and will be probably more so, from that relaxation of exertion, so natural in peace, when necessity is not felt, it became the duty of this House to resort, to a considerable extent, at least as far as is proposed, to the only remaining remedy. But to this it has been objected, that the country is not prepared, and that the result of our premature exertion would be to bring distress on it, without effecting the intended object. Were it so, however urgent the reasons in its favor, we ought to desist, as it is folly to oppose the laws of necessity. But he could not for a moment yield to the assertion; on the contrary, he firmly believed that the country is prepared, even to maturity, for the introduction of manufactures. We have abundance of resources, and things naturally tend at this moment in that direction. A prosperous commerce has poured an immense amount of commercial capital into this country. This capital has, till lately, found occupation in commerce; but that state of the world which transferred it to this country, and gave it active employment, has passed away, never to return. Where shall we now find full employment for our prodigious amount of tonnage; where markets for the numerous and abundant products of our country? This great body of active capital, which for *the moment* has found sufficient employment in supplying our markets, exhausted by the war, and measures preceding it, must find a new direction; it will not be idle. What channel can it take, but that of manufactures? This, if things continue as they are, will be its direction. It will introduce a new era in our affairs, in many respects highly advantageous, and ought to be countenanced by the government.

Besides, we have already surmounted the greatest difficulty that has ever been found in undertakings of this kind. The cotton and woollen manufactures are not to be *introduced*—they are *already* introduced to a great extent; freeing us entirely from the hazards, and, in a great measure the sacrifices experienced in giving the capital of the country a new direction. The restrictive measures and the war, though not intended for that purpose, have, by the necessary operation of things, turned a large amount of capital to this new branch of industry. He had often heard it said, both in and out of Congress, that this effect alone would indemnify the country for all of its losses. So high was this tone of feeling, when the want of these establishments were practically felt, that he remembered, during the war, when some question was agitated respecting the introduction of foreign goods, that many then opposed it on the grounds of injuring our manufactures. He then said, that war alone furnished sufficient stimulus, and perhaps too much, as it would make their growth unnaturally rapid; but, that on the return of peace, it would then be time to show our affection for them.[1] He at that time did not expect an apathy and aversion to the extent which is now seen. But it will no doubt be said, if they are so far established, and if the situation of the country is so favorable to their growth, where is the necessity of affording them protection? It is to put them beyond the reach of contingency. Besides, capital is not yet, and cannot, for some time, be adjusted to the new state of things. There is, in fact, from the operation of temporary causes, a great pressure on these establishments. They had extended so rapidly during the late war, that many, he feared, were without the requisite surplus capital, or skill to meet the present crisis. Should such prove to be the fact, it would give a back set, and might, to a great extent, endanger their ultimate success. Should the present owners be ruined, and the workmen dispersed and turn to other pursuits, the country would sustain a great loss. Such would, no doubt, be the fact to a considerable extent, if not protected. Besides, circumstances, if we act with wisdom, are favorable to attract to our country much skill and industry. The country in Europe, having the most skilful workmen, is broken up. It is to us, if wisely used, more valuable than the repeal of the Edict of Nantz was to England. She had the prudence to profit by it—let us not discover less political sagacity. Afford to ingenuity and industry immediate and ample protection, and they will not fail to give a preference to this free and happy country.

It has been objected to this bill, that it will injure our marine, and consequently impair our naval strength. How far it is fairly liable to this charge, he was not prepared to say. He hoped and believed, it would not, at least to any alarming extent, have that effect immediately; and he firmly believed, that its lasting opera-

1. See No. 99.

tion would be highly beneficial to our commerce. The trade to the East Indies would certainly be much affected; but it was stated in debate, that the whole of that trade employed but 600 sailors. But whatever might be the loss in this, or other branches of our foreign commerce, he trusted it would be amply compensated in our coasting trade; a branch of navigation wholly in our own hands. It has at all times employed a great amount of tonnage, something more he believed than one-third of the whole; nor is it liable to the imputation thrown out by a member from North Carolina, (Mr. Gaston) that it produced inferior sailors.[2] It required long and dangerous voyages; and if his information was correct, no branch of trade made better or more skilful seamen. The fact that it is wholly in our own hands, is a very important one, while every branch of our foreign trade must suffer from competition with other nations.

Other objections of a political character were made to the encouragement of manufactures. It is said they destroy the moral and physical power of the people. This might formerly have been true to a considerable extent, before the perfection of machinery, and when the success of the manufactures depended on the minute subdivision of labor. At that time it required a large portion of the population of a country to be engaged in them; and every minute sub-division of labor is undoubtedly unfavorable to the intellect; but the great perfection of machinery has in a considerable degree obviated these objections. In fact it has been stated that the manufacturing districts in England furnish the greatest number of recruits to her army, and that, as soldiers, they are not materially inferior to the rest of her population. It has been further asserted that manufactures are the fruitful cause of pauperism; and England has been referred to as furnishing conclusive evidence of its truth. For his part, he could perceive no such tendency in them, but the exact contrary, as they furnished new stimulus and means of subsistence to the laboring classes of the community. We ought not to look to the cotton and woollen establishments of Great Britain for the prodigious numbers of poor with which her population was disgraced. Causes much more efficient exist. Her poor laws and

2. AC14-1, p. 456-7.

statutes regulating the price of labor with heavy taxes, were the real causes. But if it must be so, if the mere fact that England manufactured more than any other country, explained the cause of her having more beggars, it is just as reasonable to refer her courage, spirit, and all her masculine virtues, in which she excels all other nations, with a single exception; he meant our own; in which we might without vanity challenge a pre-eminence.

Another objection had been made, which he must acknowledge was better founded, that capital employed in manufacturing produced a greater dependance on the part of the employed, than in commerce, navigation or agriculture. It is certainly an evil and to be regretted; but he did not think it a decisive objection to the system; especially when it had incidental political advantages which in his opinion more than counterpoised it. It produced an interest strictly American, as much so as agriculture; in which it had the decided advantage of commerce or navigation. The country will from this derive much advantage. Again, it is calculated to bind together more closely our widely-spread Republic. It will greatly increase our mutual dependence and intercourse; and will as a necessary consequence, excite an increased attention to internal improvement, a subject every way so intimately connected with the ultimate attainment of national strength and the perfection of our political institutions. He regarded the fact that it would make the parts adhere more closely, that it would form a new and most powerful cement, far out-weighing any political objections that might be urged against the system. In his opinion the *liberty* and the *union* of this country were inseparably[3] united! That as the destruction of the latter would most certainly involve the former; so its maintenance will with equal certainty preserve it. He did not speak lightly. He had often and long revolved it in his mind; and he had critically examined into the causes that destroyed the liberty of other states. There are none that apply to us, or apply with a force to alarm. The basis of our Republic is too broad and its structure too strong to be shaken by them. Its extension and organization will be found to afford effectual security against their operation; but let it be deeply impressed on the heart of this House and

3. In *NI* this is "inseparately"; the *AC* makes the obvious correction.

country, that while they guarded against the old they exposed us to a new and terrible danger, disunion. This single word comprehended almost the sum of our political dangers; and against it we ought to be perpetually guarded.[4]

129 NOTE: On Feb. 13 Secretary of the Treasury Dallas submitted his proposed tariff schedule (*AC*14-1, p. 960, 1674-98), which was referred to the Ways and Means Committee. On the same day Thomas Newton of Virginia, Chairman of the Committee of Commerce and Manufactures, offered a resolution for a duty on imports of cotton goods, accompanied by a report that was a glowing eulogy of the protective system (p. 960-7). On Mar. 12 (p. 1201) Lowndes, for the Ways and Means Committee, reported a bill to regulate the duties on imports. Two years before, on the occasion of the repeal of the embargo (No. 99) Calhoun had declared that "certain manufactures in cottons and woolens . . . should have a moderate but permanent protection insured to them," and he considered the tariff an essential point in his post-war program (see No. 123 NOTE), but during the early stages of this debate he had little to say. On Mar. 23 he spoke briefly in support of his colleague Lowndes, who wished to retain the committee's duty of 44 per cent on brown sugar (*AC*14-1, p. 1262).

On the 25th, as the House in Committee of the Whole debated the duty on cotton goods (p. 1270-1), Webster moved an amendment to make the duty 30 per cent for two years, 25 per cent for two years, and 20 per cent thereafter. Clay moved to make the first two years three, and the second two, one. Calhoun "hoped the amendment to the amendment would not prevail. He believed the mode proposed by the original motion was correct, and that the permanent duty of 20 per cent. was an ample protection . . . and he hoped it would be adopted in the way proposed by the amendment." (P. 1271-2).

The debate proceeded with arguments over individual items, but on Apr. 4 (p. 1329) Randolph, after making a motion to strike out the proviso which fixed the minimum price of cotton goods at 25¢ a yard, attacked the bill "avowing his willingness to encourage, as far as was proper, those manufactures of cloths conducted in the families of our citizens, and argued against the propriety of promoting the manufacturing establishments to the extent, and in the manner proposed by the bill." Calhoun followed Randolph's speech with his general defense above.

On the 8th, on the third reading of the bill (p. 1350), Randolph moved postponement to December, contending that the Dallas plan

4. See No. 151, n. 1.

had not been "maturely prepared," and that the bill had been "pre-
cipitated through the House, and the discussion on it showed a
strange and mysterious connexion between this measure" and the
bank bill. Calhoun replied (p. 1351) denying "any improper or
unfair understanding" and even declared that "the most zealous
friends of the bank were generally unfriendly to this tariff."

"After some further conversation between Mr. Randolph and
Mr. Calhoun" the question was put on the postponement and the
motion lost. After a three-hour speech by Randolph against the bill
it passed, 88 to 54 (p. 1352).

Compare Calhoun's prefatory remarks in this speech with his
1833 account of it (*Works*, II, 208-9); Crallé prefaces the speech
(*ibid.*, p. 163) with the wrong date, and erroneously gives a motion
by Tucker as the occasion. His note of the circumstances is evidently
his own enlargement of Calhoun's 1833 statement. See also Wiltse,
Calhoun, Nationalist, p. 120-4, 413, and *Life*, p. 18-20.   SOURCE:
NI, Apr. 23, 1816; AC14-1, p. 1329-36.

130. REMARKS ON THE BILL TO REQUIRE SPECIE PAYMENT

April 17, 1816

Mr. Calhoun hoped the motion to insert the 1st of February would
not prevail. He added a few remarks to those he submitted when
he first introduced the bill; and adverting to the effect of the Virginia enforcing act, observed that an attempt to compel specie
payments in a particular state, when all the surrounding banks
did not so pay, was a very different thing from a general regulation,
which would operate on every part of the country alike. He had
all along believed no single state could safely resume the payment
of specie—could not meet the consequent curtailment of discounts;
but this did not prove that specie payments were impracticable if
resumed cotemporaneously throughout the country. Mr. C. felt
very anxious for the fate of this measure; he strongly suspected the
banks did not mean voluntarily to resume specie payments, though
it was in their power to import specie from abroad. He spoke boldly
on the subject—he did not believe the banks sincere in their declarations; and if there was the least giving back here, the object
would be lost. He hoped there would be such a vote on the bill,
as would give assurance that Congress was determined to compel

the restoration of a sound currency. To this end, Mr. C. believed the last of December would afford the banks ample time; but he would not be tenacious on the subject, if the House thought otherwise.

130 NOTE: On Mar. 20 Calhoun laid before the House a letter from Secretary of the Treasury Dallas, dated Mar. 19 (*AC*14-1, p. 1229-33), answering an inquiry of the 15th in which Calhoun had asked Dallas if in his opinion it was practicable now to collect dues to the government in specie, Treasury notes, and notes of specie-paying banks, and if after Nov. 1 the stamp duties on non-specie paying banks should be increased. In his reply Dallas explained the necessity the government had been under in the summer of 1814, when the banks suspended specie payment, of accepting bank notes; he repeated the opinion, stated in his Treasury Report of Dec. 6 last, that resumption must be a slow process and required also government interposition. He declared that the establishment of a national bank would assure the government's ability to pay specie. He therefore suggested an act of Congress requiring the Treasury, after Dec. 31 next, to receive government dues only in specie or notes redeemable in specie, and to deposit government funds in no banks which did not so redeem their notes, and that the act provide for an increase of at least 200 per cent in the present stamp duties on notes of banks not resuming specie payment by that time.

On Apr. 6 Calhoun reported a bill (MS Bill, Apr. 6, 1816, *NA*, RG233, 14A-B1; *AC*14-1, p. 1345-6) "for the more effectual collection of revenue in the lawful money of the United States" which closely followed the outline proposed by Dallas, except that, contrary to Dallas' recommendation, it included Treasury notes as a means of payment. It had sections to forbid acceptance after Dec. 31 next for dues to the United States of notes of non-specie paying banks; forbade deposit of government money in those banks; required the Secretary of the Treasury to sue banks failing to pay government dues in specie; and provided for imposition of the following stamp duties on notes of such banks: up to $1, 10¢; thence to $2, 20¢; to $3, 30¢; to $5, 50¢; to $10, $1; to $20, $2; to $50, $5; to $100, $10; to $500, $50; above $500, $100.

A Letter to Mr. Calhoun, Chairman of the Committee on a National Currency. (Philadelphia, M. Carey, 1816) protested the bill, citing the duties, and proposed the use of "bank credit," instead of bank notes. The *National Intelligencer* for Apr. 13 also noted circulation of memorials protesting the "penalties" of this bill. On Apr. 11, on Calhoun's motion and before the bill came up in the

House (*AC*14-1, p. 1356), it was recommitted to his committee for the purpose of cutting out the high duties which, he declared "if retained, would probably require more discussion than, at this late period," the House would allow. Accordingly on the 12th (p. 1361) Calhoun presented the bill revised to exclude the stamp duties. On the 17th, when the bill came up for discussion in the Committee of the Whole, Calhoun "took a succinct view of the bill, and re-capitulated briefly the evils which demanded this measure" (p. 1382), presenting the case so vigorously that his fellow committee member, Henry St. George Tucker of Virginia, referred (p. 1385) to Calhoun's "strong language" and his statement that "the disease was deep-rooted." Calhoun's statement above—the only one re-corded in which he took a general view of the bill—came in the midst of the debate on the 17th. See No. 131.   SOURCE: *NI*, May 11, 1816; *AC*14-1, p. 1389-90.

131. DEBATE ON THE SPECIE PAYMENT BILL

April 23, 1816

Mr. Calhoun moved to fill the blank in the first section with *fifteen* millions; and then, in a speech of some length, stated to the committee the benefits which were anticipated from the proposed issue of Treasury notes; the aid and relief they would afford to the community, under the pressure which would unavoidably be produced by the banks in the necessary curtailment of their discounts, the withdrawal of their notes from circulation, &c. preparatory to the resumption of specie payments, which the bill would enforce. It was his opinion that the bill would be effectual in producing the payment of specie, without the aid of this feature; but there were others who doubted whether the restoration could be well or safely effected without it; and he wished to afford every facility and relief that could be with propriety given, as well to the banks as to the community.

[*The remarks of four speakers intervene at this point, opposing or defending the proposed Treasury note plan.*[1]]

Mr. Calhoun replied to the arguments against the amendment. He had no idea the banks would resume specie payments willingly; they would go into it only because they would see inevitable ruin

1. *AC*14-1, p. 1416-7.

in refusing; but as they would be compelled to embrace the measure, he wished to give them ample means.

131 NOTE: On the 22nd, when the specie bill (No. 130 NOTE) came before the House (AC14-1, p. 1413), Calhoun again moved amendments—this time in regard to the Treasury notes—which threw the bill back into the Committee of the Whole. His new amendments would have provided for an issue of Treasury notes, non-interest bearing, receivable for dues to the United States, to be lent by the Secretary of the Treasury to the Bank of the United States or to state banks, on interest to be repaid in three annual installments, or to individuals or corporations in payment for United States "stock," the whole issue of notes to be drawn in and cancelled in three years (p. 1415-6). His initial remarks above followed the reading of these amendments. He had already, on the 18th, explained that his move was to meet the objection that calling of the notes might create a "deficiency" of currency (p. 1405).

After further amendments (p. 1417-8), the additions were reported to the House, but on the 25th after a hot debate on the bill, it was finally rejected by one vote (p. 1432-7).

The next day Webster, who had voted for the bill, offered three resolutions, one of which directed the Secretary of the Treasury "to adopt such measures as he may deem necessary, to cause, as soon as may be," dues to the government to be paid in specie, Treasury notes or United States Bank notes, and that this "ought" not to be deferred later than Feb. 1 next (p. 1440). There was again heated discussion in which Calhoun engaged (p. 1449), but this resolution passed, the date being changed to Feb. 20, and became law on Apr. 30 (p. 1450, 1919-20).   SOURCE: NI, Apr. 25, 1816, and correction, Apr. 27; AC14-1, p. 1416, 1417.

132. To [HENRY WHEATON?]

Bath [S.C.] 18th May 1816

My dear Sir, I regret that your letter of the 29th of April did not reach me till after the adjournment of Congress. The business to which it relates I entirely approve. I think it of national importance to have the adjudications of the supreme court fully and fairly reported. With these sentiments, it combined with my personal friendship for you, I should have attended to the contents of your letter with much pleasure. At another session should I be able to render any service in relation to it, I will cheerfully do it.

With esteem yours &c

J. C. CALHOUN

SOURCE: Pierpont Morgan Library, Wheaton Papers.

133. To ALEX. J. DALLAS, Secretary of the Treasury, Washington

Bath [*S.C.*] 15th June 1816

Dear Sir, Mr. Mosely who has a small claim against the government on account of taking the census for one of the districts of this state, is fearful amidst the more important business of your office, that his may escape your memory.[1] He has requested me to remember you of it by letter. I spoke to you about it a few days before the end of the session, but you were at that time too much engaged to attend to it. The amount is small but as he is in moderate circumstances it is something to him.

As you took a deep interest in the proceedings of the last session, and had your full share of responsibility, I know it will afford you much pleasure, to hear that they are well received by any [consi]derable portion of the community. Since [m]y return, I have had an opportunity [of j]udging of the popular sentiment in this state. All the great measures of the session are very popular. I hear not one objection to the bank, Tariff, or taxes. I may say, I believe, with truth, that there is in Carolina, on those great subjects, substantially, but one voice. It augurs well to see the nation unite in measures of such magnitude, with so little division. It is the very essence of national strength and prosperity; and it is that which in this country would seem most difficult to be effected. I hope what has been done will not be disturbed; and that at the next session, the other great measures contemplated will be carried into effect.

Tho' the measures of Congress at the last session are so generally popular, yet, I expect, great changes in this part of the Union a[t] the coming election. The compensation bill is much objected to.[2]

1. The transcript reads "memomery."
2. No. 127; see also No. 147.

I find in my own district very considerable dissatisfaction at it. Should there be a change of representation in the fifteenth Congress it is to be hoped it will not extend to measures. That would be indeed a national misfortune.

I feel much anxiety about the national bank and the circulation of the country. I hope there is no danger of the stock being sub-scribed;[3] and that there will be no impediment to its commencing under fair auspices. I fear great difficulty will be found in restoring specie payment.[4] To the south things are in relation to that point, as fair as could be expected. The high price of our staple removes all difficulty. It is very different however in the central parts of the Union. The more I reflect on it the greater is my surprise that [th]e bank, or any other measure passed in [rela]tion to it. My best respects to Mrs. Dallas and [the] family. I shall miss them much next winter [in W]ashington.

With esteem Yours etc.

J. C. CALHOUN

SOURCE: *LC*, Carnegie Institution of Washington Transcript Collection.

134. From JOHN NOBLE

Charleston August 21st. 1816

Dear Sir I this day saw, Mr. P. Grimball, who was contractor for carrying the mail between this & Augusta, at the time you lost the $500. He requested me, to state to you, that he had written on to Washington, to know, whether he or the government must make good the money you lost, in the mail, early in the year— that if government says he must pay it, he is willing to do so, if you will give him some time—say 5 or 6 months

In my opinion, you ought to accept of any offer he may make, which will finally secure to you the whole or indeed any part of the $500. As to compulsory means, when he is unwilling, I think

3. Presumably Calhoun meant *under-subscribed*. Subscription was completed in August (Walters, *Dallas,* p. 215).
4. See No. 130.

them even worse than useless, inasmuch as I am informed & I believe correctly, that he is not worth any thing, in his own right —under these circumstances should you, bring suit—you may not only loose the debt, but have costs of suit to pay. As I have understood, it is somewhat doubtfull, whether you can recover in law, without more proof than you will be able to bring forward, as to how it was lost, whether by negligence &c., I am at a loss to account for Mr. G's proposition, unless it arises from a wish, to get more contracts from government, which I believe he is now endeavouring to obtain. He asked me, if you had written on to governmt. respecting your loss, I told him I did not know— from this question, I think it probable, he may suppose, a complaint from you to the Post. M. General, might prevent his procuring any more contracts from that quarter. Also he may suppose, that he is not likely to succeed, untill he has made satisfactory arrangements to pay you & the other person, who lost money at the same time with you. Mr. Cheves, to whom you have written on the subject, thinks with me. Mr. M. Cohen, wishes to know how & when titles can be made to him, for the house & lot he purchased from my aunt. I wd. be glad to hear from you on the subject. Your friends here, feel much anxiety, as to your reelection. They hardly deem it possible, you shd. fail. We have had some well written numbers, on the compensation bill, addressed to the people of So Carolina, published in the Patriot, they ought & I hope will have their proper influence on the electors.[1] The writer you probably know—he belongs to your election District.

We have nothing new. Banking & commercial houses, failing on the large scale, in the British Empire. The manufacturers obliged to discharge a number of their workmen—the demand for their manufactures being very much diminished. Cotton falling in Europe daily. Our present crop I fear will not command more than from 15 to 20 cents.

---

1. The compensation bill—see Nos. 127 and 147. The three articles signed "Politicus" appeared in the *Southern Patriot,* Aug. 7, 12, and 14, 1816. Calhoun was re-elected by a majority of 434 (*ibid.,* Oct. 24, 1816). Of the seven representatives from South Carolina who voted for the bill only Calhoun and Henry Middleton were re-elected (*AC*14-1, p. 1188; *BDC*; see also 1843 *Life,* p. 23).

Give my best respects to Floride &c. and believe me as usual, your sincere friend &c.

JOHN NOBLE

SOURCE: *SCL.*

135. From WILLIAM WIRT

Richmond Augt. 22d. 1816

Dear Sir I have recieved your letter of the 4h. inst. relative to the imposition practised on you by Fowler & Hicks; and find on enquiry at our council chamber that the facts which you state, have been truly reported to you—of the bond, which was given to secure the State against the return of the negroes, and which is suable therefore for the benefit of the State, *only,* you can make no advantage—but both Fowler & Hicks are represented as solvent, and I have very little doubt that you will be able to recieve a complete reimbursement both for the purchase money and damages, from them. Fowler lives in the County of Goochland and Hicks in that of Louisa in this State: both those counties are out of the range of my practise—but I have inclosed your letter to Wm G. Poindexter, a member of the profession and the Speaker of our State Senate, from whose vigor and dexterity in matters of this sort, I think you may calculate on speedily recieving your money, without the delay of a suit—the terror of a prosecution for a breach of their bond will be an engine in his hands which he will not fail to use to the best advantage. Mr. Poindexter resides near Goochland courthouse an[d] is instructed to communicate with you.

I regret that my engagements, last winter, were of such a character as to debar me from that cultivation of your acquaintance which I had promised myself on my departure from Richmond— and I fear extremely that I shall not have an opportunity of renewing the attempt this fall. But can you not do me the pleasure to see me on your passage through this place? I hope I need scarcely assure you that I shall feel myself both gratified and flattered by a call—since you would do me an act of simple justice, merely, by believing me,

With very great respect and esteem, Your Obt Servt

WM. WIRT

135 NOTE: See Wirt's Letter Book for a copy (undated) of his to Poindexter enclosing Calhoun's letter. Wirt speaks of Calhoun as "the republican champion in congress from S. Carolina." He adds: "He is said to be as rich as a jew." The Negroes had been sold from the state penitentiary.   SOURCE: *LC,* Letter Book Copy, William Wirt Papers.

136. To JAMES BARREL, Providence, R.I.

Bath [*S.C.*] 22d. Sepr. 1816

Dear Sir, Mr. John McCalla a friend of mine connected with a very able house in Charleston, is about to settle in Augusta Georgia in a few weeks, as a commission merchant. He is a good judge of cotton, very attentive and faithful to business and is very desireous to be employed by some of our manufacturers in your part of the Union in his line of business. I know not that you are connected in any degree with the cotton establishments in your vicinity, but should any of your friends feel disposed to effect purchases in Augusta, I can with confidence recommend Mr. McCalla.

With esteem &c

JOHN C. CALHOUN

136 NOTE: See No. 141.   SOURCE: John A. May, Aiken, S.C., 1953.

137. To FELIX GRUNDY, Nashville, Tenn.

Washington 12th Decr. 1816

Dear Grundy, I feel for the misfortune which you have experienced in your daughter's marrying without your consent. It is one of those events which to a father must be most afflicting.

Of Mr. Ramsay Mayson I have not the least knowledge either personally or by character. There is a family of the name of Mayson in Cambridge a village in the county in which I reside. If he is of that family, which I think probable, his connections are very respectable. They are a family as respectable as any in that part of the country.

None of my colleagues live near that part of our state. I have enquired of the one who lives the most contiguous. He is ignorant of Mr. Mayson.

I will take the liberty of addressing a letter to one of my friends in that neighbourhood, in whom I have full confidence, from whom the information you desire can be obtained. I shall of course make no allusion to you or the cause which has produced the enquiry. Your letter does not authorise me to take this step; yet I cannot doubt, it is what you would wish done were you present, and personally applying for the information. As soon as I obtain it I will forward it to you. I thank you for your kind feelings relative to my reelection; and also your opinion in relation to the compensation law.[1] I would be glad to hear from you frequently and to have your opinion on all the great political occurances of the country. From long and intimate personal acquaintance, I have been taught to pay great respect to the soundness of your judgment.

Your friend

J. C. CALHOUN

SOURCE: University of North Carolina, Southern Historical Collection, Felix Grundy Papers.

138. COMMENT ON A RESOLUTION TO REQUEST THE PRESIDENT TO SUSPEND EXECUTION OF A LAW

December 13, 1816

Mr. Calhoun of South Carolina said, the defect alledged appeared not to be in the law; but in the execution of the law. If so, it was in the power of the Executive to dismiss the officer, without the interposition of this House. Mr. C. said he felt very little disposition to give his support to any proposition, which should assume the idea of the power of this House to suspend a law. If the decisions of the commissioner were such as had been represented, no amendment of the law could have any effect whatever, because the law did not even touch the case which had been stated. The

1. See No. 127 and No. 134 n. 1.

evil appeared to be in the officer himself. It is in the President's power to remove that evil; in assuming power in this case, said Mr. C. we should act out of the line of our duty. If the President did not dismiss the officer, there was another remedy by the exercise of a power belonging to this House—that of impeachment.

138 NOTE: The Apr. 9, 1816, law for compensation for property lost in the military service provided for a commissioner to decide on claims; the ninth section brought under the act houses destroyed by the enemy while officially under American military occupation (AC14-1, p. 1806-9). On Dec. 6, 1816, (AC14-2, p. 245) President Madison sent a message to Congress saying that, the ninth section "having received a construction giving it a scope of great and uncertain extent," he had thought proper to suspend proceedings under that section till Congress could further define it. The message was referred to the Claims Committee which on the 17th reported a bill (p. 298-9) to repeal the ninth section, eliminate the commissioner and transfer all claims under the remainder of the act to the War Department (see the act as passed, p. 1345-7).

The day Madison's message was received, John Forsyth, of Georgia, moved resolutions asking the President for information and requesting that he order suspension of execution of the law pending action by Congress (p. 246).

The debate at the moment was on Forsyth's resolution for suspension of the act, but had ranged over the whole field, and several cases were cited. Other members besides Calhoun challenged the right of the House or the President to suspend a law (p. 250-1, 281, 287-8, 290). The resolution was tabled (p. 296). For further proceedings see No. 143.   SOURCE: NI, Dec. 17, 1816; AC14-2, p. 291.

139. MOTION FOR A COMMITTEE TO PLAN A FUND FOR INTERNAL IMPROVEMENTS

December 16, 1816

Mr. Calhoun, of South Carolina referring to a proposition of the same sort made at the last session,[1] but then opposed by him as being unseasonably introduced, said that, since that time, the Bank Law had passed, the subscription had been filled under auspicious

1. See AC14-1, p. 1204-5 for the motion of Bolling Hall, of Georgia, to apply the bank bonus to internal improvements, and Calhoun's reply.

circumstances, and the bank was about to go into operation. Now, he said, was a proper moment for the House to consider whether the course of internal improvement was a proper direction for the United States to give to their share of the profits of that institution. He therefore moved,

"That a committee be appointed to enquire into the expediency of setting apart the bonus, and the net annual proceeds, of the National Bank, as a permanent fund for internal improvement."

Mr. C. said, it was not his object at this period to discuss the importance of national improvement. It was sufficient to say, that it was of such importance as to have been annually recommended to the attention of Congress by the Executive. That it had not been heretofore acted on, was not to be attributed, Mr. C. said, to any impression derogating from the importance of the subject. It arose from the want of funds; from the embarrassed state of our finances, and from the critical state of our foreign relations, which demanded all our attention. We had now abundance of revenue, and were in a state of peace, giving leisure to Congress to examine subjects connected with domestic affairs—of all which, internal improvement was not exceeded in importance by any. He hoped, therefore, the resolution would pass, and the inquiry be made as proposed.

139 NOTE: In March and April, 1816, Calhoun expressed himself emphatically on the need for internal improvements (see NOTES to Nos. 123 and 128). In April, 1814, Thomas Wilson of Pennsylvania had moved appointment of a committee to report on the expediency of provision for "the progressive improvement" of land and water routes on the principle of Albert Gallatin's 1808 report (*AC*13-2, p. 1935-41; for Gallatin's report see *ASP, Miscellaneous,* I, 724-41.) Dallas in his bank letter (No. 120 NOTE) had proposed applying the bonus to the purpose.

In his special message of Dec. 23, 1811 (*AC*12-1, p. 2166-7), President Madison had transmitted the application of the New York legislature for aid for its proposed Erie Canal, and had requested that Congress consider "a general system." In his annual message of Dec. 5, 1815 (*AC*14-1, p. 16-7), Madison urged systematic provision by Congress on a national scale, remarking that "any defect of Constitutional authority" could be supplied by amendment, and in his annual message of Dec. 3, 1816 (*AC*14-2, p. 14), but with less emphasis, he repeated the recommendation. Wilson was appointed chairman of the committee on that part of Madison's message (p. 234-5), and on Feb. 8, 1817, four days after Calhoun's speech (No. 151) he presented a report (AC14-2, p. 924-33) on roads and canals. The report concentrated on canals and proposed that half the cost of $20,000,000 (which was the same as Gallatin's estimate) be borne by the states. No action was taken on this resolution, but the same day Calhoun's bonus bill (No. 142) was passed.

Calhoun's motion was unanimously agreed to, and he was appointed chairman of the committee. See No. 142.   Source: *NI*, Dec. 17, 1816; AC14-2, p. 296-7.

140. COMMENT ON A PROPOSED AMENDMENT FOR ELECTION OF PRESIDENTIAL ELECTORS

December 17, 1816

Mr. Calhoun, in acceding to this motion, took the opportunity to observe, that he considered this a question of great importance. He thought the proposed amendment to the Constitution, if adopted, would remove some evils which experience has shewn to exist, and which in future time, if uncorrected, may menace the existence of the Republic. He therefore thought this subject entitled to the most mature consideration.

140 NOTE: Congressman Israel Pickens, of North Carolina, on the 11th offered a resolution to amend the Constitution to provide that presidential electors be elected by districts (AC14-2, p. 256-7); it was now in the Committee of the Whole, and the motion was to continue consideration. The resolution failed in the committee to get the necessary two-thirds majority (p. 355).   Source: *NI*, Dec. 19, 1816; AC14-2, p. 311.

141. From ISAAC BRIGGS

Wilmington, Del. 12thmo 19th. 1816.

My dear Friend,   The following is a duplicate of a letter dated and sent, per Mail, from this place, on 10 mo. 23—1816, addressed to thee, at Willington, Abbeville County S. C.

"I have received thy favor of 22d. ultimo, respecting thy friend, John McCalla. I will attend to thy request. To be of service to thee or to any friend of thine will be to me a gr[a]tification. I believe I have considerable interest with the manufacturing classes in the middle states. I may therefore perhaps be of some service to our friend McCalla. Perhaps, with thy kind assistance, we may reciprocate the benefit.

My son-in-law, Joseph E. Bentley, has been brought up to the mercantile business. He is a young man of activity and intelligence—of sobriety and integrity. After making the necessary enquiry, if we find that a good commission-business can be carried on with the southern states in cotton and sugars, he and I propose to join in that business in Philadelphia. We should calculate on having the orders of most of the manufacturers, and should in that case be glad to correspond with John McCalla, in Augusta, and with his friends in Charleston.

Wilt thou favor me with a line respecting this prospect of ours? and request John McCalla to do the same. On thy judgement and counsel we shall greatly rely.

The Manufacturers are at present under considerable pressure, but they must rise, or the vital interests of our Country must sink. We have *imported* during the past year, I suppose, nearly, if not quite, the value of 200 millions, and the whole value of our *Exports*, of domestic articles, has not reached 60 millions of dollars.

Accept my salutations of esteem and friendship."

I should be highly gratified to receive an answer to the preceding—And may I so far tax thy kindness as to request that thou wilt mention the subject on my behalf to our mutual friends, now in Washington City, from South Carolina and Georgia? Although thy kindness may result in my private benefit, yet it *is* with some reluctance that I make the effort to withdraw any part of thy attention from those great national objects, which I, with sincere pleasure, have seen thee so usefully and ably holding up to the view of Congress.

I have been delighted with the idea of appropriating, for *internal improvements,* the Bonus, and the national share of the annual profits of the Bank of the United States. May the patriotic proposition receive the legislative sanction—and may it never be rendered abortive, by hereafter diverting the fund from its noble course! If we mean to *continue* a happy, and *become* a powerful nation, we must cultivate our internal resources—we must facilitate intercourse by roads and canals—we must diminish our dependence on other nations, by providing for most of our wants by *our own industry,* and by encreasing the value of our surplus productions, by *our own labor*—so shall we dissipate prejudice, promote harmony and cement union among ourselves, and dry up the sources of a deleterious foreign influence.

In that spirit of candor and of friendship which casteth out all fear of offending, I will just touch another subject, which I deem of immense importance to our country generally, but having an emphasis of interest as it relates to the Southern States. It is Slavery. The Morality of the question has been so often handled that it has become perfectly trite—on this point, I have not the smallest doubt, we think alike.[1] We, in common with all good citizens, lament the existence, in our otherwise happy land, of the slavery of one degraded Class of human beings; And participating in the high gratification of seeing the exalted reputation of our Country for the virtue and happiness of her citizens, and the wisdom of her political institutions, we blush the more for this *one* stain on our national character. For myself, without the smallest disposition to enquire into its origin, or to cast censure on my southern brethren, who on the contrary, have my sympathy, I, see, with deep regret, that this embarrassing evil exists—that it is a moral and political poison—it has a deleterious effect on education—and it suffers not liberty to rest on the broad basis of the rights of *man.* In its progress, it is more and more impairing your political strength—it endangers your best prosperity. How to remove this evil, consistently with *equal justice,* is a very serious question. I hope, you, my friends of the southern states, will explore the rich resources of your own minds for a remidy. These sentiments are given with entire freedom, because they are intended for the confidential eye of friendship alone, and not to be seen where they might excite dangerous discontents.

Thy sincere friend,

ISAAC BRIGGS.

1. Compare Calhoun's statement, above, p. 312.

141 NOTE: See No. 136 for McCalla; *ASP, Claims*, p. 362, 544-5 (petition of Isaac Briggs, surveyor of public lands south of Tennessee, 1803-1807); AC14-2, p. 1069; Briggs' *Statements . . . Addressed to Thomas Newton, Chairman of the Committee of Commerce and Manufactures* (Washington, 1816).   SOURCE: Maryland Historical Society, Briggs-Stabler Papers.

142. THE INTERNAL IMPROVEMENTS BILL

December 23, 1816

[Mr. Calhoun, from the committee appointed on the 16th, reported:]

A Bill to set apart and pledge as a permanent fund for internal improvements the bonus of the national bank and the United States' share of its dividends.

Sec 1st. Be it enacted . . . that the United State's Share of the dividends of the national bank and the bonus for its charter be and the same are hereby set apart and permanently pledged as a fund for constructing roads and canals; and that it be subject to such specifick appropriations, in that respect, as Congress may hereafter make.

Sec 2d Be it farther enacted that the said fund be put under the care of the secretary of the treasury for the time being; and, that it shall be his duty, unless otherwise directed, to vest the said dividend, if not spicifically appropriated by Congress, in the stock of the United States; which stock shall accrue to, and, is hereby constituted a part of, the said fund for constructing of roads and canals

Sec. 3d. Be it farther enacted that it shall also be the duty of the said Secretary unless otherwise directed to vest the bonus for the charter of said bank as it may fall due, in the stock of the United States; and also to lay before Congress at their usual session the condition of the said fund.

142 NOTE: See Nos. 139 and 151.   SOURCE: MS Bill and printed copy (with MS amendment), Dec. 23, 1816, *NA*, RG233, 14A-B2 (the MS Bill is entirely in Calhoun's hand); *NI*, Dec. 24, 1816; AC14-2, p. 361.

143. Speech on the Bill for Payment for
Lost Property

December 30, 1816

Mr. Calhoun next spoke. He said it had been remarked that the administration of the law by the commissioner was defective, and not the law itself; but Mr. C. said, in vindicating this bill, and opposing the amendment, he objected not to the administration of the law, but to the part of the law itself which was proposed to be repealed. He considered it objectionable in point of principle. There was a material difference, he said, between cases of property destroyed in the military service, and those of houses destroyed by the enemy. The one case was defined, the other not. Besides, the cases of houses destroyed were but few: whilst cases of the former description were numerous. There was therefore good reason to make a distinction between the two classes of cases. Mr. C. considered the case of the destruction of houses by an enemy as involving a great principle. He knew that the gentlemen from Louisiana and Kentucky had expressed their views, that the whole amount of property destroyed by an enemy during war should be paid for out of the public funds.[1] To this doctrine, Mr. C. objected altogether. The very declaration of war, he said, changed the value of property. If you do away with the direct effect of war by paying for property actually destroyed, ought you not to compensate individuals for indirect losses occasioned by the war? The very declaration of war, he said sunk the value of tonnage 50, 60 or 70 per cent. If you would remunerate individuals for houses destroyed by an enemy, why not for other property, whose value, equally important to the owners, is equally destroyed by the war? How will you distinguish between these cases? Other laws, besides acts of war, are frequently made by a government, which change the value of property. An embargo is laid, for instance, by which a certain description of property, to a large amount, is made wholly unproductive. The idea of the gentleman from Kentucky, Mr. C. said, went upon a misconception. All laws are made for the general good; and, whether an individual be bene-

1. Thomas B. Robertson of Louisiana and Speaker Clay (AC14-2, p. 369-70, 382-6).

fited or not, it is his duty to acquiesce, and not oppose the decision of his country. The declaration of war did on the frontier of New York produce distress; but the interior of New York it enriched with a shower of gold. It benefited them with a market which others had not. To equalize the effects of the war exactly, according to gentlemen's notions, you should take from those who were benefited by the war, and give to those who sustained loss.

The reason why, Mr. C. said, he was indisposed to submit this important class of cases to the decision of any commissioner, was, that the cases descended by imperceptible gradations from occupation that was military, to that which was not. For example, the whole of the houses on a part of the Niagara frontier had been destroyed; many of them were in the occupation of military force, but the majority were not, but were destroyed in the neighborhood of the others. Here then is a class of cases of great importance, not only as to the amount of the claims, but as to the doctrine connected with them: they were such as no commissioner could decide. If the principle was established of paying for them all, in the event of any future war it would bankrupt the nation. If a commercial town was attacked, the nation must pay for every house destroyed! Say the city of New York was destroyed—could the Treasury meet so vast a claim for reimbursement? It could not. Beware, said Mr. C. how you introduce the principle into the statute book, of destroying the distinction between public and private property! By doing so, you become the universal insurers. The enemy will make war on you in that way which will most affect your Treasury. If you adopt the principle advocated by these gentlemen, your towns may fall a sacrifice to it, in the hope thereby to bankrupt you.

It had been stated that this House was not a proper tribunal to decide on private claims.[2] Mr. C. said he regretted to hear this remark, particularly from the source from which it came. This House was as capable, Mr. C. said, as any tribunal whatever. A committee might be selected, who would attend with vigilance to the claims, as would the present Committee of Claims; and if the House was not very vigilant in superintending the reports of its committees,

2. See for instance p. 375-6 (Johnson) and p. 383, 386 (Clay).

why was it not? Because they had a confidence in the reports, which, as regarded the Committee of Claims, Mr. C. asserted to be well founded. Mr. C. said he was sorry to see acquiescence in the acts of a committee construed into inattention and want of disposition to attend to them. The gentleman from Virginia had well said, that this kind of negligence, experienced in private cases, was equally applicable to public bills.[3] It is not the fact, said Mr. C. that this acquiescence is negligence. The House *is* vigilant and attentive: and, when there is not an express division on any question before it, it only indicates that the members of the House have made up their minds on the subject, and do not desire a division.

The House of Representatives, Mr. C. said, was not, he believed a favorite body in the nation.[4] It had no patronage to bestow, no favors to grant, and could rely only on its own character to sustain it: and it was therefore the duty of members to defend the character of the House. It had been said that the power of petitioning this House was merely the power of having a petition rejected.[5] Mr. C. considered the reverse the fact; that mere importunity sometimes succeeded in obtaining claims which ought never to have been allowed. He was aware, he said, that this argument made something against the capacity of this House to decide on claims, but not in the sense in which the gentlemen from New York and Kentucky had pressed this point against the House.[6] If any failing in this respect was imputable to the House, Mr. C. said it was that they acted with too much feeling; and when the claimants came before this House, they would find ample indulgence. Mr. C. said, further, that he was clearly of opinion that where, in the cases of houses destroyed, there could be proved regular military occupation by military force, the cases would be favorably decided. But the cases changed by minute graduations from actual to accidental military occupation in such manner that he was unwilling to trust the decision of those cases to any tribunal but this House.

3. This was Randolph's comment, p. 386.
4. Compare this remark with that of Richard H. Wilde of Georgia (p. 604), and note the comment on it of Cyrus King of Massachusetts (p. 505). See Adams, *History of U.S.*, IX, 134-5.
5. This is quoted from Clay, *AC*14-2, p. 386; see No. 144, n. 2.
6. See also Thomas P. Grosvenor of New York, *AC*14-2, p. 388-90.

143 NOTE: The debate was in the Committee of the Whole on the bill of the Claims Committee (No. 138), and on the amendment of Richard M. Johnson of Kentucky (*AC*14-2, p. 374) to continue the bill as it stood but to subject the commissioner's decisions to revision by the Secretary of the Treasury. SOURCE: *NI*, Jan. 2, 1817; *AC*14-2, p. 390-2.

144. REMARKS ON THE BILL FOR PAYMENT FOR LOST PROPERTY

January 6, 1817

Mr. Calhoun, in reply to Mr. Clay, said, that he had not understood the proceeding of the British government on the Niagara frontier as an implied promise to indemnify the sufferers, but rather as an examination into the nature and extent of the loss, to be laid before the government for its consideration—a proceeding very proper, even for this government in similar circumstances. As to the conduct of the Emperor Alexander, to whom the Speaker had in a former debate referred,[1] he said it was also very doubtful what was the object of his visit to the interior, whether for the purposes of munificence, as reported on one hand, or for the administration of justice and inflicting punishment, as reported by others. Be it as it might, in either of these cases, Mr. C. said we ought not to go abroad for examples, but to regulate our conduct by the rules of reason, wherewith he could not suppose the people would be dissatisfied.

Mr. C. said, he was glad to hear the Speaker's explanation in regard to the insensibility of this House to petitions,[2] and that he had referred to a mere physical inability to decide on these claims —an objection which could be easily obviated by raising other committees, one for instance for the claims from the Canadian frontier, another for those from the South, &c. He was glad to hear that the Speaker did not mean to impute to the House hard heartedness, of which construction his remarks had been susceptible.

1. *AC*14-2, p. 384.
2. See above, p. 375, and *AC*14-2, p. 427 (Clay's reply).

Notwithstanding the remarks since made, Mr. C. said, the position taken by him a day or two ago, and so very ably supported to-day by Mr. Barbour,[3] remained unchanged: for, if he understood the qualifications of the Speaker, they denied the rule, leaving the question of remuneration to sufferers one of mere expediency. Mr. C. repeated his objection to the rule laid down by Mr. Clay:[4] that if established, all distinction between public and private property in war would be obliterated. As to the restraint of the laws of war, Mr. Calhoun said that even in the late war, the rules of civilized warfare had not been observed by our adversary to their full extent. If we were to destroy the distinction between public and private property, my word for it, said Mr. C., you would find the effect of it in any future war. Mr. C. urged the importance of adhering, in this respect, to established principles; for which reason, cases coming under the 9th section should be left to this House, that it might at once establish the rule, and decide the cases. A strict application, he said, of the rule of the law, as it exists, would not embrace many just cases, and for this reason also Congress ought to decide them, having the power to enlarge the rule. In all that had been said in favor of retaining the 9th section, a wish had been expressed, that the rule of the decision made on claims in this District, should prevail throughout the United States. Mr. C. entered his protest against it: he believed those decisions did not come within the letter of the law, within the spirit of the law, nor within the rules on which the country ought to act in this case.

144 NOTE: Clay's speech (*AC*14-2, p. 426-8) in which he had referred to the British proceedings immediately precedes this. See Nos. 138 and 143. The bill finally passed on the 10th and became law on Mar. 3 (p. 462, 1345-7). SOURCE: *NI*, Jan. 11, 1817; *AC*14-2, p. 428-9.

3. Philip P. Barbour of Virginia—p. 423-4.
4. P. 426.

145. Debate on the Specie Payments on Stock of the United States Bank

January 7, 1817

Mr. Calhoun said, the House ought not to adopt this resolution, whether it regarded its own control over the bank, or justice to the institution. He denied that the facts suggested authorized the inquiry. The regulation adopted by the Directors was, that loans might be had if stock to their amount was pledged for the faithful payment of the notes when due. This regulation, he contended, was a prudent one. Though by the charter dividends were withheld from those who failed to pay the second instalment, this penalty was no hold on the stockholders, because the dividends would be very small; and he was certain but little of the specie part of the second instalment would be paid in. The regulation of the bank would produce the payment of the greater part of the instalment, and was liberal as well as prudent. The bank, Mr. C. understood, commenced its operations on the first of this month; and it had been stated at the last session, in debate on the charter, that it would be obliged to give these accommodations, as their notes would be the same as specie.[1] Mr. C. thought the regulation fair and just, because it put all subscribers on the same footing, as all who deposited stock would be enabled to obtain a loan; but without it, a few stockholders in Philadelphia and New York, able to give security and obtain discounts, would alone have had the benefit of the aid now extended to all. It was also expedient, as without it there would have been a draft on the money market of the country of three millions of dollars, which would have produced at this time the most pernicious consequences. He repeated, that it was distinctly understood at the last session, that the second specie payment would necessarily be made by accommodations from the bank; and the House could not now say the Directors had departed from the spirit or the provisions of their charter. The bank had gone into operation, and now having a will of its own, it had a right to adopt the regulation, if they perceived it was expedient. It

1. See Catterall, *Second Bank of U.S.*, p. 41, n. 3; Calhoun may also have been referring to a portion of Forsyth's speech of Mar. 5, 1816 (*AC*14-1, p. 1143).

had not been expected the specie capital would much exceed the amount of the first instalment, and the House had no reason to doubt the willingness of the bank to provide itself with an ample amount of specie, as it was notorious it had taken measures to procure it.[2] He repeated his belief that the resolution was unnecessary, and improper.

[*Forsyth and John Ross of Pennsylvania continued the argument.*]

Mr. Calhoun replied to Mr. Ross and to Mr. Forsyth. If the resolution was not offered on a certain, or even supposable state of facts, it was a good reason for rejecting the enquiry; the House ought never to proceed but upon facts at least probable—in this instance it would be an act of caprice. But admitting as true the facts suggested, they did not justify the enquiry; because, as he contended, the Directors had acted consistently with their chartered rights; and he reminded Mr. Forsyth that he had in 1815 objected to the bank bill, then discussed that in the very nature of things, all the specie instalments would not be paid without accommodation from the bank. Mr. C. repeated his approbation of the regulation, from the impartiality it produced in the accommodations, and the unhappy effect a draft of three millions on the money market, would at this time have produced in the relation between paper and specie, which draft was obviated by the regulation.

[*At this point two members opposed the resolution, but Richard H. Wilde of Georgia, and Thomas B. Robertson of Louisiana endorsed it.*]

Mr. Calhoun thought the 9th rule of the charter, quoted by Mr. Robertson, had no reference to the regulation referred to, and argued that the deposit required by the bank was not that dealing or trading which was prohibited by the rule. He considered the notes of the bank the same as specie because they were convertible into gold and silver at pleasure. Mr. C. replied to Mr. Wilde and others, and said he was the more anxious that this motion should not be agreed to, as it was a leading case of enquiry. He thought if ever the House lost its control over the bank it would be by

2. This is a reference to the bank's reported efforts to buy specie abroad— see AC14-2, p. 433.

disturbing them on trivial questions and occasions. He had the strongest conviction that this bank, backed by the government, would in time bring about that great revolution in our currency so much desired; that it required all the support of the government in it, and he hoped that the House would not now interfere in the regulations adopted with that view.

145 NOTE: On the 6th (*AC*14-2, p. 419), John Forsyth of Georgia submitted a resolution for inquiry by the Currency Committee, of which Calhoun was chairman, as to whether the president and directors of the Bank had adopted any arrangement by which "the specie portion of the second installment can be evaded or postponed," and, in such case, the expediency of enforcing payment. This installment was, by the bank act, to include $10 in gold or silver (above, p. 292), to be paid six months after the date of the subscriptions.

The new Secretary of the Treasury, William H. Crawford, like Dallas, had failed to persuade the state banks to agree to resume specie payment by Feb. 20 (Catterall, *Second Bank of U.S.*, p. 23-4), so that the Bank, required by its charter to pay specie, and in process of collecting specie on its subscriptions, was in a critical position. Its management, faced with the prospect that subscribers would forego the first dividend—the only penalty for delay in paying installments—rather than pay specie, so that the Bank would get neither specie nor other payments on stock, had adopted the device that a person could borrow from the Bank by pledging stock as security (see the description of this, *AC*14-2, p. 434-5). The Bank's own notes, redeemable by it in specie, thus became the specie payment on the stock (see also remarks of Forsyth and Thomas P. Grosvenor, p. 432-3).

Calhoun spoke when Forsyth called up the resolution on this day. The resolution was adopted, 89 to 68 (p. 435-6); see Calhoun's report, No. 146. SOURCE: *NI*, Jan. 9, 1817; *AC*14-2, p. 431-4.

146. REPORT ON THE SPECIE PAYMENTS ON STOCK OF THE UNITED STATES BANK

January 10, 1817

The committee on the national currency to whom were refered the resolution of the house directing them to enquire, "whether the President and Directors of the bank of the United States have adopted any arrangement by which the specie portion of the second instalment can be evaded or postponed; and if such arrangement has been made, the expediency of adopting some regulation by which the payment of the specie portion of the second instalment may be enforced at the time required by the act of incorporation or within a limited time thereafter.

Reported, that they have availed themselves of the opportunity of obtaining the information required by the house through the Honble. James Loyd, one of the directors of the national bank who is now in this city. In answer to their enquires the committee received from him the letter which accompanies this report; and on mature examination of the facts disclosed by it, they are of opinion that the bank in adopting the arrangement were actuated by a sincere desire, to effect the great objects for which it was instituted; as well as a regard to its own immediate interest. The committee are unanimously of opinion that it would be inexpedient to adopt any regulation; and therefore report the following resolution.

Resolved that the committee on the national currency be discharged from farther proceeding on the above recited resolution.

[*Accompanying the report was Calhoun's letter, dated "Committee Room 9th Jan. 1817," to James Lloyd. It cited the resolution and closed with the statement that the committee* "wish it to be distinctly understood, that they do not consider it any part of their duty to inquire into the expediency of the arrangement, provided it be within the limits of the chartered powers of the bank."]

146 NOTE: This report on Forsyth's resolution (see No. 145) and the letter to Lloyd are in Calhoun's hand. Lloyd's letter, dated Washington, Jan. 9, went at length into the matter, largely traversing the ground that Calhoun covered in his argument of the 7th. Lloyd related the sending of an agent to Europe to purchase specie, and cited and explained the Dec. 18 resolution of the Directors for loans on security of stock.

Forsyth "observed the report and documents were of so singular a character" that he moved they be printed, and "after some conversation between" himself, Calhoun and others this was ordered. For other proceedings by Forsyth on the bank see *AC*14-2, p. 476, 715, and 1053. SOURCE: MS Report, Jan. 10, 1817, *NA*, RG233, 14A-D17.5; *NI*, Jan. 11, 14, 1817; *AC*14-2, p. 454-9.

147. First Speech on Amendments to the Compensation Law

January 17, 1817

Mr. Calhoun said, that he hoped the House would not agree to fill the blanks with six dollars, as reported by the Committee of the Whole. He had remained silent thus long, not that he agreed with those who thought this a trivial question, but because he was anxious, in ultimately making up his mind, to profit by the observations of others. He had, however, finally adopted the course which he intended to pursue. If the blank were filled with a sum fully equal to the present pay, he would vote for the bill on its passage, not that in itself he preferred the daily to the annual pay; for on that point his opinion remained unaltered. He believed the latter for several reasons, which would not be repeated, to be of itself preferable. The daily, however, had one advantage at present over the other mode; it had a greater prospect of being permanent. If the pay, said he, is left in its present form, it will most certainly be repealed by the next Congress, whatever may be the feelings of a majority of that body, as to the mode or the amount of pay. They will not be free agents; most of them being already committed in the canvass for a seat in this House. But should the mode be changed, and the amount retained, the very men who have turned out the most of us, who have been the agitators in the late elections, will in all probability become the pacificators. For we may be perfectly assured of one fact, that the feelings of those gentlemen are very different now, and before the elections. If you change the mode, they will seize the opportunity, and assert that you have now done what ought originally to have been done. Should the blank not be filled with an adequate sum, say nine or ten dollars a day, he would vote against the passage of the bill, so as to retain the present law; but if it must come to a repeal, he would prefer it to take place after the 4th of March, so as to leave the subject entirely open for the next Congress. Such was the course that he would pursue.

It had more than once been said, that this is not an important subject. If the observation was made in reference to the members who now composed this body, he would readily assent. To them it is a trivial subject. They are free agents, and if they find the sacrifice too considerable, they can at any moment return to those private pursuits, so much more profitable, and in many respects, desirable. We then as individuals, have no right to complain, should the pay be reduced to the smallest amount. But there is another aspect of this subject, of a very different character. The question of adequate, or inadequate pay to the members of Congress, is, if he was not greatly mistaken, intimately connected with the very essence of our liberty. This House is the foundation of the fabric of our liberty. So happy is its constitution, that in all instances of a general nature, its duty and its interest are inseparable. If he understood correctly the structure of our government, the prevailing principle is not so much a balance of power, as a well connected chain of responsibility. That responsibility commenced here, and this House is the centre of its operation. The members are elected for two years only; and at the end of that period, are responsible to their constituents for the faithful discharge of their public duties. Besides, the very structure of the House is admirably calculated to unite interest and duty. The members of Congress have in their individual capacity, no power or prerogative. These attach to the entire body assembled here, and acting under certain set forms. We then as individuals are, said Mr. C. not less amenable to the laws which we enact, than the humblest citizen. Such is the responsibility, such the structure, such the sure foundation of our liberty.

If we turn our attention to what are called the co-ordinate branches of our government, we find them very differently constructed. The Judiciary is in no degree responsible to the people immediately. To Congress, to this body, is the whole of their responsibility. Such too, in a great measure, is the theory of our government, as applied to the Executive branch. It is true the President is elected for a term of years, but that term is twice the length of ours; and, besides, his election is in point of fact, removed in all of the states three degrees from the people; the electors in many of the states are chosen by the state legislatures, and where that is not formally the case, yet it is in point of fact effected through the agency of those bodies. But what mainly distinguishes the legislative and executive branches, as it regards their *actual* responsibility to the people, is the nature of their operation. It is the duty of the former to enact laws, of the latter to execute them. Every citizen of ordinary information, is capable, in a greater or less degree, to form an opinion of the propriety of the law; and consequently to judge whether Congress has or has not done its duty; but of the execution of the laws, they are far less competent to judge. How can the community judge, whether the President, in appointing officers to execute the laws, has in all cases been governed by fair and honest motives, or by favor or corruption? How much less competent is it to judge whether the application of the public money has been made with economy and fidelity, or with waste and corruption! These are facts that can be fully investigated, and brought before the public by Congress, and Congress only. Hence, it is that the Constitution has made the President responsible to Congress. This, then, is the essence of our liberty: Congress is responsible to the people immediately, and the other branches of government are responsible to it. What then becomes of the theory of the government, if the President holds offices in his gift, which, as it regards honor or profit, are more desirable than a seat in this House, the only office immediately in the gift of the people?

Here Mr. C. checked himself. He found himself, he said, committing an unpardonable error, in presenting arguments to this body. The ear of this House on this subject, said he, is sealed against truth and reason. What has produced this magic spell? Instructions! Well then, has it come to this? Have the people of this country snatched the power of deliberation from this body? Have they resolved the government into its original elements, and resumed to themselves their primitive power of legislation? Are we then a body of individual agents, and not a deliberate one without the power, but possessing the form of legislation? If such be the fact, let gentlemen produce their instructions, properly authenticated. Let them name the time and place, at which the people assembled, and deliberated on this question. O no! they have no written, no verbal instructions; but they have implied instructions.[1] The law is unpopular, and they are bound to repeal it, in opposition to their conscience and reason. Have gentlemen reflected on

1. This may be a reference to Clay's remark, *AC*14-2, p. 496.

the consequences of this doctrine? Are we bound in all cases to do what is popular? If it is true, how are political errors, once prevalent, ever to be corrected? Suppose a party to spring up in this country, whose real views were the destruction of liberty; suppose that by management, by the patronage of offices, by the corruption of the press, they should delude the people, and obtain a majority—and surely such a state of things is not impossible—what then will be the effect of this doctrine? Ought we to sit quiet? Ought we to be dumb? Or rather ought we to approbate, though we see that liberty is to be ingulphed?

This doctrine of implied instruction, if I am not mistaken, is a new one, for the first time broached in this House; and if I am not greatly deceived, not more new than dangerous. It is very different in its character and effects, from the old doctrine that the constituents have a right to assemble and formally to instruct the representative; and though I would not hold myself bound to obey any such instructions, yet I conceive that the doctrine is not of a very dangerous character, as the good sense of the people has as yet prevented them from exercising such a right, and will, in all probability, in future prevent them. But this novel doctrine is of a far different character. Such instruction may exist any day and on any subject. It may be always at hand to justify any aberration from political duty. Mr. C. would ask its advocates in what do they differ in their actions, from the mere trimmer, the political weather cock? It is true, the one may have in view his own advancement, in consulting his popularity; and the other may be governed by a mistaken but conscientious regard to duty; yet, how is the country benefited by this difference, since they equally abandon the plain road of truth and reason, to worship at the shrine of this political idol. It was said by a member from Massachusetts (Mr. Conner) that this right of instruction is only denied in monarchies, and, as a proof of it, he cited the opinion of Mr. Burke, whom he called a pensioner, at the Bristol election.[2] So far is he from being correct, that in none of the free governments of antiquity can he point out the least trace of his doctrine. It originated in the modern govern-

2. Samuel S. Conner argued emphatically for the principle of control of the representative by his constituents, and cited Burke "pensioner of the British Crown" as advocate of the doctrine of independence (p. 538).

ments of Europe, particularly that of Great Britain. The English Parliament had, at its origin, no other power or duty, but granting money to the crown; and as the members of that body were frequently urgently pressed to enlarge their money grants, it was a pretty convenient excuse to avoid the squeeze, to say they were not instructed. The gentleman was incorrect in calling Burke a pensioner at the time he delivered the celebrated speech at the Bristol polls. Burke at that time, whatever may have been his subsequent character, was a first rate champion in the cause of liberty and of *this* country; and if the gentleman would recur to the points in which he refused to obey the instructions of his constituents, it will not greatly encrease his affection for such doctrines. That mind must be greatly different from mine, said Mr. C. who can read that speech, and not embrace its doctrines.[3]

I too, said Mr. C. am an advocate for instruction. *I am instructed. The Constitution is my letter of instruction.* Written by the hand of the people, stampt with their authority, it admits of no doubt as to its obligation. Your very acts in opposition to its authority, are null. This is the solemn voice of the people, to which I bow in perfect submission. It is here the vox populi is the vox Dei. This is the all-powerful creative voice which spoke our government into existence, and made us politically as we are. This body is the first orb in the political creation, and stands next in authority to the original creative voice of the people; and any attempt to give a different direction to its movement, from what the Constitution and the deliberate consideration of its members, point out, I consider as an innovation on the principles of our government. This is necessary to make the people really happy; and any one invested with public authority, ought to be as sensibly alive to the people's happiness, as some gentlemen wish the House to be to mere popularity. He knew that such was the structure of our government, that the permanent feeling of the community would impress itself on this House. He rejoiced that such was the fact, as there would be no security for liberty, were it otherwise. The sense of the people, said he, operating fairly and constitutionally through elections, will be felt on this very subject, at the

3. See Prior, *Memoir of . . . Edmund Burke*, p. 165-7.

very next session; but surely the question by whom the repeal is to be effected, is one of no slight importance. It can by our successors, if they think proper, be at least consistently done; by us it cannot. Should we reduce it to the old rates, when it is well known that the sense of a great majority of this House is wholly averse to it, besides the great loss of individual character which we must sustain, it is calculated to bring into suspicion all political characters, to the great injury of the public. You may rely on it, the public wish and expect us to act by the convictions of our mind and will, not to tolerate the idea that either on this or any other important occasion, you are acting a part, and that you studiously shape your conduct to catch the applause of the audience.

Mr. C. said, he hoped he would not be misunderstood; that while he combatted the idea that we are bound to do such acts as will render us popular, for such he understood the doctrine, we are to overlook the characters of those for whom we were to make laws. This was most studiously to be regarded. The laws ought, in all cases, to fit the permanent and settled character of the community. The state of public feeling, then, is a fact to be reasoned upon, and to receive the weight on any particular question to which it may fairly be entitled. But, for his part, he preferred that erectness of mind which, in all cases, felt disposed to embrace what was, in itself, just and wise. Such characters he thought more useful, under our form of government, than any other, and were more certain of the applause of after ages. If he was not mistaken, it constituted the very essence of the admired characters of antiquity, such as Cato, Phocian, and Aristides; and if we could conceive them divested of this trait, they would cease to be the objects of our admiration.

Mr. C. said, taking it for granted that he had succeeded in proving that this House was at liberty to decide on this question according to the dictates of its best judgment: he now would resume the argument where he had dropt it. He had proved that this House is the foundation of our liberty; that it is responsible to the people for the faithful discharge of its duties, and that any other branch of government is responsible to it as the immediate representatives of the people, and that it is essential to the fair operation of the principles of our constitutions, that this body should not be in any degree under the influence of the other branches of the government. How then stood the fact? He begged that no one would attribute to him factious views. He would speak in relation to no particular measure or men. He wished simply to illustrate general principles; to speak to the constituents and the laws. How then, he repeated, is the fact? Are there not in the power of the President a multitude of offices more profitable, and many both more profitable and honorable in public estimation than a seat in this House—the *only office in the general government* in the gift of the *people?* Have we not seen, in many instances, men attracted out of this House to fill subordinate executive offices, whose only temptation was pay; and what is far more dangerous, in every respect much more to be dreaded, do we not see the very best talents of the House, men of the most aspiring characters, anxious to fill the departments on foreign missions? Let me not be understood to throw blame on them—the fault is not so much in them as the system. Congress, then, is only the first step in the flight of honorable distinction. So high the people can raise the aspirant, to go beyond, to rise to the highest, the Executive must take him by the hand. On what side then must his inclination be? On the side of his constituents, who can do no more than to keep him where he is or that of the executive power on whom his future hope must depend? Setting corruption aside, which he believed had made no inroad on us, but take human nature as it is, can you expect, with ordinary virtue, that vigilant and bold oversight over the executive power which the Constitution supposes, and which is necessary to coerce a power possessed of so much *patronage?* He was aware the evil was difficult to be cured. It was the opinion of some, that no member of either House ought to be capable of being appointed to any office for the term for which the President is elected. It is worthy of reflection. For his part, but one objection occurred to him which he could not surmount. He feared, that so long as the executive offices which he had mentioned, continued to be more desirable than a seat in this House, it would tend still further to depress the legislature. The best materials for politics would systematically avoid Congress, and approach executive favour through some other avenue.

Whether this or some other plan be adopted in part, he was confident it was necessary to make a seat in Congress more desirable than what it is even at the present pay. What sum was sufficient for that purpose he stated last year in debate, and had only to regret that the country did not see the same necessity with him on this point. Gentlemen say we ought to come here for pure patriotism and honor. It sounds well; but, if the system be adopted to its full extent, there will be found neither patriotism or honor sufficient for continual privations. We must regard human nature as it is, said Mr. C. and particularly that portion for whom we legislate. Our countrymen, with many admirable qualities, are, in my opinion, greatly distinguished by the love of acquisition, I will not call it avarice, and the love of honorable distinction. He objected to neither of these traits. They both grew necessarily out of the character of our country and institutions. Our population advances beyond that of all countries; marriages in all conditions of life take place at an early period. Hence, the duty imposed on almost every one to make provision for a growing family. Hence, our love of gain, which, in most instances, is founded on the purest virtues. The love of distinction is not less deeply fixed. In a country of such blended qualities, reliance ought not to be had wholly on honor or profit. They ought to be blended in due proportion. The truth is, that no office requiring long continued privations, will be honored, unless duly rewarded, for it ceases to be an object of pursuit. If these views be correct, the effect of an adequate reward is not only to attract talent to the place where it is most needed, the legislature, but you make it more stationary there, and what is more essential, place it more beyond executive control; and thus realize the full effects of the theory of your government. The additional expense would not be felt; and he knew of no other objection, which had the least plausibility, except that we cannot plead the example of any other country, and that it is calculated to produce too much competition for a seat in Congress. He acknowledged the want of example in other countries, and he thought it worth serious investigation, what effect it had had on the permanency of their liberties. But why should we look for examples either to the state legislatures or to other countries? In what other instance has the duties of legislation involved so great a sacrifice of time and domestic pursuits? Compare our services here, with that of a judge, or most executive offices, and they will be found not less burdensome. Nor did he fear, that the competition for a seat in Congress would be too animated. He believed a sharply contested election, if corruption did not enter, was of public advantage. It brings the proceedings of this body more fully before the people, and makes them much better acquainted with their interest. It even makes a seat here more honorable in public estimation. Nor was he afraid that competitions would produce corruption. Fifteen hundred or two thousand dollars a year would not be sufficient for this purpose. An election to Congress was, in this respect, more safe than that to a state legislature; as it requires so many more to elect to the former than the latter. This security grows with the increasing growth of the country; as the number of constituents will, relatively to the representatives, increase.

There were other and important considerations connected with a just pay to the members of this body; but as they had been fairly presented by the report of the committee, he would not fully discuss them. By an inadequate pay, you close the door of public honor on some of the most deserving citizens. Talents in this country are principally from the middling and lower classes. These, in fact, constitute the great body of the community. A young man of talents spends his property and time to acquire sufficient information to pursue a profession. He proves worthy of public confidence; ought he not to receive indemnity for the application of his time and talents to the service of his country? It would be economy with a vengeance to exclude all such from the floor of legislation, or to make them mere political adventurers, who would enter here only for further promotion. The extent of our country said he, points another and powerful reason why the pay should be respectable. No one is fit for legislation, who does not constantly bear in mind that our Republic is distinguished from all other free countries that have ever existed, by the extent of our territory. While we derive from this distinction many advantages, we are liable to great and menacing dangers. While we behold our growth with pride, it must at the same time impress us with awe. It is our duty to overcome space by every effort in our power. We ought to attract suitable talents from the most distant part of our Republic by a full and generous allowance. Distance itself constitutes a great objection to many to perform the duties of this body. Should the men who by nature and study are endowed with requisite qualities for public service, be forced by a miserable parsimony either to direct their talents to private pursuits, or to affairs of the respective states, and men of inferior capacity be sent to this body who can measure the public misfortune? What could tend more powerfully to dissever this union? Some have taken up the idea, as extraordinary as it may seem, that the increased pay to the members is in its nature aristocratical. What, is it aristocratical! to compensate the public servant for his services to the public? Can it be considered as favoring the power of a few to extend the power and influence of the people in the affairs of the general government? It enables them to select the best talents for their own immediate service; it raises them in the scale of influence by causing the most shining and aspiring talents to be dependent on them for promotion and honor. It makes their service more desirable than that of executive employment; and by a simple process enables them through their immediate agents, this House, to hold a controlling power over any department of the government. Such is the aristocratical tendency of this reprobated measure.

Mr. C. said that he might extend his observations much farther on this most important subject; but so much had been well said by others that he would abstain. He must however present to the House a reason which he believed had not as yet been touched on; he meant the happy effect, which an adequate compensation would have on the tone of parties in our country. Make a seat in Congress, what it ought to be, the first post in the community, next to the Presidency, and men of the greatest distinction in any part of the country will seek it. The post then of honor and distinction being in the people, and not in the President, will be open to all parties in proportion to their ascendancy in the Union. That entire monopoly of honor and public profit by the majority will not be experienced, which must be felt, when the honors of the country are principally in the hands of the Chief Magistrate. Those who best understand our nature can the most fully appreciate the consequences. Although it may not abate the heat of party, it will greatly affect their feelings towards our happy political institutions.

147 NOTE: The 1816 compensation law (see No. 127) was
the central point in a storm that was primarily responsible for the
replacement of half the Senate and two-thirds of the House (see
Adams, *History of U.S.*, IX, 134-8, and Wiltse, *Calhoun, Nationalist*,
p. 125). On Dec. 4 Richard M. Johnson, author of the offending
bill, made his indignant protest against the vicious popular reaction
and moved a committee to consider repeal (*AC*14-2, p. 235-43).
On the 18th as chairman he brought in a bill for immediate return
to the per diem basis—but leaving it to the House to fix the rates
(p. 319-20)—together with a report (p. 312-9) which eloquently
defended the law and the claims of the members to higher pay to
maintain the power and the dignity of the legislature.

The debate was now in the House on the amendment of the
Committee of the Whole to restore the old rate of six dollars a day
(p. 574). Calhoun, who had successfully met the fire from his own
constituents (see No. 134), was here speaking first. He vigorously
defended the law, and, pointing out that the old per diem method
had the best chance of running the gauntlet of popular criticism
in the next Congress, urged that the rate be set at the equivalent
of the new law. See No. 148.

In his strictures on the right of constituents to instruct their
representatives he was joined by others, but his significant contribution to the debate was his demonstration of the fact that this was
a blow to the dignity and independence of the House. He proceeded
at once to a searching analysis of its place in the government—his
first since his first month in Congress—and likewise to an analysis
of the American character. Ignoring the Senate—equally involved
in the salary question—he declared the House to be the starting
point in the "chain of responsibility," "the prevailing principle" of
our government. Envisaging the degeneration of the House, he fore-
saw the consequent control of honor and profit in the hands of the
President to the benefit of the majority. Compare the remarks of
Thomas B. Robertson of Louisiana (p. 493-5), and see Adams, *History of U.S.*, IX, 144-6. The dramatic tribute to Calhoun, however,
came from his old opponent Thomas P. Grosvenor of New York:
"Mr. G. said, he had heard with peculiar satisfaction the able,
manly, and Constitutional speech of the honorable gentleman from
South Carolina, (Mr. Calhoun.) [Mr. G. paused a moment, when he
proceeded.] Mr. Speaker, I will not be restrained, no barriers shall
exist which I will not leap over for the purpose of offering to that
gentleman my thanks for the judicious, independent and national
course, which he has pursued in this House for the last two years,
and particularly upon the subject now before us. Let the honorable
gentleman continue with the same manly independence, aloof from
party views, and local prejudices, to pursue the great interests of

his country—and fulfil the high destiny for which it is manifest he was born. The buzz of popular applause may not cheer him on his way, but he will inevitably arrive at a high and happy elevation in the view of his country and the world; and to those who surrender their conscience, their judgment, and their independence, at the shrine of popular caprice and clamor, he shall finally hold the same relation, that the eagle in his towering flight holds to the grovelling buzzard. No gentleman had been bold enough to encounter his argument of yesterday. No gentleman could encounter it without a sure prospect of discomfiture.

"It is unnecessary to add, said Mr. G., that I agree with that gentleman in all his views of the propriety, importance, and necessity of the bill of last session." (AC14-2, p. 621-2.)

See also the comments of Richard H. Wilde of Georgia (p. 601). SOURCE: NI, Jan. 30, 1817; AC14-2, p. 574-82.

148. SECOND SPEECH ON AMENDMENTS TO THE COMPENSATION LAW

January 20, 1817

Mr. Calhoun rose to explain. The member from Massachusetts must surely have misunderstood him in attributing to him the doctrine that the voice of the people is to be disregarded. He knew too well the principles of our government, to entertain such an opinion. It had been asserted, that instructions were obligatory, and that a member might infer instructions from the mere unpopularity of a measure. This he denied. He looked for his instructions to the Constitution. This was the true voice of the people; the other, that which the gentleman sets up, cannot be considered the genuine voice of the people. In fact, he considered an attempt to make it obligatory, as a species of usurpation on the Constitution. Those who go about to please the people this way, may possibly succeed to render themselves popular, but they will not always in making the people happy and great. But, he believed, in this instance, they will not succeed even in popularity. The people like to see consistency and firmness in their public servants; and, if they disapprove of their acts, they would rather change them than to see them act contrary to their own judgment. This is the true remedy for our errors, should we fall into them. There is another course, said he, where it is the misfortune of the representative to differ from his constituents on great occasions, which I think is more manly than the one advocated; I mean for the member to resign. He did not recommend this course; but he would greatly prefer it to voting against the dictates of his conscience. The gentleman asks, said Mr. C. if I would vote for a war against the voice of the people? I, in my turn, would ask the member from Massachusetts, if he would vote for a war which, in his sincere opinion would destroy the country, merely because it happened to be popular? Without waiting for his answer, however, he would reply to the question which the gentleman had proposed. He could scarcely conceive the case that he would vote for a war of a dangerous character, without being certain of the people; but not on the ground of obeying instruction. The reason was plain. The hearty concurrence of the people in such a war, constitutes the principal force of the country. It is as essential as cannon and ball.

148 NOTE: John Tyler, of Virginia, who took his seat in December, on Jan. 18 (*AC*14-2, p. 619-21) spoke vigorously for the principle that the representative was bound by the will of his constituents, and for repeal of the law. On the 20th (p. 649-52) he undertook to reply to the strictures on his doctrine, referring to Grosvenor and Calhoun (No. 147 NOTE), but canvassing chiefly the arguments of the former. He was followed by Conner of Massachusetts (*AC*14-2, p. 652-3) who addressed his remarks entirely to Calhoun, asking: "If a land-tax, an excise, an embargo, or war are proper, levy it, whether the people coincide in its propriety or not? This is a fine theory . . . unfortunately the practice of the honorable gentleman is against it."

After Calhoun spoke Conner replied to him again (p. 654-5), insisting that "as to every purpose of practical expediency, we do and ought to obey the popular voice, where that voice is distinctly and urgently expressed." He stated "that he would by no means be understood to insinuate, that the honorable gentleman from South Carolina was the mere theorist; the nation knew him to be on all important subjects the practical politician; but on this he thought he chose to indulge himself in theoretical speculations. Sir, said Mr. C., no one respects more than myself the manly independence of the honorable gentleman, his extensive political knowledge, and his powers of eloquence. And as to the elegant comparison of the gentleman from New York, (Mr. Grosvenor,) of the eagle with the turkey-buzzard, alluding to the gentleman from South Carolina and those who opposed his doctrine, I can assure that gentleman, that

I am as willing to admit as himself, that the gentleman from South Carolina is the eagle; that he soars in an expanse above vulgar politicians, is certain; that *he* is not the bird that feeds on carrion is still more certain; nor, sir, is he the political gladiator that wields his dagger on all subjects, on all sides, just as caprice, interest, or the whim of the moment may dictate."

Grosvenor was finally able to get his version of the bill adopted—to repeal the compensation law at the close of the session, and to prevent revival of any preceding law, thus forcing the next House to act on the subject (p. 692, 701, 706, 714, 1278). Calhoun voted against it. It was passed in the Senate with a minimum of debate. SOURCE: *NI*, Feb. 18, 1817; AC14-2, p. 653-4.

149. SPEECH ON THE NEUTRALITY BILL

January 25, 1817

Mr. Calhoun expressed in common with other gentlemen his good wishes for the cause of the South American colonies against the mother country; but that such wishes would never influence him to permit a violation of our neutral obligations. The provision under discussion, however, he thought pushed the restrictions further than those obligations required—that he looked on armed vessels as much articles of trade as munitions of war, and he was unwilling to make our citizens answerable for the conduct of those who purchased their vessels. All that could be done, and what appeared necessary, was to require bond of the purchaser that he would not violate the neutrality of this country—further he could not go in legislating on the subject. He alluded to the nature of the contest existing in the Spanish provinces, acknowledged that its analogy to our own situation in '76 enlisted our sympathies—but all that could be expected of us by the patriots was that we, being neutral, should do nothing to weaken their efforts or injure their cause.

[*Randolph and Joseph Hopkinson of Pennsylvania followed with defenses of the bill.*[1]]

Mr. Calhoun said the question was, whether the bill did or did not go further than necessary, to prevent our citizens from taking part in the war between Spain and her colonies. In reply to an argument by Mr. Hopkinson, he said, he still thought to sell vessels

1. AC14-2, p. 747-52.

to either of the belligerents, was no violation of neutrality—and
that a trade in arms and munitions, or in vessels, stood on the same
footing. Spain herself purchased vessels at Havana, for the public
service, and she could not object to an act in others, which she had
done herself. Mr. C. entered somewhat at large into the question
of the legality of permitting the sale of vessels to either belligerent
party, after their departure from the United States, and in his opinion, the trade being legal, he argued that the third section went
further than necessary, in fulfilment of our neutral obligations, by
making the builder or the seller of the vessel, liable for the conduct
of the purchaser. To sell armed vessels in our own ports to a belligerent, he acknowledged would be illegal, but maintained, that
they might be transferred after their departure beyond the jurisdiction of the country.[2] The third section would he thought, operate
oppressively, inasmuch as it made the vendor in our ports, responsible for the illegal conduct of the party purchasing, and in that way
throw burthens on commerce not necessary and injurious. If this
provision were demanded by the neutral duties of the country, it
ought certainly to be resorted to, he said, but not otherwise; but
he thought it ought not to extend its penalties further than to the
conduct of the first purchaser. The experience and superiority of
our ship builders, gave to their work a value which made it more
sought after, and he thought the policy of the country required,
that the profession should be restrained as little as possible. The
law of '94, had contemplated a war between two independent
powers, not one between a mother country and its colonies;[3] and
if the defect of that law could not preserve our neutral character
in the war now existing in the South, he was willing to adopt a
remedy, but he would not go so far as to prohibit the sale of vessels,
while the encouragement of ship building was so important an
object to the country. To shew the hardships which might arise,
from holding the seller responsible for the conduct of the purchasers
of a vessel, Mr. C. supposed the case of a vessel, which being
engaged in the Northwest or China trade, should become unfit to
return home, and be sold, and afterwards converted to purposes

2. Calhoun made a motion, later in the debate, in accordance with this, but
it failed (p. 766).

3. The law of June 5, 1794.

prohibited by the bill in its present shape—to make the first seller of this vessel, responsible for the conduct of the purchasers, would be an act of oppression he could not consent to. He was willing to adopt additional restraints because the Executive had asked for them, but he did not believe any regulations could entirely prohibit the trade proposed to be suppressed.

149 NOTE: On Dec. 26 President Madison requested Congress to strengthen the neutrality laws (*AC*14-2, p. 40), and on Jan. 14 Forsyth, from the Foreign Relations Committee, presented a bill (p. 477-8) providing: Sec. 1, a fine up to $10,000 and imprisonment up to 10 years upon an American citizen knowingly fitting out a vessel for use against a friendly power; Sec. 2, for double bond for armed vessels sailing from American ports; and, Sec. 3, authorizing customs collectors to detain vessels, on reasonable evidence, and to require the bond. In the first day's debate there was much opposition to the strictness of the bill, especially Sec. 3 (Jan. 24, p. 716-45). The bill finally became law on Mar. 3 (p. 1308-10), substantially as reported, with an additional section to prevent increasing the armament of a belligerent ship. Calhoun voted against it (p. 767). SOURCE: *NI*, Jan. 30, 1817; *AC*14-2, p. 747, 752-3.

150. To COL. JOHN E. CALHOUN, Charleston, S.C.

Washington 30th Jan. 1817

Dear John, I received your letter by Mr. [Lagree?] last evening and some time ago another by mail, to which I have not as yet replied. I do not approve of Martin's offer. I would not devide the tract; nor would I take less than six dollars per acre. I think you ought to sell at that price with ease.

James left here for New Orleans by water about two weeks since.[1] He felt a good deal down. I hope he will do well. Let me hear from you. I am &c

            J. C. Calhoun

150 NOTE: See No. 155. SOURCE: *CC.*

1. Midshipman James Edward Colhoun—see No. 156 NOTE.

151. SPEECH ON INTERNAL IMPROVEMENTS

February 4, 1817

Mr. Calhoun rose and observed, that it seemed to be the fate of some measures to be praised, but not adopted. Such, he feared, would be the fate of that on which we are now deliberating. From the indisposition manifested by the House to go into committee on the bill, there was not much prospect of its success; yet it seemed to him, when he reflected how favorable was the present moment, and how confessedly important a good system of roads and canals was to our country, he might reasonably be very sanguine of success. At peace with all the world; abounding in pecuniary means; and, what was of the most importance, and at what he rejoiced, as most favorable to the country, party and sectional feelings immerged in a liberal and enlightened regard to the general concerns of the nation. Such, said he, are the favorable circumstances under which we are now deliberating. Thus situated, to what can we direct our resources and attention more important than internal improvements? What can add more to the wealth, the strength, and the political prosperity of our country? The manner in which facility and cheapness of intercourse, added to the wealth of a nation, had been so often and ably discussed by writers on political economy, that he presumed the House to be perfectly acquainted with the subject. It was sufficient to observe, that every branch of national industry, Agricultural, Manufacturing, and Commercial, was greatly stimulated and rendered by it more productive. The result is, said he, that it tends to diffuse universal opulence. It gives to the interior the advantages possessed by the parts most eligibly situated for trade. It makes the country price, whether in the sale of the raw product, or in the purchase of the articles for consumption, approximate to that of the commercial towns. In fact, if we look into the nature of wealth we will find, that nothing can be more favorable to its growth than good roads and canals. An article, to command a price, must not only be useful, but must be the subject of demand; and the better the means of commercial intercourse, the larger is the sphere of demand.

The truth of these positions, said Mr. C. is obvious; and has been tested by all countries where the experiment has been made. It has particularly been strikingly exemplified in England, and if the result there, in a country so limited and so similar in its products, has been to produce a most uncommon state of opulence, what may we not expect from the same cause in our country, abounding as it does in the greatest variety of products, and presenting the greatest facility for improvements? Let it not be said that internal improvements may be wholly left to the enterprize of the states and of individuals. He knew, he said, that much might justly be expected to be done by them; but in a country so new, and so extensive as ours, there is room enough, said he, for all the general and state governments and individuals, in which to exert their resources. But many of the improvements contemplated, said Mr. C. are on too great a scale for the resources of the states or individuals; and many of such a nature, that the rival jealousy of the states, if left alone, might prevent. They required the resources and the general superintendence of this government to effect and complete them.

But, said Mr. C. there are higher and more powerful considerations why Congress ought to take charge of this subject. If we were only to consider the pecuniary advantages of a good system of roads and canals, it might indeed admit of some doubt whether they ought not to be left wholly to individual exertions; but when we come to consider how intimately the strength and political prosperity of the Republic are connected with this subject, we find the most urgent reasons why we should apply our resources to them. In many respects, no country of equal population and wealth, possesses equal materials of power with ours. The people, in muscular power, in hardy and enterprizing habits, and in a lofty and gallant courage, are surpassed by none. In one respect, and in my opinion, in one only, are we materially weak. We occupy a surface prodigiously great in proportion to our numbers. The common strength is brought to bear with great difficulty on the point that may be menaced by an enemy. It is our duty, then, as far as in the nature of things it can be effected, to counteract this weakness. Good roads and canals judiciously laid out, are the proper remedy. In the recent war, how much did we suffer for the want of them! Besides the tardiness and the consequential inefficacy of our military movements, to what an increased expence was the country put for the article of transportation alone! In the event of another war, the saving in this particular

would go far towards indemnifying us for the expense of constructing the means of transportation.

It is not, however, in this respect only, that roads and canals
add to the strength of the country. Our power of raising revenue,
in war particularly depends, said he, mainly on them. In peace our
revenue depends principally on the imposts; in war this source, in
a great measure, fails, and internal taxes, to a great amount, become
necessary. Unless the means of commercial intercourse are rendered
much more perfect than they now are, we shall never be able in
war to raise the necessary supplies. If taxes were collected in kind;
if, for instance, the farmer and mechanic paid in their surplus produce, then the difficulty would not exist, as, in no country on earth,
is there so great a surplus, in proportion to its population, as in
ours. But such a system of taxes is impossible. They must be paid
in money; and, by the Constitution, must be laid uniformly. What
then is the effect? The taxes are raised in every part of this extensive
country, uniformly; but the expenditure must, in its nature, be
principally confined to the scene of military operations. This drains
the circulating medium from one part, and accumulates it in
another, and perhaps a very distant one. The result, said he, is
obvious. Unless it can return through the operation of trade, the
parts from which the constant drain takes place, must ultimately
be impoverished. Commercial intercourse is the true remedy to
this weakness; and the means by which that is to be effected, are
roads, canals, and the coasting trade. On these, combined with
domestic manufactures, does the monied capacity of this country,
in war, depend. Without them, not only will we be unable to raise
the necessary supplies, but the currency of the country must necessarily fall into the greatest disorder; such as we lately experienced.

But on this subject of national power, what, said Mr. C. can be
more important than a perfect unity in every part, in feelings and
sentiments? And what can tend more powerfully to produce it, than
overcoming the effects of distance? No country, enjoying freedom,
ever occupied any thing like as great an extent of country as this
Republic. One hundred years ago, the most profound philosophers
did not believe it to be even possible. They did not suppose it
possible that a pure republic could exist on as great a scale even
as the Island of Great Britain. What then was considered as

chimerical, said Mr. C. we now have the felicity to enjoy; and, what is most remarkable, such is the happy mould of our government, so well are the state and the general powers blended, that much of our political happiness draws its origin from the extent of our Republic. It has exempted us from the most of the causes which distracted the small republics of antiquity. Let it not however be forgotten; let it, said he, be forever kept in mind, that it exposes us to the greatest of all calamities, next to the loss of liberty, and even to that in its consequence—*disunion.*[1] We are great, and rapidly, he was about to say fearfully, growing. This, said he, is our pride and danger—our weakness and our strength. Little, said Mr. C. does he deserve to be entrusted with the liberties of this people, who does not raise his mind to these truths. We are under the most imperious obligation to counteract every tendency to disunion. The strongest of all cements is, undoubtedly, the wisdom, justice, and, above all, the moderation of this House; yet the great subject on which we are now deliberating, in this respect, deserves the most serious consideration. Whatever, said Mr. C. impedes the intercourse of the extremes with this, the centre of the Republic, weakens the union. The more enlarged the sphere of commercial circulation, the more extended that of social intercourse; the more strongly are we bound together; the more inseparable are our destinies. Those who understand the human heart best, know how powerfully distance tends to break the sympathies of our nature. Nothing, not even dissimilarity of language, tends more to estrange man from man. Let us then, said Mr. C. bind the Republic together with a perfect system of roads and canals. Let us conquer space. It is thus the most distant parts of the republic will be brought within a few days travel of the centre; it is thus that a citizen of the West will read the news of Boston still moist from the press. The mail and the press, said he, are the nerves of the body politic. By them, the slightest impression made on the most remote parts, is communicated to the whole system; and the more perfect the means of transportation, the more rapid and true the vibration. To aid us in this great work, to maintain the integrity of this Republic, we inhabit a country presenting the most admirable advantages.

1. See No. 129, n. 4.

Belted around, as it is, by lakes and oceans, intersected in every direction by bays and rivers, the hand of industry and art is tempted to improvement. So situated, said he, blessed with a form of government at once combining liberty and strength, we may reasonably raise our eyes to a most splendid future, if we only act in a manner worthy of our advantages. If, however, neglecting them, we permit a low, sordid, selfish, and sectional spirit to take possession of this House, this happy scene will vanish. We will divide, and in its consequences will follow misery and despotism.

To legislate for our country, said Mr. C. requires not only the most enlarged views, but a species of self-devotion, not exacted in any other. In a country so extensive, and so various in its interests, what is necessary for the common good, may apparently be opposed to the interest of particular sections. It must be submitted to as the condition of our greatness. But were we a small republic; were we confined to the ten miles square, the selfish instincts of our nature might in most cases be relied on in the management of public affairs.

Such, then, being the obvious advantages of internal improvements, why, said Mr. C. should the House hesitate to commence the system? He understood there were, with some members, constitutional objections. The power of Congress is objected to; first, that they have none to cut a road or canal through a state without its consent—and next, that the public monies can only be appropriated to effect the particular powers enumerated in the Constitution. The first of these objections, said Mr. C. it is plain does not apply to this bill. No particular road or canal is proposed to be cut through any state. The bill simply appropriates money to the general purpose of improving the means of communication. When a bill is introduced to apply the money to a particular object in any state, then, and not till then, will the question be fairly before us. Mr. C. gave no opinion on this point. In fact, he scarcely thought it worth the discussion, since the good sense of the states might be relied on. They will in all cases readily yield their assent. The fear is in a different direction: in a too great a solicitude to obtain an undue share to be expended within their respective limits. In fact, he said he understood that this was not the objection insisted on. It was mainly urged that the Congress can only apply the public money in execution of the enumerated powers. He was no advocate for refined arguments on the Constitution.[2] The instrument was not intended as a thesis for the logician to exercise his ingenuity on. It ought to be construed with plain, good sense; and what can be more express than the Constitution on this very point? The first power delegated to Congress, is comprized in these words: "to lay and collect taxes, duties, imposts and excises; to pay the debts, and provide for the common defence and general welfare of the United States; but all duties, imposts and excises shall be uniform throughout the United States." First—the power is given to lay taxes; next, the objects are enumerated to which the money accruing from the exercise of this power, may be applied—to pay the debts, provide for the defence, and promote the general welfare; and last, the rule for laying the taxes is prescribed—that all duties, imposts and excises shall be uniform. If the framers had intended to limit the use of the money to the powers afterwards enumerated and defined, nothing could be more easy than to have expressed it plainly.

He knew it was the opinion of some, that the words "to pay the debts and provide for the common defence and general welfare," which he had just cited, were not intended to be referred to the power of laying taxes, contained in the first part of the section, but that they are to be understood as distinct and independent powers, granted in general terms; and are [*qualified* [3]] by a more detailed enumeration of powers in the subsequent part of the Constitution. If such were in fact the meaning, surely nothing can be conceived more bungling and awkward than the manner in which the framers have communicated their intention. If it were their intention to make a summary of the powers of Congress in general terms, which were afterwards to be particularly defined and enumerated, they should have told us so plainly and distinctly; and if the words "to pay the debts, and provide for the common defence and general welfare," were intended for this summary, they should have headed the list of our powers, and it

---

2. Congressman Lewis Williams of North Carolina apparently was giving his recollection of this phrase when he remarked on Calhoun's brushing aside subtleties and depending on "first impressions made on his mind when reading the Constitution" (AC14-2, p. 972; see No. 153, n. 1).

3. *NI* reads "gratified." See below, Source.

should have been stated, that to effect these general objects, the following specific powers were granted. He asked the members to read the section with attention, and it would, he conceived, plainly appear that such could not be the intention. The whole section seemed to him to be about taxes. It plainly commenced and ended with it, and nothing could be more strained than to suppose the intermediate words "to pay the debts, and provide for the common defence and general welfare," were to be taken as independent and distinct powers.

Forced, however, as such a construction was, he might admit it, and urge that the words do constitute a part of the enumerated powers. The Constitution, said he, gives to Congress the power to establish post offices and post-roads. He knew the interpretation which was usually given to these words confined our power to that of designating only the post roads; but it seemed to him that the word "establish" comprehended something more. But suppose the Constitution to be silent, said Mr. C. why should we be confined in the application of money to the enumerated powers? There is nothing in the reason of the thing, that he could perceive, why it should be so restricted; and the habitual and uniform practice of the government coincided with his opinion. Our laws are full of instances of money appropriated without any reference to the enumerated powers. We granted by an unanimous vote, or nearly so, 50,000 dollars to the distressed inhabitants of Caraccas, and a very large sum, at two different times, to the Saint Domingo refugees. If we are restricted in the use of our money to the enumerated powers, on what principle, said he, can the purchase of Louisiana be justified? To pass over many other instances, the identical power, which is now the subject of discussion, has in several instances been exercised. To look no further back, at the last session a considerable sum was granted to complete the Cumberland road. In reply to this uniform course of legislation, Mr. C. expected it would be said, that our Constitution was founded on positive and written principles, and not on precedents. He did not deny the position; but he introduced these instances to prove the uniform sense of Congress, and the country, (for they had not been objected to) as to our powers; and surely, said he, they furnish better evidence of the true interpretation of the Constitution than the most refined and subtle arguments.[4]

Let it not be urged, that the construction for which he contended gave a dangerous extent to the powers of Congress. In this point of view, he conceived it to be more safe than the opposite. By giving a reasonable extent to the money power, it exempted from the necessity of giving a strained and forced construction to the other enumerated powers. For instance, he said, if the public money could be applied to the purchase of Louisiana, as he contended, then there was no constitutional difficulty in that purchase; but, if it could not, then were we compelled either to deny that we had the power to purchase, or to strain some of the enumerated powers, to prove our right. It had, for instance, been said, that we had the right to purchase, under the power to admit new states; a construction he would venture to say, far more forced than the one for which he contended. Such are my views, said he, on our right to pass this bill.

He believed that the passage of the bill would not be much endangered by a doubt of the power; as he conceived on that point there were not many who were opposed. The mode is principally objected to. A system it is contended ought to be presented before the money is appropriated. He thought differently. To set apart the fund appeared to him to be naturally the first act; at least he took it to be the only practicable course. A bill filled with details would have but a faint prospect of passing. The enemies to any possible system in detail and those who are opposed in principle, would unite and defeat it. Though he was unwilling to incorporate details in the bill, yet he was not adverse to presenting his views on that point. The first great object was to perfect the communication from Maine to Louisiana. This might be fairly considered as the principal artery of the whole system. The next was the connection of the Lakes with the Hudson River. In a political, commercial and military point of view, few objects could be more important. The next object of chief importance was

4. Pickering thought the commerce clause a better source of authority (AC14-2, p. 858-9, 916; see also p. 878-80). Daniel Sheffey of Virginia accepted this and added the general welfare and defense clauses (p. 886-91), as did Thomas R. Gold (p. 878-80). See Clay's speech for the bill and his remark on the question of its constitutionality (p. 866-8).

to connect all the great commercial points on the Atlantic, Philadelphia, Baltimore, Washington, Richmond, Charleston and Savannah, with the Western States; and finally, to perfect the intercourse between the West and New Orleans. These seem to him to be the great objects. There were others no doubt of great importance which would receive the aid of government. The fund proposed to be set apart in this bill was about 650,000 dollars a year, which was doubtless, too small to effect such great objects of itself; but it would be a good beginning; and he had no doubt when it was once begun, the great work will be finished. If the bill succeeds, at the next session the details can be arranged, and the system commenced. He could not consider those who objected merely to the mode to be very hearty in favor of the system. Every member must know that in all great measures it is necessary to concede something; as it is impossible to make all think alike in the minutiae of the measure who are agreed in principle. A deep conviction of the importance of the thing itself is almost sure to be accompanied with a liberal spirit of concession. The committee who introduced this bill gave it the shape in their opinion the most proper in itself and the most likely to succeed. If it cannot pass in its present form and under the present circumstances, it is certainly very doubtful whether it ever will. He felt a deep solicitude in relation to it. He was anxious that this Congress should have the reputation of it, and he was the more so, on account of the feelings which had been created against it. No body of men in his opinion ever better merited, than this Congress, the confidence of the country. For wisdom, firmness, and industry, it had never been excelled. To its acts he appealed for the truth of his assertions. The country already began to experience the benefit of its foresight and firmness. The diseased state of the currency, which many thought incurable, and most thought could not be healed in so short a time, begins to exhibit symptoms of speedy health. Uninfluenced by any other considerations than love of country and duty, said he, let us add this to the many useful measures already adopted. The money cannot be appropriated to a more exalted use. Every portion of the community, the farmer, mechanic and merchant will feel its good effects; and, what is of the greatest importance, the strength of the community will be augmented, and its political prosperity rendered more secure.

151 NOTE: Calhoun's speech in the Committee of the Whole on his internal improvements bill (No. 142) was the culmination of his career in the House. He dwelt on the increase of wealth that roads and canals would bring, on the service they would render in war, and, repeating phrases from the close of his tariff speech (No. 129), he urged his plan as the remedy against the republic's weakness—its vast area—and against its greatest danger—disunion. He briefly sketched the outline of the proposed system, which was largely that of Gallatin's 1808 report. The question of constitutionality of the bill perplexed him, and in his argument he resorted to the implied powers of Congress. The Committee of the Whole reported the bill after only one day's debate, with an amendment providing that the funds be paid to the states in proportion to their representation in Congress and expended by them on projects designated by that body (AC14-2, p. 866, 868, 870). In the House, on the 6th, the basis of apportionment was again changed to that of the states' representation in the House (p. 874). Calhoun apparently made no objection to this amendment, but when the motion was offered to make the present representation the permanent basis of apportionment, he opposed it as it "would destroy the bill," which was based on the principle of "a community of interest"; the motion was defeated (p. 874-5).

On the same day Timothy Pickering of Massachusetts, who played an important part in the progress of the bill through the House, offered an amendment, partly rephrased by Samuel D. Ingham, of Pennsylvania, and himself (p. 875-6), which was adopted on the 7th (p. 922), and which rewrote portions of the bill. The amendment (No. 142 SOURCE) read as follows: "That the Bonus secured to the United States, by the 'act to incorporate the subscribers to the Bank of the United States' and the dividends which shall arise from their Shares in its capital Stock, during the present term of twenty years for which the proprietors thereof have been incorporated, be and the Same are hereby set apart & pledged as a fund for constructing roads and canals and improving the navigation of water courses; in order to facilitate, promote, & give Security to internal commerce among the Several states, & to render more easy & less expensive, the means and provisions necessary for their common defence.

"Section 2. And be it further enacted, That the monies constituting the Said fund, Shall from time to time be applied in constructing, or to aid in constructing such roads or canals, or in improving the navigation of such water courses or both, in each state, as congress with the assent of such state shall by law direct, and in the manner most conducive to the general welfare. And the proportion of the said monies to be expended on the objects aforesaid, in each State, shall be in the ratio of its representation, at the time of such expenditure, in the most numerous branch of the national legislature."

Pickering seems to have been willing to concede the proviso of the consent of each state, but Calhoun "though extremely anxious to accommodate the bill to the views of others, so as to receive as much support as possible, yet felt himself obliged to object to the modification just made, and moved to restore Mr. Pickering's motion to the shape in which he first moved it." (*AC*14-2, p. 876). The next day he moved the elimination of the words "with the consent of the State," but his motion failed (p. 922).

The New York delegation supplied 24 of the 86 votes finally cast for the bill—only 3 voting against it—and Thomas R. Gold of that state thought Calhoun merited "the thanks of his country" (p. 880). On December 11 preceding, one of his colleagues had presented the petition of DeWitt Clinton and the other commissioners of the state asking help in the construction of the Erie and Champlain canals, and the phrases "Next to the . . . security of the right to self-government," and "the continuance of our Union is essential to our freedom" make an effective parallel to Calhoun's speech (p. 260-5).

On the 8th the bill, as amended by Pickering and with insignificant verbal alterations, passed the House; the final vote was 86 to 84 (p. 934). In the Senate it was reported, without amendment, by that body's Committee on Roads and Canals. The bill passed on the 27th by a vote of 22 to 16, with the apportionment ratio again set at the representation of the state in Congress (p. 109, 112, 185-8). On March 1 the House accepted the Senate amendment (p. 1051-2).

President Madison unexpectedly vetoed the bill on Mar. 3 (p. 1060-1; see 1843 *Life*, p. 21-2; Wiltse, *Calhoun, Nationalist*, p. 137) on the ground that the object of the bill did not lie in the enumerated powers of Congress, nor "within the power to make laws necessary and proper." Only 60 members—Clay, the Speaker, included— voted with Calhoun to override the veto.   SOURCE: *NI*, Feb. 22, 1817; *AC*14-2, p. 851-8. There was also a seven-page pamphlet print (n.p., n.d.), which seems to have been printed from the *National Intelligencer,* but two interesting differences ("restricted" on p. 5 for "gratified" and "system" on p. 6 for "great work") suggest the possibility of an independent printing. It was also printed in Williston, *Eloquence of the U.S.,* III, apparently from the *National Intelligencer* version, and Crallé, II, 186-96, seems to have printed from Williston (note his copying "imports" and "qualified" instead of "imposts" and "gratified"—*Works,* II, 188, 193; *Eloquence,* III, 257, 261).

152. From JOHN TRUMBULL

Washington 10th. Febry. 1817.

Sir I have the honor to acquaint you that in Consequence of the joint resolution of the two Houses of Congress on the Subject of Paintings, I have waited on the President of the United States, who appears to agree with what was suggested in the Senate respecting the Subjects proper to be chosen—and to adopt my Idea of the Size which Should be employd

But it appears that no definite agreement can be made with me on the point which is essential on my part with respect to amount and periods of payment without an appropriation. On this Subject therefore I must again put myself under the ["your" *cancelled*] protection of my friends

I enclose a Copy of what I submitted this morning to the President. The Sum which I propose, you will find is about double what I believe you mentioned in debate as the probable expense—the Sum which you named would be Satisfactory, if the Paintings were to be—6 by 9 feet which gives the principal figures near half the Size of Life—but to admit the figures to be the Size of Life, requires a Surface of 18 by 12. Which is quadruple the other—and therefore I require double the Sum which you named as the probable expense. I enclose Copy of a Letter of M Houdon on the Subject of a proposed Statue of Washington for the City of New York—which will Shew that my demand does not exceed ["I do not require anything beyond" *cancelled*] the custom of Artists in Similar cases

In addition to what I State ["have mentioned" *cancelled*] to have lately recd. from the Academy at N York permit me to mention that Sr. Frances Baring paid me many years ago for a picture of the Sortie of Gibraltar 20 inches by 30, ["the Same Size as those which" *cancelled*] you have seen 500 Guineas—& that for the picture of the Same Subject, 6 by 9 feet I refused 1200.[1]

Mr. West recd. 3000 G.—$14,000 for the picture which he intended for Phila.—which is not so large, as those which I propose for the Capitol & does not contain so many figures—besides which, the figures, & the whole Scene being imaginary. He escapes the enormous difficulty which arises from being fettered by portraits & peculiarities of dress & every accompaniment—to Say nothing of the expense which I have incurred in Collecting these materials partly in Europe partly in America

152 NOTE: On Jan. 22, 1817, Calhoun was appointed chairman of a committee on a joint resolution from the Senate to employ John Trumbull to execute four paintings for the Capitol (*AC*14-2, p. 704); it was introduced in the Senate by James Barbour of Virginia (p. 64). On the 25th Calhoun reported it favorably (p. 746), and on the 27th, when the "models from which the large paintings are to be taken" were exhibited, he, with others, defended it (p. 761-3). The resolution was finally ratified on Feb. 6 (p. 1348). See Sizer, *Autobiography of John Trumbull*, p. 257-9, for Trumbull's notes on the business, and p. 310 for Jefferson's supporting letter to Barbour.   SOURCE: The New-York Historical Society. This letter, unsigned, is apparently a retained draft, and several minor cancellations have been ignored.

153. SPEECH ON THE TRANSFER OF APPROPRIATIONS

February 14, 1817

Mr. Calhoun called the attention of the committee to the correspondence between the Committee of Ways and Means and the acting Secretary of War. It seemed by that correspondence that, besides other instances of transfers of the money appropriated by Congress, from the objects to which it was intended, to some other not contemplated, that the money appropriated to the construction of Arsenals had in part been applied to the repairing of arms and erecting accommodations for the quarter masters. These might be

1. See Sizer, *Autobiography of John Trumbull*, p. 149; it was Sir Thomas Baring.

proper objects of expenditure. This was not the point of his censure. He objected that the money had not been applied to the objects for which it was appropriated. It was a sheer abuse of power; not justified by the existing laws, as lax as they unfortunately are on this point. The law authorises a transfer (under the immediate direction of the President) of the money appropriated, from one object to another object also authorised; and in every instance, in which it is not done by his authority, or in which it is applied to an object not authorised, or where there has been a transfer of appropriation from an object, without there being a surplus of the sum appropriated to that object, he conceived it to be an abuse. The farther we progress in this business, the more apparent is the necessity of abolishing the whole power of transfers. It has and will continue to introduce confusion and abuses in the disbursements of the public money. He regretted that the Committee of Ways and Means had not acted on the resolution, which he introduced on this subject at an early period of the session; and as late as it was, he hoped that they would report before its termination.

Every one, said he, who has been a member of this House, long enough to make the observation, must be struck with the different degree of attention, which an appropriation and a tax bill excites. To the latter there is all attention, while the former excites less than most others; in fact there are few bills that excite less. What produces this difference? It is not because one is less important than the other. If in this respect there is any difference, he conceived that the former was most important. In laying a tax, there might indeed be danger of oppression, but, if the money is well applied, an adequate return is made to the country; but, if the appropriation is made to useless objects, or, what is worse, if the public officers are permitted to abuse their trust, and squander the public money, it is lost to the community. Why then the difference of interest which they excite? It is to be found in a difference of their nature. The people know and feel the amount of taxes. It is generally unpopular to lay them, and popular to repeal. Stimulated by these motives, there are many who are ready to prove their zeal in this particular service; and to move their repeal whenever they can be spared, and even when they cannot without manifest detriment to the public. Very different is the case of the disbursements of the public money. Whether that is done with a due regard to the public interest, or whether it is fairly and honestly applied, are facts that excite in the people far less interest, because they are not so open to public observation. If the member who devoted his labor to the examination of the public accounts, and the correcting of abuses, was as certain to reap the reward of popular favor, as he who moved the repeal of taxes, there would not exist so many abuses as there now are.

If the member from North Carolina (Mr. Williams) really wishes to render the public essential service, let him turn his attention to the bill now before the House; and not to the repealing of the taxes, before he knows whether they can be spared or not.[1] This is the real path of patriotism; and, as the path of duty usually is, rugged and steep. It is in the disbursements of the public money that those dangerous disorders first strike, which finally end in the destruction of liberty. Abuses of this kind cannot be permitted, without endangering the principles of our Constitution. It is in their nature to grow; and what was embezzlement at first becomes right in a few years. It is thus, if tolerated, an interest will grow in favor of abuses, which, from its nature, must ever be opposed to the power and reputation of this House. They who fatten on the public, will be persuaded that by destroying your political weight, they not only render themselves secure in their lawless gain, but that they may be greatly enlarged. Such an interest is ever in favor of the power of a single ruler. Hence is the necessity on our part, as the guardians of the community, to be vigilant, to suppress the first symptoms of abuse. We have the sole power to raise and apply money. It is the sinew of our strength. Not a cent of money ought to be applied, but by our direction, and under our control. How stands the fact? We are told that most extensive and superb stone barracks, sufficient to receive 2000 troops, have, the last

1. Lewis Williams the same day (AC14-2, p. 954) had offered a resolution for repeal of the internal duties. He resented Calhoun's strictures and on the 17th, in the course of a long speech in support of repeal, remarked of Calhoun (p. 972): "That gentleman seems to have a prescriptive right to know and expound the motives of others, when they differ from him in opinion. On many occasions he has intimated that members who differed from him were aiming at popularity!" Williams warned his critic that "such reflections" would be of no avail. Calhoun's reply appears merely a condemnation of making the motion so late in the session (p. 986).

year, been erected near Sackett's Harbor, though not a cent was appropriated to this object. It is even reported to have been done without the consent of the War Department. It is further stated that a military road is constructing from Detroit to Ohio. The barracks and road may be proper; if the soldiers are to be employed on them, it is much better than an idle garrison life. In fact, he knew not how the military can, in peace, be better employed, than in constructing of such roads as may be useful in war. It was not to the thing itself that he objected. He censured the application of the public money to such objects, without ever submitting the question to Congress. It is an evil that cannot be tolerated, unless we are ready to become mere cyphers. These were not the only abuses. There were many, he feared, particularly in the army.

In making these statements, Mr. C. was actuated by no ill will to any one. If it had been his misfortune to feel such, he could not be actuated by it in the discharge of his public duties, without forgetting all his principles. He stated them simply because he thought the best interest of the country required that they should be known and corrected. He could not agree with his friend from Kentucky (Mr. McKee) that all efforts at correcting such abuses, are hopeless. He says it has not been done; and concludes therefore that it cannot. Mr. C. thought differently. There has been nothing like a concentrated and steady effort to effect the cure; nor had the times ever been so propitious. When party spirit is high, it is very difficult to undertake reformations of this kind. Factious views are sure to be attributed, and attributed with success, to the member who attempts it. Happily for us, party spirit has in a great measure disappeared. We have peace not only abroad, but at home. Now then is the moment for this most salutary work. A proper degree of labor and firmness cannot fail of success. Very melancholy indeed would be our situation, if the evil were too inveterate to be cured, but by lopping off the whole strength of the government, as proposed by some.

What then are the means which he proposed? In the first place, Mr. C. conceived it to be indispensible that our appropriations should be made in many respects more specific. He rejoiced to see the Committee of Ways and Means commence this system in the Ordnance Department, and hoped they would extend it to

413

the Quarter-Master's, and to other heads where a general appropriation was now made. But specific appropriations were of no avail, under our present system of transfers. If that power of dispensing with law is to continue, he would be adverse to any estimates, but would put the gross amount of revenue under the direction of the President, to be used as he thought proper. It is then indispensible that the right of transferring, or rather dispensing with appropriation, be repealed, and prohibited. In the next place, the year for the appropriation and for expenditure should coincide. As it now stands, the appropriation is made for the year commencing the 1st of January, and the expenditure, for what is called the fiscal, commencing the 1st of October. The effect is, that we can never, without great labor, compare the appropriation of money to an object, with the expenditure. They both ought, in my opinion, to be made for the fiscal year; and, if we will insist that the accounts of expenditures be fully made up and laid before us early every session, it will of itself do much to reform. But to give the measures full success, we must proceed one step farther. The committees appointed at the last session, on expenditures, must go to the respective officers, and descend into the details. This is indispensible, and it ought to be their duty to report the state of the expenditure fully to this House. He regretted that they had not done so this session. If these steps be pursued, and if the members of this House will turn their displeasure against any officer, from the highest to the lowest, who permits abuses, a great and immediate reform must be the immediate effect. We shall then no longer hear of arrearages, and accounts unsettled for years. Abuses will thus be corrected in the infancy, and the purity of our institutions preserved. He could not give in to the system that to prevent abuses, the taxes must be abolished. He saw no termination to the system, but in an entire prostration of the power of government. In his opinion, our relation to the rest of the world did not admit of that system. We stand alone; all other established governments were entirely dissimilar from ours. We ought to be the strong man armed. We knew not when the whole of our strength might be needed. He was not an alarmist; but in his opinion self defence is the first of political duties. He hoped that peace, moderation and justice would ever be pursued by our councils; and that the fruit would be exemption from war.

But we ought to be prepared for the worst. His policy was to draw freely from the people when the public interest requires it; but to see that the public money be truly, wisely, and economically applied. He could not agree with the member from North Carolina, (Mr. Williams) in dispensing with the internal taxes. Instead of that system, let us maintain them, and apply as much of our revenue as possible to the discharge of the public debts. He was no friend to a debt, large or small. He wished it to be paid off to the last cent, immediately. Behold in England the ultimate effects of a debt accumulating from age to age! A population of the most unparalleled industry, bowed to the dust by the pressure. Let us profit by the example, and, in this moment of peace and prosperity, remove the public burden. Having performed this act of justice to posterity, we then may make reductions in the amount of taxes, both external and internal; and, should it be our misfortune to be involved in hostility, we would find ourselves freed from debt, and with perfect method and economy introduced into our money transactions. Thus happily situated, the full energy of the public power might be executed, and danger be met with a greater prospect of success.

153 NOTE: The House was considering, in the Committee of the Whole, the appropriation bill for the military service. "Some debate took place . . . on the practice . . . of transferring appropriations from one branch of service to another" (*AC*14-2, p. 956). Calhoun's speech is the only one given. On Dec. 30, when he offered a resolution for an inquiry by the Ways and Means Committee on the expediency of repealing the portions of the act of Mar. 3, 1809, allowing the President to make such transfers within the Treasury, War and Navy Departments, he had remarked on the "great evils" resulting, especially in the War Department, and urged the need for "rigid adherence to specific appropriations" (p. 374). The matter seems to have been dropped on receipt of a letter from Secretary of the Treasury Crawford of Jan. 1, 1817, defending the practice (p. 420-1).   SOURCE: *NI*, Feb. 22, 1817; *AC*14-2, p. 956-60.

154. To VIRGIL MAXCY, Annapolis, Md.

Washington 23d. Feb 1817

Dear Maxcy, I thank you much for your last letter. It is on a subject to me very interesting. A well regulated republick, and a good system of farming universally diffused are to me most interesting subjects. To attain each is the summit of my desires. If I can obtain the N. Caro. grape on my return I will frank it to you agreeably to your request. I have never seen the bull grape;[1] but from your discription I am inclined to think it grows in the neighbourhood of Gen. Pickens. If I can obtain it, I will bring some cuttings next fall. I am much engaged as the session is about closing and you must therefore excuse so short a letter in reply to one so long and interesting as your's. My best respects to Mrs. Maxcy.

Your friend

J. C. CALHOUN

If you could obtain for me a complete German gardner, I would esteem it a great favour. Should you find one, and an oppertunity should occur to ship to Charleston to the care of Dr. John Noble King Street, I could easily get him to my farm.

SOURCE: *LC*, Galloway–Maxcy–Markoe Papers.

155. To COL. JOHN E. CALHOUN, Charleston, S.C.

Washington 27th Feb 1817

Dear John, I received your last letter this morning and am glad that you have sold the Barony. I would return by the lower country as you request; but the condition of my family prevents. However it is not necessary as Judge DeSaussure will have to make the tittles. The legal tittle was not transfered to us by our mutual partition. If not too inconvenient you had better go to Columbia and get him to execute the tittles. The portion of the money coming to me you are authorised to receive. I have no objection to make a deduction for prompt payment, provided it does not much exceed legal interest. Should you get the money I wish you to call

1. *I.e.,* a wild grape—perhaps the muscadine, in the lower South often called the "bullace."

on Dr. MacBride and pay him what I owe him. I would not sell the other tract for one cent less than eight dollars; and would even sell at that reluctantly. I will be in Columbia about the 10th or 11th of next month. I would be very glad to meet you there. Should you conclude to meet me, you had better put up at the Stage house, so that we may not miss each other. In much haste

J. C. CALHOUN

155 NOTE: See No. 150. Roberts' Barony, listed in the schedule of lands appended to the will of Senator John Ewing Colhoun (Wills[T] Charleston, 29, p. 445-50), was not a real "barony" but merely one of several tracts bought by John Roberts of London toward the end of the Proprietory regime; this one, of 12,000 acres, was surveyed on the Eastern Branch of the Salkehatchie, in 1735 (Plat, S.C. Archives), and advertised for sale June 5, 1767 (*S.C. and American General Gazette*). May 21, 1820 (*CC*) Calhoun wrote his brother-in-law that "our Saltcatcher debtors have again disapointed us."

For definition of the South Carolina baronies, see *SCHM*, XI (1910), 75-6. SOURCE: *CC*.

156. To MIDSHIPMAN JAMES E. COLHOUN, Frigate Congress, Norfolk, Va.

Bath [S.C.] 27th Octr. 1817

Dear James, It afforded myself, your sister and all of your friends great pleasure to hear of your safe arrival at Norfolk. Your being on board the Congress gave her cruise a great additional interest with us all; and the occasional notice which the papers took of her were read with much avidity. You have indeed been fortunate, both in getting on board of a frigate, and being placed under the command of so accomplished a seaman as Cap Morris. I hope and believe that your personal merit has in some degree contributed to put you in so eligible a situation I called on your Uncle Norris on the subject of remittance, as I know you must feel a considerable anxiety in relation to it. He thinks it unsafe to send by mail as there are so many miscarriages by it; and as it is uncertain whether you would be at Norfolk by the time the remittance might arrive; and therefore thinks it more advisable to send the money by me. I will be at Washington by the first Decr. and you can draw on me for it, or if you can get a furlough come on to Washington. Your sister and the children go with me.[1] [They] have both been unwell but are now better. Our state has been very unhealthy this autum; but no deaths have tak[en] place among your relations; except Col. Calhoun [*and*] General Pickens.[2] The latter died suddenly of an apoplexy in August last. No other changes have occurred. Your mother and Mrs Miller are with us and are both well. Your mother is much hurt that you have not mentioned her in your letter; and she and Mrs. M. desire to be mentioned to you affectionately. As I expect to see you at Washington in a short time I will abstain from writing a long letter. Andrew says he wishes to see you very much; and often talks of your fighting John Bull. Your sister says you must be sure to come to Washington, as she is very anxious to see you. Your Uncle Norris and all of your friends desire to be remembered to you. Give my respect to Capt. Morris. There is none of our naval officers for whom I have a greater esteem. You must exert yourself not to disapoint expectation, which is high in your favour.

Your brother   J. C. CALHOUN

156 NOTE: James Edward Colhoun was appointed midshipman May 30, 1816, furloughed for eight months twice (June 12, 1821, April 23, 1823), commissioned Lieutenant Apr. 28, 1826, and ended his service in the navy with a leave till further orders July 21, 1829 (Dundas, *Calhoun Settlement*). Andrew Norris was Senator Colhoun's executor and presumably his half-brother.   SOURCE: *CC.*

157. To JAMES MONROE

Willington [S.C.] 1st Novr 1817
Dear Sir, By the last mail, I received your favour of the 10th of last month. I am impressed with the importance of the trust which you have tendered to me; and in determining to accept of it, I

1. Anna Maria Calhoun was born Feb. 13, 1817.
2. Joseph Calhoun died Apr. 14; General Pickens, Aug. 1, 1817 (*BDC*).

am governed by a sincere desire to add to the prosperity of the country and the reputation of your administration.

With great esteem I am yours sincerely

JOHN C. CALHOUN

157 NOTE: For Monroe's offer of the appointment as Secretary of War see Wiltse, *Calhoun, Nationalist,* p. 139-41. SOURCE: *LC,* James Monroe Papers.

158. From JAMES EDWARD COLHOUN

U S Frigate Congress. Norfolk. Nov. 10. 1817

Dear Sir I have just received your letter dated the 27th. of Oct. and am gratified to learn, all friends are well. The reported unhealthiness of the State and the death of a number of my acquaintances in Charleston, made me extremely anxious to hear from home.

You said Mother was hurt, because, I did not mention her in my letter; assure her it was because I had written to herself and thought her distant from you: my unhappy temper has sometimes made me undutiful, but I have always been affectionate.

Capt. Sinclair took command of us a few days since; he has orders to prepare the ship for sea. It is reported we are to take commissioners out, to Buenos Ayres. Should that be true, it will employ us some months; our requisitions, are made out for six months. The hope of meriting your esteem and the fear of disappointing the expectations of my friends will stimulate me to improve every opportunity of instruction that offers. No doubt we'll have a pleasant cruise, however the pleasure I anticipated of seeing yourself and family at Washington has made me more indifferent latterly about immediate service, than I was a fortnight after my arrival.

Uncle Norris has acted prudently in not remitting by mail, I think I can manage with what I have, but be sure to write the first mail and devise some plan by which I can receive it on my return, which will probably be, to this place, as Capt. Sinclair resides here.

I presume Mother is in the lower country and will write to her shortly. Tell Sister, Brother and Uncle Norris to write to me. As it is full time, congratulate Mrs. P Noble [1]

Remember me to all friends, kiss Andrew and the little stranger.

Your affectionate Brother

J E Colhoun

Source: *SCL.*

159. To Mrs. Floride Calhoun, Pendleton, S.C.

Chesterter [*Chester*] Ct. house [*S.C.*] 15th Novr 1817

Dear Mother, We arrived here this evening; and as I am certain you would be anxious to hear from us frequently, I cannot admit the opportunity of the Columbia mail going out in the morning without writing. We have thus far meet with not the least accident; and the children stand traveling much better, and are far less troublesome than we expected. The child's health is evidently better; and Andrew's chill to day was not so severe as the preceeding one; tho I think his fever was nearly the same. His appetite seems to be improving. We have made thus far 30 miles a day with ease, both to ourselves and the horses, tho the roads, particularly to day, are much the worst on the whole journey. The horses prove very true, except Jake, in going down hill, where it is very steep, is some times a little unruly. We are much better pleased with Hector as a driver than what we expected to be; in fact Floride's confidence in his driving is completely restored. I hope the children's health will be daily improving and the rest of the journey will prove as safe as the past. Floride joins in expression of affection both to yourself and Mrs. Miller, whose kindness we will long remember. Remember us to John E. the Govr. and all friends.[1]

Your affectionate son

J. C. Calh[oun]

Source: *CC.*

1. Patrick Noble married Elizabeth Bonneau Pickens Sept. 5, 1816. Their first child, Ezekiel Pickens Noble, was born Dec. 2, 1817.
1. John Ewing Colhoun; Gov. Andrew Pickens, Jr.

CALENDAR

〚

This Calendar summarizes Calhoun papers not printed in this volume and lists others not so printed to which reference is made in the editorial notes. (Compare pages xv and xxxiv-xxxviii.) Unless otherwise stated, any action noted was by Calhoun.

The location or source of each paper is cited within brackets at the beginning of the Calendar entry. The symbol *als* (autograph letter signed) indicates a letter written and signed by the same person; *ls* (letter signed) indicates a letter written by one person and signed by another; and *fc* (file copy) indicates a document preserved in the form of a letter-book or clerk's copy. Other abbreviations and symbols used in this Calendar correspond with those used elsewhere in this volume (see pages xxxix-xl).

1802

May 20: [Wills(T) Charleston, 29, p. 445-50] signature as witness to will of Senator John Ewing Colhoun.

1804

May 4: signed bond—see No. 6, n. 2.

1808

Dec. 14: [LC, Carnegie Institution of Washington, Transcript Collection] commission as aide-de-camp to governor with rank of lieutenant colonel; [S.C. Archives, Journal of the Executive] entry recording the appointment.

1812

Jan. 9: further comment on the additional military force bill—see No. 50 NOTE.

Feb. 15: [*SCL, als*] recommending Richard Oneal for appointment as midshipman.

Feb. 20: on the militia bill—see No. 46 NOTE.

Feb. 27: [*AC*12-1, p. 1108-9] opposed postponement of consideration of a report on proposed war taxes.

Apr. 1: [*AC*12-1, p. 1592-3] appealed decision of chair that Randolph could read notes of a conference of Foreign Relations Committee with Secretary of State Monroe, chair upheld; (p. 1594) disputed Randolph's version of Monroe's statement on the embargo —see also No. 59.

Apr. 8: [*AC*12-1, p. 1278, 1619] on motion of Calhoun, the House went into secret session and considered a bill which became law Apr. 14 (p. 2269-70) and prohibited, during the continuance of the embargo, exportation of specie or goods.

Apr. 14: [*NA*, RG233, 12A-B1, MS; the MS redated Apr. 28 for bill of that date] from Foreign Relations Committee introduced a bill making further provision for the army, providing for paymasters and "sub-inspectors," for pay of brigade majors, for drivers for light artillery companies, and for two additional major generals and four additional brigadier generals, and repealing all provision in the army rules act authorizing corporal punishment; after debate it was rejected on the 25th because of the section adding the generals (*AC*12-1, p. 1319, 1324, 1327, 1333-4)—see also Apr. 28 below.

Apr. 15: [*NA*, RG233, 12A-B1, MS] from Foreign Relations Committee presented a bill authorizing departure of ships from U. S. ports "in certain cases," the vessels being those on government service (*AC*12-1, p. 1321, 1323); the bill became law Apr. 27 (p. 2281).

Apr. 25: [*AC*12-1, p. 1335-6] supported a motion to adjourn for a period beginning the 9th of May, not the 29th of April, as there were "several bills" which should first be acted on; the House, however, finally declined to agree to any recess (p. 1341-2, 1352-3).

Apr. 28: [*AC*12-1, p. 1346—see also entry for April 14 above] bill making further provision for the army; re-introduced by Calhoun, with the generals section omitted; it became law on May 16 (p. 2299-2300); provision for two additional brigadier generals and for minor officers was made in an act of July 6 (p. 2361), in a bill introduced by the Military Affairs Committee (p. 1567, 1581). Apr. 28: [*NA*, RG233, 12A-B1, MS] from Foreign Relations Committee introduced (*AC*12-1, p. 1346; see also p. 1376 and 1377-8) a bill to amend the act of Mar. 28 (p. 2257-61) establishing the Quartermaster's Department; bill enacted May 22 (p. 2308-9).

May 6: on Randolph's charge of French influence—see No. 64, n. 3.

June 19: bill for repeal of embargo and specie exportation acts—see No. 69 NOTE.

June 23: [*NA*, RG233, 12A-B1, MS] from Committee of Foreign Relations presented (*AC*12-1, p. 1532) a bill to prohibit exportation of naval and military stores by land or sea to Canada; recommitted on the 27th (p. 1560-1), but reported by Calhoun on the 29th without amendment, it was rejected on the third reading on the 30th (p. 1563, 1568-70); the bill was reconsidered the next day; and on July 2 it was amended and passed (p. 1571-2, 1574) and the title changed to read "to prohibit American vessels from proceeding to, or trading with, the enemies of the United States, and for other purposes" (*House Journal*, p. 414-5); as enacted on the 6th it provided also for heavy penalties for acceptance by American citizens or residents of British licenses for trade with any port (*AC*12-1, p. 2354-6). See No. 85 NOTE.

June 30: [*AC*12-1, p. 1569] comment on bill of June 23.

Dec. 21: [*AC*12-2, p. 436] "Mr. Calhoun spoke at some length in favor of an increase of the Navy on general principles and of even a larger force than was proposed now to be added to the bill." This was in debate on the Senate bill to build 4 seventy-four-gun ships and 6 forty-fours (p. 404); the bill became law Jan. 2, 1813 (p. 1315-6); see also *Federal Republican,* Jan. 1, 1813, for Calhoun's comment on extravagance in the Navy Department.

Dec. 31: [*NA*, RG217, General Accounting Office, *fc*] to Calhoun in regard to 1808 account of Dr. John A. Casey.

1812, n.d.:   [*NA*, Naval Records Collection, Misc. Letters Rec'd., 1812, vol. 2, p. 36] to Paul Hamilton recommending Thomas W. Legge, of Charleston, for lieutenant of Marines.

1813

Jan. 5:   [*NA*, RG15, War Department, Pension Office, Letter Books: General, vol. 3, *fc*] to Calhoun answering his inquiry about pension claims.

Feb. 23, 25, 27:   on the retaliation bill—see No. 79 NOTE.

May 28:   [*SCL, als*] recommending William Calhoun for midshipman.

June 1:   comment on Richards case—see No. 80 NOTE.

June 15:   [*AC*13-1, p. 163] Calhoun defended the executive against the charge of discrimination in the distribution of arms to the militia.

JUNE 16:   [Mass. Historical Society, James Schouler Collection, *als*] to Secretary of the Navy, endorsing application of Mr. Burton.

June 17, 21:   comments on Webster's resolutions—see No. 81 NOTE.

July 7:   [*AC*13-1, p. 396] reported from the Foreign Relations Committee a Senate bill supplementary to the naturalization acts; recommitted on the third reading to another committee, it was amended and on the 19th reported and adopted (p. 433, 465-9). As finally ratified, July 30, 1813, it provided that persons resident in the United States on June 18, 1812, who had previously declared intention to become citizens or who were on that day, by existing laws, eligible for citizenship "may be admitted to become citizens" under process of the existing laws (p. 2738).

Oct. 26:   from Willington, S.C., to George Bowie—see No. 86 NOTE.

Dec. 22:   from N. A. Ware—see second entry for Jan. 25, 1814.

Dec. 30:   [*AC*13-2, p. 817] on bill authorizing a subscription to stock of the Chesapeake and Delaware Canal Co., an amendment to include the Rariton and Delaware Canal, Calhoun "expressed a doubt as to the propriety of the location of these canals in reference to a connected chain of inland communication from North to South. . . . He was not opposed to the object of the bill." Feb. 17, following, a similar bill was introduced in the Senate (p. 635), but did not pass (p. 723); see also p. 813, 822, 844, 1696, 1767, and 1881 for Va., N.C., S.C., and Ga. petitions for federal aid for "an inland water communication" from the Chesapeake to the St. Mary's River; Calhoun was appointed fourth on a committee on one of these (p. 1767).

1814

Jan. 7: [AC13-2, p. 867] moved to table a resolution by Thomas P. Grosvenor for inquiry into rules for furloughs for army officers, contending that the Northwest frontier was endangered by these leaves; Calhoun opposed the resolution as being impracticable; his motion carried (p. 870-1).

Jan. 13: [AC13-2, p. 928] Calhoun, "observing that, as the Russian mediation was at an end, there could be no objection to calling for papers" thereon, presented a resolution asking the President for them. The papers were sent, in the form of a report by Monroe, on the 18th (p. 2087-96). Jan. 13: [AC13-2, p. 930-1] William Lowndes, of South Carolina, moved to amend the bill to encourage enlistments (see No. 90 NOTE) by raising the bounty; Calhoun supported the amendment—which was adopted—as preferable to a raise in pay.

Jan. 17: [AC13-2, p. 1012] Calhoun's motion that the resolution (p. 1010) of William Reed of Massachusetts to inquire into economies effected in the navy be tabled was adopted; however, he declared his belief that the inquiry was friendly.

Jan. 21: [AC13-2, p. 1097-9] twice spoke briefly for a motion tabling a resolution (p. 1095) for a committee to consider introducing an expatriation bill lest such a move impede the pending negotiations with Great Britain; the motion carried.

Jan. 24: [AC13-2, p. 1127-8] Lyman Law of Connecticut having moved an inquiry (p. 1123-5) to relieve the citizens of New London of the reports that they were responsible for the "blue light" signals to guide the enemy, Calhoun thought the subject "too diminutive" for consideration and denied that anyone had been "cruel enough" to charge the citizens with such an act; the motion was tabled (p. 1128). Jan. 24: [AC13-2, p. 1131] Calhoun spoke for the bill "prohibiting the delivery of libelled merchandise on bonds to the owners," pending trial.

Jan. 25: [AC13-2, p. 1141] a resolution (p. 1140-1) having been offered for an inquiry into expediency of indemnifying persons on the Niagara frontier for depredations by the enemy, Calhoun "observed that this motion embraced a novel principle" and, to give time for reflection, moved that it be tabled; the motion passed. Jan. 25: [Carter, *Territorial Papers of the U. S.*, VI, p. 417] to Secretary of State recommending Nathaniel A. Ware, "a particular friend of mine," and enclosing letter of Ware (Natchez, Miss., Dec. 22, 1813) to him.

Feb. 4: [*LC*, Gideon Welles Papers, Vol. 1, *als*] from Benjamin Tallmadge, signed also by Calhoun, to William Jones, Secretary of the Navy, recommending William R. Lord of Litchfield for appointment as midshipman.

Feb. 7: [*NA*, RG28, Records of the Postmaster General, Outgoing correspondence] from G[ideon] G[ranger] on "Mr W Calhouns" inquiry on postal service in South Carolina.

Apr. 4: [*NA*, RG233, 13A-B1, MS] "A Bill to prohibit the exportation of specie, gold or silver coin or bullion" was recommended by the President in his Mar. 31 message (AC13-2, p. 694) and reported by Calhoun with his embargo report (No. 96 NOTE); in debate Calhoun expressed his doubt that export of bullion could be prevented (Apr. 12, p. 2012-3). The bill was postponed indefinitely on the third reading (p. 2017-8). Apr. 4: [AC13-2, p. 1948-9] on the ground that repeal of the embargo would make consideration unnecessary, Calhoun successfully opposed a motion to have the Senate bill (p. 1229) to prohibit importation of certain woolen goods and cane spirits (referred to Foreign Relations Committee) considered with the bill to repeal the embargo.

Apr. 6: amendment to embargo repeal bill—see No. 96, n. 1.

Apr. 12: see first entry for Apr. 4 above.

June 15: [Historical Society of Pa., Dreer Collection, *als*] to James Monroe, recommending Abner J. Lipscomb for District Attorney for Mississippi Territory; optimism in regard to the war despite the turn of affairs in Europe—"from the good sense and virtue evinced by the country nothing disastrous is to be feared."

Nov. 19, 25, 28: on the bank bill—see No. 106 NOTE.

Dec. 22: on the militia bill—see No. 107, n. 1.

Dec. 23: from James Monroe—see No. 103 NOTE.

1815

June 17: endorsement of Isaac Harby—see No. 116 NOTE.

Sept. 22: [Univ. of N.C., Southern Historical Collection, Univ. of N.C. Papers, *als*] to John Haywood, Raleigh, N.C., from Edgefield Court House, S.C., on behalf of John Lyon, in regard to an estate debt due the University of N.C. and recommending Eldred Simkins and George McDuffie "as faithful and able attornies at law."

Dec. 20: [*SCL, als*] to B. W. Crowninshield (signed by four other S. C. Congressmen) recommending Dr. William Butler.

Dec. 23: [*NA*, RG28, Records of the Postmaster General, Outgoing correspondence] from R[eturn] J. Meigs about service of "Mr. Waddle" [Moses Waddel?] as Postmaster at Willington, S.C.

Dec. 24: from A. J. Dallas quoting Calhoun's letter of Dec. 23—see No. 120 NOTE.

1816

Jan. 31: on application of Isaac Harby—see No. 116 NOTE.

Feb. 29: on the bank bill—see No. 126 NOTE.

Mar. 1, 13: on the bank bill—see No. 120, n. 3, and No. 128 NOTE.

Mar. 19: letter from A. J. Dallas—see No. 130 NOTE.

Mar. 20: [*NA*, RG233, 14A-B1, MS] from Committee on the National Currency reported (*AC*14-1, p. 1229) a bill to regulate the currency of foreign gold and silver coins, setting the value of the British and Portuguese coins at 27 grains to the dollar, the French at 27½, the Spanish at 28½, and the French crowns and five-franc pieces at $1.176 and $1.16 per ounce, respectively; ratified Apr. 29 (p. 1886).

Mar. 23, 25:   on the tariff—see No. 129 NOTE.

Apr. 4, 5:   on the bank bill—see No. 128 NOTE.

Apr. 6:   specie payment bill—see No. 130 NOTE.

Apr. 8:   on the tariff—see No. 129 NOTE.

Apr. c. 10:   *Letter to Mr. Calhoun*—see No. 130 NOTE.

Apr. 11, 12:   specie payment bill—see No. 130 NOTE.

Apr. 13 [*NA*, RG233, 14A-C17.5, MS] from Committee on the National Currency reported (*AC*14-1, p. 1365) a resolution "that it is inexpedient to prohibit the exportation of bullion or specie at the present time."

Apr. 18, 22, 26:   on specie payment bill and resolutions—see No. 131 NOTE.

Apr. 30:   [*NA*, RG45, Naval Records Collection, *als*] to B. W. Crowninshield (signed also by three other S. C. Congressmen) recommending transfer of Dr. [William] Butler to the *Washington*.

Dec. 11:   [*NA*, RG45, Naval Records Collection, *fc*] from B. W. Crowninshield, enclosing an order for Edward P. Postell.

Dec. 13:   [Historical Society of Pa., *als*] recommending Federal Judge Buckner Thurston for appointment as director if a branch of the Bank of the United States were established in Washington.

Dec. 17:   [*NA*, RG107, Records of the Office of the Secretary of War, Letters Rec'd., Unregistered Series, *als*] to G[eorge] Graham, inquiry for Wilson Whartley.

Dec. 24:   [*NA*, RG45, Naval Records Collection, *fc*] from B. W. Crowninshield, sending "copy of letter of appointment" sent to Midshipman James E. Colhoun in June last.

Dec. 26:   [*AC*14-2, p. 365] on Calhoun's motion, resolution in regard to Chickasaw lands in Kentucky tabled.

Dec. 30:   on transfer of appropriations—see No. 153 NOTE.

1816 n.d.: [Anderson Galleries Catalog, Mar. 27, 1916; original not found] to W. W. Bibb—lack of talented Republican leadership, as compared with Federalist, in Senate.

1817

Jan. 9: to James Lloyd, and his reply, on specie payments—see No. 146.

Feb. 6, 7: on internal improvements bill—see No. 151 NOTE. Feb. 6, 12, 17, 21: [*NA,* RG217, General Accounting Office, *fc*] to Calhoun about the claims of Reuben Nash and Dr. John Miller, Dr. Casey, Corporal Sample, John Bell, and Thomas Mayo.

Nov. 12: [*SCL, als*] to [Andrew Pickens, Jr.], legal opinion on division of Ezekiel Pickens' estate among his children—see No. 86 NOTE.

Nov. 24, 28: [*NA,* RG107, Records of the Office of the Secretary of War, Letters Rec'd., Registered Series, *ls* and *als*], from Daniel D. Tompkins, congratulating Calhoun on "appointment to the Department of War" and endorsing complaints by army chaplain Cave Jones; and (Nov. 28) from Jones, stating his complaints.

Dec. 6: [*LC,* Gideon Welles Papers, Vol. 2, *ls*] from Daniel D. Tompkins recommending George D. Brewerton as second lieutenant.

GENEALOGICAL TABLE

◻

This table has been prepared for the benefit of readers who find the interrelationships within the Calhoun, Noble, and Pickens families confusing. No attempt has been made to make this a complete genealogy of these families. Included are chiefly those members of the families who are mentioned elsewhere in this volume. But to this rule there is one exception: all of the children of John C. Calhoun are enumerated, whether their names appear in these pages or not.

The children of Patrick Calhoun and Catherine Montgomery are assigned Roman numerals in the order of their respective births. The Arabic numerals used for his descendants follow the same principle.

The information embodied in this table has been drawn from the following four sources: the Calhoun Family Bible at Fort Hill, Clemson, S. C.; Lewin Dwinell McPherson, compiler, *Calhoun, Hamilton, Baskin, and Related Families* (n.p., c. 1957); *The Pendleton, [S. C.], Messenger,* April 29, 1836; *SCHM,* VII (1906), p. 81-98, 153-69, and LIII (1952), p. 51-3.

Parents	Children
Patrick Calhoun (emigrant from Ireland to Pennsylvania) m. in Ireland, Catherine Montgomery (1683/4-1760) d. in Pennsylvania 1741	I. Mary (b. 1714) II. James (1716-1760) III. Ezekiel (1720-1762) IV. William (b. 1723) V. Patrick (1727-1796)

Parents	Children

I. Mary Calhoun
    m. c. 1730-31 John Noble (d. 1752)
	1. Alexander (1733-1802)
	    and four others

I-1. Alexander Noble
    m. 1768 Catherine Calhoun (III-3)
	1. John (1769-1819)
	2. Ezekiel (1774-1832)
	3. Patrick (1787-1840)
	4. Alexander (d. 1821)
	    and three others

I-1-3. Patrick Noble
    m. 1816 Elizabeth Bonneau
    Pickens (III-1-1-2)
	1. Ezekiel Pickens (1817-1891)
	    and six others

III. Ezekiel Calhoun
    m. c. 1742 Jane Ewing
	1. Rebecca (1745-1814)
	2. John Ewing (1750-1802)
	3. Catherine (1752-1803)
	    and four others

III-1. Rebecca Calhoun
    m. 1765 Andrew Pickens
    (1739-1817)
	1. Ezekiel (1768-1813)
	2. Margaret (1777-1830)
	3. Andrew (1779-1838)
	    and ten others

III-1-1. Ezekiel Pickens
    m. 1793 Elizabeth Bonneau
    (1764-1806?)
    m. 2d. 1807 Elizabeth Barksdale
    (1782-1859)
	1. Ezekiel (1794-1860)
	2. Elizabeth Bonneau (1797-
	    1834) and two others
	
	Three children

III-1-2. Margaret Pickens m. George Bowie (b. c. 1771)	

III-1-3. Andrew Pickens
    m. 1804 Susan Wilkinson
    (1788-1810)
	1. Francis Wilkinson
	    (1805-1869)
	2. Susan Calhoun
	    (1808-1878)

Parents	Children
III-2. John Ewing Colhoun m. 1786 Floride Bonneau (1765-1836)	1. John Ewing (b. 1791) 2. Floride (1792-1866) 3. James Edward (1798-1889) and three others
IV. William Calhoun m. Agnes Long (b. 1733)	1. Joseph (1750-1817) 2. Ezekiel (b. 1770) and eight others
V. Patrick Calhoun m. 2d. 1770 Martha Caldwell (1750-1801)	1. Catherine (1775-1796) 2. William (1776-1840) 3. James (1779-1843) 4. John Caldwell (1782-1850) 5. Patrick (1784-1840)
V-1. Catherine Calhoun m. 1795 Moses Waddel (1770-1840)	
V-2. William Calhoun m. 1805 Catherine Jenner deGraffenreid (1786-1829)	1. Tscharner (1806-1840) and ten others
V-3. James Calhoun m. 1802 Sara Caldwell Martin (d. 1845)	Eight children
V-4. John Caldwell Calhoun m. 1811 Floride Colhoun (III-2-2)	1. Andrew Pickens (1812-1865) 2. Floride (1814-1815) 3. Jane (1816-1816?) 4. Anna Maria (1817-1875) 5. Elizabeth (1819-1820) 6. Patrick (1821-1858) 7. John Caldwell (1823-1855) 8. Martha Cornelia (1824-1857) 9. James Edward (1826-1861) 10. William Lowndes (1829-1858)

Parents	Children

V-5. Patrick Calhoun
  m. 1803 Nancy Needham
    deGraffenreid (1787-1841)
	Six children

BIBLIOGRAPHY

▯

Acts and Resolutions of the General Assembly of the State of South Carolina Passed in December, 1808. Columbia. 1809.

Adams, Henry. *History of the United States of America during the Administrations of Thomas Jefferson and James Madison.* 9 vols. New York. 1889-91.

Appletons' Cyclopaedia of American Biography. James Grant Wilson and John Fiske, eds. 6 vols. New York. 1888-9.

Baldwin, Ebenezer. *Annals of Yale College.* 2nd edition. New Haven. 1838.

Bassett, John Spencer, ed. *Correspondence of Andrew Jackson.* 7 vols. Washington. 1926-35.

Bemis, Samuel Flagg. *A Diplomatic History of the United States.* 4th edition. New York. 1955.

Benton, Thomas H. *Thirty Years' View.* 2 vols. New York. 1854-56.

Brackett, Richard Newman. *The Old Stone Church, Oconee County, South Carolina.* Columbia. 1905.

Brant, Irving. *James Madison, President, 1809-1812.* Indianapolis. 1956.

Briggs, Isaac. *Statements . . . Addressed to Thomas Newton, Chairman of the Committee of Commerce and Manufactures.* Washington. 1816.

Carter, C. E., ed. *The Territorial Papers of the United States.* 18 vols. Washington. 1934-52.

Catterall, Ralph C. H. *Second Bank of the United States.* Chicago. 1903.

Coit, Margaret L. *John C. Calhoun, American Portrait.* Boston. 1950.

Cooper, Thomas, and David J. McCord. *The Statutes at Large of South Carolina.* 10 vols. Columbia. 1836-41.

Cross, Wilbur L. *Connecticut Yankee.* New Haven. 1943.

Dalcho, Frederick. *Historical Account of the Protestant Episcopal Church in South Carolina.* Charleston. 1820.

Debates . . . in the House of Representatives of South Carolina, on the Constitution Framed for the United States . . . . Charleston. 1831.

Directory for the District of Charleston, The. Charleston. 1809.

Drayton, John. *A View of South-Carolina as Respects Her Natural and Civil Concerns.* Charleston. 1802.

Dundas, F. deSales. *Calhoun Settlement, District of Abbeville, S.C.* n.p. [c. 1949.]

Easterby, James Harold. *Basic Documents of South Carolina: The Constitution of 1778.* Columbia. 1953.

Fisher, George P. *Life of Benjamin Silliman.* 2 vols. New York. 1866.

Hamilton, Stanislaus Murray, ed. *Writings of James Monroe.* 7 vols. New York. 1898-1903.

Heitman, Francis Bernard. *Historical Register and Dictionary of the United States Army.* 2 vols. Washington. 1903.

Howe, George. *Presbyterian Church in South Carolina.* 2 vols. Columbia. 1870, 1883.

Jameson, J. Franklin, ed. *Correspondence of John C. Calhoun* (*AHAAR*, 1899, II. Washington. 1900).

Latimer, Margaret K. "South Carolina—a Protagonist of the War of 1812," in *AHR*, LXI (July, 1956), p. 914-29.

Letter to . . . Mr. Calhoun, Chairman of the Committee on a National Currency, A. Philadelphia. 1816.

MacDonald, John. *Rules and Regulations for the Field Exercise and Manoeuvres of the French Infantry.* 2 vols. London. 1803.

Madison, James, Alexander Hamilton, and John Jay. *The Federalist.* University edition. New York. 1864.

Meigs, William M. *Life of John Caldwell Calhoun.* 2 vols. New York. 1917.

Meriwether, R. L. *Expansion of South Carolina, 1729-65.* Kingsport. 1940.

Mills, Robert. *Atlas of . . . South Carolina.* Baltimore. 1825.

Mr. Calhoun's Speech on the Loan Bill . . . February, 1814. Printed by Rapine and Elliot. Washington. [1814.]

Moragne, Mary E. *The Neglected Thread: A Journal from the Calhoun Community, 1836-1846.* Delle Mullen Craven, ed. Columbia. 1951.

Morse, Jedidiah. *American Geography.* Elizabethtown. 1789.

Niles' Weekly Register. Baltimore. 1811-49.

O'Neall, John Belton. *Biographical Sketches of the Bench and Bar of South Carolina.* 2 vols. Charleston. 1859.

Oppenheim, Samuel. *Early Congressional Debates and Reporters.* New York. 1889.

Peters, Richard, ed. *The Public Statutes at Large of the United States of America,* II. Boston. 1848.

Prior, Sir James. *Memoir of . . . Edmund Burke.* London. 1839.

Ravenel, Mrs. St. Julien. *Life and Times of William Lowndes of South Carolina, 1782-1822.* Boston. 1901.

Salley, A. S. "The Calhoun Family of South Carolina" (*SCHM,* VII [1906], p. 81-98, 153-69.

Scott, Winfield. *Memoirs of Lieut.-General Scott.* 2 vols. New York. 1864.

Sizer, Theodore. *Autobiography of Colonel John Trumbull.* New Haven. 1953.

Speeches of Messrs. Calhoun and Grosvenor, upon Mr. Webster's Resolutions, The. Charleston. 1813.

Starke, W. Pinkney. "Account of Calhoun's Early Life, Abridged from the Manuscript," in J. Franklin Jameson, ed., *Correspondence of John C. Calhoun (AHAAR,* 1899, II. Washington. 1900), p. 65-89.

Stokes, Anson Phelps. *Memorials of Eminent Yale Men.* 2 vols. New Haven. 1914.

Vattel, Emmerich de. *Law of Nations.* New York. 1796.

Waddel, John Newton. *Memorials of the Academic Life.* Richmond. 1891.

Wallace, Cranmore. *Sketch of the Life and Character of Bishop Gadsden.* New Haven. 1853.

Wallace, David Duncan. *History of South Carolina.* 4 vols. New York. 1934.

Walters, Raymond, Jr. *Alexander James Dallas.* Philadelphia. 1943.

Williston, Ebenezer Bancroft. *Eloquence of the United States.* 4 vols. New York. 1829.

Wiltse, Charles M. *John C. Calhoun.* 3 vols.: *Nationalist, 1782-1828; Nullifier, 1829-1839; Sectionalist, 1840-1850.* Indianapolis. 1944, 1949, 1951.

[Yale] *College Catalogue* . . . . 1809.

Zimmerman, James Fulton. *Impressment of American Seamen.* New York. 1925.

INDEX

◫

All numbers (except those obviously used for dates and other purposes) refer to pages, not to the 159 numbered documents in this volume. Usually, misspellings in the text are corrected without any special indication to that effect. Christian names, titles, and other identifications have usually been added when they were ascertainable; when they were not, John C. Calhoun's incomplete form of reference to a person has been reproduced in this index without other change than the addition of a blank line.

Calhoun's correspondence with any person or office is the first topical subdivision for the index entry for each such person or office. The word "letter" indicates an extant letter to or from Calhoun that has been printed or calendared in this volume; when the word is used without a modifier, it signifies a personal letter. "Answer from" indicates an extant, official reply to Calhoun as a Congressman. "Writes to" and "correspondence with" indicate mentions of personal letters that have not been located.

Entries in the Calendar that, for chronological completeness, merely repeat references made in the body of the book have not been given their Calendar page numbers, which would constitute meaningless duplication.

When the name of a state appears in parentheses after the name of a person, it indicates that the person was a member of the United States House of Representatives from the mentioned state. Three committees of the House are designated by the following abbreviations: FRC, Foreign Relations Committee; UNCC, Unified National Currency Committee; W&MC, Ways and Means Committee. An "n" appearing in connection with a page number refers to either an editorial NOTE or to a footnote appearing on that page;

439

but an "n" is not so used in the few instances in which an editorial NOTE fills the entire page. The abbreviation "JCC" indicates John Caldwell Calhoun (1782-1850).

Abbeville County, S.C., JCC's address, 365, 369. *See also* Bath; Willington.

Abbeville Courthouse and District, S.C.: xxviii, 95, 126, 274; Waddel's school in, 4n; Calhoun family home, 4n, 4, 6n, 18, 21, 26, 32, 51, 61, 63, 89; JCC on climate, health, and character of, 18, 26, 27, 32-3, 38, 44, 45, 47, 49, 57, 61; JCC at (for law studies and practice), 32, 37, 39, 42, 43, 45, 46, 48, 49, 50, 51, 51n, 53, 54, 55, 56, 57; JCC's popularity in, 37n; JCC praises, 38, 53; JCC represents, xxvi, xxvi n, 40n.

Abbeville District Meeting on *Chesapeake* Affair, xxv, 34-7n.

Adams, John, and relations with England, 318.

Admiralty courts, British: and *Essex* case, 113, 113n; and Orders in Council, 223-4.

Agriculture, U.S., JCC on: harmed by war and restrictive system, 132, 349-50; stimulated by internal improvements, 398, 406. *See also* Calhoun, John Caldwell, PERSONAL, Finances.

Albany, N.Y., petition for embargo repeal, 102-8 *passim*.

Albatross (sloop), 4.

Alexander I of Russia, 246, 376.

Alexandria, D.C., 98n.

American Revolution: and S.C., xxiii-xxiv, 26n, 133; JCC on, 36, 81, 82, 133, 156, 196, 202, 334, 395; JCC compares War of 1812 to, xxvii, 36, 67-8, 121-2n, 156, 258-9; invasion of Canada in, 82, 193; British naval policy in, 116, 215; and Armed Neutrality, 221, 222, 226, 240n.

Anderson, Mr. ———, Jr., 14.

Anderson, Jane Harris Reese (Mrs. Robert Anderson, Sr.), treatment of her stepson, 33.

Anderson, Gen. Robert, 33.

Anderson, Robert, Jr., 14(?), 33.

Annapolis, Md., 101, 416.

Appropriations, JCC on: and Jay's Treaty, 305; his speech and resolution on transfer of, 410-5n.

Archer, Stevenson (Md.), 203, 203n.

Armed Neutrality, 221, 222; JCC hopes for another, 226, 240n, 254, 258.

Armstrong, John: U.S. minister to France, 119, 171, 176; Secretary of War, 147n, 149, 149n, 162.

Army, U.S.:

In War of 1812: bills and resolutions for increase of, 68, 69n-71n, 87-8n, 149, 153, 161n, 175n, 200n, 201n, 208n, 229, 232-3, 261-2n, 271-3n, 422, 423; JCC's support of, 76, 81, 81n, 88n, 152, 185, 255-7, 260; JCC on Randolph's resolution for, 89, 89n; recruiting, 93, 95; JCC's comments and resolutions on supply and discipline, 253, 262-3n, 273, 273n, 326, 425; JCC on improvement in and victories of Brown, Jackson, Scott, xxviii, 257, 258, 261, 261n, 263, 263n, 274-5, 277, 288, 288n, 319, 322, 324. For defeats *see* War of 1812, Campaigns.

Peacetime: JCC's support for, 276-9, 316-27 *passim*, 330n; bill for peace establishment, 277-8, 279; bill for additional military academies, 287-90n; JCC's resolution and speech on transfer of appropriations for, 410-5n.

Army, U.S. (continued)
JCC on officers of: from S.C., 90, 91, 93, 96, 260; advantage of service for political career, 96; source of best, 287-8.
See also Militia, U.S.; War Department.
Asby, Thomas, 33.
Asheville, N.C., 177, 178n.
Augusta, Ga., 283, 362, 365, 370.
Austria, 23.

Backus, Rev. Azel, 19, 19n, 20; JCC's opinion of, 22.
Baldwin, Abraham, 10.
Baltimore, Md., 75n, 96, 102n, 406; American victory at, 319.
Banister, Mrs. ———, 57.
Bank of North America, 333.
Bank of Washington, 340.
Banks, national:
First U.S. (1791), as model for second, xxxi, 205n, 266n, 303n.
Proposals (1813-1815): by N.Y. petition, 204, 204n; by JCC, xxx, 204-5n; by Taylor's bill, 205n, 266n; by Dallas, xxx, 259n, 265n-6n, 275, 275n; by Fisk's bill for and debate on, 263-71n; Senate bills for, 275n.
Second U.S. (1816): bill for, provisions, and amendments, xxxi, 290-304n, 340n-7n *passim;* bonus of, 302, 304n, 346n, 370-1, 372, 407-8; debate on, 331-43, 345-7n, 357n; success of, 361, 367-8; control by Congress, 379-80; JCC's letter of recommendation to, 428. *See also* Specie payment.
Banks, state: and inflation, 334-7, 340-2; and specie payment, 357-60n *passim,* 380n.
Barbour, James, Senator from Va., 410n.
Barbour, Philip P. (Va.), 306, 306n; supports JCC, 377, 377n.
Baring, Sir Thomas (erroneously called Sir Francis), 409-10n.
Barksdale, Elizabeth, 33, 33n, 183n, 432.

Barlow, Joel, U.S. minister to France, 171, 175n, 176.
Barrel, James, letter of recommendation to, 365.
Bassano, Duc de, French Foreign Minister, 170, 171, 175n, 176.
Bath (Abbeville County), S.C., JCC's home, 51n, 182, 182n, 283, 360, 361, 365, 417. *See also* Willington.
Bell, John, answers for, 429.
Benson, Egbert (N.Y.), 180.
Bentley, Joseph E., 370.
Berlin Decree. *See* Decrees, French.
Bermuda, Lieutenant Governor of, 164n.
Bethlehem, Conn., 19, 19n, 22.
Bibb, William W. (Ga.): JCC writes to, 429; and army bill, 87, 87n; overrules JCC, 108; calls Grosvenor to order, 176; ends debate, 177n; on FRC report, 180; in Senate, 429.
Blanding, Abram, 29.
Blanding, Elizabeth Martin (Mrs. Abram Blanding), 29.
Bleecker, Harmanus (N.Y.), Federalist, opposes war, 104, 107n-8n, 154, 157.
Blockades, British: Fox's (1806), 64, 64n, 113-4, 116-7, 118, 119, 154; of Continent, 76, 80, 124, 150, 221, 222, 240; JCC on as violation of law of nations, 111, 113, 114; peacetime of U.S. coast, 116-7; wartime of U.S. coast, 181n, 206, 247, 351.
Boisseau, Mrs. ——— (sister-in-law of Mrs. Colhoun ?), 49, 54.
Boisseau, James Edward (half-brother of Mrs. Colhoun ?), 45n.
Boisseau, Wentworth (nephew of Mrs. Colhoun): writes to JCC, 53; student of Waddel, 38(?), 44(?), 45, 45n, 47, 49; "misconduct" of, 53-4, 55-6.
Bonneau, Elizabeth, 33n, 183n, 432.
Bonneau, Floride, xxiv, 433. *See also* Colhoun, Floride Bonneau.
Bonneau, Samuel, xxiv, 45n.
Bonneau's Ferry (Mrs. Colhoun's plantation, St. John's Berkeley, S.C.): JCC at, 42, 43n, 46-7, 48,

Bonneau's Ferry (continued)
51n, 51, 59n, 60, 162, 177; Mrs.
JCC at, 91, 92n, 286.
Bonus bill, 372, 407-8.
Boston, Mass., 4, 40, 97, 401; JCC
at, 13; Port Bill (1774), 202, 204n.
Bowie, Alexander, 37n; friendship
with JCC, 51n.
Bowie, George: letter to, 183n; and
Abbeville Meeting, 34, 37n; JCC in
law office of, 39; JCC mentions, 44,
47, 182, 183; marriage of, 44n, 432.
Bowie, Margaret Pickens (Mrs. George
Bowie, cousin of JCC), 44, 44n, 52,
432.
Bradley, William C. (Vt.), 242n, 251-
2n.
Brest, 113.
Brewerton, George D., 429.
Bridgewater, battle of, JCC on, 257.
Briggs, Isaac: letter of request from,
369-72; JCC writes to, 369; *State-
ments* and petition, 372n.
Bristol, England, election at, 385, 386.
Brothers in Unity (Yale literary so-
ciety), 5, 6n; JCC's reply to, 6n.
Brown, Mrs. ———, 18.
Brown, Gen. Jacob, JCC praises, 261,
261n, 263, 322.
Buenos Aires, commissioners to, 419.
Burke, Edmund, 319, 385, 385n;
JCC's opinion of, 386.
Burton, Mr. ———, 424.
Butler, Dr. William, letters of recom-
mendation for, 427, 428.

Cabinets:
British, 34, 112, 246, 247; members of, 77, 80, 93, 114, 114n, 175n,
212n, 319.
U.S.: changes in, 59, 59n, 147n,
149, 162; and War of 1812, 95,
100, 148-9n. *See also* Navy, State,
Treasury, and War Departments.
Cadore, Duc de, French Foreign Minister, letter of, 181n.
Cady, Daniel (N.Y.), 342n-3n.
Caldwell, Martha. *See* Calhoun, Martha Caldwell.

Calhoun, Agnes Long (Mrs. William
Calhoun), 433.
Calhoun, Andrew Pickens (son of
JCC), 433; birth of, 86n; JCC men-
tions, 86, 92, 135, 206, 286, 418,
420.
Calhoun, Anna Maria (daughter of
JCC), 433; birth of, 418n, 420;
JCC mentions, 418, 420.
Calhoun, Catherine (cousin of JCC),
432.
Calhoun, Catherine (sister of JCC),
433.
Calhoun, Catherine Jenner deGraffen-
reid (Mrs. William Calhoun), 433.
Calhoun, Catherine Montgomery (Mrs.
Patrick Calhoun, grandmother of
JCC), 431.
Calhoun, Elizabeth (daughter of
JCC), 433.
Calhoun, Ezekiel (uncle of JCC),
xxiv, 9, 431, 432.
Calhoun, Ezekiel (cousin of JCC),
23, 433.
Calhoun family: S.C. home of, xxiii-
xxiv, 4n; cemetery of, 4n; Bible of,
58n, 286n, 431.
Calhoun, Floride (daughter of JCC),
433; birth of, 205; death of, 205n,
283-4.
Calhoun, Floride Colhoun (wife of
JCC), 60, 364, 417, 433; letters to,
91-2, 205-6, 286; correspondence
with, 86, 92, 135, 286; health and
pregnancies of, 60, 61, 62, 86-7,
205-6, 286, 286n, 418n; disapproval
of theatre by, 60; JCC's love and
anxiety for, 86-7, 92, 205-6, 283-4,
286; goes to Washington with JCC,
xxxii, 418, 419, 420. *See also* Colhoun, Floride.
Calhoun, James (uncle of JCC), 431.
Calhoun, James (brother of JCC),
433; correspondence with JCC, 26,
28, 30, 31; business of, 4, 30, 31;
and JCC's finances, 4n, 30-1, 274.
Calhoun, James Edward (cousin of
JCC). *See* Colhoun, James Edward.
Calhoun, James Edward (son of
JCC), 433.

Calhoun, Jane (daughter of JCC), 433; birth and death of, 286n.

Calhoun, Jane Ewing (Mrs. Ezekiel Calhoun), 432.

Calhoun, John Caldwell:

PERSONAL

Private correspondence: with his brothers, 6n-7n, 11, 18, 26, 28, 29, 30, 31, 90, 149, 274; with other relatives and friends, 14, 17, 18, 21, 22, 24, 27, 53, 98n, 205, 366; business letters to JCC, 362-4. *See also* entries for members of the Bowie, Calhoun, Colhoun, De-Saussure, Macbride, Maxcy, Noble, and Pickens families. For letters of recommendation and personal correspondence with politicians *see* the subheading of this entry for Political correspondence.

Family: background and relatives, xxiii-xxv, xxvi, 3-4n, 6n, 431-4; relationship with his brothers, 4n, 6, 21, 30-1, 44, 274; relationship with Senator Colhoun, xxiv, 8-9, 421; affection for Colhoun children, 22; opinions on marriage, 55, 56, 57-8; patronage and political service to his family, 91, 96, 260, 276, 424, 426, 427, 428; misses his family, 92, 135, 348; comments on Congress and family life, 101, 344-5, 348, 390; Pickens' executor, 182-3n, 429. For his love for his wife *see* Colhoun, Floride. *See also* Colhoun, Floride Bonneau; Waddel, Moses.

Education, s t u d i e s, interests: choice of and preparation for college, xxv, 3-4n; classical training, 3, 3n, 331n; refers to ancient literature, 282, 326, 330; refers to mathematics, 8, 282; interest in history, 22; refers to ancient history, 196, 200, 211, 317, 325, 326, 385, 387, 401, 402; refers to European history, 84, 159, 194, 196, 226, 251, 317, 320-1, 353, 385-6, 400; refers to "history of republics," 156, 196, 200, 290, 355, 401; refers to Burke,

Calhoun, John Caldwell (continued)
319, 385-6; refers to American history, 72-3, 133, 144, 196, 200, 226, 305, 318; interest in science and natural history, 3, 90, 91; interest in education, 38, 40n.

Law: opinions on, 9-10, 15, 17, 22-3, 41; studies under DeSaussure, 13n, 32, 39; studies under Bowie, 33, 39; admission to bar, 39-40n, 43n; and changes in S.C. legal procedures, 40n, 46, 46n; law practice, 41, 48, 51, 51n, 55, 57, 58, 93n, 95-6n; closes practice, 48, 57; opinion on marriage settlements, 55; legal comments, 172, 211, 307-13; writes Wirt for legal assistance, 364, 365n; recommends law firm, 427; opinion on Pickens' will, 429. *See also* Law of nations; Litchfield Law School.

Finances: and his education, 4n, 12, 30-1n; "not ambitious of great wealth," 41; opinion of marriage settlements, 54-5; division of Colhoun property, 61, 416-7n; proposed purchase of home site, 50, 51n; interest in agriculture, 11, 13, 30, 44, 61, 252, 348, 362, 416; advice on farming and crop sales, 63, 135-6, 182-3, 206, 274, 416; business in Philadelphia, 101; owes money, 206, 416-7; family handling his affairs, 206, 274, 397, 416-7; loses $500 in mails, 362-3; cheated in purchase of slaves, 364-5n; report of his wealth, 365n; sale of his property, 397, 416-7.

Health: fever in S.C., 4; dysentery at Yale, 11-2; danger to in Charleston, 13, 32-3; good at Litchfield, 17, 22, 25, 26, 28; good in S.C., 32, 38; 1814 illness, 243n, 266n; exercise, 25, 25-6, 51n, 87.

POLITICAL

Political correspondence: letters to friends, 92-3, 360-2, 365-6, 427, 429; letters of recommendation and inquiry, 285n, 361, 365, 369, 422, 424, 426, 427, 428; writes to

Calhoun, John Caldwell (continued)
Cheves, 363; writes to Wirt, 364;
letter of acceptance, 418-9; answers
on Congressional business, 263n,
303n, 358n, 381n; letters of request
and recommendation, 284-5, 358n,
360, 369-71, 409-10, 426; answers
for constituents, 423, 424, 426, 427,
428, 429; letters of request and
recommendation to him as Secretary of War, 429.

Early interest: conservative leanings, xxv, xxvi, 8-9n; ambition, 8-9n;
meets Jefferson, 14, 14n; comment,
23, 23n; support of Osborn, 25, 25n.

In S.C.: Abbeville Meeting, xxv,
34, 37, 37n; in S.C. House, xxv,
40, 40n, 46, 46n; trustee of S.C.
College, 40n; speech to Republican
caucus, 41n; appointment as aide-
de-camp, 421; enemies, 61-2; election in 1816, xxxi, 362-4.

In Congress, foreign relations and
defense of the executive:

12th Congress, 1st Session:
second on FRC, 63, 69n; defense
of Nov. report, 69n, 75-86n; account of FRC meeting on Henry
affair, 92-3n; dispute with Randolph
on embargo, motion for and remarks
on secrecy of FRC proceedings,
96-8n, 422; chairman of FRC, 109n,
148; moves consideration of exportation bill introduced by Porter,
422; presents army bills, 109n, 422,
423; presents embargo modification
bill, 422; presents war report, 109,
122n; presents bill declaring war,
122n, 125-6n; presents embargo repeal bill, 134n; presents and comments on bill to prohibit trade with
enemy, 423.

12th Congress, 2nd Session:
chairman of FRC, 148; remarks on
FRC consideration of seamen's bill,
147-8n; votes for seamen's bill, 148-
9n, 162; presents export limitation
bill, 164-5n; FRC and licenses,
164n-5n; presents and comments
on retaliation bills, 165, 167.

Calhoun, John Caldwell (continued)
13th Congress, 1st Session:
chairman of FRC, 176; defends the
executive on militia, 424; defends
the executive on French Decrees,
169-77n; votes for four of Webster's
resolutions, 177n; presents Senate
naturalization bill, 424; presents report and resolutions on conduct of
the executive, 179-81n, 186n; reports against embargo, 181-2n;
speaks and votes against FRC embargo, 182n; votes for FRC license
bill, 182n; FRC and Newton's resolution, 182n.

13th Congress, 2nd Session:
chairman of FRC and votes for embargo, 184; presents and speaks for
non-importation a n d ransoming
bills, 184; remarks on discussion of
FRC report on conduct of the executive, 185-6n; defends the executive in debate on Turreau letter,
186-9n; opposes FRC consideration
of resolution, 188n; resolution on
Russian mediation papers, 425; presents and speaks for FRC bill for
repeal of restrictive system, 240-
54n; presents and comments on
specie exportation bill, 426; opposes
woolens importation bill, 426.

13th Congress, 3rd Session:
loses FRC chairmanship, 243n,
266n; is second on FRC, 266n;
speech on results of war, 279-83n.

14th Congress, 1st Session:
speech on commercial treaty, 304-
14n.

14th Congress, 2nd Session:
speech and vote on neutrality bill,
395-7n.

In Congress, armed forces:
12th Congress, 1st Session:
vote on volunteer bill, 70; vote and
comment on militia bills, 71n; comments and vote on army bill, 87-8n;
comment on Randolph's army resolution, 89, 89n; presents FRC army
bills, 109n, 422, 423; presents FRC
Quartermaster's Dept. bill, 423.

Calhoun, John Caldwell (continued)
12th Congress, 2nd Session: speech for navy bill, 423; comment and speech on army bill, 149, 150-62n.

13th Congress, 1st Session: on militia, 424.

13th Congress, 2nd Session: motion on Grosvenor's army resolution, 425; support of Lowndes on army bill, 425; speech defending military policy, 189-93, 200n; motion on Reed's navy resolution, 425; remarks on coastal defense, 206-8n.

13th Congress, 3rd Session: speech on military situation, 254-9n; remarks on volunteer bill, 261-2n; resolutions on army, 262-3n; remarks on militia bill, 271-3n; chairman of committee and report on army discipline, 273, 273n; speeches on peace establishment, 277-83n.

14th Congress, 1st Session: speeches on military academies bill, 287-90n; speech on revenue for army and navy, 316-25, 330-1n.

14th Congress, 2nd Session: resolution and speech on transfer of appropriations, 410-5n.

In Congress, restrictive system:
12th Congress, 1st Session: supports 1812 embargo, 97n; moves consideration of specie exportation bill, 422; speaks against embargo modification, 98-9n, 100-1n, 102-8n; presents FRC bill for exception to embargo, 422; presents FRC bill for repeal of embargo, 134n; speech for repeal of system, 126-35n; presents and comments on FRC bill to prohibit trade with enemy, 423.

12th Congress, 2nd Session: speech on merchants' bonds, 135-46n; comment and votes on enforcement of system, 135n, 163, 163n; presents and speaks for export limitation bill, 164-5n.

13th Congress, 1st Session:

Calhoun, John Caldwell (continued)
reports and speaks against embargo, 181-2n; votes for license bill, 182n; opposes FRC consideration of export limitation resolution, 182n.

13th Congress, 2nd Session: votes for 1813 embargo, 184; presents and speaks for non-importation and ransoming bills, 184; speaks for bill on libelled merchandise, 426; votes against resolutions against system, 184, 242n; report and bill for repeal of system, 184, 240-3n, 426; speaks for repeal of system, 243-54n; report and comment on specie exportation bill, 426.

In Congress, war finance:
12th Congress, 1st Session: war taxes, 422.

12th Congress, 2nd Session: speech against W&MC report, 136-46n; comment on Navy Dept. extravagance, 423.

13th Congress, 2nd Session: motion on war claims inquiry, 426; third on bank committee and resolution on national bank, 204-5n; speech on loan bill, 208-40n.

13th Congress, 3rd Session: speaks on bank bill, 263-71n; third on bank committee, 270-1n; comment on a bank bill, 275-6n.

14th Congress, 1st Session: comment on resolution on claims act, 366-7n; speaks on claims bill, 373-7n.

In Congress, the national program: speaks on Force Bill in 1833, 357n; speaks on treasury note bill in 1837, 266n, 275n.

13th Congress, 2nd Session: comment on canal bill, 424-5; fourth on canal committee, 425; speech on encouragement of manufactures, 252-4n.

14th Congress, 1st Session: chairman of UNCC, 266n, 290, 303n; correspondence on bank, 303n; presents and speaks for bank

Calhoun, John Caldwell (continued)
bill, 290, 303n, 331-43n, 345-7n;
speech on revenue report, 314-6n;
speech on revenue bill, 316-31n;
reports bill to regulate foreign currency, 427-8; remarks and speech
on tariff bill, 347-57n; specie payment bill, 357-60n; reports against
prohibition of specie export, 428;
speaks on Webster's specie payment
resolutions, 360n.

14th Congress, 2nd Session:
motion and chairman of committee
for bonus bill, 367-9n; writes and
reports bonus bill, 372, 372n;
speaks for bonus bill, 398-409n;
specie payment for bank stock, 378-
81n; resolution and speech on transfer of appropriations, 410-5n.

In Congress, miscellaneous:
12th Congress, 1st Session:
speech and votes on apportionment
bill, 71-4n; remarks on Louisiana
amendment, 94; speaks for Rounsavell's release, 98n; opposes adjournment, 422; comment and motion on Caracas resolution, 100-1n;
remarks on House rules, 108-9n.

12th Congress, 2nd Session:
votes against Wright's retaliation
bill, 167.

13th Congress, 1st Session:
remarks on Richards' petition, 169-
70n; comment and vote for printing
Mass. Memorial, 178, 178n.

13th Congress, 2nd Session:
votes to consider resolution on spies,
187n; speech on factious opposition,
189-201n; speaks against expatriation bill committee, 425; speaks
against Law's motion, 425-6; speaks
and votes against printing Md.
Memorial, 201-4n.

14th Congress, 1st Session:
speech for compensation bill, 343-
5n.

14th Congress, 2nd Session:
comment on constitutional amendment, 369, 369n; motion on Chickasaw lands resolution, 428; speeches

Calhoun, John Caldwell (continued)
on compensation act, 382-95n;
chairman of committee and report
for Trumbull's paintings, 410n.

Party politics:
Comments on partisanship: opposes factions in S.C., 25, 36, 61-2,
201n; seeks party unity, 99n, 146-
7n, 184, 242n-3n, 247, 248, 248n,
270n-1n; on party spirit, 100, 177,
342, 391, 398, 413; favors bipartti-
san foreign policy, 234; opposes
"legislation on party principles,"
269-70. *See also* Federalist party;
Republican party; United States,
Dangers of disunion in.

Close associates: works with
Grundy, 76, 97n, 148, 176-7n, 181n,
182n, 195, 205n, 365-6; Grundy his
"mouthpiece," 200n; support of and
by Clay, 85n, 108-9n, 148, 168-
9n, 174, 321, 324, 405n, 408; works
with Cheves and Lowndes, xxviii,
98-9n, 134n-5n, 142-6n, 161n, 163n,
230, 230n, 270n, 275n, 315n, 330n,
356n, 425; other friendships and
praise, 126, 234, 248, 266n, 345,
360, 362.

As speaker and writer: method
of preparing speeches, xxxv, xxxv n,
51, 348; comments on himself, 62,
74, 223, 230, 339, 382; authorship
of FRC reports, 69n, 97n, 122n-4,
330n; style of his speeches, xxxv,
86n, 210n, 238n-9, 282n-3n, 330n;
loan bill and bonus bill speeches
among his best, 239, 330n, 407n;
his moderation, 200n, 201n, 240n;
his contempt for idle debate, 208-9,
210, 257, 259; bill and report in
his own hand, 372n, 381n.

Publication of speeches: contemporary, xxiv, 75n, 169n, 177n, 182n,
201n, 238n, 408-9n; later, xxxv-
xxxviii, 85n. *See also* Crallé, Richard K.

Political praise of: by Bowie, 37n;
by friends, 62, 75n; by Ritchie, 85n;
by Randolph, xxx-xxxi, 331n; by
Wirt, 364; by Briggs, 370-1; by

Calhoun, John Caldwell (continued)
Grosvenor, 392-3n; by Wilde, 393n;
by Conner, xxvii, 394-5n; by Gold,
408.

As Secretary of War: accepts appointment, xxxii, 418-9, 429; travels
to Washington, 420; letters to, 429.

Calhoun, John Caldwell (son of JCC),
433.

Calhoun, Col. Joseph (cousin of JCC),
433; political career of, 23n, 40n,
58n; chairman of Abbeville Meeting, 34, 34n, 37; JCC succeeds in
Congress, 58n; death of, 418, 418n.

Calhoun, Martha Caldwell (Mrs. Patrick Calhoun, mother of JCC), 433;
letter to (alleged), 4-7n; death of,
3-4; date of death, 4, 4n, 6n.

Calhoun, Martha Cornelia (daughter
of JCC), 433.

Calhoun, Mary (aunt of JCC), 431,
432.

Calhoun, Nancy Needham deGraffenreid (Mrs. Patrick Calhoun), 434;
JCC mentions, 63, 90, 150, 274.

Calhoun, Patrick (grandfather of
JCC), 431.

Calhoun, Patrick (father of JCC), 9n,
431, 433; political career, xxiii-xxiv
n; home of, xxiii, 4n.

Calhoun, Patrick (brother of JCC),
50, 51n, 433, 434; letters to, 63,
89-90, 149-50, 274-5; writes to JCC,
274.

Calhoun, Patrick (son of JCC), 433.

Calhoun, Rebecca (cousin of JCC).
See Pickens, Rebecca Calhoun.

Calhoun, Sara Caldwell Martin (Mrs.
James Calhoun), 433.

Calhoun, Tscharner (nephew of JCC),
26, 433.

Calhoun, William (uncle of JCC),
431, 433.

Calhoun, William (brother of JCC),
26, 433; answer probably intended
for, 426; writes to JCC, 29.

Calhoun, William (probably a cousin
of JCC), 424.

Calhoun, William Lowndes (son of
JCC), 433.

Cambridge, S.C., 365.

Canada: JCC favors and Federalists
oppose U.S. war campaign against,
xxix, 82, 149, 161n, 191, 192-3,
197, 207, 231, 233, 234, 239, 376;
Revolutionary invasion of, 82, 193;
danger to U.S. in British possession
of, 92-3, 192, 277-8, 325; JCC
prophesies conquest of, 104-5, 206n,
208, 256-7, 271n, 276; illegal trade
with, 132, 423.

Canals, U.S. support for, xxxii, 89n,
368n-9n, 371, 408, 424-5. See also
Internal improvements.

Canary Islands, 101n.

Caracas, Venezuela, relief for, 100-1n,
404.

Carolina Gazette (Charleston, S.C.),
37.

Carrington, Capt. Edward, 276.

Casey, Dr. John A., answers for, 423,
429(?).

Casey, Dr. Thomas (cousin of JCC by
marriage, probably the Dr. Casey
of the following pages): writes to
JCC, 205; and the Abbeville Meeting, 34, 37; Calhoun family doctor,
205, 283.

Castlereagh, Lord, British Foreign
Secretary, 175n, 212n.

Censuses: S.C. (1809), 40; U.S., 74,
361.

Champlain Canal, 408.

Charleston, S.C.: JCC at, xxiv, 13,
13n, 30, 32-3, 44, 48, 51n, 57, 60;
JCC's family and friends at, xxiv,
5, 12, 13, 18, 26, 29-30, 33, 38, 41,
42, 43n, 46, 48, 54, 58, 86, 90,
91, 92n, 93, 99, 102n, 135, 146,
162, 178n, 283, 286, 362, 397, 416;
health and climate of, 13, 32-3, 38,
57, 419; JCC on immorality of, 28,
29, 38; port and business of, 31,
48, 59, 145n, 286, 365, 370, 406;
newspapers of, 37, 59, 75, 98n,
284; JCC on theatre in, 60.

Chatham, Earl of, 84, 196, 251.

Cheppelle, Mr. ———, 9.

Chesapeake Affair, 117; Abbeville
resolutions concerning, xxv, 34-7,

Chesapeake Affair (continued)
122n; and JCC's first public speech,
xxv, 37, 37n.

Chesapeake and Delaware Canal Company, 424-5.

Chesapeake Bay, defense of, 327.

Chester, S.C., JCC at, 420.

Cheves, Langdon (S.C.), Republican:
JCC writes to, 363; opposition to
restrictive system, xxviii, 99n, 134n,
135n, 142, 142n, 145n, 146n, 163n;
JCC calls "my friend," 142; reports as W&MC chairman, 145n,
163n; speech on army bill, 161n;
Speaker of the House, 230, 230n,
271n, 273n; out of Congress, 284,
363.

Chickasaw Indian lands, 428.

China trade, 396.

Chippawa, battle of, 257, 257n.

Christ Church Parish, S.C., 60.

Claims, U.S. Commissioner of, 366-
7, 373, 374, 376n.

Clark, James (Ky.), 266n.

Clay, Henry (Ky.), Republican,
Speaker of the House: supports war,
85n, 88n, 122n, 141, 143, 148; rules
for JCC, 108-9n, 174; JCC calls
"my friend," 141; excludes Richards, 168-9n; supports national program, 316n, 321, 324, 330n, 356n,
405n, 408; on claims and petitions,
373-7n *passim;* on implied instructions, 384n.

Clinton, DeWitt, 96, 408.

Coastal defense, U.S., JCC on, 36, 85,
192-3, 206-8n, 255-7, 323, 327.

Coastal trade, U.S., JCC on, 328, 350,
354, 400.

Cohen, Mr. M., 363.

Colhoun, Floride (cousin and wife of
JCC), 433; letter to, 57-8; correspondence with, 44, 45, 47, 48, 49,
53; JCC mentions, 16, 17, 19, 27,
29, 38; JCC's love for, xxvi, 42-58
passim; engagement rumored, 42,
43n, 47; date for wedding, 48, 50,
55, 57, 58n; her health and accident, 49, 50, 54, 56; JCC's opinion
of her character, 48, 52, 58; her

Colhoun, Floride (continued)
property, 54-5, 61, 61n, 317, 416-
7n. *See also* Calhoun, Floride Colhoun.

Colhoun, Floride Bonneau (Mrs. John
Ewing Colhoun, mother-in-law of
JCC), xxiv, 433; letters to, 11-2,
15-9, 21-2, 24-33, 37-8, 41-5, 46-57,
60-1, 86-7, 135-6, 283-4, 420; letter from, 19-21; correspondence
with, 11, 16, 18, 19, 20, 24, 26, 27,
29, 32, 38, 43, 44, 45, 49, 51, 53,
54, 56, 60, 86.

Relations with her family and
friends: her children, 12n, 16, 16n,
58-9, 60, 418, 419, 420; Pickens
family, 14, 14n, 17n, 20, 20n, 24,
33, 43n, 182(?), 183(?), 183n;
DeSaussure, 20, 21, 21n, 49, 50,
54-5.

Travel: JCC travels with, 13, 13-
4, 15, 24, 28, 30; her winter visits
to S.C., 16, 18-9, 20, 24, 28, 37-8,
41, 42, 43n, 45; JCC urges her to
visit S.C., 33, 38, 42, 44, 45, 53;
returns to S.C., 45, 55, 57, 58; goes
to New Haven, 59, 60. For JCC's
visits to her *see* Bonneau's Ferry;
Newport, R.I.

And JCC: affection between, 15,
19, 24, 27, 38, 44, 92, 206, 286,
420; JCC's comments on education
of her children, 15, 16, 16n, 17,
18-9, 19-20, 22, 24, 29, 41; JCC
loves her as a mother, 16, 45, 48,
56, 135; JCC asks loan from, 30-1n;
and JCC's courtship, xxvi, 42-5, 46-
57; JCC and her finances, 135-6,
363.

Colhoun, James Edward (cousin and
brother-in-law of JCC), xix, 428,
433; letter to, 417-8; letter from,
419-20; JCC offers to correspond
with, 52, 54; correspondence, 417,
419; changes surname to Calhoun,
12n; JCC mentions, 16, 17, 19, 24,
26, 27, 29, 38, 42, 45, 48, 50, 55,
57, 286; education, 19-20, 22, 29;
naval service, 397, 397n, 417-8n,
419, 428.

Colhoun, Senator John Ewing (cousin of JCC), xix, xxvi, 12n, 13n, 21n, 59n, 432, 433; political career, xxiv, 8-9n; will of, 20n, 417n, 418n, 421.

Colhoun, John Ewing (cousin and brother-in-law of JCC), 433; letters to, 276, 397, 416-7; correspondence with, 397, 416; JCC mentions, 16, 17, 19, 27, 29, 38, 45, 48, 57, 286, 420; education, 19-20, 22, 29, 59n; DeSaussure's letter to, 39n; sickness of, 58-61 *passim*, 92; military service, 276, 276n; JCC on their mutual property, 397, 416-7n.

Columbia, Ga., JCC at, 3.

Columbia, S.C., 50, 420; JCC at, 33, 45, 60, 61, 416.

Commerce, U.S. *See* Coastal trade; Exports, U.S.; Restrictive system; Tariff of 1816.

Congress, U.S.:

JCC on constitutional powers of: relations between Houses, 72-3, 75n; right of petition to, 102, 375; taxation and appropriation, 140, 338, 400, 403-4, 412; relations with the executive, 186, 187, 306, 311, 313, 383-4, 388; and spies, 187; right of opposition in, 198-9, 233-4; and bank, 204-5n, 244, 332, 347n; and treaties, 305-14n; function of House, 329, 387; and currency, 332-6, 338, 339n; and suspension of laws, 366-7n, 377; and internal improvements, xxxii, 368n, 402-8 *passim;* relations with judiciary, 383; as letter of instruction, 386, 393; and Louisiana Purchase, 404, 405.

Powers of granted by laws: and bank, 290, 292, 298-304n *passim*, 341n, 342n, 379-80; and internal improvements, 372, 408.

Acts of: national bank (1791), 205n, 303n; neutrality (1794), 396; protection of seamen (1796), 218, 218n; mitigation of penalties (1797), 138-40, 164; duty (1799), 164; mitigation of penalties (1800), 164; judiciary (1801), xxiv, 9n; army rules (1806), 422; foreign

Congress, U.S. (continued)
currency (1806), 270n, 334; transfer of appropriations (1809), 411, 415n. For non-intercourse acts *see* Restrictive system; for acts of the 12th, 13th, and 14th Congresses *see* House of Representatives.

Congress (U.S. frigate), 417, 419.

Connecticut, 5, 10, 15n, 39, 291n. *See also* Litchfield; New Haven.

Conner, Samuel S. (Mass.), 288n, 385, 393-4n; tribute to JCC, xxvii, 394n-5n.

Constitution, U.S.

JCC on: praises, 35, 72, 117, 146, 310; and war, 81, 82, 319; describes, 199, 233-4, 310-1, 402-5n; slave trade clause, 312; proposed amendment, 369, 369n; as letter of instruction, 386, 393.

Separation of powers in: federative character and states' rights, xxvi, 70, 311, 331n, 333, 347n; relations between branches, xxvi, 72-3, 74n, 140, 186-7, 343, 383-4. *See also* Congress, U.S.; President, U.S.

Constitutional Convention, xxiv, xxiv n, 72-3, 90, 333-4, 403.

Continental Congress, 82.

Cooper, Mr. ———, 91-2.

Cooper River, xxiv, 43n.

Cotton: culture and sale of, 83, 137, 274, 349, 362, 363, 365, 370; manufactures, 253, 274, 327, 347-8, 352-3, 356n.

Courts, state, 294n, 295n. *See also* South Carolina.

Courts, U.S.: Circuit, 295n; Supreme, 360.

Couturier, Mr. ———, 93.

Craig, Sir James, 92, 93.

Crallé, Richard K., xvii, xxxvi-xxxviii, 69n, 85n, 105n, 123, 129n, 148, 201n, 209n-39n *passim*, 282n-3n, 357n, 409n.

Crawford, William H.: minister to France, 189n; Secretary of the Treasury, 380n, 415n.

Cresswell, Robert, letter to, 92-3.

Crowninshield, Benjamin W., Secretary of the Navy: letters of recommendation to, 427, 428; answers from, 428.
Cumberland Road, 404.
Cummins, Rev. Francis, 27, 27n.
Cunningham, Mr. ———, 22.
Currency, foreign, 270n, 334, 427-8. For U.S. currency *see* Specie exportation; Specie payment.

Dallas, Alexander J.:
    Secretary of the Treasury: letter to, 361-2; answers from, 303n, 358n; his 1814 proposal for bank, xxx, 259n, 265n, 266n, 271n, 275n, 303n; his 1815 plan for bank, xxxi, 303-4n, 368n; proposal for tariff, 356n-7n; and specie payment, 358n, 380n.
    Acting Secretary of War, 276.
    Presumably Acting Secretary of State, 284, 285.
Dallas family, 362.
Darington, Mr. ———, 22, 29.
Davie, William Richardson, 90, 96, 96n.
Dearborn, Gen. Henry, 90.
Decrees, French: effect on U.S., 64, 120, 120n, 222-3; as grounds for Orders in Council, 64, 65-6, 118, 119, 120-1, 172-3, 175n, 191; pretended repeal of (1810), xxviii-xxix, 65, 69n, 83, 85n, 120, 124, 150, 154, 161n; "repeal" as cause of war, 170, 172-4, 175n, 204n.
    Berlin Decree (1806), 64, 64n, 118, 119.
    Repeal decree (1811): falsely dated, 169-70n, 175n; Webster's resolutions on, 169-77n, 179-81n.
Defense, U.S. coastal. *See* Coastal defense, U.S.
deGraffenreid, Catherine Jenner, 433.
deGraffenreid, Nancy Needham. *See* Calhoun, Nancy Needham deGraffenreid.
Dehon, Rev. Theodore, 30, 30n, 57.
Delaware canals, 424-5.

Denmark, 213, 222, 240-1, 245, 246.
DeSaussure, ———, 59.
DeSaussure, Henry A., 21, 21n.
DeSaussure, Judge Henry William: correspondence with, 20, 21, 50, 54; JCC in his law office, 13n, 32, 39-40n; as Mrs. Colhoun's attorney, 20, 21n, 43n, 59n, 61; and JCC's engagement, 49, 50, 52, 54; and Mrs. JCC's property, 54, 416-7.
DeSaussure, Mrs. Henry William, 59.
DeSaussure, William Ford, letter from, 58-9.
Deserters, British, 147n, 202, 203n-4n.
Detargney, Rev. Martin, 33.
Detroit, 278n, 413.
District of Columbia: and banks, 204-5n, 291, 300, 302, 302n, 340, 428; proposed military academy in, 289n; claims in, 377. *See also* Washington, D.C.
Disunion. *See* United States, Dangers of disunion in.
Dodge, Stephen, 31n.
Drayton, William, 91.
DuBose, Mr. ———, 44.
Dwight, Timothy, 5, 10-1.

Earthquakes (1812): in U.S., 91, 107; in Venezuela, 101.
East Indies trade, 348, 354.
Eastern states, U.S.: representation of, 73n, 74; commercial interests and opposition to war, xxvii, xxviii, 98n, 105, 164n-5n, 178n. *See also* Middle states, U.S.; New England.
Edgefield Courthouse and District, S.C.: JCC represents, xxvi n; JCC at, 427.
Edict of Nantes, 353.
Edisto River, 47n.
Elbe River, 113.
Elections: of 1806, 23n; of 1808, 41n; of 1810, xxvi, xxvi n, 58, 58n, 72; of 1812, 95-6, 98n; of 1816 and compensation law, xxxi, 361-2, 363, 363n, 366, 382, 386-7, 390, 392.
Elmore, Gen. John A., 58, 58n.
Embargo. *See* Restrictive system.

Emott, James (N.Y.), 153, 233.

England:

Commercial and maritime policy of as cause of war: JCC on (in FRC reports), xxvii, 63-7, 109-22n, 124; JCC on (in speeches), 157-8, 210-29, 239-40n, 243-4; defended by Randolph and Federalists, xxvii, 84, 92, 152, 153-4, 156, 197-8, 211-9 *passim,* 227, 260; Rule of 1756, 221-2, 251. *See also* Blockades, British; Impressment, British; Orders in Council.

JCC on wartime policy of: illegal trade and attempts for disunion, 130, 164-5n, 184, 423; violations of laws of war, 166-7, 377; 1814 plans, 254, 258; naval supremacy of and prospect of future wars with, 104, 119, 156-7, 193, 206, 214, 226, 227, 256, 277-8, 289, 315, 318, 320-3, 325, 326, 348-9.

P o s t w a r commercial relations with U.S.: cotton, 274, 363; treaty, 304-5, 313n-4n; sterling exchange, 335, 427.

JCC on as an example for U.S.: in government, 67, 73, 84, 194-6, 313, 386, 389, 415; in settlement of claims, 376, 377n; in manufactures, 354-5; in internal improvements, 398-9.

See also Imposts; Restrictive system. For British wars *see* France; War of 1812. For U.S. ministers to England *see* Monroe, James; Pinkney, William. For U.S. chargé in London *see* Russell, Jonathan. For British ministers to U.S. *see* Erskine, David M.; Foster, Augustus. For British cabinet *see* Cabinets.

Eppes, John W. (Va.), reports as chairman of W&MC, 209, 239, 259n.

Erie Canal, xxxii, 368n, 408.

Erskine, David M., British minister to U.S., 1809 negotiations, 120.

Essex case, JCC on, 110-3, 118, 121, 124, 152, 222.

Eton fag system at Yale, 5, 5n.

Europe, neutral nations of and British commercial policy, 244, 245, 246, 247, 248n-9n. For wars in *see* France.

Eustis, William, Secretary of War, 93, 95; replaced by Armstrong, 147n, 149, 149n, 162.

Eutaw, battle of, JCC on, 133.

Ewing, Jane, 432.

Executive, U.S. *See* Madison, James; President, U.S. For executive control of Congress *see* House of Representatives, U.S.

Expatriation, 230, 230n, 239, 425.

Exports, U.S., 137, 370; bills and resolutions to restrict, 78-9, 164, 165n, 182n, 422; effects of war on, 349-51. *See also* Cotton; Decrees, French; Orders in Council; Restrictive system.

Federal Republican (Georgetown, D.C.): JCC criticizes, 147n, 162, 168-9n; and Turreau letter, 188n-9n. *See also* Hanson, Alexander C.

Federalist party:

Support of and opposition to: JCC's connections and sympathy with, xxv, xxvi-xxvii, 8, 9n, 81n, 101-2n, 201n; JCC works with in opposing the restrictive system, xxviii, 97, 98n, 100-1n, 102, 104, 245; newspaper support of, 168-9n, 284-5; Webster's praise of, 254; leadership in Senate, 429. For JCC's early opposition to *see* Republican party.

And War of 1812: its opposition to, 107n-8n, 109n, 120n; JCC attacks for its opposition, 104, 147-8, 150-62n *passim,* 163, 163n, 187, 187n, 189-98 *passim,* 201-4n, 206-40n *passim,* 245, 254-9n *passim,* 260, 279-82, 288, 318; JCC defends administration against, xxviii-xxix, 88n, 169-77 *passim,* 179-81n, 185-9n, 200n, 235, 254, 259n, 321; JCC on its indifference to impressment,

Federalist party (continued)
xxix, 147, 154-5, 157, 203, 212-20
passim, 235n-6n; JCC on states'
rights and disunion sentiment in,
xxx, 151-3, 165n, 177, 178n, 200n-
1n, 260; JCC on danger of financial
control by, 268, 269-70n; JCC describes it as factious opposition,
xxix, 194-201n, 207-8, 217-8, 236-
7; Grundy charges it with moral
treason, 195, 200n. For its accusations of French influence upon
Republicans *see* Republican party.

Federalist, The: as source of JCC's
political philosophy, xxvi, 74n; on
factions, 201n, 236.

Felder, John Meyers: JCC's classmate,
15, 15n, 16, 17, 19, 20, 22, 25, 26,
27; Republican activities of, 25,
25n.

Fisheries, Atlantic, 258.

Fisk, James (Vt.), 75n, 269, 270n.

Fisk, Jonathan (N.Y.), 170; as second
on W&MC presents bank bill, 264n,
265n-6n, 271n.

Ford, Timothy, JCC in his law office,
13n, 39.

Forsyth, John (Ga.), Republican,
240n, 367n; becomes FRC chairman, 243n, 266n; on bank, 268,
381n; reports FRC bills, 313n-4n,
397n; resolution on specie payment,
378-81n.

Fort Hill, Clemson, S.C., 58n, 286n,
431.

Foster, Augustus, British minister to
U.S., 65, 96.

Fowler & Hicks, 364.

Fox, Charles James, 77, 114, 114n;
"Fox's blockade" (1806), 64, 64n,
113-4, 116-7, 118, 119, 154.

France, 77, 81, 196, 221, 222, 273,
319, 427-8.
Napoleonic wars, 14, 23, 110,
111, 113, 149-50, 158, 280, 281,
315n, 317, 352, 353; JCC on comparison of French and British aggressions, xxvii-xxviii, 64, 83, 85n,
118-20, 154, 172, 174-5, 202-3,
222-3: effects of Napoleon's defeat

France (continued)
on U.S., xxix, 202, 225-6, 239-48n
passim, 254. *See also* Blockades,
British; Decrees, French; *Essex*
case; Napoleon Bonaparte; Orders
in Council. For "French influence"
see Republican party.
For French Foreign Ministers *see*
Bassano, Duc de; Cadore, Duc de.
For French ministers to U.S. *see*
Serurier, J. M. P.; Turreau, Gen.
L. M. For U.S. ministers to France
see Armstrong, John; Barlow, Joel;
Crawford, William H.

Frazer, Mr. ——, 29-30.

Frontier defense, 255, 262n, 278, 425.
See also Canada.

Gadsden, Christopher Edwards, 5, 5n.

Gaines, Gen. Edmund P., 263n.

Gales, Joseph, xxvi, xxxvi n, xxxviii,
xxxviii n, 123, 125n.

Gallatin, Albert, Secretary of the
Treasury: report on war taxes, 89,
91; letter on tariff revenue, 134n;
letter on merchants' bonds, 137-8;
report (1808) on internal improvements, 368n, 369n, 407n.

Gaston, William (N.C.): disputes
with JCC, 169n, 201n, 201-4n, 235,
235n; JCC quotes, 232, 234, 309,
354; moves repeal of restrictive system, 242n.

Georgia, 10; canal petition of, 425.

Georgia and [South] Carolina Gazette
(Petersburg, Ga.), 37.

Germany, 240-1, 245.

Ghent, Treaty of, xxx, 307; and impressment, 279-80; instructions to
U.S. commission, 280n, 281.

Gibbs, Sir Samuel, 275.

Gibert family, 3n.

Givhans Ferry, S.C., 47, 47n.

Gold, James, 39.

Gold, Thomas R. (N.Y.), 163, 163n,
405n; praise of JCC, 408.

Goldsborough, Charles (Md.), 148-9n,
203n; his resolution, 171.

Goochland County, Va., 364.

Gourdin, Eleanor, 42, 62n. *See also* Macbride, Eleanor Gourdin.

Gourdin, Theodore, 62, 62n, 146, 163.

Graham, George, Acting Secretary of War, 410; letter of inquiry to, 428.

Graham, John, Chief Clerk of the State Dept., 188n, 189n.

Granger, Gideon, Postmaster General, answer from, 426.

Grapes, Southern varieties, 416, 416n.

Great Britain. *See* England.

Great Lakes, 258, 322, 405.

"Greenville line," 258.

Greenville, S. C., 33, 50.

Grimball, Mr. P., 362-3.

Grosvenor, Thomas P. (N.Y.), Federalist, 168n, 375, 375n, 380n; disputes with JCC, 165n, 169n, 176, 188n, 203, 206-8n, 216n, 425; attacks administration and war, 170n, 176, 188, 202, 202n, 221-2n; near-duel with JCC, 184; Cheves rules against, 235n-6n; praises JCC, 392-3, 394n-5n; his compensation bill, 394n, 395n.

Grundy, Felix (Tenn.), Republican: letter to, 365-6; correspondence for, 366; FRC member, 76, 97n, 124, 148; presents FRC bills, 148, 149n, 182n, 184, 280n; supports administration, 176-7n, 181n; charges Federalists with "moral treason," 195, 200n; JCC calls "my friend," 195; JCC's "mouthpiece," 200n; resolution and committee for bank, 205n; his daughter's marriage, 365; JCC's friendship and respect for, 365-6.

Guerrière (British frigate), 227.

Hall, Bolling (Ga.), motion on internal improvements, 346n, 367, 367n.

Hamilton, Alexander, xxxi.

Hamilton, Paul, Secretary of the Navy, 147n, 162, 180; letter of recommendation to, 424.

Hampden, John, 84.

Hanson, Alexander C. (Md.), Federalist: publisher of *Federal Repub-*

Hanson, Alexander C. (continued) *lican,* 162(?), 188n; resolutions on Turreau letter, 186, 188n, 189n; attacks JCC, 200n, 271n, 280, 280n; JCC replies to, 281-2.

Harby, Isaac: letter of request from, 284-5; letters of recommendation for, 285n.

Hardin, Benjamin (Ky.), 319n.

Harper, John A. (N.H.), 97n, 167.

Harper, Robert Goodloe, Federalist, JCC's connections with, xxiv, 23n, 81n, 102n.

Harrison, Gen. William Henry, xxviii.

Hartford, Conn., JCC at, 15.

Hartford Convention, xxx.

Havana, Cuba, 396.

Havre de Grace, Md., JCC at, 13.

Hawkins, Joseph H. (Ky.), 262n.

Haywood, John, letter to for constituent, 427.

Hector (a slave), 420.

Hemp, and War of 1812, 83.

Henry, John, British agent for disunion, 92-3n, 93-4, 96, 117-8, 118n.

Hicks, Fowler &, 364.

Holland, 196, 213, 240-1, 245, 246.

Hopkinson, Joseph (Pa.), 318, 318n, 319, 341n, 395.

Hornet (U.S. sloop), 90, 93, 94n.

Horry, Mr. ———, 32, 33.

Horry, Mrs. ———, 32.

Houdon, Jean Antoine, 409.

House of Commons, British, 73, 173. *See also* Parliament, British.

House of Representatives, U.S.:

JCC on: character of, 74-5n, 375, 376, 383, 389-91, 392, 411, 412; courtesy and rules of, 100, 101n, 105, 105n, 173-4, 176, 179-80, 235-6n, 271n, 359n; committees of and opposition to "inquisitorial committees," 103, 186, 189n, 374-5; proper form for report and resolution, 136-7, 169, 186-8; danger of executive control of, 140, 235, 305-6, 344, 384, 387-8, 391, 392. For constitutional powers of the House *see* Congress, U.S. For Speakers of the House *see* Cheves,

House of Representatives (continued)
Langdon; Clay, Henry. For chairman of the House *see* Bibb, William W.

12TH CONGRESS

Proceedings: JCC elected to, 50, 58, 58n; opening and proposed recess of first session, 63, 69n, 422; arrest of Rounsavell by, 98n; JCC on prospects for second session, 135; Goldsborough's resolution on repeal of French Decrees, 170, 171, 175n-6; close of, 162; JCC cites journal of, 232-3.

Committees:

FRC: members, 63, 69n, 75, 96, 97n, 124, 148; meetings, 63, 92, 96-8n, 422; report and resolutions on relations with Great Britain, xxvii, xxviii, 63, 63-71n, 75-6, 85n, 122n, 232-3; bills, introduced by Porter, xxvii, 70, 97n, 105-6, 109n; Henry papers referred to, 92, 93n; JCC becomes chairman and moves consideration of bill, 109n, 422; bills, introduced by JCC, 109n, 122n, 125-6, 134n, 164-5, 165-6, 167, 422, 423; Smilie and JCC as chairmen, 148; and seamen's bill, 147, 162; seamen's bill, introduced by Grundy, 148-9n, 162, 280n.

Military Affairs, bills, introduced by Williams, 69n-71n, 161n, 423.

W&MC: revenue report, 91, 91n; bills, introduced by Cheves, 134n-5n, 163n; report on merchants' bonds, 136-40, 145n-6n.

Special committees: apportionment, 74n; secrecy of proceedings, 98n; relief of Caracas and Teneriffe, 101n; retaliation, 166n-7n.

13TH CONGRESS

Proceedings: seating of stenographers, 168-9n; resolutions on French Decrees, 169-77n; orders Mass. Memorial printed, 178n; JCC on lateness of first session, 179; resolution on Russian mediation papers, 425; refuses to print Md.

House of Representatives (continued)
Memorial, 201-4n; tariff resolution, 248, 248n, 253; JCC on close of second session, 206; opening of third session, 243n, 259n, 266n; JCC's criticism of, 257-9; his return from, 283.

Committees:

Commerce and Manufactures: Newton's resolution transferred to, 182n.

FRC: members, xxix, 176, 182n, 266n; report on conduct of the executive, 179-81n; bills, introduced by JCC, 184, 241-3n, 424, 426; report on proposed embargo, 181-2n; bills, introduced by Grundy, 182n, 184; and export resolution, 182n; and Turreau letter, 188n; report for repeal of restrictive system, 240-1, 426; and woolens importation bill, 426; Forsyth becomes chairman, 243n, 266n.

Military Affairs: bills, introduced by Troup, 200n, 255, 261-2n, 263n, 271-2n, 277n; resolution to on army supply system, 262-3n.

W&MC: bills from, 177n, 205n, 209, 239, 257, 259n, 265n-6n; bank report, 204-5n; members, 205n, 239, 265n; Eppes' revenue reports and correspondence, 209, 239, 255, 257, 259n, 265n.

Special committees: proposed committee of investigation opposed by JCC, 186, 187-8, 189n; for bank in D.C., 205n; for amending Fisk's bank bill, 270-1n; for new system of army discipline, 273, 273n; on canal petition, 425.

14TH CONGRESS

JCC on: his criticism of, 318; his position in, xxx-xxxi, 331n, 392-3n, 394-5n, 408; his praise of, 361, 406; and compensation law, 382-3, 387, 392, 395n, 406.

Proceedings: publication of laws, 285n; opening of first session, 286, 286n; JCC on length and close of first session, 348, 359n, 360, 361;

House of Representatives (continued)
appropriation for Cumberland Road,
404; resolution on specie payment,
360n, 362, 378-81n; joint resolution
on Trumbull paintings, 409, 410n;
JCC on close of second session,
412n, 416, 417.

Committees:

Claims: 367n, 374-5, 376n;
supplementary committees suggested, 376.

Commerce and Manufactures:
Newton's report and resolution on
tariff, 356n; statements to, 372n.

FRC: bills from, introduced by
Forsyth, 313n-4n, 397n.

Military Affairs: bill from,
288n, 290n.

UNCC: members, xxx, 266n,
359n; bills, introduced by JCC,
290-304n, 339n, 347n, 357-9n,
427-8; resolutions, reports, and correspondence, 303n, 358n, 380-1n,
428; Forsyth's resolution to, 378-
81n *passim*.

W&MC: Lowndes' revenue report and resolutions, 314-6n, 330n;
tariff bill, 356n; and transfer of appropriations, 410-5 *passim;* JCC's
resolution to, 411, 415n.

Special committees: on compensation of members, 343-5n; on
roads and canals, 368-9n; for bonus
bill, 367-9n, 372, 406; to repeal
compensation act, 392; on Trumbull's paintings, 410n; on expenditures, 414.

15TH CONGRESS
JCC on: anxiety over his election
to, xxxi, 361-2, 363, 363n, 366, 392;
and compensation act, 382, 387,
392, 395n; and internal improvements, 406.

BILLS AND ACTS
12th Congress, 1st Session (1811-
1812): apportionment act (Dec.
21), 71-5n; army act (Dec. 24),
70, 88n; army act (Jan. 11), 70,
76, 81, 87-8n, 153, 161n, 232-3;
volunteer act (Feb. 6), 70, 161n;

House of Representatives (continued)
Quartermaster's Dept. act (Mar.
28), 423; navy act (Mar. 30), 70,
90; army bill (April), 109n, 422;
bill for importation of British goods
(April), 98-9n, 142; embargo act
(Apr. 14), xxvii, 96-8n, 100, 105-6,
109n, 175n, 422; Louisiana acts
(Apr. 8, 14), 94-5n; militia act
(Apr. 10), 70-1n; exportation of
specie act (Apr. 14), 98n, 109n,
134n, 422; embargo modification
act (Apr. 27), 422; Venezuela relief act (May 8), 101n, 404; army
act (May 16), 423; act to amend
Quartermaster's Dept. act (May
22), 423; bill for partial suspension
of non-importation (June), xxviii,
126-35n, 140, 142, 144; embargo
and specie exportation repeal bill
(June), xxviii, 134; act declaring
war (June 18), 122n, 125-6n, 307;
act prohibiting trading with the
enemy (July 6), 423; army act
(July 6), 423.

12th Congress, 2nd Session
(1812-1813): retaliation bill (November), 166n-7; acts empowering
the Secretary of the Treasury in
remission of penalties (Jan. 2, Feb.
27), 146n; navy act (Jan. 2), 149,
423; army act (Jan. 29), xxviii,
149, 149n, 150, 152, 161n-2n, 175n;
bill to enforce non-importation
(February), 135n, 163, 163n; bill
limiting exportation in foreign vessels (February), 164-5n; license
bill (February), 165n, 182n; retaliation act (Mar. 3), 165-8n, 202,
230, 230n, 239; seamen's regulation
act (Mar. 3), 147-9n, 161n, 162,
279, 280n.

13th Congress, 1st Session
(1813): embargo bill (July), 181-
2n; naturalization act (July 30),
424; license act (Aug. 2), 182n.

13th Congress, 2nd Session
(1813-1814): bill to enforce non-
importation (December), 184; bill
to prohibit ransoming of vessels

House of Representatives (continued)
(December), 184; Chesapeake and
Delaware Canal Company bill (December), 424-5; embargo act (Dec.
17), 181n, 182n, 184, 242n; bill
prohibiting delivery of libelled merchandise (January), 426; army acts
(Jan. 27, 28, Feb. 10), 200n-1n,
208n, 229, 425; Chesapeake and
Delaware Canal Company bill
(February), 425; embargo modification act (Mar. 4), 184; loan act
(Mar. 24), xxix-xxx, 208-40n;
woolens importation bill (April),
426; specie exportation bill (April),
243n, 426; embargo repeal act
(Apr. 14), 184, 240-54, 426.

13th Congress, 3rd S e s s i o n
(1814-1815): army bills (October),
xxx, 260, 261-2n, 272n; bank bills
(November, December), xxx, 259n,
263-71n, 275n-6n, 379; militia bill
(December), 271-2n; army act
(Dec. 10), 272n; army commissaries bill (January), 263n; volunteer act (Jan. 27), 261-2n, 272n;
bank bill (February), 275-6n; act
to repeal discriminatory d u t i e s
(Mar. 3), 304-5, 314n; army act
(Mar. 3), 277-9.

14th Congress, 1st S e s s i o n
(1815-1816): military academies
bill (December-January), 287-90n;
bill to regulate commerce with
Great Britain (December-January),
304-14n; revenue act (Feb. 5),
315n-6n; act to regulate commerce
with Great Britain (Mar. 1), 314n;
revenue act (Mar. 5), xxxi, 316-31n,
361; compensation act (Mar. 19),
343-5n, 361-2, 363, 363n, 366, 382-
95n; specie payment bill (April),
357-60n; act for payment for lost
property (Apr. 9), 366-7n, 373,
377; bank act (Apr. 10), 205n,
290-304n, 331-43n, 345-7n, 357,
361, 362, 367-8, 378-9n, 380n;
tariff act (Apr. 27), 347-57, 361;
currency act (Apr. 29), 427-8.

14th Congress, 2nd S e s s i o n

House of Representatives (continued)
(1816-1817): bonus bill (December), 369n, 370-1, 372, 398-409n;
act to repeal compensation act
(Feb. 6), 382-95n; army appropriation act (Mar. 3), 415n; neutrality
act (Mar. 3), 395-7n; act to amend
the payment for lost property act
(Mar. 3), 367n, 373-7n.

Housten, Lady ———, 18.

Hudson River, 405.

Hunter, James, 59.

Immigration, JCC favors, 10-1, 353.
See also Naturalized citizens, U.S.

Impeachment, 187, 188, 367.

Imposts:

Discriminatory duties on British
goods: as substitute for restrictive
system, xxviii, 99n, 127-30, 134n,
143-4, 163n, 241, 243n, 251-4n;
repeal of, 304-5, 308, 312-4n.

Chief source of U.S. revenue,
128-30, 315n-6n, 327-8, 400. *See
also* Tariff of 1816.

Impressment, British: of American
seamen, as cause for war, xxvii, xxix,
35-6, 66-7, 71n, 76, 85n, 116, 121,
122n, 124, 147, 154-7, 159, 167,
191, 192, 208, 211-4, 216, 218,
219, 220, 239, 243, 244, 250, 271n,
279, 281; of naturalized citizens and
compromise on, 147, 147n, 148n,
157, 157n, 213, 214, 215, 215n,
216, 218, 239, 281; as part of
British commercial policy, 158,
158n, 214, 227, 240n; and law of
nations, 214-5n, 239-40n; and
Treaty of Ghent, 279-82.

Indians: in S.C., xxiii; and the British,
117, 166, 166n, 167, 258, 277;
lands of, 428.

Industries. *See* Manufactures, U.S.

Ingham, Samuel D. (Pa.), 248, 248n,
407n.

Instruction, implied, of Congressmen,
JCC on, 384-7, 392, 393-4n.

*Intelligencer. See National Intelli-
gencer.*

Internal improvements: JCC favors, xxxi-xxxii, 314, 315n, 326, 398-407; use of bank bonus for, 346n, 370-1; bonus bill, 372, 407-8; and states' rights, 399, 402, 407n-8. *See also* Canals; Roads.

Jackson, Gen. Andrew, praised by JCC, 263, 263n, 322.
Jackson, John G. (Va.), 278, 278n.
Jamaica, West Indies, 14.
James, William Dobein, 39, 39n.
Java (British frigate), 227.
Jay's Treaty, 305.
Jefferson, Thomas, 122n, 410n; JCC meets, 14, 14n; his administration, 35-7, 108n, 146, 239, 320.
Johnson, Richard M. (Ky.), 95n, 108n, 145n; and compensation act, 345n, 392; JCC praises, 345n; and claims act, 374n, 376n.
Johnson, Judge William, 284.
Jones, Rev. Cave: letter of request from, 429; recommended, 429.
Jones, Samuel B., Pickens' executor, 182, 183n.
Jones, William, Secretary of the Navy, 147n, 149, 162; letter of recommendation to, 426.

Keane, Gen. John, 275.
Kentucky, Chickasaw lands in, 428.
King, Cyrus (Mass.), 375n.

Lagree (Legare ?), Mr. ———, 397.
Lake Erie, battle of, xxviii.
Langdon, John, 41n.
Latham, Capt. ———, 59.
Laurens, District and town, S.C.: JCC at, 48; JCC represents, xxvi, 58, 92.
Law, Lyman (Conn.), 425-6.
Law of nations: and rights of belligerents and neutrals, 35, 64, 67, 111-5 *passim*, 154, 223; and impressment, 214-6, 239; defined, 216, 216n.
Laws of war, 166, 167, 377.

Laws, U.S.: printing of, 284-5n; suspension of, 366-7. For specific bills and acts *see* Congress, U.S.; House of Representatives, U.S.
Legge, Thomas W., letter of recommendation for, 424.
Legislatures, state, 71n; JCC on electoral powers of, 383, 389, 390.
Leipzig, battle of, xxix.
Leopard (British frigate), 34, 35-6.
Licenses, British: bills to forbid to U.S. ships, 164n-5n, 182n, 423; and embargo, 181n.
Linonian Society (Yale literary society), 5, 6n.
Lipscomb, Abner J., letter of recommendation for, 427.
Lisbon, 274.
Litchfield, Conn.: JCC at, 15-31 *passim*; JCC on climate of, 24, 25, 26-7, 28, 29, 30; political controversy in, 25, 25n; JCC's opinion of, 25, 25n, 29, 31; JCC leaves, 32; JCC's friend from, 426.
Litchfield Law School: JCC at, xxv, 15-32, 39; schedule and lectures, 17, 27, 28, 29, 31, 32; JCC's methods at, 51n.
Liverpool, Earl of, British Secretary of War, 93.
Lloyd, James, letter to and answer from for UNCC, 381, 381n.
Locke, John, 84.
Long, Agnes, 433.
Lord, William R., letter of recommendation for, 426.
Lothrop's wharf, Charleston, S. C., 59.
Louisa County, Va., 364.
Louisiana, 94-5n, 405; constitutionality of purchase, 404, 405.
Lowndes, William (S.C.), Republican: and war party, 71n; JCC praises, 98; opposes restrictive system, 98, 99n, 135n, 142, 142n; JCC calls "my friend," 142; on army bills, 161n, 425; on bank bills, 267, 270n, 271n, 275n; on Constitution, 307, 307n, 312; chairman of W&MC, his revenue and tariff bills, 315n, 330n, 356n.

Lyon, John, letter for, 427.

Macbride, Eleanor Gourdin (Mrs. James Macbride), JCC mentions, 42, 62, 62n, 91, 94, 100, 146, 162, 163.
Macbride, Dr. James: letters to, 61-2, 90-1, 93-4, 99-100, 146-7, 162-3, 177-8; correspondence with, 61, 90, 99, 146, 162; JCC's friendship and respect for, 42, 61-2, 90, 286; engagement of, 42; visits to and from JCC, 42, 162, 177; political interests of, 61-2, 90-1, 99-100, 162; scientific interests of, 62n, 90, 91; patronage requests of, 93, 178; JCC's political confidences to, 94, 146, 177-8; to attend Mrs. JCC, 286; JCC owes money to, 416-7.
McCalla, John, letter of recommendation for, 365, 369-70, 372n.
MacDonald, John, 273, 273n.
McDuffie, George, JCC recommends, 427.
Macedonian (British frigate), 227.
McElhenny, Rev. James, 20, 20n, 33.
McGehee, ———, 206.
McKee, Samuel (Ky.), 170; JCC calls "my friend," 413.
McKim, Alexander (Md.), 252-3, 254n.
McLean, Alney (Ky.), 347n.
Macon, Nathaniel (N.C.), 100-1n, 239.
Madison, James, U.S. President:
Messages to Congress:
Nov. 5, 1811: on foreign affairs, 63, 68, 68n, 69n, 70, 85n, 88n, 122n, 161n.
Dec. 23, 1811: on internal improvements, 368n.
Mar. 9, 1812: on Henry affair, 93n.
Apr. 1, 1812: for embargo, 97n.
June 1, 1812: for war, xxvii, 109, 120n, 122n, 123, 124.
Nov. 4, 1812: on merchants' bonds, 136, 137, 145n; on impress-

Madison, James (continued)
ment compromise, 146n, 147n, 148; on army, 161n; on Indians, 166n; on repeal of French Decrees, 175n.
Feb. 24, 1813: on British licenses, 164n-5n.
July 12, 1813: reply to House resolutions, 177n, 179, 181n, 185-6n.
July 20, 1813: for embargo, 181n-2n, 184.
Dec. 7, 1813: on retaliation, 168n, 202, 202n; on cruisers, 189n.
Dec. 9, 1813: for embargo, 184.
Jan. 18, 1814: reply to House resolutions, 188n, 189n.
Mar. 31, 1814: for repeal of restrictive system, 184, 240, 242n-3n, 248n-9n.
Sept. 20, 1814: on army, 255, 261n.
Dec. 5, 1815: for military academies, 289n; on currency, 290, 303n; on internal improvements, 368n.
Dec. 3, 1816: on internal improvements, 368n-9n.
Dec. 6, 1816: on claims law, 366n.
Dec. 26, 1816: on neutrality, 397n.
His administration and War of 1812: coöperation with war party, xxvii-xxviii, 71n, 123, 124, 126n, 146, 148-9n, 161n, 239; JCC's opinions and criticism of, xxvi, 90, 95, 99-100, 146-7, 201n; JCC defends against Randolph, 105-6; armistice negotiations, 124, 147n, 147-9n, 157, 157n, 189-90n; as FRC chairman JCC defends against Federalists, xxix, 146, 147-8, 169-76n *passim*, 179-81n, 248, 254, 259n, 424; veto of bank bill, 275n.
His peacetime administration: newspaper support for, 284-5; commerce treaty, 305; and constitutionality of internal improvements, 368n, 408; veto of bonus bill, xxxii,

Madison, James (continued)
408; and Trumbull, 409.
For his executive powers *see* President, U.S.

Mail service, U.S., 416, 417-8, 419; to and in S.C., 6n, 9, 37-8, 47, 48, 50, 53, 54, 58-9, 60, 61, 126, 178, 275, 283, 362-3, 369, 418, 420, 426, 427; to and in New England, 11, 16, 18, 21n, 21, 24, 28, 38, 45, 49, 52, 57; to Washington, D.C., 86, 92, 95, 99, 205, 260, 274, 360, 369; JCC on importance of, 401.

Maine, 258, 405.

Majority and minority: JCC on rights and duties of, 78, 155, 160, 198-9, 200n, 201n, 236; and patronage, 391, 392. For the majority party *see* Republican party; for the minority party *see* Federalist party.

Manufactures, U.S., JCC on, 11, 274; importance for national defense, 238, 326, 350, 400; stimulated by war, 238, 253, 328, 352-3; effects on employees, 354-5; stimulated by internal improvements, 398, 406. *See also* Tariff of 1816.

Maria (schooner), 59.

Marines, U.S., 424.

Markley, Mr. ———, 18, 22.

Martin, ———, 397.

Martin, Elizabeth (cousin of JCC), 29.

Martin, Sara Caldwell, 433.

Martyn, John, edition of Virgil by, 3n.

Maryland, 14, 74; Memorial of its House of Delegates, 201-4n.

Massachusetts, 98n; and war, 178n, 227-8; Memorial of its legislature, 178, 178n.

Maxcy, Jonathan, 102n.

Maxcy, Mary Galloway (Mrs. Virgil Maxcy), 416.

Maxcy, Milton, 102n.

Maxcy, Virgil: letters to, 101-2, 416; correspondence with, 416; at Litchfield, 51n; and JCC's speeches, xxxv n, xxxvii-xxxviii, 75n, 282n; JCC's friendship for, 101; JCC's

Maxcy, Virgil (continued)
prospective visits to, 101, 416; Federalist, 101, 102n; law career of, 102n; and S.C. connections, 102n.

Mayo, Thomas, answers for, 429.

Mayrant, William (S.C.), 347n.

Mayson family, 365-6.

Mayson, Ramsay, 365-6.

Mediterranean Sea: and Tripolitan War, 144; commerce in, 241.

Meigs, Return J., Postmaster General, 363; answer from, 427.

Merchant marine, U.S.: and war, 69, 182n, 352, 373; and U.S. manufactures, 353-4. *See also* Decrees, French; Impressment, British; Orders in Council.

Merchants' bonds, W&MC report and JCC's speech on, xxvii n, 136-46n.

Middle states, U.S.: JCC on conditions in, 362; and the national program, xxxii, 371, 408. *See also* Eastern states, U.S.

Middleton, Henry (S.C.), 363n.

Milan Decree. *See* Decrees, French.

Military academies, JCC on bill for, 287-90n.

Militia, U.S., 36, 69, 69n, 81n, 256, 260, 288-90, 323, 327, 424; bills for, 70-1n, 261-2n, 271-3n, 288; JCC's opinions on, 81, 144, 324-5.

Miller, Mrs. ———, 418, 420.

Miller, Dr. John, answers for, 429.

Miller's Weekly Messenger (Pendleton, S.C.), 37.

Milligan, Mr. ———, 47.

Minority. *See* Majority and minority; Opposition.

Mississippi River, 274, 327.

Mississippi Territory, patronage in, 426, 427.

Monroe, James: letter of acceptance to, 418-9; letters of recommendation to, 426, 427; answer from, 263n.

U.S. minister to England, 90, 110-1, 112, 114n, 124.

Secretary of State (1811-1814), 59n; criticizes Congress, 70, 88n, 90; and war party, 71n, 123, 124, 422; and Henry affair, 92-3; and

Monroe, James (continued)
1812 embargo, 97n, 422; JCC or Monroe as author of war report, 123-4; editorials in *National Intelligencer*, 123-4; and impressment compromise, 124, 148; report on repeal of French Decrees, 176, 180, 181n, 182n; report on Turreau letter, 188n, 189n; instructs peace commission, 280n, 281; report on Russian mediation, 425.
Acting Secretary of War (Dec., 1812-Jan., 1813), asks army bills, 161n.
Secretary of War (1814-Feb., 1815): on Pickens' commission, 260; asks army bills, 262n; letter to JCC on army supply system, 263n; report on system of army discipline, 273, 273n.
Secretary of State (Feb., 1815-1816), 285.
President: JCC expects his election, 274; offers JCC the War Dept., xxxii, 418-9n.
Montgomery, Gen. Richard, 82.
Monticello (Albemarle County, Va.), 14n.
Morris, Capt. Charles, JCC's opinion of, 417, 418.
Moseley, Mr. ——— (probably Joseph, brother-in-law of Nancy Calhoun), 63, 90, 150.
Moseley, Mrs. ——— (probably Mrs. Joseph Moseley, sister of Nancy Calhoun), 63, 90, 150.
Moseley, William, 361.
Mount Dearborn, S.C., 289n.
Muscadine grapes, 416n.

Nantes, Edict of, 353.
Napoleon Bonaparte, 23; his Continental system, 65-6, 132, 143, 240, 242n, 244, 245, 246, 252n; called tyrant by JCC, 67, 132, 143, 159, 202-3; denounced by the opposition, xxviii, 85n, 109n, 159, 176, 249. For his wars *see* France. *See also* Decrees, French.

Nash, Reuben, answer for, 429.
Nashville, Tenn., 365.
Natchez, Miss., 426.
National debt, U.S., 315n; JCC's dislike of, 130, 415.
National Intelligencer: JCC mentions, 63, 96, 172; prints Clay-Randolph correspondence, 109n; Monroe's editorials in, 123-4; prints Turreau letter, 188n-9n.
Naturalized citizens, U.S.: JCC and Dwight on, 10-1; and retaliation, 167, 168n, 202, 203, 203n; and bank, 303n, 342, 342n; naturalization acts, 424. *See also* Impressment, British.
Navy, British. *See* Blockades, British; England; Impressment, British. For naval battles *see* Navy, U.S.
Navy Department: letters of recommendation to, 422, 424, 426, 427, 428; answers from, 428; JCC mentions, 274; JCC on abuses in, 415n, 423. For Secretaries of the Navy *see* Crowninshield, Benjamin W.; Hamilton, Paul; Jones, William.
Navy, U.S.: bills and resolutions for, 69, 70, 149, 232, 423, 425.
JCC on: 90, 106, 130, 192, 314, 319, 322-4, 326, 330n, 353-4, 423; battles, xxviii, 34-7, 117, 144, 227, 260, 274, 322; steam frigates for, 327; supports tariff because of U.S. naval inferiority, 348, 350, 351-2; advice on naval career, 417-8. For JCC's patronage in *see* Navy Department.
Netherlands. *See* Holland.
Neutrals: U.S. trade with, 240-2n, 244-8n; JCC on duties of, 395-7n. For rights of neutrals as cause of war *see* Essex case; Impressment, British; Law of nations; Orders in Council.
Newberry Courthouse and District, S. C.: JCC represents, xxvi; JCC at, 41.
New England, 8, 9n; JCC's opinions of, xxv, 10, 13, 53; disunion and states' rights sentiment in, xxvi,

New England (continued)
xxx, xxxii, 92-3n, 93-4, 96, 117-8,
164n-5n, 178, 178n, 200n-1n, 240,
260, 425-6. *See also* Eastern states,
U.S.; Federalist party; Litchfield,
Conn.; Newport, R.I.

New Haven, Conn., 11, 21n, 21, 60;
JCC at, 4, 6n, 7, 9, 11.

New Jersey, 291, 291n.

New London, Conn., 425-6; JCC at,
15.

New Orleans, La., 26, 137, 397, 406;
battle of, 274-5, 277, 319, 324.

New York, 22, 95, 374; delegation in
Congress, xxxii, 274, 408; legislature of, 368n.

New York Academy, 409.

New York, N.Y., 26, 30, 31, 59, 207,
260, 374, 409; JCC at, 4, 5, 24;
and bank, 204-5n, 346n, 378.

Newport, Ky., 289n.

Newport, R.I.: Mrs. Colhoun's address, 11-58 *passim;* JCC visits Mrs.
Colhoun at, xxv-xxvi, 11-3, 15, 17,
29, 31, 48, 59n; JCC's opinions of,
12-3, 22, 24, 31; JCC's comments
on climate of, 16, 21, 24, 25-6, 28,
29; JCC's friends at, 16, 17, 19,
20, 22, 24, 26, 27, 29, 30, 30n, 31,
33, 38, 55.

Newspapers, 37, 59; JCC mentions,
14, 23, 28, 29, 91, 100, 149, 401,
417; partisanship of, 25n, 168-9n,
284-5; comments on JCC, 75n, 85n,
98n, 147n, 162, 182n, 236n, 263,
275, 339, 340, 363, 363n; JCC
criticizes, 84, 106, 147n, 162, 168-
9n, 224, 280, 321, 339, 385; Rounsavell's arrest, 98n. *See also National Intelligencer.*

Newton, Isaac, 84.

Newton, Thomas (Va.), chairman of
Committee on Commerce and Manufactures, 182n, 356n, 372n.

Niagara frontier, 278; property damage on, 374, 376, 426.

Ninety-Six District, S.C., representation of, xxiii n, xxiv, xxiv n, 23n.

Noble, Alexander (1733-1802, cousin
of JCC), xxiv, 432.

Noble, Alexander (died 1821, cousin
of JCC), 432; letter to, 12-3; correspondence with, 11, 11n, 12, 26,
30.

Noble, Catherine Calhoun (Mrs. Alexander Noble, cousin of JCC), 432.

Noble, Elizabeth Pickens (Mrs. Patrick Noble). *See* Pickens, Elizabeth
Bonneau.

Noble, Ezekiel Pickens (cousin of
JCC), 420, 420n, 432.

Noble, John (died 1752), 432.

Noble, John (1769-1819, cousin of
JCC), 20, 20n, 432; letter from,
362-4; writes to JCC, 52; JCC mentions, 13, 13n, 30, 416.

Noble, Mary Calhoun (Mrs. John
Noble, aunt of JCC), 432.

Noble, Patrick (cousin of JCC), 420n,
432; letters to, 95-6, 126, 274-5;
correspondence with, 95, 96; political career, 95-6n; JCC advises on
army career, 96; JCC's law partner,
96n.

Non-importation. *See* Restrictive system.

Non-intercourse, commercial. *See* Restrictive system.

Norfolk, Va., 36, 36n, 417, 419.

Norris, Andrew (half-brother of Senator Colhoun ?), 417, 418, 418n,
419, 420.

North Carolina: petition from, 425;
University of, 427.

North, Lord, administration of, 194.

Northwest trade, 396.

Norwich, Conn., JCC at, 15.

Ohio, 291, 291n, 413.

Oneal, Richard, letter of recommendation for, 422.

Opposition: JCC on right of, 155, 198-
9; JCC defines factious and useful, xxix, 194-6. For the opposition
in Congress *see* Federalist party;
Randolph, John.

Orangeburg District, S.C., 15n.

Orders in Council, JCC on: as cause
of war, xxvii, 64, 71n, 76, 80, 154,

Orders in Council (continued) 191; and French Decrees, 65, 69n, 82, 118-9, 120-1, 170, 172-5, 175n, 179, 191; repeal of, xxix, 124, 136, 145n, 148, 150, 158-9, 175n, 176, 177n, 179, 220; part of British commercial policy, 222n, 224.
 Order of Jan. 7, 1807, 114-5, 118, 150, 154; Order of Nov. 11, 1807, 115, 119, 150-4; Orders of 1809, 154.

Ordnance Department, specific appropriations to, 413-4.

Orleans: territory of, 94; island of, 274.

Osborn, Selleck, 25n.

Pakenham, Sir Edward, 275.

Parliament, British: JCC on, 173, 224; in contrast with Congress, 73, 84, 313, 386.

Passports, 242, 242n.

Patronage: JCC on, 284-5n, 360-1, 361, 375, 384, 385, 388, 391; JCC's patronage correspondence, 426, 427, 428, 429. For his patronage correspondence and services for constituents *see* South Carolina.

Patton, Mr. ——, 24.

Peacock (U.S. sloop), 260.

Pearl River, 95n.

Pearson, Joseph (N.C.), 147, 147n, 148.

Pendleton District, S.C.: Pickens and Colhoun family home, xxiv, 7, 9, 13, 18, 20, 21, 22, 23, 44, 45, 47, 52, 53, 79, 182, 260, 420; JCC at, 51n, 61.

Pennsylvania: delegation in Congress, xxxii; legislature, 341n.

Pension Office, answer from, 424.

Perceval, Spencer, British Prime Minister, 80.

Perry, Oliver Hazard, xxviii.

Petigru, James L., 3n.

Petitions: JCC on right of, 102-3, 169n, 375n, 376; Albany Petition, 102-8n *passim;* Richards', 168-9n; Mass. Memorial, 178, 178n; Md.

Petitions (continued) Memorial, 201-4n; N.Y. and Philadelphia bank petitions, 204-5n; seamen's, 217; canal petitions, 368n, 408, 425.

Philadelphia, Pa., 11, 370, 406, 410; JCC at, 23, 32, 101; and bank, 205n, 291, 295, 296, 346n-7n, 378.

Pickens, Gen. Andrew, xxiv, 4n, 44n, 432; JCC mentions, 9, 10, 14, 53, 182, 183, 416; death of, 418, 418n.

Pickens, Col. Andrew, Jr. (cousin of JCC), 102n, 432; letters to, 3-4, 7-10, 13-4, 22-4, 260, 429; correspondence with, 3, 7, 9, 10, 22, 260; family of, 4n, 14, 14n, 17n, 43n, 47, 47n, 52, 53, 183n, 429; law career and political ambition, 8-9, 23; army career, 91, 260, 260n; Governor of S.C., 420, 420n.

Pickens, Elizabeth Barksdale (Mrs. Ezekiel Pickens): letter to, 182-3; marriage of, 33, 33n, 183n, 432.

Pickens, Elizabeth Bonneau (Mrs. Ezekiel Pickens), xxiv, 33n, 183n, 432.

Pickens, Elizabeth Bonneau (cousin of JCC), 432; JCC mentions, 17, 19, 26, 27, 29, 38, 45, 48, 50, 52, 60; educated by Mrs. Colhoun, 17n, 183n; marriage of, 420, 420n, 432.

Pickens, Ezekiel (1768-1813, cousin of JCC): writes to JCC, 92; JCC mentions, 14, 14n, 21, 44, 57, 60; marriages and family of, xxiv, 17n, 33, 33n, 60, 183n, 432; as Senator Colhoun's executor, 20n, 43n, 47, 47n, 59n, 61; JCC his executor, 182-3n, 429.

Pickens, Ezekiel (1794-1860, cousin of JCC), 183, 183n, 432.

Pickens, Francis Wilkinson (cousin of JCC), xxxvi, xxxvi n, 432.

Pickens, Israel (N.C.), 369, 369n.

Pickens, Margaret (cousin of JCC). *See* Bowie, Margaret Pickens.

Pickens, Rebecca Calhoun (Mrs. Andrew Pickens, cousin of JCC), 4n, 432; JCC mentions, 9, 10, 14, 53.

Pickens, Susan Calhoun (cousin of

Pickens, Susan Calhoun (continued) JCC), 52, 432.
Pickens, Susan Wilkinson (Mrs. Andrew Pickens, Jr.), 14, 14n, 23, 432; death of, 47, 47n.
Pickering, Timothy (Mass.), Federalist: opposes war, 178n, 209n, 217, 217n, 223n, 278n; and internal improvements, 405n, 407n-8.
Pierpont, John, 11n.
Pinckney, Thomas, 96, 96n.
Pineville, S.C., Macbride's home, 42, 61, 91, 94, 100; JCC at, 42, 61.
Pinkney, William, U.S. minister to England, 92, 92n.
Pitkin, Timothy (Conn.), 157, 157n, 343n, 347n.
Pitt, William, 84, 196, 251.
Pitt, William, the Younger, 77, 319.
Plattsburg, battle of, 319.
Plumer, William, 97n.
Poindexter, William G., 364, 365n.
Porter, Peter B. (N.Y.), chairman of FRC, 69n, 71n, 88n; his reports, 63-9, 70, 85n, 93n, 97n, 109n; JCC succeeds, xxvii, 109n; JCC moves consideration of his last bill, 422.
Portland, Me., 291n.
Portugal, 222, 241, 427.
Postell, Edward P., answer for, 428.
Postmaster General, 363; answers from, 426, 427.
Potter, Elisha R. (R.I.), 254n.
President, U.S.:
  JCC on constitutional powers of: and retaliation, 167; and diplomacy, 186; and relations with Congress, 186, 187, 306, 311, 313, 383-4, 388; election of, 342, 369, 369n, 383; as predominant branch of U.S. government, 343-4; and dismissal of officials, 366-7; and suspension of laws, 366-7n.
  His powers derived from legislation: and army, 68, 69, 70, 87n, 88n, 89, 125, 161n, 165-7, 262n, 272n, 278n; and restrictive system, 101n, 145n, 242; and bank, 205n, 264n, 265n, 268, 270n, 291-304n *passim*, 340n, 341n; and transfer of

President (continued)
  appropriations, 411, 414, 415n. For specific Presidential actions *see* Jefferson, Thomas; Madison, James.
Prince Regent, 59, 172-3n.
Prince William's Church and Parish, S.C., xxiii.
Princeton University, 21, 21n.
Prisoners of war, 166, 167.
Privateers, U.S., 125, 251, 274.
Providence, R.I., 365.
"Providence College." *See* Rhode Island College.
Purcell, Mrs. Sarah Blake, 21n.

Quan, Robert, 178n.
Quartermaster's Department: specific appropriation to, 413-4; bills for, 423.
Quincy, Josiah (Mass.), 97, 98n, 233.

Raisin River Massacre, 167.
Raleigh, N.C., JCC at, 286.
Randolph, John (Va.):
  Opposes war, 109n, 120n; disputes with JCC, xxvii, 75-85n, 89, 89n, 97, 97n, 100-1n, 102-7, 108n, 159, 422; as member opposes FRC proceedings, 85n, 96-7, 422; charges discourtesy to minority, 100-1n; dispute with Clay, 108-9n.
  In 14th Congress, 375, 375n, 395; dispute with JCC on treaties, 307n; dispute with Clay, 316n; disputes with JCC on national program, xxxi, 319-20, 331n, 342n, 346, 346n, 347n, 347-57n; his political philosophy and praise of JCC, xxxi, 331n.
Rariton and Delaware Canal, 424-5.
Reed, William (Mass.), 425.
Reeve, Judge Tapping, JCC studies under, 15, 16n, 32, 39.
Regulators in S.C., xxiii.
Representation, legislative: S.C. compromise on, xxiii-xxiv, xxv, 40n; JCC on theory of, 71-5n.
Republican party:
  Support of: by JCC and his fam-

Republican party (continued)
ily, xxiv, xxv, xxvi-xxvii, 9n, 23, 23n, 25, 25n, 41n; by newspapers, 25n, 169n, 284-5; JCC on public support, 151-2, 197, 269; in Senate, 429.

As war party in Congress, xxvii-xxx, 69n, 71n, 99n, 100, 102, 123, 124, 147n, 185, 201n, 207, 232, 239, 257, 282; Federalist charges of French influence on, 83-4, 85n, 87, 106, 159, 187, 188, 189n, 225, 227, 249-50, 251, 252n; is divided on restrictive system, xxvii, xxviii, 99n, 126, 134, 135n, 184, 242n-3n, 245, 247-52; supports administration, 147n, 148, 161n, 167, 176-7n, 181n, 185, 188n, 200n, 239, 240, 242n-3n, 248n; is divided on bank, xxx, 266n, 269-71n, 275n.

Restrictive system:

JCC on: public opinion and support for, 36, 83, 92, 113, 126-34 *passim*, 141-5, 202, 204n; as pacific policy, 64-5, 76, 90-1, 120, 224, 228, 244, 245, 246, 250-1; effects on U.S. merchants and economy, 83, 104, 105, 136-45n *passim*, 373; effects on England, 99n, 126-7, 129, 130, 150, 179; protection of U.S. manufactures by, 248, 251, 253-4n, 352-3.

Congressional opposition to: by JCC, Cheves, and Lowndes, xxvii, xxvii n, xxviii, xxx, 91, 98-9n, 126-35n, 142-6n, 163, 163n, 181-2n, 184, 243n, 245, 248n; by Federalists and Randolph, 102-8n, 228, 249, 422; repeal of, 240-3n, 243-54n, 356n.

Embargo of 1807, 64-5, 108n, 244.

Non-intercourse law of 1809, 65.
Non-importation law of 1810, 65, 134n, 172, 172n.
Non-importation law of 1811, 69n, 120, 145n, 150; proposals to modify or repeal it, 98-9n, 126-35n, 136-46n, 163, 163n, 242n; bills to enforce it, 163, 163n, 184; repeal

Restrictive system (continued)
of, 241-3n.

Embargo of 1812: as preliminary to war, xxvii, 96-8n, 100, 109n, 175n, 422; proposals and bills to modify or repeal it, 98-9n, 100-1n, 102-8 *passim*, 134n, 422.

Embargo of 1813: recommended by Madison, 181n, 184; bill fails, 182n; enacted, 182n, 184; proposals to modify or repeal, 184, 242n; repeal of, 240-3n, 426.

Retaliation: bills for, 165-8n; dangers of, 168n, 202-4n, 230, 239. For retaliation between France and England *see* Decrees, French; Orders in Council.

Rhea, John (Tenn.), Republican, 75n; supports war program and administration, 98, 98n, 107n, 169, 170.

Rhine River, 23.

Rhode Island, 11, 19; JCC's opinion of, 13. *See also* Newport.

Rhode Island College, 3, 102n.

Rice crop, 61, 135-6.

Richards, George, 168-9n.

Richardson, William M. (Mass.), 126, 134-5, 245.

Richmond, Va., 364, 406.

Righton family, 60, 60n.

Ritchie, Thomas, praises JCC, 85n.

Roads, U.S. support for, xxxii, 89n, 368n-9n, 371, 404. *See also* Internal improvements.

Roberts' Barony, 416-7n.

Roberts, John, 417n.

Roberts, Jonathan (Pa.), 188n.

Robertson, Thomas B. (La.), 230, 230n, 343n, 392; JCC calls "my friend," 341; JCC replies to, 341-2, 373, 373n, 379.

Rodgers, ———, JCC's opinion of, 62.

Rome, ancient, as example to U.S., 196, 211, 317, 326. *See also* Calhoun, John Caldwell, PERSONAL, Education, studies, interests.

Ross, John (Pa.), 379.

Rounsavell, Nathaniel, 98n, 201n.

"Rule of 1756," 221-2, 251.

Russell, Jonathan, American chargé in London, 148, 173n, 175n, 176.

Russia, 222, 244, 245, 249, 250; war in, 149-50; emperor of, 246, 376; mediation by, 425.

Sackett's Harbor, N.Y., 412-3.

"Sailors' rights" and War of 1812, 243, 244, 250, 271n, 279. *See also* Impressment, British.

St. John's Berkeley Parish, S.C. *See* Bonneau's Ferry.

St. Mary's River, 425.

St. Michael's Church, Charleston, S.C., 30n.

St. Paul's Parish, S.C., xxiv n, 33.

St. Thomas and St. Dennis Parish, S.C., Ezekiel Pickens' home, 14, 33n, 183n.

Salisbury Courthouse, N.C., 178n.

Salkehatchie River, 417n.

Sample, Cpl. ———, answer for, 429.

Santo Domingo refugees, 404.

Saratoga, battle of, JCC on, 133.

Savannah, Ga., 406.

Savannah River: JCC and his relatives living near, 4n, 30, 50, 51n, 182n; flood, 49.

Scott, Gen. Winfield, 263n; JCC praises, 257n, 288, 288n, 322.

Seamen, U.S.: bills for regulation of, 148, 161n, 162, 242, 242n, 251-2; petition of, 217, 217n; certificates, 218, 218n; and coastal trade, 353-4. *See also* Impressment, British; "Sailors' rights."

Search, right of, 215, 216n, 279.

Seaton, William, xxxvi, xxxvi n, xxxviii, 125n.

Sectionalism, JCC on: opposes, 71-4, 131, 178, 178n, 217; War of 1812 a cure for, 287, 288-9; national program a cure for, 342, 355, 361, 398-402, 407n; size of U.S. a cause of, 390-1, 399, 400-1, 407. *See also* States' rights.

Senate, U.S., 8, 9n, 123, 149, 175n, 266n, 295, 306, 311, 313, 392, 409, 410n; bills of, 70, 88n, 95n, 146n,

Senate, U.S. (continued)
165-8n *passim*, 182n, 260, 271-2n, 275n, 314n, 423, 424, 425, 426; JCC on, xxvi, 71-5n, 429; amends House bills, 71-5n, 88n, 98n, 125n-6n, 208n, 232-3, 242n, 251n, 291n-304 *passim*, 347n, 408; passes House bills, 125n, 126n, 395n; defeats House bills, 165n, 182n, 184, 263n, 272n; JCC in, 266n, 275n, 357n. For powers of *see* Congress, U.S.; for acts of *see* House of Representatives, U.S.

Seneca, S.C., 38.

Separation of powers. *See* Constitution, U.S.

Sergeant, John (Pa.), 339n, 341n.

Serurier, J. M. P., French minister to U.S., 87, 106, 106n, 171.

Shackleford, Mr. ———, 283; JCC's opinion of, 42.

Sheffey, Daniel (Va.), Federalist: fears slave revolt, 158, 237; disputes with JCC on war, 170, 172-4, 193, 200n, 201n, 206n; on bonus bill, 405n.

Shields, S. B., 34, 37.

Shipbuilding, U.S., JCC on, 395-7n.

Shipherd, Zebulon R. (N.Y.), 201n.

Silliman, Prof. Benjamin, 59, 59n.

Simkins, Eldred, xxxvi, xxxvi n, xxxvii; JCC recommends, 427.

Sinclair, Capt. Arthur, 419.

Sinking fund, 264.

Slavery, JCC and: denies danger of revolt in South, 80-1, 85n, 86n, 158, 237; his s l a v e s, 206(?), 420(?); uses simile of, 218, 229; his purchase of slaves, 312n, 364-5n; denounces slave trade, 312; Briggs on, 371.

Smilie, John (Pa.), chairman of FRC, 148.

Smith, Dr. ———, 183.

Smith, Robert, Secretary of State, 59n, 188n-9n.

Smith, Gen. Samuel (Md.), on bank, 340-3n *passim*.

Smith, William (probable identification), JCC's opinion of, 62.

Smuggling, under restrictive system, JCC on, 127-9, 132, 143, 144, 253.

Snowden, ———, 62.

South American revolutions, 330n, 395-7.

South Carolina:

State politics: JCC's family and friends in, xxiii-xxiv n, 9n, 23n, 33, 33n, 40n, 93n, 96n, 420n; sectionalism and factions, xxiii-xxv, 23, 23n, 61-2; courts, xxiii, 33, 39-40n, 41, 43n, 46n, 48, 57, 58; JCC in legislature, xxiii, xxv, 40, 40n, 46, 46n, 421; census of 1809, 40, 40n; constitution of 1778, xxiii, xxiv, xxv, 40n.

And national politics: Congressional elections and representation, xxiv, xxvi, xxvi n, xxxi, 23n, 50, 58, 58n, 72, 72n, 363, 363n; Abbeville Meeting, 34-7n; delegation in Congress, 91, 284, 285n, 286, 286n, 347n, 363n, 366, 427, 428. *See also* Calhoun, John Caldwell, POLITICAL; Cheves, Langdon; Lowndes, William.

JCC on: morality of, 10, 28, 29, 38; climate and health of, 19, 49, 50, 55, 418, 419. *See also* Abbeville Courthouse and District.

As JCC's constituency: his relations with, xxvi, 37n, 50, 93n, 362, 363, 363n; his comments on and praise of, 72, 89-90, 91, 95, 142-3, 348, 361; JCC on duties of a Congressman to, 383-94 *passim.*

JCC's patronage recommendations for citizens of: army and navy, 91, 93, 96, 260, 422, 424, 427, 428; pensions and claims, 361, 423, 424, 428, 429; miscellaneous, 178, 284-5n, 365, 369, 372n, 426, 427.

Baronies of, 417n; canal petition of, 425; postal service in, 426.

South Carolina College, 40n, 102n.

Southampton, S.C., 4; JCC at, 3, 4n.

Southern states, U.S., JCC on: relations with New England, 10, 18, 165n; representation of, 73n; agriculture and economy of, 79, 79n, 83,

Southern states, U.S. (continued) 137, 348, 362; possibility of slave revolt in, 80-1, 85n, 86n, 158, 237; and the war, 83, 131, 217, 263, 376; and slave trade, 312; and internal improvements, xxxii, 406.

Southern Patriot (Charleston, S.C.), 284-5n, 363, 363n.

Sovereignty, JCC's theory of, 74. *See also* Constitution, U.S.; States' rights.

Spain, 428; U.S. trade with colonies of, 111, 112, 118; as neutral, 213, 222, 241, 245; prospects of war with, 320; revolt of colonies of, 395-7.

Specie exportation: bills on, 98n, 243n, 422; and bank, 335-6.

Specie payment:

And War of 1812: JCC on currency disorder, 241, 350-1, 400, 406; suspension of in 1814, 255, 323, 333-8 *passim,* 341n, 358n; bill and resolutions to reëstablish, 347n, 357, 360n.

And U.S. bank, 332, 339, 339n, 342, 406; in wartime bills, 264, 264n, 265, 265n, 270n, 275n; for bank stock, 291-3n, 378-81n; required by bank bill, 301-4n *passim,* 337-8, 340, 341n, 345-6.

Stanford, Richard (N.C.), 81n.

State Department: letters of recommendation to, 284-5n, 426, 427; and Turreau letter, 188n-9n. For Secretaries of State *see* Dallas, Alexander J.; Monroe, James; Smith, Robert.

States' rights: and militia, 70-1n, 272n; JCC and Randolph on, 72, 75n, 84, 94, 129, 151, 178, 234, 311, 331n, 333, 347n; and national program, xxxii, 347n, 399, 402, 408. *See also* Sectionalism.

Steamships, JCC on: travel by, 286; for navy, 327.

Stedman, James, 13.

Stenographers, Congressional reporting by, 168-9n.

Sterling, Mrs. ———, 61.

Sterling, Micah: Yale classmate of JCC, 15, 15n; JCC recommends as tutor for Colhouns, 15, 17, 18-9, 20.

Stockton, Richard (N.J.), Federalist, disputes with JCC, 174, 190n, 201n, 279n.

Stowe, Silas (N.Y.), 160.

Strobel, Martin, 29.

Supreme Court, U.S., reporting of, 360.

Sweden, 222, 244, 245, 246.

Tallmadge, Benjamin (Conn.), letter of recommendation cosigned by JCC, 426.

Talmadge, Mr. ———, 92.

Tariff of 1816, 315n-6n, 356n, 361, 370; JCC favors, xxxi, xxxii, 248, 248n, 251-4n, 313, 326-7, 330n-1n; his speech for bill, 347-57n, 407n.

Taxes, U.S.: of 1798, JCC on, 79, 79n; direct peacetime, JCC favors, 314-6n, 328-31n, 361, 411, 412, 412n, 414-5. *See also* Congress, U.S.; Imposts; War of 1812, Finances.

Taylor, John, of Caroline, 124.

Taylor, John (S.C.), 286, 286n.

Taylor, John W. (N.Y.), his bank bill, 205n, 265n-6n.

Thames, battle of, xxviii, 345n.

Thompson, Judge Waddy, 39, 39n.

Thurston, Mr. ———, and family: JCC writes to, 24; JCC mentions, 16, 17, 19, 32, 33.

Thurston, Judge Buckner, letter of recommendation for, 428.

Tobacco crop, 349.

Tompkins, Daniel D., Vice President: letters of recommendation from, 429; presidential candidacy of, 274.

Toulon fleet, 14.

Treasury Department, 415n; powers and duties of Secretary of, 136-40, 145n, 248n, 291, 293, 300, 301, 303n, 304n, 358n, 360n, 372, 376n. For Secretaries of the Treasury *see* Crawford, William H.; Dallas, Alexander J.; Gallatin, Albert.

Treasury notes, U.S., 259n, 336; and bank, 264-71n *passim*, 275n, 293, 293n, 294, 294n, 341, 358n; JCC proposes an issue of, 359-60n; JCC's speech on bill of 1837 for, 266n, 275n.

Treasury, U.S. 255, 259n, 312, 323, 374.

Treaties: JCC on nature of treaty-making power, 304-14n *passim;* Jay's, 305; of Ghent, xxx, 279-81, 307.

Trinity Church, Newport, R.I., 30n.

Tripolitan War, JCC on, 144.

Troup, George M. (Ga.), chairman of Military Affairs Committee, 271; reports, 200, 262n, 263n, 272n, 278n.

Trumbull, John, letter of request from, 409-10.

Tucker, Henry St. George (Va.), 357n, 359n.

Tulip Hill (Maxcy's home near Annapolis, Md.), 101.

Turner, Dr. ———, 16.

Turreau, Gen. L. M., French minister to U.S., debate on letter of, 186-9n.

Tyler, John (Va.), on compensation law, 394n.

United States, JCC on:

Character of the people: pacific, 35, 67-8, 109-10, 116, 118, 119, 122n, 143, 144, 145, 153, 220, 238, 246-7; praise of, 35, 131-3, 143, 190-1, 219, 317, 328-9, 389, 399; power of public opinion, 152-3, 329, 338, 339, 384-7, 392, 393-4n; their love of gain, 219, 317-8, 389. *See also* Restrictive system; War of 1812.

Classes in: yeomanry, 89, 269; middle class, ambition and ability of, 287, 344, 390; wealthy class, 269-70, 287-8.

Destiny and mission of, 79-80, 82-3, 107-8, 133-4, 177-8, 227, 328-30, 402; true military and foreign policy for, 243-4, 249, 288,

United States (continued)
316-31n *passim;* examples for, 389-90. For further examples *see* England; Rome, ancient.

Dangers of disunion in: greatest danger to U.S., xxix, 93-4, 151, 160-1, 162, 177-8, 355-6; encouraged by factious opposition, 36, 152, 156, 195-200, 201n; encouraged by England, 92-3n, 117-8, 164n-5n; discouraged by repeal of restrictive system, 131-3, 135n, 144-5; discouraged by public opinion, xxix, 160-1, 162n, 177-8, 200, 201n, 233-4, 240n, 427; discouraged by growth of national spirit, 217, 287, 288-9; liberty and union inseparable, 355, 401; preservation of liberty, 325.

Geography and size of: encourage smuggling, 131-2, 143; effect on Congress, 344; encourage disunion, 390-1, 399, 401, 407n; advantages for internal improvements, 401-2.

Citizens of: duties and rights of, 211, 212, 216, 233-5, 289-90, 324-5; and bank, 297, 297n, 300, 303n, 342, 342n; and South American revolutions, 395, 397n. *See also* Impressment, British; Naturalized citizens, U.S.; Seamen, U.S.

United States Capitol: acoustics of first, 74; seating arrangements in first, 168; paintings for second, 409-10n.

University of North Carolina, 427.

Venezuela, relief for, 100, 101n, 404.
Vienna, S.C., 4n.
Virginia, 72, 74n, 80-1, 86n, 357; JCC in, 14; slaves sold by, 364-5n.
Virginia and Kentucky Resolutions, 151-2.
Waddel, Catherine Calhoun (Mrs. Moses Waddel, sister of JCC), 433.
Waddel, Rev. Moses: answer for, 427; writes to JCC, 27; JCC his pupil, xxv, 3, 3n, 4n; JCC mentions and

Waddel, Rev. Moses (continued)
praises his school, 38, 47, 49, 52, 53, 54.
War Department, 93, 263n, 367n; answer from, 424; letter of inquiry to, 428; official letters to JCC as Secretary of War, 429; JCC on abuses in, 410-5n. For Secretaries of War *see* Armstrong, John; Dallas, Alexander J.; Eustis, William; Graham, George; Monroe, James.
War of 1812:
JCC on causes of: *Chesapeake* Affair, 34-6, 117; British encouragement of U.S. disunion, 92-3n, 117-8. *See also* Canada; England.

JCC's opinions of: second war of independence, xxvii, 36, 67-8, 107, 122, 122n, 156, 258-9; just and expedient, 76-80, 101, 126, 153, 156, 174, 178, 179, 185, 190, 209-31 *passim,* 233, 276; beginning of new era for U.S., 90-1, 107, 133, 227, 237-8; offensive vs. defensive, 82, 190-3, 200n, 229-30; for free trade and sailors' rights, 243, 244, 246-7, 250, 271n, 279; should have been fought earlier, 245, 251.

Preparations for: FRC report, 68-9, 71n, 75; JCC on public opinion and war, 76, 78-80, 87-8, 95, 96, 126, 129-33, 160-1, 162n, 220, 235, 327-8, 394, 394n, 427; U.S. unpreparedness, xxvii, 78, 88, 99-100, 104, 131; JCC on prospective declaration of war, 85, 90, 91, 100; embargo as preliminary to war, xxvii, 96-8n, 100, 109n, 175n, 422; declaration of war, 97n, 99n, 125-6n, 141, 307, 373; war report, 109-25n; declaration of war and repeal of Orders and Decrees, 148, 172, 176, 178n.

Finances, xxviii, xxx, 89-90, 91, 108n, 130, 134n, 143-4, 145n, 208-10, 230-2, 239, 241, 254-9n, 350-1, 399-400, 422. *See also* Banks, national.

Campaigns: U.S. mismanagement and defeats, xxviii, xxix, 146-7n,

War of 1812 (continued)
148, 162, 254-5, 263, 323. *See also*
Canada. For U.S. victories *see*
Army, U.S.; Navy, U.S.

Peace negotiations: armistice proposals, 124, 147n, 147-9n, 157, 157n, 189-90n; JCC on, 146, 258, 260, 281, 425; news of peace, 273n, 275n; Treaty of Ghent, 279-80n, 307.

Results of: benefit to manufactures, 237-8; JCC calls it successful, 276, 282; effect on national spirit and prosperity, 288-9, 316, 321-2; lessons of, 315, 316, 399-400; property damage in, 367n, 373-7. For effect on U.S. finances *see* Specie payment.

Ward, Mr. ———, 15, 32.

Ware, Nathaniel A., letter of request from and letter of recommendation for, 426.

Washington (U.S. ship of the line), 428.

Washington, D.C., 137, 284, 361, 362, 381, 381n, 406, 409; JCC at, 14, 14n, 63, 86, 89, 90, 91, 92, 93, 95, 99, 101, 126, 135, 146, 149, 162, 177, 205, 260, 274, 276, 286, 362, 365, 370, 397, 416, 418, 419; JCC's friends and society in, 86-7, 362, 364; and War of 1812, xxx, 248n. *See also* District of Columbia.

Washington, George: JCC on relations with England under, 112, 221-2, 318; JCC's praise of, 151; Houdon's statute of, 409.

Wasp (U.S. sloop), 274, 274n.

Watertown, N.Y., 15n.

Webster, Daniel (N.H.), Federalist: resolutions on repeal of French Decrees, 169, 171, 172, 172n, 176, 179-81n, 185-6n, 191; attacks Republican war policy, xxix, 170n, 192, 192n, 197, 200n, 208n, 252n, 259n, 262n; on disunion, 197; JCC replies to, 206-8, 249-52, 254-9; opposes bank bill, 341n; amendment to tariff bill, 356n; on specie payment, 360n.

Wellesley, Marquis of, British Foreign Secretary, 80.

Wellington, Duke of, 322.

West, Benjamin, 410.

West Florida, 94-5n.

West Indies, 14, 53; trade with, 164n-5n. *See also Essex* case.

Western states, U.S.: insurrection in, 11; and War of 1812, 83, 131, 217, 262n; and internal improvements, xxxii, 401, 406.

Whartley, Wilson, letter of inquiry for, 428.

Wheaton, Henry: letter to, 360-1; writes request to JCC, 360.

Whiskey tax of 1794, 79n.

Wilde, Richard H. (Ga.), 375n, 379; his tribute to JCC, 393n.

Wilkinson, Susan. *See* Pickens, Susan Wilkinson.

Williams, David R. (S.C.), chairman of Military Affairs Committee, 69n, 70, 71n, 161n.

Williams, Lewis (N.C.), 412, 415; criticizes JCC, 403n, 412n.

Williamsburg District, S.C., 62n.

Willington (Abbeville County and District), S.C., 183; Waddel's school at, 4n, 427; JCC's post office, 182n, 205, 369, 418. *See also* Bath.

Wilson, Thomas (Pa.), 368n-9n.

Wirt, William: letter from, 364-5; JCC writes to, 364; comment on JCC, 365n.

Woolen manufactures, U.S., protection of, 253, 327, 347-8, 352-3, 356n.

Wright, Robert (Md.), Republican: on impressment, 85n, 212n; on restrictive system, 98, 98n, 242n; supports war, 166n, 187n, 240n; on bank bill, 267, 268.

Yale College, 59, 59n; JCC at, xxv, 3, 4-12, 39, 59n; JCC's friends at, 5, 6n, 10, 11n, 15n, 62n; JCC's studies at, 5, 7-8, 10-1n; literary societies of, 5, 6n; JCC's bond to, 12n; 1804 commencement, 12, 12n.

Yankees, JCC's opinion of, 10.

Colophon

The text type used in this volume is Caledonia. Set by Linotype, it is chiefly of the ten-points size leaded three points. The display type is Bodoni. The letterpress paper is Warren's Old Style.

The partners operating in Chicago under the name of Lee & Fawcett have served as consultants, with Eugenia Fawcett as designer of the volume and Charles E. Lee as production editor. But in the last stages of progress W. Edwin Hemphill has been responsible for some details, including the explanatory introduction to the Index.

Typesetting, presswork, and binding have been done by The R. L. Bryan Company of Columbia, South Carolina, under the supervision of its Vice-President, Robert S. Davis.

Date Due